BEGINNING PHOTOGRAPHY

BEGINNING PHOTOGRAPHY

RALPH HATTERSLEY

A complete course in photography for beginners,
combining three classic best-selling volumes in one—
Beginner's Guide to Photography,
Beginner's Guide to Darkroom Techniques, and
Beginner's Guide to Photographing People—
fully revised and updated in this new edition.

1981   Doubleday & Company, Inc., Garden City, New York

Library of Congress Cataloging in Publication Data

Hattersley, Ralph.
    Beginning photography.

    "A complete course in photography for beginners,
combining . . . Beginner's guide to photography,
Beginner's guide to darkroom techniques, and Beginner's
guide to photographing people, fully revised and updated."
    1. Photography.   I. Title.
TR146.H363   770
ISBN: 0-385-17318-0
Library of Congress Catalog Card Number 80–2741

CONTENTS

PART FIVE • PHOTOGRAPHIC SUBJECTS

BEGINNING
PHOTOGRAPHY

How To Make Pictures

THE CAMERA

• Introduction

Photography is actually a very simple craft. However, if you are just a beginner it probably looks like a jungle to you. Many of the articles in the camera magazines probably make no sense to you at all. Thus you may find them both frightening and exasperating. The truth is that some professional photographers have the same problem, for like yourself they are less interested in scientific jargon than in making interesting pictures. The technological stuff really gets them into a tizzy.

The object of this book is to remedy the situation as much as possible. I will try to provide a starting place that is truly a starting place, instead of a point already 200 miles down the road toward professional photography.

I will not try to tell you all there is to know about photography, nor will I try to convince you that I'm a hotshot and a walking encyclopedia. I will very carefully restrict myself to *basic* ideas. Furthermore, I will very carefully leave out all kinds of information you don't really need to know about. These may be interesting, but there is no sense in cluttering up your head with them in the beginning. They would only confuse you at this point and possibly lead you to despair.

Of necessity, any road through the jungle of an unfamiliar subject must be constructed of words. In our case we must use photographic terms, or jargon. If you concentrate on learning what these terms mean, you will find it is easy to learn more about photography. The photographic magazines will finally seem intelligible to you, and so will the photo books.

To help you learn the basic terms, I'm having them printed in heavy type (**bold face type**) whenever I say anything about them that will help you understand what they mean. If you encounter such a term later on in the book and have forgotten what it means, skim back over the **bold face** words and find it again. Review the definition carefully, then return to your place in the text.

Besides being a road through the photographic jungle, this book has two main objectives: (1) to prepare you for learning more about photography and (2) to get you actually involved in making pictures. Instead of taking your film to the drugstore, you will be doing everything for yourself. Furthermore, your own pictures will be much better than those the drugstore could produce for you.

• Choosing a Camera

Though there are a great many kinds of cameras, I will not attempt to survey them all. If you are a beginner, this would only confuse and frustrate you. And it would be of little use in helping you decide what kind of camera you should have. Long experience in photographic teaching has taught me that the vast majority of people now prefer to begin with 35-mm or 110 cameras. Assuming that your needs will be similar to those of the majority, I will limit my recommendations to cameras of these types. *However, the material in other sections of this book will accurately apply to all types of roll film, not just 35-mm and 110.*

This book will not apply to the **Polaroid Land camera.** However, if you have one I'd recommend keeping it, for it is marvelous within its own realm. Use it for your pictures-in-a-minute and buy another camera—perhaps a very inexpensive one—for doing the kinds of things that will be discussed here.

If you already have a regular roll-film camera of some kind, you don't need another one right now. Even if it is a very simple and inexpensive one, you can do most of the things I will tell you about. Then, if you find yourself really interested in photography, you can begin to think about buying a more sophisticated camera. But don't jump to conclusions and act hastily. If you look at your needs realistically, you may find that the simple camera will permit you to do all the things you really want to do in photography. For example, if all you really want is small family and vacation snapshots, a very cheap camera may be more than adequate.

The standard 35-mm camera is first on my list of recommendations. One reason, as I have already mentioned, is that it is the camera most people wish to use anyway. Another is that the genius of the photographic industry has focused itself on it, making it the most useful, pleasurable, and convenient-to-use camera available. The popular 110 camera, also mentioned, is not nearly as adequate.

Standard 35-mm cameras make small images (1 $\times$ 1⅜ inches); but they are large enough for beginners to cope with very adequately. They use motion-picture-type film of the 35-mm size. It is 1⅜ inches wide and has sprocket holes (perfo-

rations) along each side. In the camera these engage sprockets, which pull the film through.

Though the images are small, most people readily learn to make quality enlargement prints of 8 $\times$ 10 or even 11 $\times$ 14 inches.

I also recommend the **126 cartridge-load camera,** which makes square images 1⅛ $\times$ 1⅛ inches. You should probably limit yourself to 8 $\times$ 10 inch prints, though 11 $\times$ 14s are a possibility. Most people find that they are completely satisfied with 8 $\times$ 10 prints or smaller. Small prints are easy to fit into books, albums, and wallets. When you start making large ones you run into the problem of what to do with them. You also run into considerable expense, for photographic enlarging paper is costly.

Many very advanced photographers find that the 8 $\times$ 10 size suits them better than any other. You should be aware of this lest you begin to think there is virtue in large size per se. Many very famous photographs are quite small.

The great advantage of a **cartridge-load camera** is its extremely simple operation, especially in loading the film. There is nothing to drop into the camera but the film cartridge itself. This is no more difficult than putting a bookmark in a book. Also, this type of camera usually automates a good many other steps that nontechnical people would otherwise find frustrating.

The **126 cartridge-load camera** uses 35-mm film, though most photographers don't seem to know this. However, it only has sprocket holes along *one* side; these are spaced farther apart than those on standard 35-mm film. The idea of the cartridge is that you never have to touch the film nor hardly even think about it. You pop the cartridge into the camera, close it, and let the take-up lever do all the thinking for you.

In terms of the quality of resulting pictures, the range of 126 cameras is very wide. The least expensive models yield a quality that is fine for wallet size but not good at all for prints 5 $\times$ 7 and larger. The expensive models are almost in the professional class. Using them, a competent craftsman can easily get high-quality 11 $\times$ 14 prints. Furthermore, these very expensive 126s are even more heavily automated than the cheaper models and will do many more things.

The **110 cartridge-load camera** seems to be replacing the 126. It is very popular for those who want small color prints but is not very good for larger prints in either black-and-white or color. The problem is that the film image is only about the size of a fingernail, which is very small. If you enlarge it very much you run into a problem with **grain** (a granular appearance of surfaces). The small film is also difficult to handle and hard to get clean enough for enlarging purposes. Thus I don't recommend the 110 camera for people who want to do the kinds of things covered in this book. But for very small color prints produced by a professional photofinisher it is very adequate.

The main reason for the popularity of the **110 camera** is probably its small size. The typical model will easily fit into a shirt pocket with room to spare. Larger models with built-in flash will generally fit into coat pockets. This great portability is very attractive, of course, but you shouldn't let it overwhelm your judgment. This type of camera is good only if you want very small prints. It is true that highly skilled photographers can get decent 8 × 10 prints, but you are hardly in this class at the moment.

For those who like to get a lot of pictures per roll, the **half-frame 35-mm camera** is the answer. The film images are substantially larger than what you get with a 110 camera. The 35-mm film is loaded in standard cassettes in two lengths. One is a 20-exposure roll, the other is 36. Thus, in standard 35-mm cameras, you get either 20 or 36 images.

With the **half-frame cameras** you get either 40 or 72 pictures in a roll, for the images are only half the standard 35-mm size. However, since the images are smaller, they won't yield as good quality in large prints as the standard 35 will. A good craftsman can get quality prints up to 8 × 10 inches. Most people would be better off settling for 5 × 7s or smaller. If small prints are all you want, the half-frame may be your cup of

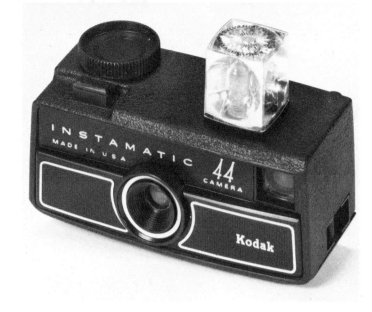

The Instamatic 44 is a cartridge camera selling for less than $10. Though easy to use, it doesn't have sophisticated features.

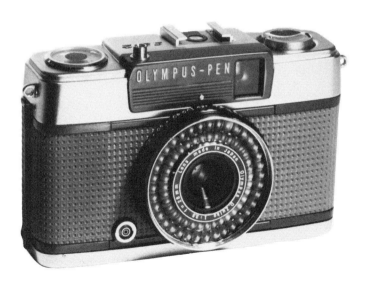

The Olympus Pen EE-2 is a half-frame 35-mm camera—small, durable, and of fine quality. It takes 72 pictures on a 36-exposure roll of film, 40 pictures on a 20-exposure roll.

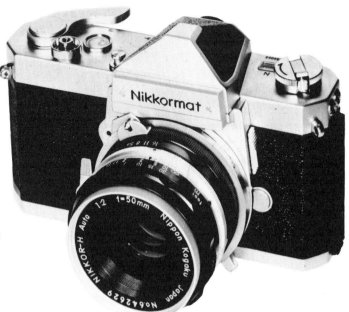

The Nikkormat is a highly reliable SLR (single-lens reflex) type of camera. This type is very popular nowadays.

tea. You can make half-frame color slides too; they are very nice indeed.

Another advantage of **half-frame cameras** is that they are very small and compact, whereas most standard-frame 35s are quite large and heavy. All the half-frame cameras will fit nicely into a man's jacket pocket or a woman's purse, while only a few of the full-frame cameras will. If you like to carry a camera with you at all times, without a shoulder strap, seriously consider the half-frame.

I've said that my primary recommendation is the standard 35-mm. It comes in two main types, called respectively **single-lens reflex** and **rangefinder.** One of the chief differences is that they employ very different means for viewing and getting the image in focus.

The **single-lens reflex camera** (called **SLR** for short) is by far the most popular type nowadays. The word "reflex" indicates that it embodies a mirror that reflects the image coming through the lens up into a viewing system that you look through when taking pictures. When you snap the shutter, the mirror flips out of the way so that the image will reach the film, then

flips down again so you can still see the picture you're getting. It usually happens so fast you're not aware of the flip and return.

The image you see in the viewing system is exactly the same as the image that reaches the film. If the viewed image is fuzzy (out-of-focus), the image on the film will also be. The placement of objects in the picture will also be the same for both images. People who buy **SLR** cameras find these factors extremely important. They are lacking in rangefinder cameras.

Rangefinder cameras take their name from the fact that they employ focusing systems similar to rangefinders on military cannon. A rangefinder simultaneously finds out how far away a pictorial subject is and adjusts the lens position to focus the subject on the film. It is very easy to use.

Rangefinder cameras have viewing windows that tell you what your subject looks like and how much of it you are including in your picture. In the center of the window is a little spot that you use for focusing. In some types of spots you have split images that come together when the subject is in focus. In others you have

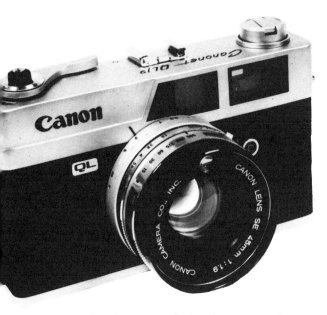

The Canon QL 19 is a rangefinder-type camera. It is automated but has manual override, so that one can pick whatever aperture setting and shutter speed he wishes.

double images that become superimposed when the focus is sharp. In both types the focusing is very accurate.

The trouble with viewing windows on rangefinder cameras is that they are actually windows. Thus, what you see through them always looks in sharp focus, whether it is near you or far away, even if the main subject of your picture is completely out of focus on the film plane. With the SLR you can tell whether something is out of focus because it clearly looks that way through the viewer. Not so with the rangefinder. *Everything always looks sharp,* whether it is or not. You can get very sharp pictures, to be sure, but only if you remember to use the rangefinder spot every time you take a picture.

Another problem with the **rangefinder camera** is that the image you see through the window

(viewfinder) and the image that the lens passes through to the film aren't quite the same. On distant objects this doesn't matter at all, for you couldn't tell the difference between the images if you tried. But on objects that are very close there can be a dramatic difference. Enough, indeed, to ruin many of your pictures.

The point is that your viewing window and your lens are looking at your subject from different positions in space. (The difference is called **parallax.**) At five feet or more it doesn't matter at all. Up close it can matter a great deal. Though there are systems for compensating for parallax (often built right into the camera), you still don't get exactly what you see through the viewfinder window. With SLRs, the viewed image and the recorded image are always identical, for they both come through the lens instead of through two different viewing systems.

These factors have made the rangefinder camera lose popularity. However, in cheaper cameras the rangefinder is a better bet than the SLR, for it is easier to make one that is sturdy. In a cheap SLR, one can't depend on the mirror mechanism (extremely delicate) holding up. In contrast, there are several economy rangefinder cameras that are quite dependable.

In terms of quality at low cost, a type of camera not yet mentioned here is recommended: the **twin-lens reflex.** Most models of this type use 120 film, which gives images 2¼ × 2¼ inches. They can easily be enlarged to 16 × 20 prints. The twin-lens has, obviously, two lenses—one above the other. The word "reflex" refers to reflection and the fact that there is a mirror behind the top, or viewing, lens.

This lens is used only for looking, so the mirror stays in place all the time. The bottom lens takes the picture. Not requiring a complex flip-and-return system, the camera can be made of good quality at low expense. Thus, if you are looking for a good inexpensive camera, the twin-lens reflex is a good bet.

However, since it is fairly bulky and takes

only 12 pictures on a roll, it is not very popular nowadays. You have, again, a **parallax** problem on looking at close-up subject matter (two lenses looking from different positions in space). And you can't conveniently use it to make 35-mm color slides, which are very popular. But in terms of durability and dependability at low cost, it is a good buy. Your best bet is to buy one second-hand, for the newer models can be quite expensive.

So far I haven't talked about **automatic cameras,** which are growing ever more popular. They usually automate only the **exposure,** though a few models also automate film advance and focus. Some cameras are so automated that all you do is point them and shoot, but this type usually has **fixed focus.** This means that photographic subjects more than five feet away are sharp, whereas closeup subjects are fuzzy (out of focus). With the auto-focus cameras this is not a problem, however. They simply focus on the closest object.

Automatic cameras have **built-in exposure meters,** which set one or both of the **exposure controls.** These controls are the **aperture** and **shutter.** Together they determine the amount of light that will be permitted to reach the film, which is called the **exposure.** With exposure automation you generally set one of the controls yourself and let the meter set the other. In a few cameras the meters do both jobs, however.

Automatic cameras usually have single-priority systems. One may have **aperture priority,** for example. This means that you set the aperture and let the meter set the shutter speed. Another camera may have **shutter priority**—you set the shutter speed and let the meter set the aperture. In either case you have one job to do, but the exposures are still automated. A few expensive cameras have **multi-mode priorities** that give you both aperture priority and shutter priority, depending on how the priority controls are set. However, I don't see any particular advantage for this.

Many **automatic cameras** can be operated in the **manual mode.** This means that you can set both exposure controls yourself. However, you use the built-in light meter to read your subject and determine what the setting should be. Most advanced photographers consider the optional manual mode a necessity, though some cameras don't have it.

You should understand the basic premise of automation, the idea behind what manufacturers have done with their cameras, the idea that the average picture maker is too stupid to read books and magazines and learn how to set exposure controls. I don't think that this is true, but it sells a lot of cameras. In this book you will learn to set the controls for yourself and may find that you don't want an automatic camera.

Fortunately, they still make nonautomatic cameras with built-in meters. They usually have **match-needle metering** embodying a moving needle and a mark that it is supposed to point at if the exposure controls are correctly set. You match the mark with the needle, so to speak. This is done when your camera is pointed at your subject, of course, for that is when you do your meter reading. Some cameras replace needles with **light-emitting diodes (LEDs** for short) that light up behind numbers or marks in the viewfinder to tell you if the exposure controls are correctly set. These nonautomatic cameras usually cost a good deal less than fully automatic cameras of the same quality, which is a good thing.

Some cameras have so many buttons, switches, and LEDs that they are confusing. You need a degree in engineering in order to know how to operate them. This often happens when manufacturers try to simplify things for you. They get carried away.

One problem with automated cameras is that they are so **battery-dependent,** which I think is a very bad feature. A given camera may need two or more batteries in order for it to function at all. The thing is that batteries wear out rapidly and even fade when they are not in use. This makes them highly undependable. The exception seems to be the button-type battery used to power exposure meters. It often holds up for a year or longer.

Most modern cameras can be used with **flash,** and some even have electronic flash built into them, which is very handy, of course. Flash exposures for built-ins are usually automated, another convenience. With some automatic flash units the exposure is determined primarily by the aperture, which is automatically set as the camera is focused. In other built-in units there are thyristor circuits combined with electronic sensors to measure the light reflected from photographic subjects. When a subject has received enough light a thyristor circuit turns off the flash lamp.

I have a warning for people who have cameras that require batteries: never leave the batteries in them when they are not in use. In time, batteries will leak and corrode the inside of your camera. The exception seems to be the button-type battery used to power built-in meters—it doesn't leak and can be left in the camera.

You may have read about **automatic cameras** with ± **two-stop exposure overrides,** which are very useful. Because a built-in meter reads both the subject and the background behind it from the shooting position, it sometimes doesn't give you the correct exposure for the subject. But this can be compensated for with the override. If the background is much darker than the subject, you will get overexposure unless you use the underexposure override. If the background is much *lighter* than the subject, you will get *underexposure* unless you use the *overexposure* override. To go two stops under you use one quarter of the exposure that the meter is reading. To go four stops *over* you use *four times* this exposure. Ordinarily you don't need an override, but sometimes the need for it is great.

There is no special trick to using a **built-in meter.** It simply reads the light reflected from whatever you see in the camera viewfinder. However, you must remember to set your film's ASA speed on the meter. This tells your camera how

sensitive the film is to light, a necessary datum.

You may have read about **center-weighted readings** with built-in meters, which is not as mysterious as it sounds. A center-weighted meter simply places emphasis on reading things that are visible at the center of the viewfinder. This is quite useful when a subject (which is usually centered) differs considerably in tonality from its background. We have seen that this could lead to over- or underexposure. Center weighting makes such exposure errors much less likely.

Before closing, a bit about price, and a word about the best source of cameras. In general, you pay for what you get. No matter how you look at it, a $100 camera is just not in the same class as a $450 one. Source is important, too. American cameras are simply not as good as those made in either Japan or Germany. Foreign manufacturers have placed emphasis on quality, whereas American ones have generally gone in for quantity. There are a few good American cameras, to be sure, but they are in the minority.

● **Camera Care**

A camera is a delicate precision instrument. Handled carefully, it will function well for years. Yet it can't take even as much rough treatment as a wristwatch.

Don't drop your camera and don't bump it into things. Don't force its levers, rings, knobs, and screws any more than you would intentionally overwind a watch. If you play strong man even once, you may ruin the camera or run up a high repair bill. Don't try to fix it yourself, or the bill will run still higher.

When not taking pictures, keep a cap on the lens. Clean it only with lens tissue, a soft sable brush, or a rubber syringe blower. Silicone polishing tissues for eyeglasses will damage its surface. So will fingerprints, which etch themselves right into the glass.

If you drop your camera in salt water, bid it a sad good-by. There is only a slim chance of saving it if you rinse it thoroughly with fresh water and take it immediately to a camera repairman.

Getting sand in it is almost as ruinous. It grinds down gears and screw threads so that they no longer mesh together snugly. Or it may lock up mechanisms so that they won't operate at all.

Don't put your camera in the glove compartment of your car or near a furnace or radiator. Don't store it in a damp place, especially in salt air.

If it has a built-in exposure meter, turn it off when it's not in use. Or if it has a cover, put it on.

If your film jams while you're advancing it, don't try to force the winding mechanism. You'll earn a fat repair bill. Just bid your pictures farewell, open the camera back, and take out the film. Load the camera again and give it another try. If it works, put in a fresh roll and start shooting again. If it doesn't, take your camera to a repairman.

Don't let your friends use it to learn photography. They are even worse than salt water.

The camera instruction manual is your bible, so keep it handy at all times. When you forget how to do something, look it up again. If you try to do it by experimentation you may seriously damage your camera.

● Exposure Meters

You ought to have a good exposure meter. A poor one isn't worth bothering with, for it will give you information that is not reliable. You can have a meter that is built into a camera or buy one that is separate. It is convenient to have both kinds if you can afford them.

With the more expensive and up-to-date cameras you can get high-quality built-in meters. Those on **SLR** cameras are extremely easy to use. On rangefinder cameras they are a lot of bother. With a good meter on either type camera, an extra meter is actually unnecessary, though handy to have at times.

Reliable meters of the separate type run from under $40 to more than $100. If your money is limited, you'd be better off to invest more in a camera with a good meter, for it will have other useful features as well. Many very good photographers have never used anything but built-in meters.

Separate meters are powered by **cadmium sulfide (CdS), silicon,** or **selenium** cells. The first two require batteries and work very well as long as the batteries are fresh. Selenium meters (sometimes called **photoelectric** meters) require no batteries. If gently treated, they will continue to give you very accurate readings for more than twenty years and require no repairs at all.

The better silicon meters, such as the Gossen Luna-Pro sbc and the Minolta Autometer II, are extremely sensitive to low levels of light, e.g., moonlight or candlelight. Cheaper meters with batteries have about the same sensitivity as selenium meters, sometimes a little less, and I don't recommend them. Either buy top-quality CdS or silicon meters or don't buy them at all.

One advantage of silicon and selenium meters is that they don't have memories. With a CdS meter, however, an old reading may be remembered as you are taking a new one and may be computed into this new reading, thus throwing it off.

In the economy-class selenium meters we have the Bower Model CP3 and the Copal/Sekonic Auto Lumi L-158. In some camera stores you can get reconditioned earlier models of more expensive meters for very little money. This is a fantastic buy, which I heartily recommend.

Except in dim light these selenium meters are accurate and dependable. Within their range they are better than even top-quality CdS meters. This is due to the memory problem with the CdS type. Silicon meters are quite all right, however, and I personally prefer the Luna-Pro sbc.

The advantage of the selenium meter is long-time dependability and no worry whether a battery is fresh enough to last through a photography field trip. With top-quality CdS and silicon

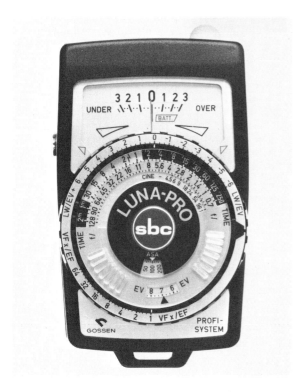

The Gossen Luna-Pro sbc is an expensive silicon-type meter that is extremely sensitive to light and can be used in very low illumination levels. It can take both incident and reflectance readings.

The Copal/Sekonic Auto-Lumi model L-158 is an inexpensive but accurate selenium-type meter used for reflectance readings.

meters it's the ability to read light so dim that the selenium meters would not read it at all.

Later I'll talk about certain problems in using meters properly, so that exposures are accurate. In terms of these problems, the best thing for the beginner is to have a high-quality SLR camera with a built-in meter. With it he can solve nearly all of them easily.

For a person who wants to experience photography at the lowest possible cost to himself, a meter, separate or built-in, isn't necessary at all. In a moment I will tell you how he can get along without one.

LENSES AND SHUTTERS

When we begin to talk about lenses and shutters the photographic jargon can easily become terribly confusing to beginners. I'll simplify as much as I can, but you need to know *some* of the jargon in order to carry forward your study of photography. You see, it was invented in the first place in order to make it possible for us to communicate with one another about photography.

● Focal Length

The technical definition of **focal length** would not make much sense to you at this point, nor do you actually need to know it. It is sufficient to know that focal length is one of the attributes of all lenses, that they may have different focal lengths, and that different focal lengths result in different pictures.

With 35-mm cameras, some common focal lengths of lenses are 21-mm, 28-mm, 35-mm, 50-mm, 90-mm, 105-mm, 135-mm, 200-mm, 250-mm, and 300-mm. As you see, we're going from small numbers to large ones. It is not surprising that the small numbers refer to **short focal lengths,** the medium numbers to **medium focal lengths,** and the large ones to **long focal lengths.** The 50-mm lens has been arbitrarily designated as the medium lens for 35-mm cameras. It is also called the **normal lens,** for most 35-mm cameras have a lens of this focal length or very close to it.

Lenses of 90-mm or longer are usually called **telephoto lenses.** Those descending in focal length from 50-mm are called **wide-angle lenses** for reasons I'll explain in a moment.

Lenses with focal lengths of 200-mm or more seem like telescopes, especially when you put them on an SLR camera and look through the viewfinder.

You can have someone stand quite a long distance from the camera and still have him fill up the whole picture. As you substitute progressively shorter focal length lenses he becomes smaller and smaller in the viewfinder. With a 21-mm lens he becomes very small indeed.

Shy photographers favor telephoto lenses, because they can sneak portraits of people without being near them. Such a lens could also be called a "narrow angle lens," though most people don't think of it this way. Like the pencil beam of a spotlight, it reaches out at a very narrow angle.

On the other hand, a 21-mm lens reaches out like a floodlight and includes a very wide angle of view—almost as much coverage as your eyes give you. The **fish-eye lens** goes another big step in coverage. Both the wide-angle and the fish-eye create a lot of image distortion, which many people find very interesting.

There are also **zoom lenses,** with variable focal length. As you look through the viewfinder and rapidly increase the focal length, you get the feeling that you are zooming out into space.

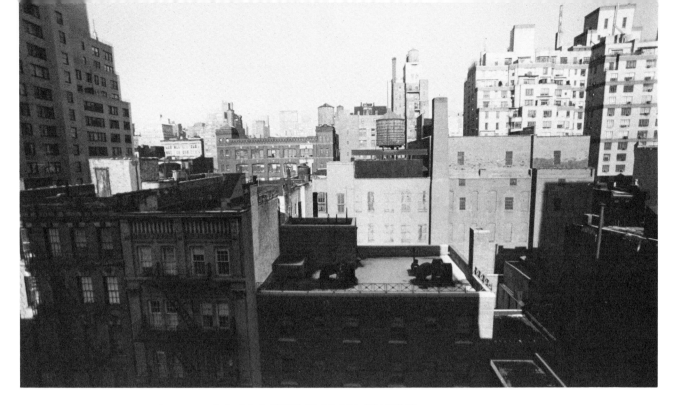

PICTURES MADE WITH LENSES OF DIFFERENT FOCAL LENGTHS.

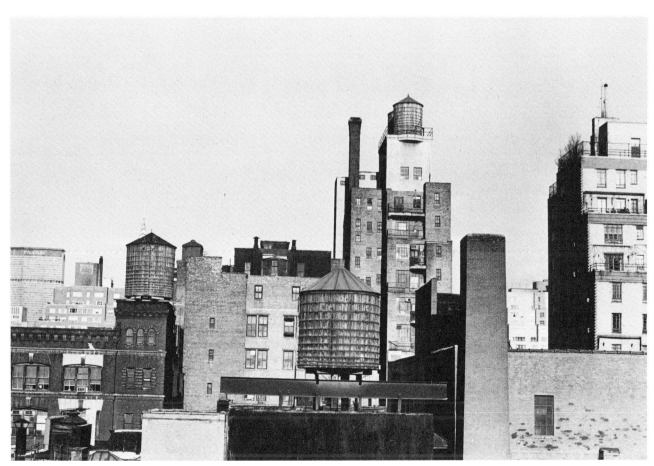

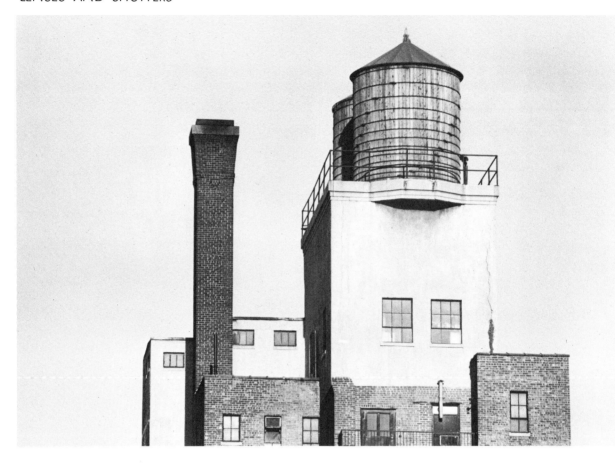

As you can see, a 21-mm lens seems to encompass nearly everything, a 50-mm lens an average amount, while a 200-mm reaches way out and takes just a small piece of the whole scene. They do many other things, too, but you should learn what these are by actually using the lenses.

Since they are heavy, expensive, and not extremely sharp, they are of interest mainly to camera buffs and professionals.

● Lens Speed

Some lenses are called "faster" than others because they let more light into the camera in the same given length of time. It's like a big bathtub drain being faster than a small one. When you look at them, you see that fast lenses are greater in diameter than slow ones. Extremely fast lenses are almost as wide as soup plates.

Lens speeds are expressed in *f*-**numbers,** which are usually marked on the lens. *The smallest f-number on the lens is its maximum speed.* On 35-mm cameras the most common lens speeds are *f*/1.4, *f*/1.8, *f*/2, and *f*/2.8.

People find it confusing because an $f/1.4$ lens is **faster** than an $f/2.8$ one. The number refers to the size of the hole, you might say. To help you keep things straight, you might remember this rule: *The larger the number, the smaller the hole.* For example, $f/16$ is quite small and $f/45$ very small indeed.

● Iris Diaphragm: Variable-size Door

The **iris diaphragm** is a circular, variable-**size** door. It opens up as wide as the lens itself but never quite closes all the way. It got its name from the iris of the eye, which also opens and closes in what appears to be the same way.

It can be compared to a variable-size bathtub drain, which can let either a little or a lot of water through in a given time. The camera diaphragm controls the amount of light that reaches the film in a given time.

The various openings of the iris diaphragm are calibrated (carefully measured) and usually inscribed on the lens barrel. These markings are called *f*-**numbers.** A typical range of *f*-numbers is $f/1.4$—2—2.8—4—5.6—8—11—16. A few

35-mm cameras go on to $f/22$. Larger cameras may go to 32—45—64—90—125. It will help you understand if you look at your camera and find these markings I'm talking about.

On most cameras you can set the iris diaphragm openings manually. Try it. Remember the rule: *The larger the number the smaller the hole.* Look at your camera and the diaphragm markings will help you remember it. If you set the diaphragm at $f/2.8$, you see that you've got a relatively large opening. Set at $f/16$ it is quite small. You will find that it is useful to memorize the series of *f*-numbers given in the last paragraph. If memory fails, look at the lens barrel. They are all marked there.

Look again at the series of *f*-numbers. As you go in one direction through the series, you progressively double the size of the aperture at each marking **(stop).** In the other direction you halve the area at each **stop.**

When you double the area of the variable-size door (diaphragm or **aperture),** twice as much light can come through in a given time. If you halve it, half as much light comes through.

Let us choose three of the *f*-**numbers** that are

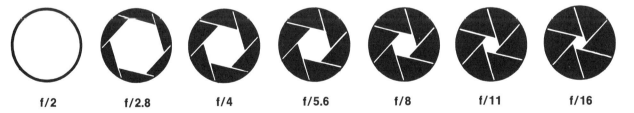

| f/2 | f/2.8 | f/4 | f/5.6 | f/8 | f/11 | f/16 |

The camera diaphragm is actually a variable-size, circular door that doesn't quite close all the way. Notice that the largest openings have the smallest numbers, and vice versa. These openings are called f-numbers, f-stops, stops, or apertures.

marked in succession on the lens barrel—$f/2$, $f/2.8$, and $f/4$. We will start by setting the aperture at $f/2.8$. If we make it smaller by resetting it to $f/4$ (this is called **stopping down),** it shuts out half the light. But if we make it larger by turning to $f/2$ (called **opening up),** it lets twice as much light in.

• Shutter: Variable-speed Door

A camera has two doors. Variable-**size:** diaphragm (or **aperture).** Variable-**speed:** shutter. Though they don't look much like doors they function like them.

The iris diaphragm controls the volume of light to reach the film. The shutter controls the length of time during which it can enter. The periods of entry are of different lengths, called **shutter speeds.**

Cameras have series of shutter speeds. Going through the series in one direction we progressively double the time interval at each new shutter setting. In the opposite direction we halve the interval each time.

The more expensive cameras have a long **shutter speed series,** for example 1 sec—$\frac{1}{2}$ sec —$\frac{1}{4}$—$\frac{1}{8}$—$\frac{1}{15}$—$\frac{1}{30}$—$\frac{1}{60}$—$\frac{1}{125}$—$\frac{1}{250}$—$\frac{1}{500}$ —$\frac{1}{1000}$. You will notice that the doubling and halving are not always exact. For example, half of $\frac{1}{60}$ is not actually $\frac{1}{125}$. It is $\frac{1}{120}$. But $\frac{1}{125}$ and $\frac{1}{120}$ are so nearly the same size that for practical purposes we can think of them as identical.

Cheaper cameras will have fewer shutter speeds, starting perhaps at $\frac{1}{30}$ and going as far as $\frac{1}{125}$ or $\frac{1}{250}$ sec.

Many cameras have an additional setting called **bulb,** a rather peculiar name dating from the early history of photography. It means that on the bulb (or "B") setting you can push down the shutter button and hold the shutter open as long as you wish—an hour, for example. When you release the button the shutter closes again. You use "B" for taking pictures in extremely dim light.

In your reading in photography you will come across two additional terms you ought to understand: **focal-plane shutter** and **between-the-lens shutter.** Most cameras will have either the first or second kind. They look very unalike but serve exactly the same function.

A **focal-plane shutter** is a sliding door positioned in the back of the camera just in front of the film. The film position is called the focal plane, because the lens focuses the image on it. The shutter gets its name because it is very near this plane.

The **between-the-lens shutter** is either positioned inside the lens itself (between its glass elements) or is just behind it. It looks something like the side view of a fist opening and closing.

The better 35-mm cameras have focal-plane shutters. The focal-plane shutter is a part of the camera, not of the lens. It means that you can have a whole series of lenses for your camera and not have to have a separate shutter for each one. This saves a lot on weight and expense. The between-the-lens shutter is usually a part of the lens.

EXPOSURE: "DOORS" WORK AS A TEAM

When you are not taking pictures, the film in your camera is in utter darkness. You take a picture by exposing the film to light. When you press the shutter release, the shutter flicks open for a moment, **exposing** the film.

When the camera shutter opens, the image of the subject you are photographing strikes the film. *This image is entirely made of light.* Thus, when I say the image strikes the film it is exactly the same as saying that light strikes it—or "exposes" it.

The film needs **correct exposure,** however. Selecting either the shutter speed or the aperture arbitrarily just won't do at all. In a moment we'll investigate as far as necessary the problem of determining correct exposure. At this point I merely wish to give you a rough idea of how the two "doors"—diaphragm and shutter—function as a team.

Using the variable-**size** door (diaphragm or aperture) you can make either a bright or dim image strike the film. At a large opening (like $f/2$) the image (light) will be bright on the film. At a small opening (like $f/16$) the image (light) will be dim.

Using the variable-**speed** door (shutter) you can have the image remain on the film for a long, medium, or short time.

To expose the film correctly means to let a certain definite **quantity** of light fall on the film.

This quantity is expressed as light intensity multiplied by time. We can get the quantity we want by letting a lot of light into the camera for a relatively short time, or a little light for a relatively long time. Using either approach we can come up with total quantities that are identical.

In photography, we call these quantities "exposures." We say that we can get the "same" exposure with a lot of light in a little time or a little light in a lot of time.

If we've gotten the correct combination of light intensity (controlled by the aperture) and time (controlled by shutter speed), we call the result "correct" exposure. This means we've permitted a carefully determined quantity of light to react on the film. Sometimes it is best to get "the" exposure with a lot of light (large aperture) and a short time (fast shutter speed). Other times it is best to use less light (smaller aperture) and a longer time (slower shutter speed). Here's how you should make your choice.

● **Subject Movement**

If your subject is moving and you photograph it at a slow shutter speed your picture will look fuzzy, or blurred. The faster it moves the higher the shutter speed required to freeze its movements and get a sharp image.

On a sunny day you can use very small apertures and very high shutter speeds at the same time. This is generally considered a very desirable situation.

On heavy overcast days, in deep shade, after sunset, or indoors, the situation is very different. The light available is relatively dim. In order to shoot at even a moderately fast shutter speed you may have to have a very fast lens with the aperture open all the way. For example, under a heavily overcast sky you might have to shoot at $\frac{1}{125}$ sec and $f/2$, even with a fast film. Many modern films are very sensitive to light and are called **fast films.** This means that for the correct exposure you don't need an enormous quantity of light to strike the film.

Indoors, the situation with respect to freezing movement is even worse, unless one has an electronic flash unit. In many rooms the best one could do for shutter speed with an $f/2$ lens might be $\frac{1}{30}$ sec—with a very fast film like Tri-X. Using a slower film you might not be able to take a picture at all.

The main point I wish to make here is that large apertures such as $f/1.4$, $f/2$, and $f/2.8$ give you opportunities to use higher shutter speeds than you could with smaller apertures. Furthermore, you may desperately desire the higher speeds in order to freeze movement.

• Body Movement

There is another factor that gives you blurred images: the movement of your own body. If you jiggle, your camera does too. You have to do the same things to counteract body movement as you do to freeze subject movement. Use fast film, fast lenses, high shutter speeds, and as bright a light as you can get.

By practicing, some people can develop such steadiness that they can hand-hold cameras and get sharp pictures at $\frac{1}{15}$ or even $\frac{1}{8}$ sec. Beginners, however, are lucky if they can get away with speeds as low as $\frac{1}{125}$. For such a person it is hopeless to try to get sharp pictures by hand-holding a camera in dim light.

There are two solutions to the problem, however: flashcubes (or electronic flash units) or tripods. Flashcubes will let you shoot at rather high shutter speeds. Electronic flash will give you the equivalent of very high shutter speeds.

With your camera on a tripod you don't need high shutter speeds. No matter how slow your shutter speed you'll get sharp pictures—as long as your *subject* isn't moving. You can even use the bulb ("B") setting and make sharp pictures with hour-long exposures.

There is a problem in seeing that the tripod itself doesn't move, however. When you press the shutter release you may jiggle both the camera and the tripod. You can prevent this by using a cable release (a wire-like tube with a spring-loaded plunger) for activating the shutter. If you bend the cable release into a half-loop it will absorb your body movement so that it doesn't reach the camera and tripod.

If you don't have a tripod it helps to rest your camera on a table, chair, or stack of books. In this case you should buy a cable release. It is quite inexpensive, and using very rickety props for your camera, you can still get sharp pictures.

The more expensive 35-mm cameras have self-timers. They also can be used to get sharp pictures when the camera is on a tripod or propped up on something. The idea is that you set the self-timer, press the shutter release, then stand away from your camera. By the time the shutter fires, all the movement in the camera and its support will have quieted down.

• Depth of Field

When you take a picture with several objects in it, the one you focus the camera on will be sharpest. Objects closer to the camera are less sharp and those *very* close to it may be totally blurred. Objects farther from the camera than your subject also get progressively less sharp.

Some of the objects in front and back of the object focused on may be *acceptably* sharp, however. This means they look sharp to the eye, though under a magnifier they would seem less so. Thus, within the picture-taking area in front of the camera there is a *zone* of acceptable sharpness. The length of this zone from front to back is called **depth of field.** Some people remember what it is if they think of it as **depth of sharpness** instead. But depth of field is the term in common use, and you ought to memorize its name and meaning.

Depth of field can be *increased* by **stopping down** (making the aperture smaller). It is *decreased* when you **open up** (make the aperture larger). The term "stopping down" comes from the fact that *f*-**numbers** are also called *f*-**stops.** Thus, to go down one stop means to make the

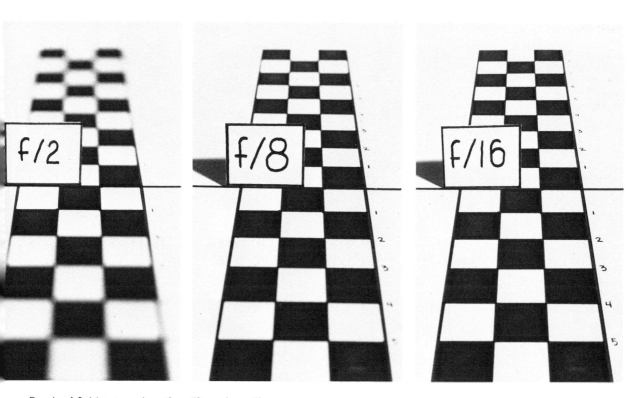

Depth of field test made with a 50-mm lens. The squares on the checkered grid are 1 × 1 inches. The f-number cards (f/2, f/8, and f/16) were about 2 feet from the camera. The measure of depth of field is the total depth of sharpness both in front and behind the card on which the lens was focused. It is obvious that when you are close to a subject there is very little at f/2, a tangible increase at f/8, and quite a bit at f/16. With distant subjects there is much more depth of field at all of these f-numbers.

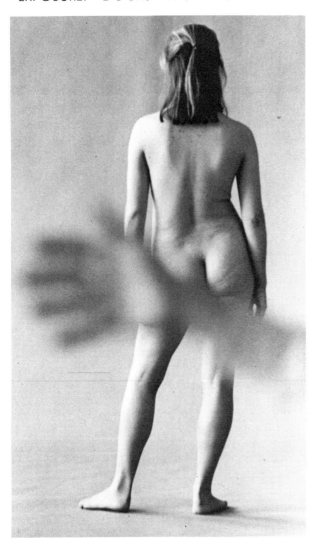
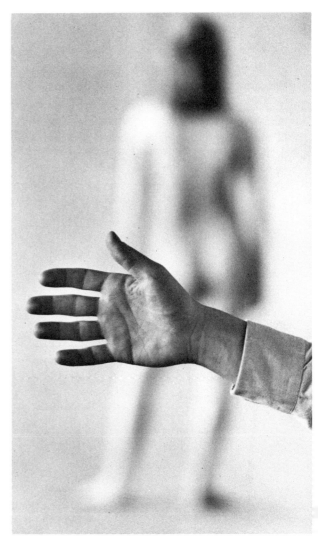

Pictures made with a 200-mm lens, one when it was
focused on the model, the other when focused on the
hand. The hand and the model are about 30 feet
apart, though the lens seems to compress the distance.
There was not enough depth of field to make both
subjects sharp. Having fuzzy areas in a picture is
called "using selective focus." That is, you select some
things to be sharp and others to be fuzzy (or out of
focus). There are a lot of interesting possibilities in
this technique, for it changes the appearance of
reality in strange and exciting ways.

aperture (diaphragm) one *f*-number smaller, for example, to change from *f*/8 to *f*/11. To open up a stop we would go from *f*/8 to *f*/5.6. This "stop" jargon is used all the time in photography, so you ought to concentrate on remembering it.

Depth of field can be *increased* in yet another way: by focusing on something farther away from the camera. In contrast, it is *decreased* by focusing on something closer. When your subject is *very* close to your camera—for example, when you are using close-up attachments on the lens—there is hardly any depth of field at all. Many cameras have **depth-of-field scales** marked on the lens barrel. They look pretty tricky but aren't really. There are two sets of numbers opposite each other. It helps if you remember what they stand for. One stands for feet (or, sometimes, meters, which are a little more than *three* feet). The other stands for *f*-numbers, or *f*-stops.

The foot (or meter) scale tells you how far away from you things are. You can use it to learn to estimate distances, a useful skill in photography. All you have to do is focus on an object, then look at the scale and read how far away it is. You can also read the depth of field without having to adjust the scale.

Say that the object is 8 feet away. The number 8 will be right across from the scale's center mark. On either side of the center mark is a duplicate series of *f*-numbers. The similar numbers on either side closest to the center mark will be the *f*-number representing the speed of the lens (the largest *f*-stop, for example, *f*/2).

As I've suggested, there will be two *f*/2s. On the scale, one will be right across from the distance (in feet or meters) that represents the *near* side of the depth of field. The other *f*/2 will be across from the number for the far distance. If you shoot your picture with the aperture set at *f*/2 this is precisely your depth of field—which includes the near and far distances within which objects are acceptably sharp and the sharpest point of all, which is approximately in the middle.

If you stop down to *f*/8 you use the two *f*/8 markings on the scale. You will find the near distance nearer, the far distance farther, and the total depth of field greater. The depth of field itself is not indicated, but you can figure it out by subtracting the near distance from the far. Subtract and you get the depth in numbers, representing either feet or meters (sometimes both, on two separate scales).

Many people are very frightened of the depth-of-field scale, because it has numbers on it. Packages of meat at the grocery store have numbers on them too, but that doesn't make them ominous. Read and reread what I've just written. Then you will find that the scale is less terrifying. Study also the picture of the lens with the depth-of-field scale—and the caption with it.

A 28-mm lens, showing the depth-of-field scale (bottom) and the *f*-number settings (top). You can see that the aperture is set at about *f*/11 and the lens focused at 4 feet. This gives us a depth of field (depth of sharpness) from about 2¾ to 8 feet. All objects falling within this range will be acceptably sharp.

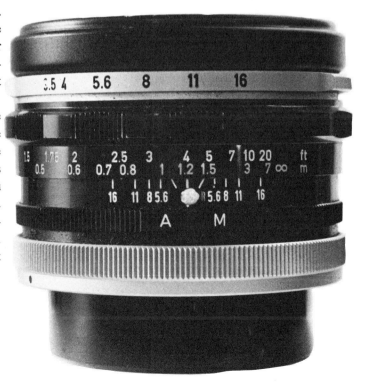

● Depth of Field and the SLR

One of the main reasons for the great popularity of the SLR (single-lens reflex) is that you can actually *see* the depth of field before you take your picture. The object you focus on looks sharp. Things in front and behind look progressively less sharp. You can't see this at all with rangefinder cameras.

You focus an SLR with the lens wide open (at the largest aperture). With this lens setting, the image is as bright as it can get, so that you can see well to focus accurately.

Unless you are working in dim light, however, you usually make your picture with the lens stopped down. This changes the depth of field, of course. With less expensive SLRs you stop the lens down to the desired *f*-number manually before shooting. Then you can see the image is perceptibly darker in the viewfinder. You can also see that the depth of field has been increased. Seeing this depth is very useful, for it tells you a good deal concerning how your picture is going to look. It won't look that dark, however.

On most SLRs the stopping down is automated. You preselect the *f*-stop you want to use and set a pointer at that marking. This doesn't actually change the aperture size. This happens when you shoot your picture and the camera stops itself down. It stops down before it permits the shutter to open.

The mirror is also lifted out of the way after the shutter release is pressed. If it weren't, no light would reach the film. After the exposure, both the mirror and the aperture return to the pre-exposure position. With the mirror back in place you can still see your subject. With the aperture fully open again it has maximum visibility. With most shutter speeds this happens so rapidly that you're hardly even aware of it. Thus, there is no perceptible break in the continuity of your seeing. This break is very disturbing in cameras that aren't automated.

With many SLRs there are ways of "previewing" your depth of field. That is, you can push a button or twist a ring and stop the lens down for a look, then open up again for maximum visibility through the viewfinder. As I've said, the final stopping down is automatic.

There are great advantages of this depth of field preview capability. One of them is that you'll get a much better idea of what your picture will look like if you are photographing things close to your camera. Or when part of your subject is nearby and the rest quite a distance away.

In these circumstances the image is often radically altered by stopping down. That is, what you see with the aperture wide open in the focusing position is not at all like the picture you'll get when stopped down. By previewing, you see what the difference will be.

● Depth of Field and the Rangefinder

You will recall that sighting through a rangefinder camera is looking through an actual window, not seeing an image passed through the camera lens into an optical system. Therefore, *everything* looks sharp *all* the time. The problem is that lenses don't see that way. You may see something as sharp and the lens may record it as out of focus on the film.

For a good many kinds of pictures this doesn't matter at all, for example, shooting subjects that are more than five feet away, in daylight. Assuming you've remembered to focus, most of the time you'll get pretty much what you see in the viewfinder. This is even more probable if you favor wide-angle lenses, which give you a great depth of field. Lenses give the very same depth of field on rangefinder cameras as they do on SLRs.

● Door Versus Door

You will recall that the diaphragm (aperture) and the shutter function as doors. They both let light into the camera. One controls its intensity, the other its duration. The sections on subject and body movement talked about sacrificing small

20

apertures in favor of large, to get as high as possible shutter speed in dim light. As you can now see, this also entails sacrificing depth of field.

Many a time photography is an either/or proposition. In moderately bright light, you can either stop movement or get great depth of field. You can't do both. In sunlight you can, of course. If you demand both indoors, you have to use either high-output tungsten or electronic-flash light sources, especially if you are using color films, which are relatively slow.

• Automated Cameras

Many of the things that have been discussed in the section on lenses and shutters are taken care of by automated cameras. To a large degree they do your thinking and remembering for you. You just point them at your subject and they choose their own shutter speeds and aperture settings. Whether you have one or not, it is still a good idea to know the problems they have to solve. Another excuse for including the lens and shutters section is that there are numerous advantages to having cameras that are not automated, or in which automation systems can be manually overridden.

If you wish to do the thinking for yourself, the information I've given is critically important. Many readers have no choice, of course, for they already have thinking cameras that can't be manually overridden or, in contrast, ordinary cameras that hardly think for themselves at all.

FILM

Photographic film consists mainly of a thin, clear, flexible plastic sheeting with gelatin coated on one side of it. Though the gelatin is the same basic stuff as Jell-O, it has been thoroughly dried, so that it is quite tough and hard.

Finely mixed in the gelatin are light-sensitive silver compounds. The gelatin functions as a glue that makes them stick to the plastic base. The mixture of gelatin with a silver compound is called an **emulsion,** which is a term you should remember.

The coated side of the film is called the **emulsion side,** or merely **the emulsion.** The uncoated side is called the **backing side,** or **backing.**

● Roll Film

For use in the cameras we've discussed, film is cut into long strips, then rolled on spools. With 35-mm films the spooled film is kept in light-tight cassettes, with one end left protruding so that the film can be attached to the mechanism that feeds it through the camera.

The 126 cartridges are completely self-contained and have two spools built into them. One is for the unexposed film. The other, called the "take-up spool," is for film with images exposed on it. The cartridge completely eliminates the confusion of threading film across sprockets and into gear systems.

Larger-size roll films such as 120 have only the spools themselves with film rolled on them. How-

ever, to keep the film from getting exposed to light, it is backed with a light-impervious strip of paper, called the **backing paper.**

The film in the 126 cartridge is also backed with paper, but the photographer never touches it until he breaks open the cartridge to remove the film for development.

In all three spooling systems the film is loaded **emulsion-side in.** Thus, if you hold a bare roll of film in your hand your fingers are touching the **backing,** *not* the **emulsion.** In a moment you'll see why it's important to know this.

● Black-and-White

If you've looked ahead you've seen that the book gets into film development and enlargement printing and that it deals with black-and-white images, not color. Do-it-yourself color developing and printing are a bit too complex for beginners. However, when you've got a good background in black-and-white work, it will be relatively easy for you to go into color.

Beginners are always advised to choose one film and stick to it. Jumping from one kind of film to another will only confuse you.

If your camera has shutter speeds as high as $\frac{1}{500}$ sec, use Kodak Tri-X (ASA 400) exclusively. If the speeds don't go that high, use either Verichrome Pan or Plus-X, which are rated at ASA 125. But choose only one of them and stick with it. The only problem with Tri-X is that it is

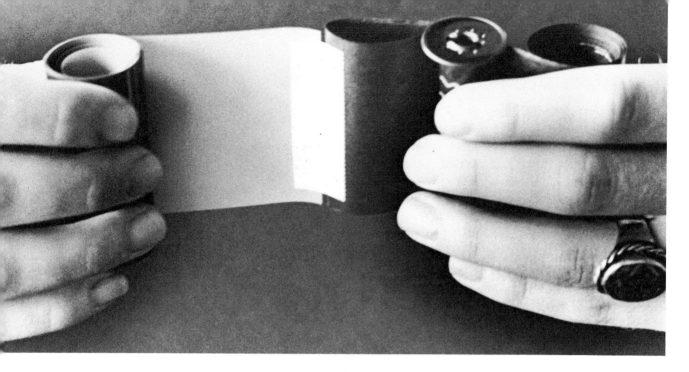

The proper way to separate roll film from its paper backing. The film is in front, the backing paper behind it. One must not touch the surface of the film; and it should be held only by the eges. This is all done in total darkness.

too fast for some cameras. Otherwise it is the world's best all-around black-and-white film.

• Film Speed

The speed of a film is its relative sensitivity to light. Thus, a fast film is very sensitive to it, a slow one less so. The sensitivity is given in numbers as the **ASA speed,** which is an international standard. Fast films have speeds around ASA 400 or higher. Medium speeds are around ASA 125. And slow films are around ASA 50 or lower.

ASA speeds are related arithmetically. Thus ASA 400 is twice as fast as ASA 200, four times as fast as ASA 100, and eight times as fast as ASA 50.

Beginners find it hard to understand just what these differences really mean. Their inclination is to think that an ASA 1600 film is *immensely* faster than one rated at ASA 400, for 1600 is a large number and 400 relatively small. Actually, the speed difference isn't much. The ASA 1600 film is only *four times* as fast as the ASA 400 film.

Let us see what difference it would make photographing in dim light, where high-speed films are much sought after. Let us say that you are already using your maximum lens aperture (say $f/2$) and a shutter speed of $\frac{1}{8}$ sec with an ASA 400 film. Since you wish to use a higher shutter speed, you think of using a faster film. An ASA 800 film will allow $\frac{1}{16}$ sec and an ASA 1600 one will only allow you to boost this up to $\frac{1}{30}$ sec. Not so much difference, is it?

You should keep this information in mind to discourage you from going gung ho for superhigh film speeds, for reasons we'll now discuss, or for pushing film speeds in development, which will be mentioned again later. Beginners should avoid both these traps like the plague.

23

FILM

● Speed and Grain

A developed film image is called a negative, because the tones of the subject come out reversed (negative). If an object is *light* it comes out *dark* on the film. *Dark* objects result in *light* (**thin** or **clear**) areas. Photographers prefer the terms "thin" or "clear." They like the term **heavy** for dark areas.

One of the characteristics of negatives is granularity, which shows up in enlargement prints as a kind of sandy look. It makes smooth objects look as if they were made of granite or sandstone.

Grain is related to film speed. With a very fast film you often get **coarse-grain,** medium speed: **medium-grain,** slow speed: **fine-grain.** This way of relating speed to grain is an ancient formula in photography. However, photographic scientists have been working for years to make fast fine-grain films.

Though it is fast, Tri-X is a fine-grain film. Those who want even finer grain should try Panatomic-X (ASA 32). However, it is not recommended for beginners, as there are certain tricks to using it properly. Furthermore, people shouldn't get hung up on grain as such. There are immensely more important things for one to concern oneself with in photography.

● Correct Exposure

Taking a picture involves exposing your film to the proper quantity (intensity × time) of light. As mentioned earlier, the light that strikes the film is in the form of an image, or light pattern. It is useful to remember that this image *is* light and is *nothing but* light.

If you are photographing John Brown, the only thing relating to him that ever gets into your camera is the light that he reflects. The lens collects the light that is reflected by various parts of his body and forms it into an image on the film plane.

There are several factors that you take into consideration in determining the correct exposure:

1. *Light intensity:* How much light is falling on your subject?

2. *Subject reflectance:* Is your subject reflecting a large percentage of the light (white rabbit), a small percentage (black cat), or an average percentage (like things you photograph most of the time)?

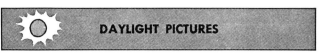

DAYLIGHT PICTURES

Set your exposure meter or automatic camera at ASA 125. If your negatives are consistently too light, increase exposure by using a lower film speed number; if too dark, reduce exposure by using a higher number.

If you don't have an exposure meter or automatic camera, use the exposures given in the following table.

DAYLIGHT EXPOSURE TABLE FOR *PLUS-X* PAN FILM			
For *average* subjects, use f-number below appropriate lighting condition.			
Shutter Speed 1/200 or 1/250 Second	**Shutter Speed 1/100 or 1/125 Second**		
Bright or Hazy Sun (Distinct Shadows)	**Cloudy Bright (No Shadows)**	**Heavy Overcast**	**Open Shade†**
f/11*	f/8	f/5.6	f/5.6

*f/16 at 1/200 or 1/250 second for brilliant scenes, such as those containing much sand or snow—OR
f/8 at 1/100 or 1/125 second for backlighted close-up subjects.
†Subject shaded from the sun but lighted by a large area of sky.

For handy reference, slip this table into your camera case.

Charts of this kind come with film or with flashbulbs. They are very carefully designed by the manufacturer and highly useful for making exposure determinations. Using them, one can get along very well most of the time without owning an exposure meter. This helps explain why so many people take successful pictures without even knowing the most fundamental facts about photography. A chart of this type has to be carefully read, however, and this takes a little effort.

3. *Angle of reflectance:* Is your subject front-lighted, sidelighted, or backlighted?

4. *Film speed:* How sensitive to light is your film? Therefore, what quantity of light is required to expose it properly?

There are several devices for helping you measure these factors and relate their effects: exposure meters, daylight exposure charts, floodlight exposure charts, and flash guides or computers. The easiest to use and quite dependable are the charts and flash guides.

• Charts and Flash Guides

Charts explaining how to use the film come in every film package. Flash guides are printed on the carton that flash bulbs or cubes come in, or on the flash gun itself. Charts and guides are very dependable—if you do *exactly* what they say you should. They have certain limitations you should know about, however.

One is that they assume you are going to photograph something that reflects an average amount of light. For 97 per cent of the time you will, but not always. If you follow charts and guides and photograph something that is very light (snow, a polar bear), you will overexpose your picture. In photographing something very dark (a black or dark gray thing) you will underexpose. Though you should be aware of this, it isn't something to worry about unduly, for practically always you'll be photographing subjects of average reflectance.

The daylight exposure chart that comes with your film is extremely reliable in certain sections. The readings it gives for "bright sun" and "hazy sun" are entirely reliable. "Cloudy bright" and "open shade" are reliable most of the time. The "heavy overcast" exposure is not reliable at all. In this case an exposure meter is a must.

The floodlight exposure charts you find in photography books are usually very safe to use. So are the flash computers built into most modern flash units. The charts for flashcubes are even more accurate. Using such data, one can get along

very well without an exposure meter, which is a fairly recent invention. Not so long ago there were no meters, and photographers got along very well indeed by relying on charts, guides, and their own experience.

• Separate Exposure Meters

All the meters mentioned earlier can be used in two distinctly different ways: one, to point at the light source—two, to point at the subject. You must understand that these approaches are *entirely* different.

A light-source reading is called an **incident reading** and requires an incident meter or having an **incident attachment** slid over, or attached to, the light-sensitive cell of a reflectance meter. It is usually an opalescent sphere.

For beginners, **incident readings** are usually the most accurate—if the light is striking the subject straight-on or at an angle no greater than 45 degrees. Taking the reading is dead easy. You just stand *in front of your subject* and point the incident sphere halfway between the light source and where you intend to stand to take your picture. Simple to do and very accurate.

However, the calibration of incident meters and meters with incident attachments assumes that your subject is reflecting an average amount of light. For very light subjects you've got to **close down** an *f*-stop or more to compensate. For very dark subjects, open up. In either case, it's best to shoot at *several* different *f*-stops to make sure that *one* of them will be the correct exposure. This is called **exposure bracketing.** It is so effective that it is very popular with advanced amateurs and professionals. It works best for static subjects such as buildings, landscapes, still lifes, and so on. Since these things aren't going anywhere, you can take as many bracketing shots as you like and know that your picture won't slip away from you. With moving subjects, exposure bracketing usually isn't practical.

The other kind of reading, where you point your meter at your subject, is called a **reflectance**

reading. You are actually measuring (reading) the light that your subject reflects. For this kind of reading be sure that the **incident attachment** has been slid aside or removed. You cannot accurately make reflectance reading with an incident attachment or make good incident readings with a meter at the reflectance setting. This is a common mistake you should avoid. Except for built-ins, most meters can be used for both incident and reflectance readings.

Even if you are a beginner, most of your reflectance readings will be fully reliable. They will not be, however, if your subject is in front of either a very light or very dark background and you are standing far enough away to read *both* the subject and background. The problem is easily solved if you move up close enough to read *only the subject*. With that exposure data you can then back up again and take your picture.

● **Built-in Meters**

Built-ins are reflectance meters and are very reliable, except when your subject is in front of a very light or very dark background. You solve this problem just as you would with a separate meter, provided that your camera can be operated manually. You move up close so that you're reading only your subject. (You can see the exact coverage in your camera viewfinder.) Then you stand back again to take your picture. This trick is probably the main secret of using a built-in on manual operation. And not using it is the main source of failure.

There is potentially a mechanical source of error with built-ins: a worn-out battery, which will give readings that are too low and lead to overexposure. Be sure your battery is fresh before starting on a vacation or camera field trip.

● **Meters in General**

Reflectance meters, either separate or built-in, take care of the angle-of-reflectance factor with-

out your having to think about it. All you have to remember (very important) is to take your reading from the same angle you intend to take your picture from. It just won't do to read the back or side of a subject, then shoot it from the front.

Incident meters do not compensate for the angle-of-reflectance factor, which is why using the incident attachment is suggested only if your subject is lighted straight-on or at an angle no greater than 45 degrees. Forgetting this rule will rapidly lead to inaccurate exposures.

All meters compensate for the film-speed factor, provided that you set the speed on the meter dial. Failure to do this completely destroys the validity of your readings. Though most separate meters can be used for both incident and reflectance readings (with different settings or attachments), people tend to use a given type mainly for just one method. For example, the Weston meters for reflectance, the Copal/Sekonic L-398 for incidence.

Darkroom Techniques

HOW TO PREPARE AND EQUIP A DARKROOM

For developing film or making prints, you need a completely darkened place in which to work, because photographic films and papers are very sensitive to light. If any light whatever falls on film it will fog (turn dark), utterly ruining any pictures that are on it. Thus it must be taken from its cassette in total darkness. If ordinary light falls on printing paper it will also fog. However, there are special colored lights (safelights) that don't affect it. Though they are dim as well as colored, they provide good visibility and solve the fog problem.

The basic requirement for a developing and printing room is that there be some way of shutting out all light from outside, which may take time and ingenuity. It is far easier to wait until dark, when there is no light around. Then almost any kind of space will make an adequate darkroom. The kitchen is often the best place, because it has running water and work surfaces for enlarger, trays, printing paper, etc. Bathrooms are popular too, but they usually lack work surfaces. However, this can be remedied by moving in a card table and putting a piece of heavy plywood on top of the bathtub.

Running water is by no means a requirement for your workroom, because you can easily carry water anywhere in the house in a plastic bucket. Those who share your home with you may not like your tying up the kitchen or bathroom all evening or having to sit around with most of the lights out, so you should consider setting up in a more remote place and transporting your chemicals in a bucket. A corner of an attic or bedroom is fine. In warm weather you can even work in the garage or on an open back porch, provided there are no street lights nearby.

You may find waiting for nightfall inconvenient —especially in summer, when the days are long. If so, you should consider making a temporary or permanent daytime darkroom, which is actually fairly easy to do. You can effectively block out the light by covering windows and doors with heavy black paper held up with staples, pushpins, carpet tacks, or black masking tape.

A cheap, readily available, and effective type of black paper is roofing paper (tar paper), which you can buy at hardware or building-supply stores. It comes in long rolls that are thirty-six inches wide, which is wider than most door or window frames. There is enough in one inexpensive roll to last a lifetime. You can even block out the doors in a double garage and have most of a roll left over.

Though roofing paper is very heavy, you can easily cut it with ordinary sewing scissors. For a temporary darkroom, cut panels that fit to the edges of the door and window frames, then hold them up with pushpins. If too much light leaks around the edges, tape them down with masking tape. When you are through printing, remove the pushpins and tape, roll up the panels, and store them away for the next time. For a permanent darkroom, use staples or tacks and black tape.

Though roofing paper is most convenient, you can use any material that will block out light, including cardboard, wallboard, plywood, heavy black felt, black Con-Tact paper, craft paper, lead-lined window-shade material, black paint (for window panes), and heavy black plastic sheeting. However, some of these materials require the use of complicated tools, whereas you need only scissors for the black paper.

For a permanent darkroom, you should systematically trace down all light leaks through or around your panels, carefully plugging each one with black paper or tape. You will soon have a room in which you can safely remove film from its cassette. For a temporary darkroom, blocking

every leak might prove inexpedient, because it could take you an hour or more each time.

For printing, it is nice to have a room that is absolutely dark until the safelights are turned on, yet this total darkness isn't really required. A *little* light leaking in won't do any harm. The question is, how much is a little? This rough check will easily tell you: Turn out all the lights in the room and wait about ten minutes, until your eyes are fully dark-adapted. If you can then *barely* make out the outlines of the things in the room, it is probably dark enough for printing. However, you shouldn't take printing paper out of its package and leave it lying around for more than a few seconds.

A darkroom made by light-trapping a window with black paper

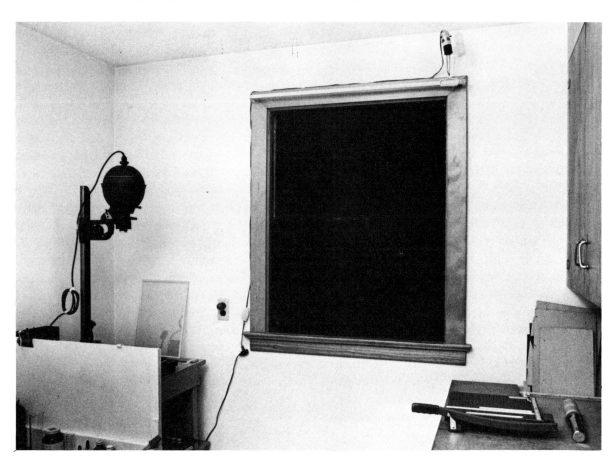

A room with this much light leaking in may or may not be dark enough for developing film, so you have to be careful, and there is a risk involved. You see, film is *much* more sensitive to light than photographic paper. Fortunately, there is a way in which we can use such a darkroom safely: by using a film-changing bag.

Since film has to be exposed to the air for only a short time when we are developing it, we need absolute darkness for just a few minutes. The critical period is when we are removing it from its cassette and putting it in a developing reel. Once it is in the developing tank it is safe, for tanks are absolutely lighttight.

With a film-changing bag, you can get through the critical steps very safely, even in a well-lighted room. It is a black, lighttight zippered bag with two elastic armholes. You put the film, reel, tank, and a beer-can opener (for opening the cassette) in it, then zipper it closed. Next, you put your hands and arms through the lighttight armholes, remove the film from its cassette, load it into the reel, put the reel in the tank, and put the cover on. Since the rest of the developing procedure can be carried out in daylight, you can see how the changing bag solves the problem of a darkroom that is not quite dark enough. However, don't buy one until you've tried to solve the problem of blacking out your workroom; you may not need it.

Most people have little choice in the room they can use for photography; they have to take whatever is available. Besides kitchens and bathrooms, people often use bedrooms, utility rooms, porches, garages, basement storage rooms, hallways, attics, and even walk-in closets. As we've seen, almost any area in a house or apartment will work, so long as the white light can be shut out.

The problem of finding work surfaces for the enlarger, trays, paper, etc., is a comparatively minor one, because almost any stable surface will do. You can use card tables, chairs, bureau tops, boards across sawhorses, wooden crates, shelves, stove and refrigerator tops, and so on. Even an ironing board will work well (for trays), provided it is shoved against the wall for stability.

Unfortunately, photographic chemicals may soften or curdle varnish and paint and can permanently stain Formica. You should therefore cover surfaces for your chemical trays with sheets of plastic, rubber, or roofing paper. Discarded plastic tablecloths, shower curtains, and tarpaulins are good and can easily be cut to any size. Saran Wrap and wax paper are fine. In a pinch you can use newspapers, but the chemicals soak through if you splash too much.

The chemicals are most destructive if they are left to stand for several days in puddles, for they will turn paint, varnish, and linoleum into a thick gravy. However, if you wipe them up right away they do no discernible damage, for they are slow-acting.

Most photographers like a darkroom to have a wet and a dry side. That is, chemicals and water are confined to one side, and things that must be

Using a film-changing bag to load film on a developing reel. In this lightproof zippered bag are a cassette of film, a beer-can opener, a developing reel, the developing tank, and the tank top. Absolute darkness prevails inside.

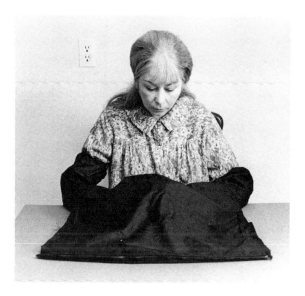

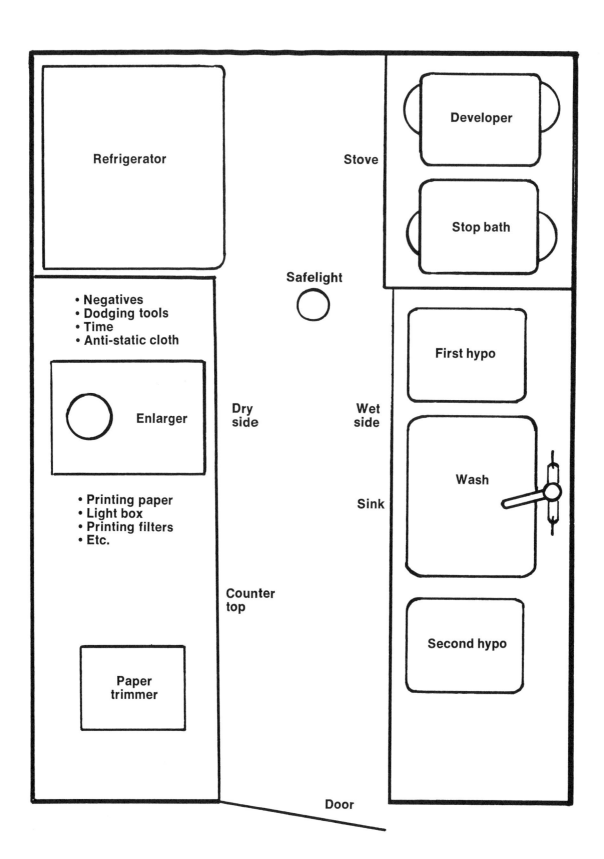

kept dry (enlarger, negatives, paper, etc.) to the other. We thus separate wet and dry things, because water and chemicals will ruin equipment and materials—even the enlarger, which only *looks* indestructible.

Unfortunately, many people haven't enough room for both a dry side and a wet side and may even have to line up their chemical trays right next to their enlargers. This is all right if you take great care to avoid any splashing whatever, though it is also a good idea to rig up high splash-boards, or partitions, with cardboard and masking tape—just in case. The big problem here is that under the dim illumination of a safelight, people invariably splash a lot more than they think. Because they can't see the splashes, they assume they are not there, and by the time they discover them the damage may be done.

If possible, it is good to have two safelights, one near the enlarger and the other positioned directly over the print-developing tray. If you buy them from a photography store, ask for ones with either OC or S55-X filters, or shields, because they can be used with variable-contrast paper as well as the regular kind. However, you can save a lot of money by buying 7½-watt red GE bulbs and using them with ordinary cords or lamps. They also can be used with any paper, but they don't light up the developer tray quite as brightly. This is a bit frustrating, yet it won't affect the quality of your prints.

Though most inexpensive enlargers on the market today are quite good, the cheapest plastic models are a little flimsy. Therefore, it is best to invest as much as you can. Your best bet may be to buy a secondhand version of an expensive machine. If the lens is unscratched and the mechanical parts are in good working order, you can usually trust it, because there is not much that tends to go wrong in a good enlarger. A little rust on

the enlarger head or scratches on the baseboard will do no harm. Defective wiring, which is most often the only thing wrong, can easily be replaced. Indeed, a disreputable-looking machine may function splendidly—and sell for a song—provided it was a good enlarger to begin with. In contrast, when a very cheap enlarger decides to fall apart, it goes all the way and there is nothing you can do about it.

For print processing, you will need five plastic trays. If you intend to make 8×10 prints you can get along fine with 8×10 trays, though they do cramp you a little bit. If you have enough money and a large enough work space, buy the 11×14 size. I will explain later what the various trays are for.

When making prints, the paper is held in place with a special hinged frame called a printing easel. It will give white print borders of any width desired. Though easels are convenient, the good ones are also expensive, so don't buy one until you have read how you can easily make one for yourself (Appendix).

In making a print, you need a way of controlling the duration of its exposure to the enlarger light, for which special electric timers are usually used. Since they are quite expensive, consider buying a cheap, hand-wound metronome from a music store. It works just as well. A clock with a sweep second hand is very good. So is a watch with a sweep second hand, but you have to rig up a little darkroom spotlight in order to see the dial. It should show light only where you want it to. You can make one by taping a four inch cylinder of black paper around the bulb end of a penlight. If you have to, you can time exposures by counting seconds under your breath, which is quite all right for many prints. However, some need more accurate timing.

For film processing, you will need a film reel and tank; a thermometer; a watch, clock, or timer, and a few other things, all of which will be discussed in the next chapter.

Most chemicals come in dry form. After they are mixed they should be stored in airtight bot-

Diagram showing how a kitchen can be used as a temporary darkroom

tles. Wine, juice, and cider bottles work very well. Plastic bottles, especially bleach containers, are not so good—unless you buy the special brown plastic bottles sold in photo stores. All in all, it is best to mix your chemicals in half-gallon quantities, unless you do a lot of work. Then you might find it more convenient to mix in gallon lots. You can also save quite a bit of money that way.

It is unnecessary at this point to explain the other things you will need for equipping your darkroom, but you will find it useful to have a partial list of them. At the appropriate time you will learn what everything is and how it should be used. Since the list is long you may find it frightening. However, most of the items aren't expensive. Though it will surely take you some time to gather everything together, you will never have to go through this particular hassle again.

A setup for making enlargements. A splashboard (on the left) protects the equipment from the chemicals.

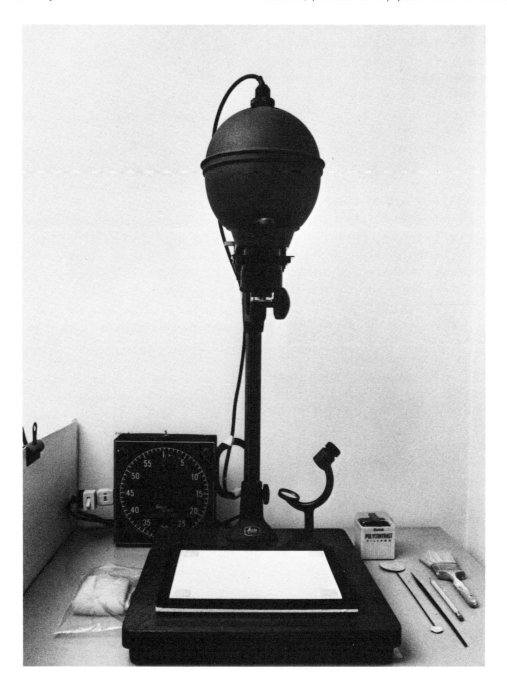

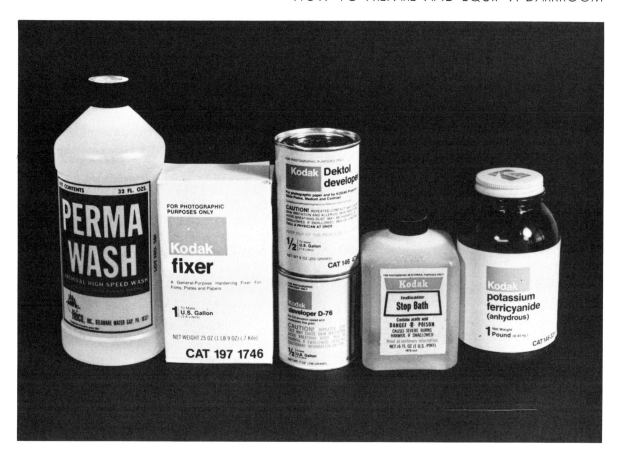

Some chemicals that are commonly used in photography

● **Photographic Equipment**

Enlarger

Enlarging easel (optional)

Photographic timer or metronome (optional)

Photographic sponge

Print-trimming board (optional)

Five print-processing trays, 8×10 or 11×14

Focus magnifier (optional)

Tray siphon (for washing prints) (optional)

Two print tongs, rubber-tipped bamboo (optional)

Photographic thermometer, preferably stainless steel

● **Photographic Chemicals**

D-76 film developer

Dektol print developer

Kodak Indicator Stop Bath

Regular acid-hardening fixing bath (hypo), in the dry form

Perma Wash (hypo eliminator), 1 quart

Potassium ferricyanide crystals (for bleaching), 1 pound

Kodak Photo-Flo solution, 1 pint

Kodak or Edwal hypo test kit (optional)

A spray can of Marshall's Film Klens (anti-static film cleaner)

• Miscellaneous Equipment

Two-gallon plastic pail (for mixing chemicals and carrying water)

Beer-can opener (for opening Kodak film cassettes)

Old turkish towels (for keeping fingers clean and dry)

Chemical stirring rod, stick, or large plastic spoon

Plastic or glass funnel, preferably with a filter

Glass or plastic measuring cup, pint or quart size

Several ordinary viscose sponges (for cleaning up)

Dodging and burning-in tools (homemade)

Lens-cleaning tissues (for cleaning enlarger lens and condenser)

Silicone negative- or record-cleaning cloth

Package of Q-Tips (for bleaching)

Package of surgical cotton (for bleaching)

Photographic spotting brush (for print retouching)

A no. 4 pointed sable brush (for cleaning negatives)

Bottle of black Spotone spotting dye

A plastic lemonade pitcher, gallon size

Four sheets of 12×16-inch single-strength glass (from the hardware store) (for making contact sheets)

Roll of 1-inch masking tape

Scissors

An 11×14-inch piece of ¾-inch plywood (for a borderless easel)

Roll of carpet tape (for easel)

White Con-Tact paper, 11×14 inches (for easel)

Two dozen rubber hose washers (for easel)

Small can of lighter fluid (for cleaning negatives)

Pint of rubbing alcohol (for cleaning negatives)

Bottles (for storing chemicals)

Comet or Ajax-type cleanser (for cleaning trays)

Paper towels (for bleaching and print retouching)

One ounce of Kodak black opaque (for negative retouching)

Depending on what you wish to do with your photography, there may be other things you will need. However, our list has already reached a terrifying length, so I will mention additional items only at the appropriate places in the book. After learning what they are for, you can decide for yourself whether to invest in them.

Be sure you understand that the things listed as optional actually *are* optional. That is, you can get along very well without them or use homemade, but very effective, substitutes, thus saving yourself a substantial amount of money. If you are ingenious you can even make your own enlarger, though it is not listed here as optional.

HOW TO DEVELOP FILM

A roll of film is a long strip of thin plastic that is coated on one side with toughened gelatin containing light-sensitive silver compounds in the form of extremely small crystals. We call them light-sensitive because they can be chemically changed by light.

When you take a picture, the light reflected by various parts of your subject passes through the camera lens, which focuses it on the film. There the light forms a visible image of your subject in complete detail. If you could stand inside your camera you would see that it looks like a projected color slide. It is important to understand that this image on the film is composed entirely of light and nothing else, and that some parts of it are brighter than others. For example, a white cat will show up brighter than a black dog.

Try to understand that the image lying on the surface of the film is *light energy,* with the white cat having a lot of it and the black dog very little or none. In the area of gelatin beneath the cat the silver compounds will be acted on by a lot of this light energy and thus be chemically changed to a considerable degree. In the area beneath the black dog there will be little or no change.

Though these chemical changes are real they aren't visible at this point. The cat, the dog, and their environment have formed a "latent image" in the gelatin, not a visible one. This means, how-

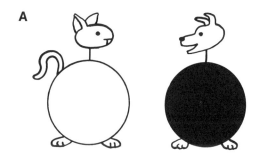

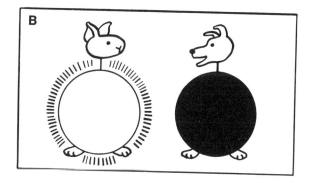

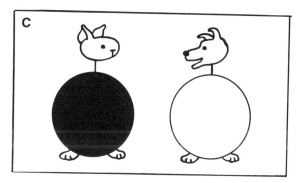

ever, that it is a *potentially* visible one, provided that it is treated with a chemical developer.

If a section of the film has been acted on by a sufficient amount of light energy it can be chemically developed. That is, a developer will break up the light-energized silver compounds, converting them into certain gases, which escape, and pure metallic silver, which happens to be black. The image, now fully visible, is made entirely of this black silver. Of course, the more silver an area contains the darker it is, and vice versa. Areas with none at all are transparent.

Crystals insufficiently exposed to light will not be developed. Since they are still light-sensitive they must be gotten rid of somehow. Otherwise, on exposure to light they will soon turn black, completely obliterating the image. It is the function of the fixing bath to take care of this problem, which it does by changing the light-sensitive silver crystals into a hypo-silver compound. This new compound is entirely insensitive to light. Furthermore, it is water-soluble, so we can rid the gelatin of it completely by washing the film in running water.

When you examine developed film you will see that the tones of your subject are reversed. For example, our white cat is now black, the black dog white (clear or transparent). For this reason we call a developed film image a "negative." Though the logic behind this is unclear, it is standard photographic jargon nonetheless. The gelatin part of film (or paper) is the "emulsion." The fixing bath is usually called "hypo."

Momentarily letting a light-image fall on the film in your camera is "exposure" or "making an exposure." When we are printing we "make exposures" by turning on the enlarger light. The light-sensitive compounds that we use are "silver halides," such as silver bromide and silver iodide.

The jargon is an important part of photography, but I am introducing it as gradually as possible. Learn the terms as fast as you can, because they will help you to read photography books and magazines, and to communicate with others interested in photography.

• Things You Need to Develop Film

Exposed film
Developing tank and reel
Photographic thermometer
Timer, clock, or watch
Funnel (glass or plastic)
Measuring cup (glass or plastic)
Photographic sponge
String
Clothespins
Towel
Scissors
Beer-can opener
Glassine negative sleeves
D-76 developer solution
Fixing solution (hypo)
Perma Wash solution (optional)
Photo-Flo solution (optional)
Water
Stirring rod, stick, or plastic spoon
Plastic bucket
Storage bottles for D-76 and hypo solutions

Developing tanks and reels: The ones most recommended for both beginners and advanced photographers are the GAF (Anscomatic), Paterson, and Nikor types. The easiest to use is the GAF, closely followed by the Paterson. The most difficult (the problem is in loading the film in the reels) is the Nikor, but it is the most popular among advanced amateurs and professionals.

You can develop only one roll of film at a time in a GAF tank, but the Paterson and Nikor tanks come in various sizes, holding up to seven reels (Paterson) and sixteen (Nikor). Developing so much film at once is quite awkward, however, so if you wish to process more than one roll at a time you should settle for either the Paterson five-reel or the Nikor four-reel. I am referring here to 35-mm reels.

The GAF and Paterson tanks and reels are plastic, the Nikor stainless steel. However, the different reels are equally fragile, so that drop-

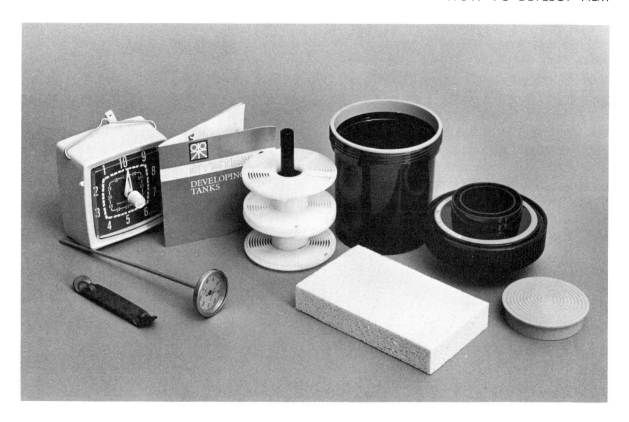

Equipment for developing film: (front) beer-can opener, photographic thermometer, photographic sponge; (rear) photographic timer, Paterson instruction manual, two Paterson "walk-in" reels, developing tank, tank top, and tank cap

ping one of them on the floor may ruin it. Nevertheless, with proper care the Nikor equipment will last for fifty years or more. Plastic tanks will last for years too, but they show signs of wear sooner, and plastics eventually deteriorate, even when not in use. You may in time have a warping problem with a GAF reel, which is made of ordinary plastic, but the Paterson nylon reel won't tend to warp.

The adjustable GAF and Paterson reels will accept various film sizes, including 120, 620, 127, 35-mm, 828, and 126 (cartridge-load). With Nikor we have non-adjustable reels in two sizes, one for 120 and 620, the other for 35-mm, 828,

and 126. As you see, Nikor reels cannot handle the 127 size, but few people use it now, anyway.

Thermometer: If you can afford it, buy a stainless-steel one. Glass thermometers break easily, and the thick ones take much too long to register changes in temperature.

Photographic sponge: Used for wiping water off processed film before hanging it up to dry. Since it has unusually fine texture it does this well, whereas ordinary viscose sponges do not.

Glassine negative envelopes: Used for storing and protecting negatives. Though you can use ordinary business envelopes or make your own negative sleeves out of typing paper, it isn't wise. In almost all papers, sulfur compounds are used as preservatives. In time they will degrade or destroy film images. So if you want your negatives to last your lifetime, buy the special envelopes, or sleeves.

Developer: Though there are numerous good developers available, the only one recommended here is Kodak D-76, a classical formula of great popularity. It is good, dependable, moderately fine-grain, and has a good "shelf life," which means that it can be stored in solution for several months without significant deterioration. In contrast, some developers "fall apart" rather rapidly. Though classified by Kodak as having "moderately fine grain," D-76 is used in certain custom labs for 35-mm film that is to be enlarged to mural size, which indicates that moderately fine is quite fine enough.

Fixing solution (hypo): Use either a regular acid-hardening fixing solution or a "rapid" (or "quick") fixer. Any brand will do, and you can buy it in either the dry chemical or solution form, though the dry form is cheaper. To save even more money, buy the one-gallon size.

Perma Wash: The best available "hypo eliminator," made by the Heico company. It will save you a good deal of time in washing both negatives and prints and help insure their longevity. By radically cutting down on the "wet time" it inhibits the development of graininess in negatives.

Photo-Flo: Like a dishwashing detergent, Photo-Flo breaks down the surface tension of water so that it will slide right off film rather than cling in large drops. Through tiny drops are all right, large ones cause ugly "drying marks" that are impossible to remove. If you soak your film in Photo-Flo just before hanging it up to dry, you don't have to use a sponge. However, you can use both if you wish.

• Getting the Developer Ready

Any kind of *film* developer that is sold in powder form should be mixed at least a day before you intend to use it, though the ones sold in liquid form can be used right away. All *paper* developers, however, can be used for printing as soon as they are mixed. D-76 comes as a powder, so mix it ahead of time. Using it too soon will lead to substantial overdevelopment, too much contrast, and a considerable amount of "grain" (a granular, or sandy, condition caused by the clumping together of silver particles).

The mixed developer is called the "stock" solution; for the "working" solution you dilute it with water 1:1 (half and half). If the D-76 is too cold (see chart), dilute it with warm water; too warm, dilute it with cold. If you wish to adjust the developer temperature *after* it has been diluted, use a one-gallon plastic food-storage bag filled with either ice cubes or hot water, stirring it around in the developer until the temperature is right. This way, you don't dilute the developer further.

Time and Temperature Film Developing Chart for D-76 Diluted 1:1

	Tri-X	Plus-X	Verichrome Pan
65F	11½ min	8½ min	9 min
68F	10	7¼	8½
70F	9	6½	7
72F	8¼	6	6¼
75F	7¼	5¼	5½

Some people prefer to make their developer dilutions right in the developing tank, others to do it in a pitcher or graduate. Since a film tank has a lighttight pour-in top, you can put the loaded film reel in a dry tank, shut out the light by putting on the top, then pour in the developer whenever you get around to it. Beginners generally prefer to do it this way, so that they won't panic in the dark. Advanced photographers do it the other way, putting the reel in the filled tank and capping it while still in the dark. This way, there is a little less chance of getting air bubbles on the film, which can cause little round spots on negatives.

● Time and Temperature

In photography, time and temperature controls are often critical, so you should never forget them. In film processing, you should combine exactly the right developing time with exactly the right developer temperature, or things will go awry. You can use different times and temperatures, but they must work together. For example, with a warm developer you use a short time, with a colder one a longer time—but you don't do this in an arbitrary way. Instead, you should carefully follow the time and temperature figures on our chart.

Do not suppose that you can accurately gauge temperature with your finger, because your judgment can easily be ten to fifteen degrees off without your noticing a thing. *Use a thermometer! Never guess,* or you will surely rue the day.

The time and temperature figures on our chart apply only to development in tanks of the types recommended in this book. For larger ones you need revised data.

The films charted are the only ones recommended. Kodak Tri-X and Plus-X are long-time favorites of the professionals, and most inexpensive cameras are specifically designed for use with either Plus-X or Verichrome Pan. So stick with these names and save yourself trouble. Whatever you do, don't buy off-brand, discount film, for it is usually years out of date and the photographic equivalent of a rotten egg.

In developing film be sure to stick within the recommended 65- to 75-degree temperature range, using the plastic-bag trick to bring your developer to temperature, if necessary. Below 65

degrees, developers lose much of their activity. Above 75, one of the ingredients (hydroquinone) may get too active, causing fog. And the emulsion gets too soft, so that it is easily damaged.

It is advisable to bring all solutions (rinse, hypo, wash water) to the same temperature as the developer, though a variation of two to three degrees in either direction is all right. You will get finer grain by thus limiting the temperature range. Once you've gotten all solutions to temperature, you can hold them there by setting their containers in a water bath, which is simply a deep tray of water at the desired temperature. Without this over-all temperature control you might have a coarse-grain problem, depending mainly on the type of film you are using and *how much* the temperatures vary from solution to solution. However, proper control takes the guesswork out of it.

● Film Handling

You have seen that film is a plastic strip with an emulsion on one side. Until the film has been processed the emulsion is sensitive to both light and your body chemistry (and numerous other things). Thus, if you touch the emulsion side you are likely to get permanent fingerprints—so don't touch it! It is all right to touch the other side (the "backing side") with clean dry hands, however.

Since both sides feel the same to your touch it is necessary to remember how film is loaded on its spool, which is always emulsion side in. Thus if you remove film from a cassette and pick up the spool, you know you are touching only the backing side, which is safe.

It would be wise to buy a practice roll at a photo store. It is out-of-date film sold at a large discount for people who wish to examine film in the daylight to see how it is spooled, then use it to practice loading their developing reels. Playing with just one roll can save you a lot of agony in the dark.

● **Loading Your Developing Reel**

Since the GAF, Paterson, and Nikor tank and reel sets come with excellent instructions it would be senseless to repeat them here. However, customers sometimes steal the instruction sheets, so make sure one is included with your purchase. And when you get it home take care not to lose it, lest after a lapse of a month or two you forget how to load and have to learn anew.

Paterson and GAF reels are of the "walk-in" type. You push one end of your film under a spring-loaded pin in the feed gate of the reel. Then you start twisting one flange of the reel back and forth, and this "walks" the film right into it, as easy as pie. Be sure to note the line in your instructions that tells you to round off the corners of the film with scissors. Otherwise, it is liable to jam.

Since the Nikor reel is considerably harder to load, you had better study the instructions carefully and be sure to work with a practice roll. First, load it several times while watching yourself in the daylight, next do it with your eyes closed, and, finally, do it several times in the dark. Without this practice you are very likely to come a cropper. If you start right out with exposed film it may jump its channels, so that some of your pictures will get stuck together in the developer. However, Nikor equipment is excellent, so don't let this dire warning make you shy away from it. But do your homework with your practice roll!

● **Agitation**

When you develop film it is necessary to "agitate" (stir up the developer) for five seconds every thirty seconds, which you do by simply moving the tank around. However, for the *first* thirty seconds of development the agitation should be continuous, mainly to get rid of air bubbles. If you let the tank just sit there you will get bubble marks ("air bells"), and the casual eddy currents in the developer will cause a disagreeable mottle on your negatives.

How you agitate can make a difference, too. The consensus among photographers is that the best method is to completely invert the developing tank, but this technique can cause development marks of another type. What we need is to randomize agitation, because random movement of the developer within the tank will give you very even development. The best bet is to use three different agitation methods. Use one for each 5-second agitation period, then repeat the sequence until the developing time is up. For the initial 30-second period, just perform the entire sequence twice.

This schedule of thirty seconds' agitation to start, followed by five seconds' agitation every thirty seconds, is a carefully worked out optimal technique. Don't agitate more than that or you'll get development marks of still another kind.

Method one: Invert the tank three or four times during the 5-second period. Method two: Rapidly spin the tank like a top, first clockwise, then counterclockwise, for the next period. Method three: Rapidly slide the tank back and forth on the table, for a distance of about one foot. When they are thus used in rotation, these three methods will give you very even development.

The GAF tank is designed so that it doesn't need to be inverted, spun, or slid back and forth. To agitate, you rapidly twist the little thermometer stirring rod that is provided. This will give you evenly developed negatives.

Film should also be agitated for its first thirty seconds in the fixing bath (hypo). Unless you do this you may have a problem with other types of processing defects. After the thirty seconds, however, you can let the tank just sit there until the fixing time is up.

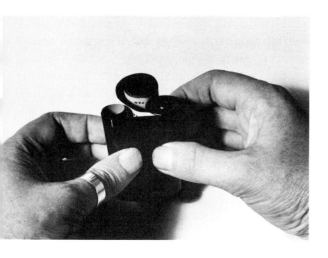

Separating roll film from its paper backing, taking care not to touch the emulsion side

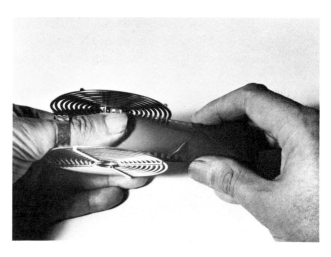

The initial step in loading a Nikor reel

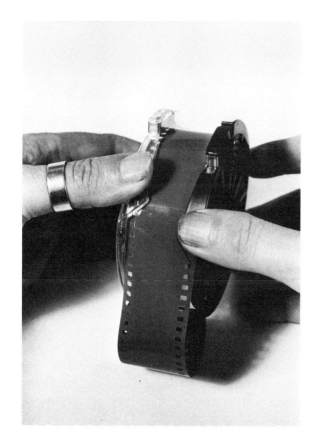

Loading film in a GAF reel. Twisting one flange of the reel "walks" the film right into it.

• Step by Step Film Processing

1. In total darkness, load the film reel and put it in the tank. Put the cover on and check to see that it is on all the way.

2. Turn on the room light.

3. Dilute the D-76 developer 1:1 and check the temperature, adjusting it if necessary.

4. Refer to the developing chart for the proper developing time and set the timer (if you are using one).

5. Put a container of water and another of hypo in a convenient place near the developing tank.

6. Pour the developer in the tank and start the timer (or check your watch).

7. Carefully following the agitation schedule and methods given, develop the film until only forty-five seconds remain of the preselected developing time.

8. Immediately pour the developer down the drain, discarding it, and fill the tank with water at the correct temperature. As soon as it is full, pour the water out again.

9. Immediately fill the tank with hypo and agitate vigorously for the first thirty seconds. After ten more minutes, pour the hypo *back into its storage bottle.* If you are using rapid fix, cut the time to five minutes. You may now take the top off the tank, because the film is no longer sensitive to light.

10. While it is still on the reel and in the tank, wash the film in rapidly running water at the right temperature for thirty seconds (or pour in five changes of water from a bucket).

11. Pour in a temperature-adjusted Perma Wash bath (¾ ounce per quart of water) and agitate ten seconds. After a total of thirty seconds, pour out the Perma Wash.

12. Wash the film for another thirty seconds in running water (or change the water five times).

13. Pour in a Photo-Flo solution, also temperature-adjusted, for one minute.

14. Hang up the film to dry.

You remove film from a Kodak 35-mm cassette by prying the end off the cassette with a beer-can opener. For a 126 plastic cartridge, twist it until it cracks open. For larger film sizes, unroll them and separate them from their paper backings. If you have done your homework with your practice roll you already know these things.

The reason for pouring out the developer when there is still forty-five seconds left of the developing time is that residual developer in the emulsion will continue to act all the way through the water rinse. Thus by the time you pour in the hypo the film will have completely developed.

If you are not using Perma Wash your film should wash for at least twenty minutes, though that is cutting the time rather short.

If you wish, you can wipe off your film with a photographic sponge and not use Photo-Flo. If so, thoroughly soak the sponge several minutes ahead of time, then squeeze it out as dry as you can get it just before use. With your hand, vigorously brush off the wiping surface to make sure there is no grit on it, because it will easily scratch wet film (so will fingernails!). Then wipe off the film three times, squeezing out the sponge after each time. Hang the film up to dry.

You make a film-drying line with string and clothespins. The best place for it is in a room where there is little dust and traffic, the bathroom usually being the best bet. If there is dust there, turn on the hot water in the tub or shower for a few minutes; a little steam will settle the dust. The problem with dust is that it easily gets embedded in wet gelatin and is hard to remove.

After hanging up a roll of film, weight its lower end with a clothespin. Check to see that there are no large water drops (tiny droplets are all right), for they make drying marks. If you find some, pick them off with your fingers or the sponge. Do this also with dust specks.

To remove film from a Nikor reel, just pull it out, letting the reel turn in your hand. With Paterson and GAF reels, pull the flanges apart a little way.

● Care of Negatives

When your film has dried, you should cut it into short strips of images (frames). Strips of five frames are convenient for 35-mm, six for 126, and three for 120. These short strips makes negatives easier to handle when you are printing them. It is also easier to make contact sheets with them (next chapter).

After cutting, you should immediately put your negatives in glassine sleeves, but only one per sleeve, because bunching them up will cause scratches.

Negatives are extremely susceptible to scratches, fingerprints, and abrasions, which show up as ugly marks on your prints. Therefore, you should always handle them by their edges, lay them down only on clean surfaces, and keep them in their sleeves when they are not being printed. Do not store film by rolling it up, because this usually causes scratches. Keep it in a cool, dry place, because heat and humidity will eventually ruin negatives.

HOW TO MAKE AND USE CONTACTS
EXPOSURE　　　　　　HOW TO PROCESS PRINTS
NEGATIVE AND PAPER CONTRAST

There are two basic ways of making prints: by projection and by contact printing. The first involves projecting a negative image onto printing paper; the resulting print is called an enlargement, or projection print. For the second way you lay the negative right on top of the paper and make an exposure. The result is called a contact, contact print, or contact proof. The contact is used mainly for previewing pictures before enlarging them and is one of the photographer's most useful tools. One usually contacts a whole roll of negatives on a single piece of printing paper and can thus see at a glance how they all stack up. Note that the word "contact" comes from the fact that the negatives and paper are in actual contact during exposure.

● **Things You Need**

Four sheets of 12×16-inch single-strength glass
Soap, hot water, and a towel
Masking tape
Enlarger
Timer, metronome, or watch
Safelight(s)

Enlarging paper (not *contact* paper), double weight
Thermometer
Dektol print developer
Kodak Indicator Stop Bath
First hypo bath
Second hypo bath
Perma Wash
Tray siphon (optional)
Photographic blotters (optional)
Five processing trays
Paper towels
Scissors
China-marker pencil
Lighter fluid
Magnifying glass or illuminated magnifier

In these lists of "Things You Need" you will often find items repeated. This is so you won't have to skip back and forth in the book looking for things when you need them.

Glass: The four sheets are used together to make a single heavy, loosely laminated plate of glass. In making contact prints there must be very close contact between the negatives and the printing paper; for sharp pictures they must be tightly squeezed together. To get good contact you put the negatives emulsion (dull side) down on the emulsion of the paper (shiny side), then press them flat with a plate of glass. One thickness of glass is enough if you hold opposite sides of it down with your hands.

However, this may be inconvenient, because you have to start holding it down before you begin the exposure, and this doesn't leave you a free hand to turn on the enlarger light. The answer is a foot switch, which you probably don't have. Another answer is to have a plate of glass heavy enough to flatten the negatives (which often curl like steel springs) all by itself. Heavy plate glass will do very nicely, but it is very expensive and easily scratched. So we create its equivalent with four sheets of ordinary single-strength glass in the standard 12×16-inch size. It is both cheap and durable.

When you are buying your glass at the hardware store, check each piece to see that it has no bubbles or scratches, because they would show up in your prints. Today's glass is very well made, so you should have no problem. The easiest way to check is to hold the glass in front of a flatly lighted section of a wall or ceiling.

Later, wash each piece carefully with soap and water (don't use a glass cleaner), then wipe it completely dry with a turkish towel. Next, stack up the plates of glass, taking great care not to get dust or lint between them. Finally, tape them together along the edges with masking tape. Don't squeeze them into the tightest possible contact while you are taping, however, for that will cause colored, irregular rings. Just let them lie there while you are doing it. Only the negatives and the printing paper need tight contact, not the individual pieces of glass.

Enlarging papers: Enlarging papers are made for use with enlarger light sources, which usually aren't very intense. Thus the papers are made very light-sensitive in order to compensate. In comparison, *contact* papers are very "slow" (relatively insensitive to light), because they are

used to make contact prints of large negatives in special contact printers that have very intense light sources. Though you intend to make contact prints, you will be using the enlarger as a light source—so use enlarging paper.

Thermometer: In making contacts or enlargements your need for a thermometer is not nearly as great as it is in film processing. In fact, most people seldom use one in printing, unless the temperatures are obviously very high or very low. The safe temperature range is from about 65 to 90 degrees F, though it is better to stay in the 65–75-degree range if you can.

Dektol print developer: Print and film developers are not the same, so don't try interchanging them unless you know exactly what you are doing. For prints, a developer has to be very alkaline and active, while lower-alkalinity film developers are much less active. Thus, if you use a paper developer for film you can easily get heavy overdevelopment. In contrast, a print in film developer may take an hour or more to develop.

Kodak Dektol is a variant of Kodak D-72, a classical formula in photography. It is dependable, has good keeping qualities, holds up for a considerable time in the developing tray, and works well with all brands and types of contact and enlarging papers. With most papers it produces a very neutral print color, which most people find desirable.

● Setting Up the Trays

Chemical trays are usually arranged touching one another in a row, or "processing line." This is convenient and cuts down the amount of splashing and dripping, but it isn't absolutely necessary. If you lack space, put your trays wherever you can, even under the enlarger table or scattered around the room.

Line up your trays in this order (if you can): (1) developer, (2) stop bath, (3) first hypo, (4) second hypo, and (5) water. Dilute the Dektol stock solution 1:2 (one part Dektol, two of water). Use one-half ounce of stock indicator stop bath per quart of water, or two ounces per gallon. The hypo stock solution should not be diluted.

As we've seen, the temperatures in a print-processing line aren't very critical. Temperature variations from tray to tray also matter little, because print emulsions are much less susceptible to damage than film emulsions; and there is no grain problem with printing paper, which is nearly grainless.

To make print handling easier, fill all the trays to within one-half inch or so of their tops. Take great care not to dribble stop bath or hypo into the developer, for they can ruin it in a jiffy. Conversely, developer will ruin both stop bath and hypo. However, the stop bath is used as an intentional sacrifice designed to save the hypo from destruction.

Here's how it works. When a print is transferred from the developer to the stop bath it carries with it some of the developer solution, which is alkaline. However, the alkali is ruinous to hypo, which can function only if it is acidic. The stop bath, a dilute acid, acidifies the print so that it won't undermine the effectiveness of the hypo. Since the stop bath itself is eventually ruined by the developer it is important to know when it is no longer functioning properly. For this we have a chemical indicator. When this yellow bath begins to turn purple (the indicator), discard it and mix a fresh one.

Concentrated indicator stop bath is very strong, so you should add it to the water—not the other way around. Pouring water into a strong acid can result in its exploding into your eyes, a very unpleasant prospect.

As far as possible, arrange your trays so as to minimize dribbling or splashing onto the work surfaces and floor. From your waist, hang a towel for keeping your fingers dry and dripless. When you *do* splash, as you most probably will, use paper towels for the wipe-up. If you use your turkish towel for this it will soon get contaminated, so that you will be wiping your fingers dirty instead of clean, thus leading you to con-

taminating everything you touch. Remember this: in photography, cleanliness is next to godliness.

● **Getting to Know Your Enlarger**

An enlarger is very much like a slide projector and can even be used for slides in a pinch. It has a light source (bulb), a light-condensing system, a focusing system, a system for raising or lowering it on its standard, and a lens with a variable aperture. Usually these systems are combined in such a simple way that it is quite obvious what they all do. If you have used an enlarger to make even one print it is unlikely you'll ever forget how it works.

The only hard thing to understand is how you are supposed to use the variable aperture. This is something you literally *have* to know, so we will go into it in some depth. The aperture is merely a variable-size hole, resembling somewhat the iris diaphragm of the eye. It is even called the diaphragm, or iris diaphragm. We can make this hole large, small, or set it to a limitless range of sizes in between. However, it is "graduated," so that if you wish you can easily set it to certain sizes that are related to one another in a very specific and accurate way. Though the relationship is extremely simple it is quite difficult to understand at first, so you will have to bear down a bit here.

These graduations—called "stops," "f/stops," or "f-numbers"—are marked on the outside of the lens barrel. Some lenses make a clicking sound as they are moved through each position and are thus said to have "click stops." It is a lot easier to hear clicks than to see the marks under a safelight. Don't let the jargon distress you, because it merely refers to a simple relationship of areas. By opening or closing the aperture we are merely changing the area of a hole.

Unfortunately, the numbers at the stop settings seem to be backward, because a large number stands for a small hole and vice versa. This is because these figures are actually ratios, which you needn't worry about right now. Though things

45

aren't backward, they seem to be, and that is what you have to get used to.

On your enlarger lens barrel you have a scale of f-number (f/stop, or aperture) settings: f/4—f/5.6—f/8—f/11—f/16. Your lens may start with f/5.6, but don't let that worry you. Changing the setting from left to right on the scale is called "stopping down," because the hole gets progressively smaller. Moving in the other direction, or "opening up," makes it larger, of course. All you have to remember is this: The larger the number the smaller the hole.

We have just seen that moving from f/4 toward f/16 is called stopping down, because the aperture (hole) gets progressively smaller. Thus, making one jump, say from f/4 to f/5.6, is "stopping down one stop." If we should go in the other direction, say all the way from f/16 to f/4, that would be "opening up *four* stops." These unfamiliar terms and numbers are an important part of the photographer's jargon, so try to get them straight.

In using the aperture settings (hole sizes), we are most interested in how their areas relate, which is as follows: As we progressively go from f/4 to f/5.6 to f/8 to f/11 to f/16 we cut the area exactly in half with each jump. Conversely, if we go in the other direction we double the area each time. Though the f-numbers themselves are ratios (fractions) and not measures of areas, the relationships just given hold true, nonetheless. And this is all we need to know.

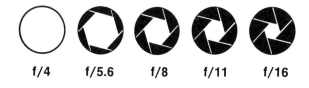

f/4   **f/5.6**   **f/8**   **f/11**   **f/16**

Diagrammatic representation of the f-number settings in your enlarger lens

• Exposure

In printing, our chief interest in the progressive doubling or halving of the area of the aperture is that it gives us some control over the "exposure." The concept of exposure is one of the most important notions in photography, so we had better look into it. It is important to remember that "exposure" (or *"an* exposure") always consists of *two* things: light intensity and time. This is usually written as: Exposure=Light Intensity×Time (or E=I×T). This is the famous "Law of Reciprocity," and all of photography is based on it.

The × in this formula merely indicates that you can get the *same* exposure with many different combinations of light intensity and time. For example, it is possible to move from using a lot of light and little time to using a little light and a lot of time without changing the exposure at all. It is like saying that 10×2 is quantitatively the *same as* 2×10, which it obviously is.

In order to make use of the Law of Reciprocity (which we do every time we make a print or shoot a picture) we must have adequate control over both light intensity and time. The intensity of the enlarger bulb itself doesn't change. However, we can use the variable aperture to control the amount of light that actually passes through the lens. With a timer or metronome we can easily control the amount of time for which the enlarger light is turned on. Thus we can have as many combinations as we wish of light intensity and time.

• Correct Exposure

At this point it is necessary to distinguish between "exposure" and *"correct* exposure," which can be miles apart in certain respects. Exposure is any combination whatever of light intensity and time. Whenever you let light fall upon film or printing paper you get an exposure, even if you don't consider the light intensity or the amount of time, and even if the images come out much too light or too dark. In contrast, "correct exposure" is the combination of light intensity and time that will make an image come out just the way you want it to. This definition is simple and subjective, as you can see, but that's really all there is to it.

● Correct Exposure in Printing

We will now see how one manipulates the light intensity and time controls in printing. Let us say you have made a test strip (pages 55ff.) and determined that the "correct exposure" for your picture is two seconds at f/4. Now, a two-second exposure is not so good, because timers and metronomes can't be used with accuracy in such a short time span, and it doesn't permit us to dodge or burn-in (pages 71ff.). So you decide that you need a longer time without changing the exposure.

The method is simple. You find that you can use longer times by merely stopping down the lens to reduce the intensity of the light passing through it. Without changing the exposure at all, this would give you the following light-intensity-and-time combinations: f/4 (two seconds)— f/5.6 (four seconds)—f/8 (eight seconds)—f/11 (sixteen seconds)—f/16 (thirty-two seconds). Both eight and sixteen seconds are convenient exposure times, while four is still too short and thirty-two tediously long.

If a print were to come out too dark or too light you would want a *different* exposure, of course. We can correct for a dark print by stopping down, cutting the time, or both. We correct for a light one by opening up, increasing the time, or both.

This rather heavy material on exposure was made necessary by the fact that beginners generally get badly confused in this area—and you can now see why. Furthermore, it is of fundamental importance in learning to see how photography actually works. The chapter on test strips will help clarify things for you, as will a little experience in making pictures.

● More About Enlargers

Before we leave this section you need to know a little more about enlargers. For example, enlarger lenses aren't very "sharp" when used "wide open" (opened to the largest aperture). That is, they produce images that are fuzzy, or diffuse, near their edges. For better sharpness it is usually good to stop down either two or three stops. However, even going down one stop is a considerable improvement. Stopping down more than three isn't wise, because enlarger lenses aren't very sharp at their smallest apertures, either.

You shouldn't leave the enlarger light turned on longer than you can help. It shortens the life of the bulb. If the bulb gets hot enough it may burn out the insulation in its socket and possibly damage the condenser or lens. A hot enlarger may destroy a negative left in it.

Photographic chemicals are excellent conductors of electricity, so if you get them on your enlarger you may short it and shock yourself cross-eyed. They will also corrode it, as will water itself.

The alignment of the enlarger standard and the baseboard is critical if you want prints that are sharp from edge to edge. Since it is easily thrown off, you shouldn't handle your enlarger roughly or drop it on the floor. Though you might be able to get it back into alignment again it could take you all day.

You should frequently clean the lens and condenser with lens tissue. In fact, you might do it every time you set up for printing.

● Exposing the Contact Sheet

Raise the enlarger head to the top of its standard, then stop the lens down two or three stops. Turn off all lights except the safelight(s). Cut off a one-inch strip of printing paper and place it *emulsion up* on the enlarger baseboard. Put a single strip of negatives *emulsion down* on top of the paper and hold them in tight contact with the glass plate.

Expose a test strip as follows: Give the *whole strip* a five-second exposure. Then start progressively *covering it up* in one-inch jumps with the printing-paper package. At each position give it an additional five-second exposure. Then process the strip (next section) and pick the step with the best-looking image, neither too light nor too dark. Count up by fives from the bottom to the selected step to find the correct exposure time. If the desired image tone would fall between two steps, average their times.

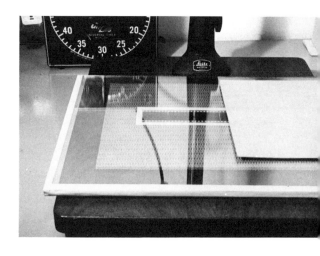

Setup for making a test strip from a single strip of film. The film is put on a two-inch strip of enlarging paper, which is resting on a sponge-rubber pad, and is then covered with a heavy, laminated plate of glass to assure good contact. As test exposures are made, the film is progressively covered up with a sheet of cardboard.

Setup for contacting a whole roll of film (seven strips) on a single sheet of 8×10 enlarging paper (the cover glass is still propped up behind the sponge-rubber pad).

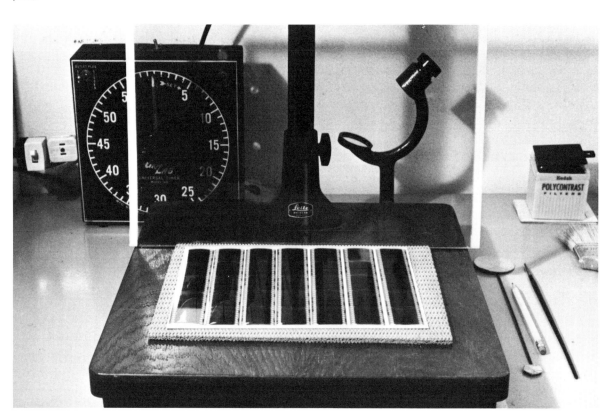

Now expose a contact using a full sheet of paper and a whole roll of film. It is a good idea to have all the strips in their original order and right side up, for this will make it easier to work with them later. Using the time obtained from the test strip, make an exposure, then process the contact.

• Processing Contacts and Enlargements

Contacts and enlargements should be handled in exactly the same way and with the same care, so the processing instructions for both will be given in this section. Some people tend to get sloppy when making contacts, but this is not good. A poorly exposed and processed contact is an offense to the aesthetic sense, which is bad for the morale. Furthermore, there is no way of extracting from it accurate information of either a technical or a pictorial nature. So heed this advice: always make the best possible contacts; if one of them doesn't come out quite right, make it over again.

Development: With a single movement, push the exposed print face down into the developer, push it around a few times, then turn it face up. Keeping it shoved under the surface, continue to move it around in the developer in a random pattern. Do this by nudging it with the tips of your fingers (or print tongs) or by lifting up the tray from different sides at random. Do not hold onto the print, because the heat from your fingers will make the developer around them more active, causing ugly brown stains.

At around 68 F the normal developing-time range for most printing papers is from 1¼ to 2¼ minutes. If a print has to be removed from the tray in less time it is definitely overexposed and should be remade. Having to develop longer than 2¼ minutes indicates definite underexposure. However, a print can sometimes be pushed to three, four, or five minutes with good results, but such extended overdevelopment *may* cause fog, stain, or mottle. You just have to try it and see. Of course, a print may be so seriously underexposed that *no* amount of time will help it.

Sometimes, and with some brands of paper, you can safely go as low as thirty to forty-five seconds, but it is not usually recommended. In such a short time, prints tend to look very mottled and muddy unless your agitation technique is superb or they are presoaked in water before development. Even then they may look bad. There is also a definite loss of image contrast (which may or may not be desirable with a given picture), and the blacks are usually not very black.

One problem with using abnormally short developing times is that you may not notice serious image degradation until your prints are dry, when it is too late to remake them easily. Just to be safe, then, remake any prints (including contacts!) that develop in less than 1¼ minutes.

Many teachers insist that their students work in a 2–2¼-minute time range, saying that this will give them the best "print quality." Any print that does not develop within that range should be automatically remade, they say. Though it is a very good discipline it goes just a bit too far. On the other hand, many really fabulous printers stick closely to this schedule.

If the developer temperature goes above 68 degrees (which is considered the ideal), cut all the times somewhat. If it is around 60 or 65, increase them. However, at 60 and below, only a heavily overexposed print will develop in a reasonable amount of time, and print quality may suffer considerably. Thus it is better to warm up the developer with the plastic-bag trick from the preceding chapter. Or you can wrap a heating pad in plastic and put it under the developer tray, turning it on from time to time.

While a print is developing do not hold it close to the safelight to examine it, because safelights are only *relatively* safe and will cause fog if too close. Using a larger than recommended bulb in a safelight will also cause fog. Of course, you would like to see the print better, but in time you will learn to judge its quality while it remains in the developer tray.

When a print has developed fully, lift it from

the developer tray by one corner and let it drain about five seconds, so that you limit the amount of developer being transferred to the stop bath. Then put it into the stop bath.

Stop bath: Constantly agitate the print for the first five to ten seconds, then leave it in the bath for a total of about thirty seconds, agitating intermittently. This bath not only acidifies your print but quickly stops its development, because the developer remaining in the emulsion and paper base can work only when it is in an alkaline state.

There is an impatient tendency to rush prints through the stop bath and into the hypo so that they can be examined under white light as soon as possible. Not so good. Remember that the function of the stop bath is to protect the hypo from the developer's alkalinity. By rushing, you will lose the protection and shorten the effective life of the hypo as much as 75 per cent or more. However, for resin-coated (RC) papers, five seconds is enough time in the stop bath.

First hypo: Agitate constantly for the first ten seconds, then briefly every thirty seconds or so. Leave regular paper in the tray from three to five minutes, resin-coated (RC) paper one minute.

Do not let prints overlap in the hypo, especially if it is fresh. It has a slight bleaching action, so the overlapping will cause obvious tonal demarcations across the prints underneath. Because of this bleaching effect you should use the shorter time with fresh hypo, gradually extending it as more and more prints are run through it. The time for RC papers should stay at one minute. However, *no* paper should fix *longer* than the suggested time in either hypo bath, unless you have prints that are too dark and in need of bleaching.

After the time is up, drain the print for about five seconds and put it into the next hypo bath.

Second hypo: Again, agitate constantly for the first ten seconds and intermittently thereafter. The total time is three to five minutes for regular paper, one for RC. When the time is up, immediately drain the print and put it in the "water holding bath" (the tray with water in it). Agitate it

there for a few seconds, too, then leave it in the water until you are ready to wash it.

The "hypo light": For accurately judging print exposure, contrast, and general quality it is good to have a white light positioned right over the hypo tray. A 150-watt bulb at a distance of three feet is about right. If the bulb is too small you will find yourself accepting prints that are actually underexposed quite a bit, while with too large a one you'll like overexposed pictures.

Print washing: Unless you use a washing aid such as Perma Wash your prints should wash for an hour in rapidly running water, even if you use the two-bath hypo system. Ideal water temperatures: 65–75 F for ordinary paper, 65–70 for RC. If you use a tray and tray siphon there should be at least twelve changes of water during the hour. To test how long it takes to make a complete change, remove the prints from the tray and drop in a few drops of food coloring; it should disappear completely within five minutes.

As an alternative to a tray you can use the bathtub, steadily filling it up and draining it, refilling it and draining, until the time is up.

With either method you should frequently agitate by pulling prints up from the bottom and putting them on top. *Constant* agitation would be even better, though very tedious.

According to the Heico chemists, with Perma Wash you can get the equivalent of an hour's ordinary wash with just a two-minute first wash, a two-minute Perma Wash bath, and a two-minute final wash. Just in case your washing techniques are a little sloppy or you are washing a lot of prints at one time, increase all the suggested times to five minutes each—which Heico says will give you the equivalent of a six-hour plain-water wash. Whichever times you use, the agitation should be constant throughout the entire process, and there should be a rapid flow of water during the washes. As you see, even with five-minute intervals you can save yourself forty-five minutes— at a time when one is usually worn out from printing.

If you use resin-coated (RC) paper you won't

need Perma Wash, however, because a four-minute ordinary wash in rapidly running water, with constant agitation, will do the job very well. The reason is that an RC emulsion is coated on plastic instead of paper. Plastic doesn't absorb hypo, and washing it out of a thin emulsion is fairly easy. However, hypo clings tenaciously to paper, making it necessary to use washing aids or to wash prints for a tediously long time. One of the main reasons for the introduction of RC was to nearly eliminate this tedium.

For all the welcome wonders of RC paper it would be a good idea to double the recommended wash time, especially if you are washing quite a few prints at once. The problem is that hypo tends to get between them, even with constant agitation, and that it takes a little time to wash it out.

Print drying: Perhaps the easiest way to dry prints made on regular printing paper is to wipe off both sides with an ordinary sponge and put them between sheets of photographic blotter paper. Blotter rolls and books aren't so good, because the lint they sometimes leave on prints is very hard to remove. Don't put your prints in telephone books, magazines, newspapers, and the like, for they all contain hypo as a paper preservative; and that is the very chemical we are trying to get rid of.

You can stack up your blotters, but not too many at once, because that will slow up drying considerably. If you lay a stack out flat the prints will tend to curl in every direction as they dry. To prevent this, prop up two opposite ends of the blotters on boxes or piles of books, so that they curve gently. Then your dried prints will curl in the same uncomplicated, easy-to-handle way.

If you have steam heat or live in an arid climate your prints may curl like steel springs no matter how you dry them, which is terribly exasperating. To counteract the curl, soak prints in a "print-flattening agent" just before drying them. This chemical helps the paper base retain some of its moisture, thus taking much of the spring out of it.

Drying is even simpler with resin-coated (RC) papers. You merely sponge them off and lay them face up on blotters, a bedspread, a clean table top, towels or sheets from the laundry hamper, or a clean stretch of the floor. It is not necessary to put anything on top of them; and in a short while they will be dry. Though they may get a little springy in very dry air it's not too bad. And they curl in just one direction.

• The Two-Bath Hypo System

You have seen that all the basic information on exposing and processing prints has been included in this chapter on contacts, because contacts and enlargements should be handled in exactly the same way. Now is also an appropriate time to explain why we use two hypo baths instead of just one. Indeed, many people *do* use just one, so you ought to know what difference it makes.

Remember that hypo changes unexposed silver halides into hypo-silver compounds not sensitive to light, so that they won't turn your pictures black. These new compounds are also water-soluble and can be eliminated from prints by washing, which is very necessary. Left in your prints, they would eventually bleach them or turn them brown, especially under conditions of high heat and humidity.

Unfortunately, these hypo-silver salts are only *relatively* soluble, which explains why, even with a two-bath system, a print should be washed a whole hour—unless a washing aid is used. It is especially hard to remove them from a paper base. Furthermore, the longer a given hypo bath is used the less soluble are the hypo-silver salts formed in it, until we eventually reach a point where even days or weeks of washing won't get rid of them. This dooms the pictures to eventual chemical destruction.

One solution is to use a single hypo bath, run just a few prints through it, then mix a fresh bath. But this would be inconvenient and expensive. A better method is the two-bath system, which is convenient, effective, and economical.

The first bath thoroughly desensitizes the print and forms the water-soluble compounds in the emulsion and paper base. With extended use of the bath, however, they become less and less soluble.

Since it has relatively little work to do, the second bath stays quite fresh and solves the solubility problem with ease. It converts the nearly insoluble salts already formed into relatively soluble ones, so that they can be eliminated by washing. Even so, the washing times already given should be followed closely, because they are based on the assumption that a two-bath system is being used. With an inefficient fixation system, we might have to extend the times from minutes to hours.

Eventually, the chemical energy of both hypo baths will be used up, but the first bath will go first because it takes the brunt of the work. So we discard it first and move the second hypo tray into its place in the processing line. Then we mix a *fresh* second hypo as a replacement. But how do we know when to shift trays?

According to Eastman Kodak, you can run two hundred regular 8×10 prints, or 350 RC prints, through the system before shifting and remixing—with trays that contain one gallon each. For smaller trays we would cut the figures proportionally. After four of these shifts, things begin to catch up with us and we have to start from scratch again with *both* baths freshly mixed.

Undoubtedly, the Kodak figures are based on using the stop bath with maximum efficiency, which means remixing it every time it starts to turn purple, leaving prints in it a long enough time, and agitating them thoroughly. There is no problem with resin-coated (RC) papers, which need only five seconds, but the thirty-second wait with regular papers will seem tedious to some people.

A reasonable compromise between impatience and impeccable technique is to process only one hundred regular prints, or 175 RC's, before shifting trays and remixing. Do this only for insurance, however, not to encourage yourself to use

sloppy technique. If you are careless enough in your use of the stop bath you can easily knock out your two-bath hypo system long before you have put even one hundred regular (175 RC) prints through it. Indeed, you can ruin it in a single printing session. And you may not even realize what you have done. In fact, you may not discover your mistake (in the form of brown or faded prints) for months or years, but it will certainly confront you · eventually. So please look ahead!

• Note Keeping

We have covered the basic information on exposure and processing and can now return to contacts per se. Assuming that the first roll you contact was normally exposed and developed, it shouldn't be necessary to go through the whole test-strip procedure with the rolls to follow. Use the same data. While you are making your first contact, keep a record as follows:

Negatives: normally exposed and developed
Paper: Kodabrome (RC), medium contrast
Enlarger position: top of standard
Aperture: stopped down two
Time: twelve seconds

When you contact rolls that are underexposed (too light) or overexposed (too dark) you have to use test strips to get different exposures, which you can add to your list for use in the future with similar rolls. Since making contacts is a bit of a drag, you might as well do it the easiest possible way, which is to work from notes.

• Dodged Contacts

Occasionally you will have a roll in which some of the five-frame strips (35-mm) are considerably lighter or darker than the rest, so that they look rather bad on a contact. Thus there is no way of telling whether they are worth enlarging, though they actually might make very good prints. However, they can be made to look very good on the contact by dodging and burning-in during exposure (pages 71ff.). To make it very easy to do, position the improperly exposed strips at the bottom of the printing paper and all the normal strips above them.

When only one or two isolated frames are off, however, it is easier to contact-print them individually on small chips of paper. When they have been washed and dried, trim them with scissors and glue them in their proper places on the front of the large contact. Elmer's Glue works fine.

● **Marking Up Contacts**

With a bright enough hypo light you can analyze a contact fairly well as soon as it has been thoroughly fixed, but for evaluation in depth it is necessary to wait until it has been washed and dried. Then you can go over it centimeter by centimeter with a magnifier—the stronger the better —and use a china marker to make notes and diagrams on it for later use.

The primary function of a contact is to help you decide whether you have actually accomplished anything on a given roll. With the magnifier you can see if the images are sharp, analyze their composition, check the expressions and poses of models, evaluate lighting patterns, look for extraneous things in pictures, and so on. While you are doing this you have an opportunity to thoroughly assess your feelings about the pictures and pick the ones you really feel like enlarging. You may choose a few for immediate enlargement, put aside others until you are in the proper mood for printing them, and decide to do nothing further with the majority.

Since rejecting your own pictures is discouraging, you will find it enheartening to hear that a professional photographer considers himself very lucky if he gets even two good pictures on a roll and is quite used to getting rolls with none at all. In this perspective you see that you shouldn't ask too much of yourself, especially in the beginning.

If you had no contact to guide you, you would probably find yourself enlarging most of the pic-

tures on a roll just to get an idea of what they look like. This is a serious waste of time, effort, and printing paper. Furthermore, people who put a lot of work into the wrong pictures usually start lying to themselves, trying very hard to believe they like them when they actually do not. However, they eventually force themselves to reject them, often motivated by adverse responses from other people. This is a much greater agony than rejecting a tiny image on a contact sheet, you may be sure. Since giving up deficient images is an everyday part of photography, you should do it in the easiest way. Bear in mind that there is no photographer in the world who can get a winner in every frame.

Another thing to consider is that looking at contacts is in many ways as great a pleasure as looking at enlargements, which is a good excuse for not feeling compelled to enlarge them all. If they are pleasing already, why gild the lily? This explains why you were asked to always make the best possible contacts: so that you can enjoy them more. Conversely, there are few things more disheartening to photographers than sloppy contact sheets.

To "mark up" a contact simply means to draw on it with a china marker, usually red because of its high visibility. With a magnifier under a bright light you can see the little images very well, so you make penciled notes to guide you when you are working under the dim illumination of safelights. Mainly, you indicate the frames you wish to enlarge and how you wish to "crop" them. Cropping means to print less than the whole image, the excess being blocked off by the edges of the printing easel. Without pencil notes and diagrams for guidance you would frequently find yourself enlarging the wrong frames or using croppings that don't work very well.

Since there is no special style used in marking up, you can do it in any way that suits your fancy and helps you remember the decisions you have made with respect to printing the frames. It would be wise to do it neatly, however, as there is no point in offending your aesthetic sense. For neatest results, sharpen the china marker with a razor blade and use a ruler or a strip of cardboard for drawing lines. Mistakes in drawing or marking up the wrong frame can easily be removed with lighter fluid and a piece of cloth or cotton.

At this point you should see that there is nothing difficult or mysterious about marking up contacts. You merely examine the images in detail, make decisions concerning how you wish to enlarge them, then record the decisions on the contacts in the form of lines and little notes to yourself.

• Evaluating the Exposure of Negatives

A contact can tell you whether your negatives are overexposed, normal, or underexposed. You can't always determine this from the pictorial quality of the contact, however, for all three types will make pleasant little pictures if the contact itself is properly exposed and developed. Unfortunately, this can lead one to enlarge images that aren't technically adequate. For example, badly underexposed negatives will sometimes make very handsome contacts, but there is little chance of making fine enlargements from them. Misled, one enlarges them anyway.

To circumvent this illusory promise of good enlargement quality, examine the areas of printing paper between the strips, not the images themselves. Look also at the film borders around the images. Assuming that the contact has been well made, the in-between areas will look dark (but not quite black) if the negatives were normally exposed. The borders of the film itself will look dark gray.

If the negatives were underexposed, these areas in between strips will be medium to light gray and the film borders even lighter. Though the little pictures may look fine it will be nearly impossible to make good enlargements from them.

With overexposed negatives the in-between

areas *and* the borders will probably look black. On the borders we find frame numbers and the name of the film, which are repeated every few inches. The numbers and letters will tend to be "blocked up." That is, the surrounding silver "bleeds" into them, making them look ragged or obliterating them entirely. Such negatives will usually make enlargements that are only barely acceptable because of coarse grain and fuzziness.

• Evaluating Negative Contrast

How well one likes a picture depends to a considerable degree on its contrast, so we have explored controls for contrast in negatives, prints, and pictorial subjects themselves.

With photographic subjects the main control is lighting, which may be contrasty, medium, or flat. However, they may also have inherent contrast, for instance a white building with a black roof.

With negatives, the controls are exposure, the contrast of the subject, the inherent contrast of a given film (which can vary greatly from type to type), the activity of a given developer (which can also vary a lot), the relative freshness of the developer, its temperature, agitation, and the developing time.

Assuming that you intend to use only the recommended films, all medium-contrast, and D-76, a medium-contrast developer, the number of contrast controls is reduced somewhat. Ordinarily, one works for medium-contrast negatives, though this is not always true. Nevertheless, the following tables assume that deviation from the average is not desirable, for this is usually the case.

A marked-up contact sheet. You make little notes and reminders to yourself in this manner. Since there are no rules for it, you can do it in any way you like.

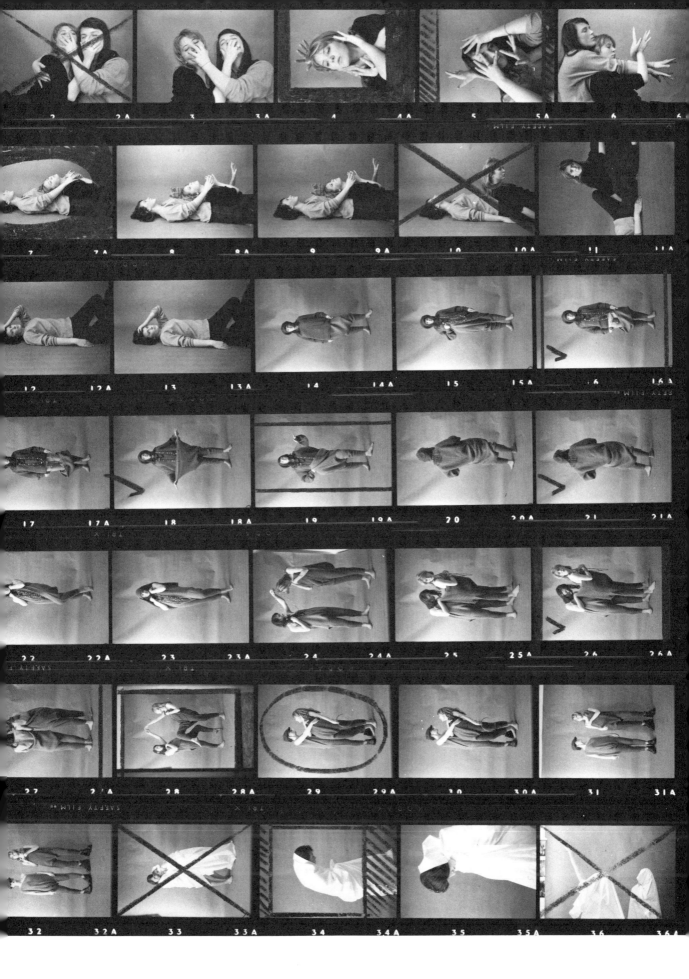

Reasons for negatives with too much contrast:

Contrasty pictorial subject matter
Processing too soon after mixing the developer
   from the dry chemical
Forgetting to dilute the developer stock solution
Too much agitation
Too high a developer temperature
Too long a developing time

Reasons for negatives with too little contrast:

Subject matter with little contrast
Underexposure
Using a chemically contaminated developer
Using an exhausted developer
Using a developer that has been stored too long
   after being mixed from the dry chemical
Diluting the developer stock solution too much
Too little agitation
Too low a developer temperature
Too short a developing time

If you wish to deliberately manipulate negative contrast it is best to change only the exposure and developing time, following the rules for everything else. For a considerable drop in contrast, try quadrupling the exposure of your negatives and cutting the developing time in half. To increase it, use a normal exposure, but increase the developing time 50 per cent. The only way to decide what these procedures can do for you is to try them, which is easy.

In printing, our contrast controls are fewer, the main one being papers with different degrees of contrast built into them. Printing papers are "graded," with numbers running from 1 (low con-trast) through 6 (very high). A no. 1 would be used for a contrasty negative, a no. 6 for a very flat one. Grades 2 and 3 are considered "normal"; a "normal negative" should fit either one or the other. However, one can get excellent prints from negatives that don't fit them.

There are also "variable-contrast" papers, with four different contrast grades inherent in them. By using different-colored "printing filters" under the enlarger lens one can get grades 1 through 4 from a single package of paper. When you have to buy only one package of paper instead of four you can buy it in one-hundred-sheet boxes and save quite a bit of money per sheet. There is also no danger of running out of any of the grades while you have any paper left at all.

When printing contacts, we use a paper of a slightly lower grade than usual, a no. 2 being considered normal, as are any negatives that contact well on it. The reason is that the smaller an image is the more contrast it has. Thus a normal negative that would look good on no. 2 in a contact might require a no. 3 paper for an 8×10 enlargement and a no. 4 for a large blow-up.

With this perspective, if you find yourself contacting on no. 3 you will know that your negatives are a bit flat. A no. 4 indicates they are not so good but probably still passable. If you have to go all the way to a 5 or 6 they are very flat indeed and will be difficult or impossible to enlarge handsomely. However, if you have to use a no. 1 paper or filter you are in no trouble, for there are several good ways of reducing print contrast. Furthermore, you probably won't even need them, unless the contact on no. 1 looks very contrasty.

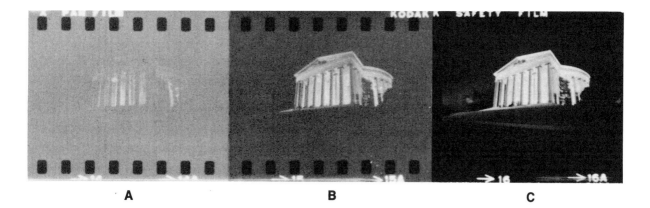

A   B   C

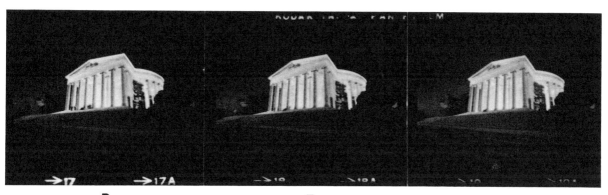

D   E   F

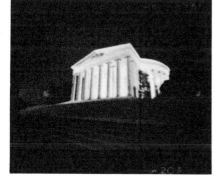

G

Individual contact prints made from a series of negatives with different exposures, adjacent prints having exposures exactly one stop apart. Negative D is the normal exposure. Thus C, B, and A are progressively one, two, and three stops underexposed. E, F, and G are progressively one, two, and three stops overexposed. Note that the overexposed negatives make better images than the underexposed ones. Note also that the film border prints gradually darker as we move from underexposure to overexposure. For the normal negative it prints dark gray, not black, though the surrounding paper is almost black. As we move toward heavy overexposure the tonal difference between the film border and the surrounding paper disappears. By examining contacts in this manner you can tell if your negatives were properly exposed, or in what direction they deviate from the normal.

print A

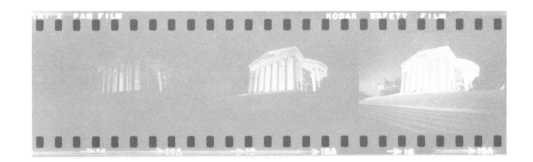

print B

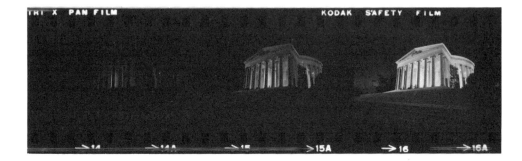

print C

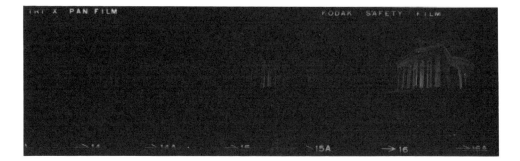

A strip of negatives one stop apart in exposure was
contact-printed in three different ways. Contact print
A was exposed to make the thinnest negative (on the
far left of the strip) reproduce as well as possible and
thus had a very short printing exposure time. Print B,
with a longer time, was printed for the normal negative
in the center of the negative strip. Print C, with a very
long exposure, was printed for the negative on the far
right end of the strip. This negative was three stops
overexposed.

   This chart suggests what can happen on any contact
sheet if the negative exposures vary considerably
from one another. Some pictures will come out too

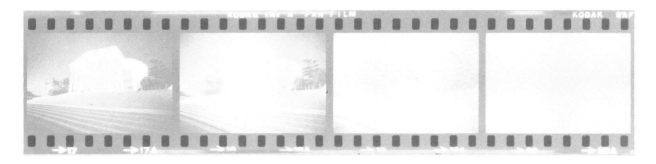

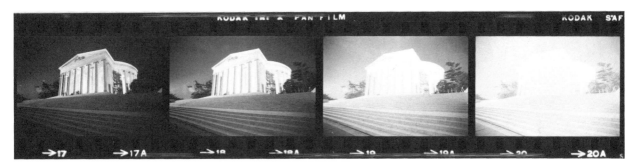

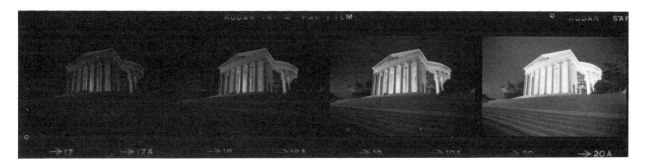

light, some just right, and some too dark. You can't really tell how the too light and too dark ones will look when enlarged. The only way you can tell is to make several contact sheets with different printing exposure times. None of these single-strip contact prints (A, B, and C) can by itself tell us which of the negatives are actually printable, but the three together tell us quite a bit. Now think of the original negative strip from which these contacts were made: The five negatives on the bottom right would all make passable prints, though the enlarged prints from the two on the far right would be quite grainy. The remaining negatives would make very poor prints.

HOW TO CLEAN NEGATIVES AND
MAKE MINOR REPAIRS
NEGATIVE DEFECTS AND THEIR CAUSES

Unless a negative is carefully cleaned just before it is put in the enlarger, the minute specks of dust and lint that cling to the back of it are likely to produce unsightly white spots and lines on the print. Though such defects can be removed from the print by retouching ("spotting"), it can be very hard and tedious work if there are a lot of them. Thus the best thing to do is to prevent them by using adequate negative-cleaning methods. However, there are things other than dust and lint that make for messy prints. They may originate in the film cassette, the camera, or the enlarger—or they may be due to faulty film processing, drying, and handling. They, too, can be prevented. If through carelessness you should get these negative defects, they can usually (but not always) be repaired or compensated for.

● **Clean Negatives Just Before Printing**

Using one or more of the methods that follow, you should clean each negative *just before* putting it in the enlarger. You may have to repeat a procedure several times in order to get a given negative clean enough. If you wish to temporarily

remove it from the enlarger, clean it *again* before putting it back. This is not overdoing it, though it may seem so. It happens that in only a second or two a cleaned negative can pick up a fresh load of dust or lint.

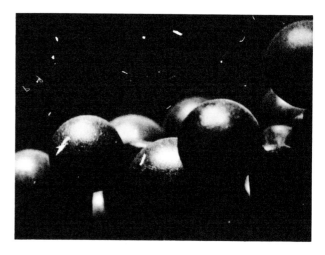

An enlargement made from a very dirty negative. It would be a long and tedious job to fill in the spots with spotting dye.

60

Static Electricity

The main problem is that the back of a negative (but not the emulsion) can readily pick up a charge of static electricity, so that like a strong magnet it will attract dust from the air, even from a distance of several inches. It also holds onto the dust when you are trying to get rid of it. We have this static problem often enough at normal room temperatures, but in a cold and dry darkroom it becomes infinitely worse.

The static charge explains why negatives can get dirty without being touched and why they should be put into the enlarger *immediately* after cleaning. The use of the anti-static materials on our list will remove the charge when used properly. Though dust will still be somewhat of a problem the negatives will at least not be attracting it magnetically.

Dust Is the Enemy

Whether you are drying freshly developed film or making prints, dust in the air will cause you lots of trouble—and there is always more of it than you think. So don't stir up more of it. Don't sweep your darkroom just before starting to work, because it will fill the air with dust particles for an hour or more. So will moving equipment and materials around too vigorously. Do your cleaning the day before, preferably with a vacuum cleaner. Instead of brushing off work surfaces, wipe them with a damp sponge. Clean your enlarger and enlarger table in the same way. On the lens and condenser use lens tissue, however, for it will not scratch their delicate surfaces. If the air in your darkroom is already filled with dust, sprinkle the floor liberally with water, then go elsewhere for an hour or two. The water will pick up much of the dust.

Materials for Negative Cleaning and Minor Repair

It is highly unlikely that you will need all the things on this list, but it is good to know about them in case you ever do. Most of the time, you can get along very well with just the sable brush, the nose grease, and the silicone cloth.

A no. 4, pointed sable (not camel-hair) brush
Nose grease
A silicone anti-static negative- or record-cleaning cloth
Marshall's Film Klens, or a similar anti-static film cleaner
A clean, well-worn handkerchief or other soft cloth
Vaseline
Surgical cotton
Q-Tips
Dektol, stop bath, and hypo
Kodak black opaque
Round toothpicks
An artist's crow-quill pen
No. 2 and 2-H pencils
Rubbing alcohol
Lighter fluid
The finest emery cloth (purple)
Hand soap

Checking for Dust

If you have processed your negatives properly, dried them in a clean place, and stored them individually in five-frame lengths (35-mm) in glassine sleeves, your cleaning problems will be minimal and the simplest cleaning methods entirely adequate. There will be no need for making repairs.

Before cleaning a negative you need a way of telling if it has dust or lint on it. Particles that will make a mess of a print may be so small that you can't see them at all in ordinary light. One way to make them stand out is to turn on the enlarger light, open up the lens all the way, and hold the negative up close to it at right angles. Then even the tiniest particles will be visible. You should make this check both before and after cleaning.

An even better method requires a kind of enlarger in which the lamp housing rests on the negative carrier and can be lifted up or tilted back. You put the cleaned negative and carrier in it and turn on the light before lowering the housing. Looking across the negative at right angles, you can easily see any dust or lint that you may have missed.

● Brush and Nose Grease

When using either checking method, one can easily pick off dust and lint particles with the sable brush, provided the negative doesn't have too high a static charge. Ordinarily, the brush would drop as much dust as it would pick up, but we use a minute amount of grease to make the dust stick to it.

To lightly grease your brush, stroke it two or three times in the oily crease at the side of your nostril. Don't use Vaseline, because you would certainly overdo it. The "nose grease system" has been popular with professional printers for years, so you don't have to look askance at it.

With either checking system some grease will be visible on the negative but won't show up on prints, because there is actually very little of it. Frequently, the brush alone will do a very adequate cleaning job, as will the following basic method.

● Thumb-and-Finger Method

On your left hand, vigorously rub together the ball of your thumb and the side of your index finger to dislodge any dust or lint on them. Then put a strip of negatives between them, with the shiny side (back) facing your thumb. While maintaining gentle pressure with finger and thumb, pull the strip slowly through with the other hand. Repeat this process two or three times. Of course, your hands should be clean and

By raising the enlarger head and turning on the light, you can see dust on the back of a negative. Then you can pick it all off with a sable brush that has a little nose grease in it.

One good way to clean a strip of negatives is to draw it gently between the ball of the thumb and the side of the index finger. The back of the strip should face the thumb. Your hands should be very clean and dry.

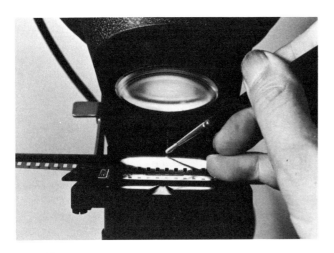

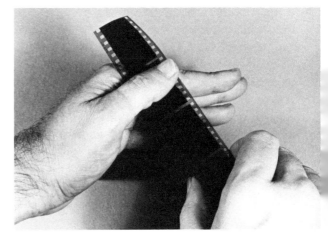

dry, or you may damage your negative. This is another old-time professional trick, and a very good one.

• Anti-static Methods

Unfortunately, neither the brush nor the finger method is very effective when used alone if a negative is highly charged. In this case one should try an anti-static cloth or spray. To use the cloth, shake it out or brush it off vigorously, to make sure there is no abrasive grit on it. Now fold it once and draw the *whole strip* through the fold, using gentle pressure. Do this two or three times. Wiping off only the frame you wish to print may not remove the charge at all, whereas the whole-strip method will remove both the static and the dust.

Unfortunately, the available anti-static cloths are so poorly made that they leave their own lint on negatives when one uses them. However, with the static charge gone the lint can be easily removed with the brush. Though this lint problem

The splotches on this print were caused by dirty rinse water, which left an oily sludge on the back of the negative. Sludge can usually be wiped off with cotton or a clean soft cloth.

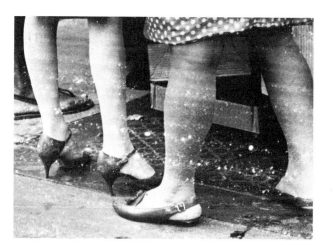

is a pain in the neck, the silicone cloth is nevertheless an excellent cleaning tool.

To use an anti-static cleaner like Marshall's, spray the entire strip of negatives on both sides, then gently wipe them off with a soft lintless cloth. Be sure the cloth has no dust or grit on it, for they can scratch negatives with ease. Take care not to inhale the Marshall's or get it in your eyes, because it contains isopropanol, which can adversely affect the heart, liver, and eye membranes. After cleaning, give the selected frame a final check and pick off any dust with the brush. If you find that dust clings to your enlarger and negative carrier it means that they are electrically charged, too. Spray them with Marshall's, then leave the room until the smell had dissipated.

• Oily Sludge

The foregoing methods should take care of your cleaning problems about 99 per cent of the time, yet you will occasionally need other techniques, too. For example, we sometimes have trouble from a very thin coating of oily sludge on the film backing (but never the emulsion). It causes a mottled effect in prints, especially if the negatives are "thin" (underexposed and/or underdeveloped). The sludge comes from the wash or final Photo-Flo rinse water, having gotten into the water pipes from a usually unknown source. Fortunately, one can gently wipe it off a negative with a soft dry cloth or cotton wool. In the unlikely event that it resists cleaning we can soak the cloth or cotton wool in lighter fluid or rubbing alcohol.

• Chewing Gum and What Not

Now and then we encounter such unlikely problems as chewing gum, the sticky coatings from masking or adhesive tape, grease, syrup, coffee, or Lord knows what. There seems to be an infinity of ways of messing up negatives when people are really determined to do it. Or when non-photographer members of the family, especially children, start handling negatives without permission. Fortunately, we have several types of solvents: water, soap and water, lighter fluid, and rubbing alcohol. Alone or together, they will take care of most problems of this sort.

• Embedded Dirt

Embedded dust is considerably harder to deal with than loose dust or lint. It gets tightly embedded in the emulsion when film is dried in a dusty room. If the emulsion is also softer than it should be, there will be even more embedded dirt. This undue softness can be caused by washing film too long. Or an overused fixer can be the culprit, because the hardener component in it may be used up, or exhausted. Ordinarily, a film emulsion is very soft all the way through processing, until it is hardened by the fixer, but with a worn-out fixer it may never get hardened at all. Too short a time in a good fixer could be the cause, as could washing in warm water.

The cure for embedded dirt may seem a bit strange, but it works well if you are patient and extremely careful. Otherwise it is an invitation to disaster. Put the negative in a clean tray of fresh print developer, handling it only by the edges. We are using the developer only for the alkali that it contains; it will thoroughly soften the emulsion in a minute or so. Let it get quite soft.

Now take a loose swatch of cotton about the size of a golf ball and get it sopping wet in the developer. Leaving the negative at the bottom of the developer (which should be about one half inch deep), gently drag the loose cotton back and forth along the strip until the dirt has been dislodged. Remember that the emulsion is *very* soft. Don't get impatient and start *rubbing,* because the dust particles, and the cotton itself, will act as abrasives and totally ruin your negative.

After this treatment, put the film in a stop bath for a few seconds, then into hypo for five to ten minutes, where it will be hardened again. Then wash and dry it in the usual way.

Don't worry: the developer won't darken the image, because there is nothing left in the emul-

sion that can develop. And there is nothing left for the fixer to fix—but the hardener component will harden the emulsion, which is all we want.

• Backing Scratches

Sometimes you will see scratch-like white lines on your prints. Indeed, they come from actual scratches on the backs of negatives. Fine and delicate though they may be, they show up on prints anyway. There are two kinds of backing scratches: straight lines running parallel to the edges of the film; and lines, either straight or curved, crossing the film in random directions.

The parallel scratches are usually caused by grit in the felt-lined slot of a film cassette, a dirty or badly designed "bulk film loader," rough spots on the camera pressure plate, or by rolling up negatives and cinching the roll tighter.

You can easily get grit in the slot by unwrapping the cassette and putting it in a pocket or camera bag instead of directly into your camera, which is the only wise thing to do. Pockets and bags are always dirtier than you think. You can use bulk loaders for 100-foot rolls of film, which you can then load into the cassette yourself. Film is much cheaper this way. However, clean or dirty, bulk loaders are prone to cause scratches—so don't use them. Ruining negatives is a poor way of economizing, don't you think?

The rectangular pressure plate is at the back of the camera and has a little spring behind it so that it can press the film flat against the film gate, which will give us pictures that are sharp from edge to edge. If its edges are a little rough they will scratch film as it is dragged across them while it is being advanced. With the finest emery cloth, smooth up any rough edges that you find.

There are a good many ways for getting random scratches on negatives, which are terribly prone to damage, anyway. Cleaning them too roughly is one way. Storing more than one in a single glassine envelope is another. A very common way of getting scratches is to pull a strip of negatives through the negative carrier while it is

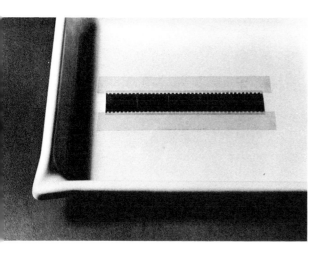

To prepare a negative for removing embedded dirt (or to bleach or intensify it—see Appendix), tape it to the bottom of a dry tray, emulsion side up, then rub the tape down hard with a thumbnail. If the tape doesn't want to stick to the tray, go over the surface first with lighter fluid, letting it dry before you put the tape down.

For removing embedded dirt, print developer has been poured over the taped-down negative. A sopping-wet wad of cotton is dragged *very gently* along the film after it has had time to get very soft in the developer. Rubbing with the cotton would ruin the negative. When the dirt is gone, discard the developer and pour hypo into the tray to harden the emulsion. Then wash and dry the film in the usual way.

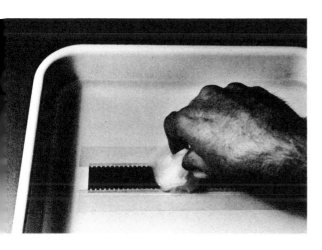

still in the enlarger. Always, one should remove the carrier, open it up, then *lift* the next frame into place.

Carrying negatives loose in pockets, purses, camera bags, or notebooks is just asking for trouble. So is letting them sit around on table tops for days. Of course, one that has been dropped on the floor and stepped on is a bad risk. We could say that the basic problem is things rubbing against negatives or negatives rubbing against things. There is *always* enough dirt around to make any rubbing whatever abrasive.

The cure for either parallel or random backing scratches is ordinary Vaseline. Remember that they make white lines on prints, which they do by scattering the enlarger light during exposure. If we could fill them in with something with about the same coefficient of refraction as the film base, they wouldn't do this. Fortunately, Vaseline fills the bill very well.

The method of application is simple. Just put a very small amount on the pad of your little finger and apply it to the back of the entire frame in small, circular patterns. What is a small amount of Vaseline? About as much as it would take to lubricate a squeaky butterfly. Not very much, you see.

Even a little Vaseline is messy, and it collects and holds dust. However, one can easily pick it off with the sable brush just before (or just after) putting the negative in the enlarger. With a thin negative, the Vaseline swirls may show up as patterns on the prints, so the Vaseline should be wiped off and a thinner coating applied. With normal or heavy (dark) negatives there is seldom any problem, unless one is using far too much Vaseline. Remember, we are only filling minute scratches, and that doesn't call for much of it.

Try not to get Vaseline on the emulsion. If you accidentally do, no harm done. Just spread it around the entire frame, then wipe it all off with a soft cloth. If there is Vaseline on only a part of the frame, it will show up on the print.

Since Vaseline is chemically inert it can be left on negatives after printing, but it is a little messy that way. Photo stores sell special "anti-scratch so-lutions," which are just as messy. However, they work exactly as Vaseline does and cost consid-erably more, so there is not much point in buying them.

• Emulsion Scratches

We don't see emulsion scratches very often, be-cause photographic gelatin is tough and scratch-resistant when it is dry. Though it is very vulnera-ble when wet it is only scratched then by gross mishandling. Emulsion scratches, which print up as *black* lines, can easily be repaired if they aren't too deep. However, deep ones may be very difficult or impossible to repair—on the negative. Then we have to use bleach on the black lines on the print, which can be an extremely intricate and tedious job, which few people would enjoy.

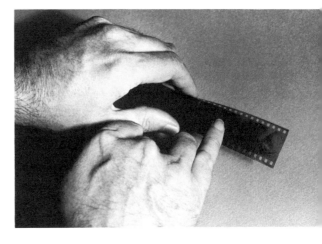

Treating a backing scratch by applying a very minute amount of Vaseline to it with the tip of the little finger.

A white line caused by a backing scratch.

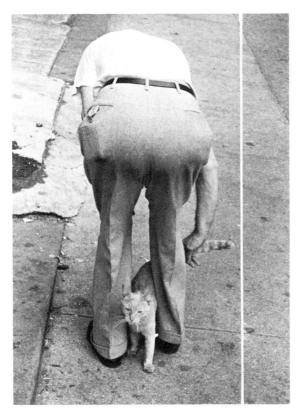

Emulsion and backing scratches are caused by the same things, except that pressure plates don't come in contact with emulsions. Instead, there may be a roughness on the camera's film gate, over which the film slides when it is advanced. Again the solution is to polish away the roughness with fine emery cloth.

Both emulsion and backing scratches are usu-ally made when the film is dry, either before or after processing, and are characterized by sharp, clean edges. Occasionally an emulsion is scratched during processing. The soft emulsion tears or digs up like old Jell-O, giving us scratches with jagged edges all the way through the gelatin. The usual culprit: long fingernails, which chop up the film as it is being removed from the developing reel. These jagged-edge scratches are so difficult to repair that only a genuine fanatic would even try, especially on small negatives.

To repair sharp-edge emulsion scratches, make a little pile of graphite dust by rubbing a no. 2 pencil on fine emery cloth. Now, make a firm lit-tle ball of cotton about the size of a dime (or use a Q-Tip). Leave the graphite dust on the emery cloth and thoroughly rub one side of the cotton ball into it, until the fibers are black and well im-pregnated with the dust. Then blow off the loose particles.

Using moderate pressure, rub the blackened cotton back and forth *across* the scratch. Even if the edges are very sharp there will usually be enough "tooth" to take graphite from the cotton fibers and fill the scratch. However, the emulsion itself also has tooth and picks up graphite. Fortunately, one can easily rub it off with a clean piece of dry cotton, still working crosswise to the scratch to avoid wiping the graphite out of it.

One can't tell when a scratch has been filled to exactly the right degree by holding the negative up to a light source, light surface, or light box. They just don't work for this purpose. The only good way to tell is to make a small test strip for the area that includes the scratch. If it prints just a little light, consider yourself lucky; when you have gotten this far it is easier to retouch the print than to remove exactly the right amount of graphite from the scratch. On the other hand, if the scratch prints too dark, work on it some more. Otherwise, you will have to do a difficult bleaching job on your print.

Though only a fanatic would work on jagged emulsion scratches, you may be working on your

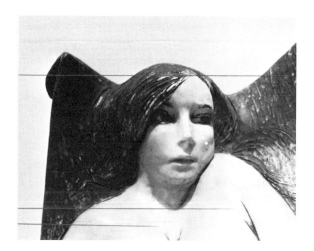

Dark lines caused by emulsion scratches on the negative. They can usually be filled in with powdered graphite, which you can make by rubbing a soft pencil on fine emery paper.

Fanatic Merit Badge. If so, try filling them in with a spotting brush and black opaque diluted with water to the consistency of ink. Or try rubbing undiluted opaque into them with a fingertip, wiping off the excess with damp cotton. There is something to be said for both systems: You can wipe off your mistakes as often as you wish without harming the negative, unless you rub on it too hard. Furthermore, the opaque has something in it that makes it stick nicely to emulsions, whereas ordinary inks and spotting colors do not.

A toothpick that has been sharpened to a needle point on emery cloth may also prove useful. Suck on it awhile to soften the point a bit, then use it for putting minute drops of very thin opaque into jagged little clear spots and torn places. For greater precision and control—but at considerable risk to your negative—you can try an artist's crow-quill pen, which has a needle-sharp point that will dig up the emulsion wherever it touches. If it touches only in the clear spots and lines you will be all right, because they will be filled with opaque, anyway.

The trick with a crow-quill is in using thin-enough opaque and getting it to feed (flow) properly. Slightly rusty or well-worn pen points work best, whereas new ones will hardly feed at all; they just won't write. The coating on the metal is the problem. Sand it off near the tip with a small piece of emery paper. It also helps if you lick the point just before sticking it in opaque. The *instant before* you intend to touch the pen to a negative you should get the flow started by writing on your thumbnail with it for a second or two. Naturally, you should practice awhile on reject negatives before digging into good ones.

Scratches and tears filled with opaque print up white, of course, which means that they have to be retouched on the print. If they fall in light image areas this is fairly easy. In medium-gray or dark areas they will drive you to the loony bin, because it takes forever to fill them in with dye. In this case, bleach on the print may prove easier than opaque in the scratch. However, some bleaching jobs are passports to the loony bin, too.

• Fuzzy, Round Blobs

Sometimes on your prints you will find round, fuzzy spots that are just a little bit lighter than the areas around them. They are caused by dirt or fingerprints on one of the lenses in the enlarger's condenser system. Breathe on the offending lens to steam it up, them wipe it clean with lens tissue. If necessary, use warm water, hand soap, and lens tissue.

• Air Bells

You may also find sharp-edged round spots on prints, but they will usually be darker than adjacent areas. Originating in the negative, they are poetically called "air bells." They are caused by faulty agitation methods during development,

Fuzzy blobs caused by dirt in the enlarger's condenser system. Cleaning these glass condensers will easily solve this problem.

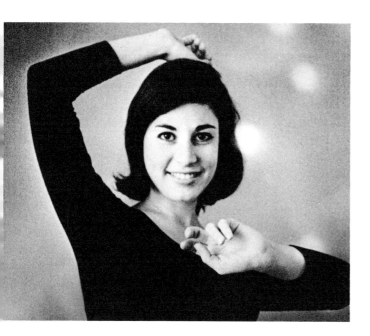

which permit air bubbles to cling to the emulsion. Wherever they touch it the developer can't reach it, so no tone is built up within them. If the bubbles are there through the whole developing time, these perfectly round spots are clear, or white. If they are there for just a minute or two the spots are grayish.

If you have a sure, steady hand you can retouch fairly large air bells with a no. 2-H pencil, provided they are of the gray type, which has a little tooth. Clear types do not. Sharpen the pencil to a long, needle point on emery cloth. Then tape one end of the negative strip to a skylit window or to a light box, holding the other end away from the surface somewhat. This puts a little spring in it so the sharp pencil point won't dig in abruptly. Now, working with only the pressure permitted by this springiness, pencil in the air bell with small, circular strokes.

For air bells too small to get into with pencil you can use opaque with the pen or sharpened toothpick. However, they are not especially hard to retouch on prints, so you might as well do the repairs at the print stage. Negatives are so small nowadays that working on them with opaque is a very tricky, frustrating business, anyway.

• Other Negative Defects

The defects that have been discussed so far have all been more or less reparable. Some of the following ones are not, yet you ought to know about them anyway. Being aware of their causes will help you avoid them.

Mottle: Most easily seen in the print, which

The black sun is actually an air bell that was caused by a bubble of air sticking to the film emulsion throughout the entire film-developing time. It prevented the developer from reaching the emulsion at that point, resulting in a round clear spot.

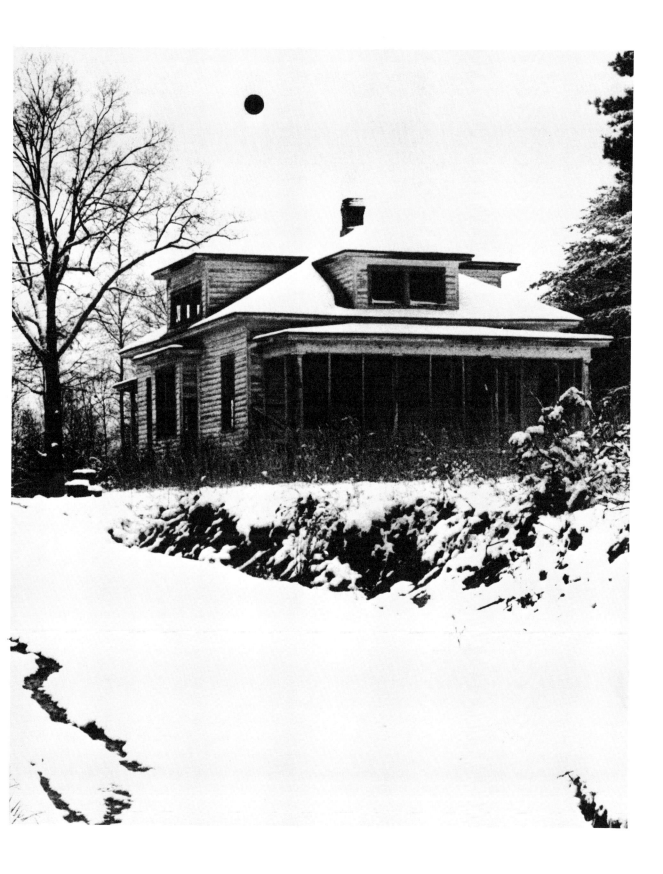

has a muddy, splotchy look. *Usual causes:* The negative was given insufficient agitation during development. May also be caused by leaving film in the developer for far too short a time. We may even get an effect that looks like a dark venetian blind. *Repair:* Both negatives and prints are usually beyond repair.

Dark edges: On a strip of negatives we see that the edge of the film is considerably darker than the center. *Usual causes:* insufficient agitation during development or using a developer that calls for too short a developing time (five minutes or less). *Repair:* on the negative, none, but dark edges can usually be corrected in printing by dodging or burning-in (pages 71ff.).

Dark streaks: Usually called "high-speed-development marks." Look for dark streaks or marks that originate on the borders of the film and go part way into the image. *Causes:* too vigorous, too frequent, or constant agitation during development. *Repair:* on the negative, none, but dark streaks can sometimes be counteracted in printing by cropping, burning-in, dodging, or retouching.

Light-struck: Dark streaks where stray light has touched the film before processing. *Usual causes:* handling film rolls or cassettes, or loading cameras, in bright sunlight; defective or worn self-load cassettes; films larger than 35-mm not wound tightly enough on their spools. *Repair:* on the negative, none, but the marks can sometimes be counteracted in printing (see "dark streaks" above).

Static marks: They usually look like black lightning flashes or fireworks displays on the negative, yet they are also found in the form of little round dots that are more or less in rows. *Causes:* Some people build up within themselves an unusual amount of static electricity, which can be discharged to unprocessed film. In cold weather or cold rooms, cameras and bulk film loaders may also build up charges if film is run through them too fast; for example, if a film advance lever or winder is used with too much vigor and haste. Some cameras and loaders are worse in this re-

spect than others. *Repair:* There is nothing one can do about static marks on negatives, but the little, round ones can be retouched on prints.

Reticulation: When printed, reticulation looks like a formal tile or mosaic pattern super-imposed on all or part of the image. *Usual causes:* washing either too long or in warm water, a great temperature difference between processing solutions, or using a fixer with an exhausted hardener. *Repair:* Though it can be neither repaired nor corrected for, it is sometimes very interesting in itself.

Water marks: Irregular marks in shapes that large drops of water would make on a surface. In a print, a water spot shows up as a little area with a vaguely defined double line around it; one of the individual lines is dark, the other light. *Cause:* leaving large drops of water on the emulsion when hanging film up to dry. Last to dry, these drops pull the emulsion out of place around their peripheries, which accounts for the lines. *Repair:* Though impossible to remove from negatives, water marks can sometimes be patched up on prints.

Grain: Hard to see on negatives, grain looks like sand or granite on prints. *Causes:* overexposure, overdevelopment, developing negatives in a print developer, processing in solutions whose temperatures vary too much from one another, using an overworked fixing bath in which the hardener is exhausted, washing too long a time, and washing in warm water. Alone, any of these factors may cause grain, but it is almost a certainty if several are combined. *Repair:* There is no way of removing grain from negatives, but it can be minimized by diffusion printing or by making prints lighter than usual.

In a sense, this chapter is a long description of the woes that possibly await you, but don't let it throw you. If you carefully follow the instructions in this book, you will never in a lifetime even see most of the defects you have just read about. Remember that about 99 per cent of the time you will be able to prepare your negatives for problemless printing by using only a brush, nose grease, and a silicone cloth.

HOW TO MAKE AND USE TEST STRIPS

Making test strips is a fast, easy, and economical way to determine the correct exposure for prints. In turn, finding the right exposure is by far the most important part of the art of printing. Without test strips, one would have to take a variety of things into account, including the relative "speed" of the printing paper, the output of the enlarger bulb, the relative density of the negative, the line voltage, and so on. However, by making test strips we neatly step around such problems and yet come up with very accurate exposure information.

Test strips are so easy to make that there is a tendency to slight them. However, the information in test strips cannot be trusted unless they are carefully exposed and processed. Furthermore, they must be examined under a light that is bright enough. For more information on these matters, review the material on pages 38–40. Remember that contacts, test strips, and prints should all be treated in the same way and with great care if they are to be effective.

• Things You Need

We will again use the list given on page 27. Since it is lengthy we won't repeat it here. However, we can eliminate the glass, soap, china marker, and lighter fluid.

• Your Processing Line and Developing Procedures

Arrange your chemical trays in the way described earlier. Carefully follow the recommended processing procedures. However, you should use one specific developing time for test strips (say $1\frac{1}{2}$ or two minutes), rather than use the time range from $1\frac{1}{4}$ to $2\frac{1}{4}$ minutes. We could say that either $1\frac{1}{2}$ or two minutes would represent the optimum, whereas there would be a slight loss in print quality with longer or shorter times that are still within the recommended range. Since we have an accurate way for determining exposure, it only makes sense to tie it in with a developing time that will give top print quality.

In making final prints, you should also aim for a specific time. Then if you miss the correct exposure somewhat you can lengthen or shorten the time to compensate for your error. You will learn that there is a fair amount of latitude. Do not do this with test strips, however! *Always* remove them from the developer after the preselected time, even if you see that they will have to be remade.

If you violate this rule and "jerk" a test strip after, say, thirty seconds, the exposure information on it will be applicable only to a print that will also be jerked in thirty seconds. Similarly, a three-minute test strip will be applicable only to a three-minute print. Though jerking and "pushing" test strips and prints are legitimate techniques for certain purposes, they are disastrous when used in ordinary printing. So don't be lazy or impatient. As a beginner, the test strip is your best friend. Treat it with respect.

• Width of Strips

Some people get carried away with the economy idea and make test strips about one half inch wide, which is much too narrow to judge with any accuracy. An exposure that looks good on such a strip may be totally wrong for an enlargement print. A one-inch strip is usually all right, a two-inch one somewhat better. Occasionally, you should use a whole sheet of paper for a test strip —just to see what things look like—and sometimes it is the only way to get all the information you need. However, narrower strips will usually suffice.

• Placement of Strips

Since a test strip will include only a section of the image, you will naturally want exposure information concerning the most important part. For accurate placement, turn on the enlarger light and lay a pencil beside the image area you deem most important. Then turn off the light and lay the strip of paper next to the pencil.

When printing pictures of people, you usually lay the strips right across their faces. For other pictures, you kind of psych them out in trying to choose areas for which correct exposure information will be applicable to the pictures as a whole. You learn to do this through experience and experimentation.

• Exposing the Strip: the Five-Second Method

Though you were given this method earlier, it will be repeated for your convenience. Stop down the enlarger lens two or three stops. Position the strip and give *all* of it a five-second exposure.

Taking care not to push it out of place, cover up about one inch of it with a sheet of cardboard and give it another five-second exposure. Continue progressively covering it up and giving five-second exposures. On the developed strip, you can tell the exposure for a given area by counting up to it by fives from the bottom.

You usually use this method when you have an approximate idea of the range in which the correct exposure will fall, say from ten to twenty-five seconds. When you are printing a lot of negatives from the same roll, you can usually guess the range pretty well after you have printed the first one or two.

• Exposing the Strip: the 5–5–10–20 Method

This method, confusing to some, has the advantage of showing what a series of tones look like when their exposures are exactly doubled (or halved). That is, adjacent tones are one stop apart. This will help you get a better quantitative idea of what exposure does to photosensitive materials.

Setup for making a test strip with a two-inch strip of printing paper. Both ends are taped to the printing easel so that it won't shift position as the cardboard is moved across it.

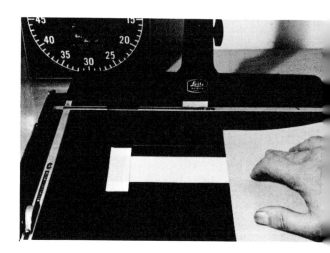

For this test, stop your lens down three or four times. As before, start by giving the whole strip an exposure, then progressively cover it up for additional exposures. However, only the *first two* exposures are alike this time. After the second one, begin progressively doubling the exposure for each succeeding step. The *individual exposures* in the series are: 5–5–10–20–40–80–160 seconds. Though you can extend the series beyond this there is usually no need to.

When we examine the developed strip we have to think of *total exposures,* which happen to add up to: 5–10–20–40–80–160–320 seconds. The exposure for a given section of a strip is its *total exposure,* not merely one of the individual exposures that were added together to make the total. Perhaps this will help you keep things straight: To tell the exposure for a particular segment, start at the bottom with 5 and count up to it by doubles: 5–10–20–etc. Or count down from 320 by halves: 320–160–80–etc. *Figure it out!*

If the *correct* exposure happens to come out long—say 80 seconds—open up two stops to make it 20. *Remember!*

An important advantage of this method is that it incorporates a much longer exposure range than the five-second system. You need this great a range when you are using unfamiliar equipment and printing materials and haven't the slightest idea where the correct exposure will fall. With a range from 5 to 320 seconds it would be hard to miss it. It will also give you a clear picture of the *tonal* range inherent in a given paper.

Many people make their test strips by uncovering the paper, though covering it is much better. Suit yourself. Warning: If you try uncovering with *this* method you will go berserk trying to figure out the total exposures.

● Remakes

There are times when it is wise to remake test strips before going on to final prints, for example when they are, all in all, either too light or too dark. This makes them relatively useless. For the light ones, open up the lens a stop or two; for the dark ones, stop down. Or you can lengthen or shorten the exposure times if you like. Since the results can be the same, do whichever is the more convenient. Remember that doubling the time is the same as opening up a stop, halving the time the same as stopping down once.

In examining a test strip, you may see that the contrast is either too high or too low for the picture. Choose another contrast of paper or printing filter and remake it. The point is that the correct exposure on one paper may be far from the correct exposure on another. In part this is because contrast and exposure depend on one another: where one varies, the other should also. Another reason is that different paper grades, or variable-contrast papers used with different filters, have different speeds, or light sensitivity. A good exposure for one paper wouldn't be right for another that is 30 per cent more sensitive to light. The general rule is: the lower the paper or filter number the greater the speed, and vice versa.

● Exposure Chips

Sometimes it is convenient to make an exposure test with a single 2×2-inch or larger chip of paper, positioning it in the most important part of the picture and making a single exposure by pure guesswork based on prior experience. Though this exposure may prove to be considerably off, one learns in time to make rather accurate exposure determinations using chips that are as much as one stop off in either direction. This is not recommended for beginners, however.

Another approach is to make two exposures on the chip, one that you estimate will be a bit too much, the other a bit too little. From analyzing the two-tone chip you can then estimate the exposure between the two that would be exactly right.

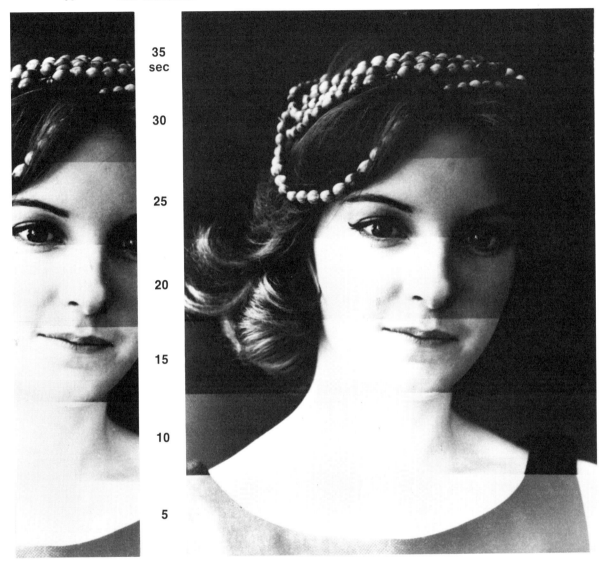

TOTAL
EXPOSURES

A   B

35
sec

30

25

20

15

10

5

C
TOTAL EXPOSURES
D

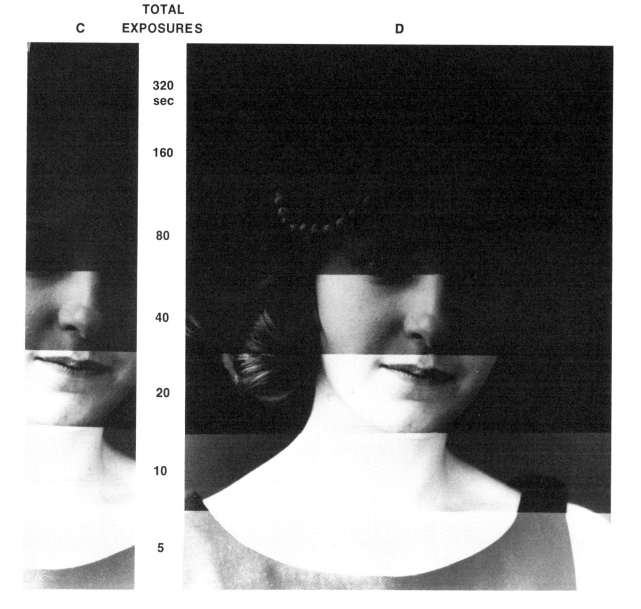

320 sec

160

80

40

20

10

5

Four test strips made from the same negative. A (two-inch) and B (full-sheet) were made with the 5–5–5–5 method (exposure increments of five seconds). C and D were made with the 5–5–10–20 system (total exposures progressively doubled). The full-sheet tests obviously give us more information than the 2-inch ones. However, the narrow ones tell us enough to permit us to successfully extrapolate from them. Note that the exposure range with the 5–5–10–20 system is much greater than with the 5–5–5–5 system.

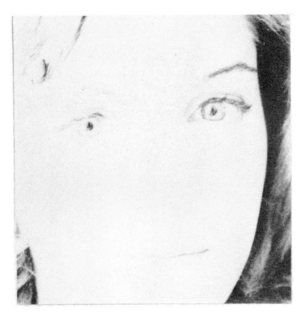

5 seconds

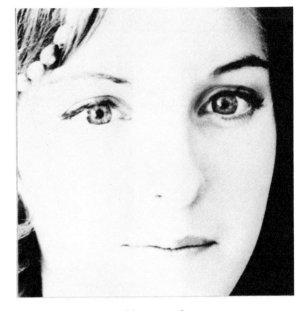

10 seconds

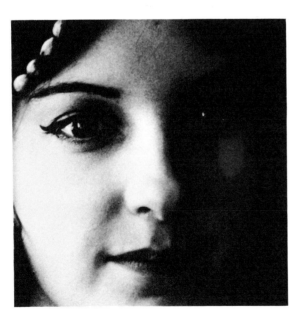

25 seconds

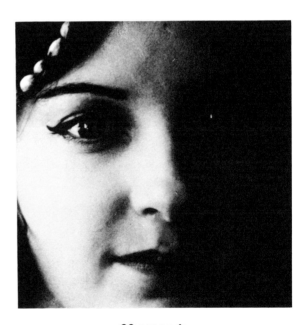

30 seconds

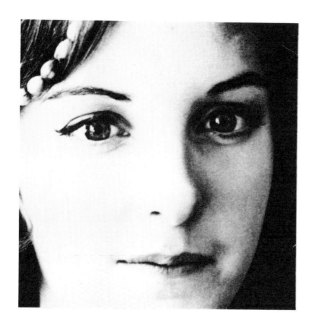

15 seconds

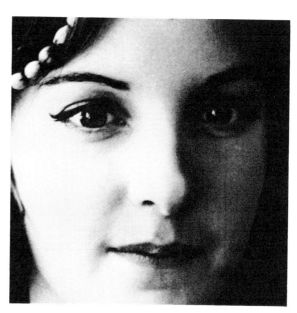

20 seconds

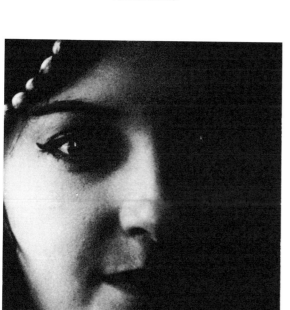

35 seconds

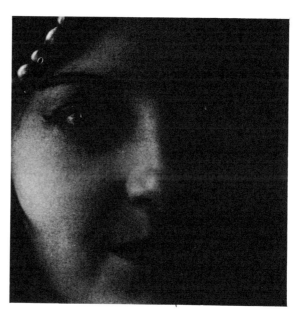

40 seconds

A series of test exposures made with three-inch pieces, or chips, of paper. You can use smaller chips, say two inches, but they won't give you as much reliable information. Chips as small as one inch are relatively useless.

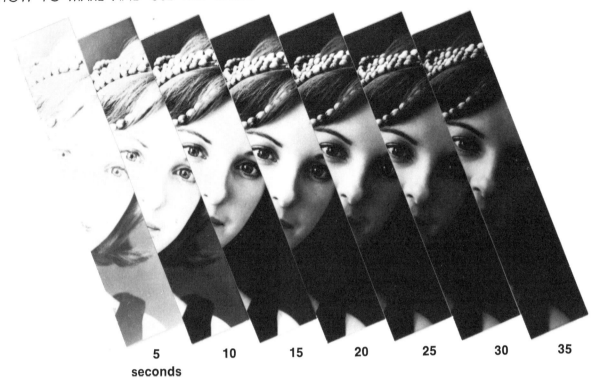

5   **10**   **15**   **20**   **25**   **30**   **35**

seconds

● Duplicate-Image Test Strips

An ordinary test strip will usually work very well, but there are times when it won't. The problem is that each of the test exposures falls in a different part of the picture. Sometimes these areas are so unlike in their exposure requirements that the best exposure on the strip might be correct for only the area in which it falls. For example, a test strip shows that step three (fifteen seconds) has exactly the right exposure, yet a full-size print proves that this is too much exposure for all the rest of the picture.

We can easily get around this difficulty by using several strips of paper instead of just one. As usual, we position a strip by running it across all the picture areas for which we think we'll need specific exposure information. We give the first strip a five-second exposure. Then we start exposing other strips in exactly the same position, giving them respectively ten, fifteen, twenty, and

Duplicate-image test strips made by exposing all the pieces of paper to the same part of the image. They were positioned at an angle to give us a good sampling of all the important tone areas of the image. They give us the basic exposure and tell us what various parts of the image would look like if they were lightened (dodged) or darkened (burned-in). These strips tell us much more than a simple two-inch strip made with the 5–5–5–5 method.

twenty-five seconds. We end up with five strips, each with a single exposure on it.

They should be developed simultaneously for a preselected optimum time. Though it is a little like playing with wet spaghetti, you should have no trouble. When you are through, you have five duplicate images, except that they vary in tone.

After the strips are fixed, lay them side by side on the back of a tray and examine them under the bright hypo light. You will probably see that none of them shows you the best exposure for the entire picture but that, among them, they tell you all you need to know. One strip might show you that ten seconds would be right for the bottom of the picture, another that twenty seconds would do for the top. Others might indicate that a certain area needs twenty-five seconds and another area five seconds. This might seem like a ridiculous situation, but it is not. The problem can easily be handled by simple dodging and burning-in (pages 71ff.). These are things we do nearly all the time in ordinary printing.

The other types of test strips wouldn't give you all this information, or even come close to it. However, these duplicate-image strips consume more paper and take more time. Even so, they are both practical and economical in the long run because of the quality of exposure information they yield. Furthermore, they will give you accurate times for dodging and burning-in, which other types of exposure strips do not.

• Full-Sheet Exposure Tests

Every now and then you should make duplicate-image tests using full sheets of paper, rather than strips. You should do it only with pictures you really care about, of course. Otherwise, you would find it hard to justify the expense and time. The idea is that by carefully studying full-size tests, you can learn many things about the finer points of printing that you might ordinarily miss. It is unnecessary to tell you not to overdo it: your wallet tells you that. Nevertheless, you should overrule this prohibition once in a while—as a useful educational expense.

A good way to use full-sheet tests is to tape them up on the wall and study them for a few days. Vary the light intensity from time to time. Look at them close up, then from various other distances until you are across the room from them. These light and distance variations can teach you a lot.

• Honor Your Test Strips

You will soon see that making test strips is so easy that you could do it in your sleep. This could lead you to treat them with disrespect, which would be a very serious mistake. You should always remember that the most important step in becoming an expert printer is making handsome test strips that are properly exposed, processed, and cared for. Furthermore, good test strips can be your teachers, because there is very little that you need to know about printing that they can't teach you. Thus, if you are serious about your creative work you will learn to honor them.

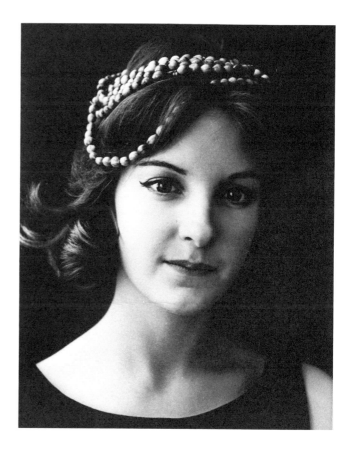

A straight print (not dodged, burned-in, or otherwise manipulated) made with a twenty-second exposure.

HOW TO MAKE AND USE A WORK PRINT

A work print is simply a preliminary study print that still needs to have work done on it in the form of cropping, dodging, burning-in, bleaching, or dye retouching. However, in terms of having the correct basic exposure and contrast it should be a high-quality picture. The idea is to have a printed image to study, for days or even weeks, before making a final commitment concerning how it will be treated in a finished print. Some people like to work this way; others don't. After you have tried it a few times, make your choice.

The purpose is to delay your decisions somewhat in order to give you a chance to see your pictures better. After you have made a few prints you will see why this is a useful idea. In our enthusiasm for seeing new pictures enlarged for the first time we often make mistakes, even to the point of producing prints of gruesome quality. At the time, however, we see them with eyes of love and utterly fail to see how awful they are. Later, we awaken, see the sorry fruits of our labors, and condemn ourselves as artistic incompetents. This is very hard on the morale, as any photographer can tell you.

The way around this morass is to be very tentative the first time you print a new roll of pictures. Instead of getting either tricky or hasty, slow yourself down and severely limit your objectives: (1) make a high-quality contact sheet and mark it up carefully, (2) make a high-quality test strip and analyze it in detail, and (3) make a high-quality basic print. This means a correctly exposed print, of the right contrast, that hasn't been dodged, burned-in, bleached, or otherwise manipulated.

By thus limiting your objectives, you greatly lessen your chances of failure. Since a work print is only a tentative way of looking ahead to what the final print will be, how can it really be wrong at this point? Indeed, some people carry this idea so far that they are quite satisfied with really sloppy work prints, finding that they can use them quite well in making decisions concerning final prints. Because these poor prints are both tentative and useful, they could hardly be considered failures.

Some people make cruddy work prints because they are lazy or can't do any better. On the other hand, skilled photographers sometimes do it when they are in a terrible hurry. With their quality standards lowered they can bang out prints almost as fast as they can move. Because of their long experience they can easily tell how a poor-quality work print will translate into a high-quality finished one.

As a beginner you are totally incapable of this, and please don't forget it. Though it will take you extra work and time, you should always make the best work prints that you possibly can. Otherwise, your sensitivity to print quality will not develop properly and you won't learn the difference between good prints and bad ones. For you a tacky work print is about as useful as a broken neck. See?

• No Cropping

It is not advisable to crop work prints, because you might crop out things that you would leave in if you had more chance to consider them. Unfortunately, many enlarger negative carriers cut off some of the image, sometimes enough to ruin certain pictures. Therefore, advanced photographers and professionals usually file out their carriers enough to permit all of the frame and some of the border to print, which gives them work prints with neat black edges. Filing out just the right amount is fairly important. When the negative is in position there should be about one sixteenth inch of border showing all the way around.

• Size of Work Print

It is easiest to assess the possibilities of a work print if you make it the same size that your finished print will be. After you have had some experience in printing, however, you will find that half size is entirely adequate—and more economical, of course. You may even want to work quarter size.

Some people go to custom labs, where they have enlargers that will project a whole roll at a time to make "enlarged contact sheets," usually 11×14 or 16×20. Though they look exactly like 8×10 contacts the images are considerably larger and easier to see. This is certainly the easiest way to get work prints, but it is more expensive than making them yourself.

• Things You Need

Though most of this list was given earlier, it seems about time to repeat it for your convenience. There are a few additions and omissions, however.

Negatives to print
Contacts
Enlarger
Enlarging easel
A no. 4 sable brush
Silicone anti-static cloth
Focusing magnifier (optional)
Focusing paper
Timer, metronome, or watch
Double-weight enlarging paper, regular or resin-coated (RC)
Printing filters (optional: for variable-contrast paper)
Scissors or paper cutter
Pencil
Note pad
Safelight(s)
Thermometer
Towel(s)
Dektol print developer
Kodak Indicator Stop Bath
First hypo
Second hypo
A hypo light
Print-inspection board
An 11×14 piece of cardboard
Tracing paper (optional)
Mount boards
Perma Wash (unless you are using RC paper)
Funnel
Chemical-storage bottles
Photographic blotters (optional)
Masking tape
A china marker

Most of these items have already been explained, but some have not.

Focusing magnifier: An optical device that you put on the focusing paper directly under the enlarger lens, to help you see when you have the negative in critically sharp focus. The useful kind is called a "high-magnification grain focuser." Other types are either useless or aggravating. If your close-up vision is not so good you will need such a magnifier, otherwise not.

Focusing paper: A sheet of printing paper that you put in the easel for focusing and cropping your pictures. Since it is of the same thickness as the paper you print on, you may be sure that the print will be in as sharp focus as the focusing paper. If you have an easel with adjustable masking blades it is convenient to draw dark-pencil frame lines on the paper, four in all, at distances of ½, 1, 1½, and 2 inches from the edge. They make setting the masking blades easy and fast.

Scissors or paper cutter: Though it is very convenient to have a paper-trimming board in the darkroom you can get along for years without one. If you use scissors to cut printing paper into halves, quarters, or strips, make yourself some little cardboard templates—5×7, 4×8, 4×5, and 1×8. For accurate trimming, put a template on the back of a sheet of printing paper, using it as a ruler for drawing a line. Even under a safelight you can see well enough to accurately cut along this line with scissors.

Pencil: When you are making test strips and work prints it is a good idea to write notes on the back of them concerning the aperture settings, exposure times, paper contrast grades, and so on. Otherwise, you may soon forget the information or get it confused. With regular paper use ordinary pencil, but *do not use* a ball-point pen or felt-tip markers. With resin-coated (RC) paper use a china marker, but write lightly with it.

Note pad: For more extensive notes, use a note pad. When you make work prints it is with the intention of duplicating them later, except for additional manipulation such as dodging and burning-in. Having good notes will make this fast and easy.

Print-inspection board: to lay prints or test strips on for examination under the hypo light. Can also be used for bleaching prints. The back of a tray will work fine, but a panel of plastic or glass is better. If you use glass, cover one side with black Con-Tact paper, the other with white. It is helpful to view prints against these colors; and the paper shatterproofs the glass.

Masking tape: In photography, masking tape

comes close to being the universal tool, so you should always have some near at hand.

● **Step by Step to Make a Work Print**

If you have made some test strips you already know how to make enlargements, because test strips *are* enlargements. However, to pull things together and make the work easier we will use this step by step schedule for making prints.

1. Assemble all the items on the list and set up the chemical processing trays.

2. Organize the negatives, contacts, printing paper, scissors, anti-static cloth, etc., on the dry side of your darkroom.

3. Select a contact sheet and examine it to refresh your mind concerning which negative you had already decided to print first.

4. Find the negative in its glassine envelope.

5. Clean it carefully, then check the effectiveness of the cleaning job, picking off remaining dust with a brush.

6. Put the negative in the enlarger.

7. Open the lens all the way.

8. Turn on the safelight(s) and turn off the white light.

9. Turn on the enlarger light.

10. Position the enlarger head and easel to give you the largest possible full-frame image on the focusing paper.

11. Focus the image sharply.

12. Turn off the enlarger light.

13. Cut a full sheet of 8×10 paper into 1×8-inch strips, returning all but one to the package.

14. Stop down the enlarger lens two or three stops.

15. Expose and process a test strip.

16. Examine the test strip under the hypo light to decide which is the best exposure on it for the work print. If the best exposure would fall between two areas, average their exposure times.

17. Set the timer for the time decided upon.

18. Change the aperture setting if necessary.

19. Put printing paper in the easel and make an exposure.

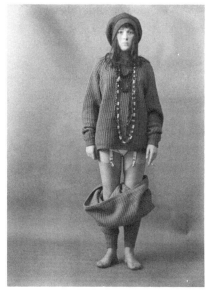

A

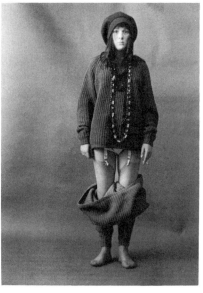

B

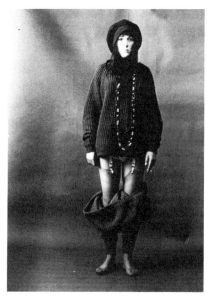

C

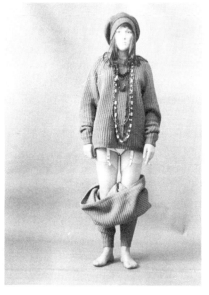

D

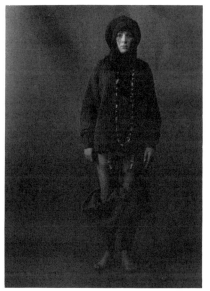

E

20. Make pencil notes on the back of it and on your note pad.

21. Process, wash, and dry the work print.

In order to make it complete, the list was made a little long, but don't let that bother you. Instead of throwing up your hands in despair, read through it line by line. You will then agree that any six-year-old could follow it.

A good work print should be properly exposed and made on paper of the right contrast grade. With one exception, B, these prints are either badly exposed or of the wrong contrast. A is properly exposed but two contrast grades too flat. C, also properly exposed, is two grades too contrasty. D and E are on the correct paper, but D is a stop underexposed, while E is one stop (100 per cent) overexposed.

● **Work Print – Finished Print**

With many a picture, you will find that a well-made work print is as far as you need to go. In such case a work print and a finished one are the same thing, a finished print merely being one that needs nothing more done to it. This is one reason you were asked to work carefully: instead of settling for a foul-ball work print you may find that you've hit a home run.

Work prints are usually called "straight prints," incidentally, but you can call them whatever you like. It is good to keep track of the twists and turns of photographic jargon, yet we are only talking here about prints that haven't been fussed with. They've been correctly exposed on the right-contrast paper, then correctly processed. That's all—no manipulation.

There are some who claim that there is no such thing as a work, or straight, print that can't be improved with a little dodging, burning-in, or bleaching. Thus it would be incorrect to say that a work print could also be a finished print at the same time. Though this view is a little precious, it happens to be a very useful one for people who are just learning the craft of photography. It would therefore be wise for you to adopt it for the time being. Assume that a work print can always be improved, no matter how good it already looks. Following this concept has turned many a person into a master printer.

A little more concerning the jargon: The terms work print, basic print, study print, first print, straight print, fast print, and trial print are synonymous. So are finished print, final print, fully realized print, and manipulated print. There is nothing precious about any of these terms, though people tend to use them as if there were. Be satisfied if they merely help you keep track of what you are reading.

● **Cropping L's**

When you set out to study a work print it is convenient to start with the cropping. If you trim one or more sides it may look better. Cropping means trimming, that's all. You can sail right into the cropping problem with a paper cutter or scissors if you like, but what if you make a mistake? What if you change your mind about how it should be cropped? Then you end up with a mutilated and useless work print. It is better not to cut it up at all. However, this still leaves you with the problem of visualizing what different croppings would look like, which is rather difficult for beginners.

The simple answer is to make yourself some visual-aid equipment in the form of "cropping L's," which are merely L shapes cut out of cardboard or paper. By laying them on a print and moving them around, you can get them to enclose a rectangle of any dimensions you like. That is, you can see what any cropping would look like without having to cut up your print.

When you find the cropping you like best you can draw it right on the print, if you like. Just use your cropping L's as rulers and draw lines with a china marker. For the sake of neatness you might sharpen the marker somewhat with a used razor

Cardboard cropping L's are used to tell what a picture will look like when its area is cut down (cropped) in various ways.

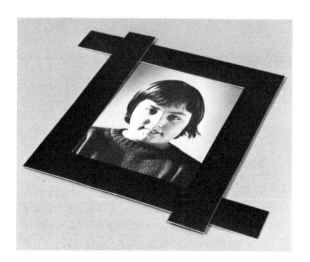

blade. If you later change your mind about the cropping, wipe it off with cotton soaked in lighter fluid.

Cut out your cropping L's neatly, or their ragged or crooked edges will throw your aesthetic judgement out of kilter. We already have enough trouble with this in photography without having to ask for it. You can make the best cropping L's from a photographic mount board that has both a white and a black side. Depending on the tone of the print, you will prefer one color or the other, but sometimes you will wish to try both. A wallboard knife and ruler are good for cutting mount board, provided you make four or five strokes for each cut. If you try to do it in one stroke the knife will go everywhere except where you want it to.

You will find that fourteen-inch cropping L's two inches wide are about right for 8×10 prints. Some people also like to have small ones to carry around with them, so they can practice cropping snapshots and pictures in magazines. It's fun.

• Use a Note Board

One makes a work print in order to have something tangible to think about while deciding how the final print should be made. It is rather like thinking up original things to think about—not so easy when you try it. One must look at the work print inch by inch, notice every single thing in it, try to decide what it does for the picture as a whole, ponder about whether it has the right tone, try to visualize what it would look like if its tone were changed, and so on. This requires genuine original thought, which we have to force ourselves into—the ego being naturally lazy. Or we can trick ourselves into it.

One of the ways of conning yourself into doing heavy-duty mental and perceptual work is to intentionally make a real production of it. An easy enough way to do this is to tape your print to the clean back of a mount board, centering it well and taking care to do a neat job of it. This gives

the work print considerable importance and prestige. The idea now is to ponder it from time to time (it's best not to do it all at once), trying to decide what you should do in making the finished print. Record your decisions neatly in pencil on the mount board around the print, judiciously making little diagrams, arrows, and asterisks, too. Take pains to make your work look important, and you will soon find yourself believing that it is. When you do come to believe, your work will be half done, even if you have to change some of your decisions later.

Except for neat cropping lines, don't write or diagram anything on the print itself, because your markings would change the visuals of your picture so radically that you wouldn't be able to make well-balanced decisions with respect to it. In effect, you would be analyzing one picture while attempting to make decisions concerning a different one.

Though you will be considering doing dodging, burning-in, bleaching, and dye retouching, they all boil down to just one thing: making certain tones either lighter or darker. The thing you must try to visualize is what difference it would make. However, until you've had quite a bit of experience in printing, you will have no substantial basis for knowing, one way or the other.

Thus you are forced to either psych out your pictures (follow your strongest whims or rely on your innate visual sensitivity) or do things arbitrarily just to see what happens. Fortunately, both approaches are quite good enough. Whatever you do, you'll make mistakes anyway, but they should be considered as textbooks from which you can learn. In a sense, the entire art of photography is founded on mistakes—so don't get uptight about them.

It would help if you were to try to see your decisions as important while you are making them and your mistakes as of no importance whatever. It is a matter of learning to cleverly con yourself.

An approach that is a little fancier may suit your legitimate need to convince yourself of the importance of thoroughly studying a work print even when you don't yet know what you are really looking for. Put a clean piece of tracing paper over the print, neatly taping it to the edge of the mount board. Now you can make impressive little diagrams right over the print without harming it any. Then when you want to see what it actually looks like again you merely lift up the tracing paper. And if you don't like your drawings you can start over again with a fresh piece of paper. Another alternative is to use a sheet of clear plastic, drawing on it with a china marker, and removing mistakes with cotton soaked in lighter fluid. It's re-usable, too.

Since you don't yet really know anything about printing, you shouldn't expect your notes and lines to embody the wisdom of Solomon. He didn't know anything about photography, anyway. But you should at least *do* the work, because it is a good habit to get into and will make it easier for you to force yourself to see better. Absurd as it may sound, all artists have to force themselves to learn to see, it is such hard work. Whoever says otherwise is telling you a fairy tale.

A work print taped to the back of a used mount board, then taped to a door, where it can be studied at leisure. As you study a work print you can make notes to yourself on the edges of the board. This will help you make up your mind with respect to what you should do when you make your final print; that is, where you should crop, dodge, burn-in, bleach, etc.

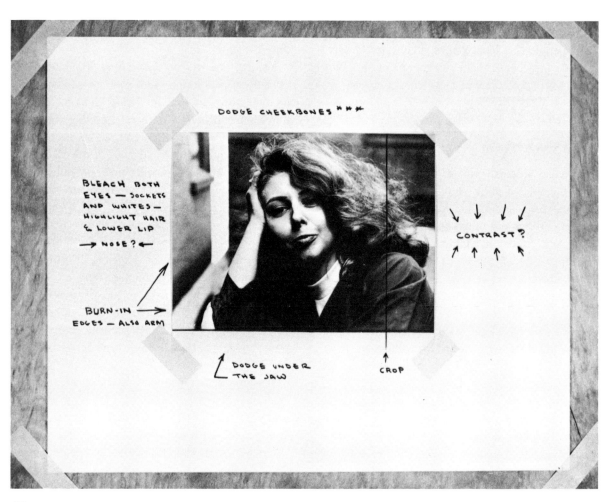

HOW AND WHEN TO DODGE AND BURN-IN

Dodging is a simple technique for lightening areas of a print, burning-in a technique for darkening them. Though this doesn't sound like much, it is the most subtle and exciting part of printing. In only an hour or so you can learn the basic skills and immediately begin using them effectively on pictures in which local tonal adjustments are obviously necessary, yet you can spend a lifetime learning their nuances. Thus we could say that both techniques are extremely easy but endlessly sophisticated, too. The results that you can get with them will keep you fascinated with printing for many years.

● Things You Need

Since you will be making enlargements again, you can use the list given in the previous chapter. However, we will add a few items that are used in making tools for dodging and burning-in.

Scissors
Pencil
A 10-inch piece of straight coat-hanger wire
Masking tape
Two round cardboard disks ¾ inch and 2 inches in diameter
Three sheets of 11×14-inch light cardboard

● Making Your Tools

To make a dodging tool, or dodger, tape the two cardboard disks to opposite ends of the wire. Though you can easily make additional dodgers using cardboard in other sizes and shapes, you will very seldom need to. If you do, the easiest thing is to temporarily tape the new shapes onto the old ones, so you won't have to go looking around for more wire.

You will need three burning-in tools made of cardboard about 11×14 inches, two with single round holes in the middle of them, one without a hole. The holes should be about three quarters of an inch and two inches in diameter. Since you will probably be looking at these cardboards for years to come, you might as well cut the holes neatly.

Though these tools are very simple, as you see, they are like clay in the hands of a master potter: amazing things can be done with them.

● How to Dodge a Print

You dodge an area in a print by temporarily blocking off the light that is falling upon it from the enlarger. You can do this by simply sticking your hand under the lens for a moment, so that a shadow is cast on the area. Indeed, many printers do most of their dodging with one or both of their hands. However, beginners should stick to dodgers, because they are easier to use with precision.

Your dodger is simply a shadow caster, and with the two disks you can get any size shadow you want by merely varying their distance from the lens. With the larger one you can even block off the light altogether, if you wish.

When you cast a shadow on an area for part of the exposure time, you lighten it in the resulting print. If you dodge it for the entire time it will come out white. By varying the proportion of

Drawing of a dodging tool in use. It casts a shadow, which should be moved around during the dodging period so that the dodged area will blend with the part of the image surrounding it. Note that the wire handle of the dodger also casts a shadow that must be blended in.

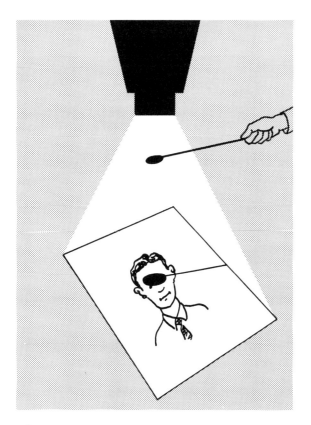

dodging time to exposure time you can lighten it to any degree you wish. However, it is usually not good to dodge a given area for more than 50 per cent of the total exposure time. If you do, it will generally come out looking flat, washed out, or muddy. If your negative is too thin, even that percentage is too high. Remember that a thin negative is one that has been underexposed and/or underdeveloped.

If you hold the dodger still while you are using it, it will make a round silhouette of itself on your picture. Occasionally this is a good idea, but usually not. Ordinarily, we want our pictures to show no evidence whatever of having been manipulated in any way, so we have to subtly blend the dodged area in with the rest of the picture. We do this by simply moving the dodger around constantly while we are using it. Easy as pie.

Perhaps the hardest thing is to learn to keep track of the dodging time while we are dodging. It is a little like the old patting-your-head-and-rubbing-your-stomach trick. The best thing is to make some dry runs, practicing until you've gotten the time problem sorted out. The easiest way is to let a photographic timer take care of the basic exposure time, while under your breath you count out seconds for dodging. Using a metronome requires a little more mental agility, a watch or clock still more. However, thousands of people time their dodging this way, so you see that it is actually possible.

You may sometimes have a problem with the shadow cast by the wire part of the dodger, because it can make light streaks on prints. The easy solution is to keep varying the angle at which this shadow crosses the image, for then it will leave no evidence of itself. Thus you must move the disk around in one pattern, the shadow of the wire in another. After a little practice you will find it easy.

● How to Burn-In a Print

To burn-in an area, you give it some extra exposure after the basic exposure time is up, at the same time blocking off this extra light from the rest of the picture, which doesn't need it. One does this with a burning-in tool, the hole letting light through, the cardboard shielding areas that already have enough exposure. For blending purposes we constantly move the cardboard around during the additional exposure.

When the enlarger light is on, the image shows up on the cardboard, its sharpness depending on the distance between the cardboard and the lens. When the board is nearly touching the printing paper the picture is so sharply defined that one can see exactly where the hole is letting light through to darken an area. In order to take advantage of this you should use a burning-in tool quite a bit larger than your printing paper, an 11×14-inch board being about the right size for an 8×10 print.

You usually don't need this precision, however, because areas that need to be darkened are generally defined rather vaguely. With the cardboard held much closer to the lens you can still see the image well enough to see what you are doing, even if it is very fuzzy. Varying this distance also permits you to control the size of the area that is being burned-in at a given moment, aided by the fact that you have holes of two sizes to work with. Using the small hole close to the printing paper, it is possible to burn-in a large area by moving it back and forth like a paintbrush or a spray gun, but this would be unduly laborious. Starting out with the right-size circle of light on the printing paper would be better. However, the paintbrush approach is good for darkening areas that are long and very narrow.

Dodging time is usually limited to about 50 per cent of the basic exposure, and there are just so many areas that can be dodged in the time available. In burning-in we don't have these limitations. You can burn-in as many areas as you like, each one for as long as you like. It is not uncommon to see a person use five to ten minutes' worth of burning-in on a single print. Frequently, individual areas are so "blocked up" that they need two to three minutes before they get any tone in them.

This means that some parts of a negative may be so heavily exposed (and dark) that light can hardly get through them at all.

It is nice to know that you can make selected parts of your prints as dark as you please, but such long burning-in times get very tedious. However, you can shorten them very considerably by opening up the enlarger lens all the way after you have given the basic exposure. There are two other problems with such long times: one is that you may heat up your enlarger too much and damage it and your negative; the answer here is to burn-in a while, let it cool off, then burn-in

Drawing of a burning-in card in use. This is a way of selectively darkening parts of the image after it has been given the basic exposure. For blending purposes the card is moved around constantly during the burning-in period. Otherwise it would create an obvious round spot with sharp edges.

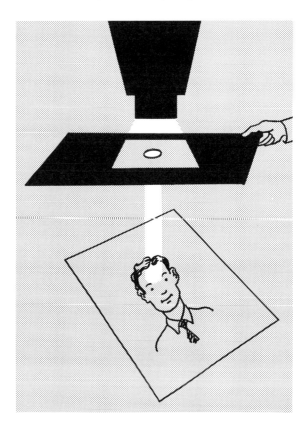

some more, etc. The other is that your negative may "pop," like a color slide popping out of focus in a slide projector. This would throw the image far out of focus and ruin the print.

There is a good answer for this, though a little time-consuming: make your print all the way through with a "prepopped" negative. Do it this way: turn on the enlarger light until the negative pops (warps), then focus the image on the focusing paper. Turn off the light and immediately put printing paper in the easel and make the basic exposure—while the negative is still popped and in focus. Then immediately do whatever burning-in you wish to do.

You use the cardboard with no hole in it to burn-in the corners and edges of pictures. You let the light shine on one edge or corner of the printing paper at a time, making a blend by constantly moving the cardboard back and forth. However, you can use a dodger instead of a cardboard and burn-in all the edges and corners at the same time. You can do this by holding the larger disk right under the lens and moving it constantly up and down between the lens and the paper.

• When to Do It

Subtly changing the tones of local areas is absurdly easy with the techniques you have just read about. The problem is in deciding which areas need changing and how far the changes should go. You do this mainly by "feel." That is, you observe and respond to your emotional reactions to pictures. You let them guide you. For example, if an area is too light you may feel it as being washed out, weak, insubstantial, unreal, or lacking in surface detail and solidity. The area simply bothers you, though you may not be able to put your feelings into words. Similarly, you may feel a too-dark area is heavy, morbid, dirty, unreal, or unduly obscure. In either case, you wish to manipulate the tone of the areas enough to change your feelings about them from negative to positive. You merely want them to look and feel right.

People usually have little trouble deciding whether they want things lighter, darker, or left alone. Most of the time, they almost automatically know whether they want to dodge or burn-in. With a little experience they learn how far they wish to go in either direction. For most of their pictures they don't need the help of a teacher. However, there are many little tricks in printing that people don't usually learn unless they are told about them. We will now look into some of them.

• Faces and Skin (Flesh) Tone

There are many things in pictures that can be too light or too dark without our minding it at all—trees, bushes, and rocks, for example. However, when it comes to such things as faces and skin tone we mind a lot. Consequently, they probably have more tone manipulation done on them than any other subject in photography, most of it done by dodging.

We will start with faces that are about two inches or longer. Usually we can dodge them with the two-inch disk, so that the skin and all the features get lightened at once. Sometimes this takes too much of the brilliance out of the eyes, however, so they must be left undodged. The solution is to use the smaller disk, moving it around above the face for the *entire* exposure, or most of it. For a two-to-three-inch face it should nearly be touching the printing paper.

A portrait may need only highlight dodging, which is very good for making skin look more alive. Just lighten the highlights that are already there, using the small dodger again. If you try to make them where none exist the dodging will look phony and the face distorted. Usually you can restrict yourself to the cheekbones, jaw line and the top two thirds of the forehead, because the large highlights usually fall in these areas.

If the eyes are sunken in shadow or have dark bags under them you may have to dodge them, even if they lose some of their brilliance. You have to make a compromise here.

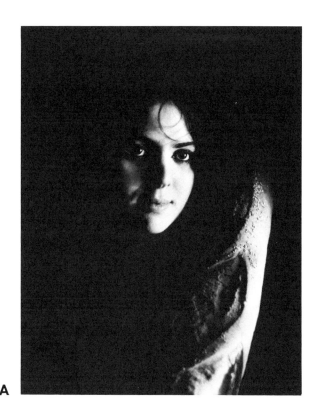

A

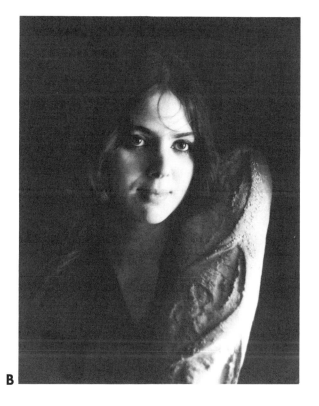

B

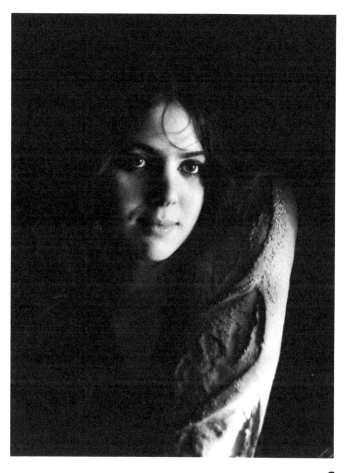

C

A is a straight print made on a no. 5 paper, which makes the face a bit too strong and harsh. Print B, on a no. 2 paper, makes the face soft enough, but the rest of the print is too gray. Print C, also on a no. 2, has the same basic exposure as B, but the edges have been heavily burned-in to make them darker.

Quite often the two sides of a face are much too far apart in tone. In this case, expose for the highlight side and dodge for the dark side. Thus the light side will take care of itself, while the other side is being lightened with the dodger. If you dodge as much as you can without making the dark side look muddy and the tonal difference between the two sides is still too great, your only other alternative is to use a lower-contrast paper. You may still need to dodge, however.

For a face smaller than an inch you will have to use the small dodger, which will dodge it all at once and wash out the eyes somewhat. However, you probably won't mind this with a face so small.

We don't use burning-in much on faces, because it is a little harder to control. It is mainly used for light-struck, washed-out ears and patches of hair. However, it is fairly easy to burn-in a whole or half face. The problem is with light-struck cheekbones and noses, for it is hard to get the burned-in tones to blend. If an ear or hair doesn't blend exactly we don't mind so much.

● **Skies**

People generally like to burn-in the skies in their landscape pictures. It makes clear skies look richer and deeper, clouded ones more dramatic with the clouds more clearly defined. With clear skies it is generally good to burn-in for a tonal gradation ranging from nearly white at the horizon to a medium gray at the top of the picture. If a sky prints too dark near the horizon you can dodge it with the shadow of a pencil during the basic exposure. Because skies are seldom lighted evenly you will probably have to burn-in one side more than the other.

Burning-in for a smooth tonal gradation is very easy. Using the cardboard without a hole, start burning-in at the top of the picture while moving the card down toward the horizon. The instant it gets there, start it back up again. Keep repeating this until the time is up. Simple enough.

You may or may not want a graded tone for a

cloudy sky; it depends on what the clouds look like. And you may wish to combine dodging with burning-in. For example, you might dodge a cloud entirely for the whole basic exposure, which would leave it a blank white if the print were developed at that point. Instead of developing, however, you could burn-in the whole sky, including the cloud. Thus the cloud would come out with its normal tone, whereas the sky around it would be darkened considerably. This would make the cloud much more dramatic. We were speaking of a cloud that was lighter than the sky to begin with, of course. Starting with a darker cloud, we could burn it in after dodging the sky, which would also be dramatic.

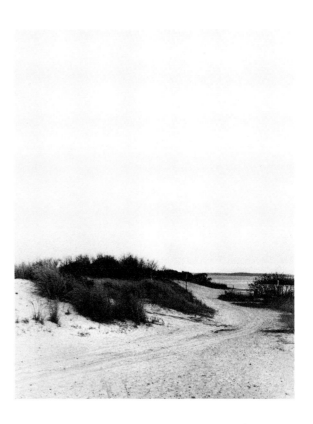

A straight print (above) of this sand dune makes a rather uninteresting picture. However, extensive burning-in brought out dramatic clouds in the sky (print at right). The lower corners of the picture were also burned-in and the center of the dune dodged somewhat.

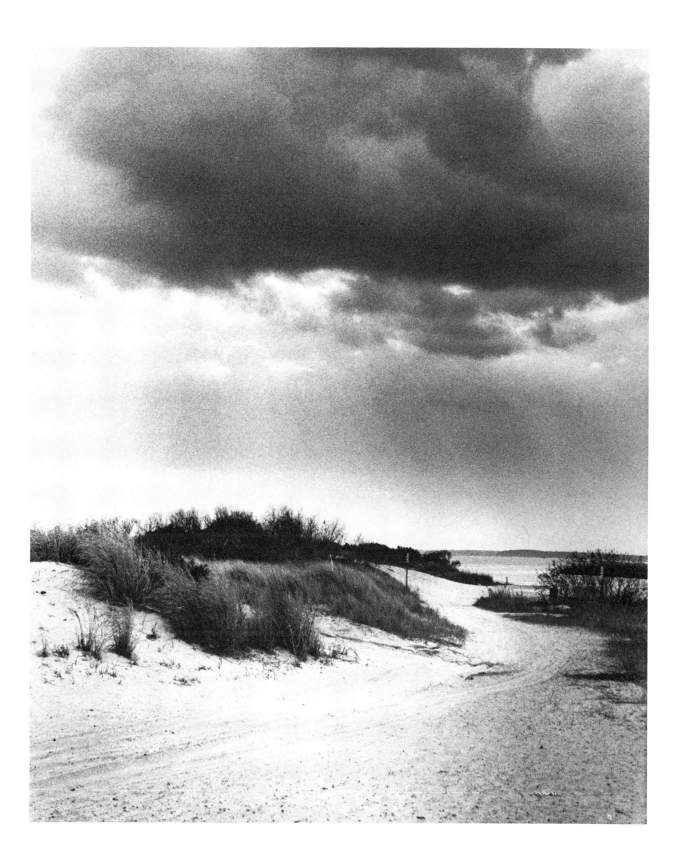

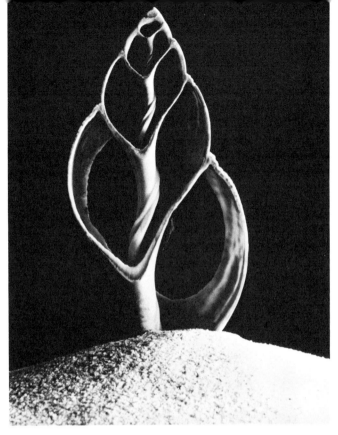

Clouds are fun to mess with, because you can make such gross mistakes without anyone being able to tell. This is a far cry from portraiture, in which your dodging and burning-in mistakes stand out like castor oil in a lemon pie.

● Corners

Some photographers like to burn-in the corners of all their pictures, but usually not very much. They sometimes call it "strengthening the corners." Burning-in strengthens corners by simply darkening them, which gives them more substance and weight (in the visual arts, tone is often equated with weight).

Darkened corners also confirm and emphasize the rectangular shape of the image, which in many pictures is a little ambiguous due to undetected optical illusions. These illusions seem to warp the pictures somewhat. However, trying to make it obvious that a picture is exactly rectangular must seem like a strange preoccupation, because rectangles per se are so totally uninteresting. Well, this is precisely why we use rectangular shapes for pictures and frames. They are such a bore that they don't distract from the pictures themselves. However, if a picture doesn't seem to be exactly rectangular our attention is attracted to its proportions rather than to the picture itself— so we remedy this distraction by burning-in the corners.

Another reason for burning-in corners is to lead the viewer's attention to the center of the picture and hold it there. We get a kind of tunnel or bull's-eye effect, in which he feels almost compelled to look where we wish him to, instead of letting his eyes wander elsewhere.

Finally, we burn-in corners to subordinate things in the picture that are too close to them.

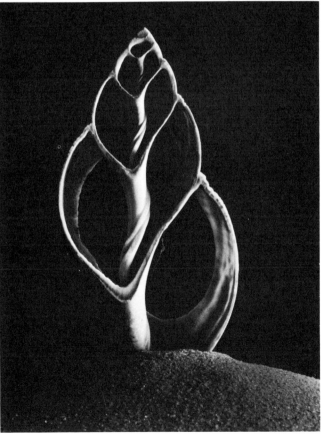

In print above the bright foreground attracts too much attention from the shell. In print below it has been heavily burned-in to make it less conspicuous.

One usually organizes a picture so that important things are somewhere near the middle and things of less importance near the edges or corners, which ordinarily guarantees that the latter won't be unduly noticed. However, strong "centers of interest" are created if things get *too* close to edges or corners. A center of interest is merely something that attracts the eye. Now, it happens that things in corners can create by far the most powerful centers.

When we burn-in things we usually lessen their visibility somewhat, because we reduce the contrast and darken the tone. Thus we have an easy way to defuse unwanted centers of interest. It sometimes doesn't work, however, because in some pictures burning-in will emphasize something rather than de-emphasize it. Then we have to resort to a special technique called "flashing." Though it is not quite the same as burning-in it is done in almost the same way. It will effectively subordinate areas near the picture corners.

You do flashing with "raw light" from the enlarger. After making the basic exposure you remove the negative, stop down the lens all the way, and burn-in the corners in the usual way. Make a record of the burning-in time, because you can use it again for other pictures.

• The Bottoms of Pictures

The bottoms of pictures frequently need burning-in, especially if they are areas of flooring, sidewalk, or roadway. When bottoms are too light they weaken pictures, make them seem insecurely balanced, and attract the eyes to the wrong places. Usually it is good to have the lighter weights (tones) near the tops of pictures, the heavier ones near their bottoms. Burning-in and dodging help us distribute weight.

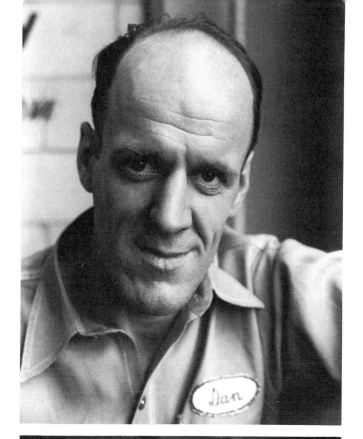

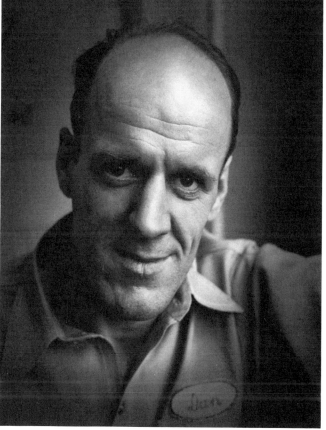

In a straight print (top) the background is a little distracting. It was toned down by flashing (below), which is simply burning-in done without a negative being in the enlarger negative carrier.

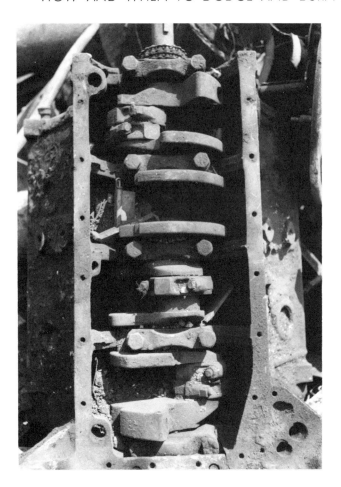 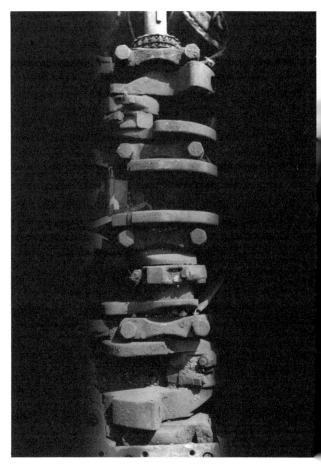

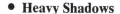

A straight print of a piece of old junk (left) makes a picture that is a bit too complicated and messy. Heavy flashing (right) simplifies and dramatizes the image.

• Heavy Shadows

Sometimes shadows get so dark that it is hard to see into them, and parts of the picture are lost in darkness. Such shadows are said to be "closed" or "blocked up." If there is good detail in the shadow areas of the negative they can be opened up (lightened) by dodging, but if they are relatively empty (clear) we can only dodge a little bit —or we'll get mud or pea soup.

• Unwanted Things

In some pictures there are things we would like to get rid of altogether. If we can't get rid of them by cropping we may be able to use dodging or burning-in; it depends mainly on the tonal areas that surround them. By heavily burning-in things in black areas we can lose them in darkness. By heavily dodging things in white areas we can lose them in lightness. Since the things we wish to eliminate may not be surrounded by either black or white we may not be able to completely obliterate them this way. However, we can lessen their visibility somewhat by making them more like their surroundings in tone. Things that are alike get lost in each other.

96

• Separation

We have just seen that when things blend together they get lost in each other, which is sometimes a good thing, because it lessens their power to distract the eye. The important things in pictures should have "good separation," however. This means that there should be good tonal contrast between them, so that you can easily tell where one leaves off and the other begins. They will also have high visibility, which is what we usually want for the most important things in our pictures. What can they accomplish if people can't see them?

To separate things, we simply make them tonally unlike—by dodging, burning-in, or both. For example, if a house in a picture blends too much with the sky, we can make one of them lighter by dodging, or one of them darker by burning-in. Or we can make one lighter and the other darker.

• Local Contrast

Earlier, we saw that graded-contrast papers and printing filters are used to give us the correct over-all contrast for a given picture. However, we often have pictures that are contrasty in some areas and flat in others, so that a single paper grade or filter cannot solve the over-all contrast problem. For example, we might have a picture calling for no. 1 contrast on the left and no. 4 on the right. This sometimes happens when we get "lens flare" from direct light striking the camera lens or from posing a subject in front of an area much brighter than itself.

The simple left-to-right problem can often be handled by "contrast dodging," in which one uses a variable-contrast paper and printing filters. You use two basic exposures, each of them given by dodging, and use a different filter for each exposure. To solve the above problem, for example,

you would use a no. 1 filter while exposing the left side of the picture and simultaneously shielding the other side from exposure by dodging. Then you would use a no. 4 filter to expose the right side while dodging the left.

To get a good blend you would move the dodging card back and forth from left to right for both exposures, just as in any other kind of dodging. Though it is an easy technique, one usually has to make a test strip for each filter, then make three or four final prints in order to get the blending just right.

Contrast dodging is a good technique, but there are few occasions for using it. One more frequently runs into local contrast problems that can be handled by ordinary dodging or burning-in on graded (single-contrast) paper. For example, try to imagine a picture of a family back yard. On one side of this picture is a sizable playhouse standing in front of a tall hedge. The contrast of the print is exactly right, except for the area around the playhouse, which is very flat. To correct for this flatness we merely dodge the house a bit (lighten it) and burn-in (darken) the shrubbery closest to it, thus building up the contrast between them.

Notice that we worked on only two things: the playhouse and the hedge. The rest of the flat side of the print wasn't touched. The point is that you can almost always liven up a whole area by selecting only a few things within it to work on. Furthermore, if you work on too many things you will nearly always give yourself away, because your dodging and burning-in will stand out like sore thumbs.

We can also *calm down* areas of a print by locally *reducing* contrast. For example, we might have another print of the same back yard in which the area around the playhouse is too contrasty instead of too flat. This could happen if it were photographed at a different time of day. In this case we would merely reverse our procedures. We would burn-in (darken) the house and dodge (lighten) the hedge, thus *reducing* the contrast between them. This would have the effect of reducing the contrast in that entire area, thus calming it down. If you have had difficulty in visualizing the material in the previous paragraphs, draw a little picture to help you. Since this is good for you, I have intentionally not provided an illustration.

● **Space and Volume**

Photography is a three-dimensional medium—some of the time. Any photograph whatever has two real dimensions, length and breadth, and the possibility of an illusional third dimension, depth. Though depth is only an illusion, we work with it all the time, like a sculptor manipulating his volumes. Illusions have their reality, too, for they are there and we can see them. We can also create, destroy, or otherwise manipulate them. Such being the reality of depth in a photograph, it makes good sense to call photography a three-dimensional medium.

Now, dodging and burning-in are two of the chief tools for depth manipulation in prints. We could say they are merely extensions of light, or lighting, which is the master tool. When we lighten or darken things in prints we are modifying the record of the effect that light was having upon them when they were photographed. Actually, we are falsifying the lighting data recorded in negatives, often to make prints look more real, more three-dimensional. In a sense, in order to tell the truth about things we have to use falsehoods. This is because we are working with illusions.

Photographs vary considerably in the amount of depth they have. When we look at some of them it is like looking through deep windows into space. We can "get into them," as they say, mentally participate in them as events taking place in space. We call them "open" prints.

However, most prints are "closed." They con-

front us with only surface, no depth, so that no amount of imagination will permit us to get into them. One characteristic of closed prints is that they are also "tight." The things in tight prints look so firmly glued into place that it is hard to imagine anything moving around or through them. Even air couldn't do it, because they have no "feeling of air space." Though the terms we are now using are intangible, stick with them, for they are an important part of the language of the visual arts. By making pictures you will come to understand them.

The first thing to do with a closed print is to open it up, which will immediately add depth to it. There is one technique so simple that even your dog could master it. It consists in using "arbitrary dodging," which simply means that you can be entirely arbitrary in choosing things to dodge, or even pay no attention to what you are dodging while you are doing it. Just wave the dodger around during the basic exposure. You can do roughly the same thing with "arbitrary burning-in," and of course you can do both. In the finished print there will be no evidence of either, except that it will be more loose, more open. These simple techniques break up the overtight structural integrity of the image, so that "the air can get between the bricks." Or we could say that they knock out some of the glue.

However, the effect may be too subtle for you to see it clearly. A sure way to guarantee a more tangible success is to be not quite so arbitrary. Follow this rule: lighten the lights and darken the darks. That is, pick out a few light areas and dodge them to make them even lighter, then pick some dark areas and burn them darker. With this formula we not only open up a print but strongly increase its three-dimensional quality. However, the lights and darks can still be selected almost arbitrarily. An important part of this trick is to not work on a total of too many areas. Just pick a few here and there. There is a related rule that you might also try: lighten the tops of things and darken their bottoms.

These techniques are often needed on prints

that seem to need nothing whatever done to them in the way of dodging or burning-in. A print may be technically excellent and still be as tight as a whale full of peanut butter. In this case, technical excellence would be equivalent to aesthetic mediocrity, so loosen it up a bit. There is no point in making pictures that you can't enter into imaginatively.

Remember the section on skies, in which we talked about graded tones. They are easy enough to create by dodging and burning-in and add a lot of depth to pictures. Graded tones are like highways into space. We grade the sky in a picture to make it look look like a real one: deep, deep, deep.

When we talked about corners we considered the tunnel effect, which is also a fast highway into the distance. Actually, the tunnel is just a special way of using tonal gradation.

You've already seen how contrast can be locally created or diminished. This knowledge can be used in depth manipulation to either increase or diminish it. In our everyday world there is a hierarchy of contrasts among things that are at various distances from us. We can use the same hierarchy in our prints. The way it works is that the closer things are to us the more they stand out (contrast). So in our prints we create contrast gradients, things that are near standing out, things at a middle distance standing out much less, and distant things nearly disappearing in their surroundings. We infrequently need to create a whole hierarchy, but we often need the knowledge for just one thing in a picture, either pushing it forward with high contrast or back with low contrast.

We mustn't forget the ancient "stepping-stone trick," which is still as good as it ever was. The idea is that the eye moves back into picture space by jumping from tone to tone as if they were stepping stones in a stream. So we add some extra tones to a picture to give the eye extra things to jump from, thus creating a stronger illusion of depth. The eye actually doesn't work this way, but the trick is very effective anyway.

The tone areas that we add don't have to be sharply defined. In fact it is better if they aren't, because they might be too obtrusive; they will create the depth illusion even if people don't notice them. It is easiest to use the trick on landscapes. For example, imagine a picture mostly filled with a vast expanse of sand or grass. Let's say that the space is flatly lighted and that the picture itself looks flat. By dodging, we can put in two or three strips of lighter tone, which will work as stepping stones even though they are long. With most pictures of this sort they would add considerably to the depth.

Totally dodging one side of the face created this unusual effect.

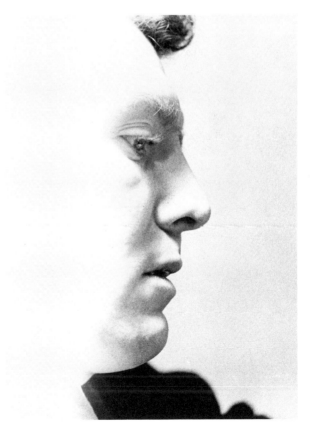

• Get the Basic Print First

Now that you've had a taste of the things that can be done by dodging and burning-in you are probably all hot to try them. They are lots of fun, friend, no doubt of that, but slow down. Slow 'way, 'way down. If you start your messing around too soon you'll never get things sorted out right.

Always start out working from the best-possible basic print: remember, it has the right contrast, the right exposure, and the right processing.

Except for needing local manipulation it is beyond improvement. If you start with a print like this it is easy to tell what your dodging and burning-in are, or are not, contributing to it. However, if you start with a sloppy work print you'll never know which is doing what to whom. And it is like a great chef spending all day frosting a stale cake. The excellence of the frosting (dodging and burning-in) won't compensate for the worms in the cake (a bad basic print).

One eye and its side of the face were dodged considerably. The other eye was burned-in to make it look like a black hole in the face.

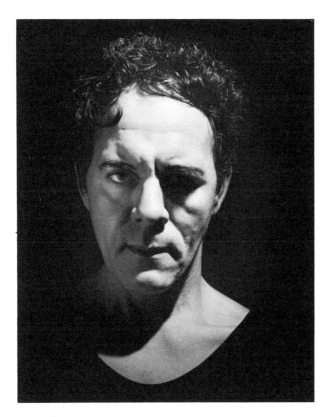

• Use Your Crystal Ball

The dodging and burning-in techniques you have just read about are not golden keys to everything whatever. They can only serve as guidelines or as clues concerning the kinds of things to look for in pictures. Therefore, look at your pictures through your crystal ball and psych your own way into seeing where and how the various tricks might apply. They work very well, you may be sure, but only if you *make* them work.

Consider the paragraphs in this chapter as puzzles, if you wish, for that may help them engage your attention. For example, you might ask yourself, "Why will lightening the tops of things and darkening their bottoms sometimes loosen up a picture and give it a strong feeling of depth?" Don't pretend you know already, for you most assuredly don't. You have to work it out by trial and error in printing. When you think you have the answer, ask yourself, "When will *darkening* the tops of things and *lightening* their bottoms do the very same things?"

Don't settle for verbal answers, which are mainly useless in photography. Answer yourself with your prints—no other way. Though this is a book for beginners, a good deal of artistic knowledge was compressed in this chapter. Don't be fooled by the fact that it read like instructions for assembling a Yo-yo. Knowledge can be concealed in simplicity, you know.

HOW TO SPOT AND RETOUCH PRINTS

No matter how well you clean your negatives, your prints will almost always have a few dust spots and hair squiggles on them, anyway. It's just one of those things we have to put up with in photography. The white spots and squiggles are unsightly, of course, so we have to get rid of them. We do this by dye spotting or retouching, which actually mean the same thing. However, "spotting" is usually associated with just dust spots and squiggles, "retouching" with more extensive repairs.

The theory is simple: blemishes caused by dust or lint on negatives stand out on prints because they are white. Ergo, we put dye in them, just enough to match the surrounding areas in tone. This makes the blemishes disappear without a trace.

We don't have to limit ourselves to dust spots and squiggles, however. There can be many other things that need to be either removed entirely or toned down. For example, in a landscape foreground we might want to get rid of paper scraps or pop bottles. In a portrait there might be an unsightly spot of light on the subject's collar. Or we may have a lovely beach picture spoiled by cigarette packages. Such things can be de-emphasized or eliminated.

Things can be altered in other ways. Say Aunt Maud's nose looks too long: it can be shortened. We don't like the white patch of skin above Albert's sock: we put dye in it, making the sock look longer. An area in a picture looks too empty: we add some extra tones to it with dye. The list of things you can do with dyes is almost endless, so if you like this kind of thing (some don't) you will find lots to amuse you.

● Things You Need

Sable spotting brush
Black Spotone dye (no. 3)—or a three-color kit
Small tube of white water color or gouache
White saucer
Eye dropper
Paper towels or napkins
Q-Tips or surgical cotton
Photo-Flo or dishwashing detergent
Magnifying glass
An envelope flap with mucilage on it
Pieces of photographic blotter

● Your Work Light

To spot prints you need good light, or you won't be able to see the tip of your brush against the darker areas of your print. This leads to missing the dust spots and getting dye in all the wrong places, which will really make a mess of a print. Work near a brightly lit window or under a 150-watt bulb about two feet away. Some people hate to spot, mainly because they can't see what they are doing. Don't let it happen to you.

If you do wreck a print, don't worry. Putting it in a tray of water for a while will wash out most of the dye. If you need to get rid of more, put it in hypo, then wash and dry it as usual. It is better to do this than tear up your print and scream bloody murder, as some people do.

• Use a Magnifier or a Reading Glass

Seeing what you are doing is so important that you may need a magnifier, even if your close-up vision is excellent and the light is strong. You need it most when you are working on thin lines from backing scratches or hairs, which are very difficult to spot without slopping the dye over onto surrounding areas. When magnified sufficiently they look as wide as sidewalks and are quite easy to spot—like parking a tricycle in a four-car garage. Follow this general rule: before you try to spot something make sure you can see it.

• Overcoming the Gelatin

If the artists of the world congregated to pick the type of surface most difficult to work on, their unanimous choice would be gelatin—and we photographers are stuck with it. Of all the things to have to put dye on evenly: photographic Jell-O! But when a print needs spotting there is no running away from it, so we have to do the best we can. There are a couple of little tricks that help, however.

The first is to put a few drops of Photo-Flo (or dishwashing detergent) in the water you work with. It flattens out those little round drops of dye that always sink into a print at the wrong time and place. It also makes it easier to lay smooth dye tones down on fairly large areas, up to an inch or two.

Another trick is to dampen local areas just before you work on them. They should be cold and a little soft but free of surface water. Damp gelatin takes dye quickly and smoothly, which can hardly be said of it when it is dry. Some people prefer to do their spotting fairly soon after processing, when their prints still aren't fully dry. They spot them first, dry them later. If you stack prints on top of each other they'll stay damp for quite a while, and it does them no harm.

Your own tongue can help you overcome the recalcitrance of dry gelatin, which doesn't want to accept dye at all. Instead of wetting your brush with water, lick it. There is just enough stickiness in saliva for it to help dye stick to the most obstinate print. The dye is harmless.

There is a related trick that is possibly more aesthetic. Wet your brush in water, stroke it a few times across the mucilage on an envelope flap, then pick up the dye with it. It doesn't work better than saliva, but it works.

There are some patient people who get a tremendous charge out of dye retouching and do a lot of it. They generally like to use non-hardening hypo, which is mixed with only hypo crystals and none of the other ingredients of an acid-hardening fixing bath. One would use about the same weight of crystals as the mixed dry chemicals (twenty-five ounces per gallon) This non-hardening fixer leaves the gelatin a little softer, less rubbery, and more acceptant of the dye—but more vulnerable too, so you have to treat it with care! Mainly you should be wary of your own fingernails.

The non-hardening hypo is all right with regular papers of all brands, though some are more fragile than others. But there are some brands of resin-coated (RC) paper that really *have* to be hardened. If not, the emulsions get as sticky as glue, get scratched at the merest touch, or slide right off the plastic base. Kodak RC papers are all right, however, so you should stick with them. Even so, you should wash and dry the prints right after processing and handle them carefully while spotting. When spotting a non-hardened print of any kind it is a good idea to lay typing paper on the part your hand will rest on. Very good protection from rings, bracelets, watch bands, and fingernails. Mostly fingernails.

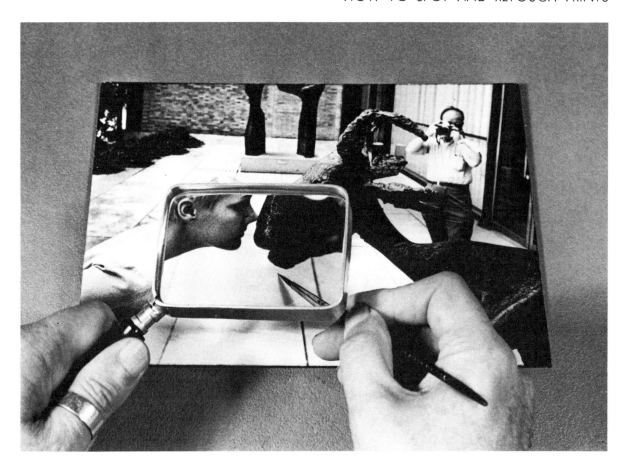

• Setting Up Your Saucer

You will use a white saucer for your palette and should prepare it in advance. Put about six or eight drops of Spotone near one edge. Across from it squeeze out about half an inch of white water color or gouache (they're about the same thing). Let them dry thoroughly. This concentrates the dye considerably, so that you can make very black dots and lines with it. It doesn't concentrate the white but makes it easier to control the amount that you get on your brush, which can be quite important. These amounts of black and white should last you for months without your adding to them.

When you are ready to use your saucer, put a match folder under one side so that you can confine a puddle of water to the other without its running into either the dye or the water color.

Print spotting is easy if you use a strong reading glass.

Lay a paper napkin or towel next to the saucer. Put a glass of water near the napkin and add a little Photo-Flo to it (eight or ten drops). Drop some water into the saucer to make your "working puddle."

• Loading and Pointing Your Brush

Spotting is much easier if you load (fill or wet) and point your brush properly. If you dip it in a glass of water you usually load it too full, which is why we use the little puddle on the saucer: one can pick up small amounts of water from the edge of it. The next step is to pick up some dye,

103

the amount depending on the tone of the area you are spotting. Against the white of the saucer, you can easily see the concentration of the dye and increase or decrease it according to your needs.

When the brush has dye in it, it may be too heavily loaded and need to be pointed. If so, use the napkin to take up the excess dye. Hold the brush almost parallel to the table and stroke the point on the napkin two or three times, or until the load seems about right. This will also give it a needle-sharp point.

If you need a slightly stickier mixture you can wet and point the brush with your lips, sometimes before you pick up dye with it, sometimes afterward. Your lips and the napkin are equally good for controlling the amount of dye.

When you are through spotting you should carefully point the brush with your lips and put it where nothing will touch the point and warp it out of shape. However, if it does get bent, load it with undiluted white water color, shape it, and let it dry. When you wash it out the point will be all right again.

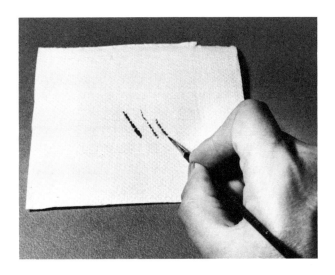

In print spotting, it is important to keep the brush sharply pointed and to control the amount of dye in it. You can do both by stroking it on a paper napkin or towel.

• Brush Patterns

Unless it is very small, don't try to fill a dust spot with just one touch of the brush, for if you do you will probably get too much dye in it. Dye sinks right into the gelatin and isn't that easy to get out. So fill in the larger spots bit by bit with little dots of dye. If the spots resist the dye, as they often do, use a little mucilage or saliva in your brush. *Don't* try to solve the problem by using a too heavily loaded brush.

To fill in white lines and hair marks, use a magnifier or a reading glass. Don't try to fill one in with a single stroke, or you will surely make a mess of it. Instead, use a lot of short lines or little dots. It isn't necessary to eliminate lines and hair marks the first time, for you can go over them several times if necessary. And it is safer to do it this way.

If at any time you lay too much dye down, wipe it up *immediately* with the napkin or your fingertip. Otherwise, you'll be stuck with it.

• Dyeing Larger Areas

No matter what we do to make gelatin a better surface to work on we can't make it take dye very evenly. We can improve matters a bit, but that is all. Thus you shouldn't try something like darkening a clear sky, because the results will look like a finger painting by a distracted monkey. This will always happen if you chose large areas of smooth, or even, tone. You can sometimes handle small smooth-tone areas, however.

It is best to restrict yourself to areas with texture in them, the more random the better. It will help cover up the mistakes you make with the dye.

To cover larger areas (one to two inches) use a brush heavily loaded with very heavily diluted dye. Put the dye on very wet, then *immediately* blot it with a photographic blotter, pressing down firmly. Repeat this process until the tone is just right.

For somewhat smaller areas, use a Q-Tip.

Load it with dye so diluted that it has hardly any color, then take off the excess by rolling it on a paper napkin. It should be just damp, so that the dye won't come off it in droplets. Rub the Q-Tip across a selected area until it is the right tone. Since the moisture will soften the gelatin, take care not to rub too hard.

There is a problem with spotting dyes: they often change color when they sink into gelatin, usually turning brown or blue. Residual hypo in the emulsion may be the cause. Most of the time, the colors are invisible against the neutral tones of a print. However, if you use too much dye, apply it in too large an area, or both, the color will stand out like carnal sin. You should therefore consider dye retouching as a way of making moderate changes in prints, not dramatic ones. And when you darken sizable areas you are doing something that could be done better by burning-in, though this is not always true.

If you already have a color problem with a retouched print, you might buy the blue and brown Spotone dyes (or start out with the three-color kit). The blue will more or less neutralize a brown on your print, and the brown neutralize a blue.

• Using the White Water Color

The white is obviously used for things that need lightening instead of darkening, but we have to use it conservatively. The reason is that the water color doesn't have the same surface sheen as the print, so that it stands out too much when the print is viewed from certain angles. However, if we use it on very small things—black spots and squiggles—it won't be too obvious, at least not as obvious as the defects themselves would be.

What we usually need in our spotting is a gray tone, not white, because the area surrounding the defect is usually a tone of gray. You can mix a gray by combining the water color with your dye, but that is not the best way. Instead, get your gray by using the white in very small amounts. Some of the dark tone underneath it will show

through, making it look gray. To load your brush, liberally wet it with your lips, then stroke it once or twice across the dried water color on the saucer. This will give you a very thin white mixture.

• Other Things You Can Do with Dye and Water Color

1. Add texture to things that need it.
2. Sharpen the edges of out-of-focus things.
3. Change facial expression by working on the corners of the mouth, nose creases, and eyes.
4. Separate things that blend too much.
5. Blend things that separate too much.
6. Fill in straggly hair.
7. Put highlights in eyes (with white) or reshape existing highlights (usually with dye alone).
8. Add detail to washed-out areas.
9. Modify the shapes of things.
10. Paint in grass, leaves, twigs, etc.
11. Strengthen weak lines and edges.
12. Even out skin blemishes somewhat.
13. Clean up the contours of things.
14. Emphasize important centers of interest.
15. Subordinate distracting areas.

It would be helpful for you to think of dye retouching as an extension of burning-in. They are often interchangeable, so that the things that can be done by burning-in can also be done (to some degree) be retouching, and vice versa.

• Take Your Time

In your first efforts at print spotting and retouching, you may feel compelled to work rapidly, with verve and dash. Don't do it! For speed is the road to catastrophe. Work *very* slowly and carefully. With a little practice you will find that you can move along like a sleepy turtle and still retouch as many as fifteen prints per hour, which is making haste slowly. So be patient and take your time. Don't pretend to yourself that you already know how to use a brush; you don't. That too will take a little time.

HOW TO IMPROVE PRINTS BY BLEACHING

One of the photographer's favorite creative tools is an easily prepared bleach made of potassium ferricyanide and water. It can also be made with hypo instead of water and is then called "Farmer's reducer," after the man who invented it. The water solution is more convenient, however, because it doesn't deteriorate quite as rapidly. Farmer's will work only for fifteen to twenty minutes before it must be discarded and remixed.

If you have made prints that came out too dark you can appreciate the value of a chemical that will lighten them to any desired degree. Though bleaching won't save all overexposed prints, it will resurrect enough of them to make it worth using. Very inexpensive in itself, it can save you a lot of money on printing paper.

Salvaging an overcooked print is just one of the handy things that bleach can do. You can also lighten selective areas in a print with it, using it as a kind of chemical dodger. If you forget to dodge an area during exposure or don't dodge it enough, you can use bleach to lighten it as much as you think necessary, even to the point of eliminating it altogether. Furthermore, with "bleach dodging" you can work on a dozen areas in a given print, which you just don't have time for with regular dodging. During a ten-second exposure, for example, you couldn't use a single dodging tool to dodge twelve different areas for five seconds each. However, they can be "dodged" (lightened) with bleach later.

Bleach is also used for "cutting out," or cleaning up, white backgrounds, which means reducing them to a pristine white. This is most often done with skies and walls, but you can whiten anything you like. Bleach can be used in print retouching for eliminating dark spots and lines, removing beer cans from scenic pictures, sharpening out-of-focus edges, lightening bags under eyes, eliminating pimples or scars, lightening the whites of eyes, brightening facial highlights, and so on.

Used as a team, bleaching (lightening) and dye retouching (darkening) will in some degree do all the things that dodging (lightening) and burning-in (darkening) do together, including adding space to prints, increasing or decreasing local contrast, emphasizing or subordinating centers of interest, etc.

In terms of what they can do for pictures it is useful to think of bleaching and dodging as being about the same thing. Similarly, dyeing and burning-in are much alike.

● **Things You Need**

Potassium ferricyanide: A fairly poisonous red-orange crystalline compound; don't get it in your mouth or eyes. In a water or hypo solution, it will bleach metallic silver.

Hypo: One can use an ordinary acid-hardening fixing bath, a rapid fixer, or simply hypo crystals in water. Use the fixer that is already in your print-processing line.

Glass or cup: A six-ounce glass or a white teacup are about the right size, because you will be mixing bleach in four-ounce quantities; it is economical that way.

Measuring spoons: Should be plastic so they won't react with the ferricyanide when you are measuring it out.

Photo-Flo: You will add five drops to each four-ounce batch of bleach. It prevents the bleach from forming little droplets, which lighten areas where they touch the print much too rapidly, making small, round white spots that require dye spotting.

Eye dropper: Buy one at a drugstore. Better yet, get half a dozen, as they are very handy.

A no. 4 sable brush: Sable only—never camel's hair or a synthetic—for precision bleaching of small areas and working around contours of all

Equipment and chemicals for bleaching include a print-inspection board, potassium ferricyanide, Photo-Flo, brush, eye dropper, Q-Tip, cotton, sponge, fixer, and a brush.

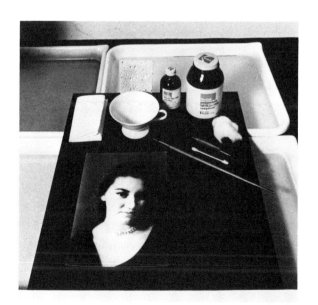

sizes and shapes. Before buying a brush, wet it with your lips to see that it makes a good point; some don't. Unsanitary but practical.

Clear nail polish: For sealing the brush ferrule against bleach, thus preventing blue stains (see Dektol, below). Wet the brush, point it with your lips, and let it thoroughly dry. Then give the ferrule two or three coats of nail polish, letting each coat dry before you apply the next one. Next put a tiny drop of it on the brush hairs at the point where they disappear into the ferrule. The lacquer should seep into the hairs, sealing off the *inside* of the ferrule from the bleach. If the brush isn't sealed, the iron in the ferrule (especially the inside) will react with the ferricyanide to form a blue stain.

Surgical cotton and Q-Tips: For applying bleach to prints.

Print-inspection board or tray bottom: Lay it right across the stop-bath tray, next to the first hypo, and make sure that the hypo light strikes it squarely. It should be a sturdy arrangement, so that you don't splash bleach all over everything including your Sunday clothes.

Ordinary viscose sponge: Prior to bleaching, prints are soaked in hypo. The sponge is for removing most of it when the print is on the inspection board, just before you start working on it. It is also for containing hypo to slow down the bleaching action in areas being treated.

Paper towels: For removing all the rest of the surface hypo (even the *tiniest* droplets) from the print just before bleaching (by itself, a sponge just won't remove enough of the hypo). Folded twice, a fresh paper towel is used as a blotter to rapidly slow down bleaching action so it won't get out of control.

Hypo light: As in dye retouching, one needs a strong work light in order to see where the brush tip is touching the print.

Magnifier or reading glass: Needed for bleaching such things as small black spots or thin black lines. Without one, you can't guide your brush accurately and will get bleach on the areas surrounding the defects you wish to lighten.

Tray: For containing a quart of solution when you wish to bleach an entire print at one time. Either an 8×10 or an 11×14 tray will do nicely.

Dektol: If there is iron or rust in your water supply you may get blue stains on your prints, either as over-all tints or as small, intensely blue spots. If you put them in Dektol, which won't harm them a bit, the stains will usually go away. Afterward, acidify them in stop bath, reharden in hypo, then wash and dry as usual. This treatment will not change their tones one iota, but it nearly always gets rid of the blue.

• Strength of Bleach Solutions

Most photographers mix bleach by eye, judging its strength by how yellow it is. Thus a weak bleach is a light lemon yellow, a strong one dark yellow. Using a white cup, you can see the color well. However, at this point in your experience you don't really know how yellow the yellow should be, so we will use some simple recipes, with bleach crystals measured in fractions of a level teaspoonful.

For bleaching all parts of a print at once, use one-eighth teaspoonful of ferricyanide per quart of water. This will give you a moderately dilute solution that is safe to work with, because it won't bleach too fast. It can also be used for local bleaching where little lightening is required.

For bleaching local areas you can work with stronger solutions, mixed in four-ounce quantities. In using them the main problem (a serious one) is to not let the bleaching action get away from you, thus ruining the print. However, stronger solutions save a lot of time.

To four ounces of water add five drops of Photo-Flo and one of the following quantities of potassium ferricyanide crystals:

Medium-strong – $\frac{1}{16}$ teaspoonful
Strong – $\frac{1}{8}$ teaspoonful
Ultra-strong – $\frac{1}{4}$ to $\frac{1}{2}$ teaspoonful

Until you have had a lot of experience with bleach, you should stick mainly to the medium-strong, using the strong rarely and avoiding the ultra-strong altogether. Unless you know your stuff the ultra-strong will simply get away from you. However, you won't really believe this until you have ruined a few prints with it, so feel free to experiment.

Unfortunately, your measuring spoons go down only to one fourth of a teaspoon. To get an idea of what one eighth of a spoon of crystals looks like, measure out one-fourth teaspoonful, put it on a piece of paper, and divide the pile in half. Divide one of the halves to get one sixteenth. When you have an approximate idea of what the quantities look like it is safe enough to guess them. As you see, it takes only small amounts to make rather strong solutions.

• Factors Affecting Speed of Bleaching

You will soon see that the fine art of print bleaching can't be learned overnight. You have to practice and you have to get used to the uncertain behavior of bleach solutions. One of the problems is that you can never predict how fast they will work on a given print. However, the speed-affecting factors are known.

Freshly mixed solutions work *much* faster than ones that have sat around for a while, even for ten minutes or so. Minerals in your water supply, and hypo that gets into the bleach solution, gradually form compounds with the ferricyanide, slowing it down until it finally won't bleach at all.

Light areas in prints bleach *much* faster than darker ones. At least, the fact that they get lighter is much more obvious, which is the same thing for practical purposes.

Naturally, strong bleach solutions work more rapidly than weak ones.

The print-developing time is an important factor. The less time you give a print the faster it will bleach. In prints developed one minute or less, the light areas bleach very rapidly, the medium and dark areas fairly rapidly. In two-minute prints the light areas bleach at a moderate rate, medium areas slowly, and dark areas very slowly. In five-minute prints only the light areas are affected at all by bleach, unless one uses a very strong solution.

Bleach applied very wet works much faster than a thin coat of it. Thus it works slowly when applied with a squeezed-out cotton wad or a brush that is damp rather than well loaded.

• Over-all Bleaching

We use over-all bleaching on prints that are overexposed but normally developed. They are thus too dark, but bleaching can often bring them back to normal tones of good quality. Prints overexposed up to 100 per cent (one stop) can usually be saved, but the less overexposure the better. Sometimes you can even rescue prints that are as much as two stops over, but you shouldn't count on it.

If overexposed prints are also *underdeveloped* the bleach will often cause a disagreeable, mottled effect. Therefore, if you see a print coming up too fast in the developer, don't "jerk" it, but let it remain in the tray for about 1½ minutes. It will be much too dark, of course, yet you *may* be able to save it by bleaching. If you jerk a print you might as well kiss it good-by.

If only half of a print is too dark, as often happens, put only that half in the bleach, moving it around so that the bleaching action will be even. Be careful not to get bleach on the part you are keeping out of the tray.

Over-all bleaching is also used to give prints extra "snap" and to increase contrast up to one paper contrast grade. To increase contrast, over-

expose the print about 20 per cent, develop it from 2 to 2½ minutes, then bleach it. In a print developed this long the darks won't bleach very much while the light areas will, thus increasing the "tonal distance" (contrast) between them. Essentially, giving a print more snap means to increase the contrast a bit.

• Over-all Bleaching Step by Step

1. Pour half a capful of Photo-Flo into a quart of water, stir it, then add one-eighth teaspoonful (level measure) of potassium ferricyanide crystals. Stir until the crystals are completely dissolved. This is very important.

2. Soak your print thoroughly in the fixing bath.

3. Pour the bleach in a tray and put the print in it.

4. Immediately start rocking the tray in an irregular way, so that the bleach flows over the print in a random pattern.

5. After ten seconds remove the print, drain it three seconds, and put it in the hypo, agitating for ten seconds or more.

6. Examine the print under the hypo light to see how much it has been bleached.

7. If more bleaching is needed, drain the print and return it to the bleach tray. If there was very little bleaching action the first time, you can safely increase the time to to twenty seconds, provided that the print is still quite obviously too dark. Then return it to the hypo and agitate as before. This process can be repeated many times, if necessary.

Doing it in stages this way is the best method for holding the bleaching action under control. If you try to bleach a print all the way the first time it is in the bleach bath, you will probably ruin it. One reason is that you will develop a compulsion to watch it bleach until it has gone too far. Another is that some of the bleaching goes on after the print goes into the hypo. Thus a print that looks just right in the bleach bath may end up being too light after the hypo has worked on it. This is why we inspect prints in the hypo, not the bleach.

After bleaching, fix the print thoroughly (for twice the time it takes for the yellow stain to disappear), then wash and dry it as usual.

The small amount of bleach that normally gets carried over into the fixing bath will neither harm it nor turn it into an effective Farmer's reducer solution. You can safely run other prints through it. However, if you dump a *lot* of bleach into it, you may have to test its bleaching action and possibly discard it. If you drain each print for three seconds after bleaching it, you should be able to work all day without harming the fixer.

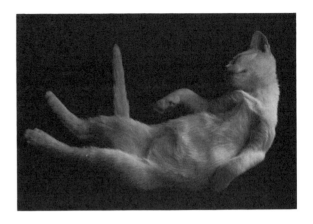

For over-all bleaching, the print is both overexposed and overdeveloped (above). The bleach lightens the whole print somewhat (below), especially the highlights, which bleach much faster than darker tones.

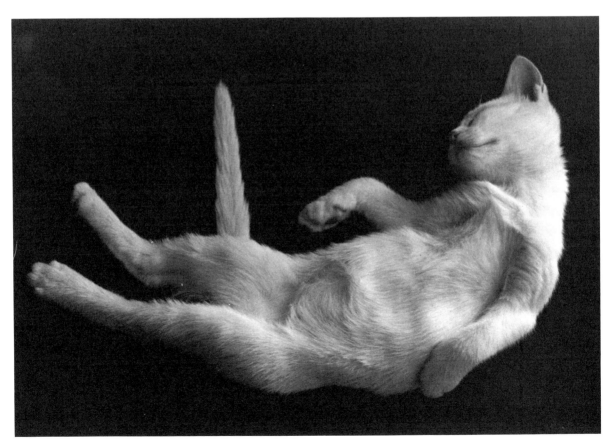

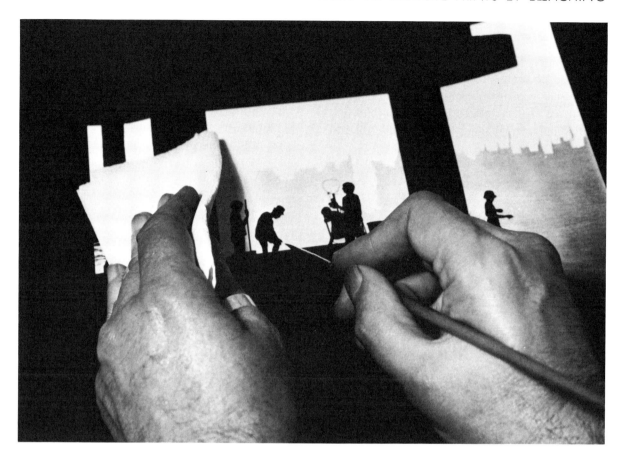

Working by the bleach-and-blot method on a print whose surface has been wiped thoroughly dry. Bleach is applied, then immediately blotted with a paper napkin. This stops it from bleaching too far or spreading. It is one of the main control methods used in print bleaching.

• Local Bleaching Step by Step

1. Put five drops of Photo-Flo into four ounces of water, stir, then add one-sixteenth teaspoonful of bleach crystals, stirring until they are completely dissolved. For stirring, you can use a small stick, a Q-Tip, or a teaspoon made of plastic or stainless steel.

2. Soak your print thoroughly in the fixing bath. It works somewhat better if the print has just been made and never dried.

3. Lay out your print-inspection board under the hypo light, next to the hypo tray. Near its top edge place the cup of bleach, the brush, a Q-Tip, a wad of cotton, the sponge, and two paper towels —one of them folded twice to serve as a blotter.

4. Drain the print, lay it on the board (or tray bottom), and wipe it thoroughly with the sponge (which has been soaked in hypo, then squeezed out).

5. Wipe the print even more thoroughly with a paper towel, so that even the *tiniest* droplets are gone.

6. Wet the brush, then point it and remove the excess bleach by stroking it on the first paper towel.

7. While holding the folded paper towel in your left hand, apply some bleach to the print and *immediately* blot it *dry* with the towel. Wait about

ten seconds for the hypo that is still in the emulsion to carry the bleaching action forward.

8. Inspect the area to determine how much bleaching occurred, then repeat the bleach-and-blot procedure as many times as necessary. *Never* wait to see what the bleach is doing, but blot first and find out later. Waiting to see is a sure road to ruin.

9. After every two or three bleach-and-blots, put some hypo on the area with a sponge, so that the continuing action of the bleach will be carried through to its end. It is also good to return the print to the hypo bath now and then—for the same reason.

10. If the area still needs bleaching, wipe off the print as before and continue with the bleaching and blotting.

11. When the print has bleached sufficiently, put it in the hypo for twice the time it takes the yellow stain (caused by the ferricyanide) to disappear.

12. Wash it and dry it as usual.

These lengthy instructions are designed to spell out the controls for you, line by line. However, print beaching isn't necessarily a slow and tedious process unless you intend to do a lot of it on a given print. Just lightening an area here and there can be a matter of only a few seconds.

A

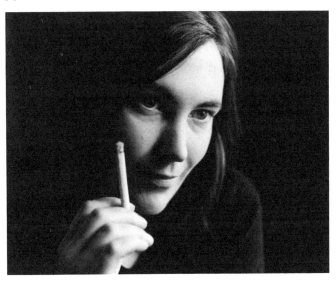

The slight bags under the eye in A can be fairly easily removed by bleaching, but pronounced ones would be very difficult to handle. In detail B we see what happens when one gets impatient and used bleach that is too strong. It could be spotted with dyes, but it would take several laborious hours. Print C shows the image after a conservative amount of bleaching.

B

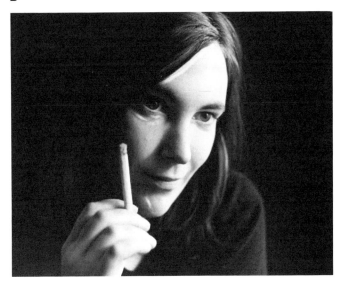

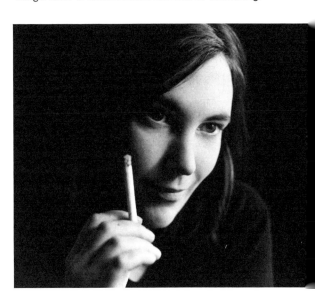

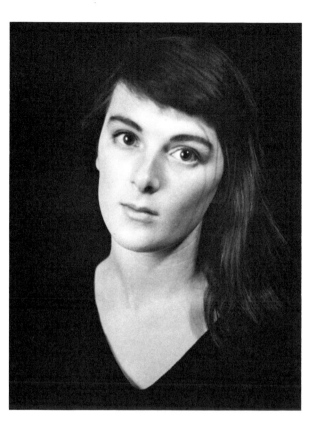 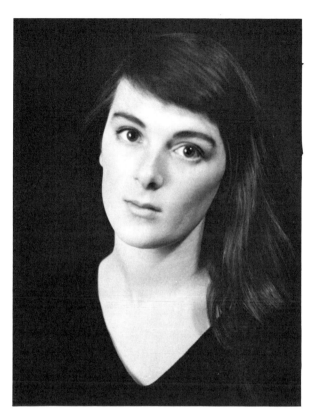

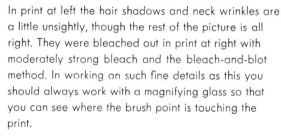

In print at left the hair shadows and neck wrinkles are a little unsightly, though the rest of the picture is all right. They were bleached out in print at right with moderately strong bleach and the bleach-and-blot method. In working on such fine details as this you should always work with a magnifying glass so that you can see where the brush point is touching the print.

● Haste Makes Waste

Though lightening a few areas may take little time, extensive bleach retouching and cutting out white backgrounds may be time-consuming and tedious. After working for perhaps twenty minutes on a print, impatience may set in and one may try to hurry things up by cutting out the print-wiping steps and using very strong bleach. You might as well know right now that this will almost invariably lead to disaster.

● A Fast-Cutting Print

If you know in advance that you are going to cut out a medium- or light-gray area, make a fast-cutting print. That is, overexpose and underdevelop it somewhat. For most papers, work for a developing time of one minute; with Kodak resin-coated (RC) papers you are usually safe in going as low as forty-five seconds. However, in both cases there will be a loss of contrast, so you should use a paper contrast grade or filter one step higher than you normally would.

When underdeveloping papers, slide them into the developer with one swift movement and maintain constant and erratic (random) agitation. Otherwise you may run into a problem with mottled tones.

You will find that the bleach works fast on prints of this type and that all areas—light, medium, and dark—are affected by it. Thus if you

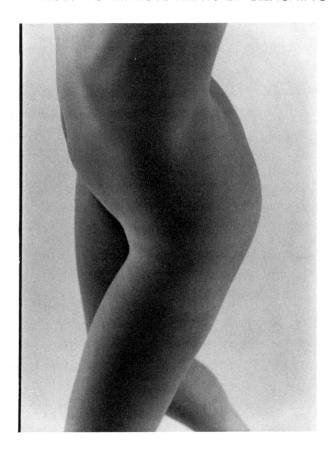

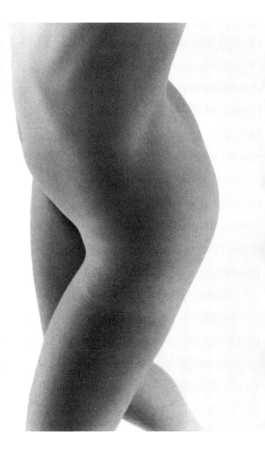

In print at left the background is a little dingy and the edge of the frame comes too close to the torso. In print at right the frame line has been dodged out and the rest of the background bleached out to a clean white.

do over-all bleaching in addition to working locally, use a very dilute or partly worn-out bleach.

• Bleach Turns Green

After it has been mixed for a while, bleach will turn green. If it is dilute the green is an indication that it is pretty well shot. However, strong bleaches can be as green as an emerald and still be very potent. The color won't get into your prints, so don't worry about it.

• Stains

You have already read about blue stains and how to deal with them, but you may also be troubled with yellow and brown stains. Either may be caused by insufficient time in the hypo, or using an exhausted hypo bath or too short a washing time.

Brown stains are often compounds of silver and ferricyanide, that is, silver that hasn't quite bleached all the way. If they fall in an area that you are cutting back to white you can generally get rid of them by alternating between strong bleach and hypo, if necessary even going to ultra-strong bleach. However, you must be careful in blotting the ultra-strong to keep it away from the rest of the image, for it will cut through tone like a knife.

Brown stains in areas that are supposed to remain medium or dark gray cannot be thus eliminated. However, they can be counteracted fairly well with light washes of blue spotting dry.

• Testing Bleaching Speed

Though the main factors influencing the speed of bleaching are known, one never knows for sure how fast a given print will bleach. If you test your bleach on light areas, it might get away from you even if it is a rather weak solution. You should therefore test it on medium or fairly dark tones, working your way gradually up to light ones.

If it should happen to work fast on medium tones you can be sure it would really clobber light ones. Thus it would be wise to dilute it considerably. On the other hand, if a bleach works too slowly, add more bleach crystals to it—but be sure to test the new mixture, too.

• Black Spots and Lines

Unless they fall in blank white areas, black spots and lines are a real agony to work on, because they take so long to disappear with medium or strong bleach, and it is so hard to keep the stuff out of adjacent areas. Though risky, it is sometimes best to turn to ultra-strong bleach. Use it in a carefully pointed *damp* brush, immediately blotting it and putting it into the hypo after each application. Remember that the ultra-strong brew is dynamite in itself, so don't take extra chances with it. However, if bleaching in areas as small as spots and lines goes a bit too far it can usually be patched up fairly easily by dye retouching—provided that you haven't slopped over into surrounding areas!

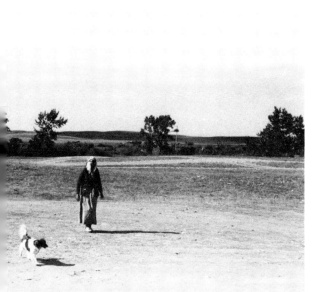 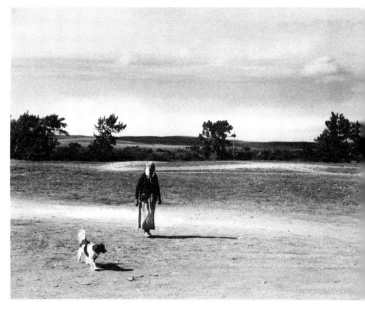

This picture of a Blackfoot Indian woman and her dog has a barren and empty feeling to it (left). In print at right the sky and foreground were burned-in and the whole picture made slightly darker. Then the lighter areas were created by bleaching.

You may find it fun to work with fast bleaches. If so, you should be willing to wipe out a few prints learning how to use the controls effectively. Work on pictures that don't quite make the grade, so you won't mind seeing them slide down the drain. But don't play fast on the draw with prints you really like.

• Keep It Moving

Sometimes it is safe to let bleach stand in an area awhile before blotting it. However, it will tend to draw into a puddle (even with Photo-Flo) so that the area isn't evenly covered. Thus the bleaching will be uneven. To counteract this, keep the bleach moving, going back and forth over the area with brush, cotton, or Q-Tip.

• Working Wet

If the edges of a lightened area don't have to be sharp, which is usually the case, you can often work on a print taken right out of the hypo and held in the palm of the left hand. Use medium-strong or strong bleach in a wad of cotton that has been well squeezed out. Blot your fingers so you won't get dribbles. After the print has drained four to five seconds, rub the area lightly with the cotton, but don't spend too long at it.

For a while, the squeezed-out cotton will simultaneously bleach the area it touches and absorb surface moisture, so that the bleach won't get loose into the surface hypo and get out of control.

After a few seconds, however, the cotton will get so full of hypo that it can't hold it any more. Along with the bleach it has picked up, the hypo will run amuck on the print. Thus when you use this method you should squeeze out the cotton again every two to three seconds, which prevents the rivulets. Though the technique sounds frightening it works well and very fast. Professional printers use it.

• You Know the Controls

The controls for successful print bleaching have been carefully spelled out so that you can start right out having fun with bleach. Many people find it one of the most fascinating tools of photography, and it could just as well be true for you.

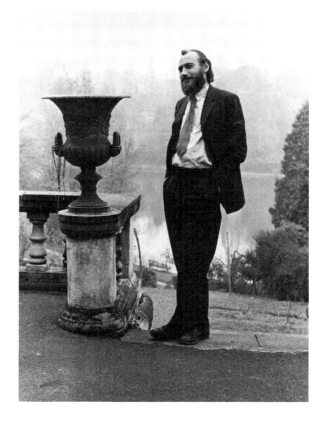

In print above the man's shirt is both dingy and wrinkled. Bleaching (right) improves it considerably. Notice that some of the wrinkles were left in; had they been entirely removed, the shirt would look like white plaster.

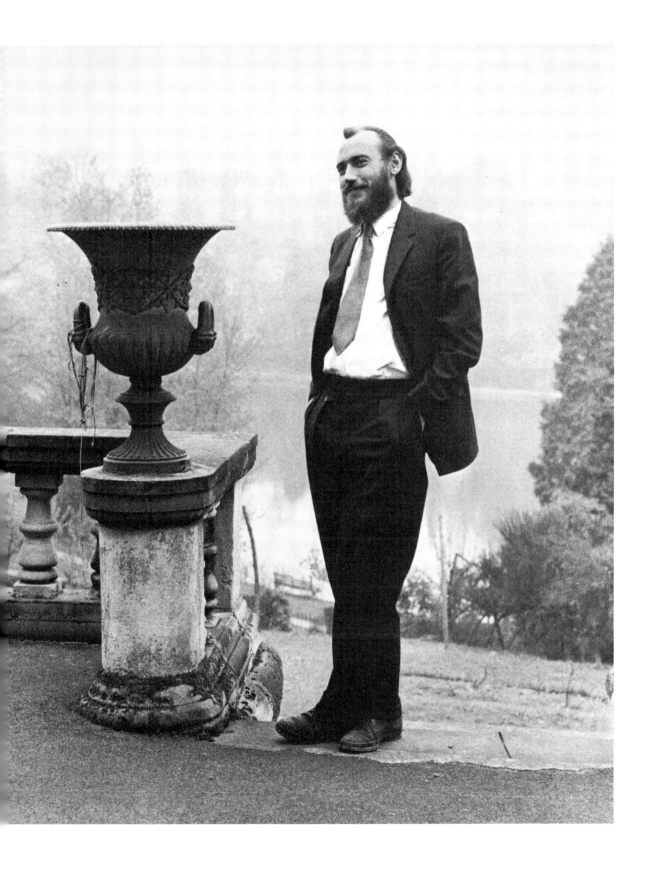

HOW TO MAKE MULTIPLE-IMAGE PRINTS FROM NEGATIVE SANDWICHES

It can be fascinating to create a multiple-image picture by printing more than one negative on a single piece of paper. Getting such an image is extremely easy, but it takes quite a bit of experimentation to come up with a really good one. Since the technique itself is so simple, you may not mind investing the materials and time required for top-notch results.

It is hard to say why we find multiple images so interesting. Perhaps it is because they are so strange; they surprise us, stimulating our minds and emotions. They tend to come across as pure symbolism, which is both unexpected and exciting. This may lead us to contemplate our personal symbolism and that which is universal, a useful step for better understanding of ourselves and others.

Frequently, multiple-image pictures have a strong resemblance to our dreams as we remember them. Indeed, for purposes of self-analysis or group discussion they can be dealt with as if they actually were dreams. The now-extensive psychology of dreams invariably fits multiple-image prints remarkably well.

However, your main motivation in working with this technique may be simply to surprise yourself as often as you can. This is as good a reason as any for playing with it.

● Things You Need

We will again use the list from page 65. Add to it the following:

Dodging and burning-in tools
Tools and materials for print bleaching

● The Basic Method

Instead of using just one negative at a time, "sandwich" (superimpose) two of them and make a print. Essentially, that is all there is to the method, though there are a few minor problems that should be dealt with.

● Picking the Negatives

The reasonable way to pick negatives is to think of all the pictures you have made and try to visualize how they would work together as multiple images. Reasonable, yes, but it just won't work. Things mentally visualized seldom work out until you have had a lot of experience.

You just have to wing it, but that is part of the fun. One way is to try all kinds of combinations of negatives in order to find ones that look good when held up to the light. The idea is that if sandwiches themselves look nice they will often make handsome pictures. On the other hand, some combinations that look unimpressive due to excessive density or flatness will make excellent prints, because these faults can be compensated for.

Beyond choosing sandwiches for their handsomeness or visual interest, the process is mainly a matter of trial and error. Some handsome superimpositions will print badly for unforeseeable reasons. And rather nondescript ones may make smashing prints. The only way to tell how a sandwich will print is to try it and find out. Since the art of photography was mainly developed by people who work this way, it would be educational for you to give it a try, too. If all it does is make you more philosophical about your mistakes in pictorial judgment, you will be a long way ahead. When you deal with the unpredictable, you should learn not to condemn your predictions.

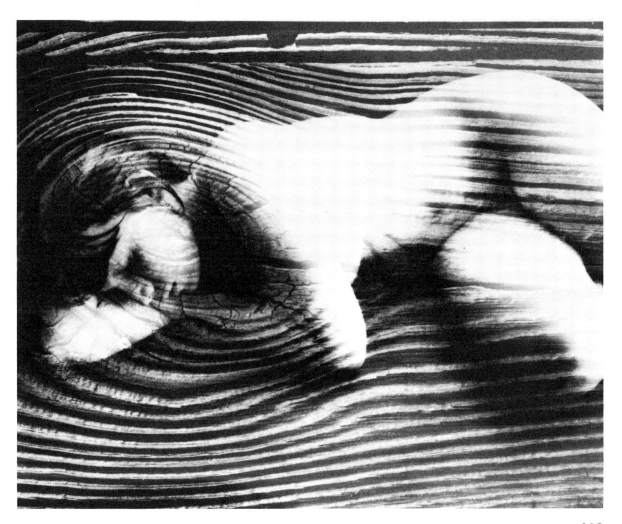

● Reversing Negatives, Flipping Them, and So On

From an innate sense of order and the rightness of things, you may feel that the two negatives in a sandwich should both be emulsion down, have their frames in register, and be oriented in the same direction from top to bottom. This would be unduly restricting yourself due to a false sense of pictorial piety. You can superimpose them this way if you like, but don't force yourself to stick to the formula. Since it is of the nature of multiple-image printing to commit mayhem on reality, you might as well add to the carnage just to see what happens.

Try sandwiching negatives emulsion to emulsion, back to back, top to bottom, and off register: you may get interesting results. You can pair negatives of two different sizes or sandwich a negative with a color slide (removed from its mount). Perhaps a fuzzy, out-of-focus negative would make a tasty sandwich when combined with a sharp one. See what you can think up, then give it a try.

● Cleaning Negatives

When you are printing a single negative, there are only two surfaces to collect dust. With sandwiched negatives there are four, so you should take great care in cleaning them (pages 44–48).

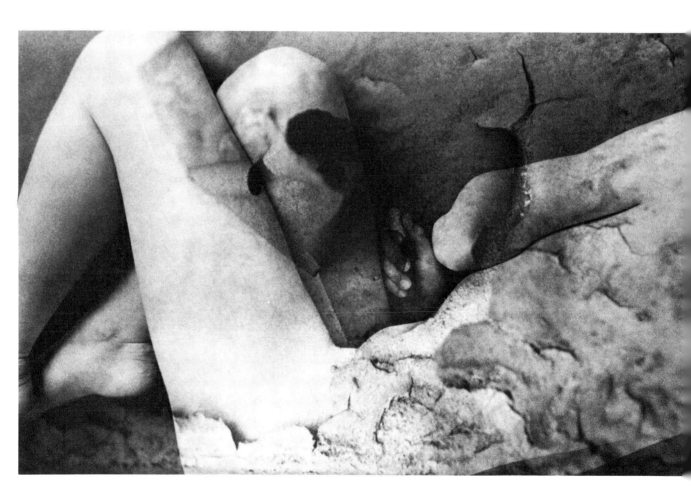

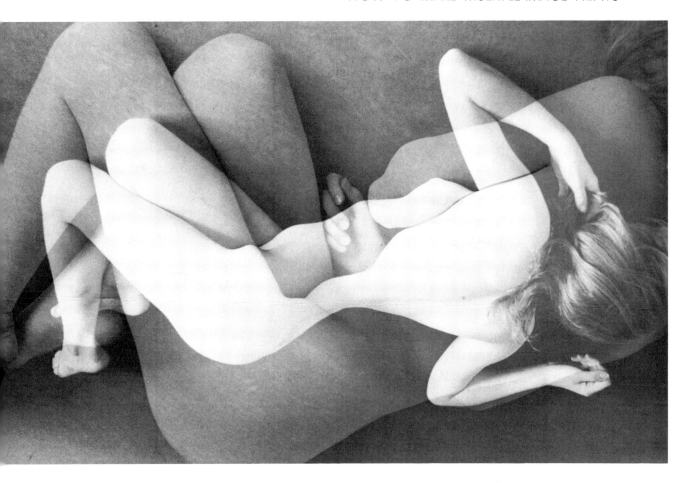

You should always clean negatives carefully, for that matter—unless you enjoy spending the lonely hours poking dye into dust spots on prints.

• Flatness and Contrast

Combined negatives often look very flat, because the light tones in one may neutralize the dark tones in the other. It can even go so far that a sandwich viewed against the light may look like a single solid expanse of gray.

Fortunately, the combinations aren't usually so totally lacking in contrast, though they lean in that direction. Most of the time, the flatness can be compensated for by using high-contrast paper or printing filters. For example, if the individual

negatives in a sandwich would print best on a no. 2 paper, the combination itself might be successfully printed on a no. 4. Thus, low contrast is not usually much of a problem.

Though most superimpositions tend toward flatness, not all of them do. Now and then, contrast is increased rather than decreased. It all depends on how the individual tones are overlapped. If the dark tones in one negative fall upon dark tones in the other, and if their light tones also overlap, there can be a considerable increase in contrast. Even so, such a sandwich will usually print well on an available contrast grade of paper (1 through 6). If it is even too contrasty for a no. 1, however, there are simple ways of flattening out the print as much as necessary (see the following chapter).

The Density Problem

You will recall that the "density" of a negative refers to how dark it looks when viewed against a light source or brightly lit surface. It depends on both exposure and development, and there is an optimum density in what we call a "normal negative." However, when we sandwich two normal negatives we may double the optimum, depending on how the tones overlap. If they are "heavy" negatives (too dense) we get even more density.

Too much density in either a single negative or a sandwich can result in a slightly fuzzy print with mushy highlights. In the enlarger the excessive silver deposit acts as a diffuser, scattering some of the light as it passes through, making a print that seems slightly unsharp. Even with dense single negatives and superimpositions that are much too dense this doesn't always happen, however, so you should make test prints before rejecting them. If sandwiched negatives are both close to normal you should have no trouble with unsharpness.

Another problem with density is that it increases the print exposure time. Even with sandwiched normal negatives you will find yourself using exposure times ranging from thirty seconds to one or two minutes when the lens is stopped down three stops. You could cut the time by opening the lens, of course, but as you will see in a moment it isn't advisable. So you may be stuck with long exposure times. Though they stretch one's patience considerably, there is nothing wrong with long exposures per se. Indeed, pictures have been made with exposures lasting a whole day or two.

However, the time can lead to a problem with heat, which can warp negatives out of focus or even damage them. Thus you may have to print with prepopped negatives (or negative sandwiches) and break up long exposures into installments to allow the enlarger to cool. If you find the installments and cooling-off periods unduly tedious, read a book while you are waiting (with a darkroom-safe spotlight, which you can make by taping a five-inch cylinder of light cardboard or black paper to an ordinary flashlight).

Stopping Down

The easiest way to sandwich two negatives is to position them both emulsion down, so they will curl together neatly like obedient spoons. Positioned emulsion to emulsion or back to back, their curl can make them as hard to handle as a greased pig. Thus if you have only the average amount of patience you will probably make most of your sandwiches the easy way.

This introduces a problem, however, in that the images on the two negatives are separated by one thickness of film base. Thus they are situated at different distances from both the lens and the printing paper, which simply means that when one image is sharp the other will be slightly out of focus—when the lens aperture is wide open for focusing. Fortunately, when we stop down three stops they will both be acceptably sharp. You can be sure of this if you focus *between* the images, rather than on one or the other. Though it sounds hard you will find it easy.

You can now see why we can't beat the problem of a long exposure time by simply opening up the lens. You may be safe in stopping down only twice, but don't count on it. With the lens wide open or stopped down only once the disparity in focus should be quite obvious. If you don't mind wrestling with a greased pig you can get around the problem by positioning the negatives emulsion to emulsion, because there will then be no separation at all between the images. However, you should stop down the lens a bit anyway, for it isn't sharp all the way to the edges at the larger aperture settings. But don't do it as a matter of rote, since some pictures look just fine with slightly soft edges.

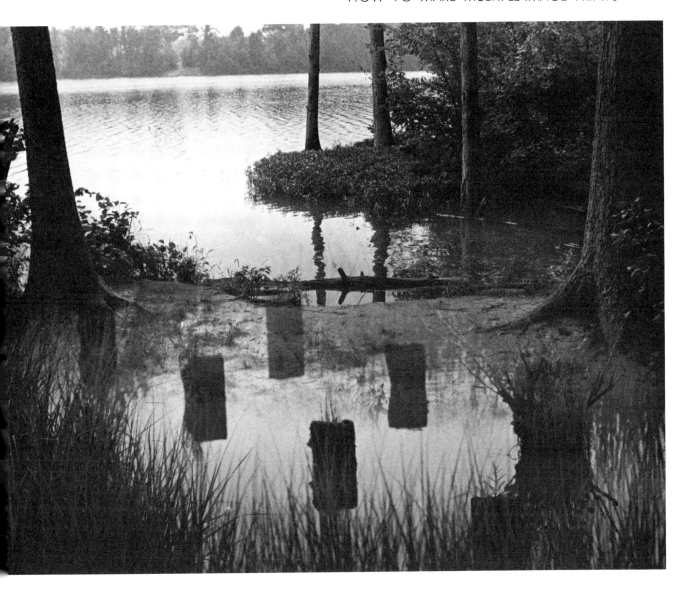

• Test Strips

When first using this unfamiliar technique, you should use an abundance of test strips and chips, both to determine exposures and to learn in the most economical way what sandwiching negatives does to prints. Since you will generally be working with heavier-than-usual densities, you can expect longer exposures, as we have seen. So increase the times for your test strips; for example, use the series 10–10–10 etc. seconds. For a very

dense sandwich, you could even use exposures of twenty or thirty seconds each.

• Dodging and Burning-In

In making multiple-image prints, you will often get dark tones where you want light ones, and vice versa, so make very liberal use of both dodging and burning-in. On account of the heavy densities, the burning-in times may be very long for certain prints. In such cases you may wish to dare the forbidden: open up the lens all the way for burning-in. With some pairs of negatives, there will be no tangible loss of quality; with others, there will be. You just have to try it and see.

You were told you should never dodge an area for more than 50 per cent of the exposure time, but this doesn't necessarily apply to printing negative sandwiches, especially if they are very dense. With the dense ones, you can sometimes dodge an area up to 80 per cent or more of the total time without its looking muddy or washed out.

• Bleaching

With multiple-image printing, you may wish to make more tone changes than you can handle with just dodging and burning-in, so wade into your prints with flourish and bleach.

• Dye Retouching

Don't forget that dyeing is an extension of burning-in; you may need it.

• Surprise!

Making multiple-image prints will probably turn out to be an emotional adventure for you, provided that you stick with it long enough to get a few passable images. Your ego will have a rough time, because it will predict numerous results that will fail to happen. Something else will always happen instead, for better or for worse. But giving your ego a hard time is the way to take the blinders off your eyes so that you can see better.

It would be wise to take the symbolism matter seriously, because this technique is a way of almost automatically bringing your hidden personal symbols to the surface, where you can see them. You will be pleased to see them, no doubt, but you are also likely to get shaken up a bit. It is like suddenly confronting yourself in a mirror in a darkened and unfamiliar house: shocking! Yet the experience will be good for you, because it will help you learn who you really are.

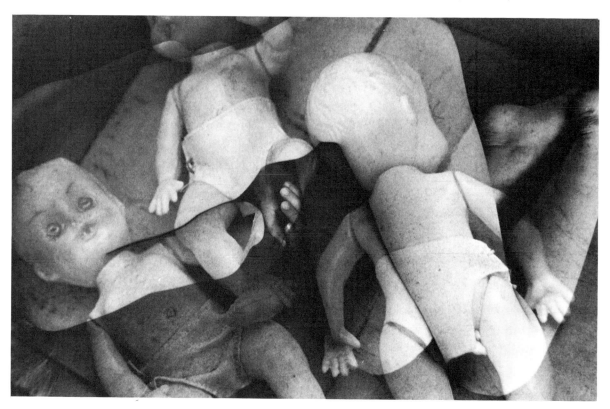

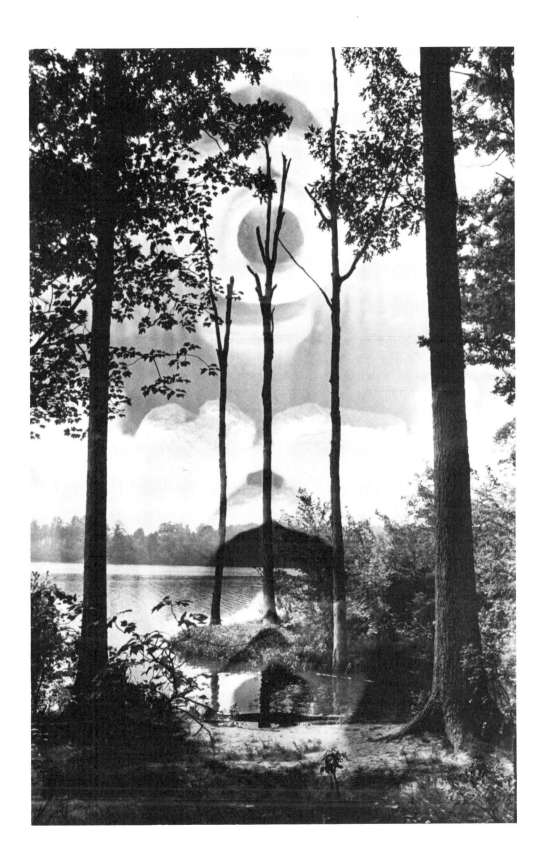

HOW TO CONTROL PRINT CONTRAST BY DEVELOPER DILUTION AND FLASHING

There are times when you may wish to reduce the contrast of a given paper as little as one contrast grade or as much as even four or five. There could be several reasons for this, for example when you have on hand only high-contrast paper and discover that your negatives require low-contrast ones. Or it may be that you can afford to buy only one package of paper, so you chose high-contrast, knowing that you can flatten it out if necessary. On the other hand, you may have negatives so contrasty that they would require a nonexistent grade of paper well below a no. 1, so you could start with a no. 1 and take it down to a minus 4 or 5.

Sometimes the reasons for flattening are strictly pictorial: you may want a print that is very flat, light, and delicate; and you can use a flattening technique not for contrast reduction as such but for bleaching, for reasons that will be explained later.

You will be given two excellent techniques, one involving intentional overexposure and under-development, the other revolving around intentional *under*exposure and flashing, or fogging. Ordinarily, these are things we wish to avoid, but under controlled conditions we can neatly turn them to our advantage.

Aside from strictly practical reasons, it is interesting to use the techniques just to see what you can do with them. Furthermore, they will lead you to many insights on how photography works.

• Things You Need

We will again use the list on page 65, since there is no point in being repetitious. To it you might add the following:

A 1-gallon juice container (optional)
An immersion heater, the size used in coffee cups (optional)
A clamp-on light fixture with a 7½-watt frosted bulb
Light dimmer or rheostat (optional)
Small graduate or measuring cup
Surgical cotton

Juice container: It should be deep enough so that you can put a curled 8×10 print in it vertically and have it covered all the way with water. If you wish, you can use a tray instead, though it is not quite as convenient.

Heater: If you have no running hot water in your darkroom you will find it handy. Otherwise,

126

you will be making frequent trips to the kitchen for hot water. In a moment you will see that hot water is very good to have on hand for purposes other than print contrast reduction.

Dimmer: for easily controlling the intensity of light falling on a print during flashing exposures. However, you can also control it by moving the light source farther away.

Measuring cup: A pint-size one used for cooking is all right. For finer measurements use one of the plastic containers that Kodak 35-mm film cassettes come in; it holds exactly one ounce.

• Developer Dilution: the Basic Method

You have already read that underdeveloping a print will reduce its contrast but that the image may come out mottled if you go too far. Therefore, underdevelopment (usually combined with overexposure) should be carefully avoided. But not always. If you can circumvent the mottle, which is easily done, you can safely underdevelop as much as you wish, thereby flattening prints up to four or five contrast grades. However, the results are usually more handsome if you settle for just one or two grades.

The basic method is to expose a test strip, soak it in warm water (100 F) for two minutes, then put it in diluted developer for two minutes. You can use any dilution you like, but 1:20 is a good starting place for a considerable reduction in contrast. The figure 1:20 is a "dilution ratio." The first number in such a ratio is always the chemical to be diluted (Dektol stock solution); the number after the colon always indicates the amount of solvent (water) to be added. In this instance, you can also express it as one part of Dektol to twenty of water, or just Dektol 1:20. Similarly, one could have a dilution of three to one (3:1) or one to fifty (1:50).

As usual with a developed test strip, the best tone tells you your exposure. In this case it will represent what one would ordinarily consider overexposure, but it will look quite normal on the strip and be the correct exposure for a finished print presoaked in warm water and developed in Dektol 1:20.

• Mottle

A print that has been underdeveloped in normally diluted Dektol (1:2) often has a disagreeable mottle, because different parts of the emulsion absorb the developer at different rates. Thus some areas will be almost fully developed and others half developed, which gives us mottle. One reason for this is that small areas of the gelatin emulsion may vary in toughness, thus varying in absorbency, too. Another is that a print developer diluted 1:2 works very rapidly and erratically. A third is uneven agitation. In a normal print these things don't matter so much, because nearly all the exposed silver halide particles are going to get reduced to metallic silver, anyway. The tones even themselves out.

Unfortunately, this is not true with prints that are deliberately overexposed and underdeveloped: a large percentage of the exposed silver halide crystals are not converted to metallic silver but remain undeveloped. This is what makes the contrast-reduction technique work. However, the uneven absorbency of the gelatin, inadequate agitation and high developer activity must be counteracted, or we will get mottle. We must therefore do three things: soften the gelatin, dilute the developer, and use a high-efficiency agitation technique.

• Warm-Water Presoak

We can help matters considerably by softening the emulsion somewhat with a two-minute presoak in warm water just before development. Then the developer can enter the gelatin at a uniform rate in all areas, provided that the agitation is adequate.

The temperature should be about 100 F. If it falls much lower than that the gelatin won't get soft enough. If it goes over 110 degrees, you may get little black specks and marks.

On some resin-coated (RC) papers the emul-

127

sions aren't tough enough and are poorly bonded to their white plastic bases, so it isn't safe to soften them. They may get sticky and even slide right off. However, Kodak RC papers are entirely safe to work with, yet they should be handled with care. Though they are very vulnerable to scratches before processing they are quite tough when wet. Nearly all regular papers can take warm water with no trouble.

● Hot-Water Burning-In

While we are on the subject of warm water, we will take a short detour, then get back to our main theme. Heat can be used to "force" parts of a print that have received an exposure that is not quite enough to permit them to develop. They are on the verge of being developable but actually won't make it. We usually see this in prints that are a little light on one side or in certain areas.

To darken a side, fill the juice container with water at about 125 F. Then curl the print and dip the light side in for about a second, repeating the treatment once or twice if necessary. If it is still too light, return the print to the developer tray for ten seconds to get the emulsion filled with developer again, then dip it another time or two. If you push the treatment any farther than this you may get fog, but not always.

To darken smaller areas, rub them gently with a wad of cotton that has been dipped in hot water and partly squeezed out (so the water won't dribble). Both tricks work best on prints that have developed 1½ minutes or more, and they will work only if the light areas are on the verge of being developable.

For a print that is *over*exposed on one side and normally exposed on the other, use a different trick. When the first side has developed far enough, slide it into the stop bath, leaving the other side sticking out so that it can continue to develop. If necessary, you can keep putting fresh developer on it with your fingertips.

End of detour.

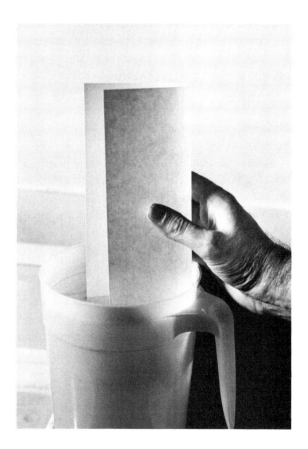

Prints to be developed in a dilute developer should be given a presoak in hot water, which can conveniently be kept in a large juice container.

● Agitation Technique

Print agitation is simple and easy if almost all of the exposed silver halide is supposed to get developed, which is usually the case. However, in developer dilution prints, the areas with *little* exposure will develop most of the way, whereas those with *heavy* exposure will remain mostly undeveloped, which is a kind of pardox. Nevertheless, the latter areas will remain so heavily prone to development that a poor developer flow pattern due to faulty agitation may result in their uneven development. For example, an area that

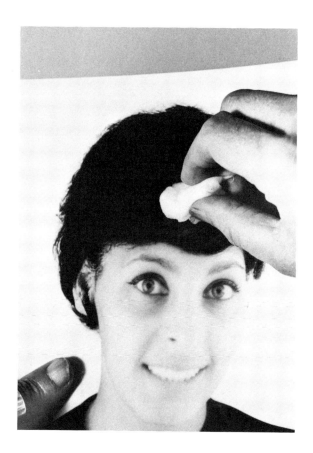

Slightly underexposed areas of a print can be darkened with hot water in a cotton swab.

• Exposure, Contrast, and Developer Dilutions

The useful range of developer dilutions is quite long. For experimenting with the technique, you might try the following: 1:5–1:10–1:15–1:20–1:50–1:100. With lower dilutions and a warm-water presoak, little or no increase in exposure is necessary, but with higher ones you may run into very long exposures—up to two or three minutes or more.

For a lower dilution, make a test strip with a series of five-second exposure times, but increase the individual exposures up to twenty or thirty seconds each for high dilutions.

As you increase the exposure and dilute the developer you get progressively less contrast, until you reach a point where there is hardly any at all. One usually goes this far only for pictorial reasons or just to see what the results will look like. If you merely wish to drop your paper one or two contrast grades, work with the 1:5 or 1:10 dilution.

• Developing Times

With all dilutions, it is probably best to use a two-minute developing time after a two-minute presoak. However, if you find that a print hasn't had enough exposure to develop up in that time you can safely increase it to five minutes or more if the developer is quite dilute. This will bring up the image, but it will also give you more contrast than you would get in only two minutes. To hold the contrast low, you should make another print, giving it more exposure.

However, you may want this extra contrast. For example, you may be using a 1:10 dilution and discover that it drops the contrast a bit more than you desire. By cutting the print exposure and extending the developing time, you can bring it back to where it should be. Indeed, if you develop long enough you can get the same contrast from a 1:10 dilution as you would get from a 1:2.

should have a flat, even tone may come out with streaks.

The ideal developer flow pattern on a print is totally random, that is, entirely erratic and unpredictable. A good way to establish such a pattern is to drag a soggy piece of cotton around the print surface during the entire developing time. Do your best to never make the same movement twice and to cover all parts of the picture about the same number of times. Make the cotton move around like an inebriated toad with a broken compass: erratically. This will give you an impeccable flow pattern and very even print tones.

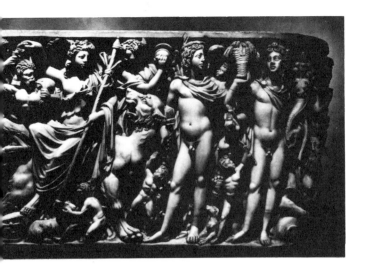

A series of prints made on no. 5 (high-contrast) paper and processed in developers at various dilutions. The idea is to show you how much contrast can be reduced with this method. The progressive dilutions were 1:2 (normal), 1:10, 1:20, 1:30, and 1:40. This gives us a contrast range much greater than one can get with graded-contrast or variable-contrast papers developed at a normal dilution.

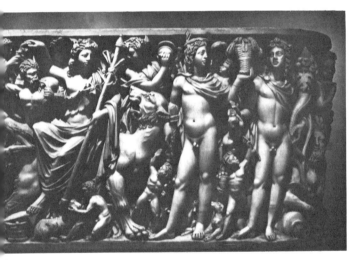

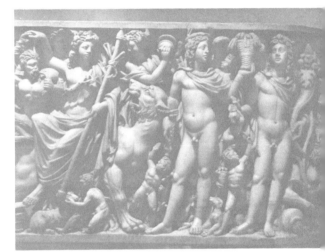

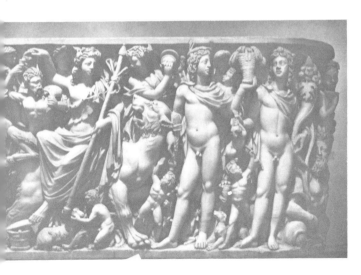

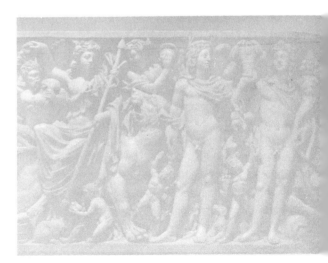

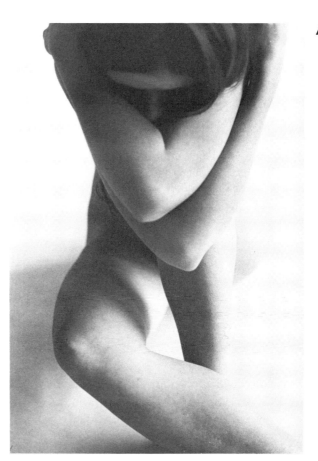

A

Overexposure and a diluted developer can be used to produce a print that will cut back very fast in potassium ferricyanide bleach. Since the contrast will be reduced, start with a paper two contrast grades too high. A, B, and C were all printed on a no. 5 paper, but A was developed in Dektol 1:2, while the dilution for B and C was 1:20. This made it easy and fast to cut out the background on C. Print C also has the desired amount of contrast.

B

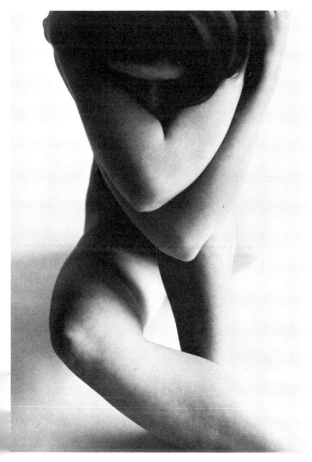

C

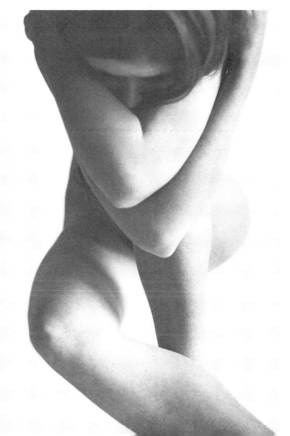

• Developer Exhaustion

Since there may be little developer in it a dilution may not hold up very long. You can probably develop half a dozen 8×10 prints in a tray of 1:20 before it weakens very much, but when you go as high as 1:50 or 1:100 it might be best to mix a new dilution after each print or two.

At the very high dilutions, the developer will get exhausted without even being used. In ten or fifteen minutes the oxygen in the air and that dissolved in the water will oxydize, or exhaust, the small amount of developing agent.

• Print Toning

Most papers change color considerably when they are processed in developers of progressively greater dilution, the particular colors that you get depending on the brand of paper you are using. A given paper may range from a slightly warmish color at 1:5 to a beautiful red-brown at, say, 1:30. The only way you can tell what colors you will get with a paper is to try it, but you can count on their being handsome. In truth, developer dilution prints often look as if they had been treated in special print "toners."

• Bleaching

When you wish to bleach areas in a print down to white, it may take quite a while, especially if the areas are fairly dark. You can speed up the bleaching action by using a developer dilution print. Try a 1:20 dilution as a starting point. Since the contrast will drop, compensate in advance by using a paper or printing filter two or three grades higher than you normally would use for the negative. The print contrast will shift neatly into place and the bleaching will be easier.

• Contrast Control by Flashing

You can reduce the contrast of a print by deliberately fogging it, but that also makes it too dark. However, if you use an underexposed print it can come out with both the right contrast and the desired tone. Actually, you expose a print twice, giving it the basic exposure with the enlarger light and a fogging (flashing) exposure with a white light. Naturally, the two exposures have to be quantitatively related in the right way, or the print won't look right. This is no problem, because we can use a special kind of test strip to determine both exposures at once.

The flashing technique will permit you to reduce contrast very dramatically; for example, you can drop an Agfa Brovira no. 6 (the highest-contrast paper available) down to a minus 4 or 5 and perhaps lower. You would seldom want to go that far, but you can if you wish.

Unlike developer dilution, there is no color change from contrast reduction by flashing, no matter how far you push it. Furthermore, there is no need to presoak the paper or use the special agitation technique just described. Ordinary procedures are quite adequate. This is not to say you should get sloppy; just use the techniques described on pages 33–35.

• Light Source for Flashing

For flashing we need a low-wattage light source, because the print is given relatively little exposure. A small bulb at the right distance from the print will permit us to use flashing exposure times that are long enough to be marked off with a metronome or an electronic exposure timer, or by counting seconds.

Fortunately, the right size and type of light source is available, a small round frosted 7½-watt bulb that will fit standard light sockets. Before using it, tape a three-inch cylinder of black paper around it, so that it won't scatter too much light around the darkroom. Then position it exactly five feet above the surface on which you will flash your prints. With most printing papers, you will then get flashing exposures that are long enough to be manageable.

However, some papers are "faster" (more sensitive to light) than others. If you should find yourself using a type too fast for the setup just described, move the light farther away or tape a few thicknesses of typing paper over the black paper

A light source for contrast reduction by flashing. It is also used for solarizing. It has a 7½-watt white bulb and a short snoot of black paper.

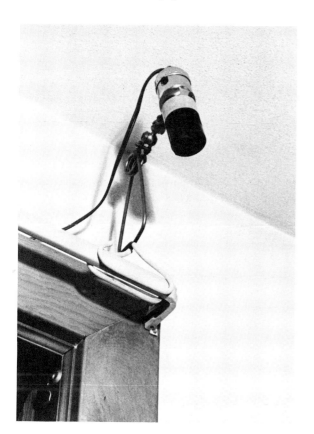

snoot. If you like, you can use a light dimmer, so that you can move the light a lot closer. Or you could use a 25-watt frosted red bulb as your light source. Red bulbs that large are no longer "safe" for papers; they have about the same effect on them as very low-wattage white bulbs.

● The Method in Brief

Make an ordinary test strip on a one-inch strip of paper, then a two-way strip on a full sheet of it. From the latter, select the combination of exposures that will give you both the over-all tone and the contrast you want for your print. Expose your print first with the enlarger, next with the flashing light. Process it in the normal way.

● The Two-Way Test Strip

The reason for making a preliminary test strip is that we only want underexposures on our two-way test, so we have to get the data for exposing it. That is, we make a small strip to get the exposures for a larger one. We don't want *over*exposed areas on the full-sheet test, because they would all be wasted. For the initial strip use the 5–5–5 method (page 56).

After processing it, calculate what you should do to make a full-sheet strip in which the darkest area would be either a normal exposure or slightly under. You might have to change the aperture, the exposure times, or both. If you are a little uncertain of what you are doing, check your exposure figures by making another one-inch strip. Don't be alarmed because some of the areas have no tone in them at all; they're supposed to be that way for this particular technique.

Now use the enlarger setting and times you have decided on and use your enlarger to make a test strip on a full sheet of paper. Next, position the paper under the flashing light and use it to expose another test strip right on top of the first one. This time, however, move the cardboard at right angles to the first strip so you will get a checkerboard effect.

For both series of exposures, you should expose by progressively covering up the paper. However, the first exposure of the basic exposure series should be made with a narrow width of the paper covered. Do this also with the flashing series. This will give you a vertical column of basic exposures that have no flashing. You can use them for comparison to the rest to see what flashing actually does. You will also have one horizontal row of flashing exposures with no basic exposures, also for comparison purposes.

For your two-way test strip, four flashing exposures of three seconds each will probably be enough—if you use the recommended lighting setup and Contrast no. 5 paper. This will give you a five-step flashing scale from zero to twelve seconds. With other papers, this flashing exposure range may be either too long or too short. If it is long, cut the exposure times or move the bulb farther away. If it's short, increase the times or the number of steps. Or you could move the flashing light closer.

After exposure, process the two-way strip normally. Remember that you should· *never* jerk a test strip or develop it too long. Even the world's most badly exposed strip has useful information on it, but only if you develop it exactly as you intend to develop your finished print.

Find the area that you like best for your final print, then count up to it from the bottom for the first exposure time, in to it from the side for the second. If your two-way strip doesn't look anything like the illustration in this chapter, figure out what is wrong and make another. It will take a whole sheet of paper, true enough, but it will save you money in the long run by simply helping you to see what you are doing.

• The Range of Usable Underexposures

How much you should underexpose with the enlarger depends on how much you want the contrast lessened: the less the first exposure the lower the contrast. The useful range is from nearly normal exposure to about three stops under. If you follow the directions in the last section you will see these data visually laid out for you in the form of a two-way test strip and won't have to bother to figure out such things as the meaning of "three stops." Indeed, test strips are especially for people who aren't good at figures.

From your two-way test strips you can see that as first exposures (enlarger) decrease, second exposures (flashing light) should increase, and vice versa. Again, instead of having to figure it out mathematically, all you have to do is look and see.

A two-way full-page test strip for determining enlarger-light and flashing-light exposures for a method of reducing picture contrast by flashing. First you make a test strip with the enlarger and the negative. Then you use the flashing light to make another test strip right on top of the first one but crosswise to it. To determine the two exposures for a given area, count up from the bottom by fives (0–5–10–15–20–etc.) for the enlarger exposure, then count in from the left by threes (0–3–6–9–etc.) for the flashing exposure. Following this procedure, we see that area Z on the test strip received a ten-second enlarger exposure and a six-second flashing exposure. In vertical column X there are only enlarger exposures; thus it is just like a regular one-inch test strip. In horizontal row Y there are only flashing exposures; therefore, it shows how long it takes to fog unexposed paper with the flashing light. We can see the fog clearly in the 12-second area on the bottom row. Although it is also in the two areas right above it it doesn't look too bad. Comparing them to the two areas to the left of them we can see there has been an improvement. Note that in column X the five- and ten-second areas have no image in them at all. As we move over to the right we can see where flashing has brought the hidden image out.

total
exposure
times
with the
enlarger

Column X

40
seconds

35

30

25

20

15

10

5

0

Row Y

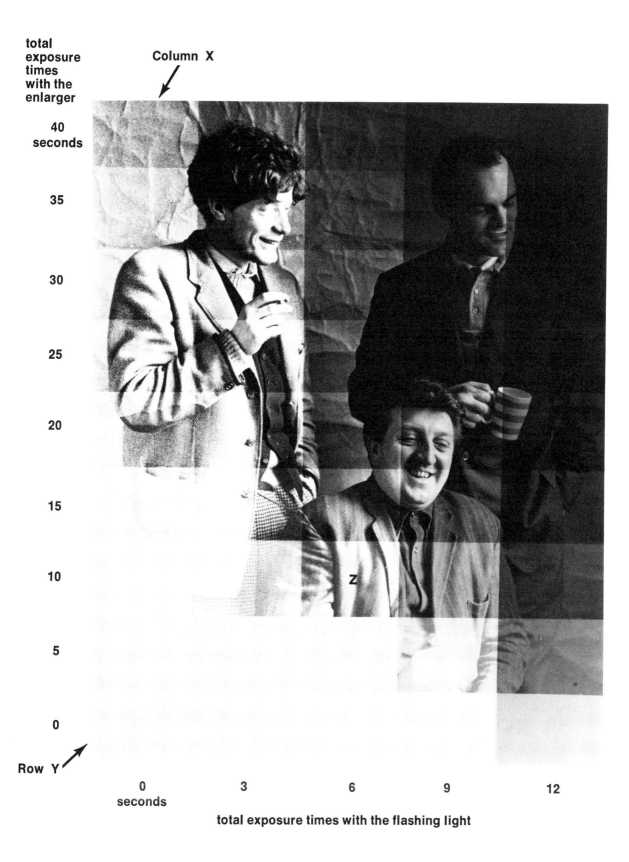

Z

0   3   6   9   12
seconds

total exposure times with the flashing light

A

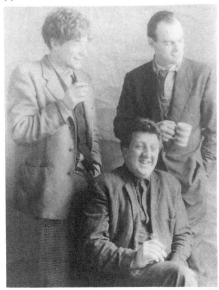

| enlarger exposures | 5 seconds |
| flashing exposures | 9 seconds |

B

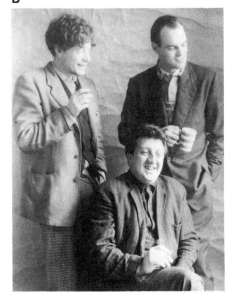

10

7½

E

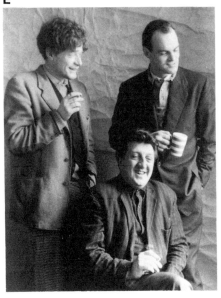

| enlarger exposures | 25 seconds |
| flashing exposures | 4½ seconds |

F

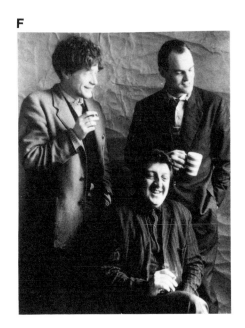

35

3

C

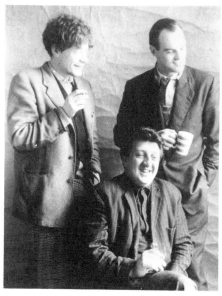

15

7

D

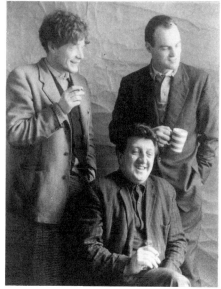

20

6

G

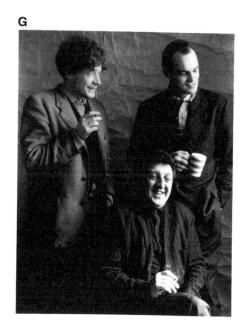

45

0

A series of prints made on Contrast no. 5, as was the two-way test strip. The range of contrasts you see here is considerably greater than you could get with graded-contrast or variable-contrast papers. In working with contrast reduction this extreme, the fogging exposure sometimes makes a print look gray and dismal. This can be corrected by over-all bleaching. We see that print A is quite a bit flatter than one would usually want, though such low contrast can sometimes have decorative possibilities. Print G, with no flashing at all, is quite a bit too contrasty. Print E seems about right; it is two or three contrast grades flatter than G.

• Preflashing

So far we have talked about postflashing, that is, doing it after the basic exposure. You can also do the flashing first, even days ahead, and use the very same flashing times. Thus you can use the same two-way test strip for both methods. Make one for every type and contrast grade of paper you intend to flash.

If you should inherit a truckload of no. 4 or 5 paper it would be good to preflash a lot of it down to grades 3, 2, 1 and possibly 0 (you need it now and then). Or you might find an army-surplus buy or a hot deal on high-contrast papers in 500-sheet quantities. On the other hand, you might try preflashing just to test your wings and see if you have learned anything from this book.

• Effective Paper Speed

In the developer dilution method, you in essence reduce the speed of a paper to practically nil; remember the long exposure times at high dilutions? With the flashing technique, we can increase it considerably, whether we postflash, preflash, or flash during development (yes). You can increase the speed of film the same way, deriving the necessary data with two-way test strips. You see, the things you are learning here can be used in more ways than you supposed.

If you don't really believe that paper speed is increased a lot by flashing, look at your full-sheet test strips. How about those areas with no image at all that develop very substantial images as the amount of flashing exposure is increased?

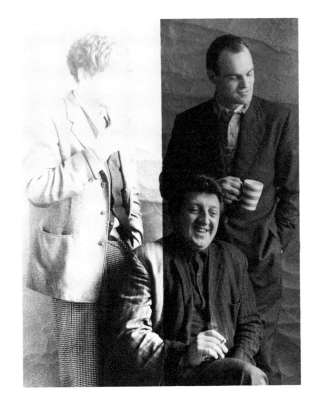

It is hard to tell the dramatic effect of flashing from looking at a test strip or at prints arranged in a series of gradually changing contrast. This print shows rather positively how much difference flashing can make. The whole print was exposed with the enlarger and negative, but only half of it was flashed. You can figure out approximately what the two exposures must have been by analyzing the two-way test strip, which was made on the same brand and contrast grade of paper.

HOW TO SOLARIZE YOUR PRINTS

In the preceding chapter, you were told that prints for contrast reduction can be flashed before the basic exposure, after it, or during development. The latter method is a little tricky, because your prints may get all or partly "solarized." However, you may want them that way, which is another matter. Solarizations are often very interesting, and the phenomenon itself is fascinating.

If a normal or underexposed print is given a brief flashing exposure about halfway through development, it will soon turn gray or black and look thoroughly "fogged." With even less exposure to white light it may merely lose contrast and not look fogged at all. As we move toward *longer* exposures, however, there is a point where some very weird things begin to happen.

By now, you know that the more exposure you give a print the darker it will be. This is a way of stating the Law of Reciprocity, upon which photography is based. But there are times when the law fails to work, for example in solarization. With exposure increases (by flashing) given during development, the print tones may come out progressively lighter instead of darker. At the same time, certain light tones may get dramatically darker. And there may be strange linear effects: along the edges between light and dark

areas we may get strong, thin lines that are either light or dark. It is not known why these things happen, but we do know how to control them.

You have seen that flashing is a technique for contrast reduction. It reduces it in solarization printing too, which is not what we want this time. So we have to compensate in advance by using a contrasty negative and a printing paper of the highest possible contrast, which happens to be Agfa's Brovira no. 6. We can also compensate later by bleaching, either local or over-all. Usually, we need to use all three methods on the same picture. It is easier to hold the contrast when we make solarizations from color slides, because they are more contrasty than negatives to begin with.

Unless you carefully control basic exposure, first development, flashing exposure, and second development, your results will prove unpredictable and unsatisfactory. One problem is to slow down both the first and the second development times, which we do by using a 1:10 developer dilution. Another is to find a dim enough light source to give us second exposures that are long enough to control. For this purpose, we use the flashing setup described in the previous chapter, except that we flash the print in a tray filled with water.

If you carefully follow the instructions, you will find that successful solarization is really quite easy. You will surely be astonished by the variety of strange results you can get from just one negative.

● Things You Need

Materials and equipment for printing (list on page 65)

Materials and equipment for print bleaching (pages 90–92)

A lighting setup for flashing (pages 110–11)

An extra tray

A preliminary test strip made on Contrast no. 5 and developed two minutes in Dektol diluted 1:10. Exposure increments of ten seconds were used. The objective was to find a lens aperture setting that would give us a "normal" exposure near the top of the strip and progressively underexposed areas below it.

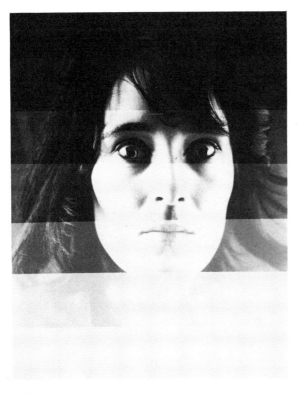

Contrast no. 5 paper

A rather contrasty negative

A color slide

● Step by Step Print Solarization

1. Fill a tray with Dektol diluted 1:10. Arrange the stop bath, first hypo, second hypo, and water holding bath in the usual way.

2. Fill the extra tray with water and position it directly under the flashing light.

3. With the enlarger and a cardboard, expose a preliminary one-inch test strip, using the 5–5–5 method. After fixation, analyze the strip and decide what aperture setting would be best for a two-way test strip. Or you may wish to change the exposure times.

4. With a whole sheet of paper, make the enlarger exposures for a two-way test strip, using the figures you have just worked out. Develop the printing paper for two minutes in Dektol 1:10.

5. Then put it in the tray of water beneath the flashing light source, agitating it for about fifteen seconds, then letting it sit there for another forty-five. Push the print to the bottom of the tray and make sure there are no air bubbles in the water.

6. Holding the piece of cardboard at right angles to the first test strip exposures, use the flashing light to make a second set of exposures. Use the exposures 3–3–3 seconds, etc. For the first exposure, cover about one inch of the paper to give yourself a column of reference tones with no flashing exposures.

7. Put the two-way strip back into the 1:10 Dektol and develop it for an additional two minutes. Process it normally the rest of the way.

8. Analyze the test strip. If it doesn't look approximately like the illustration of the two-way solarized test strip in this chapter, figure out what went wrong and make another. Remember that by remaking test strips you will save time and money in the long run.

9. If the two-way test strip is satisfactory, find the portions that look promising and use their exposure times for making finished prints.

• Don't Jerk It!

Any time that a print seems to be getting much too dark during the second development, let it go the full two minutes anyway. You can cut it back later with bleach. If you jerk it too soon you may have a problem with mottle.

On the other hand, if a print doesn't come up enough in the two minutes, you can safely extend the time even up to five or ten minutes. At ten minutes you may get fog or developer stain but, again, you may not. It is worth the risk. Since the picture will look a little peculiar anyway, a little fog shouldn't hurt it.

With Contrast no. 5 and the prescribed flashing setup, the workable range for flashing exposures should be from about three to fifteen seconds, which is about the same as the range for contrast reduction by flashing (preceding chapter).

If you prefer to use a rheostat or a 25-watt red bulb, night light, Christmas-tree light, or some other light source, you will have to determine for yourself the best exposures by making one or more two-way test strips.

The above range for flashing exposures will work on many high-contrast papers, though some of them won't solarize very well. Kodabromide, for example, will hardly solarize at all. You may have to test a variety of papers.

• Data from Other People

It would be nice if you could directly use data from photography books and magazines, but it sometimes doesn't work out very well. There are always certain differences between your equipment and materials and those used by authors in developing their figures. Thus their data will seldom apply exactly to your situation. However, you can safely use them as a starting point for your own experiments. In this book the most important thing is method; with it, you can derive accurate figures for yourself.

• Agitation for Over-all Bleaching

Solarized prints usually react well to bleach, and the methods given on pages 90–101 will work very well on them. Since you now know about "impeccable" agitation (preceding chapter), we will add it to the lore on bleaching. When you agitate by tray tipping or pushing the print around, the bleach moves over the edges of the print at a higher speed than over the rest of it. This causes the edges to bleach too fast, especially if the tones are light. If you use the randomized-toad method with a cotton swab it will even out the bleaching very nicely.

• Color Effects

The color effects that we encounter in using the higher developer dilutions can also be brought into solarization. The trick is to use Dektol 1:10 for the first development and a higher dilution, say 1:30 or 1:40, for the second, but with the same developing times. If necessary you can extend them, but don't cut them. You can also add color by using a 100 F water prebath before the first development. With either approach or both used together, you will need revised first and second exposure times. Determine them with preliminary and two-way test strips.

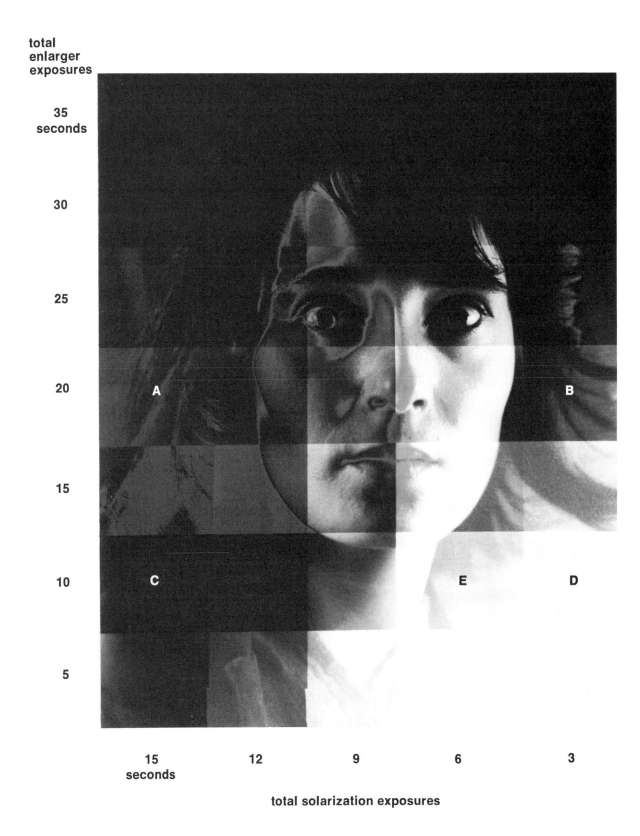

total
enlarger
exposures

35
seconds

30

25

20   A   B

15

10   C   E   D

5

15   12   9   6   3
seconds

total solarization exposures

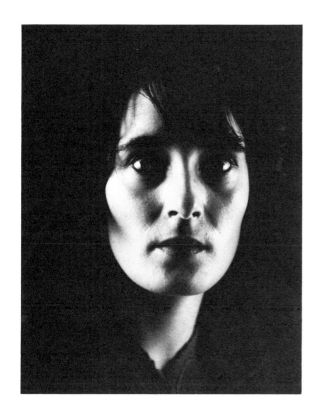

This is a normal, or reference, print made on Contrast no. 5, which is much too contrasty for this particular negative if one wishes to treat it as an ordinary portrait. It was exposed normally for this particular contrast grade and developed normally for 1½ minutes in Dektol 1:2. Having such a reference print will help you keep track of what the solarization process is doing to the image contrast.

A two-way solarization test strip made on Contrast no. 5. Such a high contrast of paper was used to compensate for an anticipated loss of contrast in the solarization process. The first series of exposures was made with the negative and the enlarger light. Then the paper was developed in Dektol diluted 1:10 for two minutes. Next it was put in a tray of clean water for a minute, after which it was given a series of solarization (flashing) exposures. Immediately afterward, it was developed another two minutes in the diluted Dektol, then run through the stop bath and fixer.

Note that Areas A and B are almost exactly alike in tone, though A got a 15-second flashing exposure and B only three seconds. C, with the same solarization exposure as A and ten seconds *less* enlarger exposure, still came out much darker than A, which is difficult to explain, though scientists are still trying. Though A and B, with the same enlarger exposure, are tonally alike, C and D, each with ten seconds' enlarger exposure, are greatly different in tone. This is also hard to explain. Area E shows a result similar to what one would get with the flashing procedure explained in the preceding chapter.

• Use Color Slides

You can make black-and-white pictures from color slides, which usually come out as "print negatives." That is, their light and dark tones are reversed. Some subjects look very good as negatives. You can also make solarizations from color slides, using the exposure-determination methods just described. You will probably discover only one real difference: some slides—mainly those with a preponderance of yellow, brown, orange, or red—will require considerably longer first exposures than negatives do, but that is an easy problem. Second exposures will be the same, as will the processing times.

In order to get sharp pictures, you must remove color transparencies from their slide mounts. Information on preparing individual frames for enlargement will be given in the next chapter.

143

A series of prints in which the ratio of enlarger exposure to solarization exposure has been varied considerably. All were made on Contrast no. 5 to compensate for loss of contrast. Note how very different the images are from each other, and how strange some of the effects are. Print E, however, merely looks as if it had been printed on a no. 0 paper and has no peculiarities of tone and line.

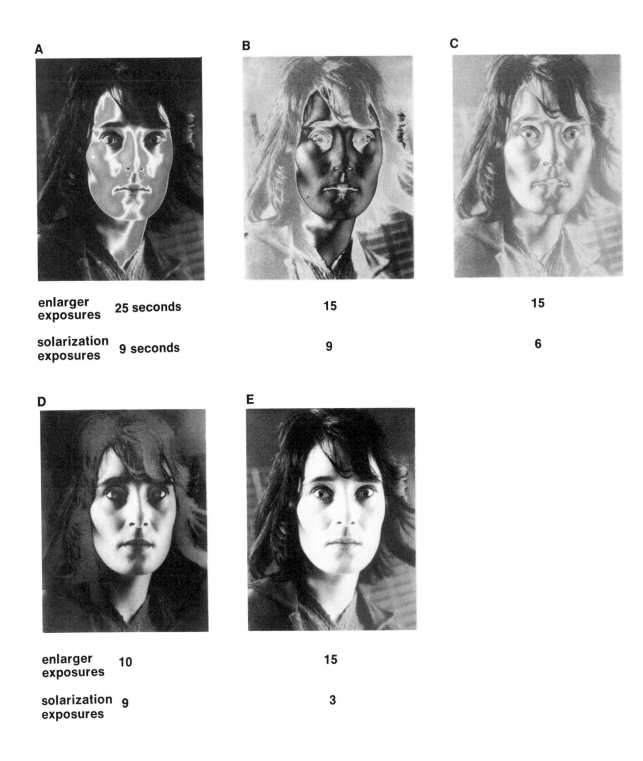

A

enlarger exposures	25 seconds
solarization exposures	9 seconds

B

15

9

C

15

6

D

enlarger exposures	10
solarization exposures	9

E

15

3

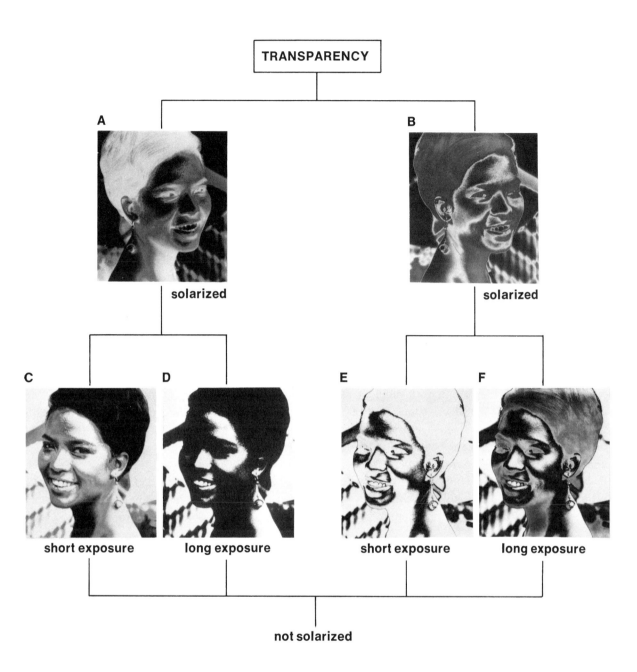

TRANSPARENCY

A

solarized

B

solarized

C

short exposure

D

long exposure

E

short exposure

F

long exposure

not solarized

A series of pictures printed on no. 5 resin-coated (RC) paper. They originate from a color slide, not a negative. A and B were made directly from the slide. Then A was used as a paper negative (next chapter) to make C and D; and E and F were contact-printed from B. A two-way solarization test strip was made to get the enlarger and solarization exposures for A and B. C, D, E, and F are straight contact prints without solarization exposures. However, you can easily solarize contact prints if you wish, after two minutes' development in Dektol 1:10.

HOW TO MAKE BLACK-AND-WHITE PRINTS FROM COLOR SLIDES   HOW TO COPY PRINTS

Can you make black-and-white pictures from color slides? Yes, you can easily make prints of the very highest quality. The method is very simple: you merely put a slide in your enlarger and make a print from it, which comes out as a "paper negative." After it has been processed and dried, you use it to make a contact print on an unexposed piece of printing paper. You go through exactly the same steps in making such a print as you would in contacting film negatives (pages 31–33). There is really nothing to it.

You can do this with any kind of enlarging paper, but there is grain in the paper base of an ordinary paper that will show up in the final positive print. In some pictures it looks very good, yet we would rather do without it most of the time. Furthermore, it takes quite a bit of fiddling around to make a paper-grain print look right, mainly because it looks like a mezzotint or lithograph. These art forms aren't too well adapted to most photographic subjects.

Fortunately, resin-coated (RC) papers are virtually grainless, because their emulsions are coated on white plasticized paper that is very thin. Thus if you use an RC paper for your paper negative you will get hardly any grain at all, except that originating in the slide itself. Now, if you should use a slide made with one of the

Kodachromes for your paper negative, it would produce a print with much finer grain than you ordinarily get by printing film negatives. Color films other than the Kodachrome type usually have quite a bit more of it, though it is seldom excessive.

If you have color negatives, you can make high-quality prints directly, without having to make intermediate paper negatives. Just handle them as if they were ordinary black-and-white negatives. They usually require longer exposure times, but that is about all.

● Things You Need

Printing materials and tools
Bleaching materials and tools
Retouching materials and tools
Kodabrome RC paper, Soft or Medium (no. 1 or no. 2)
or Polycontrast Rapid RC and printing filters
The tape-laminated glass plate used for making contacts
A sponge-rubber typewriter or area-rug pad
Ready-Mounts for color slides
Color slides
Color negatives
Scissors

146

Black paper
Ruler
Scotch tape

Most of these things have already been explained sufficiently. For 8×10 prints, the typewriter pad should be cut down to about 10×12 inches. It is to put under the unexposed paper, the paper negative, and the glass when you are making an exposure for a contact print. It helps hold the paper and the negative in tight contact, thus assuring sharpness in the final print. The other new tools and materials will be explained as we go along.

• The Contrast of Color Slides (Transparencies)

Color slides are generally quite a bit more contrasty than black-and-white negatives, though it doesn't seem as if they are. This means that you have to deliberately hold down the contrast when you are making a paper negative and again when you are making a print from it. Though you can use the contrast-reducing techniques from pages 110–22, it would be simpler if you could get along without them.

Fortunately, most slides will make fine black-and-white pictures if you make both the paper negatives and the final prints on a no. 2 (medium) RC paper or use a no. 2 printing filter with Polycontrast Rapid RC. However, some of the prints will tend to be a little on the "brilliant" side, that is, just a bit too contrasty.

We can easily get around the problem by making our negatives on no. 1 paper (soft) or using a no. 1 printing filter. If some of them should turn out to be a little too soft we can easily bring up the contrast again by printing them on a harder paper, for example a no. 3 (hard) or no. 4 (extra hard). You see, there is no rule that we have to make our paper negatives and final prints on the same grade of paper.

In this technique we need an RC paper only for making the "paper" negative, because that gets us around the paper-grain problem. Once

you have the paper negative you can print it on any kind of paper you wish with good results, because the grain problem enters in only at the negative stage.

On rare occasions you will have a color slide that is too contrasty for even a no. 1 paper negative and a no. 1 final print. In that case, remake the negative on no. 1 and reduce the contrast even more by using a 1:10 or 1:20 developer dilution, or use the flashing technique. Sometimes you may wish to use these techniques for strictly pictorial purposes or just to see what you can do with them. Since color transparencies will record a remarkable range of tones, you may merely want to know how much detail you can bring out in both the dark and highlight areas of your prints.

• Step by Step in Making a Black-and-White Print from a Color Slide

1. Remove the slide from its mount and prepare it for enlargement.

2. Clean it carefully, just as you would a negative.

3. Expose a one-inch test strip on Kodabrome RC Soft (no. 1) paper or Polycontrast Rapid RC with a no. 1 filter. Process it normally.

4. Using the exposure data obtained from the strip, expose a full sheet of the same paper and process it normally. You now have a paper negative.

5. Remove the transparency from the enlarger and open up the lens two or three stops; you need more light because it will have to go through the white base of the paper negative in order to expose the final print. Acting only as a light source, the enlarger doesn't need to be stopped down for sharpness.

6. Center the sponge-rubber pad on the enlarger baseboard directly under the lens. To make sure that the rectangle of light will cover it you may have to raise the enlarger head a few inches.

7. Make a one-inch test strip from the paper negative; put a strip of unexposed paper emulsion

up in the center of the pad and cover it with the paper negative, emulsion (image side) down. Cover both with the glass plate. Expose and process the test strip normally. If necessary, make another one.

8. Examine the test strip to decide on the exposure and the contrast of paper (or printing filter) for the final print.

9. Expose and process the final print.

• Preparing the Transparency

Color transparencies curl a little bit in their cardboard mounts. Slide projectors compensate for this but enlargers do not. Consequently, if you make a paper negative with a mounted slide it will be out of focus either in the center or around the edges. Thus it must be removed from the mount so that the negative carrier and the weight of the enlarger head will flatten it properly.

Since single frames are difficult to clean and to position in negative carriers, you should Scotch-tape narrow strips of thin black paper to two opposite ends of each transparency. They will give you something to hold onto. The black paper that comes in packages of printing paper is about the right thickness. The strips should be of the same width as the film.

After you are through printing, you will have some unmounted color transparencies, which can't be projected. Easy enough. Buy some "Ready-Mounts" from the photo store and remount them yourself. There is nothing to it.

• Clean the Glass

To prevent extra dust spots on your paper negative and final print, you should carefully clean the tape-laminated glass plate (glass sandwich). Use a lintless cloth or paper towel and detergent or ordinary soap and water. Then dust it off frequently while you are using it.

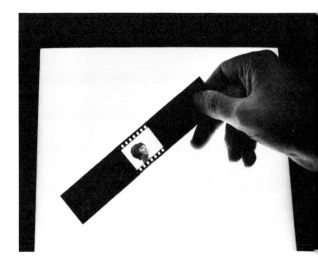

Held in front of a light box, this transparency has been removed from its slide mount and prepared for conversion into black-and-white prints. The ends are black paper taped on with Scotch tape.

• Judging Paper-Negative Quality

People who make paper negatives usually underexpose them quite a bit without being aware of it. The reason is clear enough, once you have had it explained to you. The first problem is that superficial appearances may be deceptive. For example, a paper negative that looks exactly as a perfect film negative should is actually underexposed approximately one stop (50 per cent). This doesn't seem to make sense.

What happens is that judgment is misled by the fact that we gauge the quality of a film negative by the light coming through it from behind (transmitted light), whereas we gauge a paper negative by the light falling upon it (reflected light). Though it is natural to do it this way, it just doesn't work in the case of the paper negative.

What really counts, however, is what a negative of either kind does to *transmitted* light. Therefore one should judge a paper negative by holding it up to a fairly strong (150-watt) tungsten light source or to a bright section of the sky. Viewed this way, a paper negative that looks up to one stop (100 per cent) overexposed when examined by reflected light will look (and be) just right. You have to get used to the fact that it looks too heavy by room light.

Underexposed paper negatives that look normal by room light will often make good prints, but they tend to lack brilliance and detail in the shadows. On the other hand, paper negatives that look much too heavy (dark, dense), even by transmitted light, will usually make rather good prints. With overexposed film negatives, we have a grain and sharpness problem; remember? But paper has no discernible grain, no matter how much one overexposes it. In contact printing, we burn right through any fuzziness due to heavy density, making it sharp again. This is not to encourage sloppiness in figuring out exposures but to get you over your fear of paper negatives that look too dark in room light.

A paper negative positioned partly in front of a light box, so that part of it is seen by transmitted light, the remainder by reflected light. The sections seen by reflected light seem too overexposed (dark, dense) for a good negative. However, all negatives should be judged by transmitted light. The light box shows that this paper negative has been exposed correctly, for it looks very good by transmitted light.

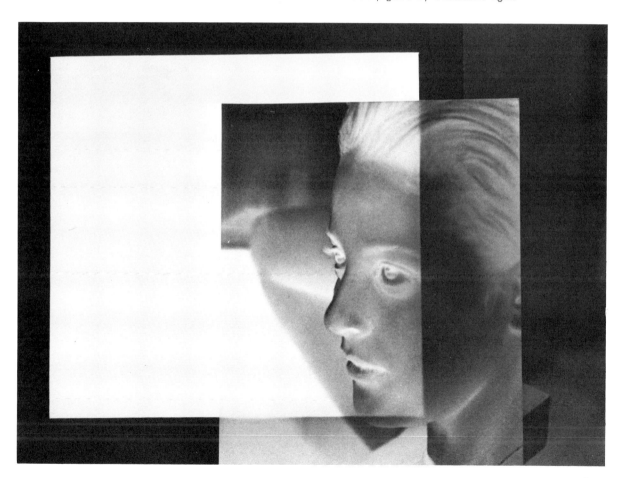

2 stops underexposed   **1 stop underexposed**   **normal negative**

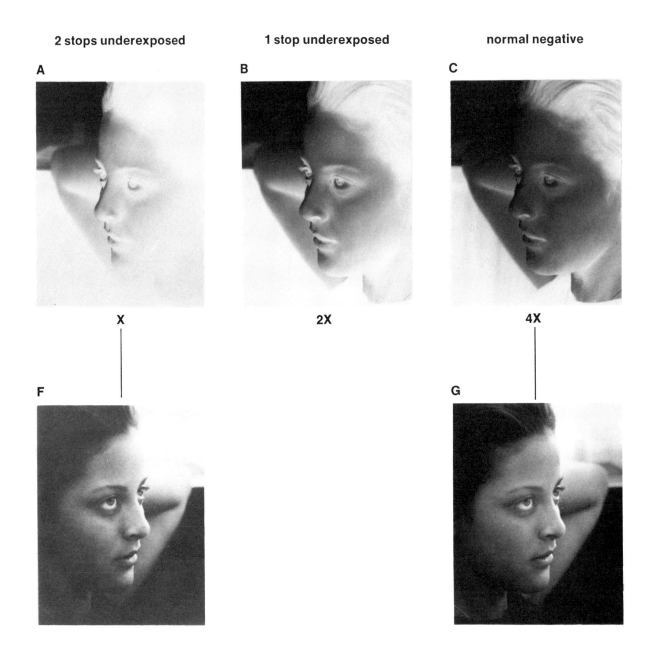

A series of paper negatives that are one stop apart in exposure. That is, starting at the left the exposures were progressively doubled. This set shows you how paper negatives look by reflected light—ordinary bright room light. Negative A is badly underexposed and hardly usable. B is also under (one stop). Though it looks too dark in room light, C is the normal negative. Though D

1 stop overexposed

2 stops overexposed

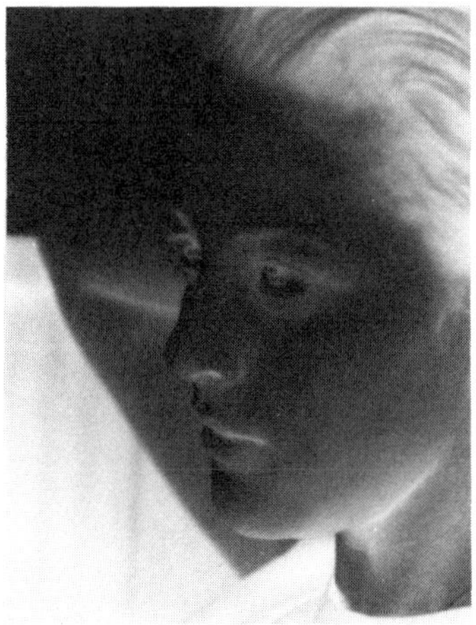

D

E

8X

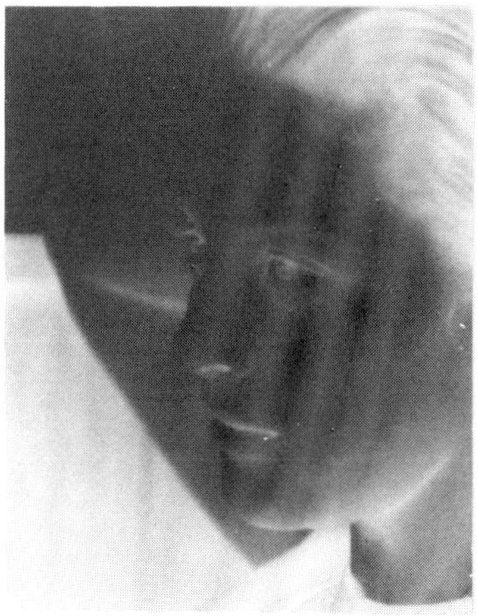

16X   **EXPOSURE (X)**

H

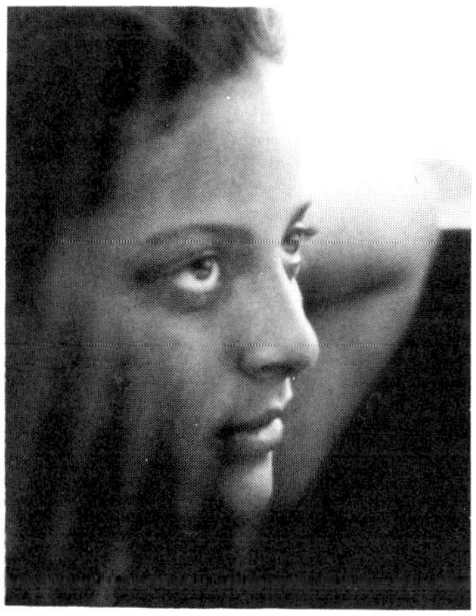

and E are overexposed, they will make good prints. However, the contact-printing exposure for E, heavily overexposed, is very long. The contact print from A (print F) is washed out, muddy, and weak. However, the print from E (print H) is hard to distinguish from the one made from negative C (print G).

● Dodging and Burning-In

You should make your first paper negative and final print without any dodging, burning-in, bleaching, or retouching. If you try doing everything at once, you will get all mixed up. In fact you will probably get thoroughly confused by the next four paragraphs.

The easiest time to do either dodging or burning-in is when you are making the paper negative from the color slide, because you can see the image projected by the enlarger onto the printing paper. However, in making the final print you see nothing but bright light shining on the white back of the paper negative, which is contact-printed, emulsion to emulsion with the unexposed paper. Things like burning-in corners and dodging the center are easy enough to do at the final print stage, but you can't even see the smaller areas that you would like to burn-in or dodge. Thus you have to estimate their position or not attempt to work on them.

On page 72 you learned that the basic exposure time limits the number of areas you can substantially dodge in a print, but that you can burn-in as much as you please. For reasons that will sound peculiar, you are not thus limited when working from color transparencies. You see, burning-in the paper negative accomplishes the same thing as dodging the final print, so you can get a myriad of areas in the final print that are lightened as much as you desire. You get them by simply burning-in the paper negative. Figure it out.

At the same time, dodging the paper negative does the same thing as burning-in the final print. To make areas come out darker on the final print, you can dodge them on the paper negative, but the amount of dodging you can do is limited by the basic exposure time. Thus only a limited number of areas in the final print can be darkened in this manner. However, when you are making the final print itself you can darken as

many areas as you like, because you now do it by burning-in.

In making prints directly from negatives, you can do an infinite amount of local darkening but only a limited amount of lightening. In making them from positive transparencies, you can do an infinite amount of both. This is confusing, of course. By the time you have it figured out, you will have considerably increased your understanding of "negative-positive processes" and your insights on what actually makes photography work.

● Which Side Is Which? Up or Down?

When we print directly from a black-and-white film negative, we position it emulsion (dull side) down in the enlarger, but a color slide should be positioned emulsion up. The image then comes out reversed from left to right in the paper negative. The final print reverses it back to its normal position.

With many color films, there is no dull side to use as a guide, but the words and numbers printed along the edges will work just as well. If they read backwards when you hold a positive transparency up to the light, it means that the emulsion side is toward you.

Use a different method for locating the emulsion of a Kodacolor-X negative. There are little arrows or pointers along one edge. When you hold the film so that the arrows are along the top edge and pointing to the right, the emulsion side is toward you.

When you make black-and-white prints from Kodacolor negatives, you don't make paper negatives. You should therefore position them emulsion down in the enlarger.

● Dye Retouching and Bleaching

All that you have learned about dye retouching and bleaching can be applied when you are making black-and-white prints from either positive or negative color transparencies. When you are working from a color positive (color slide), you also get a sizable negative to work on, which you haven't had before.

One of the easiest and most exciting things to do is to make areas come out white in the final print. You can do this by bleaching the print, of course, but it can be a tedious job if the areas are fairly dark. It is much faster and easier to just paint them out on the emulsion side of the paper negative with Kodak black opaque. Since no light will go through the opaque, they print up pristine white. Mistakes with the opaque can easily be removed with a wad of damp cotton, so you can work over an area as many times as necessary.

You can also get white lines by drawing on the paper negative with a well-pointed china marker (use a razor blade) or a nylon-tip pen. If you are careful, you can do good shading with a china marker, and you can rub off your mistakes with a dry cloth or cotton and lighter fluid. If you don't want the texture of your shading to show, do it on the back of the paper negative.

You can bleach things on the paper negative to make them come out darker in the final print; and you can put dye on them to make them come out lighter. At the paper-negative stage, the ultimate effects of bleaching and dyeing are reversed, just as are the effects of dodging and burning-in. After you have worked on the paper negative, you still have the final print to play with, if you like. An additional bonus is that mistakes in dyeing and bleaching can often be patched up on the finished print.

● Prints from Color Negatives

You have already been told enough about making black-and-white prints from color negatives to permit you to go ahead on your own. All you need to know is that they should be put into the enlarger emulsion down and that they require a

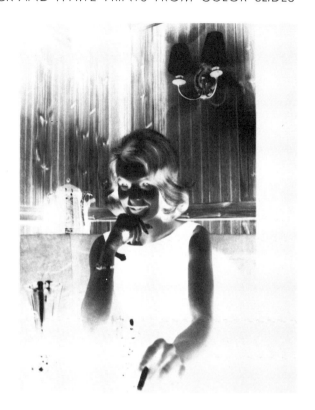

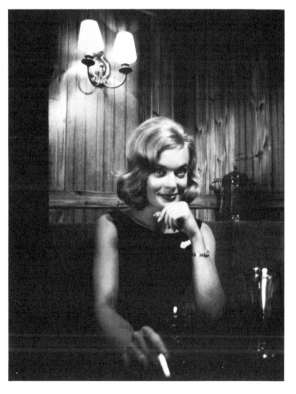

A paper negative and print from a very contrasty color transparency.

longer exposure than do black-and-white negatives.

Even so, some extra information might be helpful. The best choice for a color negative film to use would be one of the Kodacolors. The requirement for a longer exposure in black-and-white printing comes from the fact that a Kodacolor negative is orange in color. This is because it has a dye-masking layer, which we needn't explain here. The orange color is all you need to know about.

Now, black-and white printing papers are deliberately made so that they are relatively insensitive to red, yellow, yellow-green, and orange light. This is so that we can work with them under safelights of the same colors. Thus when you put a Kodacolor negative into the enlarger you are in essence putting a safelight filter in with it. With a long enough exposure, however, you overcome the effect of the orange filter layer and end up with a print of good quality.

Since you know the exposure times will be longer, you should increase the individual times in your test strips. For example, instead of using five-second exposures, you could go to ten or fifteen seconds.

• Copying Prints

In most families there are pictures that uncles and aunts want copies of, but they seldom get them, because the negatives are missing and the family photographer (you) doesn't know how to make copies. Let us solve this nagging problem.

The first thing you need is lighting that is very even, intense, and diffuse. The best source of it is skylight on a clear sunny day, so tape up your pictures on the shady side of the house or garage. Line them all up at eye level, then go down the line taking pictures with a hand-held camera. If you can't get up close enough with your camera, buy a supplementary close-up lens for it (you will find many other uses for it).

A paper negative and print from a transparency with a tremendous amount of fine detail in it. We see how the negative looks by reflected light: much too dark. However, by transmitted light (on a light box) it looks good. It preserves all the details in the shadows and darker mid tones.

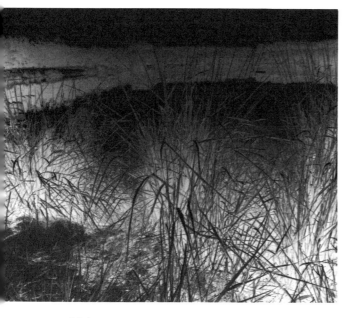

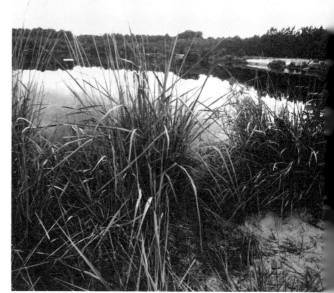

Be sure to get your camera properly squared away to each picture so that their opposite edges are parallel in the viewfinder. If you don't consciously keep track of the edges they nearly always come out skewed. Otherwise not.

Determine your exposure by reading a Kodak gray card held flat against one of the pictures. For a built-in meter, bring the camera close enough to fill the whole viewfinder with the gray card. If you have a separate meter, hold it about five inches away. If you have no meter at all, refer to the data sheet that comes with the film and use the recommendation for "open sky." Shoot at f/4 or f/5.6.

In order to get both slides and prints of all the pictures, you should use one of the Kodachromes. When you take your exposed film to the drugstore, ask them to have Kodak process it (not someone else) and send it back unmounted. Then use the paper-negative process you have just been reading about. Kodachrome contrast and fine grain are just right for it.

After you have made your first paper negative and final print, you can set up an assembly line and really rip along. Do it by using the same paper-negative and final-print exposures for all the rest of the copy transparencies.

They will be a handsome bluish color, incidentally—much prettier for projection than strictly black-and-white pictures. When you are finished printing, you can put them in Ready-Mounts.

One nice thing about having a paper negative is that you can make all the prints you wish from it. It is much less prone to scratches than a film negative. And you can dodge, burn-in, bleach, dye, and crop it.

If you don't wish to take the time to make paper negatives and are not interested in slides, make your copies on a Kodacolor. Then you can make black-and-white prints directly. Both the contrast and grain are good, though they are even better with a Kodachrome.

One reason for using skylight is that it is very bright on a sunny day, so that you can photograph at a shutter speed high enough to compen-

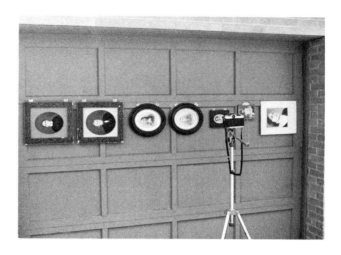

Family pictures aligned on a garage door for quick copying. If you have a steady camera hand you won't need a tripod.

sate for your quivering and shaking. Even so, you should make a deliberate effort to steady yourself and your camera. Slow down your breathing, brace the camera by jamming it tightly against your forehead, and grip it so that your index finger has no function whatever in holding onto it. This finger should be so free and independent that you can use it to slowly *squeeze* on the shutter release without jarring the fingers that are actually holding the camera.

However, if you are a really flipped character with a high-speed quiver you will have to take additional measures. You can use a tripod with a cable release to steady your camera. Or you can tape your pictures to the sunny side of the house and use a considerably higher shutter speed for hand-holding your camera. If you opt to do the latter, work at a time of day—morning or afternoon—when the sun will fall upon the pictures at an angle of about 45 degrees.

Sunlight is both bright and even, of course, but it is not diffuse. Skylight, which is highly diffused, tends to fill in or hide scratches and other blemishes on the surfaces of pictures. But direct sunlight sets them out in high relief. If your pictures are unmarred, however, you can use it all you like.

155

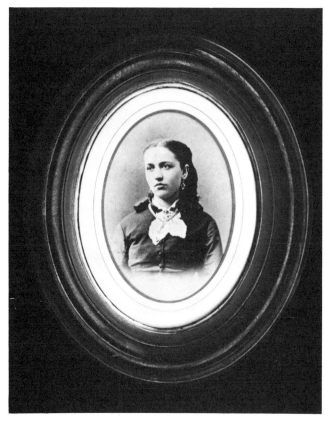

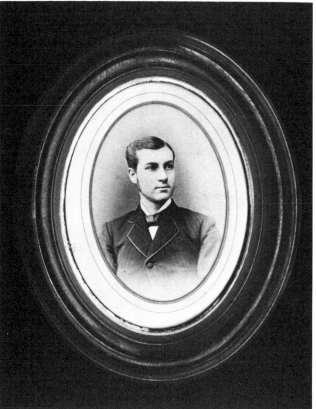

Color slides made in sunlight from black-and-white pictures won't come out so blue, but they will probably have a color cast of some hue—from little defects in manufacture or processing. Fortunately, slides look good with a bit of color.

• Ghostly Fuzzigrams

You can make rather interesting fuzzy, or diffuse, pictures in several ways. If you chose the right transparencies to make them from, they can look very good, either as negatives or positives. However, fuzziness is something we ordinarily attempt to avoid.

One method is to expose the paper negative through the back of the printing paper. That is, instead of positioning the paper emulsion up, which is the usual thing, you turn it face down. The colored image projected by the enlarger falls on the white plastic base, which diffuses it considerably before it gets through to the emulsion on the other side.

Because the plastic base prevents a lot of the enlarger light from getting through it at all, you will have to give a lot of exposure. Use longer exposure times for your test strips, say twenty or thirty seconds.

You can also get your fuzziness through contact printing by positioning a sharp paper-negative emulsion up on the printing paper; and this doesn't require any more exposure than you would generally use in making a final contact print. For even greater diffusion, position the paper negative and the unexposed paper back to back. For this you will need extra exposure, so make a test strip.

Fuzzy prints of normal contrast often look rather muddy. You can usually improve them by making them much more contrasty or very flat and light.

Family pictures that were copied on Kodachrome-X, then converted into paper negatives and contact prints.

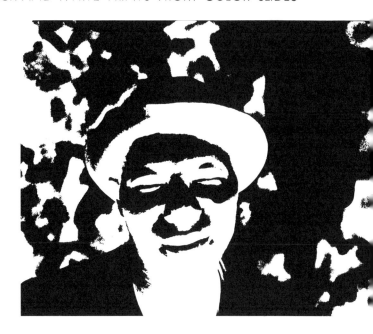

● High-Contrast Prints

One of photography's favorite sports is to convert images with an ordinary range of light, medium, and dark tones into pictures with only black and white in them. They are very dramatic and often look like wood or linoleum block prints. The trick is to work from transparencies that already have a lot of contrast and print them on high-contrast papers.

Earlier, you learned that color slides generally have a lot of contrast, though not always. We were initially concerned with holding the contrast down, but we are now faced with the problem of building it up even more. As we've seen, it is best to start with a contrasty slide. In a moment you will see that you can also use ones with only moderate contrast, though the method used with them is a bit more involved.

We must define a contrasty color transparency a little better. It is one that has both very light and very dark tones in it. It may also have a whole range of middle tones, and, again, it may not. In either case, we should call the transparency contrasty. High contrast merely means that there is a considerable tonal difference between some areas in a picture. The fact that widely contrasting light and dark tones may have mid tones between them doesn't lessen the contrast, though it seems to. In this technique we get rid of the mid tones, anyway.

With a contrasty color slide, it is dead easy to make a dramatic, high-contrast print. All you do is to make both the paper negative and the final print on Kodabrome RC Ultra Hard (no. 5) paper. Or you might try Ilford Ilfospeed no. 5. The middle tones (grays) ordinarily "drop out," so that only black and white are left. Their absence increases the feeling of contrast. If a few of the grays refuse to drop out, make a contact print from the positive. From the paper negative that you get, make another positive. One rarely has to go this far, however.

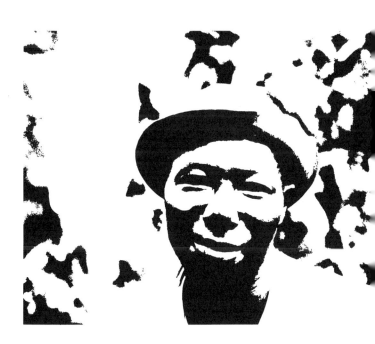

The high-contrast negative was made by printing a rather contrasty transparency on a no. 5 resin-coated (RC) paper. The high-contrast contact print was also made on a no. 5 paper. However, a no. 1 or 2 would have worked just as well, because there are no mid tones in the paper negative.

157

Since you are not familiar with high-contrast images or with making tones drop out, you should make an abundance of test strips as you go along. After making some preliminary one-inch strips, you might try a slightly different kind of two-way test. Make a full-sheet paper-negative test strip, process and dry it, then put it on a full sheet of unexposed paper and cover both with the glass plate.

Remove the negative from the enlarger, open up two or three stops, and make a second set of test exposures at right angles to the first set. As usual with two-way test strips, you will end up with a checkerboard effect and a lot of useful exposure information.

When you have made your full-sheet paper negative, it may need a bit of cleaning up with bleach and opaque, though not necessarily so. If there are some light tones that haven't quite dropped out, you can usually get rid of them easily by overall bleaching (pages 93–94). On the other hand, they may drop out automatically when you make your final print, so don't be too hasty to start bleaching.

In the white areas of the paper negative (which will print black in the finished print; remember?) there may be some black spots and lines that you wish to get rid of. They would print up as white garbage in the black areas of your final print. Eliminate them with ultra-strong bleach, but take great care not to let it get away from you.

If there are unsightly white things in the black areas of the paper negative, they will print up as black garbage in the final print. Fill them in with black opaque. Except when you are working along the contours of white areas, you can literally slosh it on, because its black surroundings are going to print up white, anyway. You can also be much freer with bleach than usual, because all the white areas around it will print up black.

Of course, you can use bleach on the final print, though it is seldom necessary. Don't use opaque, because it will show up strongly; use spotting dye instead.

When you work from transparencies of strong contrast (long tonal range), you can almost always get brilliant and clean high-contrast final prints with the above method, often without having to use bleach or opaque. When you use color slides of low or moderate contrast, you may have to add two additional steps; they are as easy as candy, so don't worry about them.

To get the extra contrast that is needed, all you do is make a contact print from the final print, as if it were a paper negative. This will give you another negative (called a "second-generation negative"). In making it you increase the contrast even more and drop out additional tones.

Then you contact-print the second-generation negative and get a second-generation positive, again increasing contrast and dropping out mid tones. You may call this positive a "final-final print," if you like. It might help you keep your head sorted out—or it might not.

Go through all the steps, the standard ones and the extras, with Kodabrome II RC Ultra Hard. This is a no. 5 contrast paper, which is very contrasty indeed. It should give you all the contrast that you want and more.

Since people seem to have a great thirst for pictorial contrast, you will probably find this whole business fascinating. And it will certainly teach you a lot about positive-negative processes in photography.

● **Conclusion**

You have come to the end of this book on laboratory techniques for the beginner. It is full of simple and workable recipes. Though the techniques were designed especially for you they are also good enough for any professional. Thus you will never have to abandon them in favor of something better.

The accent throughout has been on method, for with method you can figure out almost anything for yourself. So as you stumble along through life, remember the humble test strip with love and reverence; it is the golden key to the Law of Reciprocity, upon which all of photography is based, and the very essence of photographic method.

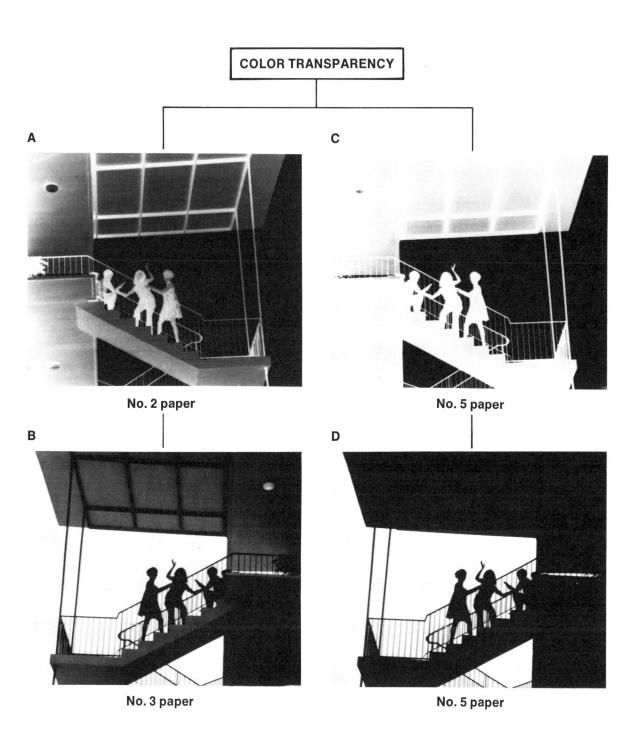

COLOR TRANSPARENCY

A

No. 2 paper

C

No. 5 paper

B

No. 3 paper

D

No. 5 paper

Frequently, you can make both a normal black-and-white print and a high-contrast one from the same color slide. You create the difference by your choice of paper contrast grades. Note that mid-tone detail disappears when no. 5 paper is used. This is called "dropping out" tones.

BITS AND PIECES

● Photographic Papers

To learn what various photographic papers look like, go to a photo store and ask to see their paper sample books. While there, buy the inexpensive booklet *Kodak Photographic Papers (G-1)*.

Contact and enlargement types: Contact papers are made only for use with contact printers, which have very bright light sources. Enlarging papers are for use with enlargers, which have relatively dim light sources; however, they can also be used for contact printing (pages 31–35, 132–42). Do not use regular contact paper for enlargements of any kind.

Paper speed: Contact papers are extremely slow (insensitive to light), which is why they shouldn't be exposed with an enlarger light source. Though they are much faster than contact papers, the different types of enlarging papers vary considerably in speed, from slow enlarging papers to fast ones.

With fast papers such as Kodabromide or Polycontrast Rapid you should make sure that your darkroom is properly light-trapped (pages 11–13) and that your safelight is actually safe. Otherwise you will get fog. There is less of a problem with slow papers, but they do require longer exposure times.

With a given type of paper, the lower contrast grades are considerably faster than the higher ones. A variable-contrast paper, such as Polycontrast Rapid, is fastest when no filter is used. A no. 1 filter cuts the speed about 30 per cent, and it drops quickly as progressively higher filters are used. To help you keep track of speed and exposure differences, there is a little enlarging computer bound into Kodak's *Darkroom Dataguide,* which is also recommended as a basic workbook.

Image tone: The so-called black-and-white papers may actually deviate quite a bit from neutral-black image tones. Contact papers are usually bluish black. The color scale for Kodak enlarging papers (recommended for quality and availability) runs from neutral-black (Kodabromide, Kodabrome RC, Polycontrast Rapid RC) to warm-black (Polycontrast, Polycontrast Rapid, Medalist, Panalure), and finally to brown-black (Opal, Ektalure, Polylure).

The tonal warmth of warm-black and brown-black papers can be varied considerably by using special developing techniques and special developers. With both paper types, Dektol produces comparatively cold tones that can be made even colder by extending the developing time. A short developing time in Dektol, or higher-than-normal developer dilutions (pages 110–16), will make them warmer. For results going even further toward brown or red-brown, one should develop warm-black and brown-black papers in Selectol, Selectol Soft, or D-52, which are usually described as "portrait developers." The brown-black papers (Opal, Ektalure, Polylure) are affected most by them.

The most popular papers are the neutral-black ones, because they will go well with many kinds of pictures. Warmer papers are used mainly for portraits and romantic landscapes.

Tint: If an emulsion is coated on a tinted-paper base, the base color will show in the image. Kodak's main paper-base colors are white, cream white, and old ivory (buff). All are handsome, but white is by far the most popular.

Weight: Photographic papers come in different thicknesses, or weights, which are usually designated by capital letters: SW (single weight), MW (medium weight), and DW (double weight). Resin-coated (RC) papers are medium weight, while regular papers are usually available in both single and double weights. Though they cost less than the others, it is best to avoid single-weight papers, because they are harder to handle, easily damaged, and produce prints that tend to curl badly and look generally scruffy.

Bases: Emulsions are usually coated on either paper or plastic bases, though materials such as glass, cloth, and metal may also be used. There is now a strong trend toward white resin-coated paper bases for photographic papers, mainly because processing, washing, and drying times are thereby considerably shortened.

Surfaces: When an emulsion is being coated on either a resin layer or paper a texture can be embossed on it. This texture, or small pattern, is called its "surface." Kodak paper surfaces are designated by the capital letters A, B, D, E, F, G, J, K, N, R, V, X, Y, and Z. Examine a sample book to see what they look like, because we will describe just a few of them here.

Surface A: A smooth, lustrous surface on a white lightweight stock (base). Because it can easily be folded without cracking the emulsion, it is often used for letters and French-fold greeting cards.

Surface F: A surface that can be given a glossy, mirror-like sheen by "ferrotyping" (drying a print face down on a chromium-plated metal sheet). Drying a print in open air or between blotters produces a high luster. This is photography's most popular surface, for both amateurs and professionals. RC papers with the F surface will come out glossy without being ferrotyped.

Surface N: A very smooth, fine matte surface that will take pencil, ink, dye, and opaque very well and is thus exceptionally good where extensive retouching is required. Since it is available in Kodak resin-coated (RC) papers, one should use it for paper negatives that require subtle retouching, which can most easily be done with chalk or pencil dust (pages 153–54).

Surface Y: Simulating silk, this is a very bright and attractive texture.

Surface Z: Simulates canvas. This surface in Opal Z paper is frequently oil-colored with opaque oils, thus creating the effect of an oil painting on canvas.

Contrast compensation: If you print the same negative on both a glossy and a matte or semi-matte paper you will see that the glossy print seems to have quite a bit more contrast. Thus a print that looks just right on a no. 2 F surface will look one or two contrast grades too flat on a no. 2 N or Z surface. There are two easy ways around this problem: buy a higher-contrast grade of paper than you usually do, or extend your negative-developing time by 50 per cent to make your negatives more contrasty.

• Print Toners

After they have been thoroughly washed, prints can be toned various colors (mostly hues of brown) in special "toners," some of them available in concentrated-liquid form, others in the powder form. In most cases, a print is put into a tray of toner, at room temperature or warmed somewhat, until the desired color arrives. However, with certain sepia toners the print is first bleached, then redeveloped in a toner. It is very easy to do.

Though most toners yield red-brown, purple-brown, and chocolate hues, there are also red, blue, and green toners available. Of the latter group, only the Kodak blue toner is worth bothering with. Kodak doesn't make red and green toners, but other companies do. Don't try them unless you like lurid colors.

Good print washing is usually very critical, so use a Perma Wash bath (pages 34–35), even with resin-coated (RC) papers, and at least quadruple the times for both the first and second washes. Use a fast flow of water and agitate the prints constantly by pulling them up from the bottom and putting them on top. The actual toning instructions—very simple—come with the bottles or packages of toner.

Since the emulsions of various kinds of paper differ chemically from one another they do not react in the same way to a given toner. Therefore, toners and papers must be paired properly (with a wrong pairing there is usually no reaction at all). In the Kodak *Darkroom Dataguide* the recommended combinations for Kodak papers are listed. They are also given with the information that comes in each package of printing paper. For example, for Kodabrome RC paper we find the following Kodak toners recommended: blue, brown, sepia, sulfide sepia T-7a, and polysulfide T-8, all of them excellent toners.

There is no way for you to learn exactly what effect you will get with a given toner until you try it for yourself, because examples of what it can do are often not available. However, you will be safe enough if you start out with Kodak toners sold in packets or as liquid concentrates.

• Summer Storage of Films and Papers

In hot and humid weather, film and paper will begin to deteriorate, especially if the packages have been opened. To prevent this, use them as soon as you can—or bundle them up in plastic food wrap and store them in the refrigerator. Stored this way, they will stay in good condition for about two years. If you wish them to last considerably longer than this, put your film and paper in the freezer section.

When you remove film from the refrigerator, the moisture in its package or cassette will condense on it, so you have to wait several hours for it to disappear—longer if the film has been frozen; don't use it until then. Unless it has been frozen, however, you can usually use paper right after taking it out of cold storage, but if you feel any moisture on the emulsion, let the paper warm up for a while.

• How to Make Borderless Easels

Easels with masking leaves (for making prints with white borders of various widths) are usually quite expensive; at least the good ones are. If you can get along without the white border, you can make yourself an effective easel for a few cents. Many people actually prefer borderless prints, because they like the way they look. They also get a lot of image size for their money, whereas borders can cut it down considerably.

The simplest easel for, say, 8×10 prints requires only a 2×12-inch strip of light cardboard, eight short lengths of masking tape, and an 8×10 piece of printing paper to focus on. First, put your negative in the enlarger and get the image size, focus, and cropping you want on the focusing paper, moving it into exactly the right position. Next, temporarily anchor the paper to the enlarger baseboard with two pieces of tape. Then butt the cardboard strip up to the ten-inch side of the paper that is farther from you and tape it there with two pieces of tape at right angles to it. Position them so that they and the cardboard strip exactly bracket two corners of the focusing paper.

Now take four pieces of tape and loop them back on themselves, sticky side out, making sticky-tabs for holding down printing paper. Remove the focusing paper and rub down a sticky-tab for each corner. You now have an effective easel. To use it, turn out the white light, fit a piece of enlarging paper into the brackets along the cardboard strip, and press its corners down fairly hard with a clean cloth (not with bare fingers!). Expose the paper and process it.

One problem with this simple easel is that you have to reposition the cardboard strip and sticky-tabs every time you make a new cropping or print another negative. You get used to it, but it does take time. Another thing is that the looped-tape tabs soon get filled with paper particles from regular papers (but not RC) and don't stay sticky very long, though you can renew the stickiness with lighter fluid. Also, they tend to pull off the baseboard when you lift up the paper after exposing it.

You can partly solve the tab problem with car-

A borderless easel constructed right on the enlarger baseboard with a strip of cardboard, two pieces of masking tape, and four masking-tape sticky-tabs.

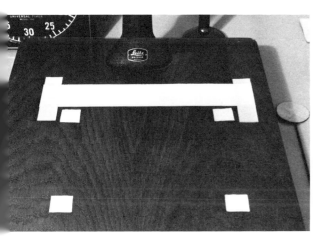

pet tape, but you have to use it carefully, because it is terribly sticky. If you rub your prints down too hard on it they may tear when you try to lift them up. Carpet-tape sticky-tabs get filled with paper particles too, but it takes a lot longer. If you rub them down hard to the baseboard with a spoon handle they won't tend to pull up with the paper, providing that you don't rub the paper down on them too hard.

You can solve the repositioning problem by making your easel mobile instead of stationary. Cover one side of an $11 \times 14 \times \frac{3}{4}$-inch piece of plywood with either white or black Con-Tact paper. If you prefer, you can use $\frac{1}{4}$-inch tempered Masonite, a piece of 1×12 board, or even an empty 100-sheet paper box that has something in it to give it weight. You will have a skidding problem, so turn your easel over and glue about two dozen rubber hose washers to the bottom.

If you use white Con-Tact, you can crop and focus your images without using a focusing paper. However, your pictures will then be out of focus by the thickness of the printing paper, though stopping down will probably take care of this. Even so, it would be better to have a 4×5 piece of paper to do your focusing on. If you use a focus magnifier, you won't need the small focusing paper. Just glue a piece of printing paper to the bottom of it. This will compensate for the focus difference between the white Con-Tact paper and a focusing paper.

After you have covered your board with Con-Tact paper and firmly rubbed it down, you can affix the cardboard strip, tape brackets, and sticky-tabs to the top of it. You will now have a mobile, all-purpose borderless easel with rubber treads.

If you use white Con-Tact paper, incidentally, it will reflect a small amount of light back through the printing paper during exposures, increasing the image contrast somewhat. Black Con-Tact won't do this, but you would find it difficult to tell what difference it makes. The surfaces of commercially made easels are black, white, or yellow, so you can see that color doesn't matter much.

A movable borderless easel made on a piece of chip board covered with Con-Tact paper. The tape borders and sticky-tabs are set for 8×10 paper. For 11×14 paper—or any other size—they would have to be moved, which takes but a moment.

Sticky-tabs made with a single piece of tape will pull up when you remove your paper from the easel. If you make each of them with two pieces of tape this won't happen nearly as often. Start with the pieces crossed, sticky side down, and do as the illustration shows.

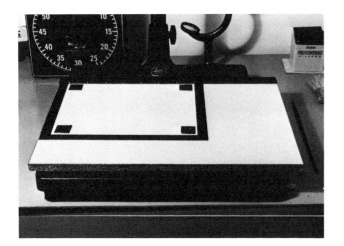

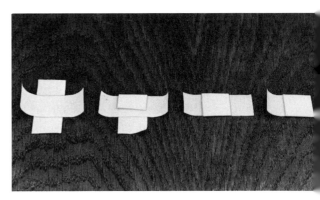

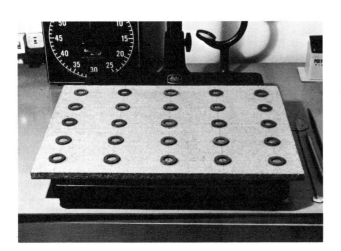

The bottom of an easel, showing rubber hose washers glued on to make a non-skid surface.

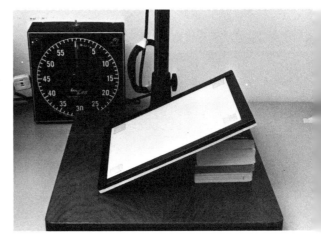

By propping one end or side of your easel up with books, you can either correct or create quite a bit of linear distortion in the image.

• How to Correct or Create Distortion

When you aim your camera either upward or downward at a rectangular shape (building, box, wall, etc.) the opposite vertical edges will converge to some degree, depending on the camera angle. This can be disturbing in a picture. However, we can make the edges parallel again by merely tilting the enlarger easel, which we can do by simply propping up one end or side of it with books or boxes. If it tends to slide we can fasten it to the enlarger baseboard with masking tape.

Try this: Put a negative in your enlarger and open the lens all the way for focusing. Put focusing paper on the easel so you can see what you are doing. Now prop up one end of the easel at an angle from twenty to thirty degrees. Position the enlarger head so that the whole frame barely fits on the paper, and focus on the center of the image. Notice that only the center is sharp, the upper and lower parts of the image getting progressively more out of focus.

Now slowly stop down the lens, stop by stop, and observe how the area of sharpness gradually expands both upward and downward. You are demonstrating "depth of field" (or depth of sharpness) to yourself and at the same time preparing to use a tilted easel and still make a picture that is acceptably sharp in all areas. Notice that there is very little depth of field when the aperture is wide open but that stopping down enough will increase it considerably.

With the lens stopped down all the way, your entire image may now be sharp—or it may not quite make it. If not, raise the enlarger head a few inches, open the lens for refocusing, and go through the whole procedure again. Depending on the easel's angle of tilt, the entire image may be sharp at the minimum aperture or even at a somewhat larger opening, because increasing the distance between the lens and the focusing paper also increases the depth of field.

Depending on the height of your enlarger standard, you may be able to raise the head high enough to permit you to get acceptably sharp pictures with the easel tilted from forty-five to seventy degrees. With many pictures, it doesn't really matter if the top and bottom edges are a bit fuzzy or out of focus.

Using a negative that has a distorted rectangular shape in it, tilt the easel just enough to make the skewed lines parallel. Note that the tilt distorts the shape of the image frame so that you have to crop some of it off in order to get a rec-

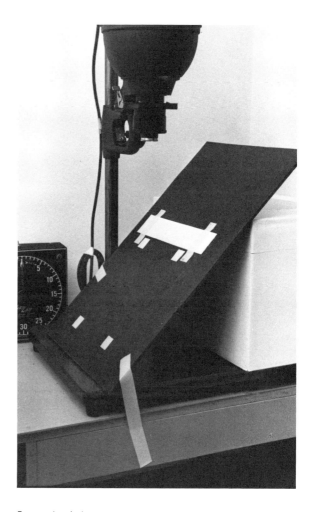

For radical distortion creation or correction, use a piece of cardboard or pressed board propped against a box. Tape it down so that it won't slide. Make a borderless easel on it for positioning and holding the printing paper.

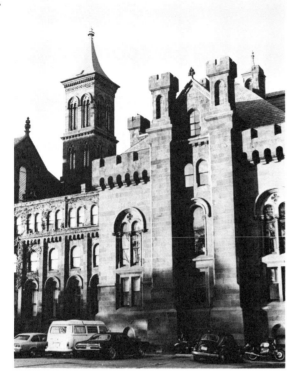

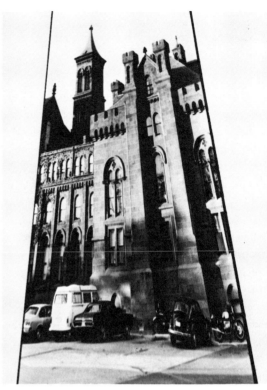

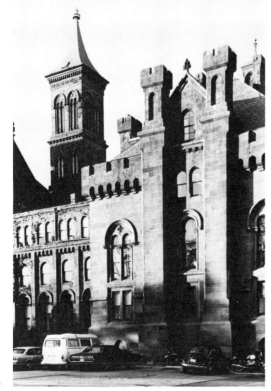

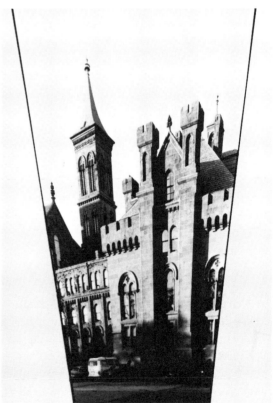

tangular picture. Now *increase* the skew of the rectangular thing in the picture, rather than trying to correct it. You may find that increasing distortion, or even introducing it, is more fun than eliminating it.

There is a minor exposure problem. With the easel tilted, the top part of the image is closer to the enlarger light than the bottom part is. Thus the top needs less exposure time. Give the whole print the basic exposure time required by the top, then give the rest of the print additional exposure by burning-in (pages 72–74).

To get the exposure times, make two one-inch test strips, positioning one across the top of the picture for the basic exposure time, the other across the bottom for the burning-in time. Expose them separately but develop them at the same time. Use five-second exposures for the top strip and ten- or fifteen-second ones for the bottom (the greater the angle of easel tilt the longer the exposure times).

The top test strip will give you the basic exposure time for the entire print. To determine the right burning-in time for the bottom of the picture, pick the best exposure in the bottom test strip and subtract the basic exposure time from it. The remainder will be the correct burning-in time. *Figure it out!*

You can also use distortion-correction and -creation techniques on subjects other than buildings.

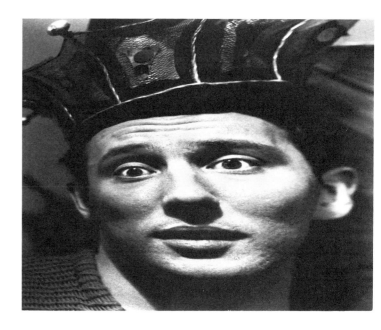

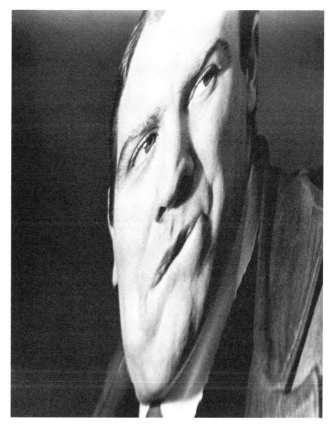

Print A, which is full-frame, is from a negative made with a 50-mm lens. Notice that the vertical parallel lines tend to converge somewhat. In print B, tipping the easel about 20 degrees corrected the convergence. However, some of the image—especially near the top—had to be trimmed off to keep the picture rectangular. Print C shows what happens when we tip the easel in the opposite direction at an angle of about 60 degrees; and print D shows a 60-degree tilt in the previous direction.

• How to Lighten and Darken Negatives

Sometimes one gets negatives that are either too dark or too light to produce good prints. The dark ones (overexposed and/or overdeveloped) make fuzzy prints with mushy, gray highlights. The light ones (underexposed and/or under-developed) make flat prints that are muddy in shadow and mid-tone areas.

Dark (heavy, dense) negatives can be reduced (lightened) with Farmer's reducer, which comes in handy packet form. Buy some packets and carefully follow the easy instructions printed on them. Review the material on print bleaching pages 90–99) because much of it will apply to bleaching negatives. Bleaching, lightening, and reduction mean the same thing.

Light (thin, too-clear) negatives can be intensified (darkened) with chromium intensifier, which also comes in convenient packets. Again, the instructions on the packets are entirely adequate. A given negative can be intensified more than once; the density gradually builds up. This is a three-solution method: bleach, clearing agent, and developer; however, it is very easy to use.

For a one-solution darkener, try Victor's Fine Grain Intensifier (in a handy vial), but don't believe the fine-grain part. Both intensifiers and reducers increase grain in negatives, and you have to learn to live with the fact. However, it is better to have a grainy negative that will print than a less grainy one that won't. As it happens, dense negatives are usually very grainy to start with, though thin ones have finer grain than usual.

With Victor's you can do local intensification, which can be fun, and the intensification can easily be removed just by soaking the negative in hypo.

Negatives that are *very* dark can often be made quite printable with Farmer's reducer, though not always. Remember that this is the same potassium ferricyanide bleach that you use on prints. There are much more restrictive limits on what

an *intensifier* will do for a *thin* negative. There has to be at least a little image detail for the intensifier to build on. Where there is none the chemical will do nothing whatever.

• How to Remove Spotting Dye

When you are learning to spot prints, you will probably botch a few jobs, usually by getting dye in the wrong places or using too much of it. Though you should practice on reject prints, you would probably rather not, which means that you will ruin some good pictures. Or will you? Perhaps you can merely remove the dye and start over.

Returning your prints to the hypo bath will remove some of it—if the bath is fresh. However, a fresh bath may also bleach some of the silver if you leave the prints in it long enough for the dye to disappear. And you have to wash and dry them again, which is a drag.

Fortunately, there is a way to safely remove dye from dry prints without having to wash them again. And you can remove just the mistakes and leave the good work untouched. All you need is clear household ammonia, surgical cotton, Q-Tips, and some small pieces of *photographic* blotter.

For bleaching lightly dyed areas, use about twenty drops of ammonia in two ounces of water. Apply the solution gently, because a wet emulsion gets soft and easily damaged. Use a well-loaded Q-Tip or cotton swab and blot the area frequently to take up the dye as the ammonia loosens it from the emulsion.

With heavily dyed areas, you will have to go to stronger ammonia, even using it full strength. This is perfectly all right as long as you work gently and patiently, though it may bleach under-developed prints somewhat. If you start rubbing you will dig up the emulsion with the cotton. Unfortunately, you may not be able to get rid of all the dye in very heavily dyed areas, yet you'll be able to lighten them considerably, which is better than nothing.

The active part of an ammonia solution (the ammonia gas itself, NH_3) disappears into the air, as you can tell by the smell. Thus there is no need to wash your prints again after getting rid of the dye. If the smell bothers you, mix the concentrated ammonia with vinegar, fifty-fifty, in two- to four-ounce quantities; then dilute the mixture with water. Warning: don't use ammonia in your spotting brush, for it will dissolve the hairs.

• How to Color Prints

Some people love to color photographs with Marshall's transparent oil colors, which are sold in photo stores. They usually color portraits that have been made on matte or semi-matte paper and treated in one of the brown toners. Such papers have a "tooth," so that the color will stick to them instead of rubbing off. The brown tone helps make the Marshall's flesh colors look real, whereas they tend to look rather greenish when applied to untoned black-and-white prints.

There is no trick whatever to using oil colors: you just rub them on and rub them off, cleaning out highlights and trimming up messy edges with a solvent. To make color cover large areas smoothly and easily, there is an oily preparation that you can rub on your prints first. The instructions with the set tell you all you will ever need to know, but most of it has just been recited here.

For more vivid colors that will work on glossy as well as matte and semi-matte surfaces, you can use transparent food and fabric dyes. They will cost you less than oils, but they are quite a bit harder to put on evenly; thus it is best to put them on pictures that have quite a bit of pattern or texture, for this will hide unevenness quite well.

For food colors, which are best because they are brightest, get a Crown Colony or McCormick four-color kit, which will give red, green, blue, and yellow. For a good purple, get gentian violet from the drugstore. Merthiolate will give you a shocking pink. All the other colors you need you can mix with this basic six. For example, Merthiolate with gentian violet will give you an excellent magenta, and green with red makes a fine brown.

Though the colors aren't very chromatic (vibrant), RIT dyes are good (and inexpensive). However, in the liquid form they aren't concentrated enough, so buy the powders. Mix a concentrated solution by dissolving one level half-teaspoonful of powder in one ounce of 70 per cent isopropyl (rubbing) alcohol or in the same amount of water heated to the simmering point. Then strain the resulting concentrate through a fine-weave cloth and put it in a dropper bottle from the drugstore.

The alcohol solution goes on very well, even on glossy prints, but it dries so fast that it is next to impossible to get it on smoothly over large areas. Thus you have to smooth colors out with ammonia (see How to Remove Spotting Dye, above). However, the alcohol mixture is very good for drawing lines and details, and coloring small areas.

The water solution dries more slowly and is thus easier to handle over larger areas (up to a square inch or two), but this is true only if you add five drops of Photo-Flo per ounce to the dye; add a similar amount to the water you rinse your brush in, and use it for diluting the dye concentrate.

You can apply dye with a spotting brush, a Q-Tip, or a cotton ball. You can also put water in a tray, add some dye concentrate, and dip all or part of a presoaked print in it—to get a light, smooth tint. Add five drops of Photo-Flo per ounce to the dilute dye. Remove unwanted dye with ammonia.

• How to Do Pencil and Chalk Retouching

If you have tried dye retouching (pages 85–89) you have no doubt found it frustrating, especially if you have worked on glossy-surface prints. Pencil and chalk retouching are much easier to do, but you have to work on matte or semi-matte surfaces. The ideal for this purpose is the Kodak N surface (see Photographic Papers, above).

You can start with a well-sharpened ordinary no. 2 pencil. If you hold it lightly in your hand the lead will go onto the print smoothly. To make the penciling even smoother, rub it with a dry Q-Tip or a small ball of cotton. To clean up the edges of areas, use an artgum eraser that has been cut into a sharp wedge. Use a soft brush to get rid of the eraser crumbs; if you do it with your hand they will leave marks. Or use an artist's kneaded rubber eraser, which leaves no crumbs.

The main shortcomings of this technique are that too much pencil will make a shiny area on your print and that retouched areas can pick up fingerprints. However, a steam treatment will usually solve both problems. If not, you will have to put your print in a picture frame under glass, which will both protect it and minimize the shine.

Steam treatment is most often used for chalked prints (see below). The technique is simple. You merely hold a retouched print face down over a pan of boiling water until the chalked or penciled areas have been thoroughly steamed. Then immediately plunge it into a tray of cold water and lay it out to dry.

The steam softens the emulsion, so that the pencil or chalk particles become embedded in it. Since the gelatin is like a very tough glue, they get stuck so tightly that they won't rub off or shine very much. The cold water merely sets the gelatin before you have a chance to get fingerprints on the chalked or penciled areas. This is an old trick of the so-called salon photographers.

For chalking prints, you need a stick of artist's black chalk, a piece of the finest black sandpaper, dental pumice, surgical cotton, and an artgum eraser. It is also handy to have artist's paper stumps, Q-Tips, and lighter fluid. All these materials are inexpensive.

We start with a little chalk dust, which we make by rubbing the chalk stick on the sandpaper. To the pile, we add an equal amount of pumice and mix them together. If you are working with a toned print, you can add other colors of chalk dust to the mixture to get the right color. The pumice gives the chalk a little "tooth," so that it will bite into the print surface and stick there. Use dental pumice from an old-fashioned drugstore or "technical" pumice from a printers' supply store. Bon Ami is also good, if you can find it.

Rub a ball of cotton, a Q-Tip, or a paper stump into the mixture, then rub it into the print surface with small, circular movements. If the area doesn't get dark enough, apply more of the mixture until it does. If it gets too dark, wipe off the excess with clean cotton. To remove chalk or pencil dust altogether, use cotton and lighter fluid.

Clean up the edges with the wedge-shaped eraser. For "picking out" minute details, you might use lighter fluid and a "mini-Q-Tip," made with a tiny wisp of cotton and a round toothpick. You can also *scratch* out small highlights with a long-pointed X-acto knife or a single-edge razor blade. For merely lightening areas somewhat you might try white chalk dust. White and black can be used on different parts of the same print.

If you wish, you can make pencil dust and use it in the same manner as you would chalk dust. Conte-crayon dust is also very good, and you can get it in black and brown.

For merely filling in dust spots, a no. 2 pencil is too soft and smeary, so get a 3-H and sharpen it to a needle point on fine black sandpaper. The trick is to handle it delicately enough. You should hold it loosely in your hand so it won't dig the print surface, then lift one end of the print off the table while you are penciling. This gives it a little spring. Use the pencil only on areas of light or medium tone, because the shine will show up in dark areas, which should be dye-spotted. Pencil and dye spotting go well together on the same print.

After a picture has been treated, blow off all the chalk or pencil particles (or use a soft brush) and give it the steam-and-cold-water treatment.

• Use a Comparison Patch

Under safelight illumination it is hard to clearly see how your prints are coming along in the developer tray. If you can decide how light the lights are and how dark the darks, it will help you decide when they have developed long enough. Having something to compare the print tones to would be very helpful in the dim light.

For this purpose make a comparison patch by exposing a 4×4-inch piece of photographic paper to the room light and putting it in the developer tray. For judging the dark areas of a print under the safelight, lay the patch across them with the black side up, and use the white side to judge the light areas.

When you are through printing, fix, wash, and dry the patch, so you can use it again.

• How to Demagnetize Your Negatives and Equipment

In the chapter on cleaning negatives, you learned what a headache static electricity can be and were told about anti-static cloths and sprays. Unfortunately, the spray recommended, Marshall's, contains isopropanol and leaves a greasy residue. Like anti-static cloths it is good, but with some shortcomings.

It would be easier to live with isopropanol if we weren't spraying it into the air, as we do with Film Klens. Well, there is an effective anti-static rinse and wetting agent that also appears to contain this chemical but there is no way of spraying it into your own eyes, which should make it considerably safer. This compound is Ecco ✕121, which is made by the Electro-Chemical Products Corporation and is available in photo stores.

The function of this product is to effectively demagnetize (degauss, remove the static charge from) your film during processing in such a manner that it will stay demagnetized as long as possible. For this purpose the degaussing agent was

incorporated in a wetting agent that has the same purpose as Photo-Flo. So before you hang your films up to dry, merely substitute Ecco ✕121 for Photo-Flo, using one ounce of the concentrate per gallon of water. When your films have finished washing, soak them for thirty seconds or more in the stuff and hang them right up to dry without wiping them. It works just fine, so good-by static—for a while, at least.

You use this same dilution in a cloth to wipe down negative carriers, film holders, enlargers, easels, work surfaces, and so on. So, you can spray on your isopropanol with Marshall's and wipe it on with Electro-Chemical's. You pays your money and you takes your choice. Happily, both products do a good job, but you should not add them to your menu or use them as a gin substitute in martinis.

• Testing the Stop Bath or Hypo

You should not permit your stop bath to lose its acidity, because it will lead to the ruin, or exhaustion, of the fixing bath in either a one- or a two-bath system. A ruined fixer frequently leads to stains and markings on prints, though they may become evident only after a period of time.

If you use an indicator stop bath it will warn you when it has been used up by turning purplish. However, plain acetic-acid baths have no indicators in them. After they have been in use for a while, such baths should be tested frequently to make sure they haven't conked out.

If you follow the hypo-use schedule given on page 36 you will have no need to test the hypo bath(s). However, you may lose track of how many prints you have run through the system, or you may suspect contamination of some kind, usually from developer carried over from an exhausted stop bath. In such cases the hypo should be tested.

For testing the stop bath and a one- or two-bath fixing system, Kodak makes a little testing outfit accompanied by simple and effective instructions. It takes about a minute to test both a stop bath and a fixer. If you have any doubts about your baths, buy the kit—it should last you for years.

Making a hypo test with the Kodak kit, a simple and fast procedure.

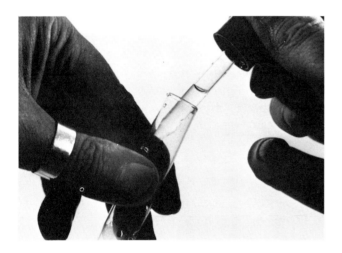

• How to Make Fog Tests

If you are using a non-standard safelight or have a lot of outside light leaking into your darkroom, you ought to run some simple fog tests. You may have a serious fog problem without realizing it, because it may not show up in the white areas and borders of your prints and yet be degrading your images very considerably.

Test the safelight(s) as follows: Make a test strip (pages 55–57) with no negative in the enlarger and the lens stopped down three or four times. You will get a strip of flat tones, and you want the exposure time for a light-to-medium gray. Now turn out the safelight(s) and give another strip of paper single exposure: for this desired tone. Still in the dark, line up six nickels or quarters on the strip.

Turn on the safelight(s) and after one minute remove a coin. Every minute thereafter remove

another coin, until they are all gone. Then turn off the safelight(s) and process the strip in the dark, using a two-minute developing time. After fixing, see how many coin silhouettes there are on the strip. If there are none it means your safelight is safe for at least six minutes with the type of paper used for making the test. If you see three the light is safe for only three minutes or a little more, etc.

Ordinarily, three or four minutes is all the safe time you need for exposing and developing a print, especially if you learn to work fast.

If you have a serious light-leak problem, test the safelight(s) first—at night, when you know there is no light leaking in. Then, in the daytime, run another safelight test to see if the leaking light and the safelight *together* are causing fog. If you get fog in less than three or four minutes, run another test for the light leak alone, with the safelight(s) turned off during the whole procedure. If you still get fog too soon it means that your darkroom isn't very safe to work in during the daytime, but there are things you can do to improve matters.

If you are getting fog from a light leak, from a safelight, or from the two working together, here are some things you can do:

Plug the light leak better
Work only at night
Use a slower enlarging paper
Get a lower-wattage bulb for your safelight
Take less time to get your paper exposed and into
    the developer
Develop your prints face down in the tray
Develop them in the dark, turning on the safelight
    only for periodic inspections
Use an anti-fogging agent in the developer

Benzotriazole is the commonly used anti-fogging agent. It is sold as Kodak Anti-Fog no. 1 in both pill and powder form. The powder is by far the more economical, though the initial cost (for four ounces) is a bit higher. It is used for paper that has been fogged over all by age, heat, and humidity—also to help solve the light-leak and safelight problem. It works very well indeed, but one shouldn't overwork the idea.

With fog tests to check their efficacy, you can use some or all of these tricks and work successfully in an area with quite a bit of light spilling in, though it might be easier to light-trap it properly (pages 11–12).

Use the same techniques to see if there is too much light leaking in to permit you to develop film, but stop the lens all the way down for the multiple-tone test strip, making your exposures on a strip of film instead of on paper. You can pull out lengths of it without opening the cassette, and use the rest for shooting pictures. If you use roll film or cartridge load, buy a 35-mm cassette of discount, out-of-date film for your tests. Ask your dealer for some with the same speed as the film you generally use.

With film, the safelight(s) should be turned off during the whole procedure, because we already know that it would cause fog and are only interested in what the leaking light will do. Use Dektol 1:2 again (at 68 to 75 F for film) and develop for a minute and a half. Again, the number of visible coin silhouettes will tell you how much safe time you have, if any. If you have as much as three or four minutes, you should be all right, provided that you pop your film right into the developing tank as soon as it has been loaded onto the reel.

However, you can get by with even more light leakage if you take precautionary steps. Of course you can use a changing bag (page 13) but that costs money. If you work in a room as dark as you can get it, with just a moderate amount of leakage, there are two effective substitutes for such a bag; and they will cost you nothing. One, load your film reels and put them in the tank under a dark coat or blanket. Two, get a stout cardboard grocery box with a top that is in good shape and cut two tight armholes in adjacent sides, one per side. Put your film cassettes, bottle opener, reels, and developing tank in it, then tape down the top. Shove your arms through the holes, load the reels, put them in the tank, and

put the top on. Then you can safely open the box. With these two systems you can counteract a rather serious light-leak problem, but it wouldn't be smart to push your luck too far.

● Developing Film by Inspection

There will be times when you know or strongly suspect that you have made rather large errors in exposing your film. Two common reasons for this are forgetting to set the correct film-speed number on your exposure meter and having to guess the correct exposure in light so dim that the meter in your camera won't register it. In the first case, you can easily figure out whether all of your film is over- or underexposed, but your guesswork exposures may go either way. In either case, you don't know what developing time you should use, because the normal time should be paired only with normal exposures. It will make overexposures too dense (dark, or heavy) and underexposures too thin (clear, or light), so you have to abandon the normal time. But then what do you do?

You simply develop the film by inspection, that is by looking at it periodically for short intervals under a Kodak no. 3 (dark-green) safelight with a 15-watt bulb in it. Even though film is sensitive to green light (panchromatic film, that is) you can do this safely because it loses much of its light sensitivity during development and the green light is very dim. The rule is that you shouldn't start inspecting until half of the normal development time has elapsed. However, if you think that the film is heavily overexposed you may have to start a bit sooner, for you may wish to put it in the fixer before the halfway point.

For a considerably brighter green light, also quite safe, you might buy a "Fotopanhandler," made by Erco. As the name telegraphically implies, one uses it for handling (inspecting) panchromatic photosensitive materials. Since it has solid-state circuitry, there are no bulbs to replace and it will probably work for years without giving difficulty. Furthermore, it initially costs very little more than the Kodak safelight setup and just a few pennies a year to operate.

If you intend to develop some film by inspection you should set up an auxiliary *tray* of developer, filled to the very top, diluted 1:1, and at the right temperature. Also have a tray of hypo (fixer) handy. If necessary, you can then pull the whole roll of film off the developing reel at the halfway time. With scissors, you can start cutting off the frames (or strips of frames) that have developed long enough and immediately putting them in the hypo. You can continue developing the remainder of the film spaghetti fashion in the developer tray, just stirring it around gently to insure even development. If you guard against fingernails, this technique will give you excellent results, so don't worry about the incongruity of it.

As another preliminary to inspecting film, you should turn off all lights except the inspection light several minutes before the midway point, in order to get your eyes dark-accommodated. Even with the Erco light the illumination level is low, so doing this is a must. By prior experimentation you can learn precisely how long it takes your eyes to fully adapt.

Now we come to the hard part: how can you tell in such dim light when a frame or roll has developed long enough? The sad, tough answer is that you can learn only through experience. You have to find out by *doing*. However, there are some general guidelines. If a roll has developed long enough, all the frames will usually (but not always) show up clearly under the green light as dark rectangles when viewed from the emulsion side. When you look at the other side they may show up a little bit, and there may be some little dark details showing here and there. These record the highlights in your pictures and will print as whites or near whites.

The best way to learn what the negatives should look like under green light is to get some practice on film you know to be normally exposed. Use both the time-and-temperature method and development by inspection for the same roll, but rely on the time to tell you when to discard the devel-

oper and pour in the hypo. Thus when you inspect the film at the halfway point you will know you are looking at frames that haven't developed far enough. When you examine it at the end of the time, just before fixation, you will know you are inspecting frames that are just right. Inspecting film after fixation isn't the same thing at all, but you might try it just to see what the difference is.

Lots of people, including many professionals and custom-lab technicians, do development by inspection, and this is the way they all learned how. There is just no other way to learn except by doing.

You now need to know approximately how far you can go with "jerking" film or "pushing" it —with cutting the developing time or extending it. It is quite safe to either cut the time in half or double it, though you can actually go further in both directions. However, there can be a serious quality fall-off with extended pushing, but this depends to a large degree on the visual graphics of your subject matter. By doubling the time or more, you may end up with contrasty and grainy negatives that are difficult or impossible to print well, even if the exposure and developing times are correctly paired.

With a half-normal developing time or less, correctly paired with overexposure, there is no such problem, though your negatives may be quite flat and require a contrasty printing paper (contrast increases with developing time, temperature, and agitation—and vice versa).

If you would like to know rather accurately the ranges of over- and underexposure that can be compensated for by shorter or longer developing times, you should run tests such as the one described on pages 63 through 66 in my book *Beginner's Guide to Photography*. To describe the test in detail here would go beyond the intended scope of this Appendix. However, we can make some rough pairings of exposure and developing time:

For $4\times$ to $16\times$ *over*exposure (two to four stops), develop one half the normal time. For the

16× you might even go as low as one third the time.

For 4× to 16× *under*exposure (two to four stops), develop twice the normal time. For the 16× under you might even go as high as two and one half times.

These data will serve well as a rough guide, which is about all that you can use anyway, because when you *have* to use inspection development you are dealing mainly with exposures of unknown quantity. In order to learn to recognize these unknown quantities, it would be wise to do quite a bit of practice developing on correctly exposed rolls and deliberately under- and overexposing on a roll or two just for practice in seeing what comes out.

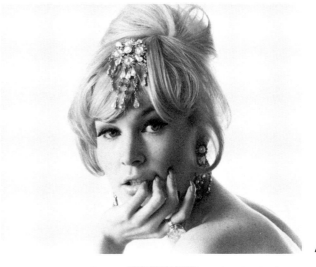

A

• How to Diffuse (Soften) Prints

Some prints look a little better if the fine details aren't too sharp. This is particularly true of delicate portraits of children and young women. If they are just a little bit soft, the blemishes (pimples, blackheads, and acne scars) tend to disappear or lose their power to attract our attention. Graininess is either lessened or eliminated altogether. Skin takes on a kind of creamy smoothness that is quite attractive. Fortunately, getting this diffuse softness is no problem at all.

The only tool you need is a small piece of cellophane, such as plastic food wrap or the wrapping from a package of cigarettes. You wad it into a tight ball, then flatten it out again, which leaves it very wrinkled. During the print expo-

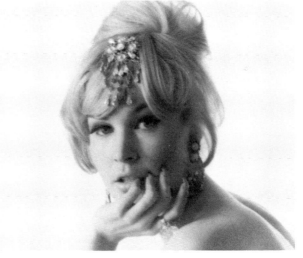

B

Print A is a low-contrast print that has had no diffusion whatever. Print B was diffused with cellophane for half of the printing exposure time, print C for the entire time.

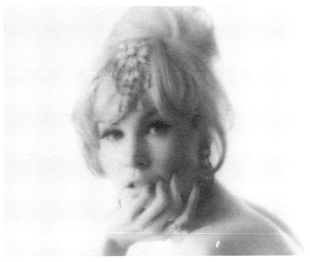

C

175

sure, you wave it around under the lens, at a distance of about two inches, for all or part of the exposure time.

Part-time diffusion gives us a moderate softening and blurring effect, which is usually (but not always) best, while full-time gives us considerably more. For even greater diffusion, use two or three layers of wrinkled plastic for the whole time. The technique is just as simple as it sounds, so don't complicate it in your mind.

Diffusion not only softens a print but flattens it, too. A flat, soft print that is not very dark may look good, while one that is too dark may look muddy. However, if you want softness without a loss of contrast you can use a printing paper one or two contrast grades higher than you would usually use for your negative. You could even print a no. 2 negative on a Brovira no. 6 and bring down the contrast to the desired level by cellophane diffusion.

You can also do local diffusion if you like, sof-tening selected parts of an image and letting the remainder print straight. Again, the technique is very easy. Make yourself a special diffusion dodger, using a wrinkled cellophane shape instead of a cardboard disk. Also, make yourself a wrinkled cellophane "burning-in card," using a piece of plastic quite a bit larger. You can make it easier to handle by taping it to a frame made of light cardboard. Cut a hole in the middle so that you can do straight printing through it while the rest of the image is being diffused and flattened. With the dodger, you can diffuse small areas, for all or part of the exposure time, while the rest of the picture prints straight.

Though cellophane diffusion is used mainly for portraits, it also goes well with gothic or romantic landscapes. It also adapts itself to communicating the ideas of spring and youth, and well fits ethereal and dreamy concepts. Happily, it is about as easy a technique as you can find in photography.

The Aesthetics of Photography

JUDGING YOUR PICTURES

● Good Pictures, Bad Pictures

After you've developed and printed a few rolls of film, you'll begin worrying over whether your pictures are any good. It never fails to happen. This problem is so difficult that many photographers worry about it for years. I hope that by giving you some ideas about pictures I can shorten your worrying time.

One of the biggest troubles with photographs is that people don't really know what to make of them (true of both photographers and non-photographers). They are fun to look at without thought or comment—everyone knows this—but when we try to analyze them the suffering begins.

Photography is like a trap, for it gets people deeply involved in it. This intense involvement inescapably forces us to think about pictures. When we find ourselves examining photographs, we discover with dismay that we don't know how. It is confusing and frustrating that we can't think about photographs the way we do about other things.

Perhaps the basic reason people fail in thinking about photographs is that they've never really tried to make sense of the reality they depict. We go through our daily lives seeing hundreds and thousands of things we hardly think about at all. In fact, if we were forced to think about them we couldn't survive, for there wouldn't be time for anything else. Photographs thrust these half-ignored things into our attention, demanding that we consider them. Though non-photographers can easily ignore the pictures we cannot.

Once we've been trapped by the medium we are automatically compelled to consider the contents of all the pictures we see, especially our own. Never having thought about them before, we find ourselves in a quandary concerning what and how to think.

Ordinary thinking won't work with photographs. It is not really thinking, anyway, but a type of remembering. Other people's ideas—from school, books, newspapers, TV, etc.—flit through our minds and we call it thought. From such sources there is a vast reservoir of second-hand ideation we can call to mind any time we like. It's different with photographs, for there is no handy reservoir. It is useless to search the memory. The things that have been said about photographs aren't very accessible. You really have to dig hard to find them. Thus, a person who has to cope with a picture has to think for himself, which can sometimes be difficult.

Despite the tribulations, one of the great attractions of photography is that it can promote original thought. However, most people need a little help in the form of concepts concerning what the medium is and what it does. We can start by showing how photographers talk about pictures.

● Like and Dislike

When experienced photographers discuss pictures the words like and dislike are often heard. Indeed, some photographers rarely employ any other terms. Used carefully, like and dislike are a great help in photographic thinking. Used sloppily, they confuse it. To preserve these two very useful terms and avoid confusion we should remember certain things every time we use them or hear them used:

1. They are words which describe *emotions,* not objective facts outside of people;

2. the people who use them are mainly unaware of how they really feel, even to the point of getting their likes and dislikes confused;

3. people know even less concerning *why* they have these feelings;

4. a person's feelings for a picture may have little or nothing to do with the picture itself;

5. they may have nothing to do with whether the photographer achieved his purpose;

6. they may relate to the photographer but not to his picture; and

7. these feelings may not agree with what anyone else feels about the picture. Despite appearances, I don't think there is any exaggeration here.

Though it's a chore to remember all these things when we think with the terms like and dislike, they are nonetheless useful in helping us examine our pictures. In truth, they take us so close to the center of our involvement we couldn't get along without them if we tried. After all, the whole point is to make pictures we like and respect and we can't help judging whether we've been successful. Thus, like and dislike are terms that are here to stay, though they must be treated with suspicion.

Few people will be satisfied in deciding whether they like a picture. Most will go on to ask themselves why. This is a fruitful question that can be pursued to great depth. Carried far enough, it leads us into a very useful form of self-analysis, for photography is one of the finest self-analytical tools we have. Nowadays, many people are using it this way. They carefully ascertain whether they like or dislike pictures, then persistently dig

for the reasons. The reward, of course, is self-discovery. There is little more one could ask for. The majority, however, avoid using photography to help them dig into themselves. They wish to avoid the pain it brings, not understanding that pain is necessary for growth.

What if a person refuses to pry into his psyche to learn why he likes or dislikes his pictures? Can he learn to criticize them expertly? No, for such a skill is earned only through years of the most intense self-examination. But is it necessary to be an expert critic? No, it isn't. One merely has to be moving in the right direction. With time and experience he will reap many rewards from photography. The great majority of photographers are rather poor critics, though very capable in judging photographic technique. Despite this shortcoming they've gotten much from photography.

Technique brings us back to the question of like and dislike, for good technique is simply the type that all competent photographers have learned to like. If they like the technique in a picture, it's good. If not, it's bad. It is as simple as that. Through the years, this idea of good technique has been turned into an absolute which has been formulized. Thus, people can use the ideas embodied in the formula as an external standard for judging their work. They don't even have to make up their minds whether they like it but can rely on the judgment of others as it has been preserved in the formula.

I suspect that the majority of photographers do this, but they are still left with the questions whether they like something and why. Only full answers will leave one entirely satisfied; and each of us must answer for himself. Ultimately, each of us must also decide for himself what makes a good picture. No outsider can tell us in a way we can understand.

● **Good and Bad, Effective and Ineffective**

Good and bad are terms commonly used in discussing photographs. Most photographers couldn't get along without them. However, one should avoid them rigorously in thought and speech unless he carefully qualifies them with each use. We shouldn't say, "This is a good picture," but "It is good *because* . . ." We must always make sure to have a substantial list following the "because," for no picture should be considered good (or bad) for just one reason. Unless thoroughly qualified, good and bad are words without meaning or with too many meanings. Useless for clear thinking. Even if we do qualify them it is better to do without them, for they have a long history of blanking out thought and distorting reason. Anyone who uses them a lot ought to be very suspicious of himself.

When most people look at pictures and say good or bad they actually mean they do or do not like them. This often has nothing to do with the worth (relative goodness) of the photographs. It is a personal emotional reaction disguised with words to sound like objective evaluation. It is also the most common use for good and bad. For people who do this, the wise thing is to discard the terms in favor of like and dislike, which makes it obvious that comments are personal and emotional. Though it may make them feel too exposed in the presence of others, it leads to more accurate thinking.

It is also useful to substitute effective or ineffective for good and bad, though they don't always mean the same thing. The new words lead us to another way of looking at photographs: in terms of their relative effectiveness in doing things to (or for) people. All photographs are made to be looked at. And photographers generally hope for fairly specific reactions in their viewers, whether the pictures be scientific, documentary, photojournalistic, or pictorial. This is even true of the photographer who keeps his pictures entirely to himself; he wants to react to them himself in a certain way.

Using effective and ineffective also leads to the question of purpose. It is not enough to say something is effective; we must also say for what pur-

pose. Many of the photographers I've known seem to thrive on thinking about pictures in terms of purpose and relative effectiveness in achieving it. Therefore, I suggest it might work equally well for you. Certainly, it is better than incautiously using the terms good and bad.

It is good to keep in mind that an effective picture may not be one people should like. For example, a poster urging you to protest destruction of the ecology: The more it stirs your ire and revulsion the more effective it is. Consider this when you're distressed at disliking one of your pictures. Perhaps it wouldn't make sense to like it. Remember, you can explore the negative side of life as well as the positive. You should explore, also, both sides in order to develop fully your creative potential.

We should also be aware that effective pictures may be bad ones. They may achieve their purposes very well, but these purposes may be bad. The Adolf Hitler regime was expert in using photography in support of virulent Nazism. Merchants often use it effectively in selling inferior merchandise. For politicians, it is sometimes a means for lying about a candidate's qualifications.

Perhaps the important thing for the beginner is to understand that the worth of his pictures depends both on their effectiveness and the relative goodness of their purposes. On the other hand, he can safely sidestep such questions until he is well advanced in photography. His first problem is to learn how the medium works.

● What Photographs Do

When we get tired of using effective, ineffective, and purpose (which are formal terms and are a bit stuffy), we can adopt the word *do*. It's a short word that gets right to the point: What do photographs *do?* As you'll see in a moment, they do lots of things. It will help you measure your progress if you learn what some of them are.

This awareness is useful, because the diversity of photography creates problems for beginners. Without even thinking about it, they wander all over the photographic map, shooting pictures of all types. Not recognizing the types or knowing what they are traditionally supposed to do, they fall into confusion. However, if you are aware of them it is less likely to happen to you.

Another common problem is that the beginner often sets out to make one kind of picture and accidentally creates another instead. He then compounds his difficulty by failing to see what he has done. All he knows is that he didn't get the effect he wanted. He doesn't understand that his picture may be quite good from another point of view.

The student often attempts to make a specific type of picture without giving any thought to what it is supposed to do. Some beginners, for example, like to make fashion photographs, but seldom realize that the function of such photographs is to sell garments, jewelry, perfume, etc. They usually end up with bastard crosses between glamour and fashion pictures, then wonder why they don't like them very much.

The solution to problems such as these is to think about the various types of pictures and what they can and cannot do. Though it takes a while to get everything clear in mind, it is not something to worry about. Time and effort will take care of everything.

● The Functions of Photographs

We will now see what photographs do. Though there are dozens of types and subtypes, we will limit the discussion to thirteen. This is quite enough for people just getting started in photography.

Stimulate memory: Photography is used more to stimulate memory than for any other reason. The family snapshot is the primary example of this. We snap our loved ones in order to remember our experiences with them. However, as memory stimulators, photographs can be much more sophisticated than snapshots. Some are even masterpieces.

Pictures made to help memory shouldn't be judged too completely right away, for only time will tell how well they've worked. Sometimes you'll find that a picture you dislike now will be a favorite in ten years because of the memories it evokes.

Pictures made to aid recall don't necessarily have to be pretty. In fact, pictorialism may be extraneous and even work against their main purpose. Too, we may have good reasons for wishing to remember some very unaesthetic things, such as a memorable night in a shoddy motel, the mess a hurricane made in the back yard, and Uncle George's broken leg. These things aren't pretty, but they are a part of life and interesting to recall when the pain has been forgotten.

Provoke an aesthetic response: Many photographers concentrate entirely on making pretty or beautiful pictures. If successful, they evoke aesthetic feelings or appreciation. These photographers often think of themselves as pictorialists and specialize in pretty girls, handsome landscapes, and similar subjects. The best of them have a powerful command of the medium, especially print quality, which is considered a thing of beauty in itself.

Because pictorialism has a long history in photography, a long list of rules and principles has grown up around it. They work rather well in making handsome pictures, though they tend to limit the imagination somewhat. The best place to learn about them is in camera clubs, which have for many years specialized in pictorialism.

Beauty is a complex subject and one doesn't learn to understand it in a day. Beginners trying to make beautiful pictures may be disappointed by results which are not pretty at all. Or if they do capture beauty now and then, it is hard to recognize. They may not have learned to see, or not developed through experience an appreciation of the aesthetics of their medium. One must understand that seeing well as a photographer is a difficult art. It takes a while to learn,

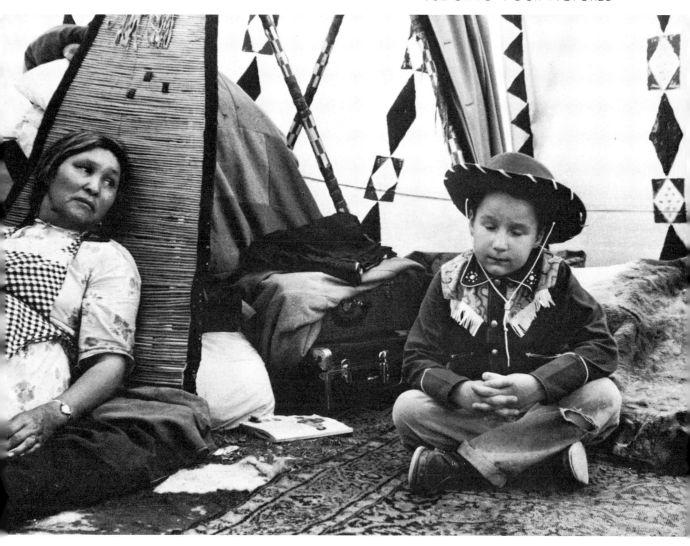

The author's son, Craig, photographed inside an
Indian tepee with an Indian woman. It was during the
very last medicine dance of the once-great Blackfoot
Indian tribe in northern Montana. Craig was so
excited he kept his eyes closed. This is a personal
photograph, a stimulus for tender memories.

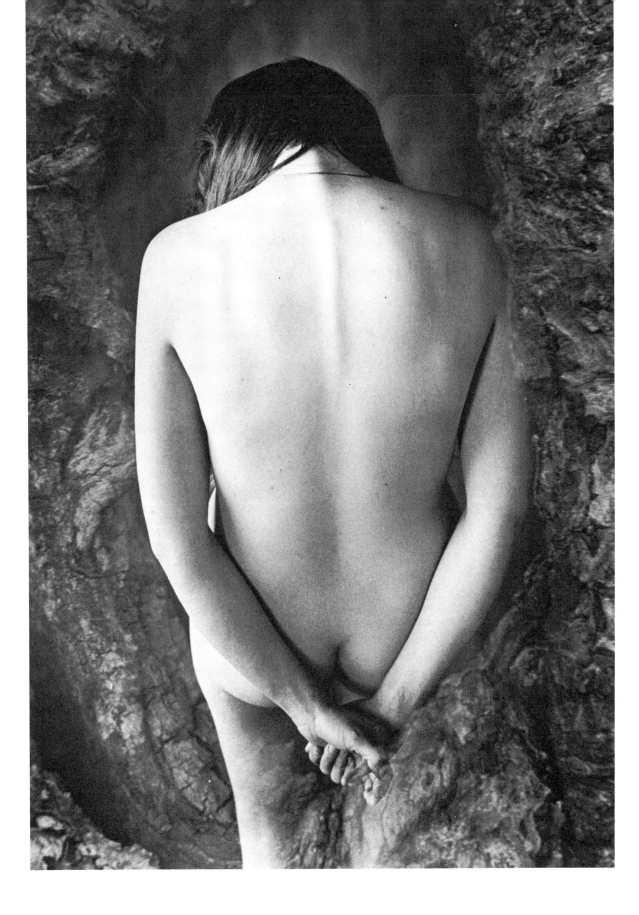

A montage of a young woman's back and a knothole in a tree. The primary purpose here is to stimulate an aesthetic response in the viewer. That is, one is supposed to be moved by the beauty of the tender young back in its rustic frame. The girl's pose should also lead the viewer to wonder how she feels and what she's thinking about.

and failures must be expected in the beginning. Instead of condemning inadequate work, the student should respect it for where it is leading him. When he arrives, he will be able to create beauty almost at will.

Arouse emotion: One of the most popular objectives in photography is to make pictures that really flip people out. The choice of subject is all-important here, though technique should be handled well too. The favorite subjects are people showing strong emotions, such as anger, lust, jealousy, fear, resentment, and pride. The idea is that one can record such things in photographs and use them to provoke emotional responses in viewers.

The all-time favorite is love, or affection. The genuine thing is a bit hard to find, but it does survive here and there. It is most often seen in parent-child relationships. If photographed well, it evokes strong responses in the viewer.

When a beginner starts to photograph in this area he is usually beset with ethical questions. How far should he intrude into the emotional lives of others? Is it right to use people's emotions to create photographs for one's personal use? Is it O.K. to photograph them without their knowledge and, without asking their permission, show the pictures to others? Questions like these plague the photographer until he answers them for himself. If he tries to push them aside and go against his ethics, he'll spoil photography for himself.

Another problem is the photographer's shyness. It is difficult to approach people who are expressing strong emotions, for they may react adversely to being photographed. The answer is to go places where people don't mind being photographed, such as protest marches, festivals, athletic events, folk rock concerts, parks, etc. There, people's natural exhibitionism comes out and they don't care if they are photographed while expressing themselves. For synthetic emotion, theater groups have much to offer. With a little skill, a photographer can make it look like the real thing. Sometimes there is a lot of real emotion in such groups.

The beginner should understand that really good emotional pictures are fairly rare; one cannot expect to get one on every roll of film. Even the world's best professionals can't do it.

Prove that one has done something: A popular use of pictures is to prove one has climbed Mount Everest alone, walked on the water across Lake Michigan, baked a wedding cake thirty feet tall, or convinced his mother-in-law she should leave on the second day of her visit. The vacationer's camera helps him prove unequivocally where he went and what he did. The home handyman takes before and after pictures of the den to prove he made a mare's nest into a beautiful place.

Photographic proof often turns into a form of bragging. It's harmless, people like to do it, and there are some things worth bragging about. Why shouldn't a proud father show pictures of his baby, silently bragging that he helped produce a healthy child? Does it matter if a young man shows pictures of his pretty girl friend to help build himself up in the eyes of others?

The proof picture only has to make its point.

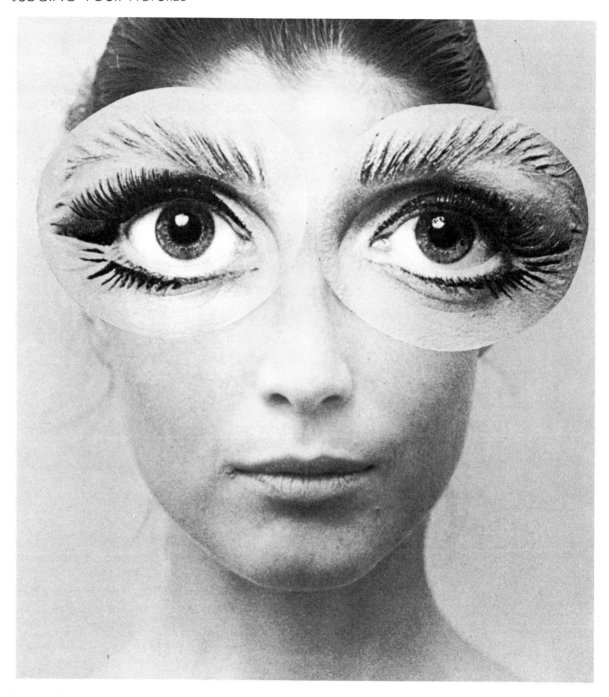

Eyes cut from one photograph were pasted onto
another, then the resulting picture was rephotographed
and reprinted. The objective was to arouse a strong
emotional response in the viewer. Nearly always,
people react to being stared at, even by a person in
a photograph. The eyes were enlarged to intensify the
feeling.

It doesn't have to be pretty, convey a message of importance, or demonstrate splendid craftsmanship. The beginner should understand that proof as such may be enough and not feel ashamed that he hasn't gilded the lily. Had he done it he might have weakened his proof, for simple, straightforward pictures are much more believable than artistic, pictorial ones.

Help one learn to see: Most photographs fall into this category, for the very process of making them tends to sharpen vision. The person just starting in photography doesn't see much at all. He doesn't really have a clue what his camera records—until he sees it all in his prints. Looking at them carefully helps him see better the next time he looks through the camera viewfinder. If photography really turns him on, he'll start seeing better *all* the time, as if he were in constant search for subjects for pictures. With experience, he develops a thoroughly disciplined vision.

For the purpose of developing vision, it doesn't matter much whether a picture is good or bad. If it is good, we search for the things that made it

This is one of the five or six thousand pictures taken by the author at the Birmingham (England) Repertory Theatre about twelve years ago. They could be used to prove beyond a doubt that he actually did cover the Rep in considerable depth. Photographs can be (and are) used to prove any number of things.

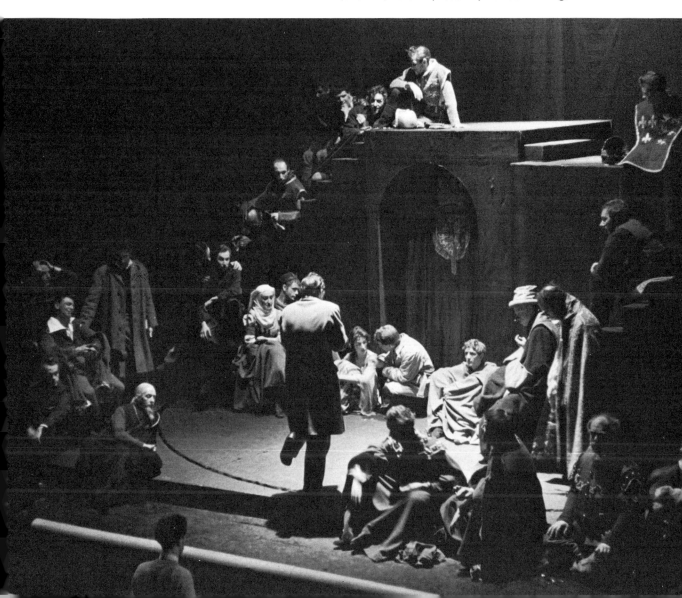

that way. If bad, for the negative, ineffective elements. Both experiences expand and sensitize vision. In this light, early failures aren't so bad. Instead of attempting suicide over pictures that bomb, the student should regard them as opportunities. It is true they cause griping of the gut, but that is always the price of artistic growth.

Amuse or entertain: What is more natural than photographing things that are amusing? A lot of people do it. The important thing is to not expect too much, for the truly hilarious photograph is extremely rare. Indeed, many top professionals have tried it and failed. Instead of setting our sights too high we should settle for modestly amusing pictures. Then we're not disappointed. The picture with modest wit is a lot of fun and worthy of everyone's respect.

The way to find amusing shots is to develop new points of view for looking at life, finding humor in the things that happen around you. Contrived humor usually fails. Stay close to home and the life familiar to you.

Entertainment photographs may not be amusing but interesting in some other way. They can record intriguing events, things, and places. Or they may use the photographic medium in an exciting way. Don't ask too much of such pictures, but let them be modestly entertaining. And don't be too upset if people refuse to let themselves be turned on by them. That is their problem. Many find photographs uncomfortably close to reality. Such people find their entertainment in things that offer an escape from it.

Record information of personal interest or value: One of photography's greatest strengths is as an information recording and storage medium. Once you've got data on film it is there forever. By data we mean a place, event, or thing; in fact, anything that will record on film is data of some sort. If you find something interesting or useful, that alone is good reason to record it. It is impor-

When the waiter saw the camera he made a face which expressed his feelings marvelously well. Though the picture has no merits beyond its humor, it needs none. Were we to judge it on its aesthetic qualities, the importance of its message, its photographic techniques, etc., we would overlook its real value.

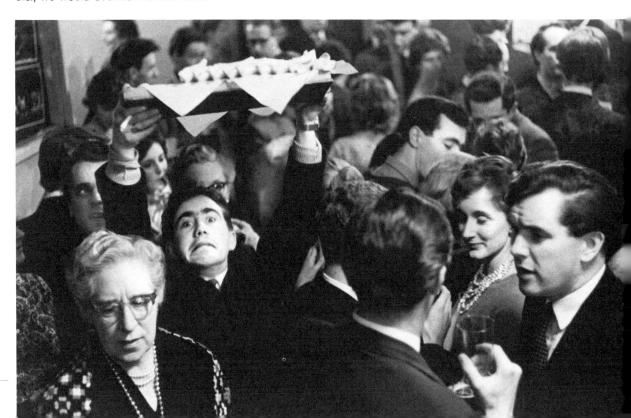

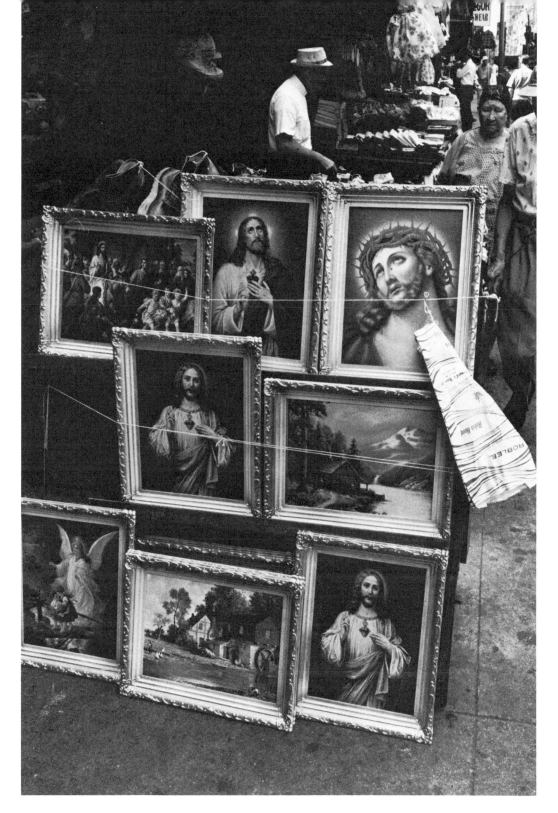

Several years ago the author was interested in the way
pictures and statues of Jesus were displayed for sale in
New York City, and made a rather extensive record
of it. One could say that the objective was to
document things of personal interest or value, an
entirely defensible reason for taking pictures. More
people should try it.

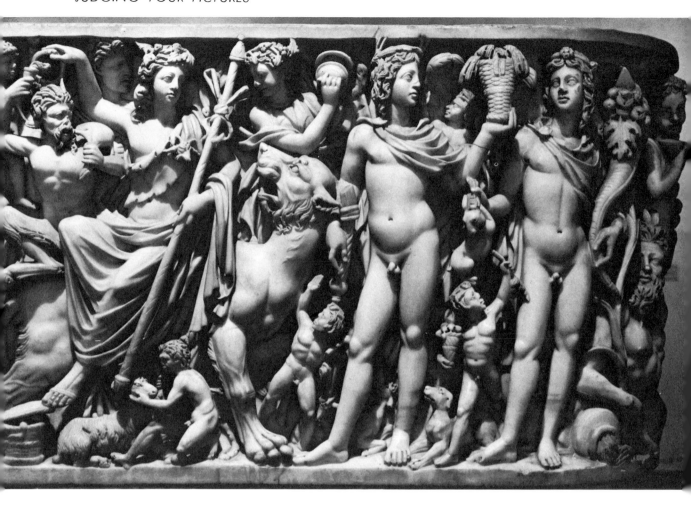

This photographic record might be of interest to archeologists and art historians. It is a detail of a Roman sarcophagus in New York's Metropolitan Museum. It should be judged as a record of someone else's art (the sculptor's), not as original art in itself. Records of this sort can easily be justified.

tant not to confuse information storage with pictorialism, for they are usually entirely different. Neither type of picture is better or worse than the other. They're just different.

Record scientific data: It has often been said that science couldn't survive without photography, which is its main means for recording and storing data. Whatever interests science, photography records. It may be the traces of atomic particles in a cloud chamber, the underside of a starfish, or an aerial view of an alluvial flat.

The non-scientist can make scientific use of photography, too. Perhaps you would like to make a study of the bugs or weeds in your back yard. Would you like to collect sea shells and photograph them? Perhaps you would like to study the behavior of white mice or frogs. In photography of this sort the important things are image sharpness, visual clarity, and selectivity (choice of the right thing, right moment, right distance, right camera angle, etc.).

If you go in this direction you should understand that other photographers won't understand your work very well, because most of them can't appreciate a picture unless it is pictorial. That's *their* problem. If *you* know what you are doing, all is well.

Record social-science information: A surprising number of people are amateur social scientists with their cameras. Primarily, this involves using photography to take a critical look at the human condition, especially in areas where people aren't faring very well. The camera asks, what is going on here, what is the cause, and how can it be improved?

In the cities, the most popular subjects are slums, settlement houses, welfare projects, and special schools. Rural conditions offer challenges too, for example, the welfare of migrant farm workers, the problems of small farmers today, the sad state of the American Indian, etc.

The person who gets into this kind of thing ought to carefully plan what he's going to do with his photographs. They accomplish nothing at all if the right people don't see them. He should do research to learn who they are, then plan his project in terms of how he wants them to react to what he has to tell them through photography.

In social-science photography it is important to accurately report what one sees, with a minimum of pictorial selectivity, trick camera angles, editorializing, and slick printing techniques. The objective is to record reality, not use the medium to make it look different. If you should do this kind of photography, ask yourself only if your pictures are real. Don't worry if they are not pretty, dramatic, or persuasive. As you build confidence in yourself and a command of the medium, you

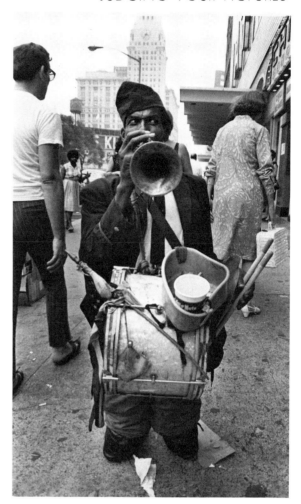

Pictures like this interest social scientists, who use them to illustrate theses, articles, and books. It shows a familiar figure on Fourteenth Street in New York and a little bit of the street itself. Besides being a street musician and beggar, this man claims to be an ordained minister. He is a bright, optimistic person.

will find it difficult to restrain yourself from visually tampering with what you see. Nonetheless, you must record things as they are.

Stimulate thought: The beginner may think his pictures should incorporate answers, but sometimes it is more important to raise questions—

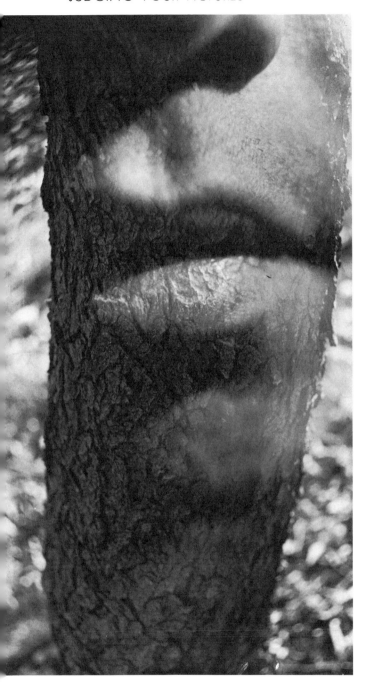

One of the main purposes of this picture is to stimulate thought. It practically insists that we speculate on its meaning. Why should there be lips on a tree? In what sense can a tree speak to us? What kind of a "person" is this tree? What is the photographer trying to say? How did he get the lips onto the tree?

190

even if he himself doesn't know the answers. Pictures that leave a viewer up in the air do him a favor, for they stimulate his thinking. A viewer will soon lose interest in a picture with a well-made, explicit point. In contrast, one that is strong and ambivalent may hold his interest for years, pushing him to solve its meaning each time he looks at it.

It is important for the photographer to stimulate his own thought, too. Perhaps the easiest way is to photograph mysterious subjects which the photographer does not completely understand. People who are honest with themselves realize they do this most of the time without even trying. It is bound to happen if one photographs other people. When one has puzzled himself with his pictures he then has the opportunity to use them in sorting through his thoughts and feelings about them. Thus, photography becomes a tool for self-discovery. It is more comfortable not to be puzzled, but this is an option we usually don't have.

If one of your pictures leads you toward self-discovery, you shouldn't demand that it do anything else for you. For you, it is a fine picture, even if it is technically weak and an aesthetic disaster. Pictorial failures may be of great worth to their makers; the wise student will take them seriously.

Freeze a moving event for examination later: Many of the events we experience change so fast we don't really get a chance to see them. This happens a lot on vacations, because people want to cover a lot of ground in very little time. The country speeds by, half unseen. A child's birthday party is another example: ten children running in twenty directions, mother crawling up the wall. By freezing time, photography will let us leisurely examine both the country and the party. Mother can joyfully look at her child when she doesn't have murder in her heart.

Often, we experience things that can be enjoyed more in retrospect than while they are happening. We may even blind ourselves to avoid discomfort. Social gatherings frequently fall in this category. In the name of fun and good will, people get together to unintentionally make each other miserable. Viewed later, pictures of such gatherings can be fascinating. A delayed look can even contribute to understanding.

Extend vision beyond its normal limits: This category is filled mainly by scientific photography, with its electron microscopes, ultrahigh-speed cameras, X rays, etc. Science extends vision dramatically, making visible the submolecular and the galactic. It makes photographs with energy waves invisible to the eye, freezes the motion of things moving too fast to see, looks inside things never before accessible to vision, etc.

For the amateur photographer there are not too many ways to extend vision. Photomicroscopy

My friend wanted me to photograph him doing his crazy act so he could look at the picture and see if he really looked crazy. Freezing action for later inspection is one of the common uses of photography, though this particular action is rather unusual. A sharper image would have served my friend's purpose better.

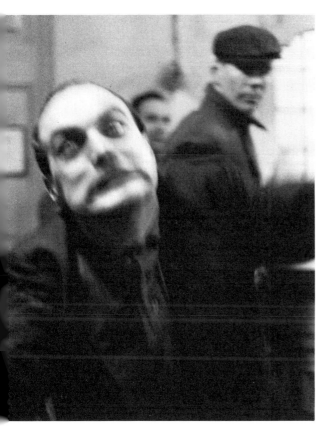

is one, for the equipment is simple, readily available, and comparatively cheap. It magnifies things enough to open vistas unseen before, creating fascinating new worlds of vision. Or by using infrared film we can change the appearance of things or show how much infrared light is radiated by different kinds of objects. Even a simple red filter will extend vision somewhat. It will penetrate fog and haze to clearly record distant objects hitherto obscured.

You will probably not find yourself making pictures in this category, but you ought to be aware of it.

Prove that certain things exist: Had Marco Polo owned a camera it would have saved him a lot of trouble. To his dying day, people wouldn't believe what he had seen in the Orient, though they later learned he had spoken the truth. With photographic evidence it wouldn't have taken so long.

To a certain degree, each of us is a Marco Polo, for we see things that wouldn't be believed without documentary evidence. For example, I know a man who can stretch his spinal column five inches and another who occasionally unstraps his wooden leg and clubs people with it. Do you believe me? Of course not, you haven't seen the photographic evidence.

There are practical uses for this kind of evidence. You can use a photograph to prove to your landlord that the bathroom plumbing is faulty. A picture may be used in evidence to help collect insurance. You can mail a picture to your vacationing neighbor to prove that his fence has fallen on your corn patch. The things you can prove with photographs are almost innumerable.

The basic function of photography is communication. Simply by recording external reality we can communicate the reality behind what is seen —the condition things are in, what is happening to them, their environment, how people relate to them, etc. And on the human side, we can show people's health, age, state of mind, occupation, recreation, etc. The possibilities are unlimited.

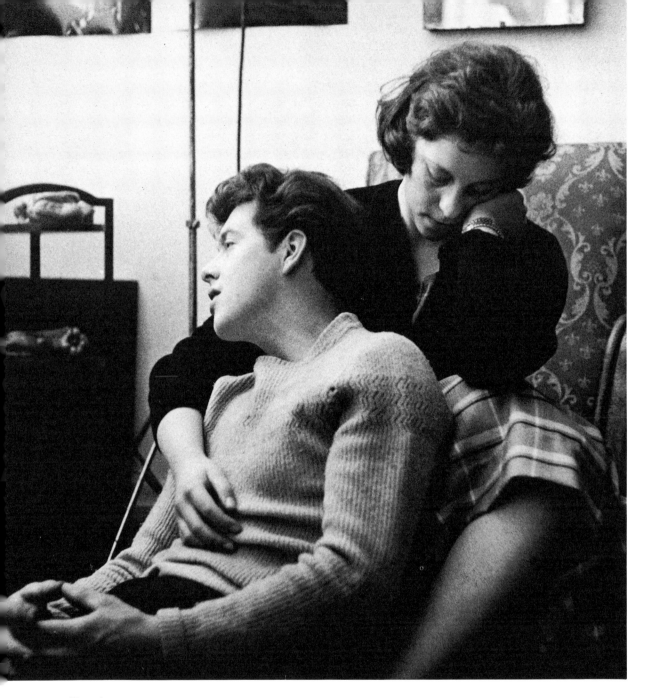

The photographer's primary aim may be communication. In my opinion, this picture says a lot about Tom
and Betty and all other young lovers. In it there is near-
ness and distance, hope and hopelessness, sweetness
and bitterness. It shows that a man's mind roves while a
woman's mind patiently waits—sometimes forever.

Anything, large or small, when reproduced in a photograph, becomes a statement in visual form.

Emotion, states of mind, and abstract ideas can also be communicated, though this is sometimes difficult to do. It is far easier to show what things look like and let people draw any inferences they wish.

Even though you may approach photography as a personal pasttime, its most fulfilling aspect is the ability to communicate with others. This may lead to disappointments, because people may fail to read the messages you so carefully put into your photographs. This is because photographs communicate much too much. You want a picture to say one thing and it says fifty; the viewer hasn't an inkling which one he is supposed to choose. Even if he does get the message the chances are high it will be on the unconscious level, so that he can't let you know what he learned.

This problem is only partly solvable. The best thing to do with your photography is to eliminate everything that doesn't contribute to your message, give pictorial emphasis to the things that do, and use captions to help you say what you mean. However, it takes a while to learn to do this well. In the meantime you should learn that visual communication is a tricky business and not let yourself get uptight about it.

As you've just seen, there are numerous types of pictures, some of them very unalike. The list could be expanded considerably. Knowing something about different types will help you decide on what kinds of pictures you are making. In striving to make pictures of quality this is important, for the criteria for quality vary according to picture type. There may be little overlap. For example, a good scientific picture may have little in common with a pictorial. An amusing photograph doesn't necessarily relate to photography as history.

You may find it educational to fit all the pictures you see into one or more of the type categories given. A few will fit a lot of them, most

pictures just one or two. As you continue to categorize you will gradually get a feeling for what constitutes quality in each area. Naturally, this will influence your photography. You must be patient, however, for it takes time to develop as a picturemaker.

You may wonder why the criteria for excellence were not spelled out when the types were discussed. In a sense, they were. It should be obvious that the humorous picture is measured by whether it makes one laugh or chuckle. The scientific picture must capture the particular data needed by a scientist. And so on.

To many, the transvestite theme is unpleasant, yet this young man at a costume party gave it a certain beauty and dignity. Is this picture primarily of interest to psychologists? Perhaps. However, it has a droll, slightly goofy quality that many folk might find attractive. Maybe we should classify it as humor.

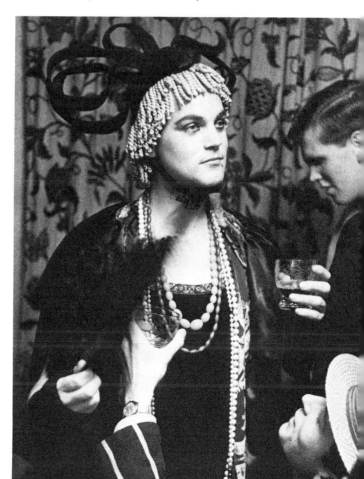

● Beautiful and Ugly

Many picturemakers find themselves concerned with only two things: beauty and ugliness. They wish to create one and eliminate the other. Their desire is simple but the problem is not. It is difficult for the beginner to even differentiate between the two, for the borders between them aren't clearly defined. Furthermore, many things in the world are both beautiful and ugly. Some vacillate back and forth between the two. Photography can make certain ugly things beautiful, and vice versa. Our cultural ideas concerning beauty and ugliness keep changing. All this makes for confusion and despair in the heart of the student.

The trouble is compounded by the fact the learner hasn't developed a sensitivity to either beauty or ugliness. Unless they are greatly exaggerated you may not recognize either quality when you see it. Or you may detect it in one type of thing—people, for example—but in nothing else. This is a very commonplace situation.

Even recognizing beauty or ugliness doesn't mean one can capture them in photographs. You must know what they are made of in terms of their visual elements, such as line, contour, form, texture, and color. Only by knowing their anatomy can one with assurance set out to make a beautiful (or ugly) picture.

In the face of these problems, what can a beginner do? The most important thing is to jump into photography and swim like mad. Try it. Make picture after picture until your innate aesthetic sense begins to assert itself.

It will help you to look at photography magazines and annuals. Visit galleries where photographs are shown. You will see the work of experienced photographers who have solved the beauty-ugliness problem in a variety of ways. Experienced photographers believe there is much beauty displayed in these places. Though you may disagree with them at first, you will find that studying the work of others expands your photographic horizons.

Working hard to make fine prints will do much to enliven your awareness of the beautiful and the ugly. Before long you will discover numerous little tricks for changing a picture in either direction. You will see what darkness and lightness or contrast and flatness do. You'll discover the effects of different croppings. Soon you'll see that sharp images and fuzzy ones have different effects and that dodging and burning-in contribute significantly. As you work you'll learn to see prints better and, in turn, everything else. In time, you'll differentiate almost instantly between the pretty and the homely, the beautiful and the ugly.

Learning to see what light does to things (next section) will help your awareness of the subtle nuances of ugliness and beauty, for light is the ultimate source of both in photography. Without light we see neither of them.

In the beauty-ugliness sphere of photography there are several paths you can choose. My advice is to try them all. One way is to devote yourself entirely to making beautiful or pretty pictures. Many photographers do. This is easily justified, for mankind has a great need for beauty. It is also a challenge, because the majority of things aren't very pretty unless we make them that way.

A few photographers concentrate on showing the ugliness in ugly things. This is justified by our need to recognize and change them. It is hard on the photographer's stomach, however, as ugliness is very upsetting. I recommend that you try a few pictures in this vein, just to help you recognize visual ugliness when you see it and understand its visual components. This will help you keep it out of your pictures if you don't want it there.

The third path is the most interesting one, where beauty and ugliness coexist in the same picture. It creates an ambivalence that can be intellectually and emotionally stimulating. It is an interesting problem to get the two in the right balance. Usually, it is best to let beauty hold the winning hand.

The most popular approach to this kind of picture is to take something ugly or homely and use one's skill to beautify it as much as possible. Sometimes it is possible to remove the ugliness altogether, but it may be a better picture with some left in.

● The Photographer Is Affected by His Work

When people start judging their progress in photography they usually concentrate entirely on their pictures as ends in themselves, ignoring the process through which they were created. Though an obvious thing to do, it is severely limited, for it ignores the most important question: What does the creation of art do for the artist? If one is to reasonably assess his progress in photography he must find an answer. From a higher perspective we can see that pictures aren't very important, after all, but the people who make them are. Furthermore, the history of art has shown that artists have always been profoundly affected by being artists and that this is what attracted them to the arts in the first place. It should be worth our time to examine some of the things that may happen to you as you become a photographic artist.

I've mentioned photography as a way of learning to see, which has long been considered one of man's most important goals. Any artist can tell you that heightened perception is wonderful. Nearly everything that is beautiful in our culture derives from it. Thus, if you find that your vision is beginning to expand, that you are seeing more things in greater detail, you have good reason to be pleased with your progress in photography. You can't expect to have the fully developed vision right away, but signs of its coming should be welcomed with joy.

Looking at photographs can stimulate thought, but making them does so even more. The photographer thinks deeply before and during the time he photographs. He meditates when he is printing. When he shows his prints to others he ponders them in a different way. Certainly, you must consider an increase in deeply reflective thinking as a good thing, so if you find yourself thinking more you must also accept the fact that you are making good progress in photography. Remember that progress is an attribute of human beings, not of pictures, which are only tones and lines on sensitized paper. Please respect what is happening in yourself and remember that one of man's greatest problems is that he doesn't think enough about the outside world. As a consequence, his psyche becomes warped. Learning to turn thought outward heals and expands it. Remember that when you ponder something outside yourself you're doing more than merely sizing up a picture possibility.

When we search for meaning in our pictures we also ponder ourselves and thought itself. In the process, we batter down inner doors that block understanding. We open up the channels for feeling. We re-examine old opinions to make way for new ones. This kind of search is often painful, which may lead us to think we're getting nowhere with our work. The reasonable thing, however, is to see that the pain itself is a good sign of progress. It is always the price one must pay to become an artist.

One of the challenges is to understand photography as a scientific process—intricate, well thought out, workable. Seen at first as a massive confusion, it gradually becomes a thing of beauty and harmony. If you find that your comprehension is growing, it is a very good sign of progress. It will give you confidence you can understand other processes if you try, which is a wonderful thing. You may find that you are now able to look on the whole world of science with less fear and suspicion. This is certainly progress of a high order.

Most photographs are of people. If we photograph people quite a bit it may profoundly change our relationship to them in a good way. In fact, many young photographers use their medium primarily for this purpose. Usually, they are trying to overcome their fear of others. I've seen it work dozens of times, so I gladly recommend it. When fear gradually disappears there is then room for love and understanding. Though this surely happens, I don't know why—perhaps because studying pictures of people encourages us to think about them and ourselves in solitude. This gives us a chance to work out things that we couldn't emotionally handle if we were with them.

If you find yourself thinking more about people, you can be sure you are making progress. If you think about them with affection, even better. Remember, it is much more important to care for one's fellow men than to make prize-winning photographs.

Many sad people see little beauty in the world, though it is all around us in great abundance. One of the prime virtues of photography is that it opens our eyes to beauty. We find glory in chunks or in tasty little bits almost everywhere we turn, for by looking for beauty we learn to see it. Perhaps you have found yourself seeing more beauty recently, though not necessarily capturing it in your pictures yet. You are doing well, as the most important thing is in seeing beauty at all. The ability to capture it in your pictures will develop in time; just be patient with yourself.

In this affluent society, many people have never experienced really hard, creative work. They can't understand its importance and how creative labor shapes the soul. However, most people who become enchanted by photography find themselves working extremely hard but enjoying every minute. Yet there are times when the gut seems about to burst. Failures bury us in pits of despair, and learning to control the medium seems a hopeless task. Nonetheless, a shred of hope carries us on to more hard labor. For creative people, even the pain is a kind of pleasure, for there is a point to the whole process.

If your involvement is like this you may rest assured that you're doing well. You have the great opportunity to learn the meaning of work and struggle. You've joined the battle against blindness, inner fear, and laziness. There is no other way to grow as a creative person.

In this section I've tried to show that preoccupation with an art medium changes people. Most artists seem to know this, but few outsiders. In assessing your progress in the photographic medium you should certainly measure its influence on you. Photography can easily turn your psyche into a great arena for debating and resolving important personal problems. This is good. It doesn't all happen in a day, so be patient with yourself. The possibilities are always open if you'll just take your time.

● Print Quality

Print quality is the most frequently used measure of progress in photography. It indicates how well one has mastered craftsmanship and the degree of development in photographic vision. It is tangible and can be talked about easily. And it is the only thing upon which photographers universally agree. If a print is thought good in Oshkosh, Wisconsin, the photographers of the world will agree.

Photographers have a tremendous respect for print quality. Indeed, they usually go overboard and think that any picture that has been beautifully printed must be good, even if they see nothing else to commend it. Many people have seen that the quickest way to earn the respect of photographers is to learn to make splendid prints. Some pursue print quality so persistently that they ignore everything else, so that their pictures are otherwise meaningless. They get trapped in technique for technique's sake and can't get out.

Learning an art is always a process of walking into traps and fighting one's way out again. It is even necessary. To get anywhere in photography, the beginner has to eat, think, and breathe print quality, to the exclusion of almost everything else. When you have mastered the art you should worry about fighting your way out of it. At this point, I doubt if you are trapped. When it happens don't worry, for it's a necessary part of the game.

There is only one good way to talk about print quality and that is by discussing original prints with the person who made them. The work of other people doesn't help much. Reproductions in books don't either, for they don't look much like original prints. Words by themselves are of limited value. Nonetheless, they can communicate some general principles.

Cleanliness: The quality print is clean in several ways: (1) no fingerprints on image or print border, (2) no scratches, spots, or squiggles from a dirty negative, (3) no chemical stains from image or border, and (4) no scum or other residue on the print surface.

Abrasions: The quality print is free of: (1) cracks in the emulsion, (2) creases, (3) indentations, (4) punctures, and (5) rubbed or scuffed places on the emulsion.

Fog: The quality print is free of fog caused by: (1) out-of-date paper, (2) too long a developing time, (3) too warm a developer, (4) accidental exposure to white light, (5) being held too close to a safelight, (6) a safelight with a larger bulb than recommended, (7) a developer contaminated with stop bath or hypo, (8) an exhausted (worn out) hypo, (9) paper that has been stored in hot and/or humid conditions, or (10) light leaks in the printing room.

Print color: The quality print is recognized by its color, which is influenced by developing time and temperature. In black-and-white prints the color is subtle, usually just a warmish or coldish look. Among quality printers, the favorite developing temperature is 68° F., plus or minus about 3 degrees. The favorite developing-time range is from 1¾ to 2¼ minutes. With many printing papers, the color tends to be warmish with short developing times, gradually getting colder as the time is increased. Most craftsman photographers like to get as cold a print as possible. However, they are leery of going too far over the maximum time for fear of getting fog.

Some papers are made with built-in warmness, though its degree is controlled somewhat by developing time. Some images look best timed at around 1 minute, others around 2. The important thing is to have the print color go well with the image, a characteristic of quality prints.

Exposure: The exposure of a quality print always satisfies exactly the requirements of the image by being neither too light nor too dark for it. One test for this is that the developed image usually looks good in bright, medium, or dim light. If it looks good only in bright light, it is overexposed. If good only in dim light, it is underexposed. Correct exposure is gauged only by the image, not by light readings and calculations. If an exposure makes the image work it is always correct.

Tonal range: The tonal range of a quality print satisfies exactly the tonal-range requirements of the image. Some people follow the rule that every print should have a tonal range from white to the blackest black the paper will produce. For some images this is all right, and learning to follow the rule teaches one the tonal possibilities of printing papers. However, it would ruin many images, for they may not need blacks or whites. Some should go from gray to black, some from gray to white, and others should range entirely in the grays. The amount of tonal range doesn't matter. The important thing is that it should make the image look just right, which is always true in the quality print.

Contrast: In a quality print the contrast always satisfies exactly the contrast requirements of the image. In most fine photographs the contrast is such that the image resembles the original subject as much as possible. Looking at such pictures is sometimes like looking through a window at the subject itself. However, such realism is not always desired, and effective contrast can range from very flat to very contrasty. The important thing is that it goes well with the image and idea of the picture.

Burning-in and dodging: In a quality print the burning-in and dodging always satisfy exactly the requirements of the image. A large percentage of negatives require one or both of these techniques.

The problem is to do it in the right places for the right amount of time. If they are overdone they make the image paint-sprayed or phony, and distract viewers from paying attention to the picture itself. In the quality print there is seldom any evidence that either burning-in or dodging has been done, though they may have been employed extensively.

Cropping: In a quality print the image has been cropped (proportioned and sized) to exactly fit the image requirements. There is neither too little nor too much picture space around the subject. The relation of picture height to width is exactly as it should be.

Sharpness: Unless pictorial requirements dictate unsharpness, the quality print is always sharp from edge to edge. This is often called grain sharpness, for many photographers use optical devices for focusing the grain present in all negatives. This is to make sure their prints are sharp. It is hard to tell when some images are in focus. However, when the grain is sharp you know they are. It can't be otherwise. Lots of photographers have a strong prejudice about grain sharpness and won't accept a print that doesn't have it.

If an enlarger lens isn't stopped down enough it will focus the image only in the center of the easel. The rest of it goes progressively out of focus toward the edges. Many cheap lenses will never give sharpness across the easel, even if they are stopped down.

These are the main criteria for print quality. You've probably seen that you'll need some experience in photography in order to understand them well. The concept "satisfy the requirements of the image" is a deceptive (and necessarily vague) oversimplification. If you sustain your interest in photography, you'll spend the rest of your life learning what it means. I'm sorry I couldn't give it all to you in a nutshell, but life just does not work that way. We seldom understand the answers it gives us until we no longer need to question.

This whole section on pictures should have opened up some avenues of investigation for you, possibly even answered a question or two. Do not be dismayed that photography has turned out to be a large subject. Each day you are somehow coping with a much larger one: life itself. Give yourself some time and you'll learn to handle photography very well indeed.

Learning to See

LIGHT

• What Light Does to Things

Early in the book you learned that light causes the chemical coating on film to react and form a latent image. Developing agents then make the latent image visible. Quantitatively, this is the entire basis of photography. If a sufficient quantity of light reaches the film it causes a reaction. For this purpose, light *quality* doesn't matter and any old light will do. However, there is more to photography than this. The secret to making fine pictures is to learn to handle light *quality*. Exposure meters can be relied on to cope with the quantity problem.

When we speak of light quality we are concerned with types of light sources and what they do to the world. That is, how do they make it look? Each type of light source has a different effect. And the appearance of each type of object is modified in a different way. For example, there is considerable difference between photographing something in sunlight or in the diffuse light streaming through a window. Depending on what it is, the diffuse light can enhance appearance and the sunlight degrade it, or vice versa. Thus, one must make the right choice for the picture to come out right.

The people most concerned with light quality are those who wish to make pictures that are aesthetically effective. However, even those who use photography as a recording medium should be aware of the many ways in which the appearance of things is affected by different light sources. This knowledge will help them make records which have greater visual clarity.

We have to understand what light does in order to consistently make visually coherent pictures. It is dead easy to make a photograph that is a visual morass, even to the point where we can't tell what its subject was. Making it clear, visually coherent, and meaningful is a difficult matter. We can count on luck some of the time, but more often photography is a skill largely dependent on our ability to see what light does to things.

Fortunately, the light problem does handle itself much of the time, so that beginners can make fairly commendable pictures without even being aware of light. They only get into trouble when they get more deeply involved in photography. Attempting more difficult things, they find their inability to cope with light quality defeating them at every turn. This is usually a low point in their experience in photography, sometimes even the lowest.

• Why We Have Trouble Seeing Light

When experienced photographers talk of seeing what light does to things they shorten the expression to "seeing light," which means the same thing. They universally declare that learning to see light is the most important thing in becoming an expert in photography (which is sometimes even referred to as the "art of light"). Having struggled with the problem themselves, they usually rate it as the most difficult one in photography.

Strongly dependent as we are on vision, it is odd that we have so little natural skill in seeing light. Without light there would be no visual world at all and we would have little knowledge of our environment. Photography wouldn't exist, of course, for there would be no way for making images or for looking at them if there were. There would probably be no country and no culture, for the absence of light would indeed be a disaster. Considering its importance, why do we see it so poorly?

One problem is that there are too many things in the world, and light affects them in too many ways, for us to keep track of them. We have enough trouble coping with the things themselves and don't wish to concern ourselves with what light is doing to them. It is quite enough that it makes them visible.

Light creates absolutely everything we see, for we see only images formed of light which has been reflected by things in our surroundings, or our eyes form images of the lights themselves. Every texture, detail, contour, color, tone, shape, volume, or brightness that is communicated to our brains comes from light. And almost everything we see has all these attributes. Certainly, this makes for great complexity. Learning to see better only adds to it.

Perhaps the main difficulty with our vision is that we never think that we're responding only to light-created electrical impulses traveling through the optic nerve. Instead, we respond directly to the things that reflect the light to us. Through the psychological phenomenon of projection we find ourselves out there with the objects, not in our own heads reacting to their reflected light energy. We are filled with their "thingness" and strongly disinclined to make ourselves aware that their appearance is in totality created by light. As long as we can see as well as we like we would rather ignore light most of the time. Furthermore, it is our nature to apprehend our surroundings in large *gestalts,* not in terms of discrete visual qualities like tone, line, and texture.

These are some of the things that must be overcome or compensated for in learning to see light. Despite the confusion, it is possible to confront the great complexity of the visible world and learn to see what light does to all of it. Following ordinary paths, this is very difficult to do. However, there are special paths that have been worked out for photographers and other artists. They involve ways of simplifying things in order to see them better.

● White-on-White

Simplification helps beginners in all of the visual arts. They start their education by drawing or photographing simple things, gradually working their way toward complexity.

Photographers usually deal with objects of one kind or another. Fortunately, there is a very easy way to simplify many of them: It is to paint them white. This simplifies by elimination, for it gets rid of color, color differences, tone (except white), and tone differences. Though these things are also caused by light, they are too much for the beginner when added to everything else he's trying to see. Temporarily eliminated, they can be dealt with later. In the meantime the less distracted student can learn to see other important things that light does.

This approach to learning to see is a very old one once used to train painters. Students were given white plaster objects, usually sculptures of heads or parts of the body, and were expected to spend several years drawing them carefully. At first they would find it very difficult to see the light and shade patterns on the objects, but after a time would eventually become quite adept at drawing them. By that time they would be experts at seeing some of the most important things that light does.

Long ago, photographers borrowed this idea from the painters, replacing charcoal or pencil with the camera. They added the idea of a movable light source, making it possible to change at will the light and shade patterns on white objects. Some teachers of photography simplified the visual problem even more by using objects of extreme structural simplicity, for example cubes, cylinders, spheres, and pyramids. In some photography schools these simple forms are used in teaching basic lighting.

The problem with such simple objects is that they make rather dull pictures. Because the project isn't very pictorial, the student slops through it, entirely forgetting he's supposed to learn to see something. Thus he gets a cruddy picture and wastes an opportunity to see better what light does to things. For people with a modicum of self-discipline these simple objects are very informative; photographers have been learning to see with them for many years. For the undisciplined they are a complete waste of time.

All is not lost, however, for some white objects are pictorially interesting. The plaster heads used by painters are, for they are usually good copies of Roman portraits in marble. Nowadays, there are many interesting things that are already painted white or made of white plastic. When painted, some fruits and vegetables look swell; even a boiled lobster becomes an interesting white subject. For many years, photographers have used white eggs for lighting practice, since they are cheap, available, and sculpturally perfect. One person stripped a discarded TV set and found many things that looked good painted white.

Finding interesting objects to paint is a part of the challenge. If you pick stupid, dull, or lumpy things, your innate aesthetic sense will rebel and you won't be able to force yourself to experiment adequately with lighting. Be sure to pick things for their form, not for their color, tone, or texture. They should be interesting in themselves, not for some other reason. To illustrate,

a lobster is interesting in itself, even though it's also good to eat, but a football is interesting only for what one does with it.

If you are going to do the experiments in this section you ought to select a variety of items to photograph, for you would soon get tired of playing with just one. Also, different kinds of objects are modified by light in different ways. If you wish to learn about light you have to give it a chance to do a few things.

Your objects should have a certain amount of bulk to them, like a bowl or jar. Things like straws, sticks, and flower stems are so thin you can't make light do much to them; and what little it does do you can't see very well. Things that lie flat on the surface are also a disappointment, so stay away from them. However, objects with bulk (body, volume) stand up from the surface where you can get at them with your lightings. They will help you see light.

Paint your collection carefully, preferably with matte-white spray enamel. Glossy enamel is not as good. If you use a brush, work wet enough to prevent brush strokes from showing. If you don't paint carefully, the results of your messiness will distract your vision so much you won't see what light is doing, which is the whole point of the work. Furthermore, they will spoil any picture you make. It is the photographer's nature that he wants to make good pictures while he's experimenting and if he doesn't he soon loses interest. Only a sustained interest in light will lead one to learn much about it. Don't let sloppiness interfere with your interest.

● **White Background**

Your background should be white too—all of it. When you look at your setups through the camera viewfinder you should see nothing whatsoever but things that are white in nature. The lightings may give them some other tone, but they have to be white to begin with. Then if tones other than white show up, as they certainly will, you will

LIGHT

know for sure they are caused by something you've done with light. You can trace down the causes, thereby learning how to handle lighting.

A piece of white paper or lightweight cardboard is convenient for a background, the larger the better. Small pieces cramp you, so you can't work with very many lighting variables. For small objects, a useful size is about 36 × 52 inches, though it's nice to have a larger one if you can find it. The paper should be spotlessly clean and free of creases, wrinkles, and scuff marks. Though you may not notice them while you are working, you'll discover them with dismay in your pictures.

Laid flat on a table, paper is good only for high-angle camera shots. However, you can curve it up a wall and get almost any angle you wish. Do this by pushing a small table (or ironing board, box, bureau, etc.) against a wall. Put one end of the paper flat on the table and let the other curve up the wall. Then tape down the four corners to hold it in place. It's usually best if the curve is fairly gentle. If it is too sharp it will show up in your pictures, which is not usually desirable.

When you put objects on the paper to light them, they should be fairly close to the front edge of the paper. If they are back near the wall you lose certain possibilities from the lightings. With really large background papers the distance from subject to wall can be quite long. It gives the photographer lighting control over the tonal relationship of subject and background, which is highly desirable. Though both are white, he can use lightings that will make the object white and the background black, and vice versa, or create tonal relationships that will fall somewhere between these extremes. If a beginner sees such things happen he can begin to understand that light (and nothing else) creates tonality.

Another convenient background is a white wall. Since it is large, the subject can be positioned far in front of it, giving the photographer tremendous control over the subject-background tonal relationship. If it is dirty, it can be far enough

away from the subject to be completely out of focus, thus preventing smudge marks and fingerprints in the image.

When we use only paper for backgrounds we get in the habit of placing our objects on a surface. Though it works most of the time, it can also be limiting. With walls, we can have subjects thrust up in the air, thus enabling ourselves to see them from fresh viewpoints. Using walls also teaches us how to make-do with something readily available. The better photographers are expert at this.

● **A Necessary Detour**

Enough has been said about white-on-white to present the experiments. However, there are many factors which haven't been discussed at all. Though the experiments involve simplification of objects with white paint, they themselves are quite complex. Without additional information you wouldn't really understand what you are supposed to learn from them.

Another reason for temporarily pulling away from white-on-white is that the things you will read will apply to photography in general, not just to making pictures of white objects. If they were presented only in the context of white-on-white you might find it difficult to see this.

● **Camera Equipment**

For working indoors, certain equipment is desirable, such as tripods, exposure meters, lights and so forth. Since indoor lightings are not very bright, exposure times are liable to be long. Few people have steady hands in the ½ to ¹⁄₆₀ seconds exposure range and this creates a problem of camera movement. The problem is easily solved with a tripod, provided one also uses a cable release.

Separate exposure meters are desirable, because built-in meters aren't sensitive enough to register many of the lightings you may wish to use. The best bet is a cadmium-sulfide meter like the

202

Gossen Luna-Pro, for it will even read moonlight. However, selenium meters like the Sekonic will do the job most of the time.

Working indoors, we frequently wish to photograph small objects, but they are minute in the camera viewfinder, and if we move the camera closer they go out of focus. However, if one uses a close-up lens they are magnified enough to fill the whole frame. They can also be magnified with an enlarger, but there is always a severe loss of quality if we push enlarging too far.

Photographers usually like to crop tight with their cameras, so that additional cropping while printing is unnecessary. This gives them the best quality possible with a given film-developer combination. Follow their lead and make your image fill up the frame. Close-up lenses are inexpensive and useful for many kinds of pictures. I recommend that you get one (or more) early in your career in photography.

• Lights

If you are to learn about light you must work with lightings for which you are entirely responsible. They give you the opportunity to study your subjects and figure out why light affects them the way it does. If the light is not under your control, this may be very hard to do.

The type of light you should dispense with immediately is ordinary room light or that which comes through the window. Though they are very useful in photography, you must bid them a temporary good-by. Together, they are often referred to as "available light." They are available in the sense they are already doing their thing for the photographer, and he doesn't have to manipulate them or use additional light sources.

Oddly, beginners invariably get better pictures with available light than with controlled, but it is because they haven't learned to see what light does. In positioning light sources under their control, they make serious visual mistakes, simply because they can't see them happening. When they use available light they are hardly aware of

light at all, and it automatically takes care of many of their visual problems. Working with available light, people can photograph for years without ever becoming aware of light as such.

Since controlled light may spoil some of your pictures, you may be tempted to avoid it. Don't. To learn, you need to make some mistakes. Without trial and error you may stall-out permanently on a plateau. By sticking for a while to light entirely under your control you will soon begin to understand the proper use of light. You will make good lightings and see them well. Furthermore, you will soon find you are also seeing available light better and understanding how you can modify it when desirable. No longer will you have to depend on gratuitous offerings from your visual environment.

We employ the white-on-white experiments to reduce visual complexity and make seeing easier. Further simplification is necessary for students. We are ordinarily confronted with too many light sources, except when we're in the sunlight. Too many sources makes it very difficult to see what each one is doing, which is precisely what we are trying to learn.

Beginners need months of drill in using only one light source. If there is only one it is much easier to sort out what it is doing. Such a limitation is not, as one might suppose, a pictorial liability to prevent your making fine pictures. On the contrary, it will make them much more probable. Thousands of fine pictures are made each year with just one light source. Indeed, many top-flight photographers rarely use more.

The most adaptable light source for photography is a photoflood bulb in a regular reflector. Clamp-on reflectors are all right, but reflectors on regular light stands are much better. There are also reflector bulbs, which have reflectors built into the back of them. Clamps can be put on them. If you have no light stand you can create one from a Christmas tree stand and a long stick. Clamp-on reflectors or bulbs can be positioned easily on the stick.

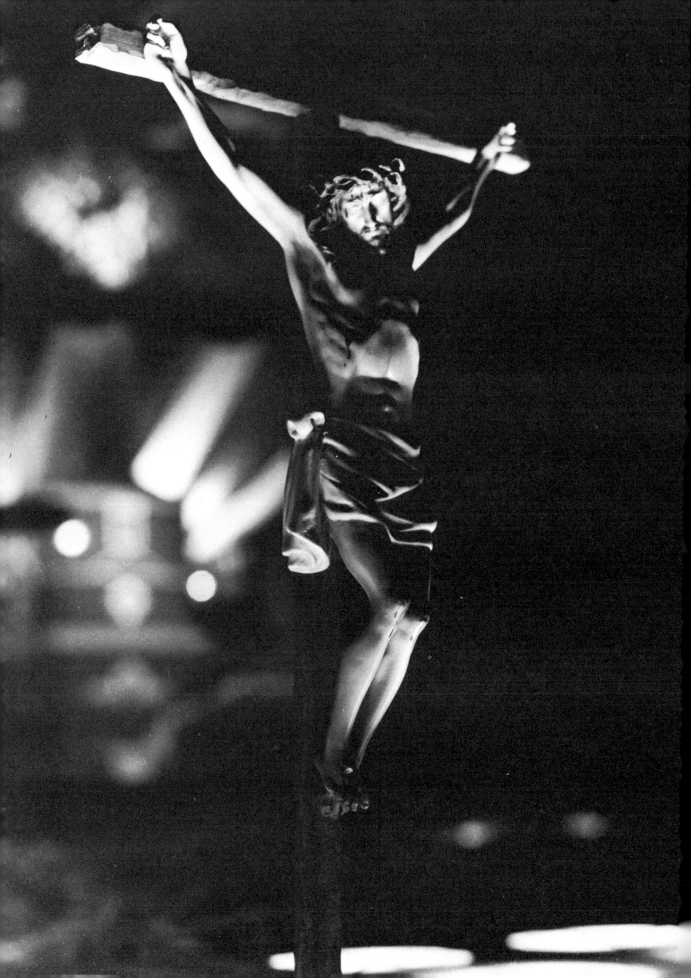

Most reflectors are round, which is good. Avoid the rectangular ones, because they limit you considerably. The round ones project the most useful light pattern: round, bright in the middle, fading out imperceptibly at the edges, until it disappears. You can see the pattern by pointing a light at a nearby wall. Rectangular reflectors cast patterns that break off sharply at the edges, which can ruin many a picture. They often have barn doors (light-control flaps or shades), which are used to change the shape of the light pattern. Though the idea is good, the barn doors cast irritating shadows. With a round reflector you can make really workable barn doors with pieces of cardboard held in place with masking tape or clothespins. The lighting patterns are good.

Because mobility is important in lighting control, it is desirable to have a lightweight light stand that can easily be moved around. Its standard should telescope from a rather low to a high position. The reflector should swivel easily on both its horizontal and vertical axes. Without such mobility one is severely limited in putting light through its paces. With experience, you can learn to do without some of it, but in the beginning you should have as much of it as possible.

• Direct, Bounce, and Edge Light

A light pointed right at a subject is called direct light. Pointed at a wall or other type of reflecting surface, it is bounce light. If it is aimed in front or behind the subject it is edge light, for only the edge of its light pattern strikes the subject. These are three of the most important lighting variables.

The easiest to use in making successful pictures is bounce light, followed at some distance by edge light. Direct light is very tricky and poison to all beginners, but they use it to slaughter pictures by the hundreds. Beginners cling to direct light because they find it impossible to believe that it is good to point the light everywhere but directly at a subject. Nobody but an expert can use direct light well.

Another reason people go for direct light is that it is much brighter than bounce or edge light, making it possible to use shorter exposure times. If we use tripods these shorter times aren't necessary, but beginners don't understand this. Thus, they feel compelled to use direct light and are very leery of bounce and edge light, which they should actually prefer.

When we do bounce or edge lightings with one floodlight, the shutter speeds 1, $\frac{1}{2}$, $\frac{1}{4}$, $\frac{1}{8}$, and $\frac{1}{15}$ are often necessary, yet they are entirely adequate if one uses a tripod. Longer exposures made with the B setting are frequently used, too. It really doesn't matter how long the exposure is. Objects sitting on tables or paper backgrounds aren't going anywhere, so you don't need fast shutter speeds to freeze their movements. Furthermore, even portraits can be made with speeds as low as $\frac{1}{2}$ or $\frac{1}{4}$ second. All you have to do is tell people to sit still or say nothing and wait for the moments of stillness that always occur naturally.

The figure was illuminated by bounce light striking it from both sides from below. The lights behind it were the mundane light sources one can see by looking out any city window at night. Putting them out of focus gave them a romantic and mysterious feeling. In sharp focus they would have ruined the picture.

• Light-Source Size

What a light source does to things is largely dependent on its size. The quality of shadows, for example, varies greatly with different sizes. Because shadows are of great importance pictorially, we'll look into what happens to them. There are two types: cast shadows and form shadows. The first are cast on surfaces by objects blocking off their light. Form shadows are on objects themselves on the surfaces that are turned part or all the way from the light.

Shadows create their pictorial effects through several means: their size, relative darkness, placement, shape, number, degree of connectedness with other shadows, edge quality, and so on. As you experiment with lighting you will gradually see what all these things do. The size of the light source mainly affects edge quality. It can create sharp-edge form and cast shadows, or soft-edge ones. In a given picture, the selection of type makes a considerable difference pictorially, for these types of shadow have very unalike qualities.

Sharp-edge form and cast shadows are created by small light sources, soft-edge ones from large sources. The sun, small in relation to our surroundings, creates sharp shadows. An overcast sky, which is huge, gives us extremely soft ones. A floodlight is relatively small, making fairly sharp shadows. However, if you point it at a wall, the wall itself (or part of it) becomes the (secondary) light source. Being larger than the diameter of the floodlight reflector, it creates softer shadows.

The percentage of the wall acting as light source depends entirely on the size of the circle of illumination created by the floodlight. If the light is up close it is small, but if it is far enough back it turns the entire wall into a source. Most walls are large enough to create shadows that are very soft indeed.

● Shadows

Without shadows, sharp or soft, most pictures would be very dull. Without them, especially form shadows, things tend to look unreal. Absence of shadows can even make things disappear altogether. In the white-on-white experiments, for example, a certain shadowless lighting will make white objects almost invisible in the camera viewfinder. Unbelievable, but true.

Shadows, especially in pictures, help us see space. Remove them all and the space disappears. However, shadows can also confuse space in

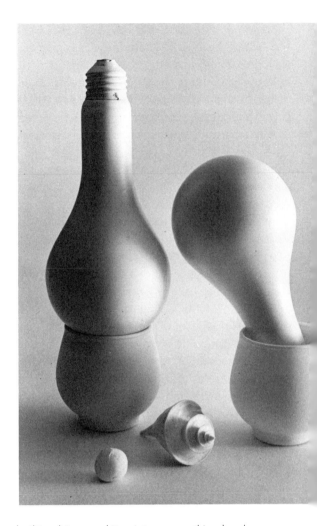

In this white-on-white picture everything has been sprayed with matte-white enamel. The grays and the strong tonal range have been created by the lighting (bounce light from the right). You can see that paint has turned cheap glassware and worn-out light bulbs into minor works of art. The shell didn't need this help.

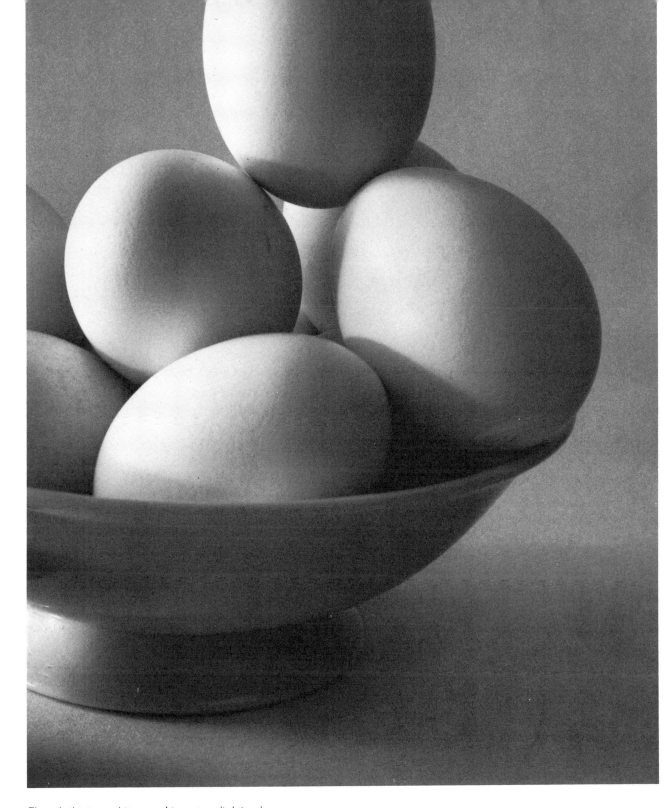

Though this is a white-on-white setup, lighting has
made gray the predominant tone. Can you look at the
shadows and tell what kind of a lighting it was? Notice
that the form shadows on the eggs have very soft
edges; so do the cast shadows in the foreground.
How many light sources were used? What are your
reasons for thinking this?

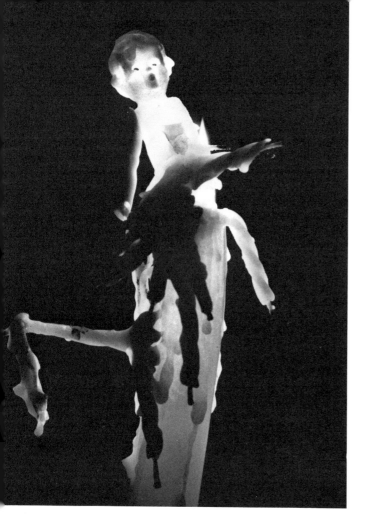

A plastic doll and white candle in front of a black background. The challenge was to make the subject look as if it were illuminated from within. The light source for the picture, another candle, was hidden behind the subject, just the tip of its flame showing.

pictures, turning it upside down, warping it, or eliminating it altogether. The culprits in this case are nearly always sharp-edge shadows. Though the space distortion in a picture is usually only partial, it happens so often that we should always be suspicious of sharp shadows. In contrast, soft-edge shadows rarely distort space, though they frequently lessen it.

Form shadows in pictures can create the illusion of form, or volume, but they can also destroy it. Pictorially, both things are useful; sometimes you want volume, sometimes not. Soft-edge form shadows are by far the best volume creators, yet they can also be used to diminish it. Sharp-edge form shadows are consistent volume destroyers.

When we return to the white-on-white experiments I will tell you how to see all these things

for yourself. Their very nature will make this kind of seeing much easier than usual. It is also why they were invented for students.

Shadows have an influence on visual complexity. Shadowless, a picture is as simple as its subject will allow it to be. Add a bunch of shadows and it gets much more complex. However, soft-edge shadows seldom complicate things much, whereas sharp-edge ones often do. They may even double or treble the number of shapes in a picture. This can make for great confusion, especially in black-and-white pictures. In color pictures the color itself helps sort out the confusion.

As a rule, photographers prefer soft shadows for almost all their pictures, for they reduce problems very considerably. In contrast, sharp-edge shadows are always a problem in themselves. For portraits in particular, soft-edge shadows are desirable. In consequence, photographers tend to limit themselves to fairly large light sources. Skylight has long been a favorite for portraiture, as have bounce and edge light.

Sharp-edge shadows can be especially disastrous on faces, which is why one should avoid small light sources, including the direct sun. These small sources also dramatize every minute textural detail on a face. Unless the skin is absolutely perfect this usually looks bad. Large sources diffuse these details, a cosmetically desirable effect. Sharp-edge shadows on faces frequently look like dark scars or paint slashes. When the whole figure is photographed they often create the illusion that its parts aren't stuck on right, for they tend to distort and twist form. All-in-all, one can do very well without small light sources and their sharp-edge shadows.

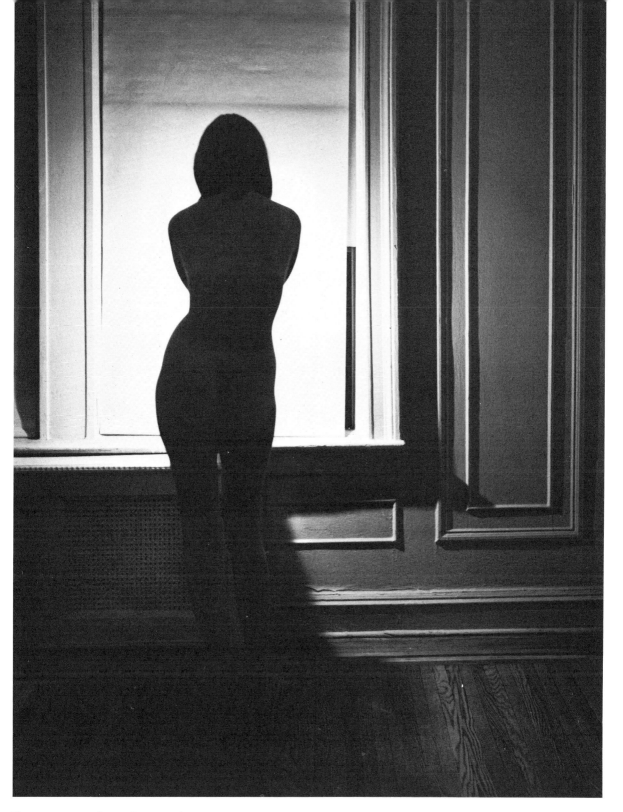

This was essentially a white-on-white project, even though the fair-skinned girl had brown hair and the floor was oak-colored. The walls and the window shade were bright white. The light source (small) is behind the girl, of course, and it is the only one in the room. The idea was to use light to create a certain mood.

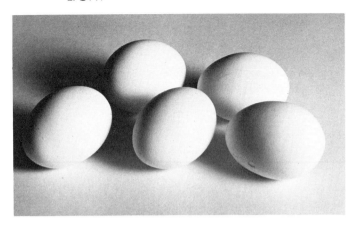

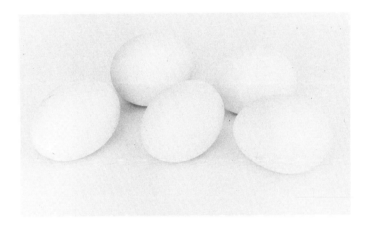

Two lightings of the same white-on-white setup.
Notice how the feeling of volume in the eggs differs
in the two pictures. In the top one they're solid and
round, in the bottom one flat and dimensionless.
Both pictures were made with bounce light, but it came
from different angles. As you see, the angle makes a
difference.

• Front, Side, and Back Lighting

The direction from which light strikes a subject
makes a lot of difference in the pictorial effect.
We generally describe the directions as front, side,
and back lighting. Beginners generally use the
least desirable, front lighting, because it is the
most obvious thing to do with a floodlight. Front
lighting doesn't give light a chance to do anything
interesting, like creating form and space. Instead,
it flattens everything out. Coming from behind the
photographer (or from between him and the subject), front lighting illuminates things too fully,
thus depriving them of their visual mystery. Thus
deprived, many things are dull and uninteresting.
Almost always it eliminates the "mood" from pictures.

As its name suggests, back lighting strikes the
subject from behind, often creating a full- or
semisilhouette effect. Sometimes you see just a
bright line around the edge of the subject. This
lighting is usually dramatic, because the picture
contrast is high and there may be areas of dramatically dark obscurity on the subject. However,
it is overdramatic for many types of pictures and
the obscure areas too extensive. Beginners should
experiment with it extensively, nonetheless, for it
helps reveal to them the unexpected possibilities
of photography. It also helps them break the bad
habit of wanting to light everything from the
front. Perhaps the most important thing to see is
that visual drama can be created at will in photography.

Side lighting is by far the most useful type,
especially if it is from a large source like the sky,
a picture window, or a wall used as a reflector.
It is very good for creating the illusions of form
and space and controlling the degree to which
they are realized. That is, you can have a lot of
both, or just a little. Side lighting gives us strong
control over the degree to which things are re-
vealed or obscured; and this is very important in
taking command of the medium. It enables us to
control pictorial mood, which most photographers
consider an absolute necessity.

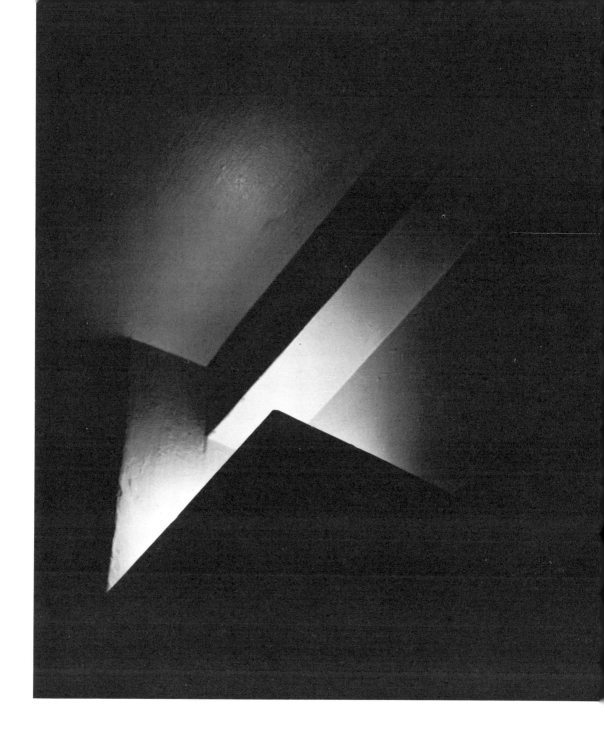

An all-white arrangement of walls and ceiling,
illuminated by a candle on top of a white cupboard.
It should prove that brilliant tonal contrasts can be
created by light alone. It also shows that we can
create a predominantly dark picture with a light
subject. Through lighting we can get any tones we
want.

With all three lightings we can use direct, bounce, or edge light. Remember, I told you to avoid direct light until you really know your stuff. Used from the side or back, it can be interesting at times, but from the front it is a disaster. In all three positions, bounce light is pictorially the safest. Edge light has to be fiddled with quite a bit with each subject, yet it has interesting possibilities from all positions.

● Light-to-Subject Distance

The beginner usually plops down a light stand near his subject and lets it just sit there. The expert moves it back and forth a lot. If it is pointed at a wall or reflector, he still moves it around in as many ways as he can think of, to see what he can make it do to his subject. Since the wall or reflector becomes the source in bounce light, he experiments with various positions for the reflector or moves his subject nearer, or farther away from, the wall.

Sometimes, subject and light source should be nearly rubbing noses. At others, they should be far apart, even ten feet or more. The only way to see which distance works best is to try them all. I haven't tried to tell you exactly what effects you'll get each time you manipulate a light, for that depends a lot on your subject and its background. There can be no absolute rules. The important thing is to try positions, distances, types of light sources, etc., so that you can see for yourself. Even knowing that you can do these things will give you a good start.

You should be convinced that there are innumerable experiments to perform with a light. Whether you try them is up to you. Certainly,

A white-on-white setup of hard-boiled eggs with their yokes removed. There was one white cardboard on the table top and another on the wall three feet away. The single photoflood was between the two and below table level. This accounts for the strange lighting on the eggs and the blackness of the foreground.

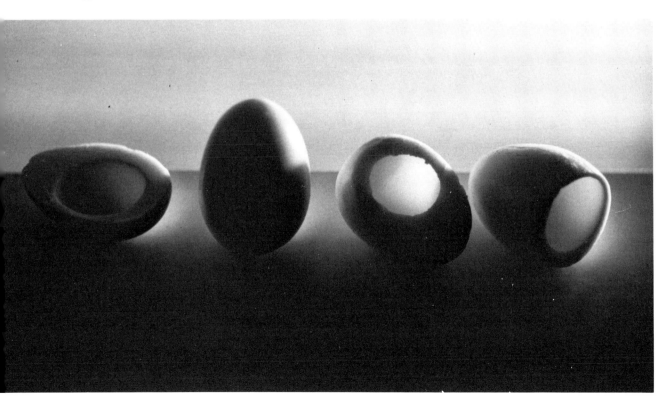

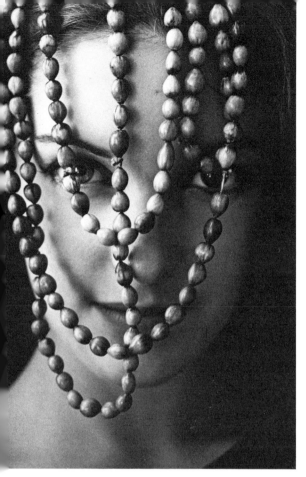
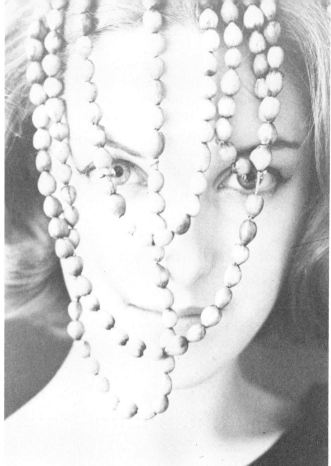

Both black and white obscurity are mentioned in the text. You get the first by losing things in blackness, the second by losing them in whiteness. It can be done either through lighting or printing. These two prints from the same negative show the two kinds of obscurity and the different feelings they create in images.

you should not just plop a light stand down and let it sit there forever, the way some beginners do. You should feel compelled to do *something* with it, even if you have great difficulty in really seeing the effects it creates. Stick to this struggle valiantly, if you can, for it is the very heart of the problem of becoming a photographer. Eventually, you will find that you can see, a wonderful thing.

● **Relative Obscurity**

Though the terms are used loosely, light and lighting don't mean quite the same thing. Light is the raw energy we work with. A lighting is what we do with it. Light always reveals, if there is anything to reflect it. However, a lighting may obscure more than it reveals. For example, a candle by a tree in a night forest is a lighting, yet we can only see three feet of bark and the rest of the forest is invisible. A spotlight on a dark stage is also an obscuring lighting, for it reveals just one actor and obscures everything else. Replace it with a match and the relative obscurity is even greater.

213

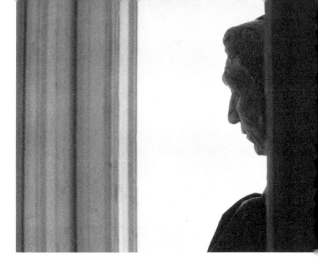

Without relative obscurity, photography would have far fewer expressive possibilities. Thus, becoming a photographer means learning to manipulate it, to make things more or less obscure at will. We should know how to reveal things as much as possible, obscure them to the same degree, or place them anywhere else we like in between. This is one of the most important skills involved in picture control.

There are several ways of obscuring something in a photograph. One is to underexpose the thing in the print, so there is nothing to see but white or very light gray. Another is to throw it far out of focus when photographing it, so that it turns into an undefinable blob in the picture. In printing, the thing and its surroundings can be burned-in to a full black, making it very obscure indeed. Cropping some of it off with the printing easel will make it partly obscure.

Though photographers use these methods a lot, their most important tool is lighting. An expert in lighting can make things as obvious or as obscure as he wishes. You will seldom need to totally obscure or totally reveal an object, but will always want it somewhere in between. The nuances of placement have a large influence on the success of pictures.

In general, large light sources reveal things, a bright overcast sky being one of the best examples. Striking a subject from just one side, large sources reveal less, for there are obscuring shadows. From the front, large sources reveal nearly everything.

Because they cast dark, sharp-edge shadows, small light sources obscure things a lot more

Though it seems not, this also was a white-on-white setup. The white-plaster head was near a white wall in one room, and the bright area behind it is a wall in another one. The large gray area shows details of a connecting hallway. The challenge was to use selective obscurity to make the sculpture come to life.

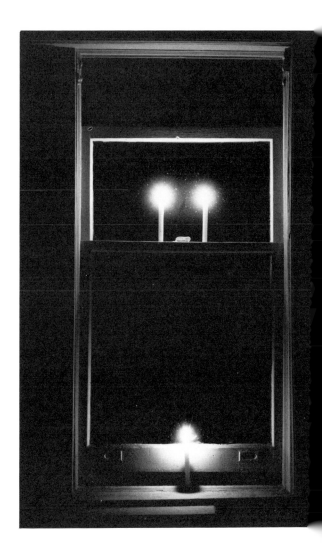

A picture made at night in a white-walled room, demonstrating that black obscurity is indeed easy to create if one knows how. It can be both dramatic and pictorial. The simple secret of making something black is to not let any light, direct or reflected, fall upon it. Blocking it off is the main problem.

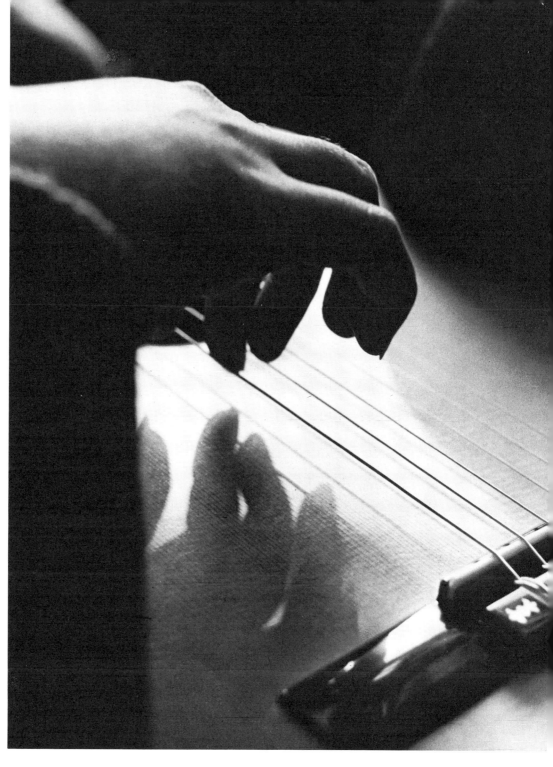

The homemade spotlight mentioned in the text was
used to make this picture. It shows that spotlights
create selective obscurity with ease and that they can
simplify subjects greatly. There is visual drama, of
course, and a detached and eerie feeling. It should be
obvious that a lighting creates both black and white.

than large sources. Not so much from the front, but from the back or side. Small sources in the form of spotlights obscure even more, for light is channeled into a beam that illuminates only the objects it is aimed at. Everything else is consigned to black obscurity.

Using a spotlight is a good experience, because it proves beyond a doubt that a lighting can create and control obscurity. However, it tends to make pictures overdramatic and is thus of limited use. You can make one by wrapping a foot-long cylinder of black paper around a 15-watt light bulb (a larger bulb would create a fire hazard). With this spotlight you can see all the basic effects and even take pictures, if you wish.

In learning to control relative obscurity it is best to work with side lightings, using medium to large light sources. Bounce light is good for this, because you can control its size by varying its distance from the wall. Combine this with varying the distance of the subject from the same wall; this will vary the lighting contrast.

• Contrast Control with Light Reflectors and Absorbers

An important factor in obscurity control is lighting contrast, which hasn't been mentioned before. High contrast with side or back lightings obscures things. Low contrast in all lightings reveals them. Mainly through contrast control we place things where we wish to on the revealed-obscured continuum.

One of the main reasons for working with just one light is to simplify the problem of seeing lighting contrast and learning simple ways of controlling it. Though an additional light can be used to control the degree of contrast, it isn't necessary. Furthermore, it would befuddle the beginner's head so that he wouldn't learn to see what either of his lights was doing.

Imagine light striking only one side of an object, leaving the other side in total shadow. The tonal difference between the two sides is called lighting contrast. The side with no light at all will look entirely black, even if the subject itself is light in tonality. Obviously, I've been describing a very high lighting contrast. It can be reduced simply by making some light strike the dark side. There are numerous ways of doing it. One way is to point another light at the dark side of the object. By moving it close or pulling it back, we can get any desired degree of lighting contrast, or eliminate it altogether. Though effective in contrast control, the second light is not desirable for a number of reasons.

Another way to reduce the contrast is to *reflect* some light onto the dark side. For this we use a light reflector, which isn't necessarily a special device for photographers only. A reflector is anything that reflects light; it's as simple as that. Most things do in some degree, even a piece of coal. Naturally, the best reflectors are things of light tone, preferably white, though light colors are also all right.

Walls are usually good reflectors; if they weren't, homes would be very dismal. Sheets and light-colored towels reflect well, as do white rugs and blankets. Aluminum foil that has been wadded up, then straightened out again, is popular with photographers. White window shades are often used. So are pieces of ordinary white paper or cardboard. The cardboards are especially useful when you are working with table top setups, because you can prop them up on the table near your subjects, just out of camera sight. Sometimes pieces only two or three inches square are useful as reflectors.

The degree of contrast on the subject depends on the closeness of the reflector and the amount of light striking it. Unlike a second light source, the reflector cannot entirely eliminate contrast. Since this is not desirable anyway, it is nothing to worry about.

You may find it hard to understand how reflectors are secondary sources of light, that light is actually coming from them. It isn't enough to know they wouldn't look white if this weren't so. Only direct experience will illustrate the point.

216

One way to see it is to point a light at an object and bring it very close. The other side will then look very dark. Next, bring a white cardboard up close to the dark side, positioning it to aim at the object but catch the full brightness of the light, too. You will see a dramatic lightening of the dark side. If you still need convincing, remove the card and put it back again several times, watching the object all the while. Until you've tried an experiment like this you may not believe that a reflector actually reflects.

It is even more difficult to see that a room is a multifaceted reflector: four walls, a ceiling, and a floor. Using all these reflecting surfaces we can create many lightings; it is just a matter of moving the floodlight around—here, there, up, down, sideways, etc. Contrast can be manipulated by the subject's positional relationship to the walls. For example, if you bounce a light from a wall and have the subject close to the light that is reflected, the contrast will be high. However, if you move the object slowly toward the opposite wall it will gradually lose contrast, because light reflecting from this wall will "fill in" the shadows. It does this even though there is no light source near it, for white or light-colored walls pick up light very readily. Experienced photographers use this knowledge about walls all the time.

Occasionally, we wish to reduce contrast entirely and eliminate as many shadows as possible. Using the room as a multifaceted reflector, there is an easy way. Standing in front of his subject, the photographer merely points his light back over his own shoulders, aimed partly at the ceiling and partly at the wall behind. This does a very effective job of flattening the lighting on the subject and filling in all the shadows. Because of the way light is reflected from the walls, ceiling, and floor, it strikes the subject evenly on all sides.

Sometimes the walls reflect more light than we like, for example, when we want our subject to have deep shadows. By reflection, the walls fill in the dark areas and we must find ways to stop them. This is the time to use a light absorber.

Placed near the subject, it makes one side perceptibly darker, because it blocks off light reflected from the walls and refuses to reflect any light itself.

Anything that is dark in tone is a light absorber, though this is hard to believe. It is dark *because* it absorbs light instead of reflecting it. We tend to think a black object is black because it is black and don't comprehend that it does something to light. It actually soaks up light like a sponge. As you've seen, there are times when this quality is useful in photography.

Black paper and cardboard are convenient light absorbers. Black cloth is good but not quite as adaptable. For the ultimate in blackness (light absorption), black velvet is the thing. In a pinch, one can use any dark thing that is available, even an overcoat. In some studios there are flats (small, movable walls) that are painted black on one side and white on the other. They help photographers reflect or absorb light at will, working very swiftly if they wish.

Bear in mind that this information on light reflection and absorption is mainly concerned with contrast control and that one of the important reasons for it is to control relative obscurity. Another significant effect is volume and space control. With no contrast, the feeling of space or volume in pictures is diminished or even obliterated. With too much contrast, the same thing may happen. However, just the right amount of it, in the right places, can create very strong illusions of volume and form.

• Evenness of Illumination

A lighting is said to be even if the light striking the subject is of the same intensity at all points. Sometimes this is desirable, sometimes not. In discussing the light pattern of a floodlight, I said that it is bright in the middle, gradually fading out toward the edges. Though the gradation is smooth, it still gives us uneven lighting. The photographer uses this smooth unevenness for pictorial effects.

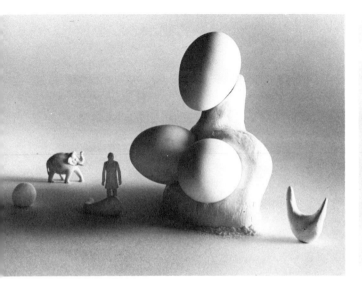
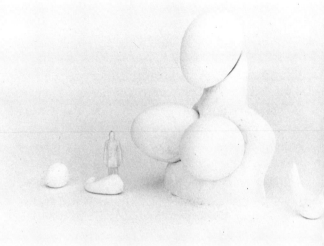

The purpose of these two white-on-white pictures is to show that light can both create and destroy space (depth, distance, dimension). Except for the lightings (and the elephant) the pictures are identical. The above one was made with bounce light, with a light absorber on the other side. For the picture on right, light was bounced from above and behind the camera position.

The challenge was to photograph five eggs, making one dominant and the others subordinate. Through lighting and clever arrangement, it could have been done in a white-on-white setup. However, a different approach was used. Four eggs were painted gray to match a gray background. Naturally, the white egg was bound to dominate.

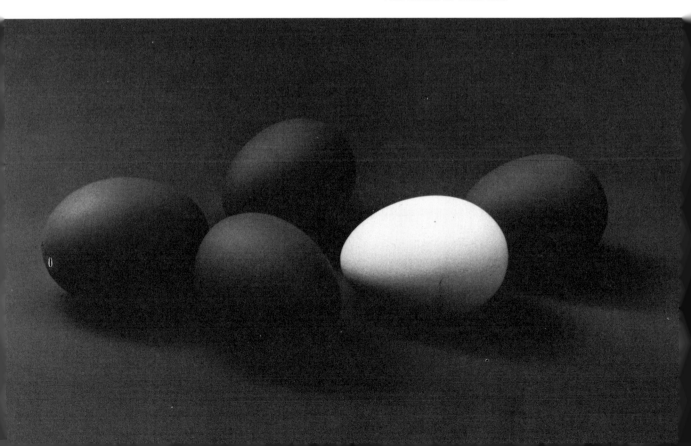

He even increases it considerably when he uses edge lighting.

The light pattern can be made very even if the floodlight is backed away from the subject; the greater the distance, the more even the illumination. Conversely, the closer the light the greater the unevenness. Front lightings, with bounce or direct light, with small light sources or large, can be made extremely even. Sunlight, open shade, and a bright overcast are the very best sources of evenness.

Because I've mentioned the subject, some readers will soon get themselves hung up on evenness, struggling to get it all the time in their lightings. There is no better way to limit oneself as a picturemaker. Evenness of illumination is good *sometimes,* but definitely *not* always. As a general rule, unevenness is much more useful.

The greatest need for even light is for making photographic copies of charts, posters, paintings, photographic prints, etc. Without it, prints come out with unsightly tones in the wrong places. They really look scruffy. However, when one is aware of the illumination problem and its simple solution, it is very easy to make good copies. Those in doubt should go outside and use the sun, open shade, or an overcast sky for making their copies. In sunlight, the copy material should be approximately perpendicular to an imaginary line drawn to the sun. If sunlight strikes it from the side it will emphasize all its surface defects; illuminated by a small light source, they cast unsightly shadows.

Sometimes we want even lighting in part of a setup, but not all of it. It is usually the background that we would like that way. Getting the background illumination *fairly* even is usually sufficient, because we can easily go the rest of the way by burning-in or dodging while printing. For some types of lighting this is necessary anyway, for example, side lightings with large light sources; there is almost always an unavoidable lighting fall off from one side of the set to the other. Often, such pictures look better if the background tone is *not* evened out, for the very unevenness may create a feeling of light and light direction that is very pictorial. In printing, the degree of this unevenness is easily controlled; one can have as much or as little as he likes.

Judging the evenness of illumination on a set is trickier than one might suppose, so that it is wise to depend on an exposure meter (as a brightness measuring device). To illustrate the problem, on a setup four feet across, the light on one side of the background may be two, four, or even eight times brighter than the light on the other side. At the same time, the photographer may not notice this difference, even though he is looking very hard to see it, it is there. Though it sounds ridiculous, this unevenness is quite common. It helps explain why experienced photographers check the corners of their sets with exposure meters. They can then make dozens of prints from one negative, without having to waste time on burning-in and dodging. With the light balance perfect in the setup, further tonal manipulation at the printing stage is unnecessary.

Though it is dangerous to generalize, there is an all-purpose trick you can use. There are few times when it won't work for pictures made with indoor setups, especially with simple backgrounds like a wall or paper. Either in your lighting or your printing, match the top two corners of your picture. Also match the bottom two. It is seldom necessary for the tones of the top corners to match the bottom ones. For unknown reasons, people like this tonal matching in their indoor pictures. But it is a studio trick that can become monotonous if used in every picture you make, indoors and out.

• Separation

Separation is one of photography's favorite terms. It refers to the tone difference (contrast) between two things that overlap in the camera viewfinder—for example, an object and its background. A substantial tone difference is called good separation. Little or no difference is called poor separation.

Far more often than not, it is good to have separation between all the overlapping things in a picture. When it is absent, things blend together in the print, spatial relations are confused and space lessened, and the apparent volume of objects diminished or destroyed. Things may even lose their identity. All of this ruins visual clarity in pictures.

The causes of separation are lighting and the natural difference in tone of objects. For example, two things of identical tone will separate easily if one is more brightly illuminated than the other. In even illumination, a gray object separates easily from black or white things.

In natural-light photography, separation is seldom a problem, for natural-light patterns are usually of fairly even intensity. However, when a problem does exist, little can be done about it except to look for another picture. In controlled-light photography, separation is frequently a problem, yet it can be solved easily through light manipulation.

In an even-light pattern, things usually separate themselves, because of their natural difference in tone. Variable-intensity light patterns (from a floodlight, for example) often blend things of a different tone together. To illustrate, if a light object is placed in front of a darker one, they will separate easily if they receive the same amount of illumination. However, in a variable-intensity light pattern the darker object may be more brightly illuminated, making it match the lighter object in tone. Naturally, this is called poor separation, or a blend.

In the white-on-white experiments, that begin on page 104, the separation problem is artificially exaggerated, because everything on the set is white and there is no natural tone difference to separate things. The only tool for creating separation is the light-intensity differential. At first, you may see this problem as hopeless. With enough experience, you'll see you can create good separation at will and that by exaggerating the separation problem you are able to find all its solutions.

Offhand, one would think that having things of different color and tone in a picture would automatically solve the separation problem, but it just doesn't work out that way. I've said that the intensity of light striking an object will affect its tone; the angle of illumination will do it too, for it affects the degree of light absorption.

In sunlight or open shade the illumination angle is no problem; things are all illuminated from the same angle. In a controlled lighting, the light source will not only be closer to some things than others but will strike them at different angles. For both reasons, the separation between lighter and darker things often disappears, and if one isn't looking for it he may not see it. It shows up strongly in prints, when it is too late to correct the problem.

Photographing things of different colors will guarantee separation only if we are using color film. With black-and-white photography it is no insurance at all. In this case, tone difference is all that counts. Black-and-white work makes it necessary to see colored things in terms of their tone, intentionally disregarding their hue and brilliance. It is hard to do this, especially with very strong colors, for we are so distracted by their vibrancy we can't decide whether they are dark, medium, or light in tone. However, our film can; if colors don't separate tonally it will automatically blend them together.

It is usually good to have the majority of the overlapping areas in a picture well separated, but have quite a few tonal blends, too. Most of the illustrations show this. It's just that the latter shouldn't predominate. A little blending here and there adds space to a picture and volume to the objects in it. Separation and blending work as a team. Separation for its own sake is not good. If you have it all the way around the edge of everything it usually creates a strong feeling of artificiality, as if things were pasted onto the picture.

For the student, the important things are to be aware of separation as an element in pictures, to learn to see it, and to try to comprehend its pictorial effect. It is not something to worship, as many photographers do, but a useful tool to be used in two directions. That is, one should learn how to both increase and decrease it, for each effect can be useful in picturemaking.

• Tone Is Relative

We strongly tend to believe that the source of an object's tone is the object itself. It is a primitive way of thinking developed early in life. We say a thing is dark because it *is* dark or light because it *is* light, and that's all there is to it. This explains nothing, of course. There is actually only one source of tone: light. By falling on things, light creates their tone; and as light intensity changes, tone does too. Thus the objects in our world are changing tone all the time, because light intensity is constantly varying, affected by time of day or year, weather conditions, indoor or outdoor environments, etc. We are strongly aware of the light variations but only casually aware of how they change tone. The photographer should make himself acutely aware of tone change, though it isn't easy to do.

For the beginner, the problem is to see that a black cat isn't always a black cat, a challenge trickier than it seems. According to how he is illuminated, it is sometimes black, more frequently dark gray, and occasionally medium gray. Though we always see it as black, the camera sees the variations. Depending on his tonal environment, it can even see the cat as a light gray.

Stated another way, the problem is to learn to see that the tone of an object is relative to light intensity and the object's reflection-absorption characteristics. The latter is easy to see; we know very well that a black cat is black (high light absorption, little reflection), a white rabbit white (high reflection, little absorption), and a gray goose gray (average reflection and absorption). The difficulty is that the cat, the rabbit, and the goose are changing tone all the time and we hardly see it.

One of the reasons is that we usually see things in familiar contexts. That is, we experience the same things and environments each day. Part of each context is a light-to-dark tonal hierarchy into which everything fits. We see each thing in terms of this tonal context and decide whether it is light, dark, or medium in tone. However, the label we give it is relative only to the context, not to the actual amount of light being reflected at a given time. We are little interested in the fact that the entire group of things shifts up and down in tone with variations in light intensity. As long as things within the group keep their places in the tonal hierarchy we are entirely satisfied.

If we can make ourselves more aware of tonal contexts and learn to think of tone as relative, it greatly helps our understanding of light. Through variable-intensity lightings, tonal contexts can be changed considerably. The tonal relationships of objects within the context naturally change, too. Thus, in a particular lighting a gray duck becomes white and a white rabbit gray. The camera viewfinder confirms it and so does the final print.

Though what I've said may seem self-evident, it isn't when you try to see it happening. For many years I've watched students struggling with the problem. One has to work hard and cleverly to irrefutably prove to himself that the tone of an object is mainly dependent on the intensity of the light falling upon it.

Mechanically, it is simple to set up the proof. For example, it is dead easy to put, say, a sugar lump in front of a sheet of black paper and make a picture in which the sugar is dark gray and the background dead white. From near the camera they will look this way, also through the viewfinder. The final print will strongly confirm it. All this evidence should certainly prove that a white thing has turned gray and a black thing

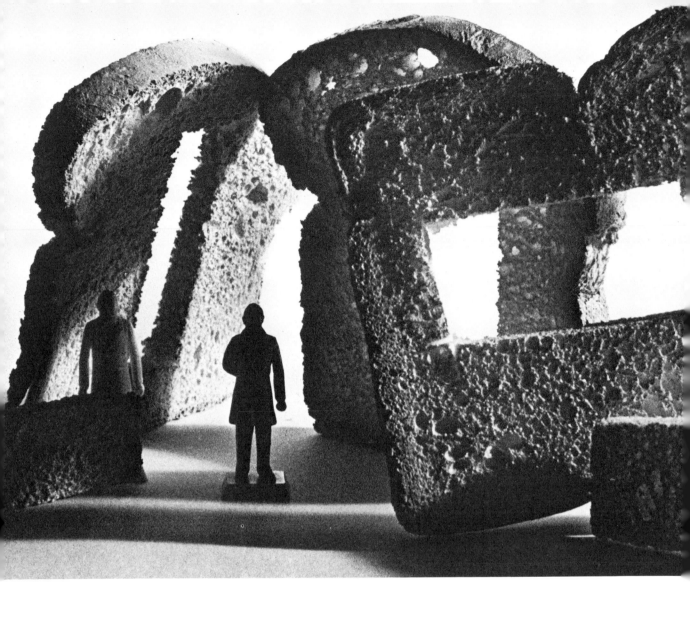

white. Nonetheless, people can't see it while they are staring right at it.

Considering all the information given on light and lighting, you should be able to guess how to do the sugar-lump experiment. Put the sugar on a black piece of paper and separate sugar and black background by several feet. Turn out all the lights but one photoflood, which should be close to the background paper and pointed right at it. Be sure that none of its light hits the sugar. Surround the sugar lump on two sides and top with black paper. You can make it dark gray, and with a

little fiddling, you can even make the sugar as black as coal. Your problem is in believing what you see.

Except for forcing yourself to see something, it is not especially useful to know how to make black sugar lumps. The important thing is to know how to make *subtle* tone changes and to clearly see them happening. Even knowing that tones *can* be changed at will is a great help. Obviously, the primary tool is light. Increase its intensity in part of a set, the tone is lightened. Decrease the intensity and the tone is darkened.

One of the primary reasons for the white-on-white experiments is to see without a doubt that tone is mainly relative to light intensity. By doing the lightings you will create a multiplicity of tones —from black through a variety of grays to white —in settings that are entirely white in nature. These tones will be inescapably there and their relationship to light intensity will be equally inescapable. Let us hope you don't escape the inescapable by refusing to see it when you are making it happen.

To make sure that everything started out as a flat white in this setup, I sprayed the bread slices with white enamel. The center of the light pattern was on the background, only its edges striking the bread and the figurines. My idea was to show that a dramatic, dark picture can be created with a white-on-white setup.

• Cast Shadows for Light Control

In the foregoing sections you learned that light of variable intensity is very useful for controlling tonal relationships. The light source recommended, a single photoflood, casts an illumination pattern varying from bright in the center to very dim at the edges. With this variation alone, a tremendous number of things can be done. Bounce and edge light offer many additional possibilities. Nonetheless, it is desirable to have even more control over lightings.

Cast shadows are frequently useful for control; by falling on part of a subject they darken it relative to the other parts, a fact quite obvious. It is less obvious that the darkening can be so subtle it doesn't even look as if shadows were involved. Though shadows that look like shadows are sometimes useful, subtle shadows can do a lot more things.

Subtlety depends on the location of the shadow caster (the object that obstructs the light) relative

A white egg with white pushpins on a white table top in a white-walled room. The light comes from the window, which is out of focus behind the egg. This picture makes it obvious that a lighting can create blacks as well as whites. It should also be clear that black is merely the absence of light.

to the light source and the subject. If it is very close to the light source and well away from the subject, it will create subtle shadows with very soft edges. They won't even look like shadows especially, but they will effectively alter tonal relationships in the set. They can be made large or small, depending on the size of the shadow caster.

Shadows become less subtle as the light source is moved back from the set and the shadow caster toward it. We reach a point where they are very dark with sharp edges. Though they are obviously shadows then, they can be very useful at times. Whether one should use obvious cast shadows depends mainly on what the lighting is already . doing to the subject. If there are strong shadow patterns, additional sharp shadows wouldn't be unduly noticeable. A carefully positioned shadow caster of the right shape will create shadows that will fit in well with those already there.

Anything that blocks light can be used to cast shadows. In small setups, one can often use a book stood on end, controlling the width of the shadow by angling the book. For larger shadows, sheets of cardboard are useful. One can use a simple dodger, like the type used in printing, but much larger. Some photographers put them on light stands and call them head screens. Sometimes a photographer makes a shadow with one hand, using the other to trip the cable release. I've even seen people used as shadow casters.

For subtly darkening large areas, it is often good to work with shadow casters close to the light source, or even fastened to it with tape or clothespins. For this purpose, sheets of light cardboard are very convenient, either whole or cut into smaller shapes.

● The Peephole-and-Squint Trick

Only an experienced visual artist can look at something and easily see all the things that light is doing to it, and even he can't do it all the time. Occasionally, he has to rely on tricks to help him.

Beginners need them most of the time, once they've learned how to use them. The most important ones have been around for years and are thoroughly proven.

One of the reasons we can't see very well is that there is much too much happening in our visual environment. When we try to see an object or visual quality we are distracted by dozens of other things bidding strongly for our attention. It happens indoors and out, and even if we are looking at an isolated object sitting on a paper background, the distractions are invariably there in quantity. Furthermore, parts of an object may prevent us from seeing other parts, or within a given part conflicting visual qualities may confuse our perception. Worst of all, we are not even aware that all these distractions exist, though without our knowing it they plague us all the time. They make us relatively blind to the world we live in.

The solution, of course, is to temporarily eliminate distractions from our field of vision, since they are making it difficult for us to see. Though there are numerous ways to do it, the easiest is to use the fingers to make a peephole to look through. (The opening should be about the size of a dime.) When we look through it, most of the visual environment is excluded. The trick is to have one eye closed and the one at the peephole squinted nearly closed.

Squinting through the peephole, a photographer examines his subject several times area by area, each time concentrating on a different visual quality. One time color, the second time contrast, the third time separation, etc. Dividing the subject into areas and separate visual qualities helps you see each of them better. Though he also tries to see it as a whole, it is a much more difficult problem.

The reason for squinting is to eliminate some more of the visual distractions. In squinting we look through our eyelashes, which then obscure eye-catching details. This frees our attention to devote itself to other things. It helps us see shadow patterns, contrast, the tonal relationship of colored objects, composition, the edge quality (sharp or soft) of shadows, tonal blending, and separation. It also helps us see which parts of a subject are visually dominant (very eye-attracting) and which are subordinate (making little bid for our attention). Squinting can be used with or without the peephole, for both serve the same purpose. One can also learn to do it with both eyes at once, though perception is more complex that way.

At first, using the peephole and squint trick doesn't help very much, because we let our attention wander a lot and don't quite know what we are looking for. It is also hard to squint steadily for periods of twenty or thirty seconds with the eyes closed exactly the right degree. Learning to concentrate is the more difficult task, but using the peephole trick helps us to do it. This is good, for learning to see is largely a matter of bringing wandering attention under tight control.

A person teaching himself to see should be squinting much of the time. It takes strenuous effort and the eye muscles get very tired. However, no harm is done and one gets used to it. There is no escaping the fact that very hard work is necessary for developing better vision. Perhaps the hardest part is to decide what one is looking for.

● The Picture-Frame Trick

Some photographers use black paper or cardboard frames for viewing their subjects. Like peepholes, frames isolate things from surrounding distractions. They can be used with the eye either open or squinted. If a frame is held motionless in front of a subject, it gives the feeling of looking at a framed picture, especially if the head is also motionless and one eye closed. With the image neatly isolated, it is easier to look at it analytically.

The effect is like looking through the camera viewfinder, but the frame is much faster to use. If the camera is on a tripod, using the viewfinder to examine the subject from different positions is a very cumbersome process. The image in the

paper frame is also much larger and easier to see. Lighting phenomena that might escape attention in the viewfinder stand out clearly in the frame.

A convenient size is an 11 × 14-inch cardboard with a 4 × 5-inch rectangular hole cut in it. It should be neatly cut, or the frame itself will distract attention, the very thing we are trying to eliminate. Holding the frame close to the eye gives us a wide view, at arm's length we get a narrow one. For an area-by-area check of a subject, we move up close to it with the frame held at arm's length. We use the frame in basically the same way as the peephole and try to see the same things: shadow patterns, contrast, separation, etc.

When using the various tricks for examining a subject it is important to stand along the line of sight of the camera lens, either in front of the camera or behind it. We want to see the same things that the camera does. If we examine the subject from the side we get a poor idea of how the picture will come out and can make big mistakes in our lighting. For example, overlapping parts of the subject may be well separated when viewed from the side but totally blended together in the viewfinder. For many pictures this would spell disaster, and other things equally bad could happen. So always stay near the lens axis when sizing up a subject. It is hard to remember at first, but one gets used to doing it in time.

● Polaroid Check Pictures

For those who can afford a second camera, a Polaroid Land camera is very good to have. Professional studio photographers often use it to check their exposure calculations, compositions, and over-all lighting patterns. Though one could make area by area checks on a subject by making numerous Polaroid close-ups, it would be a very expensive procedure. It is best to make just one shot of the entire setup to get an impression of it as a whole.

Sometimes, a photographer has several lightings in mind but can't decide which one he likes best. If he takes a Polaroid of each he can compare them side by side, instead of relying on his memory of what they all looked like. Most people's visual memory is rather poor, and this includes photographers.

Polaroid shots are too small to be of much use in seeing details, but their very smallness makes them very good for seeing the over-all light and shadow pattern, composition, cropping, and the illumination balance from one side of the set to the other. Sometimes such things are harder to see in larger pictures.

● The Moving-Light Trick

We all know that moving things attract our attention and that it is hard to concentrate on things that are sitting still. These facts can be applied to the problem of seeing what light does. When we've made a lighting on a set we may shirk analyzing it carefully. It is very hard work for the eyes and they rebel. However, if we swing the light source back and forth, the resulting movement in the light and shade patterns makes it easier for the eyes to concentrate on what light is doing to the subject. The movement also shows us a variety of lightings to choose from.

If we do two lightings at 10-minute intervals, it is hard to compare them for quality. The visual effects of the first one have slipped from memory. However, if we move the light source rapidly from one to the other, comparison is much easier. It is also less fatiguing. We must always remember that learning to see is very hard work, sometimes to the point of causing nausea, and do what we can to make it easier for ourselves.

Though the moving-light trick is used for comparing different lightings and make seeing less laborious, it is also excellent for the same things as the peephole, the frame, and the Polaroid picture. Movement as such attracts our attention to all the effects created by light.

The tricks can all be combined in various ways. If one of them isn't working well for you, try it with another. Say you are using a frame in an attempt to see the separation in a part of a setup and are having no luck at all; the separation is there but you can't see it. Start moving the light source. It constantly increases and decreases the separation, making it easier to see—especially through a frame. Or say a moving light source isn't making things clear to you; squinting may be just the addition needed. In fact, the two tricks are often combined.

You must understand that trying a trick only once or twice won't do a thing for you and that each time you use it you should repeat it many times. Even a lighting expert does. Using the moving-light trick on a difficult and unfamiliar subject, you might switch the light back and forth twenty or thirty times. This gives you ample opportunity to analyze your subject and see everything that light does to it. With a familiar subject you may have to move the light only four or five times, however.

Repeating a trick many, many times is especially important for the beginner, because you still don't know for sure what you are looking for. With sufficient repetition, the trick itself helps you learn. This is naturally very fatiguing at first, but it is the price for learning to see.

● The On-and-Off Trick

This trick is useful when you are using more than the one light source recommended for beginners. The problem with a second (or third or fourth) light source is that an inexperienced photographer can't see what it does to the light and shadow pattern already created on the subject by the first light. In consequence, the additional light source destroys all the good qualities carefully created with the first one.

However, there is a simple way for learning to see what the second light is doing. It is to snap it on and off many times while making an area-by-area examination of the subject. One looks for *changes* in shadow pattern, contrast, separation, dominance and subordination, etc. With all the tricks we look for the same things; it's just that there are different ways of doing it.

It is generally a good idea to combine this trick with squinting through a frame or peephole, though experienced photographers usually just squint. They do it automatically whenever they are creating lightings.

The tricks I've described are the main ones used in photography. With practice, you can learn what you are supposed to see with them, then learn to see it well. The over-all objective, of course, is to learn to see light.

• Some Observable Qualities of the Visual World

One of the beginner's toughest problems is to learn what to look for when creating lightings, using available light of various kinds, choosing and arranging subjects for pictures, using tricks for seeing better, making prints, etc. In all these cases you are looking for the very same things, but don't know what they are. Ignorance makes learning to see a laborious and frustrating problem. However, when you have learned what to look for, the task is much easier. This book can go only so far in helping you, because seeing and understanding depend so much on personal experience and inner growth.

Many of the visible qualities that light creates in things have already been discussed. Most of them can also be observed in photographs. They are being repeated now in concise form, as well as some not mentioned before, which will be discussed at greater length.

The qualities differ considerably, for some can be measured objectively, while others can only be assessed subjectively. We could call the former "objective visible qualities," for they can be measured or mapped with instruments; and many people can observe them and arrive at identical conclusions concerning what they've seen. Some examples are separation, contrast, dominance, and visibility.

We could call the others "semisubjective visible qualities," because the observer is always a part of the thing observed. That is, these qualities are simultaneously things in the visual world and reactions to them in the observer. This complicates the problem of learning how to see, for it means having to turn one's attention inward and outward at the same time. Though it would simplify matters to dispense with semisubjective visible qualities, it would also make it impossible to learn to see. We cannot eliminate the subjective factor, for seeing the world involves seeing oneself, and vice versa.

Some of the semisubjective qualities are beauty, pictorialism, and clarity. Though they are things that we can see, our perception of them is strongly influenced by experience, taste, and sensitivity. Thus, people's reactions to them vary. We can say that such qualities have both subjective and objective components. For example, an object is beautiful only because people think that it is (subjective), but it has certain visible qualities that make it that way (objective). However, not everyone will agree it is beautiful (subjective).

Listed below are forty visible qualities in pairs, each of which is a continuum. If you always think of them this way it will help you to see. For example, you should remember there are all degrees of separation and blending, sharpness and softness, contrast and flatness, etc. In handling light, the objective is to create the degree of, say, contrast that satisfies the requirements of a given picture. It could be a lot or very little, for there is nothing good about contrast as such. It is merely a visible quality that can be manipulated for a variety of reasons.

The photographer's problem is to place visible qualities in suitable places on their continua, not to try to move them to the extremes. For example, pictures seldom need extreme contrast or flatness, for something in between is usually more appropriate.

The pairs are not opposites in terms of their "goodness" and "badness," though it may appear that desirable qualities are paired with undesirable ones. Certainly, we prefer clarity to confusion, strength to weakness, and beauty to ugliness. However, confusion, weakness, and ugliness can make important contributions to pictures. Indeed, some pictures wouldn't make any sense without them.

Usually, both sides of a continuum are in a picture, each acting as a foil for the other. For example, a static surface helps a dynamic object, unimportant subordinate things help an important thing achieve necessary dominance, and so on. The problem is not to rid pictures of opposites, but to use them well. Playing opposites against each other is an important part of the photographer's art. It involves learning to move at will in either direction on all of the continua.

Light is not entirely responsible for the visible qualities, because things make their own contributions, too. Skillful lighting will not make a thing of beauty of a dead crocodile, but it will help us tolerate it. It can't make a beautiful woman look like an old witch, though it can dim her glory somewhat. The important thing is that lightings have an affect on all the qualities listed.

All the continua interrelate and overlap, so that working on one of them, say, contrast and flatness, may affect ten others. If a person is adjusting the contrast of a subject he should watch how the other things change, too. Though this complicates the problem of learning to see, we learn to live with it in time.

- **Visible Qualities, Objective and Semisubjective**

1. separation—blending
2. contrast—flatness
3. dominance—subordination
4. sharpness—softness
5. simplicity—complexity
6. volume—flatness
7. space—two-dimensionality
8. visibility—obscurity
9. clarity—confusion
10. diffuse—specular
11. heaviness—lightness
12. strength—weakness
13. obvious—subtle
14. dynamic—static
15. evocative—non-evocative
16. pictorial—non-pictorial
17. reality—unreality
18. beauty—ugliness
19. interesting—uninteresting
20. rational—irrational

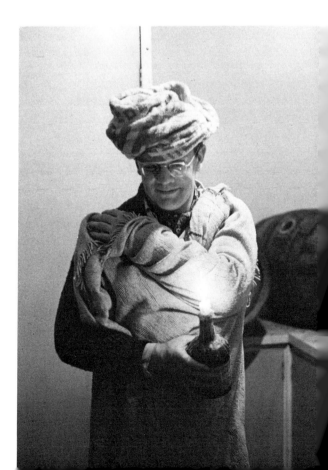

Working by itself, the ceiling light would turn this man into a silhouette, for it is well behind him. However, the candle is just barely strong enough to lighten his face and pick up highlights on his hands and clothing. Nonetheless, there is still a semisilhouette effect, which separates him from the background.

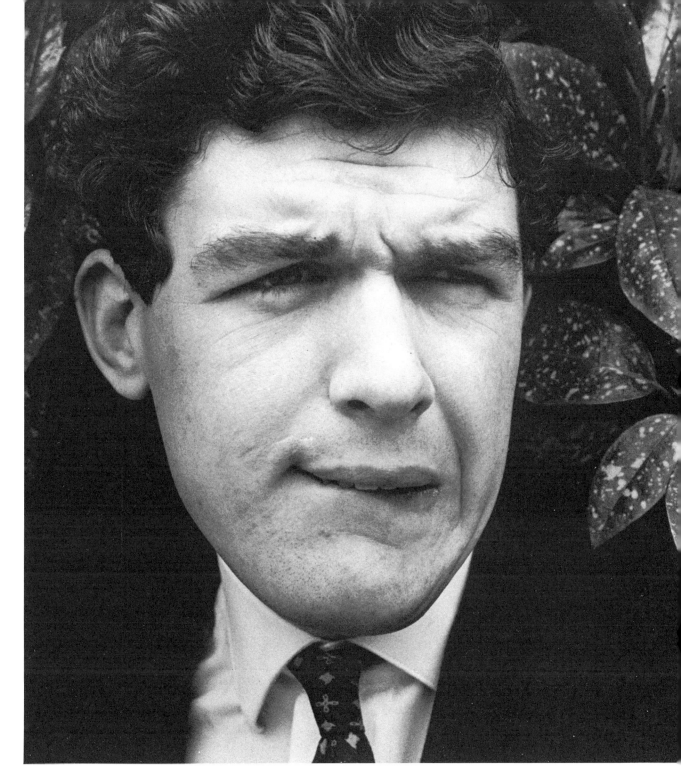

This young actor was lit by a very large light source: a huge skylight. Such a lighting is very, very flat. It gives the many form shadows on his face such soft edges that they don't even look like shadows at all. It also eliminates lighting contrast to a large degree. However, we have "natural" contrast here.

1. *Separation and blending:* The degree of tone difference (contrast) between things that overlap in the viewfinder. Separation and blending can be changed by using another angle of illumination, changing the distance between the things that are overlapping, choosing between an even or a variable-intensity light pattern, and using reflectors, light absorbers, or shadow casters.

2. *Contrast and flatness:* The degree of tone difference between parts of a subject. High contrast generally comes from small light sources (including spotlights), side lightings, and lack of fill light from reflectors or walls. Flatness comes from large light sources, front lightings, and maximum reflection from walls or reflectors on the shadow side of the subject.

3. *Dominance and subordination:* The degree to which things attract and hold our attention. Dominance depends a lot on uniqueness; the more unique things are to us the greater their attraction. Subordination leans heavily on familiarity and similarity. A thing that we're used to, that is surrounded by others like itself, doesn't attract the eye. Lighting can make a thing *tonally* unique or similar to other things in its environment, thus affecting the degree of its dominance or subordination. The two qualities work as a team. The usual idea is to make important things dominant, less important ones subordinate. Subordinate things act as a foil for those that are dominant.

4. *Sharpness and softness:* This category is concerned with the apparent sharpness of subjects, not of images. Apparent sharpness is strongly influenced by contrast and the edges of cast and form shadows. Small light sources create dark, sharp-edge shadows and high contrast, thus causing an over-all feeling of sharpness. Large light sources create lighter shadows, softer edges, and lower contrast, causing a feeling of softness. The ultimate in sharpness would come from an infinitely small light source, the ultimate in softness from a very diffuse one large enough to entirely surround the subject.

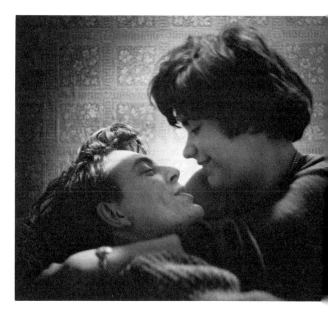

From the very soft tonal gradations on their faces, you can tell that the lovers were being struck by light bounced from somewhere in the room. The bright spot comes from a table lamp behind them. The wallpaper was extremely garish, but the dim light toned it down very nicely. We call this effect "subordination."

5. *Simplicity and complexity:* The simplicity or complexity of a subject is mainly determined by the number, size, and variations in contour of the shapes it contains. Objects are shapes (or groups of them). Shadows are also shapes, though soft-edge ones are sometimes so subtle we can barely see them as such. Sharp-edge shadows (from small light sources) are easily perceived as shapes and usually add to the complexity of a subject by increasing the number of shapes in it. Soft-edge shadows (from large light sources) contribute to simplicity, especially if they are very light.

Bounce light coming from above and behind the camera removes nearly all shadows; if all parts of the subject are of the same natural tone, the simplicity is nearly total. A lighting that makes most of the shadows join together is also a simplifier, for it diminishes their number. Though it causes sharp shadows, a spotlight can simplify greatly by leaving almost everything obscured in deep shadow.

6. *Volume and flatness:* Depending on what light is doing to it, a solid opaque object may look either like a volume or a flat shape. Though we *know* it is a volume, it doesn't always *look* like one. In photographs especially, objects can look as flat as pancakes, which may or may not be desirable. To convey a strong feeling of volume, an object should be quite a bit lighter on one side and well-separated from its background. There should be a smooth tonal gradation from light to dark, not a sharp break between highlight and shadow.

Side lighting with medium to large light sources usually creates the feeling of volume. Most front lightings and all low-contrast lightings create flat-

A white body, white walls, and two white candles—but we have a dramatic picture that is predominantly black. Because they are small light sources, candles create strong shadows and high contrast. Though they are a lot of fun to work with, one needs an ultrasensitive meter like the Luna-Pro for reading exposures.

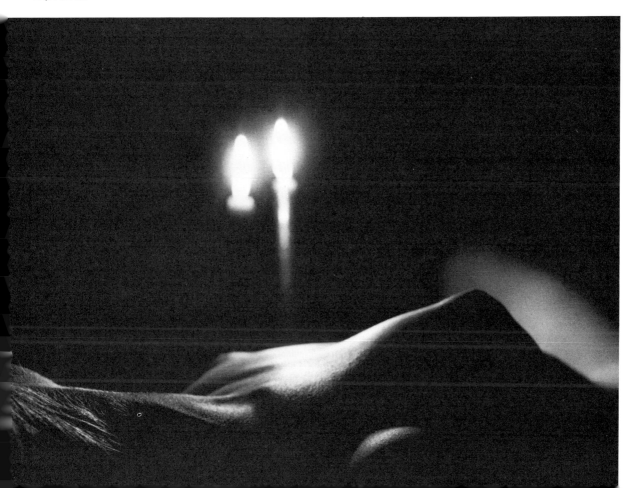

LIGHT

ness. By creating sharp-edge shadows, small light sources often cause subtle optical illusions that confuse or distort the appearance of volume.

7. *Space and two-dimensionality:* Settings or scenes may appear to include more or less space (or depth or distance) than they actually do. The appearance can range from infinite space to total two-dimensionality.

The things in a picture affect its feeling of space. Objects with a strong appearance of volume contribute to it, flat objects to two-dimensionality. Side lightings with fairly strong contrast add depth to a setting or scene, though too

The lighting situation in this large, bare room was utterly desolate—except for the soft glow of light on the floor. As a photographer, I recognized the floor as my salvation and decided to silhouette my model against it. When one sees light doing something interesting, he should always take advantage of it.

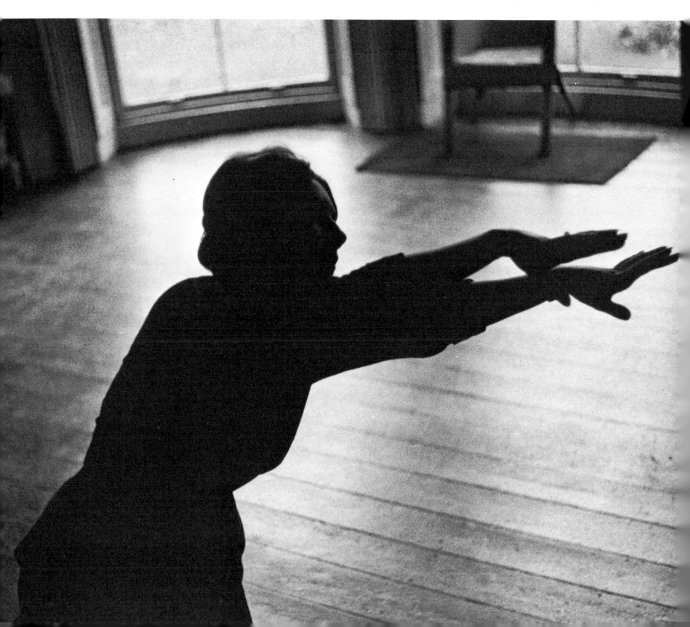

much contrast can destroy it. Little or no lighting contrast leads to flatness, or two-dimensionality. Therefore, a broad light source surrounding the subject or right in front of it will make it very flat.

8. *Visibility and obscurity:* When we are shooting pictures, everything is usually very discernible to us, though the tonal range in our subject may be as high as a thousand to one. We can easily see into the brightest highlights and the very darkest shadows. Photographs won't record all we see, however, for they have a much shorter tonal range. This means that dark things may disappear into blackness in the print, light things into whiteness. Though this is sometimes inconvenient, it gives you the opportunity to let people see only what you want them to.

Through control of lighting, you can make things visible or obscure to any degree you wish. You can lose them in whiteness or blackness, or place them anywhere you like in between. Where you place them depends on their function and relative importance in the picture. Two of your main controls for visibility and obscurity are lighting contrast and the angle of illumination.

9. *Clarity and confusion:* Numerous factors determine whether a picture is clear or visually confused. Lighting is one of the important ones. If a subject is visually confusing to start with, a lighting that creates numerous sharp-edge shadows and intricate shadow patterns will make it more so. However, lighting that creates soft-edge shadows that blend together gently will add nothing to the confusion already existing.

Sometimes confusion is desirable, though usually not. However, we should know how to increase or lessen it at will. Sinking parts of a subject into black or white oblivion is often the best way to reduce confusion, the idea being that the removal of visually disturbing and extraneous elements will naturally contribute to pictorial clarity. Or it may be that only stronger separation is needed. Just about everything that one can do with light affects the clarity-confusion continuum to some degree.

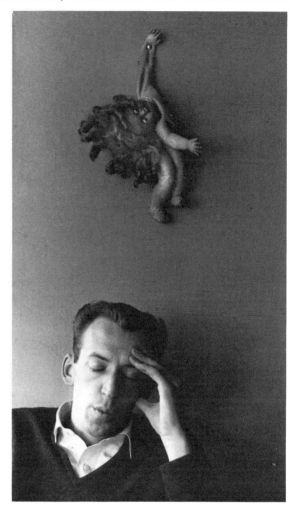

There was a moderately large light source (two adjacent windows). The light struck the pale yellow wall at such an angle as to turn it quite dark. The man was at a considerable distance from the side wall to his left, so little light reflected from it to fill in the dark shadows on the side of his face.

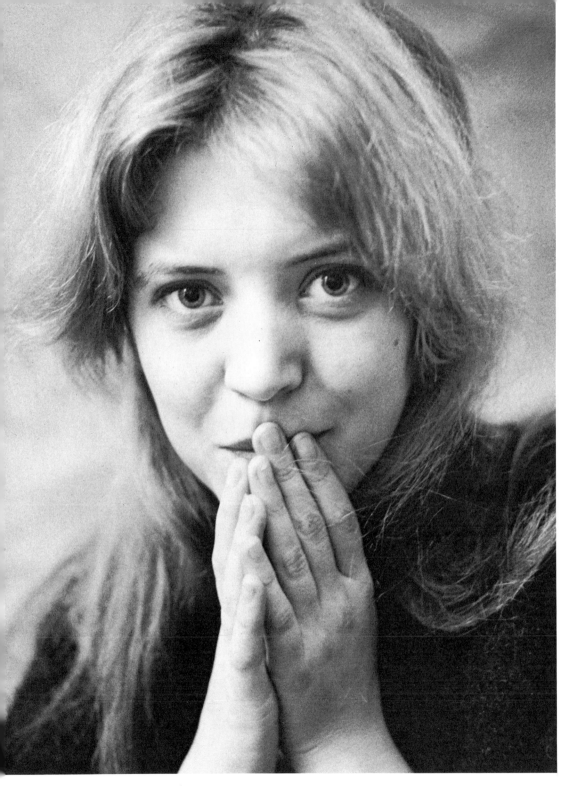

A very soft bounce lighting made with the light source about six feet from the side wall. Bounce lightings not only treat faces well but create a good feeling in the room. They make everything look soft, round, and handsome. Naturally, this contributes to the model's feeling of well-being, which is good.

10. *Diffuse and specular:* This category is concerned with the highlight qualities of matte and shiny surfaces. Light reflected from a matte surface is diffuse, from a shiny surface specular. A matte surface scatters light rays in all directions, while a shiny one reflects all parallel rays in the same direction. Because it is being scattered, light makes the matte surface look smooth and creamy. When it is reflected from a shiny surface we see the reflected image of the light source itself. Undiffused, it is usually strong enough to heavily overexpose the portion of the film it strikes. Furthermore, the image of the source often confuses or distorts the shape of the object which is reflecting it.

Both problems are solved by using very broad light sources for photographing shiny objects.

Struck by the fact that light created an interesting pattern on the floor, I asked this dancer to use it as a little stage. From the soft reflections on her neck, one can tell she was lit by a very large light source from the right side of the picture. It was a long, high wall. The opposite wall was very dark.

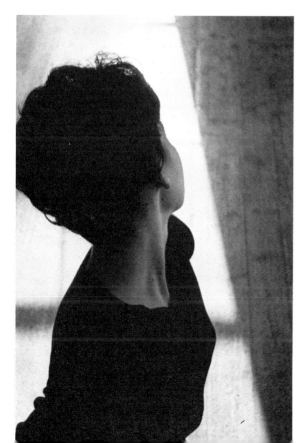

Polished metal things are often entirely surrounded with paper or plastic "tents," which, when illuminated from outside, become secondary light sources. The image of such a source is still reflected by a shiny surface, but it is quite large—not a small, too-bright spot.

11. *Heaviness and lightness:* These are rather intangible qualities, as are the others remaining on the list. They are qualities more felt than seen. That is, one picture may *feel* heavy, another light. However, there is a close correlation between feeling and seeing, because dark things are always felt as heavy and light things as light.

Lightings that produce a preponderance of dark shadow might be called heavy. If light areas predominate they are light. Any change in lighting might affect the lightness or heaviness of a subject, so it is a good idea to be on the lookout for changes. Pictures may have heavy, medium, or light themes. Naturally, themes and visual qualities should match in weight. The beauty of a young child is an example of a light theme, the tragedy of war a heavy one.

12. *Strength and weakness:* The appearance of strength or weakness in subjects depends considerably on how they are illuminated, though other factors are also involved. High contrast goes with strength, low contrast with weakness. The feeling of volume contributes to strength, flatness goes with weakness. Abrupt tone changes are strong, subtle ones weak. Some photographers reserve visual strength for masculine themes, visual weakness for feminine ones. However, it is also interesting when they are switched around.

13. *Obvious and subtle:* Light can do all the things I've mentioned in either an obvious or subtle way. For example, the apparent volume of an object may be so obviously realized that it seems one could reach into the picture and pick it up. Subtly realized solidity would sometimes seem real, sometimes not, and would demand much more of the imagination.

Remember that all the tricks of lighting can be used in both obvious and subtle ways. You should make your choice in terms of what you want your pictures to express.

14. *Dynamic and static:* This category is closely related to the two previous ones, in that strong, obvious, and dynamic are nearly synonymous. So are weak, subtle, and static. However, I keep them in separate categories, because they lead to fairly different ways of looking at things. For example, dynamic and static are good terms for helping us think of "movement" in pictures, which is an indirect way of describing their impact on our eyes.

A picture with strong or busy movement is called dynamic, and it jars our perceptual systems. A picture with little or no movement is so static it leaves us unaffected. The qualities we should seek depends on our pictorial objectives. A picture of thunder and damnation should be very dynamic; one expressing peace and quiet should be relatively static. From what has been already said you should be able to create both dynamic and static lightings.

15. *Evocative and non-evocative:* These terms describe both visible qualities and our reactions to them. Saying that something is evocative means that it stirs us emotionally. We want our pictures to do this, too. We are stirred by things because of their qualities and our prior experiences with them. In creating lightings, we do our very best to identify, analyze, and recreate the visible qualities that have aroused us in the past, using our memories and feelings as a guide.

Though our eyes are vital for the task, only our guts can tell us how well we are doing. Some lightings are evocative because they remind us of such things as dawn, sunset, campfires, candlelight, spring mornings, or young love by moonlight. Though they will enhance many subjects they work best on the ones most appropriate. For example, candlelight will do nice things for a cabbage but immensely more for a pretty girl. With the information you have, you should be able to create lightings of the evocative kind.

16. *Pictorial and non-pictorial:* A photograph

236

is pictorial if it looks like we think a picture should look. Depending a lot on the subject itself, a given lighting makes it look pictorial, nonpictorial, or something in between. It is a very subjective quality, of course, though it is strongly influenced by our experience in looking at photographs and paintings. If we see a thing that resembles what we've seen in pictures, we feel justified in making a picture of it. If that quality is absent we are very reluctant to click the shutter. Very narrow at first, our concept of pictorialism gradually broadens with experience.

Standing right under a directional ceiling fixture, this man is very strongly lighted. The heavy contrast and harshly defined shadows on his face are in keeping with the agony he appears to be experiencing. It is only appearance, however, for he is actually as happy as a clam and singing a gay song at a party.

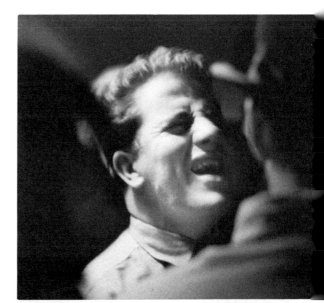

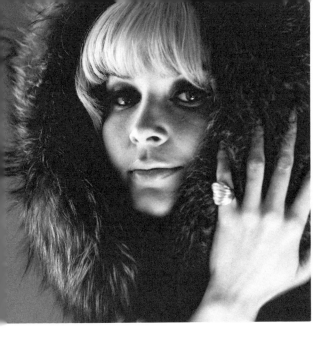

The interesting and delicate facial tones come from light that was bounced from the floor in front of the girl. You can tell this because the undersurfaces on her face are light, the top surfaces dark. Little light reached the white background, so it came out gray. This lighting is often useful for portraits.

The light source was a ceiling fixture that functioned rather like a spotlight. You can see it caused sharp-edge shadows and high contrast. The nearby light-colored background wall photographed almost black, because so little of the light hit it. The lighting makes this living room look as if it were a nightclub.

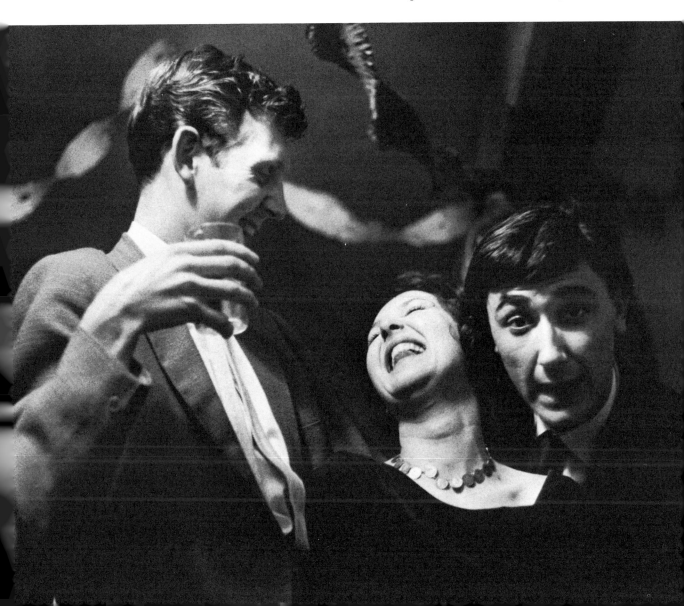

These young pirates are cavorting on the parental bed
—dirty shoes and all. In the small, white-painted
bedroom, sky light from windows on two sides bounces
all around, making everything look soft and bright.
Sky light in small, bright rooms is very good for family
photography and very easy to use.

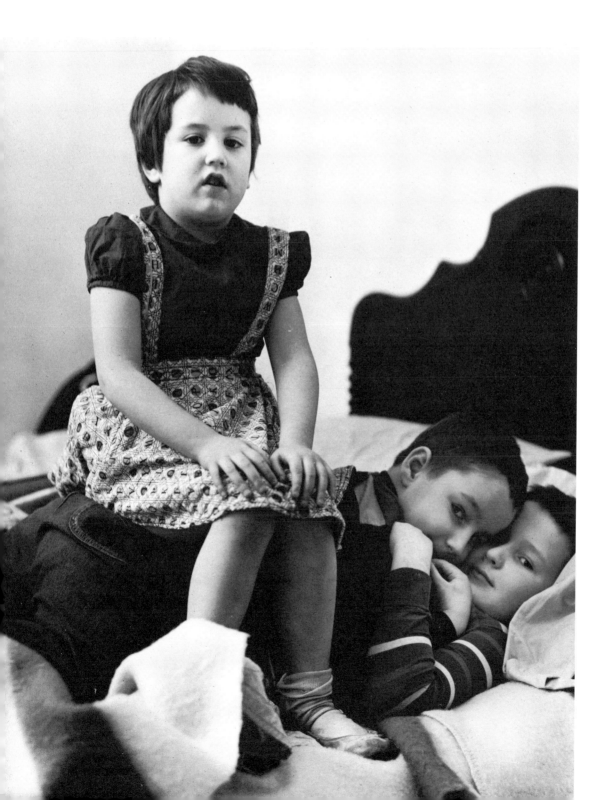

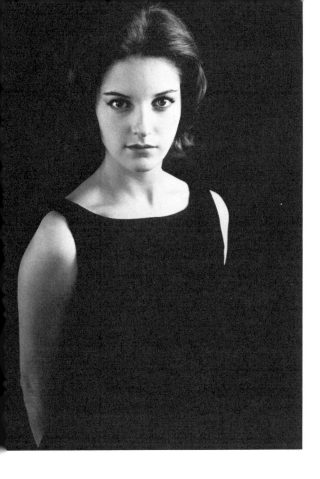

The lighting concept was to make the girl's skin look luminous and beautiful. On the theory that blacks make whites look lighter and brighter, I chose a black background. Her black gown and dark hair contributed additional black tones. The main light was bounced from the right. There is a strong reflection from the left.

As we are working with light it is important to see that our perception is filtered through our experience with pictures. We call a lighting good only because we've seen it before. We see what we've learned to see, respect what we've learned to respect, and perceive only the things we are looking for. As students, we should attempt to identify and analyze the qualities that, in our opinion, make a thing look pictorial or not, then carefully track down our reasons for thinking so. This inner exploration is a part of the process of learning to see.

17. *Reality and unreality:* Our experience mainly determines whether a lighting makes things seem real or unreal to us. For most of us, for example, a shadowless lighting makes things look unreal by robbing them of lighting contrast, volume, and space. However, they wouldn't look unreal to an Eskimo who has often trudged over snow fields under bright overcast skies. He is used to a world with no dimension.

Photographers get entranced by the problem of realism. They try to make pictures that are more real than life, turn reality into fantasy, or record the world exactly as it is. Light is an important tool for this purpose, though not the only one. As you are working with it, remember that each lighting change may make things either more or less real than before. The problem is to put your fingers on the specific qualities that account for the difference.

18. *Beauty and ugliness:* The visible qualities of an object make it beautiful, ugly, or something in between. Its nature limits what light can do to it, yet within the limits light can create dramatic changes. It can make pretty things prettier and homely things more homely. Sometimes it can make pretty things homely, homely things pretty. However, light can rarely reduce real beauty to ugliness or elevate ugliness to beauty, though it does happen now and then.

All the lightings I've described here shift the

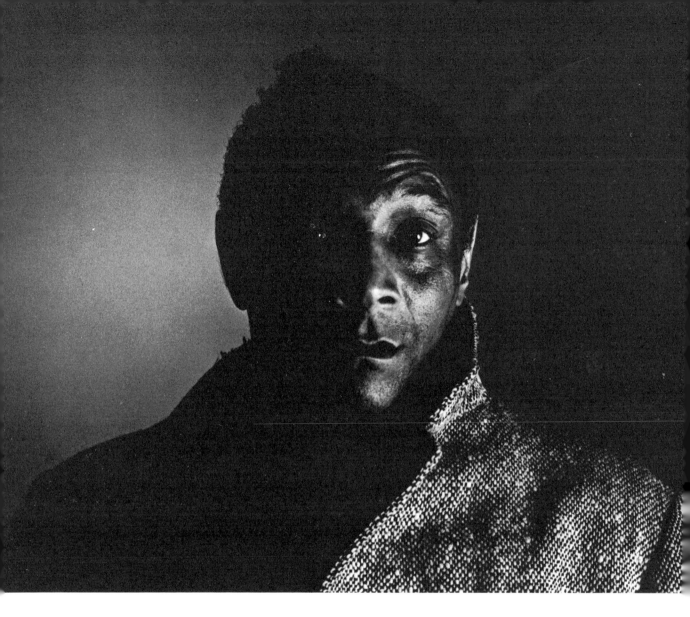

I used two light sources here: edge light from the man's left and a small bulb pointed at the background well below the height of his shoulders. The background light was used to give barely minimal separation. The reason for this darkness and obscurity was to communicate the idea that this man is essentially a mystery.

position of things along the beauty-ugliness continuum, the direction of the move depending on the nature of individual subjects. For example, a side lighting will add beauty to one subject and ugliness to another. The problem, of course, is to see clearly in which direction they move.

Changes in a lighting often shift a subject's position on the continuum. Having determined the direction it has moved, we must identify the visible elements responsible for the shift. We must also dig into ourselves to discover and analyze our unconscious concepts of beauty and ugliness.

19. *Interesting and uninteresting:* Our degree of interest in something is determined by numerous factors, not all of them visible or obvious, such as our experience with it or knowledge concerning it. However, a subject can also be interesting or not in a strictly visual sense. Its shape, for example, can be intriguing or dull. So can its color, design, shadow patterns, highlight patterns, etc. In fact, each separate visible quality can occupy either end of the continuum. Added together, they make a picture a success or a failure.

Though we're unaccustomed to judging the relative interest of contours, tonal ranges, textures, shadow patterns, and separations, we can teach ourselves to do it well. Gradually, we learn the merits of each kind of lighting, what it can contribute to pictorial interest. We also learn how much jazzing up each kind of subject requires. Fascinating things require very little, of course, uninteresting things a lot.

20. *Rational and irrational:* When we make pictures we always wonder whether they make any sense. We suspect, often with good reason, that many of them don't. Naturally, we want them all to be a product of rationality.

There are many factors that contribute to making a picture appear sensible. Lighting is one of the important ones. Well done, it can make a picture everything we think it should be. Poorly done, it can turn it into nonsense.

This category is closely related to several others. To illustrate, if a picture is evocative, pictorial, beautiful, and interesting, we are sure it makes good sense. However, if it is non-evocative, non-pictorial, ugly, and uninteresting, it usually strikes us as nonsense. Many changes in lighting can affect the meaningfulness and good sense of a picture. The student's job is to learn to detect this as it happens.

● The Tricks Will Help You

Earlier, when the basic tricks for aiding vision were described, I mentioned only a few of the things you should be looking for when composing or evaluating a picture subject, or in a lighting setup. Now, however, you know of many visible qualities that you should make yourself aware of. Developing this awareness is a big and important job. Using the tricks can help you understand what was said about the qualities and can also help you see them better. You won't develop this sensitivity all at once, so you must be patient with yourself.

Use the tricks all the time, not just when you are making pictures. Wherever you are, light is always available for study without your having to lift a finger. Take advantage of its generous availability and analyze it constantly. Light creates the visual world you live in. As a photographer you have a vested interest in all the aspects of light.

● A Bonus Trick for Hard-Working Students

An important part of the art of seeing is knowing all the visible effects and their causes. You now know quite a bit about both, though mainly in a verbal way. If you were to see a sharp-edge shadow you would probably look for a small light source; low contrast would lead you to a large light source, such as a reflecting surface that fills in shadows, or a front lighting. You now have the knowledge, because this section of the book has actually been an essay on causes and effects.

However, we haven't discussed the problem of telling where light is coming from. If an effect has been created, we need to know where it originated. But sometimes tracing the origin can pose quite a problem. This is not always true, of course, for some sources of light are obvious. For instance, if we look at a subject with fairly strong lighting contrast we can readily see that the bright highlights come from a floodlight, a bright pattern of bounce light, a window, or some other light source we couldn't miss if we tried.

It is much harder to tell the origin of light striking a shadow area of a subject. If we can see anything at all in the area, we know that *something* is reflecting light into it; the question is what? It is usually safe to assume that a wall or the ceiling is doing it, but not always. There is a simple way for locating the source. It is to hold a hand (or finger) close enough to the area to cast a shadow. An imaginary line drawn from the shadow through the finger will point right at the source of light.

If the shadow is very delicate, with soft edges, it means the source is large. A darker, sharp-edge shadow indicates a smaller source. A double shadow comes from two sources. Absence of a shadow tells us the light source is off to one side of the hand.

Using the hand-and-shadow trick, you will often detect light coming from surprising places, such as other areas in the subject itself or from a white shirt you are wearing. Of course, the reason for locating all the sources for the light falling on a subject is to make them subject to control if desirable. They can be blocked off, shifted to a different location, brightened, dimmed, etc. However, if we don't know where light is coming from there is not much we can do about it.

LIGHTING EXPERIMENTS

We've nearly reached the end of our detour, and you can now proceed to experiment with light. Before doing so, please reread the sections entitled "Why We Have Trouble Seeing Light," "White-on-White," "White Background," and "A Necessary Detour."

When people do experiments they naturally have certain expectations. Those who expect the right things tend to do them correctly, learn what they were supposed to learn, and enjoy the work. For those who expect the wrong things, experiments become a misery and a waste of time. This being the case, I will say what one can reasonably expect from doing the experiments described:

1. Only a small percentage of the possible lightings on an average subject would make good pictures.

2. Part of the problem of learning to see is to unravel the secret of what makes bad lightings bad. We have the equally difficult task of deciding what makes good lightings good. The results of the experiments have not been given in advance. You must detect both kinds for yourself.

3. A lighting that is bad for one subject may be good for another. The student's problem is to discover why. And which lighting is good for what.

4. There are no mechanical differentiating devices built into experiments to automatically in-

form us which lightings are effective on a subject and which aren't.

5. Visible qualities like separation and blending, contrast and flatness, and space and two-dimensionality are neither good nor bad in themselves. The only question is, what do they accomplish in a given picture?

6. You should take a picture of everything that happens—good, bad, and indifferent—in each of the steps of your lighting experiments. For moral support, you must remember that most lightings on an average subject aren't very exciting.

7. It is likely that you'll sense when a lighting isn't doing anything worth while and you will be reluctant to photograph it. Force yourself to. Unless you are an expert, you will miss most of what light is doing when you're looking right at a subject, but pick up much of it later when you look at your prints. It isn't enough to merely sense that a lighting is ineffective; you must also pinpoint the exact causes.

8. The prints don't have to be large, but they should be made with great care if you want to learn anything from them. Poorly made prints are so psychologically depressing that they badly distort perception. Furthermore, beginners get confused between lighting and printing defects, not knowing which is which. It takes considerable will power to force oneself to make good prints of badly lighted subjects. Nonetheless, they are

necessary for helping us see why the lightings aren't working well.

9. Hurrying through experiments destroys their value. Though you could probably rush through them all in an hour or two, it would be a total waste of time and the end to your hope of benefiting from them. Take your time and carefully study each step along the way.

10. Doing an experiment just once is seldom enough. Most of the ones given here should be done many times, using different kinds of subjects and groupings thereof.

11. The purpose of the white-on-white experiments is not to teach people how to photograph white objects, no more than cancer research with mice is for learning how to cure mouse cancer. The only reason for using white objects is that they give us a remarkable opportunity to see clearly some of the important things that light does.

12. The success of the experiments depends very heavily on the care with which you select and prepare the subjects for your lightings and photographs.

● **Equipment and Materials**

1. one photoflood light on an adjustable stand
2. table
3. large sheets of white, gray, and black background paper
4. a variety of white-painted objects
5. a variety of unpainted objects
6. camera and film
7. tripod and cable release
8. exposure meter
9. masking tape and clothespins
10. one or more close-up lenses
11. black and white cardboards for light absorption and reflection
12. smaller pieces of cardboard for shadow casting
13. a white-painted, seven-inch juice can
14. three white eggs
15. a workroom with white or light-colored walls

● **Preparing the Basic Setup**

1. Shove the table against a wall, about four feet from the corner of the room. Move all other furniture out of the vicinity.

2. Put the white background paper on the table, curving one end of it up the wall. Tape it in place.

3. Position the camera and tripod so that the only thing visible in the viewfinder is the whiteness of the background.

● **Exploring Contrast and Flatness**

1. Place a white object on the white background.

2. Position the floodlight on the side of the table nearest a side wall. Point it directly at the object from such an angle that from the camera position the shadow line bisects the object. Observe how much contrast is created.

3. With one light absorber, the black cardboard, near the dark side of the object, see how much you can increase the contrast. Using several absorbers, see if you can make the side pitch black.

4. With one or more *reflectors* on the dark side, see how much you can *diminish* the contrast. Eliminate it altogether if you can.

5. Edge the photoflood now, so that the bright part of the light pattern is pointed between the object and the camera, with just the edge of the light striking the object. If necessary, reposition the light so that the shadow line bisects the object once again. With the reflector(s), try again to eliminate the contrast, making sure they are reflecting a bright part of the light pattern.

6. Move the floodlight to the other side of the table and, using direct light, center the shadow line again. Is there more or less contrast than in step 2? How do you account for the difference, if there is any?

7. With light absorbers, increase the contrast as much as possible. Is it as easy as before? Will absorbers of the same size do the job?

8. With edge light alone, and light reflected from the nearby corner wall, see how much you can diminish the contrast. Move the light around quite a bit to find the most effective position for it.

9. Return the light to the side of the table nearest the corner wall, then swing the reflector around to point at that wall. It should be about three feet from it. Observe the contrast on the object. Swing the light slowly back and forth in a 180-degree arc, carefully observing the contrast changes. Now move the light to within a foot of the wall. What happens to the contrast on the object? Slowly swing it again, observing the changes.

10. With the light at the side of the table, choose the bounce-light position that creates the most contrast, then use a reflector to diminish it as much as possible, then an absorber to increase it to the maximum. Compared with what happened when you were using direct and edge light, how successful are your efforts?

11. Once again, move the light stand to the other side of the table and point the light at the far side wall. How much contrast do you get? How do you account for what you see? With a light absorber, see how much you can increase the contrast.

12. Now raise the light source up high on its stand and point it at a spot on the ceiling directly over the table. Where is the break-off line between light and shadow now? Is there much contrast? How do you account for the light you see in the shadow areas? Tip the light down sharply to point directly at the object. What do you observe now?

13. Now create a lighting that wipes out contrast altogether. Play around with it until the effect is indeed total. If you don't remember how, refer to the text again.

14. Quickly run through all the lightings again and decide which ones make the object look best, which ones worst. Be sure to make photographs of the two extremes.

15. Replace the white object with an un-painted one. Carefully repeat the entire project, taking judicious note of the contrast changes you see. If you like, repeat it again with a person as your subject. Whether they are photographing people or objects, photographers run through the same lighting maneuvers. They insist on lighting equipment mobility, so that they can run through all possible lighting variations as quickly as possible. Having done this experiment, I think you can now understand why.

● Exploring Separation and Blending

1. Place three white objects on a white background in such a way that they overlap in the viewfinder. Measuring along the lens axis, they should be about three inches apart.

2. Position the floodlight by the side of the table nearest a side wall. Point it at the objects from such an angle that their highlight sides blend with each other and the background, too. Maneuver the light until the blending is absolute when viewed from the camera position. You should see no highlight separation at all in the viewfinder.

3. Continuing to point it at the objects, move the light back and forth, sideways, and up and down until the highlight sides separate. You may have to do a good deal of maneuvering.

4. Use edge light with the light stand by the nearest wall, to see how much separation you can get. Don't hesitate to edge the light very radically. You can also bring it very close to the objects, for it won't hurt them to get a little warm.

5. Use bounce light from the same side of the table to blend the highlight edges together as completely as you can. Move the floodlight up and down, along the wall in both directions, and at various distances from it.

6. Still using bounce light, create as much separation as you can. Use all of your imagination in finding ways to bounce the light. In addition to using the wall, try bouncing it from a cardboard reflector right on the table with the objects.

Try bouncing it from the floor or from a reflector propped up below the level of the table.

7. Using direct, edge, and bounce light consecutively, try reducing and increasing separation by casting shadows on one or more of the objects. Try different sizes and shapes of shadow casters, and use them in a variety of positions. Find combinations that won't produce obvious shadows. Don't take much time making shadow casters, because crude ones work very well.

8. Move the objects eight inches apart and repeat all the steps. What difference, if any, does the greater distance make?

9. Replace the objects with three that aren't white. Carefully repeat all the steps. As a photographer, your real concern is with ordinary things, not white-painted ones; so take special pains with this part of the experiment.

10. Have a friend sit himself in front of the background, profile to the camera, facing the nearest side wall. With edge light, then bounce light, blend the edge of his face with the background. Next, use a shadow caster to create separation. Then, without using shadows, use both edge and bounce light to create as much separation as possible.

11. Quickly run through all the lightings again, with white objects, ordinary objects, and your friend. Decide which ones did most justice to your subjects and what, if anything, separation or blending had to do with it.

● Checking Out the Background

People tend to ignore what light is doing to their backgrounds, and this gets them into numerous difficulties. This project will draw your attention to it and tell you what things you should be aware of. Always, the background is an important part of a picture. You should certainly know what it is doing at all times.

1. With bounce light from above or behind the camera, establish an absolutely flat light pattern on both the horizontal and vertical parts of

the background paper. If you are successful you should get identical meter readings from all four corners.

2. Experiment with bounce light from the nearest side wall to get as large as possible a difference in meter readings between the two top corners. Experiment some more with side bounce light to get the corners as much alike as possible.

3. Bounce the light from the farthest side wall and see what that does to the evenness of the background.

4. Center the floodlight in front of the background, four feet away, moving aside the camera if it is in the way. Now get as even a lighting as you can. Take meter readings of the four corners and the center. Can you get all the readings to match? Back the light away a few more feet and try it again. Can you detect tone differences as well as your meter can?

5. With the light still about four feet from the background, edge it so that the middle of the light pattern cuts the edge of the paper. With the meter, measure the brightness difference between the two sides. Move the light closer and do it again. How far back do you have to move it to make the brightness difference negligible?

6. With light bounced from the floor, see how great a tone difference you can make between the horizontal and vertical parts of the background. With the center of the photoflood below table level, try the same thing with direct light.

7. The curve in the paper sometimes shows up in pictures as a shadow, a highlight, or a combination of both. Though this is usually undesirable, it is sometimes useful. With a fairly tight curve, run through all the lightings you've learned about to see what they do to it. Repeat the series with a moderate curve and a very gentle one. Which lightings tended to erase the curves, which made them stand out?

8. Working with direct light, use a shadow caster to make a soft-edge gray tone across the entire top half of the background; then do the same thing to the bottom half. Repeat the ex-

periment with bounce light from the near wall and with edge light. Do it in such a way that the shadow caster doesn't show in the viewfinder. Casting shadows accurately in bounce light can be quite difficult, but they can really pay off pictorially.

• Controlling the Subject-Background Tonal Relationship

One of the most important areas for control in photography is the subject-background tonal relationship. Properly handled, it contributes much to photographs. Mishandled, it often ruins them.

1. Position a white object on the table so that it is the maximum distance from the vertical part of the background paper.

2. With direct, edge, and bounce light consecutively, make the object much lighter than the vertical part of the background.

3. With the same types of light, make it much darker than the background.

4. Aiming the light source from below the level of the table top, use direct, edge, and bounce light consecutively to make the object much lighter than the background again. In this and previous steps you may wish to use reflectors, light absorbers, or shadow casters.

5. Using direct, edge, and bounce light, try to make the major part of the object match the background in tone.

6. Move the object to within five inches of the vertical part of the background. Repeat steps 2, 3, 4, and 5. How do you account for the difficulty (or impossibility) of creating the desired tonal relationships?

7. Quickly run through all the lightings again and decide which of them would make the best, and the worst, pictures.

8. Replace the white background with medium-gray paper. Repeat all the lightings, attempting to get the subject-background tonal relationships that were requested. It's not as hard as it sounds.

9. Now use a black background and create the same effects. You'll have to use all your ingenuity for this problem.

10. Still using the black background, replace your object with an unpainted one and go through the entire experiment.

11. With the same object, go through it again with a gray background.

12. And go through it once more with a white background.

13. Replace both objects with a willing friend, so that you can do head and shoulders portraits. This time use the whole wall as a background. To help control his tonal relationship to the wall, move him sideways along it. This will control the amount of fill light reaching him from side walls. Also, vary his distance from the background wall, from one foot to ten feet (if you have enough room).

14. Using direct, edge, and bounce light, make his face much darker than the background, then much lighter. Where necessary, have him shift positions in the room.

15. With all three types of light, make his face a tonal match for the background.

16. Bounce the light off the floor in front of him to see how that affects his tonal relationship to the background.

17. For the same reason, bounce it from the ceiling directly over his head. Do it once when he is standing two feet from the background wall and again when he's as far away from it as he can get in your workroom.

18. Quickly, run through all the lightings and positions again and decide which were most, and least, flattering to your model.

• Lighting to Specifications: Creating and Destroying Volume

You have been told a lot about getting various visible effects, so at this point you should be able to create them to order without being told how to do it. The purpose of this project is to test how well you've learned. It will also teach you more about lighting and seeing light.

● Creating Volume

1. For this project, use a white-painted, seven-inch juice can, one floodlight, and a white background paper that has been curved up the wall. Decide for yourself the size of the paper, the position of the can, the type of lighting, and whether to use reflectors, light absorbers, shadow casters, etc.

2. The image will be vertical, the cylinder filling a little more than half of the frame. Its top will appear as a well-defined elipse. Nothing will appear in the viewfinder except the cylinder and white paper.

3. Tonal relationships: One side and the top of the can will be white, the other side nearly black—the blacker the better. The top of the can will be a brighter white than the light side. The vertical part of the background will be a rich gray.

4. Shadows: The form shadow and the cast shadow will have soft edges but be very dark. Seen from the camera position, the edge of the form shadow will bisect the can vertically.

5. Gradation: The tone change from light to dark on the front of the can will be very smooth. There will be no sign of a sharp tone break.

6. The foreground will be substantially darker than the light side of the cylinder, but considerably lighter than its dark side.

7. Insofar as it's humanly possible, you will make the two top corners of the background match in tone, testing the match with meter readings. The nature of the other requirements may make it impossible to get an exact match.

When you've met the specifications, replace the white can with an unpainted one to see what it looks like. Try it with any other cylindrical things available, including your fingers and your arm. The question you should ask is, do they have a feeling of volume?

● Destroying Volume

1. Use the white can and background again.

2. Tonal relationships: The top and both sides of the can will match. The whole can will exactly match both the horizontal and vertical parts of the background. It is easy to make all these things match fairly well, but to make them go all the way is quite a job.

3. Shadows: none.

4. Gradation: none. Check the four corners and the center of the background with a meter. You should get identical readings.

When you've satisfied the requirements, observe other cylindrical things in the same setting to see what they look like. Your question: Does the lighting make them look flat or like they have volume?

● Manipulating Simplicity and Complexity

1. Make a white-on-white still-life arrangement with five or six objects. Position them fairly close together in a pleasing composition.

2. Create a lighting that will complicate the picture as much as possible. Don't be satisfied with anything less than visual chaos. If you don't remember how to do such a lighting, refer to the text again.

3. Establish another lighting that will simplify the picture as much as possible. Go all the way on this.

4. In steps 2 and 3 you will probably get images you won't like very much, so do a third lighting, halfway between the extremes, that will make your subject as handsome as possible.

5. Repeat the entire experiment with an arrangement of things that aren't white.

● Exploring Strength and Weakness

1. Choose a subject, not necessarily white, that you see as being boldly fashioned, or very masculine. Create as strong a lighting for it as you can.

2. Now light it as weakly as possible. How does this change the feeling you get from looking at it?

3. Replace it with a very delicate subject and use a very strong lighting again, going as far as possible to make the delicate thing look strongly virile.

4. Now set up a lighting that makes it look delicate to the very extreme.

5. Finally, do lightings for both subjects that make them look just right.

• Exploring Space and Two-Dimensionality

1. Put three white eggs on a white background, positioning them about ten inches apart and at a 45-degree angle to the lens axis.

2. Using just the floodlight (direct, edge, or bounce), see how far apart you can make them seem when they are looked at through the viewfinder.

3. With the help of one or more shadow casters, see how much you can increase the apparent depth.

4. Using only the floodlight, try to destroy all the apparent depth.

5. With the help of any means available, create an apparent depth about halfway between the extremes.

(If necessary, refer to the text to refresh your memory on how to accomplish these steps.)

• Exploring Dominance
and Subordination

1. Put five or six white things of approximately equal size on a white background. Make a pleasing arrangement, but one in which none of the things seems dominant when examined through the viewfinder. This by itself will take a little doing.

2. Set up a lighting that will make one of the things dominant. Use any lighting trick in the book.

3. Rearrange the objects so that, without the help of special lighting, one of them seems domi-

nant. Arrange a lighting that lessens its dominance.

4. Now create a lighting that greatly increases it. Do this either by making it stand out more or by making all the other objects more subordinate.

5. Rearrange the objects and illuminate them so that all but one are lost in dark oblivion. You'll have to be pretty tricky to solve this problem.

6. Now lose all but one of them in white oblivion. You'll probably break your back figuring out how to do this one.

7. Substitute unpainted objects and repeat the experiments.

8. Using these same objects and a gray background paper, do the experiments again.

9. And repeat them yet again, using a black background.

10. Abandon the setup for a while and go to another part of the room with the photoflood. See what you can do to make pieces of furniture and other things either dominant or subordinate.

• Exploring Confusion

1. Choose a hodgepodge of unpainted things and arrange them in a disorderly way. Make the composition in the viewfinder as chaotic as you can. And don't settle for just ordinary chaos.

2. Through experimentation, find the lighting that adds most to the confusion. If you wish, use shadow casters, reflectors, light absorbers, or anything else you can think of.

3. Through experimentation find the lighting that reduces the chaos to the lowest possible level. Use your imagination on this. Your lighting may or may not turn the original disorder into something pictorial. It probably won't.

4. If it doesn't, see if you can find a point between maximum and minimum confusion that has pictorial possibilities, but don't be surprised if you can't. After all, you started with a hodgepodge and it may be impossible to overcome it through the use of lighting alone. Since a project like this offers little hope of a good picture, you may have

to talk yourself into doing it. The important thing to remember is that you are learning principles that can be applied to good pictures later.

● Exploring Beauty and Ugliness

1. Find a subject you consider beautiful, or at least very pretty. It doesn't matter what it is, painted or unpainted, large or small, animate or inanimate, etc. Using any or all of the lighting tricks you've read about, make this pretty thing as homely as you can. However, don't be surprised if it is a difficult task.

2. Now find the lighting that does the most to embellish your subject's beauty. Use all the tricks in the book, if necessary.

3. Find the ugliest thing available and light it so that it would make a handsome picture. Such a thing is possible, but you really have to sweat to win this game.

4. Through experimentation, find the lighting that does the most to increase your subject's ugliness. Use all or any of the tricks you've read about. It isn't as easy as it sounds, for you have to discover what ugliness actually consists of if you are going to effectively increase it. Finding the basic visible elements that make up either beauty or ugliness is a long-time job.

● Illumination from Within

1. Arrange three white eggs on a white background. Find a lighting that will make them appear as if they were illuminated from within, like light bulbs. In this project you must follow the old rule that light makes dark, and vice versa. This means that a dark area makes a light area seem lighter, and a light area makes a dark one seem darker. You'll certainly have to use this concept to make eggs look like burning light bulbs.

2. Try to do the same thing with a smooth, unpainted object (like a rock) on a gray background.

3. Using the same object, try it again on a black background. Try it with the eggs, too. Don't let the apparent simplicity of this project fool you, for it is one of the most difficult lighting problems in photography. However, some photographers can consistently make their subjects seem to radiate from within, which gives their photographs a wonderful beauty.

● Postscript to the Lighting Experiments

The assignments in this book are not like those usually given students in photography. Most teachers tell their pupils to make good pictures of certain subjects or to handsomely illustrate various themes. Such projects are very reasonable. However, they are not basic enough in some respects, because they seldom deal directly with the student's fundamental problem of learning to see.

In contrast, the experiments you've just read about are primarily concerned with helping you see better, and the problem of making good pictures is temporarily put aside. I assume that after you've learned to recognize and manipulate the visible elements of your environment and your photographs, you will naturally wish to apply this knowledge to improving your photography. You'll certainly wish to do *something* with your new set of tools.

A careful reading of the experiments will give you a sound knowledge of the practical methods used to determine the pictorial potentials of the basic tools used in handling light—light sources, reflectors, walls, shadow casters, etc. The same methods are used for assessing all lighting equipment, no matter how sophisticated it is. They are even used by professionals with equipment worth hundreds of thousands of dollars.

The techniques discussed in the experiments work anywhere, not just in indoor workrooms. I've explained my reasons for asking you to work temporarily indoors. Once you've successfully done the projects, it is time to take your new understanding out into a larger world. Whatever you do, don't let yourself become dependent on controlled light and your workroom. Unfortunately, many people do.

In a sense, doing the assignments will turn your workroom into a microcosm of the whole visual world. The lightings you will create will duplicate in miniature most of the lighting phenomena in your environment. The important thing is to see that this is actually true and to intentionally relate everything you do indoors to something happening elsewhere. It won't happen automatically, so you will have to make a determined effort to see the relationships.

Earlier, I said you could probably rush through all the experiments in an hour or two, but that it would be a complete waste of time. It makes better educational sense to use all your spare time for a month or more. Even a highly skilled photographer would have to devote time, because some parts of the experiments are quite difficult. When you try them you may think they're impossible, though this is not true.

Despite occasional tough spots, the projects were carefully designed for the rank beginner. Even rushing through them disinterestedly, one can assuredly pick up information of value.

● Conclusion

The text is for people with no prior experience in photography, though it is filled with material it took me thirty years to gather. I hope I've managed to keep my promise to myself by writing about it in a way you find both simple and useful.

The book's first line says that photography is actually a very simple craft. I trust you can wade through all the complications I've introduced and see that this is really true. I've merely tried to take the simplicity apart so you can see how it works.

This is basically a treatise on causes and effects in photography. I hope it helps you become a master at controlling causes and a true artist at seeing and understanding the effects, however subtle they may be. May photography be an unending source of pleasure and excitement for you.

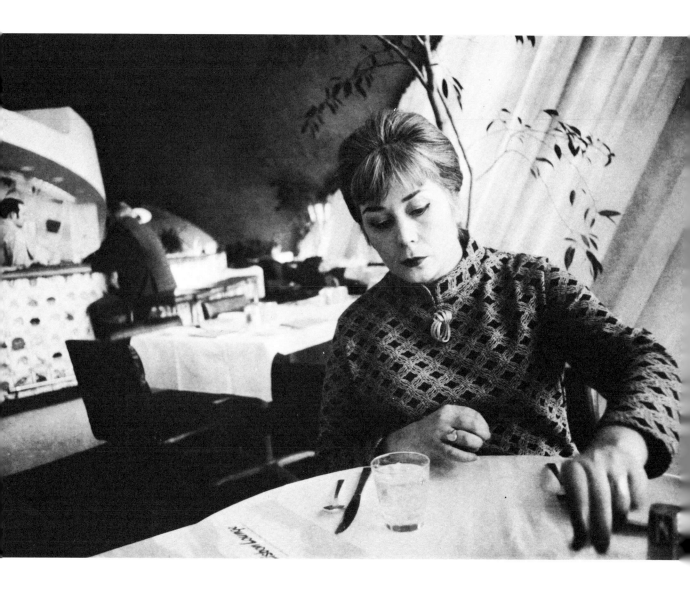

My wife Lisa Lu contemplates an extra-dry martini on the rocks at the airport restaurant in New York where we began our vacation. Daytime with natural (or available) light, shot with a 28mm lens, from an incident light reading. This is an elegant young lady, you can bet your life.

Photographic Subjects

HOW TO SHOOT CANDID PORTRAITS

The term "candid portrait" usually refers to informal pictures of people—as distinct from formal portraits, such as those made by professional portrait photographers. Candid portraits are said to have special virtues that formal portraits don't have, and they have long been popular with the public. Basically, the word candid means open, frank, unguarded, honest, or truthful. Ideally, candid portraits should have these qualities, and they very often do. They should reveal the inner person, not the outward role-playing.

● **The Ethical Foundation**

Unless your photography is based on attitudes and behavior which your inner self recognizes as deeply ethical, you are very unlikely to get any happiness from it. Such happiness as you do achieve will certainly be spurious and fleeting. The truth of this is most obvious when one sets out to make portraits: if you do it for the wrong reasons you will surely pay the price in inner conflict and self-condemnation.

Many photographers seem to think that making candid portraits is entirely a matter of clever tactics: you simply scheme to catch people off guard in self-revealing situations, then photograph them when they are not looking. And then, of course, you make dead sure they never see the photographs, though you display them for everyone else.

Interesting candids can be made in this manner, but doing it with such an attitude is a serious offense against the inner ethical self—if you still have one, and let us hope that you do. For reasons that will be made clear later, it is quite all right to photograph people who are unaware that you are doing it—but not for the wrong reasons or with the wrong attitudes, for this is a crime against the inner self. It can spoil your photography for you and even damage your life.

Fortunately, there are approaches to candid portraiture in which there is much less risk of offending your own ethics, so we will devote ourselves to them in this chapter. Indeed, portraiture of any kind, rightly seen, can be (and should be) a practice of ethics.

The starting point for any of the approaches is to examine your attitudes concerning the people you wish to photograph and see if you fully respect yourself for them. Make up your mind, and stick to it, that you will never photograph anyone (or even any *thing*) until you respect your reasons for wanting to do it. Search deeply into yourself, don't accept phony ego answers, and you will soon find yourself approaching photography in a deeper, more satisfying way.

With respect to your subjects, do your best to reach this goal: use your photography to help them like themselves better for reasons that they can accept in their inner selves.

• Some Wrong Reasons for Portraiture

Though the average person can find literally hundreds of wrong reasons for doing almost anything, I will mention just a few of the ones related to portraiture. You should not make pictures of people for reasons such as these:

1. in order to have a feeling of power over them.

2. to hold them up to ridicule, either in your own mind or in the minds of others.

3. to use the pictures, especially of people of the opposite sex, to stimulate farfetched fantasy in yourself.

4. to strip your subjects of privacy by showing things in them that they wish to keep hidden.

5. to make a reputation for yourself as photography's big game hunter, with many heads to your credit.

6. to prove to yourself, with unflattering pictures, that the human race is no damned good.

7. to see if you can outwit unwary models and get them to unintentionally reveal themselves in your pictures.

8. to use other people's faces to make pictures of your personal hangups.

9. to use the photographer-model relationship as a disguised sexual encounter and as a stimulus to sexual fantasy.

10. to undermine the confidence of your subjects in their personality and appearance.

If you will examine yourself very closely you will probably discover at least some of these bad habits: get rid of them! There are many others—get rid of them too!

• Some Right Reasons

In the long run it is much easier to photograph people for the right reasons than for the wrong ones—and it doesn't burden the conscience and lead to self-conflict. Having the right intentions is what counts most, even if you don't always measure up to them. You should make pictures of people for reasons such as these:

1. to show that you care enough for them to want their pictures.

2. to let them know that you find them interesting or handsome.

3. to make pictures to aid your memory in holding people close to your heart.

4. to use images of people to show them things of value in themselves about which they may have been unaware or uncertain.

5. to show your subjects you are trying to see them in an accurate and kindly way.

6. to show them that you are intentionally using photography as a way of honoring them.

7. to let them know they are contributing to

My mother, the late Ruth Claire Hattersley, gazing upon her elder son with a fond look. The light source was a bare photoflood bulb positioned close to the ceiling. Mom put on her best party dress and necklace especially for the shooting session. With Dad around she felt uncomfortable (he had a criticizing eye), so we went into the next room, where this picture was made. I didn't tell her why we moved, but I think she knew.

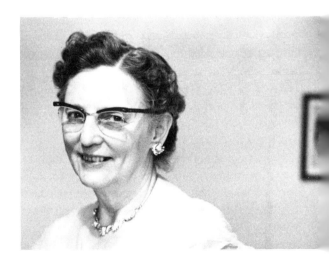

your understanding by permitting you to look at them carefully.

8. to let people know that photographing them is helping you overcome your fear of people.

9. to make images of people that will help them respect and like themselves more.

10. to try to make pictures that will contribute to the humanity of all who see them.

There is an immediate payoff for taking people pictures for the right reasons, provided that you believe in them: your subjects will sense your good will, drop as much of their role-playing as they dare, and reveal something of their inner selves to you and your camera. You can then take portraits that are truly candid, that are open, frank, unguarded, honest, or truthful. Furthermore, you can really believe in such pictures as descriptions of the true nature of the human race, instead of having to fantasize about images made by trickery and motivated by your own egotism.

• **Unconscious Telepathy**

You may have wondered why this book starts with the request that you make photography, especially of people, a practice of ethics. After all, isn't photography simply a matter of mechanics? Well, you know better than that, don't you? Photography is actually many things, including a relationship between people in which one person attempts to define the other. Unless such a relationship is ethically conducted it can only lead to grief. Ethics asks that we care for people, but liking one or two is not enough. You should do your very best to learn to like the whole world, yourself included, for that is the basic ethical imperative.

Some people think that this good will, this caring, can be faked and that a clever bedside manner is the only requirement for fine portraiture. Well, it ain't that easy, and clever fakers usually end up making dull, superficial portraits and ruining photography or themselves. Perhaps the main

reason for the superficial portraits is that subjects who are being lied to are well aware of it on the unconscious level and respond to the lies projecting only masks for the photographer.

I don't ask you to believe that people are fully telepathic on the unconscious level, but it is true nevertheless. Even as a nonbeliever you can make good use of this information if you will go so far as accepting it as at least a remote possibility and behave accordingly. Assuming that people can actually tell whether your motives are good or bad, despite your skill as an actor, examine these motives with great care and gradually replace the negative ones with positive. Whether you believe in unconscious telepathy or not you will find that this procedure will add immensely to the meaning and joy of making people pictures.

My father, the late Judge Ralph M. Hattersley, Sr., a kindly man with an eagle eye. I think I unconsciously knew he wouldn't live much longer, though I didn't suspect this till later. So I shot literally hundreds of pictures of him that summer. Here he is in his office in one of his four county seats, waiting for court to get into session. Light coming from the sky, entering from a large window to his left. Hand-held Kodak Medalist, a splendid but awkward camera, at f/3.5.

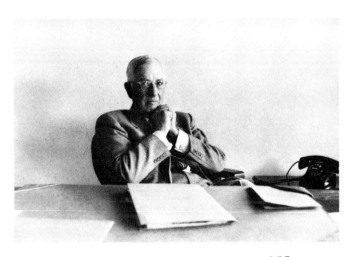

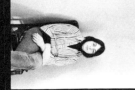
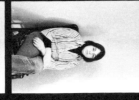
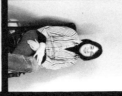
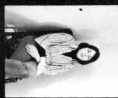
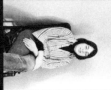
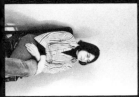
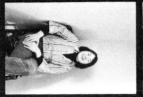
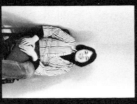
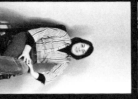
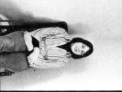
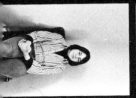
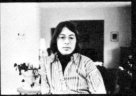
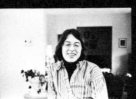
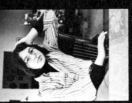
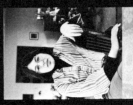
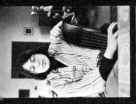
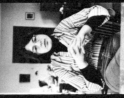
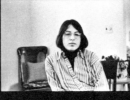
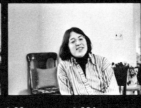
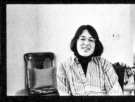

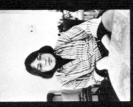
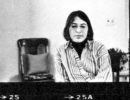
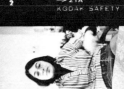
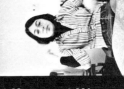
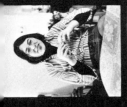
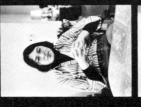
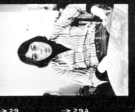
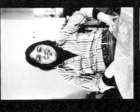
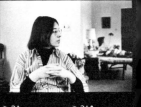
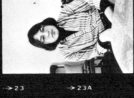
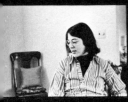
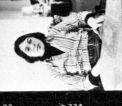
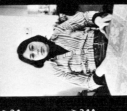
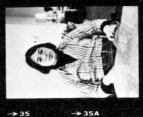
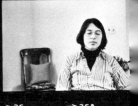

● People Are Mirrors

For a moment I will stretch your credulity still further, then pass on to more everyday matters. One strange consequence of unconscious telepathy is that it enables people to act as mirrors for one another—in fact, they do it more often than not. We do this mainly with gestures and facial expressions very carefully but unconsciously selected for what they can communicate to people who are looking at us. The objective is to inform these people very specifically concerning their own feelings, motives, and attitudes, which are mainly unconscious and not easily uncovered otherwise. In doing this we are mirrors of a sort.

This has an important bearing on photography, because when we portray other people they are simultaneously portraying us. Thus every people picture is a double portrait, though this may not be true of snapshots. Many experienced serious photographers are well aware of this, but it is also something you should know as a beginner.

Reading a photograph as a mirror may be difficult, though sometimes the mirroring is obvious. For example, I once had an extremely paranoid student who every week brought to me dozens of people pictures shot on the streets of New York. Without exception, every one of them

My stepdaughter Kathi Turner, visiting us during a vacation during her senior year at the University of Rochester in upstate New York. This contact sheet shows rather well how I shot—very fast, almost with my eyes closed—running through the 36-exposure roll in about ten minutes. This was for a reason: she didn't like the pictures I had shot of her the year before—"too mature, too sexy, too much like Sophia Loren" (yeah, she actually looked that way). So I worked very fast so as not to superimpose my visual opinions on her face, and Kathi was very pleased with the results. The pictures fitted her self-image well. As for the sexy pictures—well, it wouldn't be nice of me to print them against her wishes, would it?

looked as paranoid as he. And I remember a lonely, morose, alienated photographer—well known in the field—whose pictures reflected no feelings but these. On the other hand, there have been numerous happy people, whose pictures reflected nothing but joy and good will for the world. I remember one, call him Tom, who could make a dirty garbage can look like the throne of England. The thing is that all kinds of photographs can be mirrors, not merely portraits.

The reason for people mirroring us is simple enough, though you may find it hard to accept. At that level of being at which we are all fully telepathic we all wish well of one another as spiritual brothers and sisters. And what greater kindness can you do for a kindred soul than to operate as a mirror in which he can see himself better? Racially, we have always accepted this mirroring as a spiritual duty, so that every person you really look at, in life or in pictures, is telling you something you need to know about yourself, the knowledge of your need having come telepathically from you.

There are literally thousands of experienced photographers who know that they are reflected accurately in their work, but many wouldn't accept the explanation given here. It doesn't really matter one way or the other. Whatever be the truth, such a photographer can often look at another person's photographs and tell very well what kind of a human being he is. Many have learned to do this without questioning how it could even be possible. In this so-called visual age, many who are not even photographers are also onto the trick, probably as a useful by-product of years spent in front of the television set.

So, you leave clear tracks whenever you make pictures and will instantly be found out by all who have really learned to see—all the more incentive for making pictures for the right reasons. And consider this: if you want to know what kind of a person you are, look at your own photographs. Singly or together, they are all mirrors of your life.

257

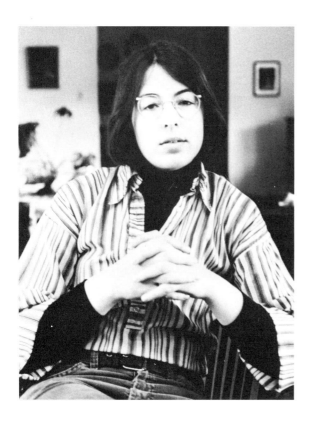

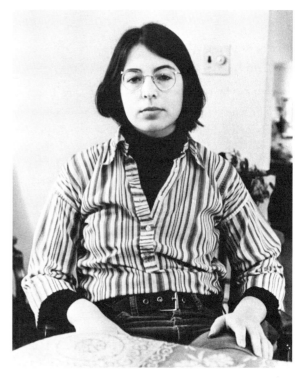

I told Kathi she could pick four of the images for enlargement, and here are her choices. Would you have picked the same ones if you were she? You can tell a lot about people by the pictures of themselves that they pick. Here we see a young woman healthy in body, mind, and spirit, reasonably pleased with herself in a very sensible way. I see this in her choices.

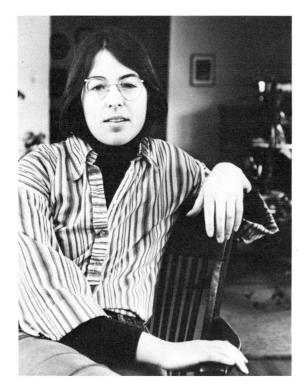

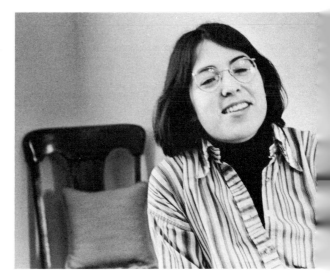

• The Fear of Being Photographed

Except for children, most people are afraid of being photographed, though they may not be consciously aware of it. Many *are* aware, however, but this doesn't help matters a bit. Since the photographer himself may be afraid too, you can see that the fear must be dealt with in some manner. The first step is to examine its nature; we will start with the model's fear.

By its very nature, visual perception is a process of criticizing visual reality, and photographing something is the act of bringing your critical faculties to bear on it. The process involves mental dissection and analysis, for when you photograph something you want to know what it is (to give the act meaning), and this is the customary way of finding out.

But people don't want to be dissected, analyzed, and accurately seen—for fear of being found out. Once found out, they will certainly be reviled and rejected. This is the unconscious supposition that many people make, based primarily on their own lack of respect for themselves. Thus a person who sees them well must necessarily come to share the disrespect.

Most people fear visual aggression, and a camera can be used for this purpose. They feel that an aggressor may discover their fear and use it to further lower their self-esteem. With respect to eye contact, a primary source of the fear, most of us are abject cowards and very unwilling to have others see it. Though we repress the fear of eye contact as best we can, trying to never even think of it at all, it affects all our relationships with other people. Naturally, it affects people being photographed, for this involves being looked at. Since photography can arouse so much fear in people, numerous photographers have looked into the problem in depth. Some feel there may be good reason for the fear, because very powerful psychological forces operate through the eyes. If this be the truth, the photographer should take great care not to bring these forces into play, for

example in visual conflicts of will with his subjects.

Half-conscious fear of the photographer's fear may be the greatest problem of all, for people unconsciously interpret it as sheer hostility, repressed but still capable of wreaking havoc on the emotional level. Since most people are afraid of those whom they photograph (if they really try to look at them), the average adult in the course of a few years has the opportunity to experience at least one emotional beating from this fear which he perceives as hostility. Naturally, he doesn't look forward to more of it.

And fear infects many, many levels of the self, sometimes even ancient fear carried over in the racial memory. I consider it highly probable that we have all preserved the atavistic fear that photographers can capture our souls in their cameras; and many people seem to respond to this particular fear when they are being photographed. Whether one believes in them or not, such ancient terrors linger in people, influence their feelings and behavior, and make them skittish when confronted with cameras.

So, what to do about all this? Perhaps the most important thing is to always remember that people tend to apprehend the camera as an instrument of visual aggression and regard being really looked at as a form of torture. Though the photographer can hide behind his or her camera, the subject must stand naked and defenseless. The act of photographing people gives you a certain power over them. The thing to do is to surrender this power as quickly and quietly as you can.

• The Meek Shall Inherit

You won't have to involve yourself very deeply in portraiture before beginning to suspect that the things you have just read may be true. As you will see, repressed fear is the big bugaboo. Some would-be photographers naïvely suppose that the way to deal with the problem of reciprocated fear is to come on to their subjects with bravado and fancy talk. Not so. This only forces models to hide within certain protective roles they have learned to adopt in times of emotional distress.

The real solution, the opposite of bravado, is to come on meek and mild—even at the grave risk of not absolutely astonishing people with your charisma. If you are a true scare cat, as so many beginners in portraiture are, it may even be wise to permit yourself a short line of patter—but *never* say it unless you really mean it:

> "I'm sorry, but I'm afraid of people, including you. If you are willing to put up with my fear —which is a lot to ask of you—I would really like to photograph you. It would help me overcome my fear, and I think you would like this."

Well, this kind of talk won't get you elected captain of the football team, but it will do wonders in encouraging people to lower their defenses and take you into their hearts. But you have got to mean it: remember that.

If you are not a scare cat—which I don't really believe—you should still come on meek and mild out of courtesy to others. Then you don't force them to don their armor and pick up their spears. The fact that you hold a camera and may be directing another person puts you in the psychologically dominant position, whether you are afraid or not. Surrender this dominance as quickly as possible. If your ego doesn't like the lesser role, tell it to go jump in the lake. However, it will like the pictures that result when fear is banished from a shooting session. With fear, you get pictures of masks; without it, a real human being.

My elder stepson Jonathan Turner in the dining room, where I do most of my portraiture. Chairs and things are already there, and I don't get in anyone's way. Now, this Jon is really some cat—I call him the King of Con. He has his elbow propped on the dining room table, in case you want to know. Bounce floodlight from his right. Shot with a hand-held Nikkormat, though I frequently use it on a tripod, too. Beautiful young man, this Jonathan.

260

• The Virtues of Snapshots

Now, the very best solution to the fear problem is the simple snapshot. Though it is said to be beyond definition, I will try it anyway. A snapshot is: (1) any photograph that *looks* like a snapshot (which assumes that you can easily recognize one without being taught); (2) a print that looks like it belongs in somebody's wallet; (3) the kind of picture that you mount in a family album with photo corners; (4) the type of photograph that Uncle Jack always makes of Aunt Gertie on their annual trip to Yosemite. You get the idea.

The snapshot is the typical output of an amateur who knows practically nothing whatever about photography. Of this person we can safely say:

1. He never really looks at the people he photographs.

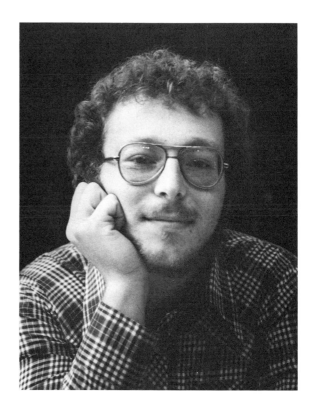

2. Even if he wished to he wouldn't know what to look for.

3. It hasn't even occurred to him that really looking might be an important part of photography, though it doesn't have to be.

4. Even if he thought of it, fear would prevent him from trying it.

5. For similar reasons, he doesn't really think about people at the same time he is not really looking at them.

6. He photographs with the unconscious and self-binding promise to his subjects that he will neither look at them nor think about them.

The things would seem to guarantee the mediocrity of the snapshot, yet it is by far the world's favorite kind of photograph. Many professional photographers and some of our greatest photographic artists adore it. There is even a "school" of so-called serious photographers devoted to trying to make snapshots, though its members—usually very advanced photographers—have had little success. How can we account for all this?

For enlightenment we will turn briefly to neo-Jungian psychology, which has an answer that you may find acceptable. It is as follows: on the level of the racial unconscious (a single great state of superconsciousness shared by all) there is a universal agreement among all people concerning the nature of "reality," including what it really looks like. Without this basic agreement, human communication would be impossible, despite the existence of languages.

One of the truly significant things about snapshots is that they constantly confirm, support, and describe this racial reality agreement, while most other types of photographs do not. That is, snapshots tell us that the world is exactly what we have agreed to think it is. In contrast, most other kinds of pictures are doubles, or mirror images of their makers superimposed on the things that were photographed. This mirroring results in very considerable distortion of the reality agreement. Thus snapshots support our faith in our ability to see reality for what it really is, which is terribly important to us, while other photographs tend to

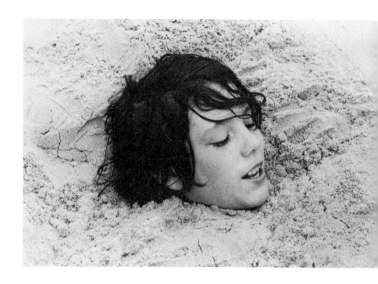

My younger stepson Bob Turner freshly buried on his first visit to the Atlantic several years ago, interment conducted by his brother and sister. I'd call this candid, wouldn't you? Kind of interesting to see a happy head floating around with no body attached.

undermine it. Actually, these things are equally good and necessary, but a full explanation of this fact is beyond the objectives of this book, and a partial one would get us nowhere.

Because the snapshot is just about the only type of photograph that conforms with the unconscious racial decision to see reality in a certain way (as a survival function of the race), it is nearly the only kind of picture that people feel safe in permitting themselves to totally believe in. If they see something in a snapshot they are unafraid to totally believe the following: the thing actually does (or did) exist; when the picture was made it looked exactly like this; it was behaving precisely in the manner indicated by the snapshot; its true nature (in terms of the reality agreement) is accurately recorded; and the snapshot itself is not a contrivance of the photographer, i.e., a mirror of his attitudes, beliefs, and experience superimposed on an image of the exterior world and possibly distorting it considerably.

A later picture of Bob, who is obviously turning ugly in his old age. I could have fixed him with a little paint, window trimming, a hammer, and a few nails, but I decided to photograph him as is. Too bad, Bob, you ugly rat. Overhead bounce light from photoflood in a reflector.

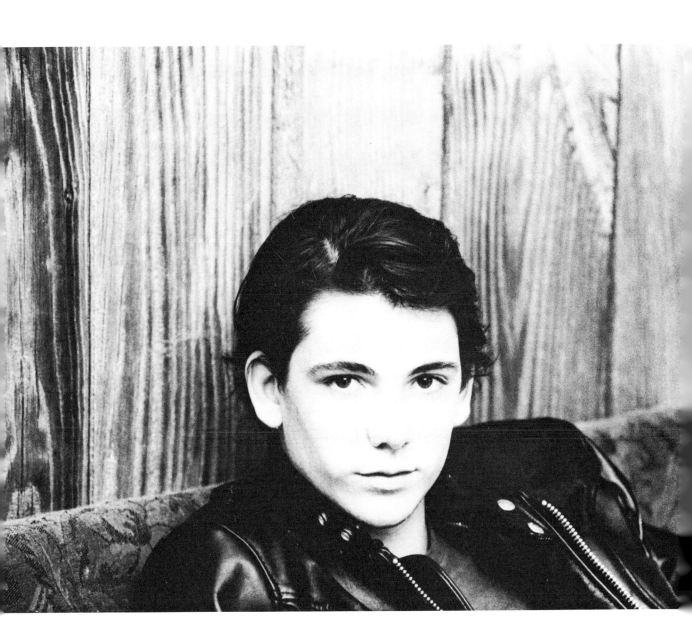

All of this happens because the snapshooter (and this includes most people who take pictures) doesn't really look at or think about his subjects. Furthermore, he simply doesn't know enough about the photographic medium to use stylistic tricks (composition, camera angle, focus control, lens tricks, etc.) to impose his personality on photographic images. Due to shyness and ignorance, reinforced by an unconscious promise, he literally *has* to leave his subjects alone. Left alone, they behave according to the reality agreement, instead of acting as mirrors. Oddly, this is true of both people and things.

Seen in this light, the snapshot surely represents the candid portrait ideal: open, frank, unguarded, honest, or truthful. Only a person who has been left entirely alone feels safe in such self-revelation in front of a camera. Thus we can now state a rule: *don't meddle with your subjects! Leave them entirely alone!*

As a beginner, this shouldn't be hard for you, as you haven't yet learned to use photography as a tool for meddling and changing people around. That will come in time, and you will lose the ability to make snapshots. Start mourning the loss right now, for it will be a large one, and few who have lost the ability have ever earned it back, though many have tried. The road back has but one signpost: *leave people alone!* You will learn that this is a most difficult art.

• The Technique of the Snapshot

1. Stand over there, please.
2. Click!
3. Thank you.

• Environments

It is now time to turn to more technical matters, so we will start with the problem of selecting environments in which to pose people. One approach is to be nonselective and photograph them wherever they happen to be. Though it is a good idea and used by photographers at all levels of at-

tainment, it can be quite difficult for the beginner. Oh, he can get his pictures easily enough, but they tend to be filled with visual distractions, things that get into the viewfinder unnoticed that don't look good in pictures, pictorial garbage that detracts from the people photographed. For the beginner, then, the answer is to be more selective concerning environments.

Indoors or out, the first thing is to check out backgrounds to find ones that are potentially useful. A background is everything that will be behind a model in a photograph, and the questions you should ask yourself are, "Do I really want it there?" and "Why?" While doing this it is helpful to think of backgrounds as having these main pictorial functions: to display your subjects, explain them, or both.

One of the classical tricks for displaying something is to remove everything else from its surroundings to lessen possible distraction. Thus plain walls, skies, lawns, roadways, and the like make good display backgrounds—there is nothing in them to distract from the people you are photographing. However, there are numerous other good display backgrounds, such as doorways, windows, patios, hallways, staircases, and so on. The important thing is to examine backgrounds carefully (through your camera viewfinder) and decide whether you really want to use them.

An explanatory background is one that helps communicate what your subject is or does. For example, if you photograph your mother in the kitchen it communicates the idea that she is both a cook and housewife, whether she actually is or not. If you photograph a man working on his car it suggests that he has a flair for mechanics. There are some people that you don't wish to separate from what they are or do when you photograph them. In such cases explanatory backgrounds may be necessary. Furthermore, the backgrounds may be interesting in themselves.

Whatever kind of background or general environment you use, it is wise to look for visual simplicity. Though visual complexity can be interesting, it is often hard to handle in portraits. You

263

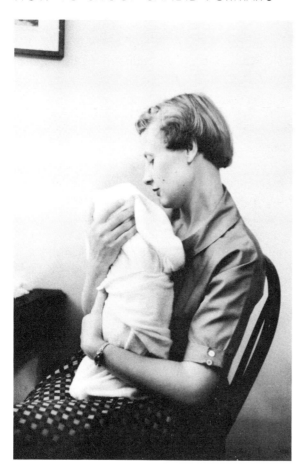

Kris Myers and new youngun. Overhead bounce floodlight. Shot with a primordial Retina II from back in the days when cameras all had wheels and were started by spinning their cranks. Double-X film, yet—ever even heard of it? ASA 200, which wasn't so bad. This picture is somewhat like a painting, but so what?

may end up with pictures that look like battle scenes from World War III.

Now, you have just been told that environmental simplicity is generally good for portraits, but for the Lord's sake don't make it into an ironclad rule. Simplicity is easier to work with, that is all. Don't make it any more than that. As for what you should put in your pictures, Picasso had the right answer: "I put the things I like in my pictures."

In choosing backgrounds you should certainly consider whether your subjects would be comfortable posing in them. The ceiling of the living room might make a very good background for Grandma, but would she be happy hanging from the chandelier?

• Outdoor Lighting

In portraiture, lightings are very important, so you should look into what they do. Direct sunlight is often cruel in what it does to people. It makes them squint until their faces look like raisins and casts sharp-edged shadows that make flesh look as hard as stone. These shadows sometimes even look like sword cuts, and facial highlights tend to look pitted and greasy. Even so, you can use direct sunlight for candid portraits, but you had better be on the alert for what it is doing to your subjects.

The lightings most often used for outdoor portraiture are hazy sun, light or heavy overcast sky, and open shade. They all treat faces gently and are comfortable for your subjects. Some beginners feel that they aren't bright enough, but this is simply not true. For modern black-and-white films, which are usually quite fast, there is an amplitude of light. Even for color films, which are usually much slower, there is plenty. Though color films will take on a bluish cast, most people don't mind it. If you do you can correct for it by using a skylight filter.

• Flash

Indoors, the light may not be bright enough for portraiture, so many people resort to flash, usually clipped right onto their cameras. This is called "direct flash." Though professionals and advanced amateurs often think that direct flash is rather gross, it is actually a good thing. To use it is very easy: just follow the instructions with the flash cubes or printed on your flash unit. It really works: if you do what you are told you can hardly fail, provided your flash unit doesn't cop out. It doesn't frighten people: direct flash is the mark of the snapshooter, and no one is afraid of him. It doesn't stir things up: at parties, family gatherings, and so on, nobody gives a hoot how many flashes go off, for everyone is used to them. For these reasons, direct flash is excellent for candid pictures, and I personally use it quite often.

However, the objections to direct flash are valid enough, though you shouldn't permit yourself to be limited by them. Go ahead and use it if you like. One objection is that it *is* direct: that is, the light rays shoot out parallel to the lens axis, fill in all the shadows on faces and things, and leave dark cast shadows behind them or slightly off to one side.

It happens that shadows on faces are mainly what make them look the way they do. Because shadows constantly change, faces do too, which is one of the most wonderful things about faces. Direct flash cancels out this kind of change by wiping out the shadows. There may still be changes of facial expression and pose, of course, but the total number of possibilities for change is indeed severely limited, which some photographers see almost as a crime. It isn't, but that's what they think.

Some facial shadows look best if they *are* filled in, for example, those caused by bags under the eyes, wrinkles, a heavily pitted skin, long noses, abnormally deep eye sockets, and long chins.

People who have such things are often made to look very good by direct flash.

Another main objection is that a direct flash picture "falsifies" the lighting in the room in which it was made. That is, the lighting displayed in the picture has little resemblance to the room lighting before and after the flash went off. And the lighting in a room does much to give it its character. You can worry about this if you like, but there is really no point to it. Direct flash looks like direct flash, room light like room light. There is room in this universe for both.

Fortunately, a simple technique called "bounce flash" will mainly overcome the objections. You bounce light by pointing your flash unit at the ceiling or a nearby wall, instead of directly at your subject. The light then reflected illuminates your subject and the room in a way acceptably close to room lighting.

Bounce flash isn't nearly as bright as direct flash, so you should use fast films, for example, Tri-X for black-and-white. For color, use a blue flashbulb or electronic flash with either Ektachrome 200 or Kodacolor 400 (the numbers represent their ASA speeds). With the Ektachrome, which is relatively slow, you will prob-

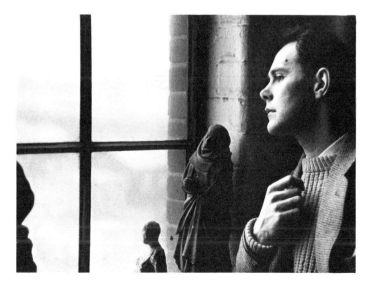

Actor Paul Williams looking down that long, long, long, long road. Window light is swell for candid portraiture, as you can plainly see. Also, windows have a variety of symbolic meanings, which is one reason they are used so often in art and photography. The little figure to Paul's right is obviously painfully constipated—but that's what art does to one.

ably need to use rather large lens openings, usually ranging from f/2.8 to f/5.6, but they are quite satisfactory for indoor portraiture.

With bounce flash the instructions with your flash cubes or flash unit will no longer work, because they are designed only for direct flash. It is necessary to personally work out new aperture settings for a given house or apartment. Once you have done this you will be able to estimate the correct settings for other locations. For overhead bounce, which is most often used, the main factor in determining the aperture is the distance of the ceiling from the flash unit. Fortunately, the ceilings in homes and apartments mostly tend to be about the same height, which means that you can use the same setting for nearly all of them. Provided that they are all white, that is. A dark ceiling would require more exposure and a larger setting.

It should be sufficient to work out settings for just one room, say the den or living room. It is quite easy to do. Just stand up and shoot a series of pictures one stop apart of a family member or friend, recording all the apertures used. The picture that comes out with the best exposure will indicate the best aperture setting for a standing shot in that room. When shooting from a seated position, open up an additional stop. This method of determining settings may seem a little guess and by golly, but thousands have used it with success.

So far I haven't differentiated between regular and electronic flash: the things you have read will apply to both. But in the realm of bounce flash some of the electronic types will do things that bulbs and flash cubes can't do. These are the types that embody sensor units and thyristor circuits and that are specially designed for semi-automatic operation for both direct and bounce flash.

With such a unit you don't have to worry very much about your distance from the ceiling or a reflecting wall. Functioning as a sensing computer, it does your worrying for you. It controls the exposure by limiting the duration of the flash

discharge, which is very bright. When the unit flashes the sensor starts measuring the light reflected from the subject to discover the point at which there has been enough of it to properly expose the film. At that point the thyristor circuit takes over and instantly turns off the flash. Thus the flash duration for a given unit may vary from, say, 1/500 to 1/10,000 of a second. This gives the photographer a very considerable range of exposures, selected for him electronically.

The sensor couldn't care less where the light reflected by the subject comes from—direct from the flash tube, or from the ceiling, wall, or floor —because it only measures quantity. Thus it makes no differentiation whatever between direct and bounce flash. Your flash unit is a sensor-computer that works out and controls your exposures for you, which is very reassuring and convenient. These outfits are real beauties and they work like a charm, but they still come with instructions that must be read and followed. We

C. B. Neblette, photography's great educator, in his old office at the Rochester Institute of Technology. Overhead bounce flash.

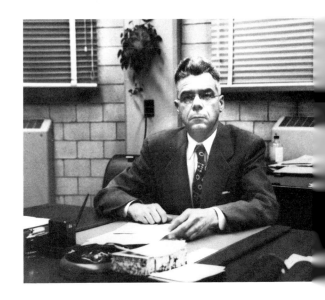

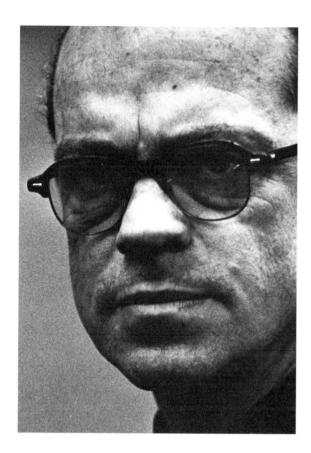

Frank Harris looking like the man who clobbered Attila the Hun. Now, the overhead bounce flash hitting the ceiling directly over his head has given us this very strong lighting. And Frank has a strong face, too, of course. Bouncing the light from more of an angle would have filled the shadows in (see next chapter).

creates on the faces of your subjects and thus cannot know how they will look in pictures. A way around this is to own an electronic unit with a built-in modeling light but such units are usually large, expensive, and cumbersome. Thus if you really want to see what light is doing—a commendable idea—it might be best to turn to floodlight or natural light.

• Floodlight

The main reason for floodlight is to raise the level of indoor light to a point where you can stop your camera lens down a bit and use fairly fast shutter speeds. You can do this best by having your light, say a 500 watt photoflood, very close to your subjects and pointed right at them. However, this is very disconcerting to people, because the light is very hot and extremely bright. Furthermore, you will probably get ugly light and shadow patterns on faces, unless you already know how to "see light," which takes quite a while to learn.

In terms of doing justice to the faces and bodies of your subjects, the best bet is to bounce your floodlight (one is usually enough) from the ceiling or a wall—any surface that is light in color will do if it is large enough. However, if you use a fast film such as Tri-X you should be able to expose around 1/60 of a second at f/2.8, which is not at all bad for candid portraiture.

You can even shoot color, using High Speed Ektachrome B (balanced for tungsten light), but you should use it only with a 3200 K lamp. This lamp gives off exactly the right color of light for this brand of film. With an ASA speed of 160, this film is quite a bit slower than Tri-X (ASA 400), so you may find yourself using shutter speeds as slow as 1/15 second. But this doesn't have to be a problem, as you will see in a moment. The answer may be a tripod.

At a speed of 1/30 second you should be able to use your camera hand-held, provided that you

have yet to see a unit that a bona fide moron can operate. Sorry.

Because people are used to it nowadays and don't seem to mind it at all, flash (ordinary or electronic) is especially good for portraiture. Since it will stop action, you don't have to ask people to hold still but can catch them moving around. Equally important, it creates no tumult. It's just on, off, and goodbye.

One problem with flash is that you can't actually see the light and shadow patterns that it

brace it tightly against your forehead, slow down your breathing a bit, and depress the shutter release by gradually *squeezing* it, not by punching at it. Such things counteract camera movement and make for sharper pictures.

At f/2.8 you will get enough depth of field to get a full or half figure acceptably sharp at the distance required to fit such figures into your viewfinder. It is also a small enough aperture for a close-up, or head shot, provided that you focus on the eye closest to your camera. If you focus on the farther eye or the contour of the head, the front of the face will be out of focus. Even if you decide to stop down to f/4 or f/5.6 you should still focus on the nearest eye—unless the eyes are equidistant from you, of course, in which case either one will do.

The safest kind of floodlighting is bounce from the ceiling, for it is gently flattering to nearly everyone. Furthermore, it distributes light rather evenly over a fairly large area, so that you don't have to take a new light reading every time a subject moves a foot or two. As you move away from the light stand the illumination will gradually fall off, of course. Even so, there is a circle of illumination around it about eight feet across in which you can stick with just one aperture and shutter speed setting. Not having to constantly change the settings will make it possible for you to be more casual and relaxed about what you are doing, which is just the thing for candid portraiture.

Light bounced from a side wall is generally more dramatic, with the drama gradually increasing as you move your subject closer and closer to the wall. However, by moving him or her away from the wall you can lessen the drama (contrast, really) to any degree you wish. Side bounce usually produces pictures with a much more three-dimensional feeling than those made by overhead bounce, mainly due to the effects of lighting contrast.

With side bounce you should take a new exposure reading every time your subject changes position more than a foot or two. It is usually safe to read the face, provided that the meter reading covers both the light and dark side of it at the same time. If you read only the light side you will get underexposure. And reading only the dark side will give you overexposure. For overhead bounce a good way to get a dependable reading is with a Kodak Gray Card. Just hold it up to your model's face and slant it slightly upward toward the ceiling. Then take a reading from it and use the camera settings indicated by your meter. This system works because the gray on the card was selected because it reflects an average amount of light, and people (including their hair, clothing, highlights, and shadows) reflect an average amount, too. Thus reading a gray card is equivalent to reading all parts of a person within view of your camera and averaging them, another good way of determining exposure. The card reading is simply faster and usually more accurate. You can use it with either a separate meter or one built into your camera.

Concerning people's reactions to rooms brightly lit by photoflood, they usually don't mind once they get used to it, which may take ten minutes or so. And children couldn't care less. However, there are adults who don't like bright light at all, especially mature women who are aware that dim light treats them more gracefully and gently. Such a person may get uptight when you drag out your floodlight, so in this case you should leave it in the closet and settle for natural light.

• Natural Light

In photography, natural light is often referred to as "available light," meaning whatever light you encounter indoors when you decide to photograph somebody there—light from doors, windows, table and floor lamps, ceiling fixtures, and so on. Each room or interior area has its own unique lighting scheme, usually created after a lot of thought, and the natural light photographer chooses to pay his respects to the creator by using the lighting as is, though he may turn on a floor lamp or raise a window shade.

Now, a thoroughly familiar lighting gives people a great deal of comfort and security, and a radical change is not always welcome, even though temporary. And it is for this reason that many candid portraitists choose to leave the lighting undisturbed, though it may make things difficult for them. However, they also know that many kinds of fine pictures can be made with natural light and that it often does wonderful things they themselves would never think of doing with light sources fully under their own control.

In terms of what it does to faces and figures, the available light indoors varies considerably in quality from one location to another. For example, near a certain window it may be wonderful, in the center of the living room just so-so, and in

Hollis N. Todd, that rarity—a master teacher. Though I could have draped something over Hollis' rusty radiator I preferred to leave his environment alone. Concern over having pictorial environments is legitimate, surely, but you can easily get carried away by it and miss many a good shot as a consequence. I like this picture of Todd, and I'm the guy I made the picture for.

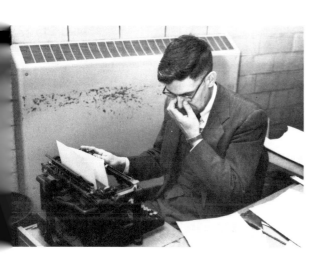

the utility room downright awful. Aware of this, the skilled photographer tries to stay constantly alert to what light is doing to people, wherever they may be, so that when it comes time to photograph them he already knows the best places for it.

Unfortunately, the light available in many places isn't very bright, because a lot of people like it that way. They may feel that low light levels promote feelings of warmth, security, intimacy, or mystery. For others it may mean privacy. At any rate, the light is dim and we find ourselves with an exposure problem. Color positive films may be entirely out, because they are so slow, but an ASA 400 color negative film is just fine.

Even with fast black-and-white films such as Tri-X we may find ourselves using exposures in the order of 1/4 second at f/2. At 1/4 second it is difficult to hold a camera steady, and f/2 gives us little depth of field. Another difficulty is that many of the meters built into cameras won't give readings in dim light, while some types of separate meters give readings too low on the meter scales to be dependable.

The best answer to this exposure problem is to have a supersensitive light meter such as the Gossen Luna-Pro, which will produce accurate readings even by moonlight. However, there is a special metering technique that will work with separate and built-in meters of less sensitivity. It is called a white card reading and the technique is easy. You divide the ASA speed of your film by five to get its "white card speed," then set this new speed on your meter. Then hold an 8×10-inch sheet of white cardboard or paper in front of your model and take a reading from it; its whiteness will help you get a good reading. Then use the exposure setting (aperture and shutter speed) registered on the meter. Or with a built-in adjust the shutter speed and/or the aperture until the needle is positioned correctly. That is all you have to do, because dividing by five compensates in advance for the fact that models are much darker than white cards.

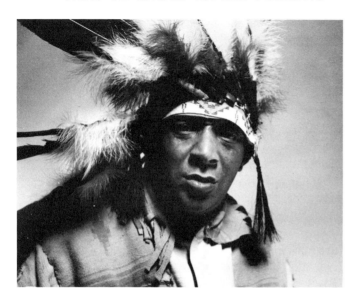

My good friend Arion Chief Suwarrow, who has spent thirty years trying to prove he is a full-blood Indian—which he ain't. For about five years I was his press agent. Studio shot: one very large floodlight bounced off a reflector on the right side of the picture. No fill light. The Chief made the headdress himself.

The slow shutter speed may cause fuzzy pictures due to camera movement, subject movement, or both. The camera movement can easily be eliminated with a tripod (which every dedicated photographer should most certainly have), provided that one uses it with a cable release. This is a thin, flexible tube-like device embodying a plunger for depressing the shutter release without jarring the camera. However, the cable release should be at least ten inches long, and you should make a loop in it before depressing the plunger. Acting as a shock absorber, the loop absorbs your body movement so that it won't be transmitted to the camera.

Having to tie yourself down with a tripod will slow up a shooting session very considerably, but it is sometimes all that you can do. It may also force you to ask a subject to hold a position while you adjust the tripod, focus, and shoot. Then if you take too long at it he or she may stiffen up from muscle fatigue and start looking very pained. With practice, however, you won't have to ask people to hold still. You will just wait patiently until they settle down for a moment, then immediately focus and shoot. Unless a person has St. Vitus dance or burrs in his britches he is bound to hold still every now and then, so you just wait. You can even do this with children, no matter how bouncy they are.

In addition to using a tripod when necessary you should also work to develop a steady camera hand, because you can photograph much more flexibly with a hand-held camera. Three of the secrets for this have already been mentioned: breath control, *squeezing* the shutter release, and pressing the camera very firmly against your forehead. In addition, brace your elbows firmly against your rib cage (instead of letting them stick out like wings). Whether standing, seated, or lying down, take a position that you think you could comfortably hold for five minutes; it will very probably be a posture steady enough for good camera handling. Also, wrap the camera neck strap around the hand that carries most of the weight of the camera in such a fashion as to virtually weld the hand and camera together.

Hold your camera in such a way that the finger or thumb used for depressing the shutter release carries none of the camera's weight; the finger's sole function should be to move freely in squeezing the release. Use any available supports to help you brace yourself: lean against a doorjamb; sit in a chair and brace your elbows on your knees; prop your elbows on a table; rest your camera on a friend's shoulder, using him as a mobile tripod; and so on.

A proper mental attitude is possibly the most important camera-steadying trick of all. Don't permit yourself to feel like the avid young cave man getting his first shot at a pterodactyl; you will surely get the shakes if you do. Remember that the people you photograph won't be going anywhere right away, so if you miss three or four shots there will be lots of others that you don't miss. So when you are ready to shoot, think about something quieting, such as grocery lists. A thought that I have personally used with good effect for self-calming goes something like this in the expurgated version: "Bugger all, I don't really want this blank blank picture anyway." Another one, again addressed to myself, is: "Look, you bloody idiot, you won't actually drop dead if you miss this shot." Sometimes you have to talk roughly to yourself to catch your own attention.

Before leaving the frustrating problem of camera steadying we must pay tribute to the humble martini, for it has steadied even more hands than virtue has. And so have Miltown and its cousins, of course. As for avoidances, be sure to steer away from strong coffee and other stimulants—if you are more interested in shooting pictures than in climbing the wall.

With practice in using these steadying tricks you will frequently find yourself using a hand-held camera at speeds below 1/30 second, sometimes as low as 1/4 or 1/2. When you are well braced and in the right frame of mind you may even be able to use the B (bulb) setting for exposures as long as two or three seconds.

Let us return to dim illumination and the need for large f/stops, such as f/1.4 or f/2. Using a tripod, you can generally stop down a bit (to f/2.8, f/4, or f/5.6) and safely use shutter speeds as low as one second. Even at this slow speed you don't necessarily have to ask people to sit still, though it is easier if you do. If you watch a person for a while you will see that his or her movement and stillness alternate in a kind of rhythm. This permits you to anticipate moments of quiet so that you can shoot pictures when they occur. This may sound difficult, but it isn't—and it is an interesting little game to play.

Another problem in low illumination levels is a nervous and fidgety model—you can't use a fast enough shutter speed to stop the movement. We will get to this problem in the next section.

• You and Your Models

In candid portraiture it is important to make your models feel comfortable and relaxed. To help in this you should learn to recognize the signs of nervousness, try to understand its causes, and accept the possibility that you yourself may be the chief cause. For example, you may be talking too

Art Gorman, when he was a student of mine about ninety years ago. For candid portraits, distractions are very useful, music being one of the best, closely followed by naked women. Art couldn't have cared less what I was up to, so I bounce flashed his picture without disturbing his mood or expression.

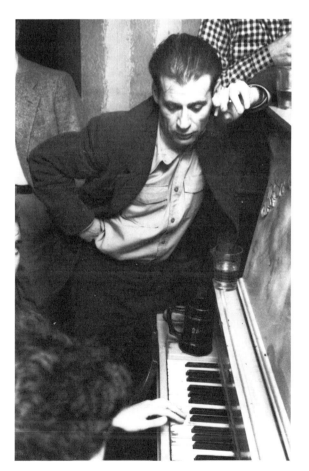

fast, coming on too hard, and hopping around like an agitated rabbit—to demonstrate your competence as a photographer and cover up your own nervousness. Such behavior will make your model as nervous as yourself.

The solution to this particular problem? Slow your speech way way down, abandon your sales pitch, and imitate the slow, deliberate movements of a tortoise. Such behavior is very, very calming to another person.

Do your best to be a downright bore for a while. Oddly, being a deliberate bore is a very effective move used even in professional photography. Ken Heyman, one of our finest photographers, is the master. He can be so boring that his models actually forget he is in the room with them. The thing is that bores practically never come on as threats, so that they are easily forgotten.

In yet another way you may cause your subjects to squirm—if you move inside their invisible defense perimeters. Unconsciously, each person draws an imaginary circle around himself, marking the minimum distance he feels he must keep between himself and others for his own emotional security. By observation you can usually tell how far a person's perimeter has been extended for you at a given moment. Then it is your duty to respect the defense perimeter and stay outside of it. In order to do this you might shoot half-figure poses instead of head shots. Or you could use a lens of fairly long focal length, such as a 90mm lens (very popular for portraiture) on a 35mm camera.

I once had a female student who was very leery of me as a threatening father figure, so her perimeter was very important to her when I was around (it was a minimum of four feet in radius). Whenever I would intentionally invade it she would make a two-foot backward jump, like a sparrow hopping along a branch. One day when I was paying very little real attention to anyone I managed to jump her the length of a large room before I awoke to what I was doing.

Well, it is usually not this easy to discover the radius of someone's perimeter, but you can usually figure it out if you keep track of such things in your model as rapid eye blinking, a sound of dryness in the voice, speeded-up speech, compulsive yawning, clenched fingers, strained neck muscles, stiffness in the back position, knees pressed tightly together, evasive eye movements, and so on. All are indicators of nervousness, often caused by the invasion of one's perimeter.

Even better, you can learn to detect nervousness in another person by its effect on your solar plexus. Anxiety is broadcast like radio waves and human glands are excellent receivers, especially those in the head, neck, and solar plexus. If you learn to listen to your glands they will tell you how your models feel. If they really hurt you have got a problem with someone.

And be sure to remember that adults are generally afraid of being really looked at, especially if it involves eye contact. When you *do* look someone in the eye, *always* look down first. *Always* be the loser in the unspoken contest for visual dominance. If you want to really look at a subject, do it through your camera viewfinder. Otherwise, confine yourself to briefly glancing at facial features other than the eyes—forehead, nose, chin, cheekbones, hair, and so on.

Earlier, you read about the great importance of making portraits for the right reasons, which includes the correct attitudes. For their self-assurance your models need to be constantly told where they stand with you, and you can tell them in subtle, indirect ways. Taking lots of pictures is one way. Another is to frequently use the word "yes" and other little sounds of approval or satisfaction (mmm, yeah, yep, fine, etc.). Though muttered half under the breath they give a model assurance that everything is all right.

Though you may not believe in unconscious telepathy, you would be wise to behave as if you did by controlling your thoughts. Thus when you are photographing people you should be on the constant lookout for things you like about them—in their appearance, personality, behavior, attitudes, or whatever—and mulling them over in your mind. Such thinking is somehow communicated, and it will do much to reassure your models and make shooting sessions relaxed and joyous.

On the other hand, when you see things in others that you dislike, don't dwell on them in your mind, for that too is communicated. As an aid in dismissing such thoughts, remember this psychological law: the things that we dislike in others are almost invariably reflections of the very same things in ourselves. Otherwise, they wouldn't bother us so much. If this doesn't work and your thoughts are still negative, try remembering something you liked very much, for example, a joyous walk in the woods with your dog. Though this has nothing to do with your model it will give a positive emotional charge to the atmosphere, which is what you both need.

Now, you must realize that there are times in a shooting session when you shouldn't take pictures, even though that is its purpose. You may have to refrain from taking some really interesting shots, possibly the best of all. But you should give them up anyway. This is the problem: most people constantly do things they don't want recorded in pictures, and you should respect their wishes in this. For example, they frown, scowl, grimace, pick at their faces, make ugly gestures, rub their eyes, stretch, cough, sneeze, pick their noses, and so on. And they are instantly aware of it if a photographer photographs such behavior. Doing so is a violation of a confidence and your model's right to select the facial expression he or she wishes to present to the world. If you do it even once your model will lose all trust in you, though nothing will be said—and the whole shooting session will slide right down the drain.

In a more positive vein, it often helps a shooting session if your model is accompanied by a friend or two. Then you can shoot your subject while he or she and the friends are talking and enjoying one another. You can get some really wonderful pictures this way.

● Poses

In formal portraiture, standardized poses are of some importance, because they are an accepted part of the game. This is not true of candid portraiture, however. Here you should be ruled by a single axiom: if the subject is comfortable the pose is just fine. You can ask people to do things —sit, stand, lie down, lean, etc.—but encourage them to be comfortable while doing so.

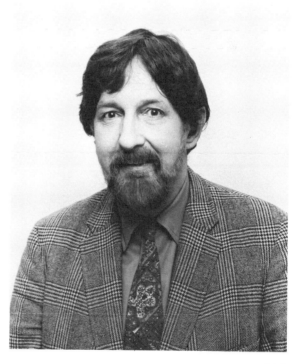

The author as a young man. Or: old author with young wig, beard darkened with eyebrow pencil. I asked Dennis Martin to snap some shots of the rejuvenated me—studio electronic flash with an umbrella—and this one I found most beguiling.

Now, many subjects will assume that you want poses as stiff as boards and will do their best to look like wooden Indians. With such a person try this approach, which is much better than a lengthy explanation of what you want from him or her: "Relax in this chair while I work on my camera a while." Then start fiddling with the camera and muttering good-naturedly to yourself, watching your subject out of the corner of your eye.

As soon as he or she tires of being a wooden Indian and relaxes into a comfortable position, make your next move. "Aha, very good pose; hold it for just a second while I get a picture." And, of course, you should be all prepared to do it just that quickly.

Even if you don't like the pose, make a picture of it anyway—film is cheap. Indeed, you should take a picture of every pose the model takes, provided that it is a comfortable one. The important thing is that this teaches your subjects in the quickest possible way that you are more interested in their comfort than in poses out of *Vogue* or *Captain Marvel*.

An even easier way to work is to say nothing whatever about poses. When you have permission, spoken or unspoken, to photograph someone, just wait around quietly and unobtrusively until he or she is doing something you like. Then walk up and make your pictures. When you work in this manner people soon get the idea that you are interested in them as they really are, not as actors playing roles from grade B movies.

Returning to the idea of pictures full of wooden Indians: there is nothing really wrong with them; most people shoot such pictures; and you should go right ahead and shoot as many as you like. However, you may also be interested in people behaving more naturally. So why not take both kinds?

If you are inclined to be shy and find that the information in this chapter makes portraiture more a threat to you than an interesting challenge, why just forget all of it—except for the comments on the snapshot. If you prefer to photograph people without really looking at them or even thinking about them, go right ahead—you will probably make excellent snapshots. And that is nothing to sniff at.

Kip Petticolas says that eyeteeth are sexy and has grown a new pair just to prove it. Portraits don't *all* have to be serious, you know. Available (natural) light from lamps and windows.

FORMAL PORTRAITURE: LIGHTING

Formal portraiture is the kind practiced by commercial portrait photographers, who have in many ways refined the art to a high degree. Certainly, they know what people like in portraits, for their livings depend on it. Thus their knowledge should be of interest to you. Their work is formal in the sense that it follows set forms, or ways of doing things, that are in universal use throughout the world. That is, they all use the same tricks and techniques, mainly because customers have found them pleasing. For you, the most useful of them is their approach to portrait lighting, which we will deal with in this chapter. Since you probably do not have professional lighting equipment, the techniques will be explained in terms of light sources that you can afford. However, the things that you will learn can also be used with more expensive equipment.

In the last chapter you were introduced to bounce light, that is, a light source pointed at a wall, ceiling, or other reflecting surface. For beginners, this is a very good start, because it doesn't demand acute perceptual awareness, or the ability to "see light." Even if you are not very conscious of what you are seeing, your pictures will usually come out pretty good, your subjects looking as you think they ought to.

However, the lightings in this chapter practically insist that you begin developing your ability to see and will be a great help for you in this direction. If you do not, your subjects may look

very bad in their pictures and may even seem like strangers. Do not avoid these lightings, however, because they are very good ones and are an important part of the living tradition of photography. As the philosopher said: "He who manages to avoid all mistakes learns nothing, for mistakes are our teachers. Anyway, complete avoidance is only possible after your funeral." So, you will certainly make mistakes with the lightings, but they will really help your visual perception.

Most of the lightings involve pointing one or more light sources right at the model or in that general direction. The effect on his or her appearance is usually very different from that of bounce light. The amount of light that falls upon your subject is considerably increased, so that you can use faster shutter speeds and/or smaller f-stops. It is also easier to work with the slower color films. In contrast, when light is bounced from a wall or reflector, much of it is absorbed or scattered, which reduces the intensity of the part that reaches the model.

The chief difference in visual quality between direct and bounce lighting can be explained in terms of shadows and shadow patterns. In terms of learning to see better, shadows give us something rather tangible to work with. In bounce lighting you are usually not very aware of either shadows or their patterns, because the shadows have such soft edges. Without well-defined edges to attach your perceptions to, you may not even be aware of any shadows at all, though there actually may be an abundance of them. And if you can't see the shadows, you will certainly be oblivious to the patterns they make. This is the problem with bounce lighting.

In comparison, direct lighting may produce shadows with edges ranging from fairly sharp to extremely sharp. Then you will have no doubt that the shadows are actually there, both on your living subject and in your pictures of him or her. Once you know they are there for sure, you can start to learn what they *do*. You will even learn to see the shadows and shadow patterns in subtle bounce lighting.

(The model for the illustrations in this chapter was my younger stepson, Bob Turner. My objective was to show shadows and shadow patterns in such an unmistakable way that you would be sure to see them and to sense how they affect the appearance of Bob's face in various ways. The pictures work well enough as portraits, to be sure, but their main function is to describe what light does to a face.)

The factors that determine the edge sharpness of shadows are the size of the light source and its distance from your subject. The *smaller* the source—and the *greater* the distance—the sharper will be the shadow edge. Conversely, the *larger* the light source—and the *less* the distance —the *softer* will be the shadow edge.

For example, small sources such as a candle, flashlight, miniature spotlight, or the sun are naturally good for producing sharp-edge shadows. However, as they are moved progressively closer to your subject the sharpness is gradually diminished, whereas increasing the distance adds to the sharpness of the edges.

Large sources such as big reflectors (or walls used as reflectors for bounce lighting), large skylights or windows, an overcast sky, or the blue sky when the sun is not in sight, are naturally good for producing soft-edge shadows. Closeness to the subject increases this softness, while distance adds sharpness.

The light sources best for beginners (3200 K bulbs in reflectors—good for both black-and-white film and Ektachrome 160 color film) fall in between the large and small sizes and in some situations can be used for either soft or sharp shadow edges. For example, if such a unit is used within one or two feet of a subject it will make soft-edge shadows. However, at a distance of four or five feet the edges become more obviously defined, and at ten feet or more they are very sharp.

Lighting contrast affects the apparent sharpness of shadow edges and is the main factor controlling how obvious the shadows will be, on your living model and in your pictures. High contrast increases our awareness of shadows and their edges, thus making them seem sharper. With moderate contrast we are less aware, and with very low contrast we are hardly aware of shadows at all (all of these things can be seen in the illustrations if you examine them closely).

Furthermore, shadows have a considerable influence in making things look the way they do (notice how Bob Turner's face changes with the lightings). And they are primary creative tools in all stages of photography, from beginning to very advanced.

Earlier, I said that bounce lightings (most of them) don't require much visual perception in the photographer. Because they usually combine very soft-edge shadows with moderate to low lighting contrast, they treat human faces very gently. No matter how your subjects are positioned geometrically with respect to the light source (a reflecting surface), they come out looking pretty good, even if you don't really see what they look like while snapping your pictures.

When we shift to direct lighting with light sources much smaller than the ceilings and reflecting walls used in bounce light, the situation changes drastically, especially if we use fairly high contrast. Now the geometric relationship of subject and light source become very important. If the head is turned in one position, it may look good; in another, it may look awful. Sometimes the difference between good and awful is represented by a very slight turning (or raising or lowering) of the head, perhaps an inch or less. The thing is that with direct lighting you are working with fairly obvious shadows on your subject's face. With your two light sources (recommended here) you can create many shadow patterns, but relatively few will look pleasant and flattering to your subject.

The question now arises, why bother trying something in which the risk of failure is so high? Well, we *learn* from failures—remember? Another answer is that you will find your successes very rewarding after you have earned them. Again, experimenting with these lightings will enable you to see for the first time in your life what a face really looks like. And you will tend to develop a much better grasp of the difference between the beautiful and the ugly, an important factor in learning photography and a much more sophisticated problem than you might suppose.

Perhaps the most important possibility is that you may find a way of drawing on your emotional energies in your efforts to learn to see better. This is a tremendous help. In photographing friends or family you make an unspoken promise to see the best in them and express it in your pictures, which would make failure very embarrassing. The fear of this will build up enough emotional tension to motivate an effort to really see. This requires a lot of energy and is very difficult and tiring.

Your emotional commitment can also help you confront your photographic failures long enough to analyze their nature and figure out how to correct them. Otherwise, you might not even notice them. As the Chinese sage Chuantze once said, "Man learns mainly from his errors, but he isn't even aware of them until they bite his nose, steal his purse, or turn his friends against him."

● The Functions of Portrait Lights

Portrait lights are used mainly in a traditional way, so we will use classical terminology (photographic jargon) in naming them and describing their functions. In a standard portraiture lighting setup the light sources are called, in order of their importance, the key light, fill light, background light, and hair light. You should work only with the key light and the fill, because the others are not especially necessary and would add to your equipment costs. The two are identical light fixtures, but the ones you will omit are different and sometimes quite specialized.

The key light gets its name from the fact that it is positioned closer to the model than the fill, thus it has a stronger effect on his or her appearance. We can say, therefore, that the key to what your picture will look like is in what the key light does to your subject's face. The higher the lighting contrast, the more this is true.

The experienced photographer always begins his lighting procedure with the fill light turned off, using the key light alone. With it he tries different light positions and asks the model to change the pose (or the tilt or turn of the head) in various ways, until he is satisfied that he has found the best combination for the particular type of face he is photographing.

Without the fill light the shadows are dark and obvious, so that the light and shade patterns created by the key light are very easy to see. Furthermore, the difference in patterns caused by shifting the light position or changing the pose is also fairly obvious. With quite a bit of experimentation it is easy enough to see that some combinations are more becoming to the model than others, so be sure to experiment enough. Only when you are satisfied that the key light and the pose are working together in the very best way should you then turn on the fill light; this is the way the professional works.

We call it the fill light because its primary function is to fill the shadows on the face and figure, which means to lighten them to some degree. The fill light gives us control over lighting contrast, which in turn permits us to make dynamic (high contrast) or static (low contrast) pictures—or something in between.

We get high contrast by using no fill light at all,

by having the fill light fixture far away from the model, or by using just the edge light. This means to point a light in front of, or behind, a subject in such a way that only the edge of its light pattern falls upon him or her. Since the edge light is relatively dim it doesn't lighten the shadows very much. To gradually *lower* the contrast we move the fill light toward the subject. When the key light and the fill light are equidistant from the model, the lighting contrast disappears altogether, so that both sides of the face and figure are of the same tone, or brightness.

• Some Functions of Lighting Contrast

Lighting contrast is very important in photography, because it mainly controls the dimensional feeling in pictures and has a strong effect on the apparent solidity and realness of our subjects. These qualities are usually created with contrast ranging from average to fairly high. However, extreme contrast wipes out both three-dimensionality and the feeling of realness. Very low contrast may also do this, but in a different way.

Another thing governed by lighting contrast is the relative obscurity of shadow areas. With black shadows the obscurity is complete, for we can see none of the things within these areas (here I refer to areas in pictures). As progressively more fill light is added, the obscurity gradually disappears, until we can see everything. You should experiment with lights to see how this works. Learn both to reveal and obscure.

Beginners often think that pictures should reveal everything, but this just isn't so. An important part of the art of photography is to know how to reveal some things while simultaneously obscuring others. This is sometimes called "emphasis and subordination." In portraiture, we usually emphasize the front of the face, especially

the eyes and mouth, then subordinate everything else to some degree. Through emphasis we lead people to see what we want them to. Through subordination we divert them from distractions.

• The Names of the Lightings

We started on the nomenclature (or jargon) with the terms key light and fill light. The lightings themselves are usually called narrow lighting, broad lighting, front lighting, split lighting, double back lighting, ghoul lighting, overhead bounce lighting, and side bounce lighting. There are a few additional types used in photographic portraiture, but these are the main ones. In this chapter you will find them defined in four ways: in terms of words, lighting diagrams, photographs of actual lighting setups, and portraits in which they were used.

Remember that the main function of the portraits is to show you in a rather bold way what different lightings will do to a face. If the lightings had been used with more subtlety you might not be able to see this.

• Narrow Lighting

For a three-quarter pose (the model's face at an angle to the camera, somewhere between full profile and full front). The key light falls only on the narrow part of the face (the front). From the camera position, the side of the nose, the side of the forehead, and most of the cheek and jaw are in shadow. In a *very* narrow lighting (sometimes called Rembrandt lighting) the shadows are connected, so that the light pattern on the part of the face nearest the camera is in the shape of a triangle.

NARROW LIGHTING

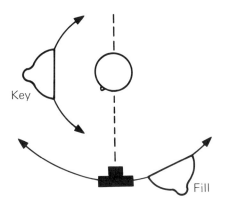

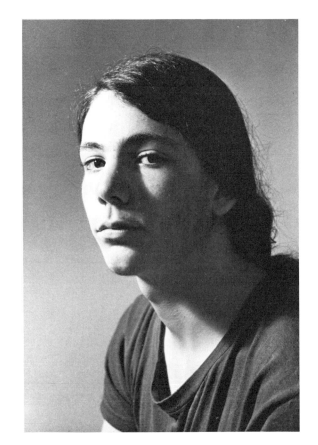

This technique, often called Rembrandt lighting, creates obvious shadow patterns and high contrast without fill light (photo top). With both lights (bottom), shadows are softer. Key light, pointed at camera, is above and slightly behind subject. Fill falls on side of face.

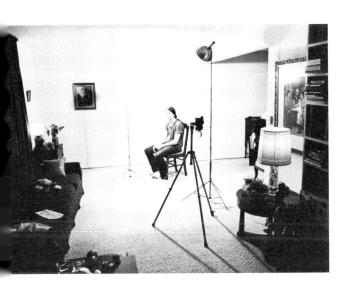

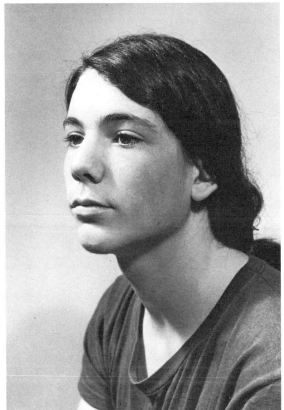

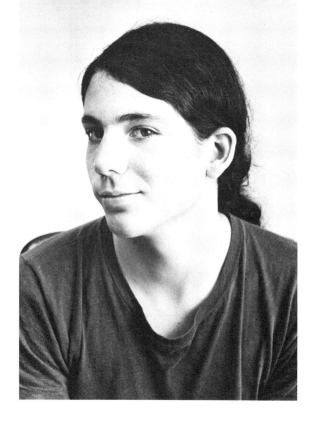

• Broad Lighting

For a three-quarter pose. The key light falls on that whole hemisphere of the head and face that is closest to the camera, which makes up a very broad area. The turned-away part of the face may also be illuminated somewhat. To prevent the face from looking too flat, the key light may be positioned high on its standard and angled sharply downward at the model.

Broad lighting fills out thin faces and reduces blemishes. Key light, angled down, is above and near subject. Fill is quite a distance away. Photo (above) was made by using both lights. Shadow edges are soft. More dramatic effect shown without fill (below).

BROAD LIGHTING

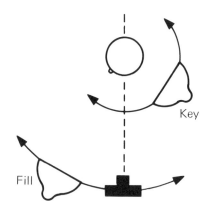

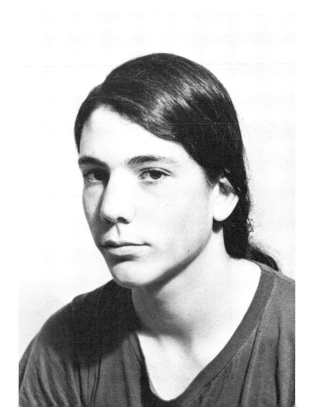

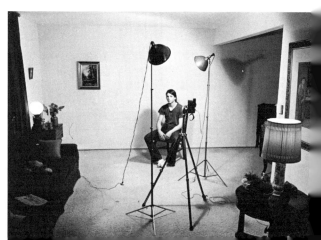

• Front Lighting

For a full-front pose (the model's face centered directly on the camera). This lighting has two variations: high-front and low-front. For high-front, the key light is usually very high on its standard and angled sharply downward. The standard may be within one or two feet of the model and positioned very close to the camera axis, so that the light falls squarely on the front part of the face. This lighting creates obvious shadows under the eyebrows, nose, lips, chin, and jaw. For low front lighting, the key light is backed up toward the camera (or even positioned behind it) and lowered on its stand. It minimizes the amount of shadow area on the face, as does also the broad lighting.

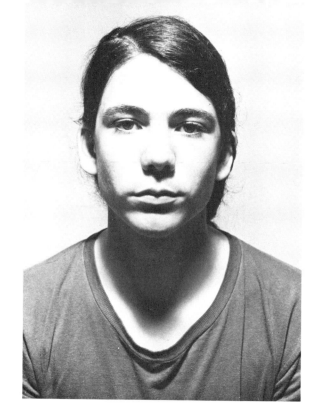

HIGH FRONTLIGHTING

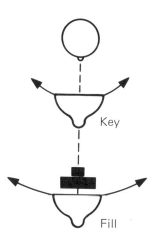

Key

Fill

High front lighting emphasizes blemishes—so use with caution. No fill light (photo above) stresses blemishes more. Fill softens contrast, gives warmer skin tones. Key light, close to subject, is shown above model. Fill, almost same height as subject, is pointed toward him.

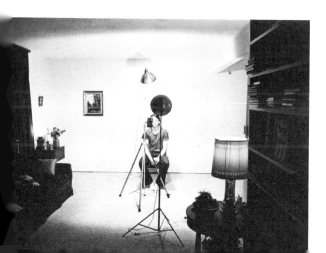

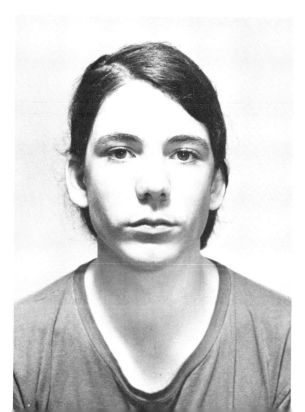

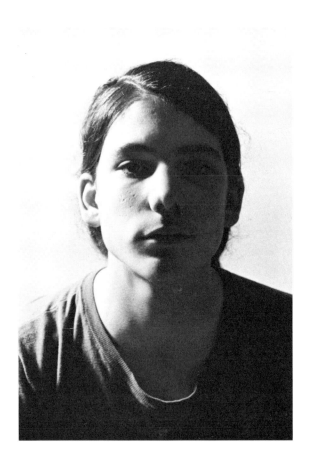

• Split Lighting

For a full-front pose. The key light is at the side of the model, and quite a bit behind, so that it strikes only one side of the face. Thus the face is "split" between highlight and shadow. Since the light may also be pointed in the general direction of the camera, there could be a problem with lens flare (strange blobs or shapes in pictures, caused by light hitting the lens). To prevent it, raise the light high on its standard and angle it downward; or use a deep lens shade; or shade the lens with a piece of cardboard while making the exposure.

SPLIT LIGHTING

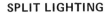

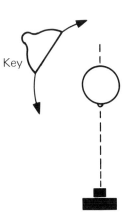

Key

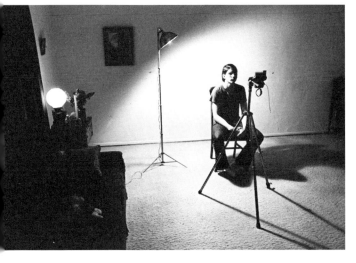

Split lighting is used mainly for interpretive portraiture. The key light splits the face in two, one half shadows, the other highlights. The key light stands above and to one side of the subject, angled down. The shadows can be lightened with either direct fill light or bounce light.

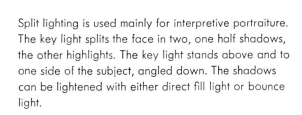

• Double Back Lighting

For a full-front pose. Use both of your light sources as kcy lights, with one on each side of, and well behind, your model. To prevent lens flare, follow the instructions given for split lighting. If you should want some fill light in the shadows you will need an additional light source. However, your picture will be more dramatic without one.

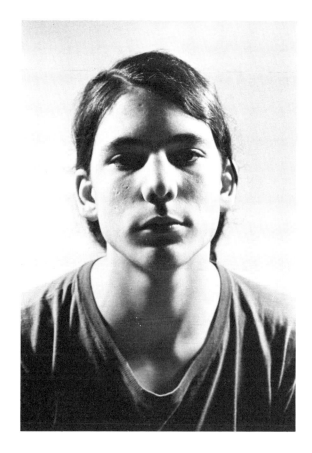

DOUBLE BACKLIGHTING

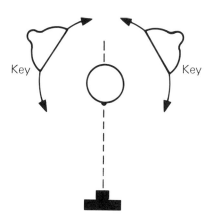

Double back lighting should not be used for everyday portraiture, because it exaggerates facial structures that are seldom seen. Note that both lights are in back of the subject and angled forward in the direction of the camera. This means that in order to prevent lens flare a lens shade should be used.

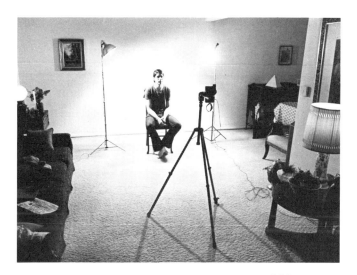

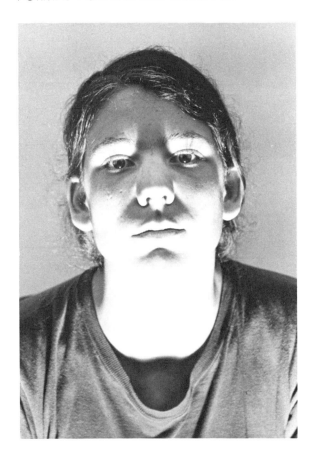

• Ghoul Lighting

Usually for full-front poses, but will also work for three-quarter poses. Remove the reflector from the light stand and prop it up in a saucepan (or something) so that its heat won't scorch the floor or carpet. Then shove it up very close to your model—but not close enough to burn!

LOW FRONTLIGHTING

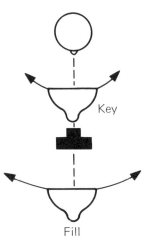

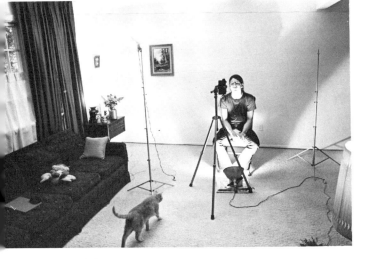

"Ghoul Lighting" is an exaggerated version of low front lighting. The key light is propped up in a saucepan on top of some newspapers—to keep the rug from getting scorched. Fill light is bounced from ceiling. This reduces light's intensity and eliminates sharp-edge shadows.

• Side Bounce Light

Best for full-front and three-quarter-front poses. A fill light is seldom used with this lighting, though it can be. There should be a wall or large reflecting surface at one side of the model, and the key light is pointed at it. Then the wall itself takes over the duty of being the key light. Variations in shadow patterns on the face are created by moving the light source back and forth along the wall. Lighting contrast is controlled by the model's distance from this side wall. Within one or two feet of it the contrast is very high, but it gets progressively less as your model moves away.

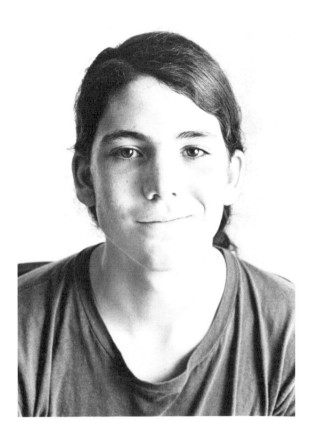

SIDE BOUNCELIGHTING

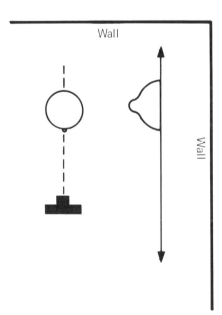

For side bounce lighting the subject is posed next to a wall and the key light is pointed at the wall. The wall itself then functions as the key light. Variations in the shadow patterns on the face are created by moving the light source back and forth along the wall.

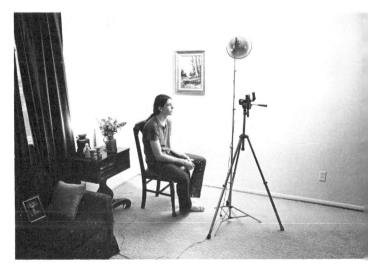

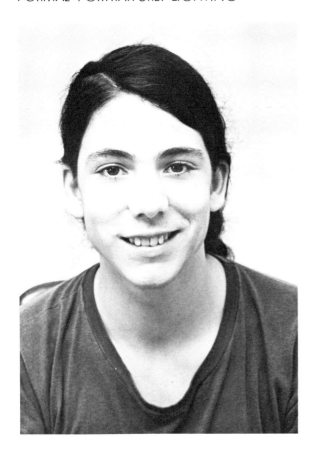

● Overhead Bounce Light

Good for almost any pose. It seldom requires a fill light, because the light reflected from the surrounding walls usually lightens the shadows as much as necessary. For a feeling of solidity and dimension, the key light is positioned within two or three feet of the model and rather high on its standard. It is pointed at the ceiling. For a flatter look it should be farther back, even behind the camera, and on the camera-to-model axis. For even greater flatness, bounce the light off the wall behind the camera.

Overhead bounce lighting produces the softest edge shadows. Note that the light source is close to the subject, positioned above his head, and pointed at the ceiling.

OVERHEAD BOUNCELIGHTING

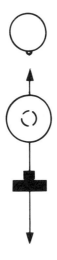

● Consider the Fill Light

So far, I have said nothing about the fill light, because its main function is to control contrast and the relative brightness of shadow areas. It has nothing much to do with the basic design (in terms of light patterns) of the picture. Using it well is very important, however. The fill light is nearly always positioned close to the camera-to-model axis and can be used on either side of it. The amount of fill that it provides is controlled by moving it forward or back along this axis, toward or away from the model. However, pointing it at an angle away from the model (edging it) will lessen the amount of fill, and so will bouncing it from a wall or the ceiling.

• Shooting Space

If you work in your home you may have a problem of finding shooting space, unless you are willing to move some furniture. If you can clear about three or four feet of wall space it should provide you a large enough background for head-and-shoulder portraits. However, having even more space is much better.

• Model-Background Tonal Relationship

It is a good thing if you can clear lots of wall space for a background, because it permits you to move your model five feet or more from the wall. This gives you quite a bit of control over the tonal relationship between your model and the backgrounds and helps you prevent unwanted shadows from falling on the background.

With enough subject-to-background distance, the center of the light patterns from both the key and fill lights can be kept off the background and be made to fall on, or in front of, your model. This darkens the background in comparison with your model's face (you can even make a white background wall come out black in a picture).

Or you can get the reverse effect by using edge light on your subjects while pointing the centers of the light patterns at the background. You can even make people come out coal black in pictures, though one usually doesn't go quite this far.

The shadow of a model can be kept off the background by positioning both the key and fill lights high on their standards and angling them downward. Though there will still be shadows on the wall, they will be down out of sight behind your subject's body.

• The Model Holds Still

I've said that direct lightings (not bounce) create fairly obvious shadow patterns on faces, and that good patterns can be utterly ruined if models move around. This means that you should ask a model to hold still after you have established a direct lighting, until you can focus and shoot your picture. Or you can tell him or her to relax, then move back into position when you are ready to shoot. When you are actually shooting, the model should be holding still, of course, and you might as well freeze your camera too—to get sharper pictures. Put it on a tripod and use a cable release for clicking the shutter.

Always remember that holding still can be very hard work, so don't ask your subjects to do it for long. Otherwise, they will stiffen up and start looking pained, which is very bad for good portraiture.

• Cosmetic Lighting

Skilled portrait photographers are adept at using lighting for cosmetic purposes, that is, for improving the faces of their models by correcting supposed defects of all kinds. Since this is very interesting to try and would contribute much to your learning to see better, we will go into the matter briefly. If you develop some expertise in cosmetic lighting you will also please your models more, and that will prove rewarding for you, too.

For any given cosmetic problem there may be quite a few answers, but one or two will be enough to get you started.

Rough or pockmarked skin: The best bet is overhead bounce light, with the light stand positioned behind the camera. Low contrast side bounce is also good. Broad lighting may be good, if you tape diffusers (sheets of white paper, tracing paper, or matte acetate) over both the key and fill lights. These lightings, all very diffuse, will fill in the tiny shadows made by the skin's roughness, smoothing it out very considerably.

Long noses: Use fairly low camera angles and low front lightings with quite a bit of fill. Overhead bounce with the light stand positioned well behind the camera may also be good. These lightings tend to blend the sides to the nose into the face, so that it doesn't stand out very much.

Fat cheeks: Narrow lightings are often best—the narrower the better—with fairly high lighting contrast. The cheek nearest the camera is partly lost in darkness, the other one turned away out of sight. Side bounce lightings, also contrasty, may be good with three-quarter poses.

Very thin faces: They can be nicely fattened up with broad lightings—with quite a bit of fill if necessary. Still using a three-quarter pose, you might also try an overhead bounce lighting, with the light stand positioned well behind the camera.

Eyeglasses: The problem is that they reflect your lights. This can usually be corrected by positioning the lights very high on their standards and angling them sharply downward.

Double chins and neck wrinkles: Lose them in the shadows created by narrow and high front lightings that are quite contrasty (little fill light used). Use diffusers on your lights.

Very deep eye sockets: The problem is to get light into them so that the eyes will show up well. Try low front and broad lightings, also side bounce light.

Protruding ears: Use a three-quarter pose, which puts one ear out of sight. Deal with the other by putting it in the shadow created by a narrow or side bounce lighting.

Very lopsided faces: Use three-quarter poses, so that the two sides of a face can't be compared straight on, with whatever lightings look best.

Heavily wrinkled faces: Use overhead bounce, with the light well behind the camera and possibly bounced off the rear wall instead of the ceiling. Also try a very low contrast side bounce lighting. These lightings provide very diffuse illumination, which will fill in and soften wrinkles considerably.

Weak chins: If you get sufficient light on a weak chin it won't look so small, so use your light sources low on their standards, or try a side bounce lighting.

Shiny bald heads: A bit of face powder or pancake makeup may be the best bet, but you can also calm down a glittering dome with narrow, broad, and low front lightings, provided your

light sources are positioned very low on their standards. Side bounce lighting may be even better. With direct lightings, a professional trick is to cast a light shadow on the top of the head with a head screen, which is exactly like a dodger used in printing, only larger. Make one with a round piece of cardboard and a stick.

Pimples: Use no direct lightings whatever, unless your light sources are heavily diffused. Because they are very diffuse to begin with, low contrast bounce lightings are a much better bet, anyway. Diffuse light takes the shine out of pimples and scatters enough light into them to make them considerably less dark.

Well, you now have an idea of what cosmetic lighting is all about. Since it will sharpen your visual perception and help you please your models, you will find it fascinating to work with. It offers more difficulties than you may think, however. For example, you will often photograph people who have more than one of the defects listed, perhaps three or four, and the ways of correcting them may be contradictory. In such cases you just have to move your lights around until something good happens. Fortunately, it usually does in time.

• What, No Poses?

This chapter is about formal portraiture, the kind mainly done by commercial photographers, so you may wonder why nothing has been said about formal poses. Well, most of them are heavily stereotyped and work well only for photographers who have had a lot of experience in using them. Furthermore, they fit into a highly specialized framework for commercial portraiture, which involves such things as special backgrounds, posing furniture, props, heavily stylized but expert lightings, extensive retouching, and soft-focus printing, all working together in a heavily formalized system. Without the whole system, formal poses may not work very well. Used by a beginner, they often look strained, unnatural, and even ludicrous. Even so, it wouldn't hurt to experiment with them, for you will not always be a beginner.

You can learn what the formal poses look like easily enough. Simply visit a couple portrait studios and look in their display windows. There is no need to visit more, because nearly all commercial portraitists use the same poses (and lightings, backgrounds, printing papers, printing techniques, toners, retouching styles, frames, and so on), though some are better at it than others. For further study, look into the work of the world's great painters prior to 1900, because the poses all originated with them.

For the beginner, the posing instructions in the last chapter are quite sufficient for a while. The main idea is that people usually look their best when they are comfortable and that the photographer should help them be that way. Pose people, yes, but help them be comfortable. And you can also just let models be themselves, and work with whatever poses they naturally fall into. The commercial portraitist might shudder at the last idea, but his problems aren't the same as yours. His subjects expect and want formal, or stylized, poses; yours may not.

• What About Electronic Flash?

Because most commercial portraitists use electronic flash, many beginners assume it is necessary for good portrait lightings. Not so. It works very well, of course, or professionals wouldn't use it, but they were making excellent portraits long before electronic flash was even invented. However, for beginners it can actually be a bad thing.

Perhaps the very most important thing in photography is to learn to see light, that is, to see how it affects the things that it falls upon. You can learn best with simple tungsten lighting equipment—photoflood bulbs, round metal reflectors, and light stands. But it is very hard to learn with electronic equipment, because you can't actually see what the light is doing. Though some larger units have built-in modeling lights, they are usually so dim that you still can't see what they are doing—unless you are already an expert at seeing light.

For these reasons it is not wise to start out with only electronic equipment—you may never learn to see what light actually does. First, improve your visual perception by using tungsten light, which will make light patterns that you can easily see, *then* turn to electronic flash.

• Using the Information

Probably the best way to use all the information in this chapter is to just wing it freely. Shoot lots of pictures so that you will have plenty of lightings to compare with one another, because this is a very good way to learn. You have been warned that some of your pictures may be bloody awful, but that is part of playing the game. Remember that some lightings just don't look good on some kinds of faces, but it is not a crime to make a bad combination. Your job is to discover the lightings that *do* work well on various faces and to learn to see light while you are doing it.

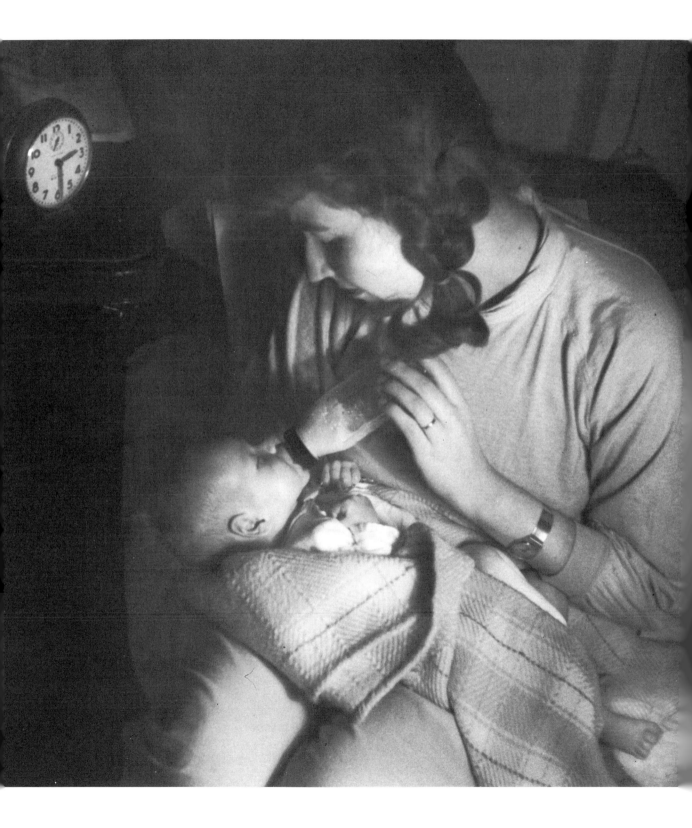

HOW TO PHOTOGRAPH BABIES

Photographing babies is not very difficult, because they are not usually going anywhere or doing much of anything while you are trying to get them in focus. They just lie there, sleeping, eating, gurgling, or trying to find their toes, and they don't mind you at all, unless you frighten them. And they are not at all critical of your attempts to get your camera to work. All the same, they can be very disagreeable, too, as any mother can tell you.

• The All-Important Schedule

The thing is to catch babies (and their mothers too) at the right times. Otherwise, making photographs may be the emotional equivalent of being run over by a Mack truck. The wrong time, of course, is when a baby has just turned his mother into the creature from the deep lagoon by trying to make his shrieks and howls heard all the way to Oshkosh, Wisconsin. So, when babies are hungry, tired, teething, croupy, or just generally ticked off it is best to be elsewhere.

My elder son Cleve and his mother Mitzi (my first wife). As you can see, the hour was late. The lighting was a single photoflood bulb in a reflector, pointed more in front of the pair than upon them. This was both for a lighting effect and to preserve Cleve's young eyes from glare. Shot with an ancient Ciroflex, hand-held. The young man is now nearly thirty.

Mother knows the best times for Baby—she gives thanks for them in her prayers—so just ask her about them and fit yourself into the happy-time schedule. It may be in the morning after Baby has just had a nap and bottle. Afternoons may be all right too, but many a mother is half-shot by that time. The point is that both Mother and Baby should be in top shape if you want your shooting session to be a happy one.

If you want to photograph your own child you don't have to ask about schedules, though husbands would be wise to consult with wives. You just fit yourself into happy times whenever they occur, make your shots, and retreat whenever the emotional weather begins to close in. Fathers aren't especially good at this, because they usually don't pay that much attention to babies, but mothers are real pros. Some incidental advice for Dad: give Mom a Polaroid camera, lots of film, and an instruction book—then stay the hell out of her way. And please refrain from criticizing her pictures.

• This Chapter Is for Men

It is actually quite unnecessary to tell women how to photograph babies, especially their own. Except for a few technical details, they already know. You see, they truly know what babies *look* like, which most men do not, because they look at them, listen to them, think about them, feel them, and live them much of the time. Above all, women have a profound emotional contact with babies, which extends their perceptions of them very considerably, whereas men don't usually have good emotional contact with much of anything, least of all themselves. One result of this female emotional contact with things is a heightened visual perception well beyond male visual perception, so you can see why a male author refuses to tell women how to look at their children.

A particular woman may need to be checked out on a camera and shown a couple of basic lightings, but a particular man may need the same things. A camera store clerk can do the checkout, and there are enough basic lightings in this book for any young mother.

So, this chapter is for men and boys, because women and girls simply don't need it.

Every parent without exception should have a picture like this of the baby (in this case, Lissa Ann) in a bathinette. It is par for the course, you might say. Overhead bounce flash, shot with a Kodak Medalist. Note how the two are really digging each other, a wonderful thing to remember through photography.

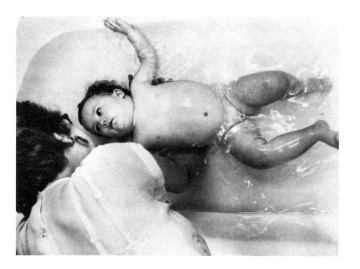

• Please the Mother

I have a friend who took many pictures of his infant son that made him look like something from under a very slimy rock. Well and good, he got revenge on Junior for displacing him in his wife's affections, but can't we do a bit better than that? We should have pictorial objectives, no doubt, but they could be a little more noble.

Well, men, pleasing a baby's mother ought to be noble enough, and it is a real challenge, too. Many women think that most men are as blind as bats, and I most sincerely agree with them. So the objective is for a blind man to make pictures of a baby that will convince the mother that he has really seen the child. Takes a bit of doing, wouldn't you say? Enough of a challenge for any man or boy.

• Watch the Mother

Another friend of mine makes beautiful pictures of babies and small children, but he is a very tricky rascal. When he is photographing a family or individual child he keeps one eye glued firmly on the mother all the while. What is he looking for? Little cues from her—happy expressions, gestures, and sounds—that tell him when to click the camera shutter. A commercial portraitist, he learned long ago that a mother would buy only the picture that had her imprimatur, her personal O.K. It is not a bad trick if you want to please a mother, and you could hardly do better than that.

On the other hand there are mothers so frantic that the best way to watch them is on their way out of the room, but you should only send a mother away after you have shown her that you can handle her baby as skillfully and gently as she. Otherwise, it would be foolish of her to leave and cruel of you to ask her to.

A wonderfully soft place on which to squirm—Mother's tummy. And seeing things upside down is a lot of fun too. Straight, direct flash. A good trick is to dodge the middle of a direct flash picture and burn in the edges quite a bit. This gives a more dimensional feeling than straight printing would. Direct flash pictures are often flat, but we have gotten around this problem very well here.

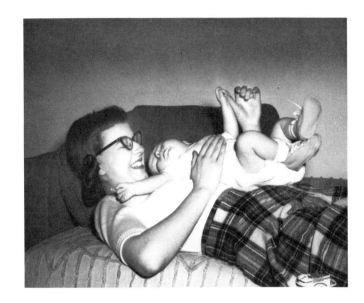

● **Early Show Points**

Tiny babies do certain things that mothers find especially cute or charming: photograph them. Following are a tiny baby's special accomplishments, or show points:

1. lifts head while lying on tummy
2. smiles (because of gas pain or being tickled)
3. discovers toes and examines them minutely
4. grasps a parental finger tightly
5. sits up more-or-less straight when propped up in an easy chair
6. looks positively cherubic while sleeping
7. handles nursing bottle with great authority
8. yawns vigorously
9. sucks on thumb
10. rolls head around to look at things
11. waves feet around in air when diaper is changed
12. makes little bubbles with mouth
13. gets an amazed look on face
14. learns to focus eyes
15. shows interest in a toy

You may think that babies look interesting when they cry, but most mothers won't like that kind of picture. Neither do they care much for scowls, which babies can manage now and then.

● **Later Show Points**

As a baby gets older he or she grows more accomplished:

1. crawls around on the floor
2. pulls self to standing position in crib or play pen
3. cheered on by adults, takes first tentative steps
4. bounces vigorously up and down in little bouncy chair
5. makes tremendous mess of self in early attempts to use a spoon
6. becomes wedded to a teething ring
7. adopts a security blanket and won't be without it
8. pounds toys on floor or high chair until they fall apart
9. dumps food on floor
10. makes grotesque faces when offered certain foods
11. tries to look between legs to see if the back side is the same as the front
12. sucks on big toe
13. splashes joyfully in the bathinette
14. sits with authority on potty seat and resists all pleas to get down to business

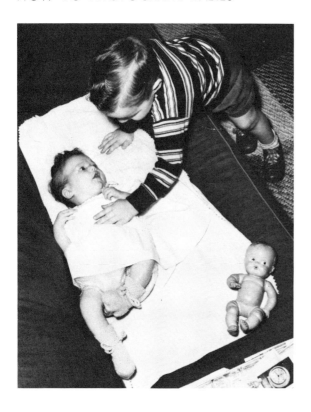

My younger son Craig making nice to his sister, Lissa Ann. He didn't start to tease and aggravate her until she was old enough to fight back. Straight flash (flash gun on camera, pointed directly at subjects). Though straight flash is considered pretty awful by photographers, you can see that it works very well indeed.

15. reacts to kitten or puppy with great suspicion

16. laughs at Mother when she nibbles on Baby's finger

17. laughs at Mother while poking her in the face

18. sits in play pen, up to waist in toys

19. throws toys out of play pen, wants them back again

20. burps when held on Mother's shoulder after being fed

These may not seem like special show points to you, but you must remember that babies haven't **had time to learn** very much. Furthermore, such activities as these bring a sparkle to parental eyes, and this sparkle should tell you when to make your pictures. Photographing them will mainly get you the kinds of pictures that parents like to put in albums, but not necessarily on walls.

● **Wall Pictures**

For pictures for display in their homes, parents generally like their babies to look their very best —sparkling clean, all dressed up, smiling or looking amazed at the world, making cute gestures, and being generally angelic. The little rascals may actually be far from angelic, but parents like to see them looking that way now and then, anyway. Furthermore, when a howling baby has nearly destroyed Mother before finally going to sleep, she likes to rest her eyes on a peaceful picture of him and remember that she really does love him after all.

● **Backgrounds**

You can more or less forget about backgrounds for the types of pictures listed under "show points." Don't be choosy; just photograph the babies wherever they happen to be. This will help you fit into the household routine, so that you won't drive Mother up the wall.

However, for display-type pictures you *do* have to be choosy, because parents want them to have a certain feeling of formality. A plain (no pattern), unwrinkled, fairly dark woolen blanket stretched smoothly across the parental bed makes a fine background for reclining shots of tiny babies, and does well for older ones, too. Use the same blanket draped neatly over an easy chair if Mother wants Baby sitting up.

Mothers and fathers make good posing furniture too—just have them hold their babies and stand in front of uncluttered walls. Professional baby photographers often carry portable backgrounds with them in the form of collapsible screens. A projection screen for viewing color slides will work about as well, if you have one.

An older baby can be posed on a sturdy blanket-draped table, provided Mother stands nearby in case of a tumble. If the baby hasn't beaten them up too much, high chairs and kiddy chairs of almost any kind are just fine. You can shove a table up to a blank wall space and put a small chair on top of it.

If you are really interested in making display-type pictures of babies you should certainly study pictures made by professional baby photographers, for they have all the answers down cold. They generally use plain backgrounds or ones painted with a certain special texture that many of them like (it helps make photographs look more like paintings). And they use the simplest posing furniture—little chairs, draped boxes and tables, little gadgets for propping babies up, and the like.

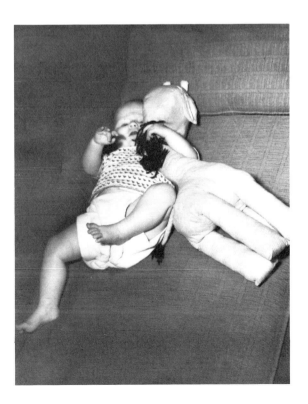

Pictorial show point for a Teeny Weenie—fed with a spoon for the first time, manages very well. A must in every mother's picture book. Overhead bounce flash; though the depth of field isn't too great, it doesn't really matter if things get a little fuzzy around the edges, does it?

Three especially good backgrounds for baby photography are beds, overstuffed chairs, and sofas such as this one. They offer simplicity for visuals and good support and protection for babies. In short, they are easy to work with. In this picture: direct flash—center dodged, edges burned in—center also brightened up by bleaching, which makes the highlights even lighter. Farmer's Reducer on highlights is a good standard tool for work on direct flash pictures.

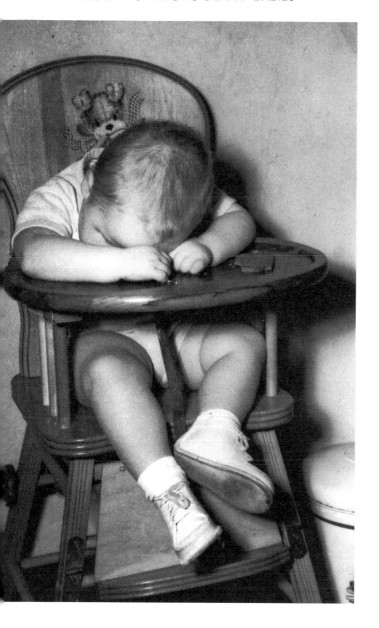

• Posing Babies

Don't even try—just take them however they come. Except for laying them down or propping them up there is not much else you can do. When they get old enough to take poses and navigate for themselves they are no longer babies but small children, and we will get to them in the following chapter.

• Light Sources

Nearly any light source will work well for making baby pictures—flash, electronic flash, floodlight, and natural light. Tiny babies don't move around very much, so you have little need for intense light and fast shutter speeds. This also makes it easy to work with a tripod. Since older babies can get pretty quick on the draw, you may need electronic flash for good action shots.

Because the eyes of tiny babies haven't as yet learned to adapt to bright lights you should never point floodlights right at them, though bounced floods are okay. It is quite all right to use ordinary and electronic flash. Though they produce very intense light the flashes are of extremely brief duration.

Cleve wasn't exactly a tiny baby, was he?—and he used that big head as a battering ram, jarring loose more than one parental tooth. Direct flash is said to "wash out" (flatten) flesh tones, but if you print your flash pictures carefully this doesn't have to happen. As you can see, Cleve looks as round and solid as can be, which means his skin isn't washed out.

• Lightings

Provided that you use ordinary or electronic flash, you can use all the direct lightings described in the last chapter. For best results you need two units—for a key light and a fill light. Direct lightings will permit you to use small apertures, even with color film, and thus get a lot of depth of field. Unless you really know your lighting, however, they are probably more bother than they are worth. You see, if you don't really know what a light will do you may position it badly and get really godawful results.

Because babies are so soft and delicate it is usually a good thing to go for lightings which communicate these qualities, which brings us to bounce lightings. All of them soft and extremely diffuse, they help us make babies look as we think they should. Use bounce flash or bounce floodlight.

Flash-on-camera works well enough on babies, as many a parent can testify, but it really doesn't flatter them very much. It flattens out their heads and faces and casts harsh black shadows behind them. Even so, many a parent is completely satisfied with this lighting, which indicates that

A bright Sunday morning coming into a pale yellow bedroom gave us this soft and delicate lighting, making flash or floodlight quite unnecessary. Any sane parent can tell you that holding a squirming baby on top of you, wet diaper or not, is one of the world's greatest aesthetic experiences. Lissa Ann and Mitzi, mother of three.

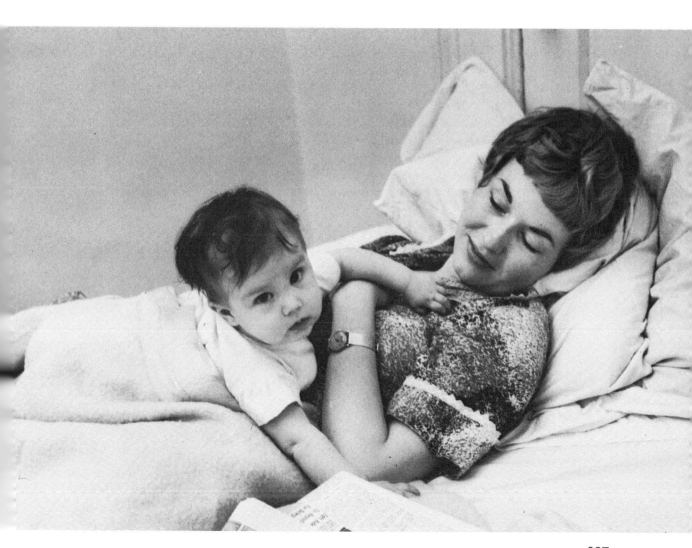

there is nothing greatly wrong with flash-on-camera. But it is not good when a baby's skin is blotchy. A baby's very tender skin does sometimes become patchy, blotchy, or reddened in spots. Unfortunately, direct flash tends to bring this out. What is needed is a very diffuse lighting to blend the blotches together and lighten them as much as possible, so overhead bounce is a good bet.

Another good thing about overhead bounce lighting is that you can put your light stand in one place and leave it there while you make pictures all around the room. And, as you read earlier, there is an eight-foot circle around the stand in which you can work without having to change your aperture and shutter speed settings. This makes it much easier for you and cuts down on the fuss and bother that might disturb the family routine.

Natural, or available, light is also fine—babies' rooms are usually bright and cheery. And if the light happens to be dim you can use a tripod. This is no inconvenience with tiny babies, because they don't move very much. Older babies don't either, though they bounce around and gesticulate more. Since slow shutter speeds are usually used with a tripod, this means that you have to wait for moments of inaction and have to give up many of the good action shots. This is too bad, of course, but you will soon learn in photography that you can't have everything.

Direct flash: note the dark shadow behind Cleve that characterizes flash-on-camera pictures. Such a shadow can be ugly, but it isn't here. Obviously the baby bed isn't going to hold this young mastodon much longer, but for a while it will hold him in one place long enough for pictures. The highlights were both dodged and bleached, one technique implementing the other.

298

• Posing Play

Photographers often play with babies—or have their mothers do it—in order to get pleasing expressions and gestures. With their lively curiosities, babies respond well to unfamiliar toys and quirky sounds, and everyone knows that they like to be tickled under their chins. If you are a stranger in the house, however, you should approach the idea of play with care. Otherwise, your little model may respond to your advances with outright terror, and after that it is all screams and tears.

It would be a lot easier to photograph babies just as they come, but parents place a high premium on those happy smiles and gestures. So someone may have to play with Baby—let Mother do it if you don't know how.

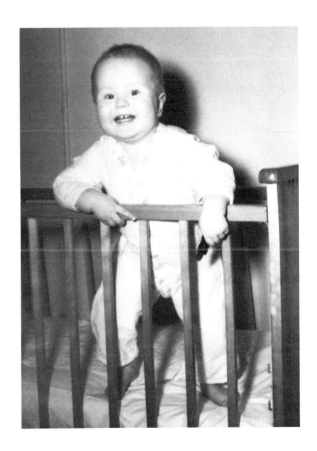

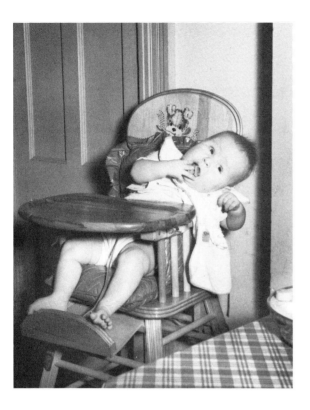

Cleve did his idiot act at least once a day, usually smearing everything within ten feet of himself with food, of which he was inordinately fond. Since he grew up to be 6'5" he must have needed a lot.

1. Any picture of your own baby is a good one.

2. If it pleases the parents a picture is good.

3. Baby pictures that look like paintings are good.

4. If the picture looks like the baby it is good.

5. If it looks like a professional picture it is good.

6. It is also good if it looks like a snapshot.

7. If a picture is in sharp focus it is good.

8. It may also be good if it is not in sharp focus.

9. A picture is good if it shows what babies are like.

10. If it makes the baby look pretty it is good.

11. If it makes the baby look bright and alert it is good.

12. If a baby picture has a baby in it it is good.

From this rather abbreviated list you might get the impression that it is hard to make a bad baby picture, for anything you shoot will fit at least one of the criteria. True enough. So why not just bang away and enjoy yourself, perhaps trying to make pictures that will please Mother?

• The Distortion Problem

In adult terms, babies are all out of proportion, because they have very large heads and small bodies. With the wrong camera angle and/or a wide angle lens this "disproportion" can be greatly increased, until we have enormous heads and hardly any bodies at all. You might find this interesting because of its oddness, but don't expect mothers to care for it at all. They prefer shots made from very ordinary angles with normal lenses or ones that are slightly telephoto.

• Good Baby Pictures

If you are going to make baby pictures you will probably need some criteria with which to measure yourself. Otherwise, you won't know whether to be pleased or discouraged with the results—people interested in photography get this way. From among the following critical concepts, choose the ones that suit you best:

The pictures on the following two pages are of Amanda Goodwin and were made by her Uncle Mike Goodwin, who obviously thinks highly of this tender sprite. He has shot literally thousands of them, but these few are a tasty sample. Mike is a photographer, painter, and graphic designer. He is also Curator of Photography at the Chrysler Museum in Norfolk, Virginia, one of the major museums of the South. His pictures show you a fruitful attitude and an approach for photography of babies. Mike himself shows up later as a ghost in Chapter Eleven.

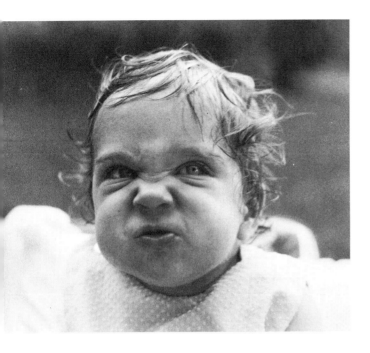

Somebody put frogs in my pants.

Teething is a solemn and serious business.

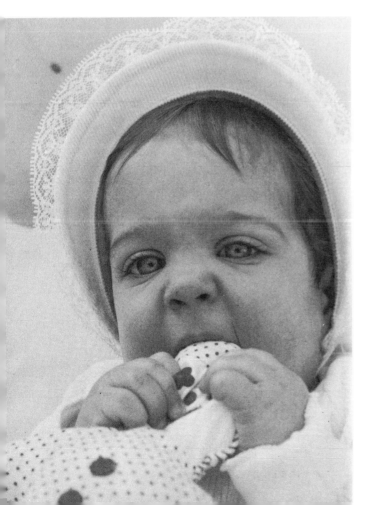

To what Voice does she listen, and what stars does she see?

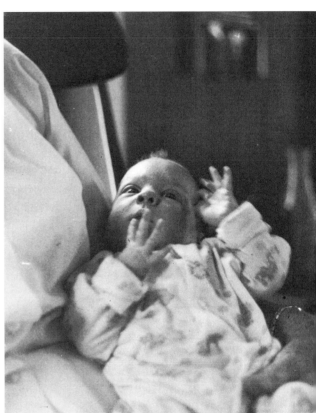

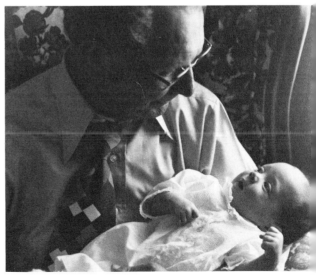

Grandpa and Amanda: reciprocal astonishment.

They say tiny babies don't laugh and chortle—*who sez?*

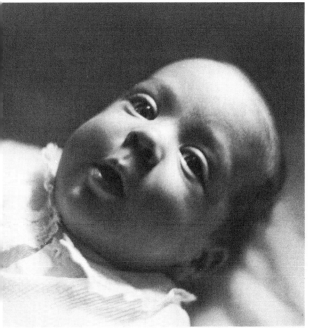

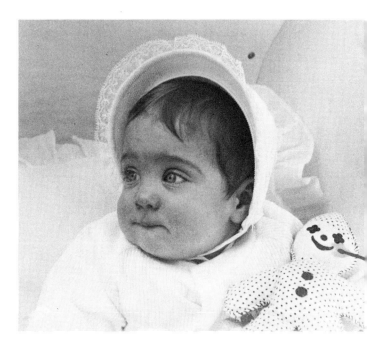

Sunday-go-to-meeting hat and guardian clown friend, Tooky.

A love child, shining in the sun.

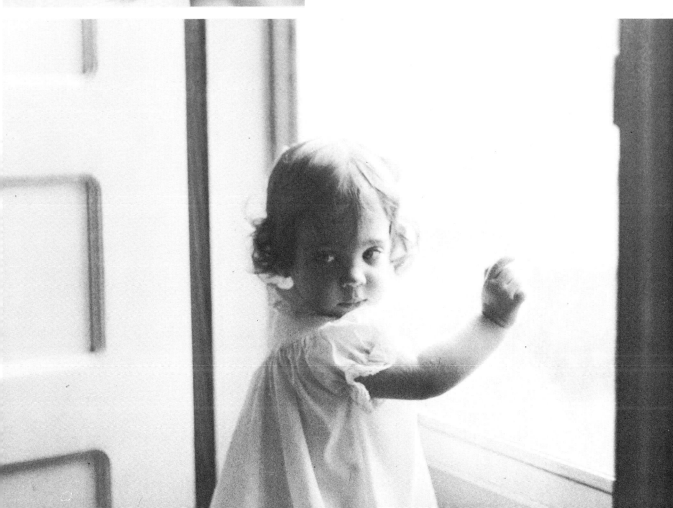

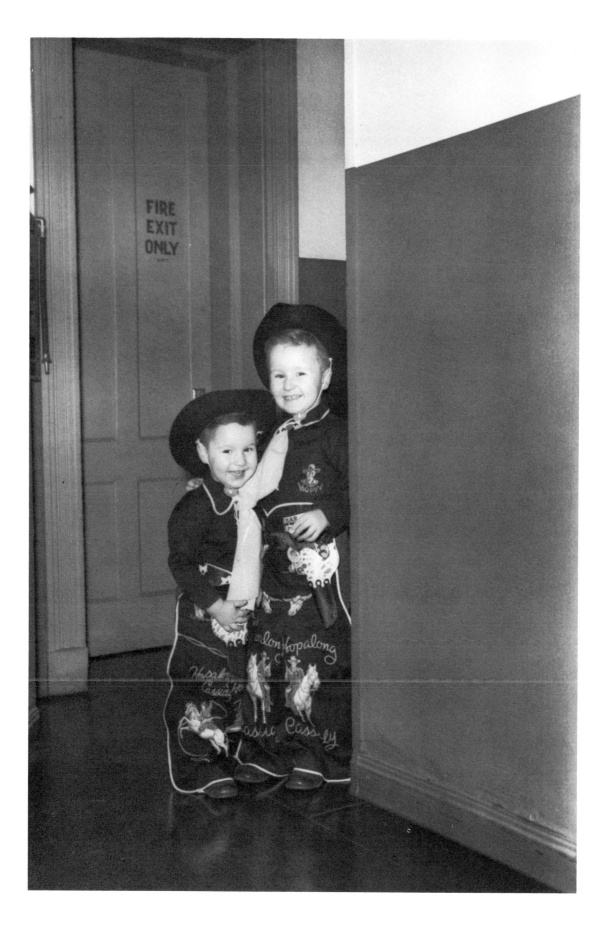

PHOTOGRAPHING CHILDREN

Having an accepting, unprejudiced, and noncritical attitude toward children is perhaps the major requirement for photographing them well (the technical side is easy). With this outlook you will find nearly everything they do interesting and worthy of your attention, which is as it should be.

Feeling this way about small children is easy enough, because they have little egotism, which is the hardest thing to put up with in people. And it is not impossibly difficult to see their occasional orneriness as cute, especially when it looks good in the camera viewfinder. Not least, they fit into our preconceptions of children by doing pretty much what we think they will, which makes us feel quite omniscient.

Older children are another matter. Though they may seem shy they are all Cossacks at heart, with abundant and as yet untamed egotism, long experience in family infighting, and a profound suspicion of adults, especially their parents. Naturally, getting around such a maverick may take quite a bit of doing, for you may be one of the enemy.

Cherubs Craig (left) and Cleve (right) and their new Christmas hoot-and-holler outfits. Direct flash. You want to know what a snapshot is? *This* is a snapshot. You just raise the camera, close your eyes, and shoot—and get real pictures of your kids instead of projections of your own ego. The noble snapshot: the most believable (and rightly so) kind of photograph that there is.

As part of your tactics you should take great care when you look at older children. Please understand this: they are highly sensitive to visual criticism and know very well when they are being looked at, measured, and found wanting—which in many families is a good part of the time. Naturally, you should use your camera with care also —don't let it become a weapon.

To get close to older children (young ones aren't a problem), you must overcome their suspicion of adults by showing that you accept them for what they actually are, not for what you think they ought to be. When you look at them, directly or through the camera viewfinder, they need to feel that you do it with approval. Whatever you do, don't lie to children about things. If you don't like a kid, say so—he won't mind. But adult lying is very hard for children to take, and they can spot adult phonies from a hundred yards.

● **The Snapshot, the Noncriticizing Picture**

You may recall that snapshooters never really look at or think about their subjects. Thus when parents make snapshots it provides a very real refuge for beleaguered children. A child feels safe from the critical parent eye, because said eye is being used mainly in a desperate effort to figure out which end of the camera is up. He knows very well that he is not being visually dissected,

303

analyzed, and judged unworthy; he knows he is being left entirely alone.

For the subject, the snapshot is the safest possible kind of photograph to be involved in. Thus the majority of family pictures—ninety per cent or more—ought to be snapshots. Just raise your camera, close your eyes, and click. Left alone emotionally, your subjects will come on as they really are—and what more could you ask for than that?

The Age of Innocence comes crashing to a close when a snapshooter gets really interested in photography and starts to think that he should stare at everything until it reveals all its secrets. Not so. The art of not looking is even more important, even for a photographer.

He played his new phonograph all day long, day after day, and even took his naps with it. More than once the family was awakened long after midnight by Burl Ives sweetly singing "The Little Engine That Could." The lovely lighting on Craig comes from a large skylit window which is just behind the sofa. The darks around him make the light really seem to shine. Hence we have the classic formula in the visual arts: darks make lights, and lights make darks. A thing is either light or dark by comparison with something else. Makes sense?

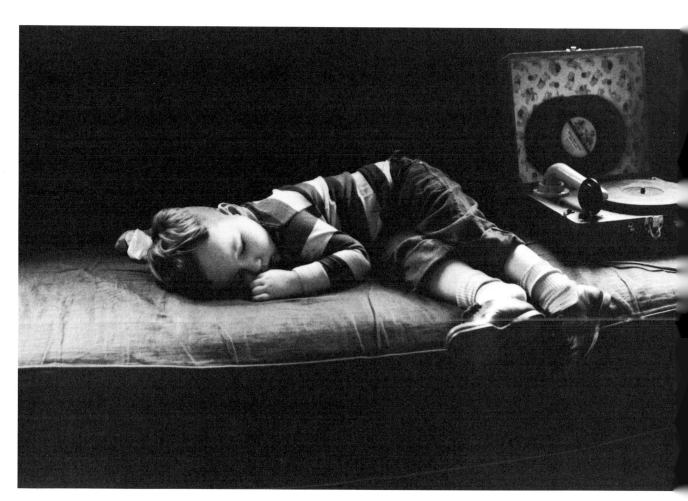

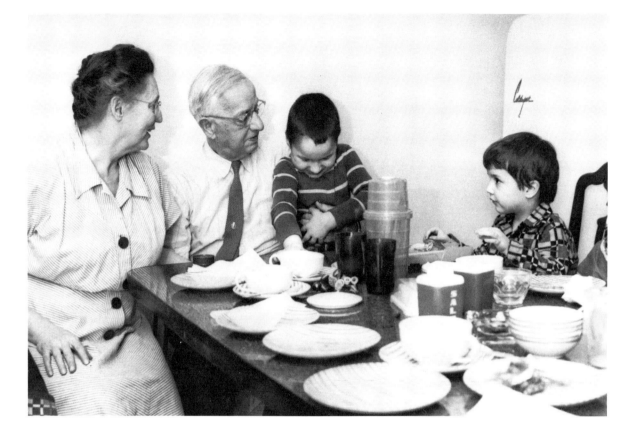

When grandparents come to visit there is a certain amount of delicate teasing or joshing that goes on with the young sprouts. As we see, Craig takes to it with shy delight. This is another snapshot, though it doesn't look so much like one. I made no effort at all to shoot a meaningful, artistic picture that is definitive of American family life and all such assorted balderdash. I just snapped several pictures, and this is one of them. What it says, if anything, is that there is a lot of love in some families. Bounce flash.

● The Noncritical Eye: A Credo

Though snapshooting is an excellent way for making pictures that do not criticize, it involves a partial mental blackout, which is not always convenient or even possible. Fortunately, there is a way of doing the same thing—developing a noncritical eye—without having to black oneself out. It involves adopting a working credo and conscientiously sticking to it. If you do this long enough you actually may learn to believe it. With respect to making pictures of children, the following credo ought to work pretty well:

1. I will shoot the pictures they want as well as those I want.

2. I will not look at them analytically unless they are obviously willing for me to do it.

3. If my behavior as a photographer threatens to intrude on a child's personal domain I will settle for making snapshots or make no pictures at all.

4. I will try to see and photograph children as they are, not as I think they ought to be.

5. I will not make pictures that undermine children's sense of dignity—as defined in their terms, not mine.

6. I will try to respect the ways in which children offer themselves to my camera, even though I might prefer other behavior.

Well, that is the general idea—ordinary everyday ethical behavior consciously extended to children. Are they worth it? You know, Jesus described children as our spiritual superiors. Thus if they aren't worth good treatment, who is?

• **Poses**

The advice on poses in Chapter One is especially good for children of all ages. The gist of it is to wait until they fall into poses you like, then walk up and shoot your pictures. If they think they should pose stiffly (as many do), shoot those poses too, then simply wait for something more relaxed. If it is obvious that they think their relaxed poses are undignified (a commonplace notion), shoot them as they wish, stiff and staring, and hope that they will eventually change their minds. You have to grant children certain rights, you know. One is to have the world see them as they wish to be seen.

Still don't know what a genuine snapshot is? Well, try this one on for size. The critical test: are these ego projections of a father or are they projecting themselves in their own right? Raise your camera, close your eyes, and shoot: that's how to get real children on film. Lissa Ann, Cleve Marshall, and Craig Robert. Real bums. A hard crew. Overhead bounce flash.

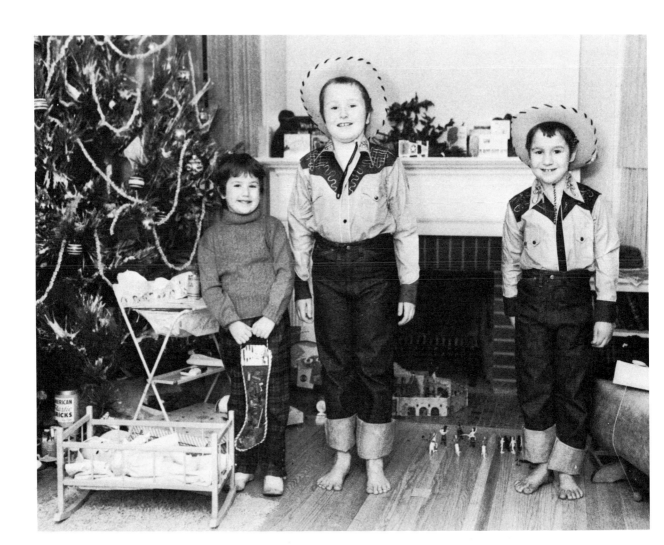

I had a special deal with Lissy's Mom: I could let ol' Lissy Pooh make as much of a mess in the bathroom as she liked while I took pictures—provided I supervised getting the mucho spilled gallons cleaned up. This usually meant that I did it, which was much easier on me than having to yell at Young Miss Nightingale here. It also meant that Lissa had a whee of a time whenever her ex-sailor father was around with his trusty mop so that she could really let herself go. The ancient law: if you want kid pictures you have got to let kids be kids.

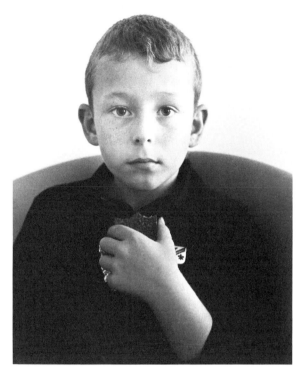

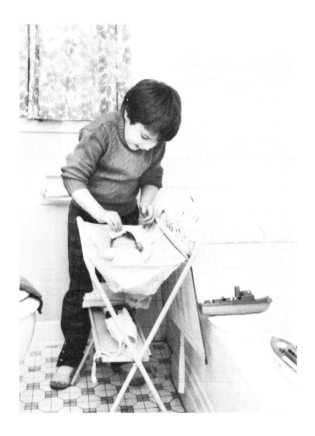

My stepson Jonathan while he was still the neighborhood angel and some years before he became the Con Man of the Western world. He has a chocolate thing in his hand, which he is nibbling at in a conservative and fastidious way. A smart, sweet kid, I'll tell you. Bounce floodlight from both sides, with the light from the right being stronger. If you want a kid to get an expression like this on his face, just let your love pour out. Let it *pour* out.

A year later, Jon again with his feline pal, Arthur, named after Arthur Freed, who didn't appreciate the compliment. We also had a cat named Bumsy, whom I rescued from a wino bar down on the Bowery. When a cat is held this way he ain't going to stay there very long, so you've got to work fast to get your shot. Window light from one side, a little reflected light on the other side of the face from a nearby wall.

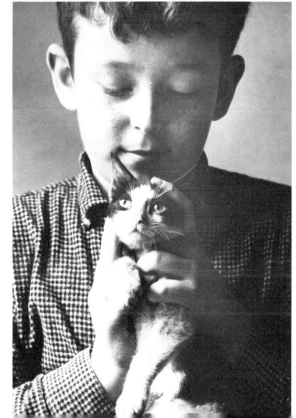

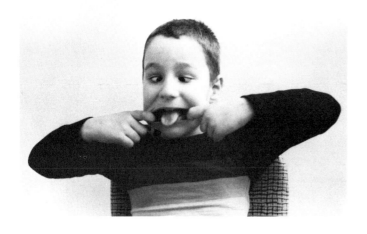

For two years Craig did this every time he thought I was going to take his picture. An editor at *Life* magazine told me that kids don't do this. Oh *yeaaaaaah*? Well, what the hell, you take what you can get in family photography.

If kids want to set up your pictures for you, let them. If you want images of kids looking and acting like kids, that's what you will get. Now, the Easter basket hats and bows are obviously supposed to be hilariously funny; so is giving the strong arm to a loudly complaining little sister. She got even later, you may be sure. Overhead bounce flash.

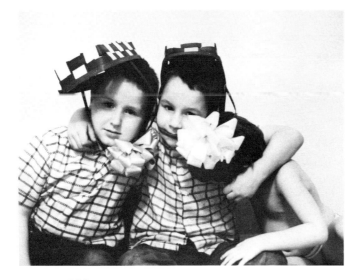

• Mug Shots

Some children automatically make horrible faces whenever they see a camera and may keep it up even into adulthood. That is a very severe situation, and if you can't talk them out of it you can't talk them out of it. So shoot their horrendous mugs and be thankful you could get anything at all. From the age of eight my younger son did nothing but mug shots for two years, laughing at me all the while. So?

• Tying Children Down

Once children learn to run the only ways to keep them in place while you focus your camera are to feed them ice cream or tie them hand and foot. Well, it's not that bad, but almost. Of course, you can always command children to stay put, yet there are better ways of getting them planted.

The best way to tie children down is to give them interesting things to do. Now, they say that the interest span of children is very short, which means that some activities won't keep them planted very long—you have to work fast. On the other hand, they can stay endlessly involved with things that interest them more, for example, television and the bathtub.

TV is the all-time kid demobilizer, of course, but you may be tired of seeing children sprawled in front of it. Though they fall into myriads of interesting poses worthy of circus performers, you eventually get them all on film. The bathtub is a little more interesting (until kids learn to be shy), because children create all of the action instead of just watching it—with the help of numerous floating toys, to be sure. Overhead bounce light (flash or flood) is just great for this scene, but you should tape the wires to the ceiling to keep them far from either children or water.

There are other things that will keep kids corralled for a while, and you should be on the lookout for them—creating juvenile art, baking a cake with Mother's help, building a real or imaginary playhouse, weaving potholders, tearing up magazines, looking at a new puppy, and so on. Until children are ready to move into their teens there is always at least *something* that will help to keep them in focus. After that they either sit around most of the time (usually locked up in their rooms) or take themselves elsewhere.

● The Focus Problem

When a child is sitting down or standing for you your problems are easy—you simply focus and shoot—but children on the go are something else, because they are always moving out of focus. The problem is especially aggravating indoors, because focusing in relatively dim light is difficult, anyway.

The consequence is that you will miss many of your best shots, things that kids do before you can focus again. Well, don't ask kids to repeat their actions—that never seems to work well— but be philosophical about it and wait for something else to happen. If you can get even one tenth of what you see you will be very lucky indeed, so count your blessings.

● Zone Focusing

Outdoors, zone focusing provides a partial answer to the focus problem, and you should surely try to master its principles. It involves taking advantage of depth of field, or the zone of image sharpness that extends both behind and in front of something that you have focused on. You might call it depth of sharpness, if you like. Stopping down increases the depth of this zone, which reaches its maximum when the lens aperture is closed all the way. In order to stop down this far, however, you must either have a lot of light or use a very slow shutter speed, or your film will be underexposed.

Fortunately, outdoor light under a hazy sun or full sunlight is so very bright that you can stop down all the way *and* use a high shutter speed—if you use a fast film like Tri-X and Kodacolor 400. Even with slower films such as Plus-X, Veri-

chrome Pan, and Ektachrome 200 you will be in good shape. The high shutter speed will help you freeze the action when Sally screams past on her skate board. The small aperture will help to keep her in sharp focus.

To use the focusing zone method you mentally stake out the area in which you think the most action is going to take place, then use your cam-

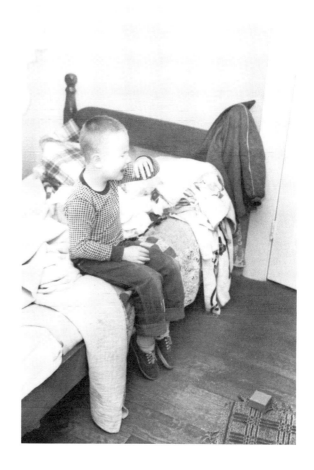

A good way to make yourself acutely unpopular with a kid: photograph him when he is bawling. The fact that the punishment—temporary banishment—is fully justified is entirely beside the point. So shoot your picture swiftly and without comment, then quickly leave his presence and leave him to his angry grief. But do this very seldom, or he will start distrusting you all the time. Overhead bounce flash.

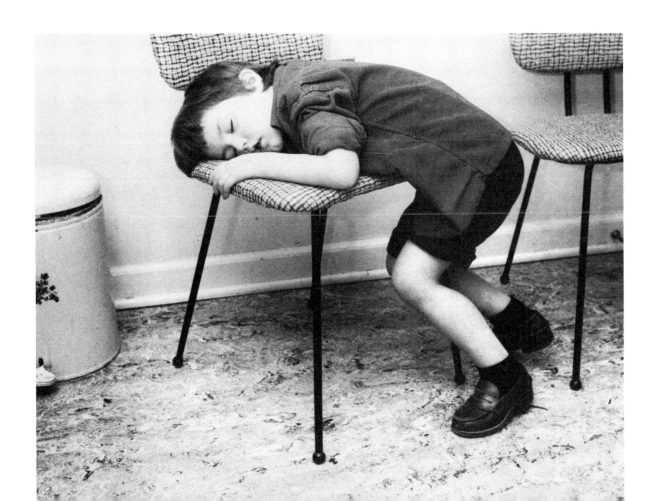

A bit uncomfortable, no doubt, but a better compromise than having to undress and get into bed, for then the day is surely done. I had to work fast here, for her mother soon bundled her off to bed, tearful complaints notwithstanding. Though the bounce flash made it look like daytime, it was actually well after dark. I knew this would happen but naturally took the picture anyway. When you feel the tug on your heartstrings, shoot—then worry about minor matters later.

You just have to photograph them while they are sleeping, they look like such little angels. But don't straighten out the bedclothes. Just let them be the poignant tangle they usually are. They were printed a little dark here so that they wouldn't look visually busy. Dig those hands, Friend, dig those hands. Bounce flash.

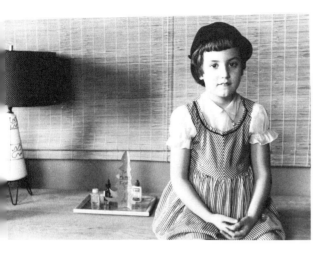

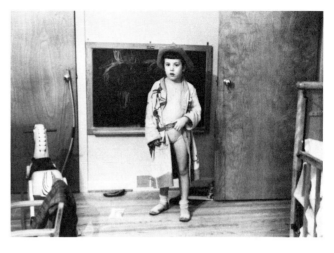

Lissa Ann sitting in my favorite spot for formal portraits, modeling her new outfit. This is a long table in the master bedroom; Lissy is lit by a soft light from a side window. She made me get my camera, and set up the picture by posing in just this way. She is obviously looking at her dad with more than a little fondness, a picture to warm the cockles of the heart.

Lissa Pooh Hattersley, the fastest gun in the West. She wanted a picture of herself posed with her latest art (behind her), which I take to be a bearded tomato and a squashed felt hat. She cleaned up her room especially for the occasion. Side bounce light.

era to actually measure the distances to the near and far borders of the area. Do this by focusing on each in turn and noting the distance in feet on the lens barrel across from the focusing mark.

Also on the lens barrel is a depth of field indicator that tells you how much depth of sharpness (in terms of the near and far distances) you will get at each f-stop (for example, f/11 or f/16) at a given focusing distance. The depth of field increases with distance.

Then instead of focusing on something you simply twist the focusing ring until the near and far distances that you have measured for your area of maximum action fall within the near and far distances marked on the lens barrel across from the particular f-stop you have decided to use.

After you have done this you no longer have to focus on anything happening within the preselected area, because it will all be acceptably

sharp due to falling within the depth of field. Not having to focus at all will permit you to pay more attention to what is happening in the arena of action and help you be ready to shoot at the very instant your Cossacks streak by.

Since most of your good shots are lost while you are focusing, the zone focusing system can be a saving grace. But you may be addicted to focusing, a great way to lose pictures, and may be constantly focusing, even when you don't have to. If this is the case, tape down the focusing ring so that it won't move and frequently remind yourself that you are using the zone focusing system.

This arena of action that you have visually staked out and actually measure is portable—you don't have to stay in one place. As you move around, all you have to do is to mentally project it out in front of you, knowing that things included within its near and far limits will come out sharp in your pictures.

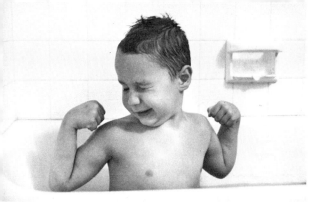

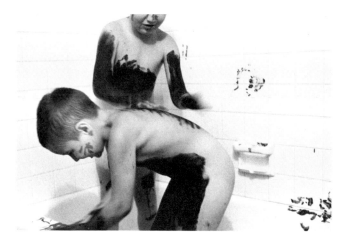

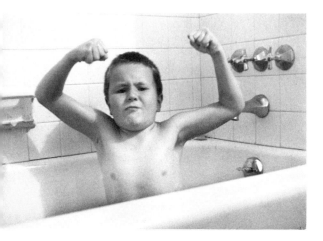

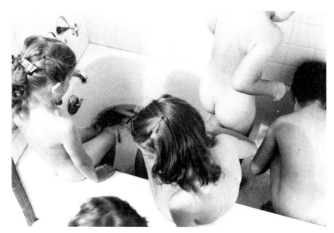

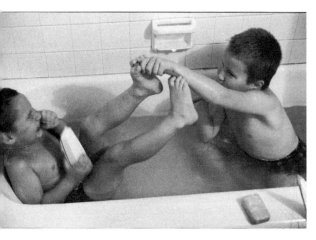

One problem with children is to keep them tied down long enough for you to get your camera in focus. Now, a bathtub serves the tie-down function very well, for it will keep them in one place for hours, will handle from one to six, and has endless possibilities for diversion. It is hard to talk children into a tub, of course, but ten times harder to talk them out of it. Bounce floodlight; the wires were taped up overhead, well out of the way of water and children. Shot with a hand-held Retina II.

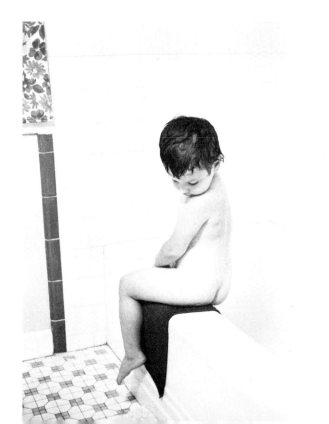

• Outdoor Lighting: Great for Kids

You have seen that outdoor light will permit you to use zone focusing, with hazy sun and direct sunlight being best for this, because they allow one to use fast shutter speeds and small f-stops. There is another great advantage, too: under a hazy sun or a cloudless sky you can usually take a single exposure reading and use it for an hour or more without having to take others. This helps simplify matters considerably, especially when you are chasing downhill after wild Indians.

If the sun is moving in and out of clouds the exposure situation deteriorates rapidly, because the correct exposure can vary by two or more f-stops in a matter of seconds. So you take a fresh reading, and by the time you are ready to shoot the clouds have moved again.

Instead of going crazy taking readings, the best bet is to estimate the light intensities. Set your camera for bright or hazy sun (distinct but fuzzy shadows), then reset the aperture according to your estimates. For example, if the sun moves behind a fairly small cloud and is still quite bright but doesn't cast shadows, open up two stops. If the cloud is large and the sun really blocked out, open up three stops.

Following children in and out of sunlight and shade is another severe hazard for photographers. The intensity of sunlight doesn't change, but shade varies all over the place. Only near the edge of a patch of shade, with lots of sky in view, can you depend on an estimate. This is called "open shade," and you open up three stops. Elsewhere in the shade you may have to open up quite a bit more (or use slower shutter speeds), depending on how deep it is. And in this case guesswork won't help much, unless you are already an expert at it.

Many times, the best solution to the shade problem is to work out an exposure plot before starting to shoot. Walk around taking readings in various patches of shade, recording the correct exposures on a little card. Then when you start shooting you can refer quickly to the card as your subjects move from place to place. This advice is mostly for people who use separate meters, because with many of the built-ins you can work fast enough to make it unnecessary.

• The Bounce Light Stakeout

Shooting action indoors isn't nearly as easy as outdoors, but having an electronic flash unit, especially one with a rather high output, will help things considerably. With a miniature unit the best bet is direct flash, but you must remember to use different f-stops for different subject-to-camera distances (to get correct exposures). With one of the larger units that embodies a sensor and a thyristor circuit you don't have this problem, of course. You can just let the unit itself take care of the exposure problem while you concentrate on keeping your subjects in focus.

With a larger unit, which includes many of the thyristor jobs, the easiest thing may be a lighting stakeout, so to speak. Plant a light stand in the middle of the room, tie it fast to a heavy piece of furniture so the Cossacks won't knock it over, and fasten your unit to the top of it, pointed at the ceiling (overhead bounce lighting).

Then you can just loaf around all day, if you like, shooting anything of interest that happens within the area covered by the sensor unit. You need an electrical connection between your camera and the unit, naturally, but a ten-foot cord will take care of that very nicely. You can use regular flash in the same way, though you have to put in a new bulb after each shot.

Though you can't freeze action with it, a stakeout with a photoflood bulb also works very nicely (if you use it without a reflector you will get quite a bit more light). Fortunately, kids aren't on the move all the time—they sit, stand still, or lie down just like anyone else. Or if you like blurred movement pictures, as some people do, you can get them easily enough with the shutter speeds permitted by overhead bounce with a photoflood.

313

The lamp will make the room very bright, but children don't mind this at all until they become teenagers, and even then they may not care. Unlike some adults, most children are fully heliotropic.

• If You Don't Know What to Do with Children

If you are photographing children and stalled for ideas, let them in on your problem, because after the age of four or five they have all kinds of ideas concerning what photography is good for. They will come up with ideas such as these: acting out the comic books, doing the King Kong bit, poor little Frankenstein, Mother nags Father, Starsky murders Hutch, disciplining bad dolls, nursing good ones back to health, wearing Mother's clothes, training the dog, teachers and students, and so on.

If you ask kids to come up with ideas you are more or less obligated to photograph everything they come up with short of mayhem. It is just the decent thing to do. Since they run through ideas rapidly (a one-minute act is very long for a child), you won't have time to get bored with anything they do. They'll get bored first, unless, perhaps, you can keep them well fed on pictures from a Polaroid camera or its Kodak equivalent.

Feeding people, young and old, on Polaroids has gotten to be a time-honored professional trick, incidentally. Many pros shoot them for their subjects, later doing their own work with Nikons, Canons, or Leicas. These prints help people see what you are up to and make them more willing to be involved in it. And for an amateur photographer (sometimes even a pro) there is no reason why a Polaroid print can't be the end product.

Well, so much for photographing children. As you can see, the subject has hardly been touched on, yet you may have read enough to get you started.

The pictures of children on the following pages are selections from several hundred that I shot during a summer vacation from teaching. I decided to use photography as a means for getting closer to my children and coming to know them better. For both purposes it worked very well indeed.

Deadeye Cleve, the rottenest gun in town.

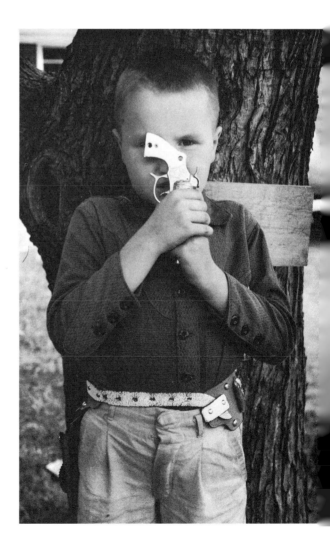

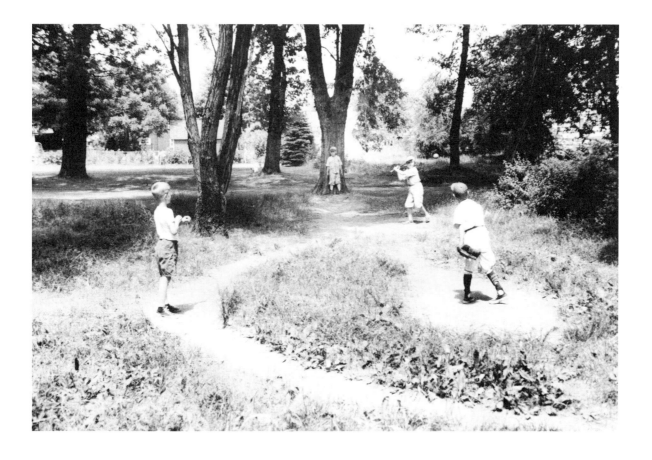

Serving up a home run.

Injured party and not-quite-so-innocent bystander.

Checking out the wild blackberry harvest.

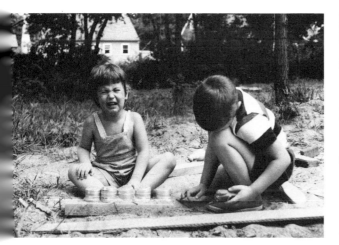

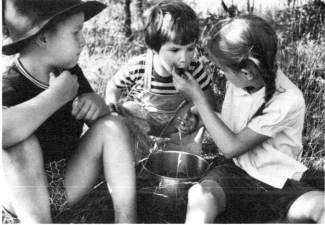

A most serious business: marriage.

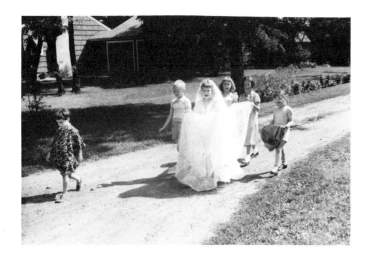

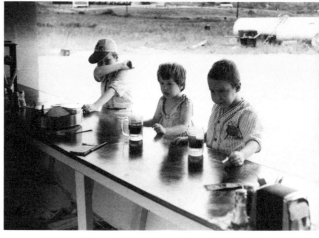

Root beer for the parched and desperate.

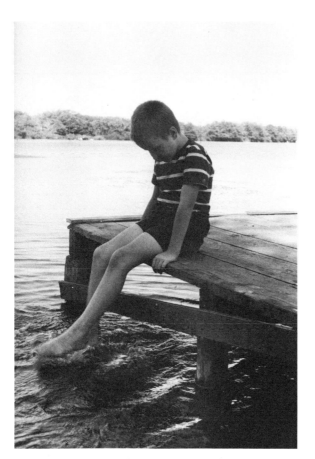

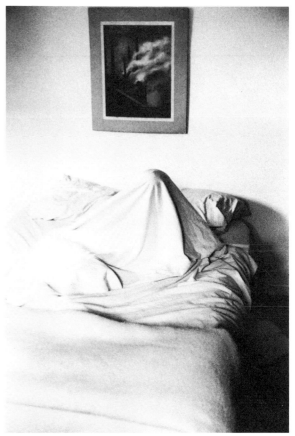

Posing for picture as a youthful contemplative.

Sick in bed, recovery phase two.

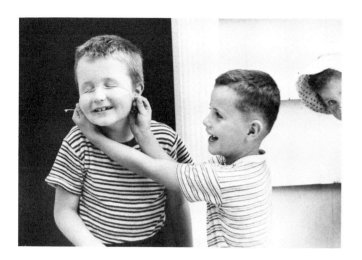

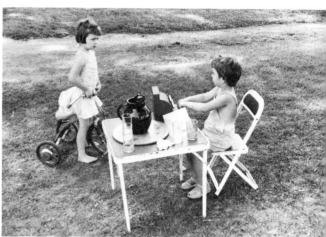

No, you can't have a free glass of Kool-Aid.

I'm tying a string around your eyes so they won't fall out.

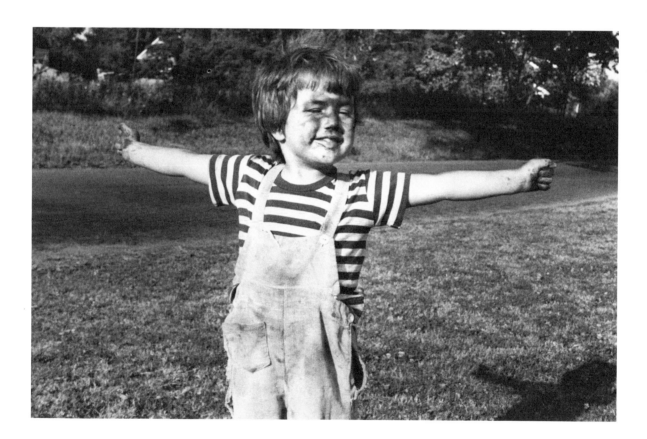

Mud, mud, glorious mud—
Keeps off mosquitoes
And good for the blood.

Nude babe watching boob tube.

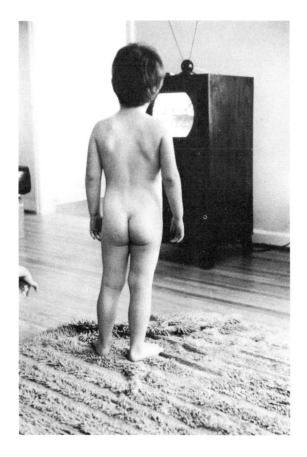

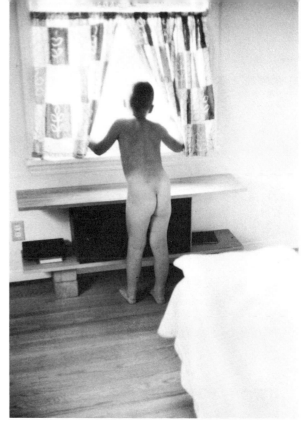

Hello, Morning Sunshine.

If *I* sat in the mud my mother would spank me.

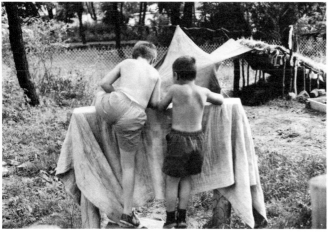

Preparing tents for a circus.

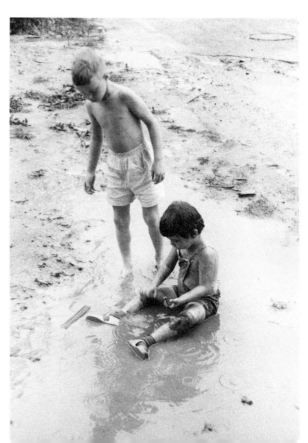

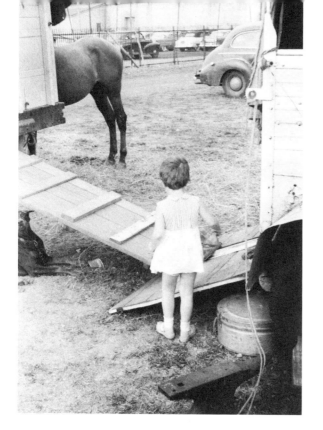

Abandoned outhouse still works.

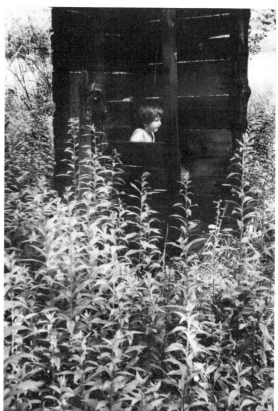

Backstage at the rodeo.

Seller of dreams and ice cream.

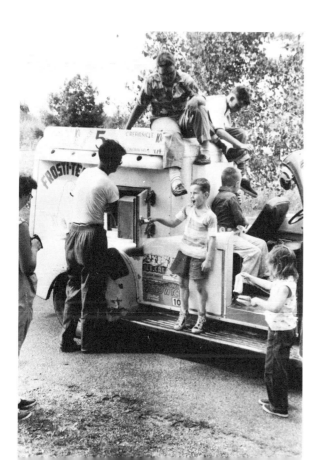

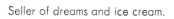

Fallen asleep while watching TV.

Efficiency expert.

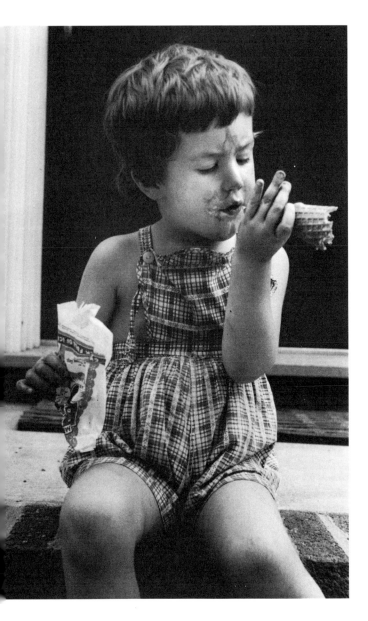

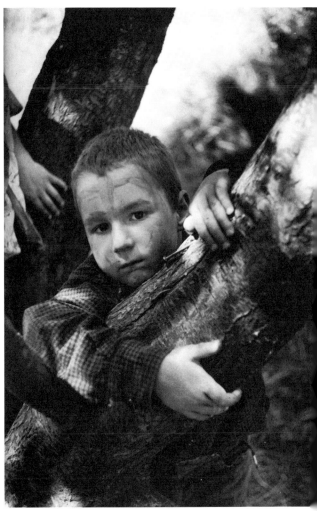

Craig Robert—also known as Keggy Bobbert.

HOW TO PHOTOGRAPH A PARTY

Photographing children's parties is dead easy—you just click away and nobody gives a hoot—except the little child who is crying. At an adult party you should carefully size things up first. If people are feeling friendly and in no pain your camera will be welcome. If the hostess is climbing the wall and the guests look strained beyond endurance, better forget about it.

Parties for adolescents are strictly off-limits for adults, except for those busily at work in the kitchen. You may be able to bang out a few quick snapshots at the beginning of a teenage fray, but then it is time to beat a hasty retreat, for sticking around just isn't cool.

Also off-limits are parties for women who have reached that age and don't wish to be reminded of it by your pictures. Family parties are usually snapshot heaven, so be sure to buy plenty of film.

Indoors: with just a few kids, all quite young, the overhead bounce light stakeout is a good idea. With more kids, or older ones, it is a hazard. One of them will manage to knock over the light stand and clobber Deborah Jones with it. So use flash on the camera. If you have a type of unit that can be bounced while it is attached to the camera, all the better. And if you have an automatic thyristor unit you are really in clover.

It is dead easy to photograph children's parties outdoors, because you can use a fast shutter speed, stop the lens way down, and use zone focusing. Just help deliver cake and ice cream, stay out of the way, and bang away like mad with your camera. With Tri-X film, the exposure here was about 1/250 at f/11.

• Children's Parties

Outdoors: remember zone focusing, how to estimate exposures when clouds are crossing the sun, and how to solve the shade problem by making an exposure plot, which should only take ten minutes. Then just snap away at whatever is going on, using up lots of film. Don't try to make great photographic art, for that can turn you into an overselective and grumpy critic. Just get all the kids on film, then go help with the ice cream.

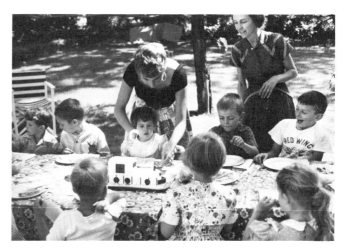

● Adolescents' Parties

I repeat: off-limits for adults. Let the teenage photographer in the family photograph them. If you haven't got one, Mother may get away with making a few fast snapshots, then leaving. But Father may be a bit too much to take. "Say, Man, your father just isn't with it." A kid doesn't want to hear that at his own party. Yet there are fathers who know how to get along with adolescents.

● Adult Parties: the General Situation

Most parties are tailored by women, who give a lot of thought to who goes with whom, the appropriate food and drink, and such matters. One of their favorite ploys is to have the lights turned down nice and warm and low, which doesn't make a party pig heaven for a natural light pho-

tographer, but does help the guests relax after a harrowing day in home or office. So here we come to an ironbound rule: don't fool around with the lighting set up by the hostess. Don't you dare touch even one light switch.

If you can't hand-hold a camera steady for long exposures, your only out is flash, direct or bounce—but don't overdo that, either. Your hostess is having a party, not putting on a circus. And be sure to ask her if it is all right to make a few snaps before you bring out your camera.

Even when it brings old friends together, a party is always a tricky business and often in danger of failure—because so many adults have forgotten how to have fun. So respect this unhappy fact and use your camera with discretion.

And remember the virtues of the snapshot, the photograph that doesn't criticize. Raise your camera, close your eyes, and click. People don't go to parties to be visually dissected; they just want to enjoy themselves—if they can.

Bounce flash has falsified the lighting of this party, for the room was very softly lit in low key. However, it shows what everyone looked like and that they were having a good time together. Furthermore, the available light was just too dim for making pictures. Thus a compromise (direct or bounce flash) was necessary.

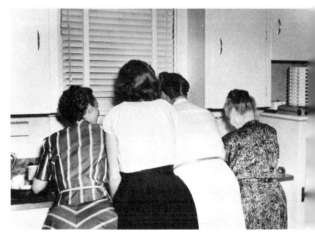

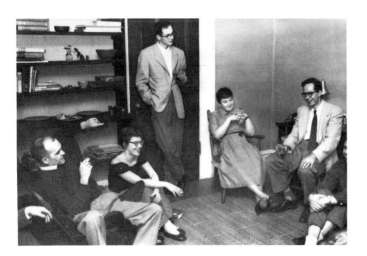

When you are shooting a party, don't neglect to catch the people who are working backstage to keep it going well. Straight flash. The harsh shadows usually associated with straight flash have mostly dropped out of sight behind the figures.

• Bashes

When the fruit of the vine flows freely and the cupids on the wallpaper start to blush, the situation for photography loosens up a bit. Even so, stick to flash or natural light pictures and continue to leave the light switches alone. Plenty of people will be making faces or doing hijinks for your camera, so you won't lack for interesting photographs. However, there is a certain etiquette that you ought to follow, or you may get punched in the nose. The point is that people are never as far gone as they seem to be, so they know very well when you are up to something.

Refrain from trying to make people look as sozzled as they actually are; don't try to sneak shots when people aren't looking; leave people who are engaged in forbidden flirtations alone; and don't photograph the guy trying to stick a whirling douche in his ear. This is paparazzi stuff,

and you just don't have to indulge in it. You should never try to make people look silly or stupid, even when they are behaving that way. However, if they *want* pictures of themselves playing the fool, that's O.K.

• Passing the Polaroids

A fine approach to party photography, one that many people naturally take, is to make a Polaroid snapshot of everyone present, passing all the pictures around as soon as they are made. This is not interpretive photography, to be sure, but as the years go by you will greatly enjoy having a visual head count of all your friends. Truthfully, snapshots look better and better with the passage of time, while interpretive photographs often begin to look empty and sterile.

Passing the Polaroids has gotten to be an American party pastime that everyone enjoys, so it is not likely that you will upset the flow of a

The life of many a party, Dick still managed to look as if he were on the way to his own funeral, with no one else bothering to come. Overhead bounce flash. Electronic flash freezes action nicely.

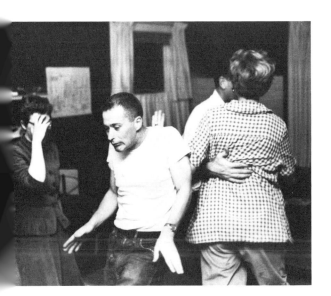

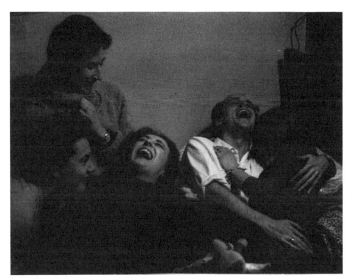

As you can see, my English friends got into a laughing jag, though the laughter looked suspiciously close to despair. It often does, doesn't it? I photographed by the available light, which was very dim, using an exposure of 1/8 second at f/4.

323

party by making them. If you lacquer them before passing them around, you can always wipe off the drink stains later. Of course, the XL-70 color print doesn't need the lacquer.

Incidentally, the Polaroid company markets a kind of film that produces both snapshots and excellent negatives, which can be enlarged later to any size you want. It comes in two sizes—Type 55 P/N (4×5) and Type 105 P/N (3¼×4¼). Kodak is now on the market with an "instant" color film and cameras for shooting it. Though they are bulkier than, say, the Polaroid Pronto! they seem to work quite well. The color is roughly comparable to Polaroid XL-70 color. Both Polaroid and Kodak instant color films produce pictures very much like color TV, which doesn't say much for their quality. However, people seem to like them just fine.

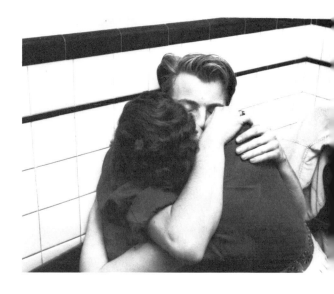

Though the party went on for hours, Jerry never once strayed from his young lady. Pestered by one and all, they finally moved to the bathroom, hoping to escape attention. However, this picture is proof that they did not. Bounce flash.

The singing was more energetic than harmonious, but no one seemed to mind. Harris reached for notes that would make a lyric soprano quail and missed them by five miles each. He didn't care. Bounce flash.

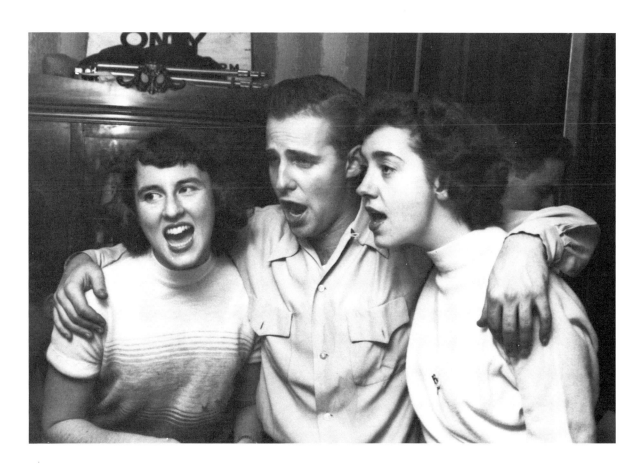

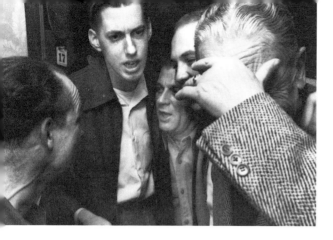

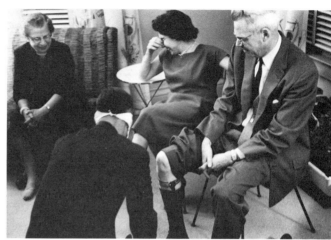

The boys had a way of wrenching a song out of shape that put Mr. Shawcross right up the wall. Fortunately, he survived the encounter and chaperoned many more noisy parties as the years went by. Bounce flash.

Don Smith was supposed to recognize his wife by the feel of her stockinged leg, but we brought in C. B. Neblette as a ringer. Don wasn't fooled. Available light.

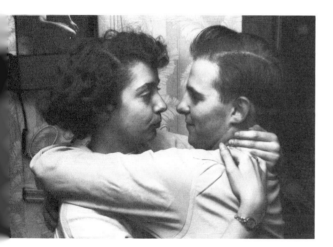

"Hello, I am here." "Hello, so am I." Bounce flash again.

They tried to catch Dave's attention, but it was already thoroughly caught. Bounce flash.

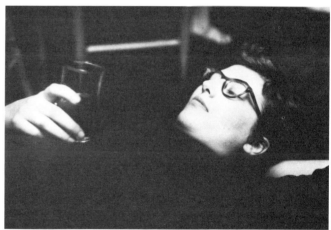

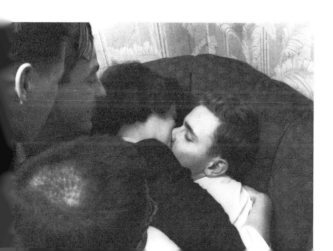

At many a party we just listened to music and had a few quiet drinks. Barbara usually stretched out on the floor, finding it very peaceful down there. Available light.

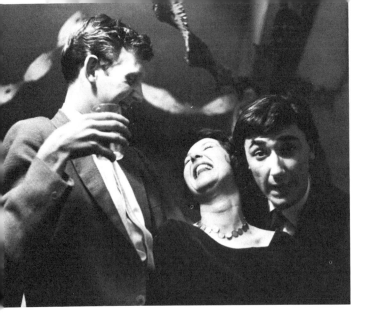

I gave a party for the entire acting company and backstage crew of the Birmingham (England) Repertory Theater. Numerous barrels of good English beer were consumed. Available light.

Pat always took off her shoes and socks and parked herself on the floor. The cracked cup was merely the least cracked cup in the house. Available light.

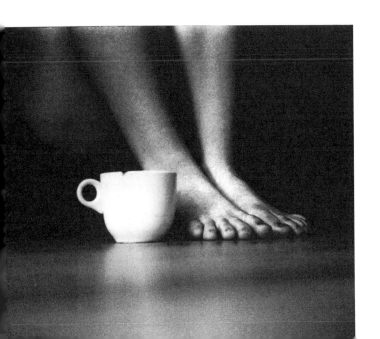

• Ideal Party Cameras

Since I have no idea what kind of a camera you have, I can't very well tell you how to use it for photographing parties. And you probably have just the one camera and have to stick with it, come what may. Even so, you may be interested in what I consider to be the ideal party cameras. They are the 110 cartridge-load types with built-in electronic flash, such as the Vivitar Point'n Shoot cameras. And that is just about all you do: point 'em and shoot—no focusing, no nothing.

Now, 110 color transparencies and negatives are only about the size of your thumbnail (13×17mm), yet they will produce very good wallet- and album-size prints. When projected the slides show excellent quality. Verichrome Pan, a black-and-white film, will permit rather good enlargements up to about 11×14 inches when it is developed in Microdol-X (diluted 1:3—develop 10 to 12 minutes at 68° F). The grain is surprisingly fine.

Though blow-ups of 20X and larger are mainly of interest to fine-grain buffs and technicians, they do suggest that 110 cameras are not mere toys. However, the fact that they *look* like toys makes them work all the better as party cameras. When you point them at people they pay little attention, undoubtedly thinking that a camera that small couldn't possibly do anything but turn out fuzzy snapshots. In other words, they are very harmless and nonthreatening in appearance.

In the 35mm format the Konica C35-EF looks very good. It, too, has a built-in electronic flash unit, which pops up when you are ready to use it. Focusing the camera changes the aperture setting, thus determining the flash exposure automatically. Since getting the exposure right is one of the primary problems in photography, this automatic system is very useful. When you are shooting without flash a cds electric eye sets your exposures automatically, which also is handy.

I will say no more about cameras, because a

The room was so dark that I could hardly see my own hand, but I shot pictures anyway and was quite surprised at who showed up in them. The exposures were about one-half second at f/2.8—f/2.8 being my favorite f-stop for indoor available light.

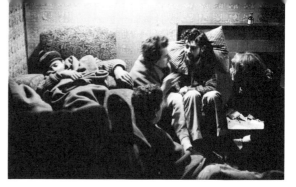

book is not the best place for information on photographic equipment, a field that is in a constant state of change. The best sources are the photography magazines, especially *Popular Photography* and *Modern Photography*. They make a strong point of keeping up on developments as they come along.

My only reason for mentioning Vivitar and Konica cameras was to give you an idea of the ideal party camera: a small, inconspicuous device that looks like nothing more than a child's toy, the more toy-like the better.

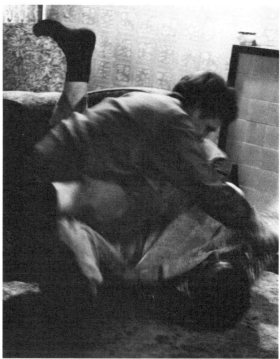

• Poses

Asking people at parties to pose is often an imposition on them—they just want to be left alone to have a good time. However, if they obviously want to pose, just shoot without hesitation any poses they present to you, even if you don't like what they look like. This is the kindly thing to do. Now, if people want *you* to pose them you can do that, too—just don't make a production out of it. If they *want* a production, that's something else; go ahead and stir one up.

Perhaps the important thing to remember about parties is that people go to them to have a good time. Therefore, you should make your behavior as a photographer a part of the fun, not an inhibition against it. Don't try to turn people into photographic art: just let them relax and come across as themselves.

They were only fighting for fun, yet the fight was very vigorous anyway. One-half second at f/2.8, which is pretty slow for a fight. Available light.

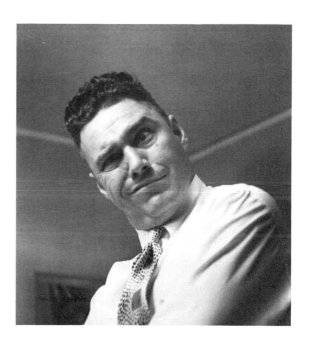

Host Hal Bolton surveys his party and finds it a roaring success. Hal is the inventor of the world's wickedest Gibson. Available light.

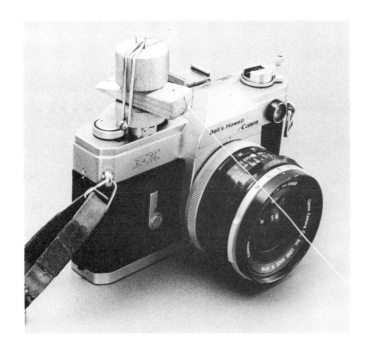

A gadget for tripping a shutter release from a distance, useful in self-portraiture, especially if your camera doesn't have a self-timer (this one does). It can also be used to hold the shutter open when the "B" (bulb setting) is used; this is convenient when you are painting with light. You operate the device by pulling gently on a linen thread, which can be of any length desired. This pulls the slotted wedge out of the assembly, thus permitting the rubber bands to force a firing pin into the shutter release mechanism and fire the shutter. The pressure is gentle, and absolutely no harm is done to the mechanism.

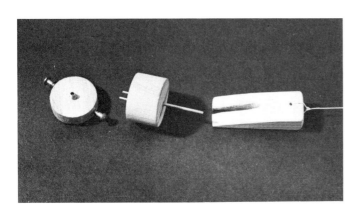

Here we see the three main parts of the shutter tripping device. Parts A and B are pieces cut from a one-inch dowel; part C was whittled from a scrap of wood and the slot put in with a saw. In part A, the two screws on the perimeter are for attaching the rubber bands. The screw in the center, rescued from a worn-out cable release, permits the device to be screwed into the camera shutter release. In part B, the two pins on the left are for holding the rubber bands in place. The longer pin on the right, made from a small finishing nail, is the firing pin. The trigger mechanism is made in a wedge shape so that as it is gently withdrawn the force of the rubber bands will come to bear on the firing pin very gradually. This is to prevent camera shake. As a further precaution against camera movement the wedge is rounded on both its top and bottom so that it will slide out of the assembly with a very light pull on the thread.

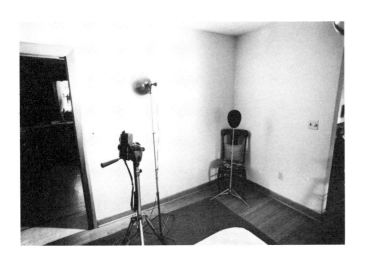

A corner of my dining room that I often use for portraiture, always using just one light bounced off the wall and ceiling in various ways. This particular lighting is the one I use most for a person sitting on the chair. Notice that the "hot" part of the light pattern on the wall doesn't extend as far as the corner of the room. The lens on the camera has a focal length of 55mm, which I find quite good for portraiture. The strange object in front of the chair is a focus and cropping target useful for self-portraiture (see text).

HOW TO MAKE SELF-PORTRAITS

Shooting a self-portrait is very easy, though you can make it difficult if you try. There are several ways of going about it, one as good as another. I suggest that you start with the easy ways, then work your way up to the harder ones.

• Equipment

Tripod: you really need one so that your camera will hold a steady position while you pose in front of it. However, you could prop up the camera on a table, chair, stack of books, or something.

Self-timer: this mechanism on a camera is made especially for self-portraits. When you set it and activate it you have from about eight to ten seconds to get into position before the shutter goes off. A self-timer makes self-protraiture dead easy, though there are ways of getting along without one.

Remote releases: if your camera has no self-timer you may wish to get an air or electronic release. An air release is a long rubber tube with a cable release plunger on one end and a squeeze bulb on the other; you squeeze the bulb to activate the plunger, which depresses the shutter release. An electronic release embodies an electrical device for depressing the shutter. You can use either type of release when you are sitting in front of your camera at some distance from it.

Shaving mirror (about 8×10 inches): if you are sitting in front of your camera and want to know how you look in the lighting you have set up, hold up the mirror to yourself, making sure it isn't reflecting light into your face and changing the lighting.

Focus and framing target: for making a self-portrait it would be nice to have an identical twin in the form of a mannequin. You could light it, pose it, focus on it, then push it aside and take its place for a self-portrait, knowing in advance exactly what the picture would look like. For a focus and framing target a little less fancy, try taping an egg-shaped piece of cardboard (about ten inches long) to the top of an adjustable-height light stand. Simple as it is you can use it as a stand-in for yourself.

Measured string: for getting yourself in focus if you are not using a focusing target. Fasten a length of it to your camera and tie a knot in it to mark off the distance on which your camera is focused. If it is, say, four feet the knot would be four feet from the back of the camera and the focusing scale would be set at four feet. Just sit squarely in front of the camera, pull the string taut, and move your head forward until your forehead touches the knot. You will then be in focus.

• Mirror Self-Portraits

The easiest way to shoot into a mirror is with a hand-held camera. Focus on your image in the mirror, then lower the camera until it is just below

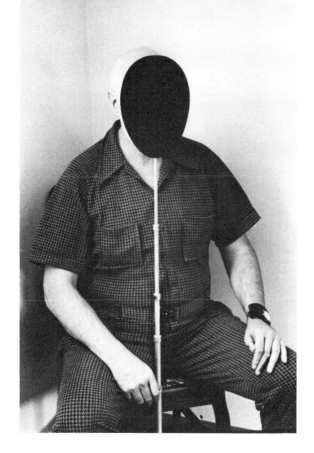

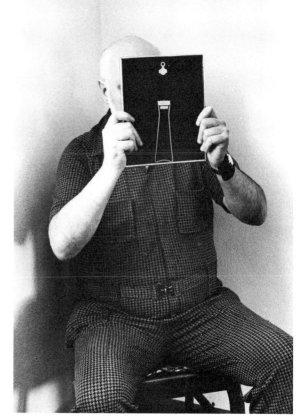

Here I am sitting behind the focus and cropping target, which has been set at the same height as my head. The black-paper egg shape has the same outside dimensions as my head; my nose is touching the back of it. Before actually shooting a picture I would set the height and position of the target, crop with my camera, focus on the target, sit behind it, touch it with my nose, then push it aside and shoot the picture. Thus the picture would be sharp and properly framed.

When you are shooting a self-portrait you can check the lighting on your face (to see if it looks good) by holding up a mirror. However, you should hold it at such an angle that it doesn't reflect light into your face, for that would give you a false picture of the results that you would get.

A self-portrait I made using the focus and cropping target and a mirror lighting check. I'm not actually as grouchy as I look, but the picture is Ralph Hattersley all right.

your chin and shoot the picture. Since you won't know exactly what the camera will be seeing, it's a good idea not to crop your head too tight; so back up and leave plenty of space around it in the viewfinder. Then if your camera isn't aimed quite right you will still be in the picture.

If you don't want a self-portrait with a camera in it you can get rid of it by aiming at the mirror at an angle, either from below or from one side. In this case you will have to work with a focus and framing target, such as the one described in the last section. Pose yourself, standing or seated,

and set the target with the back of the egg shape touching your nose and at the same height as your head. Then set the camera angle so that the target is well positioned in the viewfinder. Then focus on the target. To get your posing position, move up behind the target until your nose touches it. Then push it to one side and shoot your picture, in which you will be in sharp focus. (The

330

string-focus idea won't work very well with mirror pictures, incidentally, because the focusing distance is the mirror-to-camera distance plus the mirror-to-subject distance, which is a little hard to work out with a string.)

To make a mirror picture with a hand-held camera you obviously don't need a self-timer or a remote release. You probably won't need them for head-and-shoulder angle shots, either, though you should use a tripod and cable release. For a shot angled from below the camera will probably be about waist level and easily reached. When you are angling from one side you should still be able to reach the cable release easily enough, though it might be handy to have an extra-long release.

When you take pictures by pointing your camera in a mirror they naturally come out as reversed, or mirror, images. The chances are that you will like self-portraits better that way, because that is how you are used to seeing yourself. If not, you can give your pictures the correct orientation by putting your negatives or transparencies wrong-side down in the enlarger.

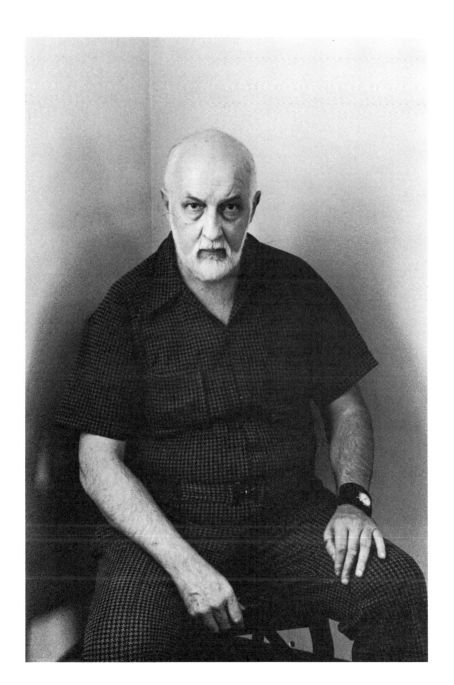

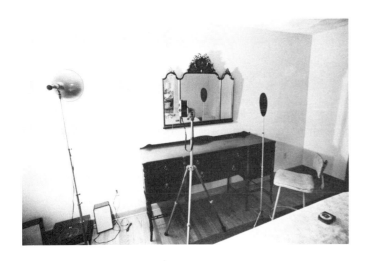

A setup in my dining room for making a mirror self-portrait when the camera is off to one side of the mirror, the focus and cropping target off to the other side. The advantage to this system is that you can see pretty well what you look like just before you take the picture. Later, I sat on the stool behind the target, touched the black egg with my nose, pushed the target aside, and made my own picture.

A picture made with the camera and myself at opposite sides of the mirror. I was looking at the reflection of the lens in the mirror, which makes it seem that I am looking right at you. This is a mirror image showing what I see when I brush my hair—when I bother to look. To get a normal image I would reverse the negative, printing it emulsion up.

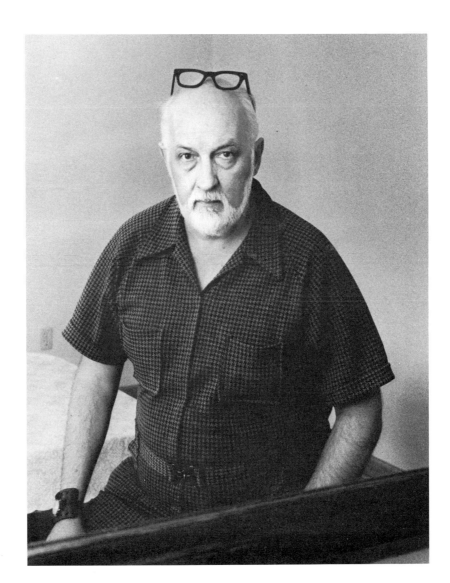

A setup for making a picture with the camera below the mirror and the subject standing well above the camera. The advantages are that you can see what you will look like and can easily reach the cable release to take the picture.

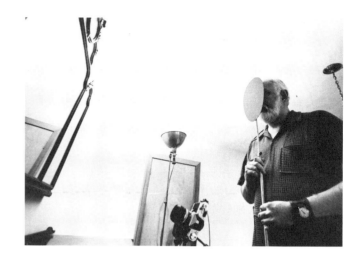

A self-portrait made with the camera below the level of the mirror and angled upward. My head tilted forward somewhat and I was looking directly at the mirrored image of the camera lens, which makes it seem that I am now looking at you. The thing growing from my head is the chain-support for a light fixture. I would rather it weren't there, but what can one do?

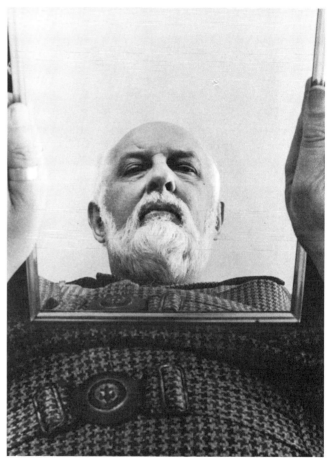

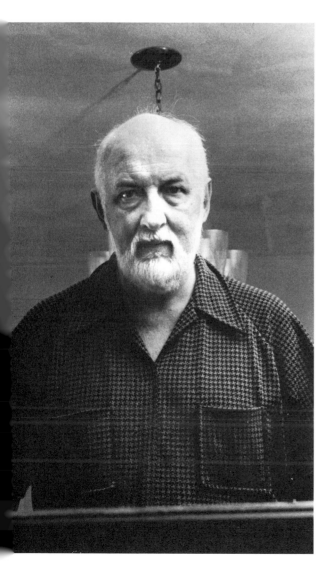

I sat on a chair with a mirror in my lap (you can see my belt buckle). The camera (on a tripod) was right in front of me and angled downward at the mirror. I moved the mirror around until the camera lens was centered in it, then activated the self-timer to take the picture. I don't know any particular advantage to this system, but it does work.

Self-portrait with John Boy in his usual position on the east end of the dining room table. Here I used a 19mm lens (very wide angle) stopped down to f/16, which gave me a tremendous depth of field. Thus I could use zone focusing (see text), getting everything sharp from John Boy's tail to the far end of the living room. I used the natural light that was coming through the dining room window.

• Depth of Field

Even if you are using a focusing target or a measured length of string it is a good idea to stop down quite a bit, in fact as much as you can. This increases the depth of field (depth of sharpness) and will help keep you in focus if you accidentally move a little bit out of position. In order to stop down quite a bit when shooting indoors you may find yourself using shutter speeds as slow as one-half second, but that is quite all right—as long as you are also using a tripod and a cable release, remote release, or self-timer. All you

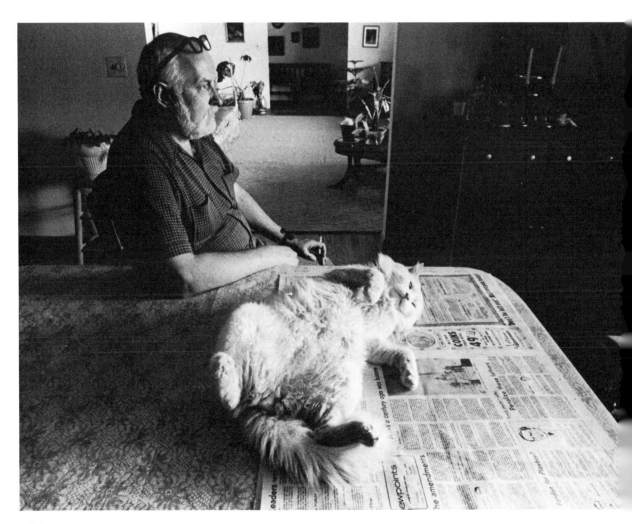

have to do is hold still for that long, which is easy enough.

Outdoors (still using a tripod) it is nearly always possible to stop down your camera all the way (for sunny bright, hazy sun, light overcast, and even heavy overcast lighting conditions). For a 35mm head shot with a normal lens this would give you roughly a foot of depth of field at f/16, which gives you quite a bit of latitude for getting positioned at the right distance from your camera. For a half-figure pose you would have about two and one-half feet, which is even better. In either case, touching your nose to a sharply focused target, or using a measured string, should guarantee a sharp picture.

If you are using a wide-angle lens for portraiture (or a telephoto, for that matter) you will get the same depth of field for head shots and half figures of the same size. Due to the distortion, however, one generally works for smaller figures when using wide-angles, and then the depth of field can be very considerable. For example, using a 19mm lens at f/16 would give us a depth of field extending from about one foot to infinity.

With depths of field this great you might just as well use zone focusing, realizing that if you position yourself anywhere within the zone you will come out sharp. You can figure out how *large* you will be at different distances by checking them out with your focusing and framing target.

Mainly because of the depth of field that you can use (with wide-angle, normal, or telephoto lenses) it is considerably easier to shoot self-portraits outdoors than in. However, if you have a modest command of the photographic medium it is easy to do indoors, too.

This was shot in the master bedroom with me sitting on a step stool. The light was coming from windows on two sides of the room. Notice the back of my head and the camera in the mirror. I shot this with the aid of the little focus and framing target, a very handy little gadget for self-portraiture. The face looks pretty dissipated to me, but I guess this is how I look.

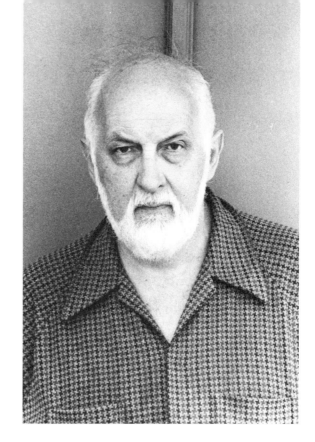

Old Grouch-Puss rides again, this time in an outdoor self-portrait lit only by skylight, which is extremely diffuse. Its very diffuseness fills in a lot of lines and wrinkles on the face, making it look somewhat younger than its actual ninety-seven years.

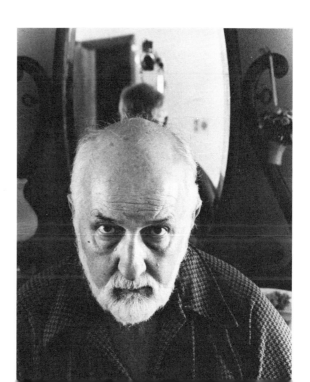

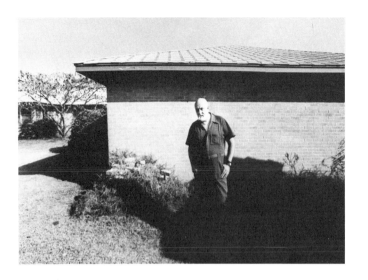

The Lord of the Manor standing behind his garage and straining hard to see his camera, which is buzzing its self-timer on a tripod in front of him. Used a 28mm lens, which permitted zone focusing and produced a very considerable depth of field or sharpness. The idea was to make use of the groovy shadow patterns that were happening in the back yard.

The Troll of the Tree gazing out at the world with more than a little suspicion. I used a 19mm lens stopped down to f/16 and zone focusing and thus got everything sharp from A to Izzard. Now hear this: until you have taken your own picture as a tree frog you really haven't lived.

• For Total Picture Control

One problem with most self-portraits (if it is a problem) is that you don't know exactly what you look like when the shutter goes off. This shouldn't matter very much, but some people just don't like to be surprised. One way to solve the difficulty is to stand a large mirror right next to the camera, angling it slightly so that you can see yourself in it when you are posed. The mirror won't see quite what the camera does, but it should come close enough for your desires.

I once knew a man who was greatly disliked for his contemptuous attitude and extreme egotism, which were written all over his face. He needed some portraits of himself one time, but he knew what he would get if he asked one of his colleagues (all of them photographers) to make them: pictures of a self-adoring young fool. So he used the mirror trick and made them himself. And what did they look like? St. Francis couldn't have looked so sweet, Clark Gable so handsome, or Einstein so intelligent. Considering the model, I was flabbergasted by the effectiveness of his self-canonization. But it does show how far you

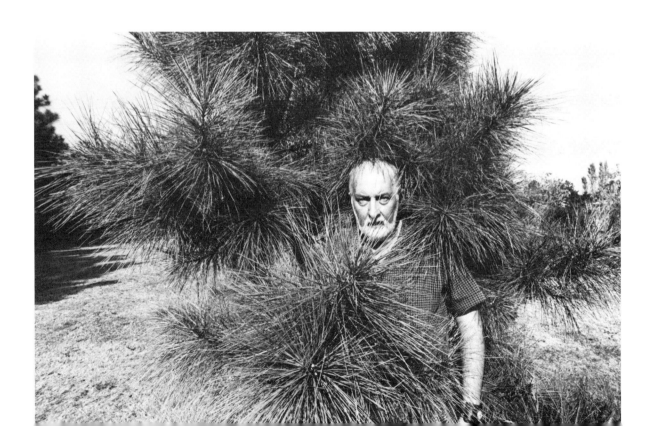

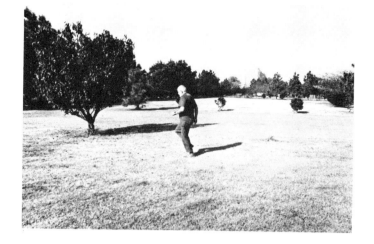

Getting in shape for the races—I'm actually a rather speedy guy, though a bit on the fat side. I used a 19mm lens and zone focusing and was actually only ten feet from the camera, though the distance seems greater.

can go toward total picture control by using this method.

There are other possibilities for mirrors, if you have a mind for such things. For example, you might cut a circular hole in the center of a mirror and poke the camera lens through it. Or you might center the lens behind a two-way mirror—the kind that is transparent like a window from the back. Both systems would give you a reflection almost identical with the image in the camera viewfinder. With a two-way glass there is a certain amount of light loss, but you can compensate for it with longer exposures or brighter lightings. The important thing with either system is that you can see almost exactly what you look like.

For total control it would be best not to use a self-timer, which gives you only eight or ten seconds to bring your facial expression under control. Use either an air or electronic shutter release, and trip the shutter whenever you feel ready.

As you have probably surmised, making a self-portrait is very easy, though you can make it hard for yourself if you wish. You may wonder why you should photograph yourself. Well, a lot of people do it and claim that it is a very meaningful experience. There is just one way to find out if this is true: try it.

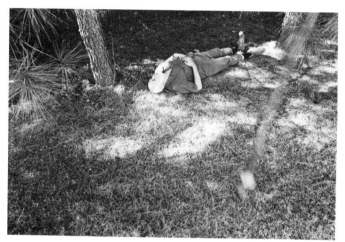

While you are at it you might as well take a picture of yourself as a corpse. At this very minute you are as good a cadaver as you'll ever be. Or maybe we are talking about too many mint juleps in this picture.

Hard shadows caused by direct sunlight make this friendly lumberjack look as tough as he really is. Made with a 19mm lens at f/16 and zone focusing. The focus and framing target was used to get the head framed in the center of the picture.

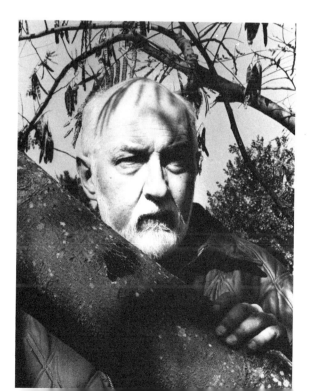

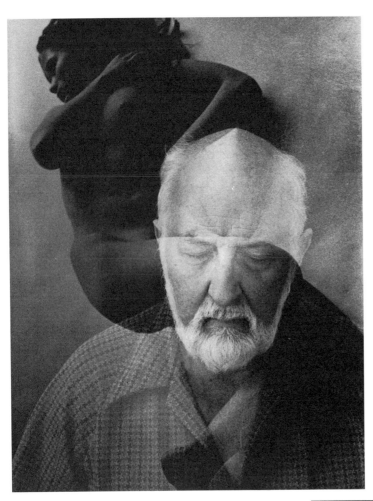

I took a picture of myself in front of a large piece of black paper, then photographed a print on the same frame of film. My camera has a bypass system (many cameras have), so that I can cock the shutter without advancing the film to the next frame. For each exposure I used half of the total exposure.

A face and a print photographed on the same frame of film. I find it rather amusing in a gross sort of way.

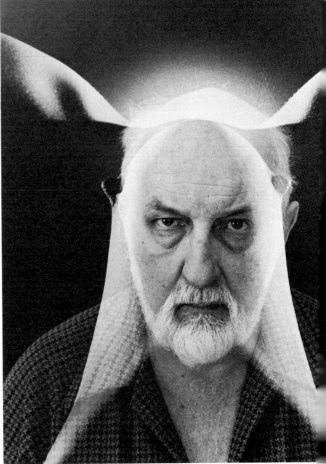

HOW TO MAKE STAGED CANDID PICTURES

If you are tired of people lining up like bowling pins in your pictures you might like to try shooting staged candids. The idea is to pose people—more or less—in such a way that your pictures look entirely unposed, or natural. In this way you can get a slice of life effect, not a bunch of wooden dummies. Once you get the idea, setting up a staged candid is easy enough to do. Of course, wooden dummies in pictures are all right, too—it is just that you might like a change of pace.

● Non-Pose Poses

There is only a limited number of things that people do that look like poses for a camera. If you ask them to do other things instead they tend to look unposed, or natural. For example, when setting up a group candid you might give instructions such as these: "When I say, 'Go'—and not until then—I want you to look away from the camera and to start doing the following things. Bill—lean back, put both arms on top of your head, and chew on your lips. Claire—lean toward the coffee table and push the candy dish slowly back and forth. Dan—prop up your chin on your left hand and leaf through this magazine, looking at the pictures. Mary—slide way down in your chair, cross your legs in front of the coffee table, and twiddle your thumbs."

You can make your shots at several points: (1) as soon as they start moving into position but before they actually get there, (2) when they have settled into position and are waiting expectantly for you to shoot, and (3) after they have become bored with you, the charade, and the camera and are chatting with one another. The chances are that shots (1) and (3) would be best and that the one in which they are actually following your instructions (2) wouldn't amount to much. But you don't have to tell them that you plan things this way as a diversionary tactic. If your models get their instructions all confused, so much the better. At least they won't be looking like wooden Indians.

I asked Brent to prop up his feet on Sam's chair and got this very informal posed candid picture, which doesn't look in the least posed.

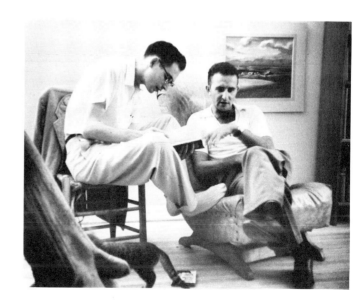

• Diversionary Tactics

1. Put your camera on a tripod (it looks very harmless there, especially if you walk away from it). Tell your models to make themselves comfortable while you run a couple of tests on your shutter (or electronic flash, self-timer, remote shutter release, etc.). Move slowly. Be a complete bore, if possible. Don't look at your subjects at all, except out of the corner of your eye, even though you are actually making pictures with your "tests." Shoot some of your pictures with your back to your subjects. After you have gotten the pictures you wanted with your "tests" and "fumbling around," make the picture that your models have been expecting—for them, not yourself.

2. Put your camera on a tripod, line up your picture the way you want it, then turn the camera over to an assistant, who will trip the shutter whenever you give an unobtrusive signal. Then distract your subjects by talking to them, pushing equipment or furniture around, bringing in drinks, turning on the hi-fi, and so on, all the while giving your assistant signals at appropriate times.

If you have a long enough remote release cable, you can do more or less the same thing without an assistant. Or you might use the self-timer on your camera, though it makes a distracting sound. Cover it up with loud music or conversation, and it won't be so bad. In shooting, activate the timer, walk away from the camera, and engage in distracting your subjects until the shutter goes off, doing this as many times as necessary to get the pictures you want. Since neither you nor your models will know exactly when the shutter will click, there is a good chance that the pictures will look truly candid. There is also the possibility that some of them won't come out very well, but you can cover yourself by shooting lots of frames.

3. Use someone (or several people) as a spe-

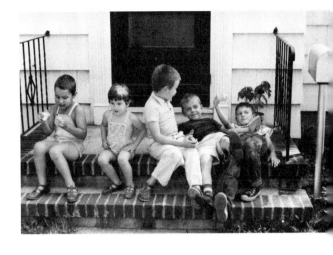

The children were all lined up stiff as starch, so I waited around until they relaxed a little bit. The posed candid trick is to pose people more-or-less, then wait around until they break the pose.

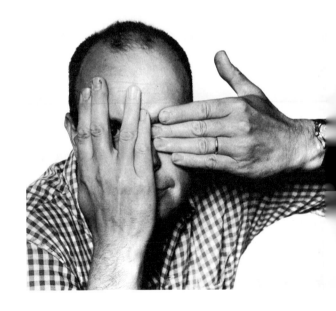

Charley Arnold likes to do things with his hands, which gives pictures of him an impromptu, candid feeling. We see the unexpected.

340

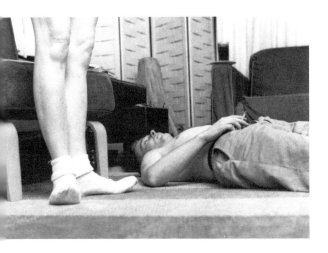

This picture looks candid because it is rather improbable—not the kind of thing people ordinarily do when posing for the camera. However, it was very carefully set up this way.

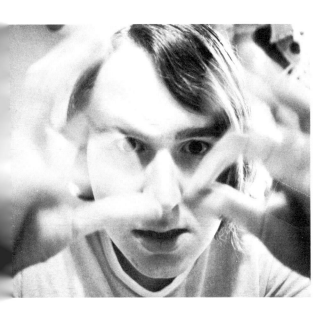

My son Cleve also likes to do things with his hands. I had intended to make just an ordinary candid snapshot, but see what happened—nothing ordinary at all about the picture.

cial distractor. For example, if you wish to photograph a young woman you could ask her to have several good friends with her. Then, having posed her in a non-pose pose, you could ask them to stand or sit just out of camera range and chat with her. While they are getting used to the idea, disappear for a minute or two or bury your head in your equipment, taking pains not to listen to what they are talking about. Well, good friends like to talk, so they will easily enough forget you as you unobtrusively make your pictures, even if you are using flash. The click of your camera shutter will tell them that everything is all right and that they don't have to worry. So reassuring is this sound that some photographers start out with empty cameras, clicking merrily away until everyone has relaxed. Then they load up and start shooting pictures, though they don't let their models know what they have been up to.

• Staged Emotion

One of the surest signs that a photograph is truly candid, or real, is a display of genuine emotion on the model's face. You may think that emotion can't be faked—but don't be too sure. It is true that if you ask someone to express a certain emotion it will probably look as unrealistic as wheels on a bat. So don't ask people to do this. Instead, ask them to do certain specific things with their faces, hands, and bodies. If you pick the right things the emotions will be there—fake but real. That is, no one could look at your pictures and tell them from the real thing.

In all fairness to your models, you should tell them roughly what you are up to but not the specific emotions that you are going for. They will usually be able to tell, anyway, so don't worry about it. The important thing is that they understand that they merely have to push their bodies and faces around at your direction, nothing more.

Following are some tried and true instructions that you might try giving to a model to see what "emotions" you will get:

1. Open your eyes as wide as you possibly can and see how long you can hold them that way.

2. Tense your neck muscles until they stand out like strings.

3. Put your hand on your forehead about an inch above your eyebrows and try to push the skin down over your eyes.

4. Put your hand to your face, with your thumb on one cheek and your fingers on the other, and push the skin up into your eyes.

5. Put your hands to your temples and press until it hurts.

6. Put a bit of this snuff on the back of one hand and sniff it up your nose.

7. Try eating this dill pickle.

8. Put an index finger in each corner of your mouth and push it up into a great big smile.

9. Put these two wads of paper between your back teeth and clamp down on them as hard as you can.

10. With your eyes closed, face right into this very bright light (such as a 500 watt photoflood), screwing your face up as much as necessary to make the light intensity tolerable.

11. Close your mouth tight and puff out your cheeks as far as you possibly can.

12. With your thumb on one cheek and your fingers on the other, twist your face as much as you can.

13. Press your chin against your chest as hard as you can.

14. Open your mouth as wide as you can.

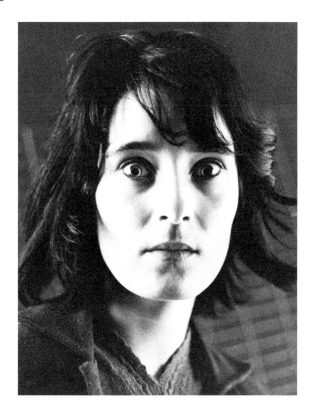

The candid emotion in this picture was carefully fabricated from a special lighting and from having Anne Lawrence open her eyes as wide as she could. There was bounce light coming from each side of her. The pattern in the background helps make the setting look real, though the picture was shot in a studio.

If you remember your childhood and the things you used to do with your face it should be obvious that having a model do these things could lead to some ridiculous pictures. On the other hand, the very gestures that are the most ridiculous will also produce all the "genuine" emotions you want—the idea is to click the shutter at just the right time. For example, from a sneeze we can get sorrow, dismay, and terror in addition to the expression normally expected, depending on how soon we shoot after the sneeze has started.

Some of the above gestures are already as-sociated with various emotions, being the things we often do when we have certain feelings. Oddly, merely doing them mechanically tends to arouse the emotions, real ones recovered from memory. It is often said that sneezing is almost exactly like dying, which might explain why genuine emotion is briefly but violently aroused by a sneeze. The point I am getting at here is that your "faked" emotions may not be as phony as you think.

Peg and Dick just horsing around. The candid feeling comes from the fact that neither of them cared a hoot what they looked like in front of the camera. They could just relax and be themselves.

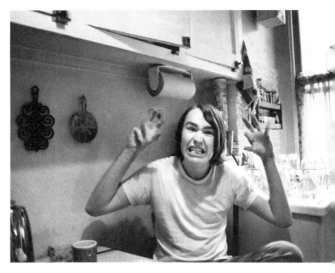

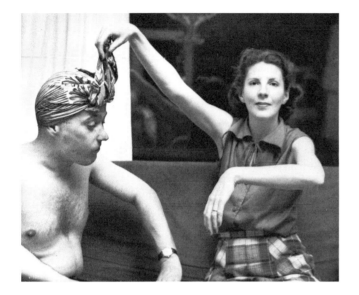

My son Cleve explaining why he is tougher than King Kong and all the lesser apes put together. Since it doesn't look like a posed studio portrait or a fashion picture, we might as well call the picture candid. What else to call it?

I asked this Spanish musician to look Satanical, and this is what happened. Reality can be faked, for he is a very gentle person. We might call this a faked-emotion posed candid picture.

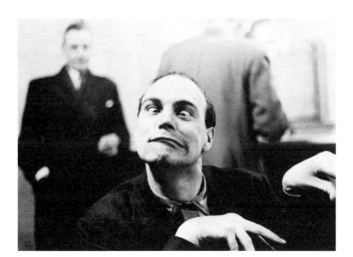

More often than not, Eddy Mole would make a terrible face for my camera. I guess you call this picture candid.

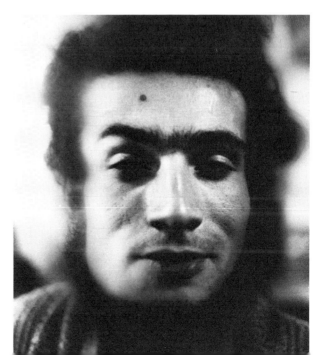

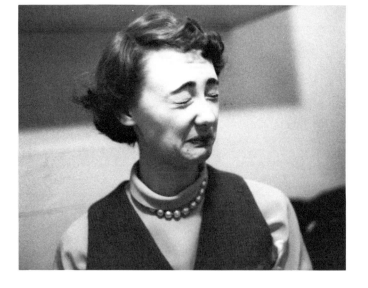

Deep and candid emotion caused by the first taste of a dill pickle.

• Psycho-Drama

With the techniques discussed so far it is easy enough to make staged candid pictures making people look as they ordinarily do when they are not in front of cameras. However, you may wish to construct your pictures around a theme, or concept, and not have people come on in an ordinary way at all. Even so, pictures built around themes can look very realistic.

One way to do it is to get your models involved in a psycho-drama, which many people see as a very interesting thing to do. You create such a drama by describing a hypothetical situation, usually traumatic, that everyone is presumably involved in, tell each person how he or she fits into it, then ask them all to act out the situation (while you shoot pictures).

For example, the drama might revolve around the hypothetical necessity of telling Ellen (one of your subjects) the bitter truth about herself. You might assign the roles as follows: "Ellen, you're a beautiful bitch in angel's clothing, but you are the only one fooled by the clothes. Tom, you're her third husband and have just learned that she is having an affair with her boss, who is very handsome and extremely rich. You are the long-suffer-

ing type. Alma, you are Ellen's homely younger sister, whom she has never really paid any attention to, which you deeply resent. You think you could help her by telling her what kind of person she really is, but you are afraid that your temper will get away from you." Et cetera.

Another way to do it is to simply suggest the theme—telling Ellen (or someone) the truth—and let people choose and define roles they would like to play. As the roles are acted out the theme may be changed considerably, or even turned upside down. But who cares? And there may be some who would rather be bystanders than participants (psycho-drama can get *very* emotional), but that is all right too.

As in any theatrical enterprise, the casting ought to have a reasonable amount of believability. For example, fiftyish-Fred might work out well as Ellen's father but not as her lover or younger brother. However, people have a natural eye for the incongruous, so they are not likely to risk ridicule by badly miscasting themselves.

As the photographer, you can also produce a psycho-drama with just one other person, taking a role yourself. I myself used to do such things when I was young. For example, I once photographed a young actress who wanted some pictures with real emotion in them for a change, so I laid out the drama for her as follows: "I am going to play your counselor, but everything I tell you will be a lie—as far as I know. Even so, I will say it in the most positive and believable manner, so stand warned. (pause) You know, your parents have been terribly disappointed in you for years. Do you even remember that they exist? Do you care for them at all? Yeah, that presumably 'warm' look in your eyes is just as phony as anything else about you. As an actress you have the emotive talents of a dead mackerel." Et cetera. My barbs got through to her— which we both wanted—simply because I accused her of things that would probably be true of almost anyone.

Well, this is heavy-duty stuff, as you have probably seen for yourself. However, actors and

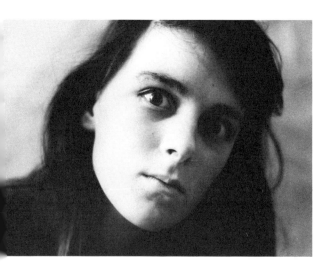

Actress Sue Jamieson and I were involved in a little psycho-drama in which I was telling her deliberately convincing lies concerning her relationship to her parents. Actors and actresses like psycho-drama, because it helps them understand emotion better.

A bit of impromptu psycho-drama in which Phillip, who is a little naïve, is telling Kim that he sees her as an angel and wants to photograph her with the wings he'll make for her.

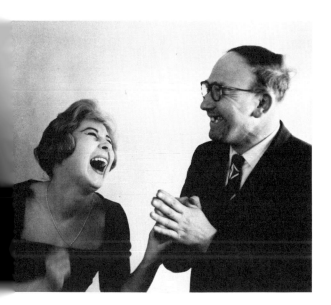

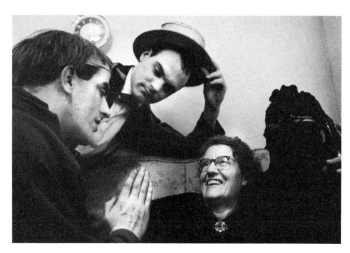

"Father" Dale has decided to save Mrs. Pritchard's soul, with Eddy Mole and a masked stranger in attendance. The salvation efforts were tightly structured, but the picture came out loose and candid. This happened at a costume party, of course.

actresses intentionally go through this kind of thing many times when they are trying to learn what emotion is all about. And the pictures? Oh, they were a great success—our young lady far transcended herself and gave an Academy Award performance. One of her photos is printed in this chapter.

Now, psycho-dramas are just not for everyone, because the tension does get awfully thick. If this is not your cup of tea, simply forget about it and use less emotional methods for staging candids, such as the one that follows.

• The Walkaway Technique

Perhaps the easiest way to stage a candid is to simply group people roughly the way you want them, then simply walk away from them for a while—ostensibly to check out equipment, bring in another light, or something of that ilk. If they are all friends, anyway, they won't really care where the photographer has gone off to. Watch them from the corner of your eye until you see that they have tired of acting like wooden dummies and have disposed themselves more comfortably. Then walk up and start making your pictures.

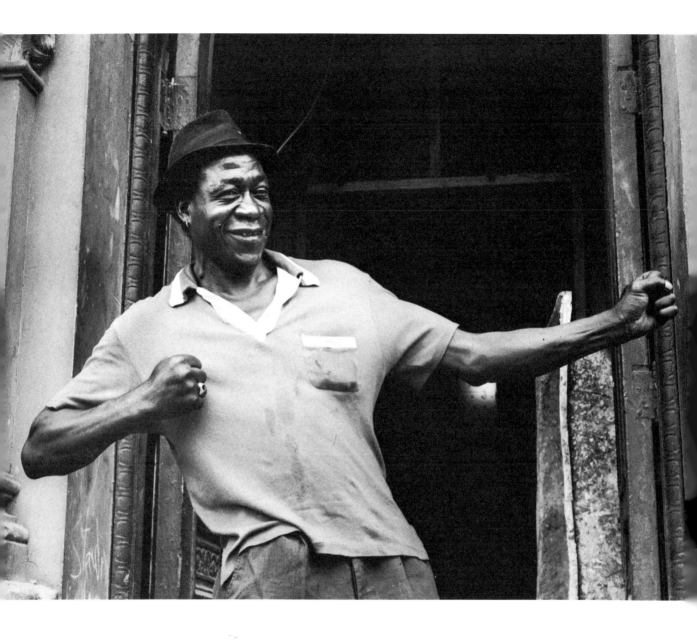

Though men frequently take this fighting pose, this man apparently knows how to use it. From the scar tissue on his face and his oft-broken right fist I would say he is no stranger to the prize ring.

HOW TO PHOTOGRAPH STRANGERS
ON THE STREET

We tend to think of the people in our pictures as friends, even if we don't know them at all. Thus street photography is a way of making friends and cherishing them without having to struggle through the formidable barriers that separate people from one another. It is also many other things, of course, including the hunter's way of collecting trophy heads, a means for recording one's contempt of other people, and a method for using other people without having to ask their permission or thank them. Let us just say that you can do street photography for both good and bad reasons.

Shooting the pictures is easy enough—just focus, frame, and click—but that is not really what bothers inexperienced photographers. They want to know how to do it without getting hassled or harmed by the strangers they photograph. Well, there are some excellent techniques for avoiding such problems, and this is what the chapter will be mainly about.

● Shoot for the Right Reasons

Remember that people are telepathic on the unconscious level and always know when you are photographing them; and if they don't like your reasons for doing it they can often shift this awareness to the conscious level and may then act on it. When they then hassle or threaten you they are, unbeknown to themselves, trying to

teach you a lesson: don't think about people in the wrong way or photograph them for the wrong reasons.

Unfortunately, your reasons (good or bad) for doing things are mainly buried in the unconscious, where you can't examine them in detail. Even so, you know whether they are positive or negative, and that should be enough to guide your behavior. For example, a feeling of guilt, whatever be its source, is enough to tell you that you have negative reasons for wanting to photograph a certain person or negative feelings concerning the way you intend to do it. The easiest thing at this point is to simply refrain from making the picture, because shooting it would violate your own inner ethics and possibly bring on a hassle.

However, a better idea would be to dig up your motives, replace negative motives with positive ones, and go ahead and shoot your picture. Simply start thinking good thoughts about your subject. It is easy enough to tell when the replacement has been successful: the guilt feeling goes away. This brings us to the ethics of taking pictures of strangers without their knowledge—should one do it at all? For the right reasons, yes. For the wrong ones, no. And your conscience is an excellent guide in this matter, so be sure to listen to it.

Furthermore, on the level of soul or higher self, people are delighted to have you think about them, look at them, and photograph them—provided that you try hard to do it in a way worthy of your own higher self (the *trying* is what counts). Much of the important spiritual work of the world gets done in this manner, with people permitting themselves to be used by others. And so it is with street photography: if you try to use people well in your mind and heart you honor them, whether they are *consciously* aware of you or not.

On the ego level it is often another story, unfortunately, because many egos are like spoiled and selfish children, always afraid that someone will try to diminish their inflated, yet fragile, self-esteem. So you might find yourself in the following situation: a stranger's higher self applauds your reasons for wanting to photograph him, while his ego, suspecting the worst, wants to take you apart.

One solution to the problem is to outwit egos, using some of the basic shooting techniques of street photography. There is no chance whatever of outwitting a higher self, because you are telepathically linked with it—so just forget about trying. Remember that if a person's higher self doesn't like your reasons for photographing him it may awaken his ego to what is going on. And egos throw rocks, Brother or Sister, and egos throw rocks.

● The See-Through Technique

If you are convinced that it is ethically permissible to fool egos in a harmless way for commendable reasons, you should enjoy the rest of this chapter, including this first technique. Our first good street photography ploy depends on the fact that you can make people think that they are transparent—really. For example, I wish to photograph a woman standing about four feet from me, so I look over her head and, never looking at her at all, bring up my camera and shoot. Lowering the camera (the follow-through is important), I look over her head again (still not looking at her), then make another shot and turn slightly away, still paying no attention.

348

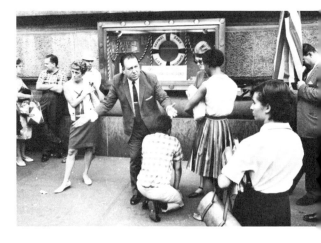

In trying to make himself heard above the roar of traffic on Forty-second Street the preacher lost his voice, yet he managed to save at least one soul, anyway. No one was aware I was taking pictures, though I made no attempt to hide my actions. If a distraction is strong enough the photographer is virtually invisible.

He calls himself the King of St. Marks Place, and the girl has just moved into the neighborhood. I simply pointed my camera at them and raised my eyebrows in questioning. As you see, they gladly posed.

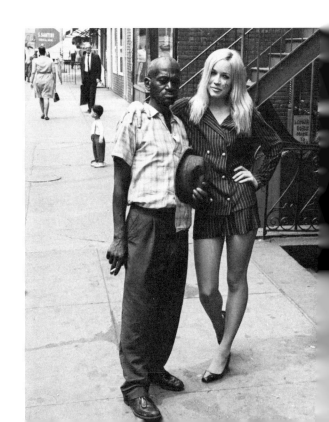

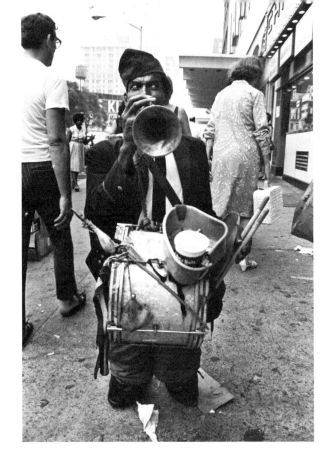

Both a street musician and an ordained minister, this man gladly posed for me. I had but to ask him courteously.

A couple of New York's finest return the smile of a pretty young mother. I just stood there, shot the picture, then went on my way.

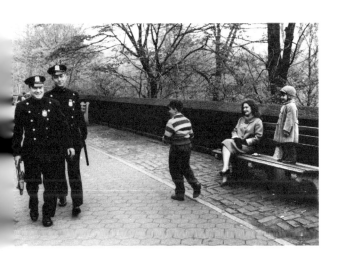

Now, the odd thing is that she seems to think she is transparent, for two compelling reasons: (1) the photographer is so little concerned about her being in the way that he doesn't even see her and (2) he goes right ahead and shoots his pictures. If she were not transparent, why would he behave this way and be so entirely casual about it? Of course, she isn't aware of her assumption, for it is only half-conscious, yet it controls her behavior, anyway.

Though not a dedicated street photographer I have used this technique numerous times, and it has always worked. Incidentally, you can usually tell when a given ploy will work: it is when you think that it will, simple as that.

• Don't Look at People

Eyes emit some form of energy to which people —and apparently many animals—are highly sensitive. Whatever it is, this energy doesn't pass through glass very well. Whether you believe in this energy or not, something very definitely happens when people make eye contact, and everyone knows it, so you shouldn't make such contact when doing street photography. First of all, it is a violation of an unwritten covenant among strangers that there will be no eye contact. Secondly, it is like hitting someone in the stomach. Finally, once you have made eye contact with strangers they know that you have singled them out for some reason and your objective of photographing them without being noticed goes right down the drain.

Eye contact through a camera viewfinding system is usually not the same at all, because the radiated energy is mainly absorbed by the glass which makes up the system. So if you have to look at a stranger, do it through your lens, not directly. There are a few people who give off so much of this visual energy that a large amount of it will get through a viewfinding system in either direction—from a photographer to a subject, or from a subject to a photographer—but I wouldn't worry about it. Such a heavy charge is not commonplace.

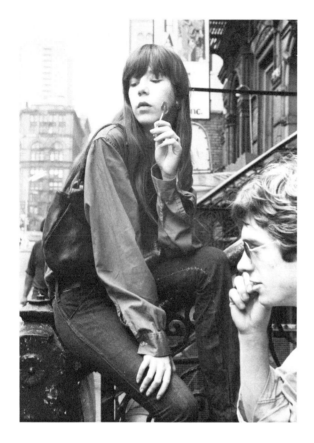

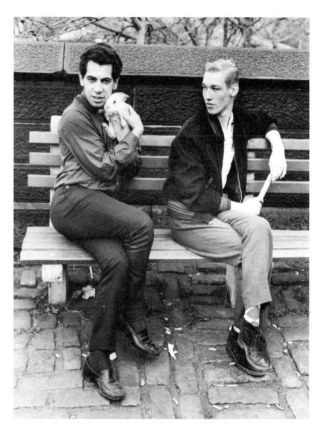

Young people used to like to go down to St. Marks Place in New York just to hang around and to see and be seen. Strangers would sit or stand together for hours, never saying a word. In that particular neighborhood people generally liked to be photographed and were very used to it. There are such pig heavens for photographers in most cities.

Once they learned I wasn't trying to put them down the young men were pleased to be photographed. The older man and his grandson (?) just happened to fall into the range of my wide angle lens, so I gladly incorporated them in the picture.

We fell into a brief conversation, and one of the young men offered to show me his bunny rabbit, which he produced from a handsome brief case. I would take his pose to be provocative, but that is apparently just his way.

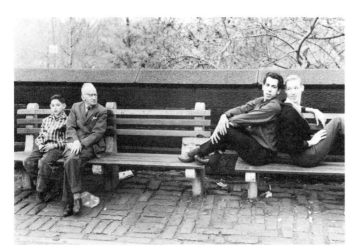

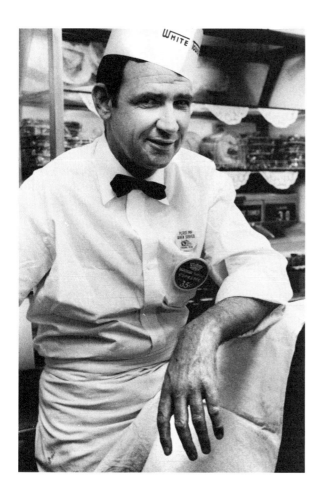

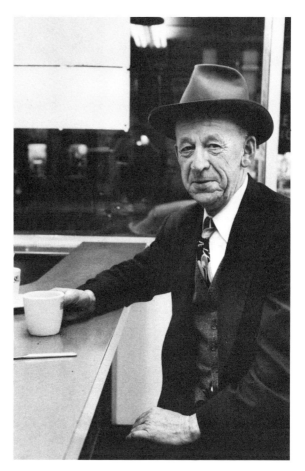

Also in the White Tower was this gentle and engaging man, who found it amusing to be photographed by an eager stranger. I liked what the years had done to his face, what he had done to it, in fact.

The chef from the White Tower Restaurant posed for me when I asked him for a picture. Strictly speaking, this is not a street picture, though the street is only six feet away.

On Broadway and Forty-second Street people are likely to be suspicious when they see you photograph them. It is just that way: one part of a city isn't the same as another. Though I was playing at playing with my camera I still got this suspicious look and didn't fool anyone. Some New Yorkers are hard to fool.

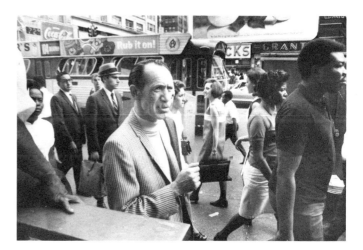

● The Catcher's Mitt Trick

Perhaps you have noticed how baseball catchers grab bad pitches and instantly center them right behind the plate in order to convince umpires that they were actually strikes. You can do this with a camera, too, and it works a lot better than trying to fool an umpire. Just shoot someone, then point your camera a little to one side and hold it there for a couple of seconds. Then lower it and look elsewhere. It is hard to understand why people can get taken in by a dodge as old and obvious as this, but they certainly do.

● The Swing Shot

The idea here is to look through the viewfinder, pointing the camera here, there, and everywhere, as if you were checking out the lens or merely killing time. However, using a fast shutter speed you may shoot your picture right in the middle of a swing—without interrupting it, to be sure.

Don't advance your film right after shooting, for that tips off what you are up to. Wait for a few seconds. With most of the tricks, waiting is a good idea, because advancing the film tells people you have just taken a picture. You don't want them to know *when* you do it or even *that* you did it.

● Shoot from the Waist

A favorite ploy in street photography is to shoot from the waist with a wide-angle lens (a 28mm is possibly the most popular, followed by a 35mm). Such a lens will give you so much depth of field that you can use zone focusing and not have to focus for each shot, which makes it much easier

He lived right around the corner from me and I often saw him with his dog, but I didn't want to disturb him with my presence as a photographer and possibly a threat. So I made a swing shot. As if just goofing around, I swung my camera in a 180° arc, clicking the shutter when he was in range but never looking at him directly. Then I made off down the street, still not looking at him.

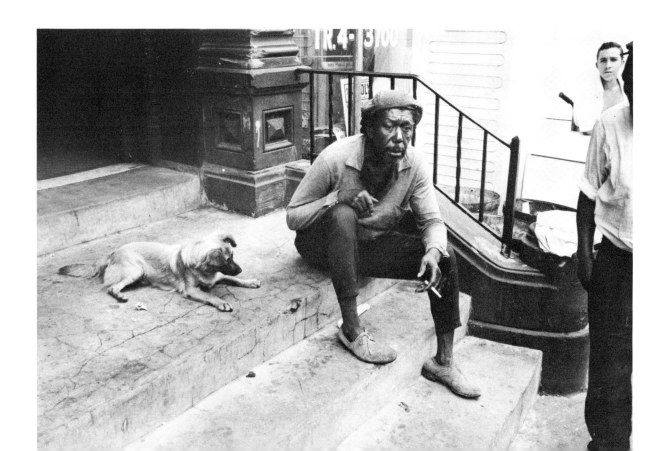

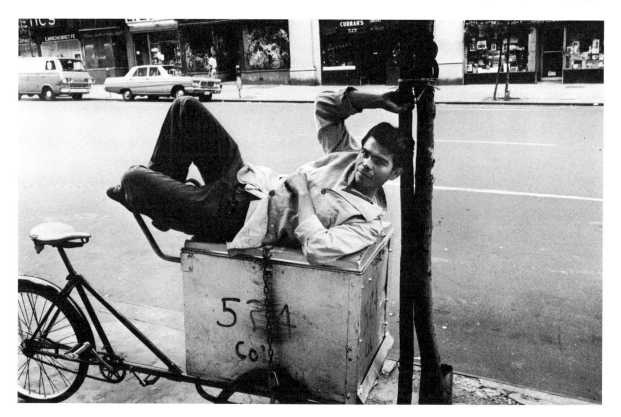

to work fast. Once you have set the zone on the focusing scale, just leave the camera hanging at your waist. A wide angle will generally give you enough extra picture space around your subjects so that you can easily crop your pictures to compensate for camera aiming errors.

A part of the trick is to not look at your camera at all when you are shooting pictures or advancing the film. And, as always, don't look directly at your subjects. With a fast enough shutter speed (e.g., 1/500 second with Tri-X) you can shoot from the waist while walking down the street toward your subjects.

• Fake Camera Tests

It seems to be a well-known fact that many people are more interested in tinkering with their cameras than in taking pictures with them. And many of those who want to take pictures have to fiddle a lot with their cameras in order to figure out how they work. Thus a person playing with a

Street photography is easy when a person asks you to take his picture, as this young man did. He is a delivery boy from one of the grocery stores in the New York neighborhood in which I formerly lived.

camera is a very familiar figure and not likely to attract much attention.

So, while you are "fiddling" you can be taking pictures without anyone being the wiser. With your apparent fumbling and bumbling you can also use the see-through technique, the catcher's mitt trick, make swing shots, and shoot from the waist. And another trick that always works is to "listen to the shutter." That is, hold the camera up to your ear, look down at the ground, and shoot your picture. Since people will assume that no one but a complete idiot would try to make a picture this way, you will be beyond suspicion.

• Mirror Attachments

A very ancient trick for street photography is to cover your lens with a special mirror attachment that will permit you to take pictures of people who are at a right angle to the lens axis. I suppose that some people would recognize such a device if they saw you using it. On the other hand, people have a strongly conditioned tendency to believe that a photographer always faces the thing he is taking a picture of, so even if they recognize your gadget they won't believe what they are seeing. Indeed, a mirror attachment is one of the safest tricks for street photography.

• Telephoto Lens

With most of the tricks presented so far there is some risk of detection—if you don't use them properly. But with a telephoto lens there is considerably less chance of being found out, though I have seen photographers being threatened by people fifty yards from them. Even so, a telephoto—the longer the better—is almost always a very safe bet.

• Substitute Exposure Readings and Focus Target

Unfortunately, you cannot walk up to a stranger, stick your camera in his or her face, and take an exposure reading. 'Tain't done. Instead, hold the palm of your hand vertical to the ground and take a reading from it, making sure that your hand is facing in the same direction as your subject so that they both get the same light. Since one piece of skin reflects about the same amount of light as another, your hand reading should also be accurate for your subject's face. For a person with a very dark skin, tilt down your hand until the palm is equally dark before taking your reading. As long as you and your subjects are in the same light you don't even have to be close to them when you take your palm reading.

Taking time to focus on people may tip them off to what you are up to, especially if you can never remember in which direction you are supposed to twist the focusing ring. So find a suitable target (a lamppost, for example) that is at the same distance from you as your subjects, focus on it, then swing around and shoot your picture. It will be sharp. Though zone focusing is an even better idea, there may not be enough light to permit you to stop down far enough, for example, at dusk.

• The Problem with Fear

Perhaps you are a paranoid, a person afraid of nearly everything that exists and especially of people. Well, most of us are this way now and then. Despite their fears, some paranoids try street photography, often being rewarded with gratuitous insults and threats from the people they try to photograph. Since this can happen to any of us we ought to look into it.

The thing is that people are like broadcasting stations, and fear is a very disruptive high energy emission. Thus the human receivers who pick it up react to it in a very negative, angry way. Unfortunately, the best receivers for fear are those who are themselves filled with it. They react in such a negative way because they confuse fear with anger and feel that the anger is being directed against themselves. The confusion shouldn't be surprising, because fear and anger are essentially the same thing.

Fear can be broadcast in all directions or focused mainly on a single point by means of the mind or the eyes. For example, if you are fearfully looking at or thinking about someone whom you intend to photograph it will focus your fear on this person, who may unconsciously interpret it as an assault. Especially if he or she also happens to be paranoid at the moment. So, you have a person who is angry at you, perhaps even before seeing you at all, and strongly predisposed to give you a hard time on any pretext whatever. You should understand that being afraid is an invitation to assault and battery by others who are also afraid.

Therefore, it should be obvious that you shouldn't try street photography (especially in large cities) when you are frightened, for there is a good chance that you will get hassled. On the other hand, some chronic paranoids deliberately turn to street photography as a way of confronting and overcoming their fears with the help of strangers. No harm is done, and on the level of the soul the strangers are glad to help. On the ego level, however, they can be quite a problem, especially if they too are paranoids.

It is too bad that people's fear of your fear comes out as anger, but that is just the way things are. And the fact that fear is broadcast and can be focused doesn't help much, either. There is just no escaping the consequences of being afraid.

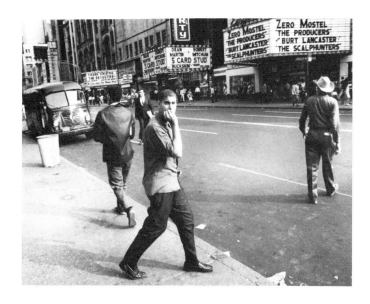

This was a grab shot made quite openly, but the young man, who obviously has things on his mind, didn't seem to care.

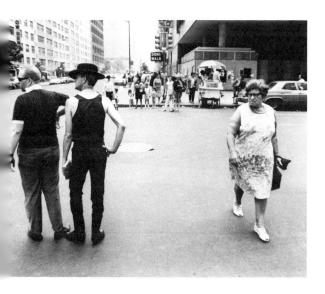

I just stood on the corner of Fourteenth Street and Fifth Avenue and photographed everyone who came along with a camera equipped with a 28mm lens, which is very good for street photography. I was so obviously standing there and shooting "dumb pictures" that no one paid any attention to me. And I took care to look at none of them directly, which further directed attention away from myself.

● You Ask Them or They Ask You

Though the tricks in this chapter are some of the favorites of experienced street photographers, you may feel guilty about using them—simply because they *are* tricks. And guilt goes hand in hand with fear, which sets up the strong negative vibration. So don't use tricks. Simply ask people if you can photograph them.

But it is not quite that simple, is it? Especially if you are shy. The best you can do in this case is to hope that some people will ask you to take their pictures. Young people often do this, and even some older ones now and then. If they ask you, just photograph them in whatever way they present themselves—posing stiffly, teasing you, hamming it up, and so on. Because such behavior is catching, you may find other people also wanting to pose for you a minute or two later.

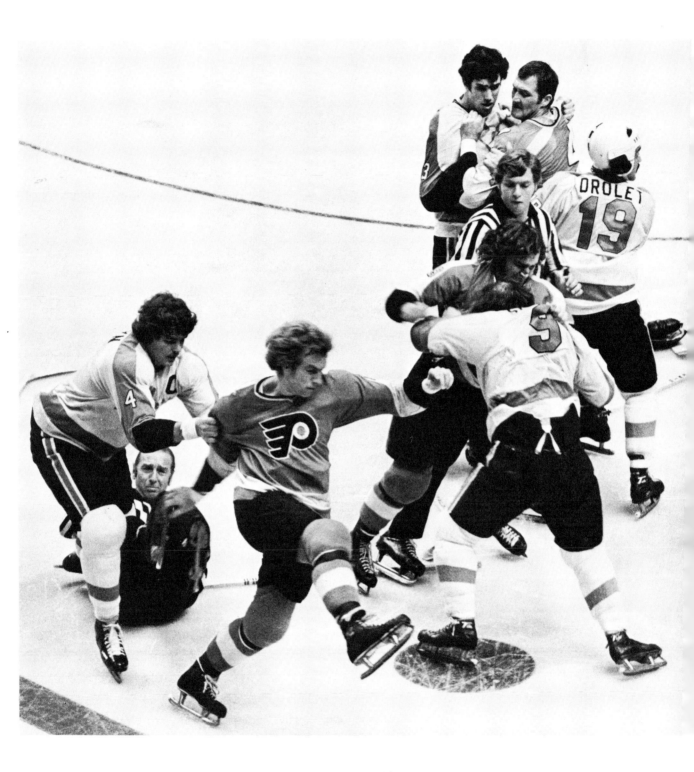

(Photo by Jim Jennings)
A proper hassle at a hockey game, but about par for
the course. This was one of Jim's first pictures as a
full-time press photographer. Shot with a 200mm f/3.5
lens with Tri-X rated at ASA 2400—exposure 1/500 at
f/8. Processed normally in Diafine for that film speed.

HOW TO PHOTOGRAPH SPORTS

Since there are a great many sports I obviously can't tell you how to photograph them all in a single chapter. The subject is simply too large. However, there are certain basic problems that occur in many kinds of sports photography, and they can be discussed in the space available. Perhaps the main problems are getting yourself within range of the action and freezing the action.

● Picking Your Spot and Laying Claim to It

It should be obvious that some photographic vantage points are better than others. For example, at a boxing or wrestling match it is handier to be at ringside than fifty yards out in the audience. At a horse race a spot near the finish line is considered best. Ski jumpers are photographed from below, so that they look like great black birds. And so on.

Perhaps the easiest way to select vantage points is to analyze sports pictures in newspapers and figure out where the photographers must have been standing when they were shot. By now the vantage points are traditional, and most sports photographers use the same ones, often in the form of press boxes. Another approach is to try to locate the pros before the start of an event to see how they have spotted themselves. They are usually the people with the very long telephoto lenses, heavy-duty tripods, and three or four cameras hanging from their necks.

Finding a good spot and getting permission to use it are two different matters. The people who conduct most sporting events just don't want you getting in the way—unless you represent the press, on whose continued favor their welfare often depends. Thus a standard ploy among sports photography nuts is to persuade newspaper editors to issue them official press photography passes, usually with the understanding that the photographers will bring in their really good shots.

So many of my students have gotten such passes for themselves that I assume that any good con artist who is also a good photographer can talk himself into one. Some have had their own passes printed, with dubious results, and others have gotten police department passes—just to copper their bets, so to speak. Even with a pass, bona fide or fake, you may still have to be a very clever con in order to gain occupancy of your vantage point. Genuine press photographers are old hands at this sort of thing.

● Telephoto and Tele-Zoom Lenses

Even with the best of vantage points you will still be very far from the action during many kinds of sporting events. For example, you might con your way right up to the sidelines for a college or high school football game, but what can you do about action across the field from you? The obvious answer is a telephoto lens, which will bring distant things up close. I suspect that most pros are now using the zoom telephoto, which is an even better answer, though a very expensive one.

A zoom lens has many focal lengths built into one, as it were—for example, 50mm all the way to 200mm. Such a zoom lens can be used as a 50mm lens, as a 200mm lens, or as a lens of any focal length in between. For sports photography it would be desirable to have a 50mm–5000mm zoom, but there is as yet no such beast. If there were it would probably cost $10,000 or more.

However, there are certain compromises possible, also expensive. For example, you could use the Nikon 50–300mm zoom (about $1,000) with a teleconverter which will convert it to 100–600mm. This would give you a range of from 50mm to 600mm, which is a lot of zoom in the present state of the art. However, the lens is very heavy, and the teleconverter cuts off the corners of the image. If that is the lens you need —and you can afford it—that's okay.

One way to get the cost closer to the $100–$200 range is to buy a fixed focus 200mm lens with a teleconverter, which would stretch it out to 400mm. If you want to buy a lens without a converter, 300mm looks like the best compromise for sports photography. It won't work for all sports, but it will work for many. Fortunately, many of the cheaper telephoto lenses on the market nowadays are quite good, mainly because lens design and manufacture on all cost levels is heavily computerized.

• Tripods, Bipods, Unipods, Rifle Stocks, and Bean Bags

Unfortunately, many a person finds it impossible to hold steady any lens that throws his camera off balance, which includes most tele-zoom lenses and fixed focus lenses beyond 90mm—the heavier the lens, the greater the problem. This makes for fuzzy pictures. If there is enough light for you to shoot at 1/500 or 1/1000 second this may solve the problem by counteracting lens and camera movement, but being able to use only these shutter speeds is a severe restriction.

The natural answer is to use as heavy a tripod as you can carry—light ones aren't much good with a heavy lens. Many professional sports photographers prefer the very heaviest Mitchell, Linhoof, or Gitzo tripods made for use with professional 35mm movie cameras, which weigh a lot. You can get them with very smooth oil-friction pan heads, which are very good for following sports action. However, tripods of this sort are very expensive, so you might consider a lighter one such as the Soligor Quick-Set Husky ($55–$95), which is quite a sturdy model.

Since it is very unhandy to work with tripods in many situations—in crowds, for example—you might consider supporting your camera and lens with a bipod, unipod, "rifle stock," or bean bag. A bipod is a two-legged "tripod," a unipod a one-

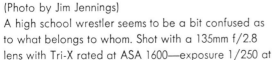
(Photo by Jim Jennings)
A high school wrestler seems to be a bit confused as to what belongs to whom. Shot with a 135mm f/2.8 lens with Tri-X rated at ASA 1600—exposure 1/250 at f/2.8. Developed for 10 minutes in Acufine.

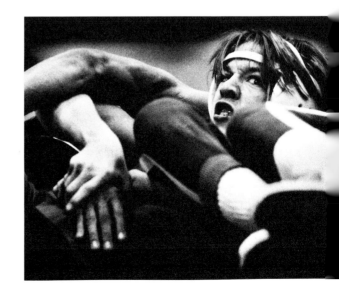

legged one. Both will give a long lens a surprising amount of support. With a special rifle stock bolted to your camera you can aim it much as you would a rifle, which is immensely better than hand-holding without the stock. A bean bag is simply a small sack three quarters filled with dried beans; you put it on a railing and rest your lens on it. You can make one with a man's sock, two pounds of beans, and a length of string for tying up the open end of the sock.

• Stopping Action: Shutter Speeds, Electronic Flash, Panning

Most photographers prefer to stop or freeze the sports action that they photograph, though we do see blurred-action pictures now and then. The first step when working either indoors or out is to use the fastest film available, and for indoor work to possibly push its ASA speed from one to three stops (see later section). The next step is to use the fastest available lens (for indoor work), which happens to be very expensive when it comes to telephotos and tele-zooms. Indoors, with the speed advantages provided by a fast film, film speed pushing, and a fast lens, you then use the fastest shutter speed that you can, usually trying to stay within the 1/250–1/1000 second range. Outdoors in strong natural light, the main

things are a fast film and a camera with high shutter speeds; you can use a *much* slower lens and simply don't need film speed pushing.

One of the best ways for freezing indoor sports action is to use electronic flash, the heavy-duty professional thyristor unit being the best bet. Depending on your distance from the action you are photographing, such a unit will produce a flash duration varying from, say, 1/500–1/50,000 second—the closer the action the shorter the duration. With electronic units the flash itself freezes the action; 1/500 will freeze most action, 1/50,000 will freeze almost anything. However, for the very fastest flashes you have to be almost within touching distance of your subjects.

With most modern cameras (single lens reflexes and other cameras with focal plane shutters) the shutters synchronize with electronic flash at relatively slow speeds, which means that the shutter speed must be set on a low number, usually 1/125 or 1/60 or less. If the flash goes off at a higher shutter speed setting with such a camera it will expose only a portion for the film frame, the rest of it being covered by part of the shutter curtain.

With cameras that synch at speeds that are too slow, electronic flash for sports photography is mainly restricted to working indoors or shooting outdoors at night. In sunlight the slow shutter speeds would simply overexpose fast films. For example, with Tri-X and a camera synched for

(Photo by Jim Jennings)
An experiment to see how long a lens could be used successfully for basketball—300mm seeming to be the practical limit. Shot with a 300mm f/4.5 lens with Tri-X rated at ASA 3200—exposure 1/250 at f/4.5. Developed in a mixture of LPS and Ethol 90 at 75° F for 4 minutes.

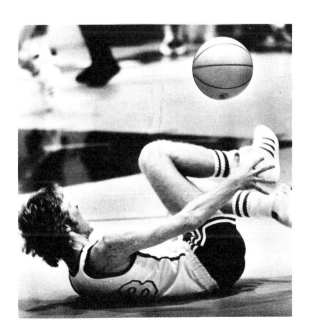

1/30 second you would overexpose (from the sunlight alone) by 4 stops (16 times) by setting the aperture at f/16, the smallest opening that most cameras have. Add to this the light from the flash itself and you can see that the overexposure would be very severe.

Cameras having between-the-lens or compur-type shutters will often synch at high enough shutter speeds to work well with electronic flash and fast films outdoors in daytime, especially if they have the apertures f/22 and f/32. However, the main function of a flash unit is for flash fill (for lightening the shadows somewhat). If your camera has fast enough shutter speeds you simply don't need flash to freeze action in sunlight, or even on overcast days.

A classical action-stopping technique called "panning" dates back to the days before fast films and high-speed shutters, and it works as well now as ever. It is used most for such things as race cars, horses, and sprinters speeding across your line of vision. The idea is to pick a target, say a running horse, and follow it with your camera just as you would follow a clay pigeon with a shotgun. When it reaches the right position you shoot your picture—while still moving the camera to keep the horse framed in the viewfinder. This follow-through is an important part of the technique, yet you can master it in one or two tries. Even better, make a bunch of dry runs without film in the camera, just to get used to the idea. With panning you can stop action at shutter speeds below 1/100 second, though your horse's legs will be blurred in the picture.

• Film Speed Pushing

The main reason for film speed pushing is to make it possible to shoot by available light indoors at faster shutter speeds than you could normally use with a given film. The idea is to use the fastest film available and to increase the effective ASA speed of the film as much as possible by overdeveloping it. This can be done with both black-and-white and color films. The best bets for

pushing are probably Tri-X, Kodacolor 400, and Fujicolor F-II (a color negative or print film), all three rated at ASA 400 and capable of having their speed pushed by several f-stops.

The ASA speed of a film is actually a constant, determined by the manufacturer, that can be neither increased nor decreased. However, it can be used *as if* it had a higher speed, which is what we really mean by saying we "increase" the ASA speed. That is, you can set a higher number on your exposure meter, shoot your pictures, overdevelop the film to the appropriate degree, and get printable negatives (black-and-white or color) or acceptable color transparencies. For example, before shooting Tri-X you can set the number 1600 on your meter and say that you are shooting it at ASA 1600. Yes, this is precisely what you are doing—a kind of *as-if* proposition—though the actual ASA speed itself remains a constant 400.

However, it is not quite this simple, because pushing the speed of a film nearly always results in a loss of image quality, the higher the push the greater the image deterioration. With more and more pushing you get a progressive loss of detail in shadow (or even midtone) areas, increase of graininess, increase of contrast, and blocking up (blurring together) of highlight details. These things happen with both color and black-and-white films, but with color film there is an additional problem—a color shift or change that can make an image look like badly tuned color TV. Despite all these difficulties, film pushing is used a lot for indoor sports photography.

You can readily see why you should consider speed pushing as strictly an emergency measure and therefore continue to expose films at their rated ASA speeds whenever possible. Unfortunately you sometimes *have* to push the speeds. Say you decide to shoot a basketball game with an f/2.8 135mm lens and either Tri-X or Kodacolor 400, both rated at ASA 400. You may find that the best you can do in the available light is to shoot at 1/60 second at f/2.8, which won't permit you to freeze much action.

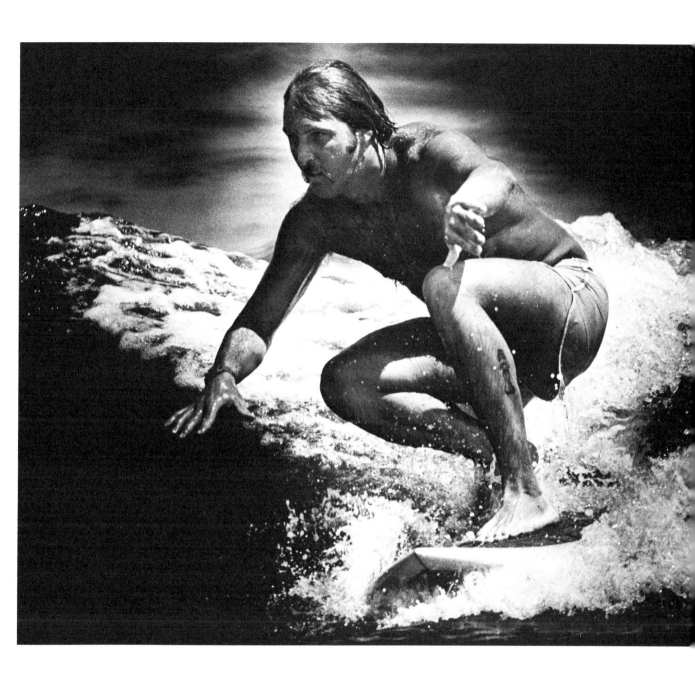

(Photo by Jim Jennings)
The East Coast Surfing Championships at Virginia
Beach, Virginia. Shot with a 500mm f/8 mirror optics
lens with Tri-X rated at ASA 400—exposure 1/1000 at
f/8. Processed normally in straight D-76.

So consider the faster shutter speeds that pushing will enable you to use: with a one-stop push (to ASA 800)—1/125. With a two-stop push (to ASA 1600)—1/250. With a three-stop push (to ASA 3200)—1/500. And with a four-stop push (to ASA 6400)—1/1000. Unfortunately, by the time you reach ASA 1600, or a two-stop gain, your images will probably be falling apart rather badly, though not always. Even so, a shutter speed of 1/250 is a great improvement over 1/60 second.

One of the decisive factors determining how far you can safely push a film is the contrast of your subject matter. Contrast means difference between tones (or values), high contrast meaning a great difference, low contrast very little difference. With a high contrast subject all the details will vanish from the dark areas of the image with even a one-stop push. Indeed, you may even lose these details when using a film at its rated speed. Naturally, the loss is even greater with pushes of two, three, and four stops. With rare exceptions, the pictures aren't even printable.

On the other hand, with very low-contrast or flat subject matter (such as you would find at an indoor swimming meet, where the preponderant tones are all about the same) you may be able to safely push to ASA 1600, 3200, or even 6400, though the 6400 negatives (black-and-white or color) might be barely printable. However, a part of this pushing game is to learn to make acceptable prints from very bad negatives. Though it takes a while you can learn to do it if you try hard enough.

In this country, very little is known at this time about Fujicolor F-II, though the Japanese tell us that it can be pushed quite a bit. At any rate, I can't give you the details right now. At this writing I have no data on pushing Kodacolor 400. The chances are that you would want to have your pushing done by a professional color lab anyway. The situation with respect to black-and-white film is different, and I can tell you what to do. For film pushing, Tri-X is the overwhelming favorite of all films, simply because it gives the best results and, of course, it has a high ASA rating to begin

with. Two of the most popular film developers for this purpose are D-76 diluted 1:1 and Acufine. For a speed up to 800 use D-76 with Tri-X. For 1200 and above use Acufine (1200 would be a 1½-stop push). The people at Acufine Incorporated insist that 1200 is the *normal* (or real or actual) ASA speed for Tri-X developed in Acufine, so you can see that you run little risk in exposing it at that speed.

Before moving to the how-to-do-it of film pushing we should consider Kodak 2475 Recording Film, which is rated at ASA 1000 by Kodak. Because of its speed it is of considerable interest to sports photographers, and you can determine its "push speeds" with the techniques that follow. Though it is a little grainy, the grains are very small and very sharp. When you decide to start pushing films you will just have to learn to live with grain, anyhow. It is better to get a grainy image under adverse lighting conditions than no image at all.

The overdevelopment required for film pushing is done by increasing the developing time while at the same time using the recommended temperature and agitation schedule. Unfortunately, if you were given a developing time chart for various degrees of pushing in either D-76 or Acufine it would be of no use whatever to you. This also applies to the chart furnished with their developer by Acufine Incorporated. You (or any other photographer, amateur or professional) simply have to figure out times for yourself. The reason for this is that photographers have different kinds of exposure meters, built-in or separate, and they vary considerably in the way they use them. Meters vary a lot with respect to their accuracy. And the degree of shutter speed accuracy is not at all the same from camera to camera. Thus if five experienced photographers were asked to photograph the very same subject at ASA 1600 we would find them getting quite different results, even if all the rolls were to be developed simultaneously in the same film tank at a custom lab. Though all the photographers would think they were shooting at 1600 we might later discover that the speed ratings actually used ranged all the way from 800 to 3200. The managers of Modernage, the world's largest custom lab, tell me that such wide deviations are not at all unusual for the professional photographers who use the lab.

A chart that gives you the developing time for a push up to ASA 1600 will be of little use to you if you actually expose at 800 or 3200 instead. At 800 you would get overdeveloped negatives, at 3200 underdeveloped ones. In either case they might be quite unprintable. To get around this problem you don't have to have your shutter speeds and meter sensitivity checked (though it wouldn't be a bad idea), nor do you have to change the way you do your metering. Indeed, if your method of using a meter has been giving you good results all along it would be unwise to change it, even if you are doing things backward or upside down.

The thing to do is to experimentally establish personal "push speeds" and developing times, working in your usual way with the equipment that you ordinarily use. If you stick to the method that follows the results will compensate for faulty equipment and errors in metering technique.

You must run some simple exposure and development tests. Make your exposures (test pictures) at the location you are most interested in, say an indoor skating rink, basketball court, or swimming pool. Since these particular places are rather flatly lighted, you will find rather low subject contrast. So let us say you want to go for broke on pushing Tri-X and decide to find out what it will do at both 1600 and 3200 (with 2475 Recording Film you might try 3200 and 6400).

Go to your chosen location during a practice session and set up your tripod at the vantage point you will use during a regular game or meet. Center your camera on the area in which the most interesting action ordinarily occurs, take an exposure reading with the meter set at 1600, and shoot a whole 36 exposure roll without moving the camera. Alternate back and forth from shot to shot between 1600 and 3200. For example, shoot a picture with an aperture and shutter

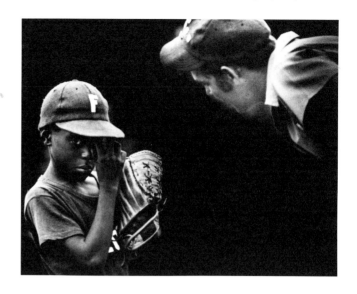

(Photo by Jim Jennings)
Crisis on the mound: a Little League baseball coach pulls his pitcher after five walks in a row in the first inning. Shot with a 300mm f/4.5 lens with Tri-X rated at ASA 800—exposure 1/500 at f/4.5. Given 1½ times normal developing time in straight D-76.

speed indicated by your meter—you will be shooting at ASA 1600. Then stop down one more stop and shoot another—you will be shooting at ASA 3200. Or instead of stopping down you can switch to the next fastest shutter speed—again, you will be shooting at ASA 3200. Thus you switch back and forth between two f-numbers or between two shutter speeds.

This is a very simple business, but beginners find it terribly confusing, so I will go over it again in a slightly different way. Say your exposure reading (with your meter set at 1600) indicates that 1/125 second at f/2.8 is the correct exposure. Leave the shutter speed set at 1/125 and make exposures in which the f-number alternates between f/2.8 and f/4. Or leave the aperture set at f/2.8 and make exposures in which the shutter speed alternates between 1/125 and 1/250 second. Either way you will end up with the same final results.

The idea of immobilizing your camera on a

363

tripod is to get a series of images as much alike as possible, so that pictorial differences won't throw off your judgment later when you are examining your test negatives. For this same reason you should try to get approximately the same kind of sports action in each shot. Since games, meets, and practice sessions tend to be quite repetitive, this shouldn't be too hard. If you rehearse your actions before shooting you may be able to expose the whole roll within 10 minutes. On the other hand it may take you an hour to get a series of shots that will look approximately the same.

Since we have taken Tri-X as an example and you are pushing it to 1600 and 3200, you should develop it in Acufine. Refer to the Acufine time and temperature chart (it comes with the developer) to get the correct developing time for the temperature at which you intend to process your film. For example, if you wish to develop at 68° F you would find that the recommended time for Tri-X (rated at ASA 1200) is 5¼ minutes. This is a good starting place. Give 5 seconds agitation every 30 seconds.

Develop the whole roll for 3 minutes, then remove the film reel from the developing tank, cut off a 5-inch length of film, and drop this short piece into a fixing bath. Return the reel to the developing tank. Every minute thereafter, cut off and fix another length, until the whole roll has been used up.

Then wash and dry the 5-inch lengths and examine the frames. Each length will contain at least one whole 1600 frame and at least one 3200 frame. The range of developing times that the strips represent should cover the entire usable developing time range for Acufine. With longer times we would expect altogether too much grain and fog.

The next step is to choose the most printable 1600 and 3200 frames, which you can only do by making test enlargements. Remember not to expect really good negatives—there just won't be any. The problem is to get the best possible prints from bad ones, which many a sports photographer has learned to do. From the frames that

print best you can check back to get the developing times, which you can then use after shooting Tri-X at 1600 or 3200 at your test location. Though your figures will be totally reliable for that place alone, you may be safe in using them for other locations that have similar lighting contrast.

These tests won't tell you anything about the accuracy of your shutter or meter, or whether you use your meter correctly. And they won't tell you at what actual ASA speeds you expose your film when you think you are shooting at 1600 or 3200. However, if you go to a game at your test location and use the very same exposures that you used for your tests, you can safely predict what kind of negatives you will get when you use the developing times that worked best in your tests. And that is all you really *need* to know.

However, if you are going to have a professional color lab push color film for you, you will have to find out whether you actually expose at the ASA speeds you think you are using. If a lab tells you they can push Fujicolor F-II to ASA 1600 you have to know whether the lab's 1600 is the same as yours. If their 1600 turns out to be your 3200, then you should expose this film at your 3200 when you expect to send it to this particular lab. When they see the developed film they will assume that you exposed it at 1600.

The way to find out how your ASA speeds compare with the lab's is to set your meter at 1600 and make test shots at several locations that interest you, bracketing the exposures in each place. To bracket means to make a series of exposures ranging from underexposure to normal exposure to overexposure, the normal exposure being the one that your chosen ASA speed, meter, and metering technique identify as the best one. For such a test you should bracket with a sufficient range of exposures, for example, with underexposures of 1, 2, 3, and 4 stops, a normal exposure, and overexposures of 1, 2, and 3 stops.

When the film comes back from the lab you may find that their 1600 is the same as yours, that their processing made the frames that you presumably exposed at 1600 come out best. Since you may not know how to judge color negatives (in the case of Fujicolor F-II), you should ask the lab people to select the best exposures (with color transparencies you can judge well enough for yourself). If the best exposures happen to be at your ASA 800 or 3200, simply set your meter with the number that worked best and continue using the same metering methods as before. Indeed, in your test locations use the very same exposures, which is even better. It doesn't really matter what push-speed numbers you use as long as you get usable exposures.

Though many sports photographers use film speed pushing as an everyday technique, it is only because they have to in order to get the kind of shots they want. Never use it except as an emergency measure. Remember, the further you push film the greater the image degradation. (There is more information on film pushing in the chapter on available light photography, p. 155).

• Motorized Cameras and Special Film Backs

Because sports action often breaks very fast and is hard to capture at its peak, many sports photographers have taken to using motorized cameras with which they can shoot pictures in rapid sequence, say at 4 or 5 frames per second. The idea is that one of the frames in a 5 or 10 frame series will probably catch the action at its height. As you might surmise, it doesn't take many sequences to use up a 36 exposure roll.

Thus there are special backs for handling longer rolls of film. A good example is the motorized Nikon MF-2 back, which will take a 100-foot roll of 35mm film, permit you to make single exposures, or give you sequence exposures at rates ranging from 1 to 4 frames per second.

Aside from their initial cost, which is usually considerable, the problem with motorized cameras and backs is that you can use an enormous amount of film without even thinking about it. And with a back like the MF-2 you also need special processing equipment in order to process

the extra-long rolls. Since I don't envision readers who are prepared to cope with such problems, I'll say no more about this highly specialized equipment.

• More About Electronic Flash

Earlier, I said that using electronic flash is a very good way for freezing indoor sports action, but many of the smaller units aren't powerful enough to be generally useful. Unfortunately, broad utility is usually a function of price—if you can lay out enough money you can get a unit that will do the job.

The best bets are the automated professional units with thyristor circuits and independent sensors, provided that they have enough range when operated on automatic. The automatic range for the better units may be anywhere from 40 to 50 feet, depending on the make, which is all right for many sports. Most of them can be manually operated for greater distances.

One of the most interesting models available is the Vivitar 283 Auto Thyristor, which costs less than $100 without accessories. The automatic range is 43 feet, which means that at that distance you can shoot Tri-X at f/5.6. This also means that you can shoot at the same distance with an f/5.6 telephoto instead of a fast (and very expensive) f/2.8 or f/3.5.

One of the problems in using flash with a telephoto lens is that the angle of the beam distributes most of the light over an area outside the area covered by the lens. Thus much of the light is wasted and the maximum distance from which you can photograph a subject is unduly limited. Vivitar solves this problem with special lenses to slip over the flash head to make the angle of the light beam match up with the angles of lenses of various focal lengths. For example, one of them is for use with camera lenses that are 135mm or longer. If you operate the flash manually it will permit a maximum range with Tri-X of 60 feet with an f/5.6 lens or 85 feet with an f/4 lens.

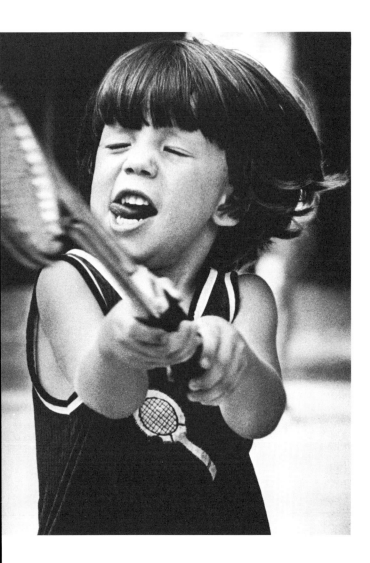

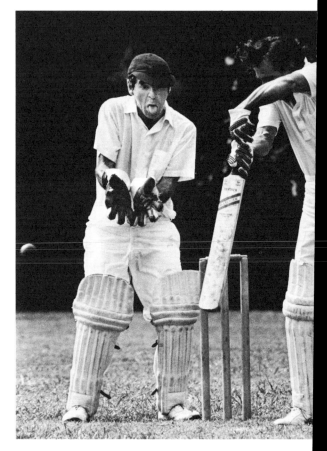

(Photo by Jim Jennings)
You are never too young to develop a two-handed forearm smash—if you can keep your eyes closed long enough. Shot with a 100mm f/2.5 lens with Tri-X rated at ASA 400—exposure 1/1000 at f/8. Processed normally in straight D-76.

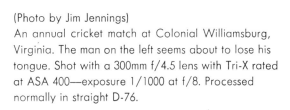

(Photo by Jim Jennings)
An annual cricket match at Colonial Williamsburg, Virginia. The man on the left seems about to lose his tongue. Shot with a 300mm f/4.5 lens with Tri-X rated at ASA 400—exposure 1/1000 at f/8. Processed normally in straight D-76.

(Photo by Jim Jennings)
In the last thirty seconds of a city championship game
the boy in the center missed a two-foot jump shot with
no one near him. His team lost by one point. Shot with
an 85mm f/1.8 lens with Tri-X rated at ASA
2400—exposure 1/500 at f/3.5. Processed in a mixture
of LPD and Ethol 90 for 4 minutes at 75° F.

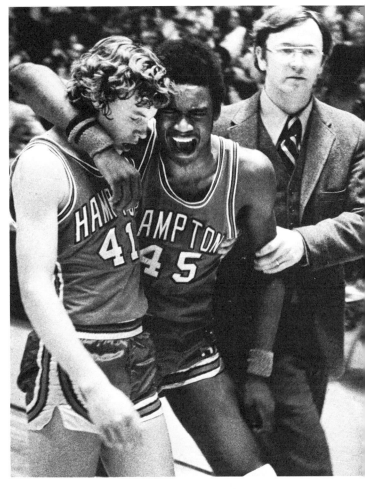

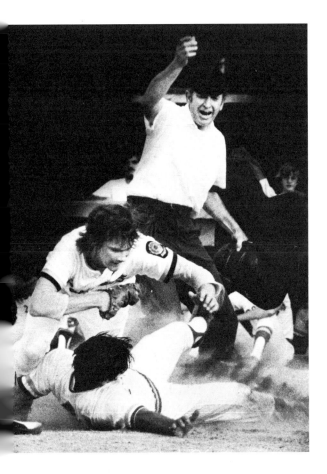

(Photo by Jim Jennings)
Some home plate action in American Legion Baseball.
Shot with a 300mm f/4.5 lens with Tri-X rated at ASA
800—exposure 1/1000 at f/11. Given 1½ times the
normal developing time in straight D-76.

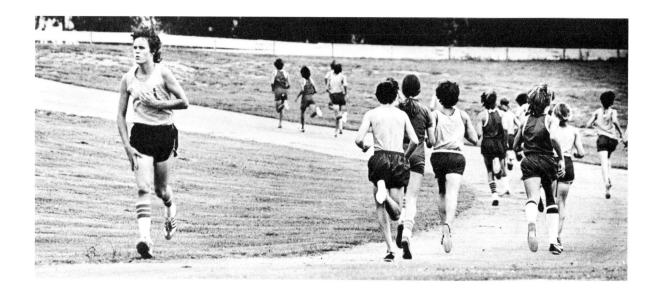

The boy on the left is still in the race, though it doesn't seem so. He is the last runner in the first heat of a high school cross-country meet, heading to finish as the second heat starts. Shot with an 80–200mm f/4.5 zoom lens with Tri-X rated at ASA 400. Processed normally in straight D-76.

That is, by concentrating the light beam the light lens makes possible more light at a given distance than you would get with a wider angle beam. This in turn extends the range of the flash unit.

To operate a unit manually you ought to know the so-called guide number for the film you are using so that you can use the number to determine the f-number setting for any given distance. The computer dial or chart on your flash unit may not include the ASA speed of this particular film. Now, when a unit can be used either with or without a lens slipped over the flash head there will be *two* guide numbers for a given film, each film having different guide numbers according to its ASA speed. For example, with the Vivitar 283 and Tri-X film the guide numbers are 240 (without the lens over the light) and 340 (with the lens).

You make use of a guide number by dividing it by the focus distance (in feet), which will give you the f-number you should use for that distance. As an example we will try the 340 Vivitar guide number for Tri-X and a focus distance of 100 feet. Thus we divide 340 by 100, which gives us 3.4 or f/3.4. There is no f/3.4 but we are close enough if we call it f/3.5 (this is a half-stop setting between f/2.8 and f/4). In short, you should set the lens aperture at f/3.5 when focused at 100 feet.

In advertisements and technical writeups in photography magazines the guide numbers for flash units are given only for 25 ASA films, which erroneously assumes that readers will know how to interpret this information. You should understand, first of all, that the number is a way of describing the light output of a unit in terms of the f-stops you can use with an ASA 25 film at various distances. It is convenient to check out a guide number at a distance of 10 feet, because 10 is an easy figure to work with. For example, we will see what we could do with a guide number of 60 at this distance, i.e., what f-stop could we use? So we divide 60 by 10 and see that we could use f/6 (or f/6.3, which is a half stop between f/5.6 and f/8). The larger the guide number the smaller the aperture that you can use—and the more powerful the flash unit.

Technical writers also assume that readers will be able to start with the guide numbers for 25 ASA films and figure out the guide numbers for

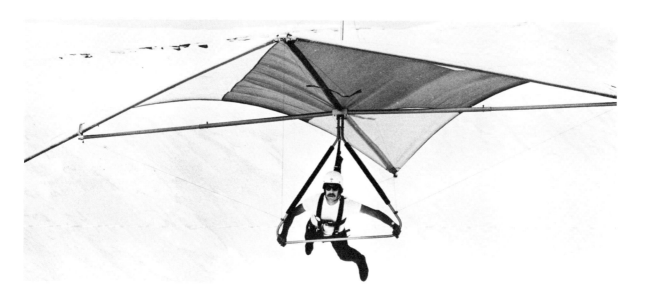

(Photo by Jim Jennings)
A hang glider at Jockey Ridge, a sand dune near Nags Head, North Carolina. A long lens makes the glider seem much higher up than it actually was, which was just a few feet. Shot with a 300mm f/4.5 lens with Tri-X rated at ASA 400—exposure 1/1000 at f/8. Processed normally in straight D-76.

faster films, though this isn't necessarily so. However, there is an easy way to do it: divide the ASA 25 guide number in half and multiply the result by each of the f-numbers, starting with f/2.8.

Let us again use a guide number of 60 for an ASA 25 film and see what guide numbers we would get for faster films. Halving the 60 gives us 30, which we multiply by each of the f-numbers, starting with f/2.8—2.8, 4, 5.6, 8, 11, and 16. We come up with the following new guide numbers: 84 (for an ASA 50 film), 120 (for ASA 100), 168 (ASA 200), 240 (ASA 400), 330 (ASA 800), and 480 (ASA 1600). If the rated ASA speed of the film you are using falls between two of these speeds it is quite safe to simply estimate what the guide number would be.

Unfortunately, manufacturers often publish guide numbers that are higher than they should be, because this makes their units appear to be more powerful than they actually are. If you use these inflated guide numbers you will underexpose your film. Thus if you buy a unit you would be wise to personally establish the basic ASA 25 guide number for yourself, then use the preceding system to get any other guide numbers that you need.

Use color film and laboratory processing for making your determination, because both are so standardized nowadays that the results will be highly dependable. Using an ASA 25 color film (e.g., Kodachrome 25), set up an average subject (including at least one person) at a distance of exactly 10 feet from your flash unit and camera, which should be on a tripod. Next shoot a series of pictures that are identical except for exposure, shooting each one at a different f-number, and starting with the largest aperture that your camera has. For example, you might shoot at f/2, f/2.8, f/4, f/5.6, f/8, f/11, and f/16. Then take the film to the drug store or a color lab.

When you get your film back, pick the best exposure in the series and figure out the f-number at which it was exposed. Then determine the ASA 25 guide number with this formula: f-number × distance (10 feet) = guide number. For example, f/4 may give you your best image, which would give you a guide number of 40, just as f/2.8 would give you a guide number of 28.

If you are testing a miniature flash unit, or

your camera doesn't have the larger apertures, 10 feet may be too great a distance for making your tests. Therefore, use a distance of 5 feet and substitute 5 for the 10 in the formula just given.

Before leaving electronic flash we will deal with one more problem. Many black-and-white films produce negatives with too little contrast when they are exposed by electronic flash, the shorter the flash duration the lower the contrast. You can put the contrast back in by simply extending the film developing time by 20 to 50 per cent. This will increase the grain somewhat, but with a film such as Tri-X the increased graininess is hardly noticeable.

• Flash or Push?

Since we have covered two of the main methods for freezing sports action indoors—film pushing or using electronic flash—you may wonder which you should use. Should you freeze action with a high shutter speed made possible by pushing, or should you freeze it with flashes of extremely short duration? Well, there is no way for me to know what *you* should do, but I can tell you the method that most professionals seem to prefer.

Whenever they can the pros try to get along without electronic flash, getting their high shutter speeds with very fast lenses, fast films like Tri-X and 2475 Recording Film, and film speed pushing. However, they back themselves up with flash equipment, using it if absolutely necessary—which it sometimes is.

Their objection to electronic flash is that they usually have to point it right at their subjects, which flattens out all the shadows on figures and makes backgrounds black. Though bounce flash would solve the problem, the high ceilings of indoor sports arenas make it impossible to use it. So we are stuck with direct flash, which gives us lightings entirely unlike the ambient light in arenas. This makes the professional unhappy, because he wants to as nearly as possible capture the entire flavor of events, including what they actually look like to the spectators attending them.

One way around the synthetic nonrealism of direct flash is a multiple-flash setup in which you use two or more off-camera flash units fired by remote control. Such arrangements can be very effective, and they have been used many times. But setting one up and testing it can be quite a production. The average newspaper pro just doesn't have time; he has to dash in, get his shots, and return to his paper in time to process them for the morning edition, which is already well under way by the time he returns. So he uses available light and push speeds when he can, or turns to direct electronic flash when he has to.

The chances are that you just don't have the equipment for multiple-flash. If you do have there is still the problem of getting permission to set it up for an event.

So what should *you* do? Whatever your experience, equipment, and ability as a con artist will permit you to do. As for electronic flash and film pushing, why not try them both if you can?

• What Should You Shoot?

You may have noticed that you haven't been told what you should shoot—what sports, what specific action within each sport, and so on. For very simple reasons you don't have to be told. For example, if you are enough of a football nut to want to shoot some games you already know what football is all about and wherein the visual excitement lies. And with many sports the key moments are self-evident—when a high diver looks most like a swan, when a pole vaulter clears the bar, when a racing driver spins out or goes over the wall, when a horse wins a race, etc.

Such things you already know without being told due to a lifetime spent in a sports-oriented country. Sports are mainly about winning and losing, and both winners and losers make interesting pictures.

As you have seen, the emphasis in this chapter has been on how to use some of the primary tools of sports photography. However, this knowledge has a great many additional uses in photography.

HOW TO PHOTOGRAPH THE NUDE

A nude is generally a picture of a totally un-clothed person, male or female, that has rather obviously been made for artistic rather than grossly sexual purposes. That is, nudes are made with the intention that they shall be art. This is the traditional way of thinking about photo-graphic nudes, and it is wise to keep it in mind. The term "nude" is also a euphemism for "naked body."

● Art and Pornography

Though pictorial nudity is now commonplace, many people are still very touchy about pictures of bare skin and strongly inclined to condemn the photographers who make them. For this reason it may be best to attempt to produce only tradi-tional nudes and to avoid trying anything that might be labeled pornography.

We have seen that a photographic nude is sup-posed to be art, meaning that to some people it should *look* like art, which isn't the same thing at all. Looking like art usually means to look like a handsome painting of a nude person, the idea being that people who paint pretty pictures are somehow proper custodians of public virtue and aesthetics. But this definition is very restrictive. Furthermore, when something looks like art it usually isn't. For a better viewpoint we should ask ourselves, What is art? Well, it is hard to say,

but it is surely an abundant embodiment of such things as beauty, hope, meaning, and truth.

If a photograph of one or more unclothed peo-ple has all these things it is surely art, whether it looks like a painting or not. Photographers gener-ally settle for beauty alone and strive very hard to create or record it. When they are successful it is quite good enough—their pictures should cer-tainly be called art. You see, each of these terms —beauty, hope, meaning, and truth—basically includes all the others.

Essentially, pornography is simply failed art, an attempt at art that doesn't come off. The ques-tion isn't whether a picture is sensual, for real art can be very sensual indeed. Art can be about people tenderly and beautifully making love, for example, or about sensually glorious human bod-ies. No, the question is whether a picture, sensual or not, embodies beauty, hope, meaning, and truth.

In other words, was the photographer able to see and understand such things and project them into a picture? In short, is he or she a sensitive, perceptive, healthy, and sane human being? The law is that you can only see what you are; thus to *create* art you have to *be* art. You have to be sane, for example.

Most definitions of pornography are very sick, yet people will hold them over you like a club—so you should know what some of them are. A photograph of human nudity may be called por-nographic if it shows:

1. the sex act in any of its many forms
2. people of opposite sexes
3. two or more people of the same sex
4. pubic hair
5. genitals
6. a nude man
7. a pose even vaguely reminiscent of one used for sex
8. any mixture of clothed and unclothed people
9. an ordinary everyday environment (living room, kitchen, bathroom, back yard, etc.)

The list could be extended indefinitely, because nudity as such—in pictures or out—is pornographic to some people. Oddly, the nude male figure is seen as very pornographic, especially to men. Through the years the female figure has been depersonalized to a great degree, but the male figure has not.

Though it is possible to consider figure photography without thinking of pornography, it is better to keep it in mind. You see, every time you do figure studies you must skirt the pornography problem, and if your pictures don't come out well you are right in the middle of it. Remember that pornography is simply failed art. You must also deal with the fact that art and pornography are often confused, one being taken for the other. Since you yourself may make this mistake you should at least consider both sides of the coin. But more: pornography mainly arises from the inability to see the world as wonderful; you should remember this, too.

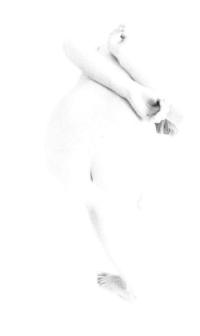

Prints from the same negative shot with a white no-seam paper background, which creates certain interesting problems for the photographer (see text). One of them comes from the insistence that white always stays white and should be printed that way, which led to the print above that is pretty well falling apart, the body almost disappearing into the whiteness. The better print below accepts the fact that a particular lighting and model have turned a white background into gray (by comparison with everything else), so it has been printed as gray. The girl's body now has a feeling of volume and space.

• **The Figure as Sculpture**

One of the long-accepted ways to deal with the pornography question is to treat the figure, male or female, as an art object—as sculpture, for example. Since many sculptors have managed to see the human body as beautiful, emulating them is a way to learn to see beauty. You could start by using sculptors' poses and could also use the same kinds of models. However, many sculptors

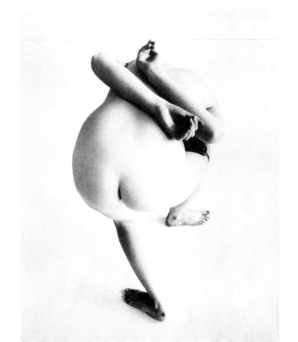

have used chunky women who would look simply fat in photographs, though their male models are usually trim and well muscled.

In treating figures as sculpture it is important to use the right backgrounds and lightings. Those mentioned later in the chapter will work very well, for I am taking you through an essentially sculptural approach to photography of the nude.

• Finding Models

If you are not too shy, the easiest way to get a model is to ask a friend to pose. Nowadays, a man and a woman will often make a trade, each posing for the other. Taking figure drawing courses in an art school is a way to contact models, though the men and women who pose there are often pretty beat up. The bedraggled ones usually refuse to pose for photographers, anyway, but the handsome ones sometimes will. Photography courses that deal with the nude are an even better bet, and there is the advantage of working under experienced instructors.

Some newspapers will accept advertising for models if it is clear that your purposes are legitimate. Though the models that one contacts in this manner often have very miscellaneous faces and figures and are out for kicks, there is always a chance of getting one or two good ones. Furthermore, it is excellent experience to work with faces and figures that are far from perfect. There is always a considerable amount of beauty in them, and you should learn to see it.

Advertising on an art school bulletin board is a good idea, because the men and women students are long-accustomed to nudity and often in need of extra money. Make it very clear in your ads that you are not a sexual pervert in search of sexual kicks, for art students are extremely leary of such people. Offer a modeling fee of around ten dollars an hour, plus a promise of modeling sessions at least two hours long. Nowadays, it is hardly worth crossing the street for less than twenty bucks, and modeling can be very hard work.

Joining a camera club may bring you in contact with photographers who know figure models willing to work for a reasonable fee, but you should investigate this possibility before joining.

Joining a little theater group is also a good idea, because many young actors and actresses think that the experience of being nude in front of others will fit into their training very well. Some of them also like to be daring. And some will pose to satisfy their vanity, theater people being well endowed with it.

The main problem in getting models is suspicion: the people you approach may think you are an uptight voyeur or that you are stupid enough to have sexual seduction in mind. There are many such people, you know. If you ask a model to bring a friend to a modeling session or to pose for a small group of photographers (instead of just yourself) the suspicion will generally lessen. Since they are not voyeurs and generally prefer to have real love as a prerequisite of sex, women photographers are not often suspected. However, the men whom they ask to model are often surprisingly shy—terrified, in fact. Though he may not know it, the average man is scared to death of women.

• Emotion and Ritual

Confronting nude persons of either sex with the intention of really looking at them is usually quite a traumatic event, though most of the emotion will drain out of a modeling session in a few minutes. Since emotion can make you as blind as a bat you should control it by establishing a matter-of-fact, businesslike ritual and sticking to it:

1. When your model arrives, review the terms for posing—the posing fee, the length of the coming session, the amount of time between rest breaks, the kinds of pictures you wish to make, whether you will want model releases, and what you intend to use your pictures for.

2. Take your model to a place where he or she can undress in privacy and return to during rest breaks.

3. Have a clearly established place where the posing will be done, for example, on a no-seam paper background. Suggest that the model wear a dressing gown during rest breaks and at other times when not in the posing area.

4. When you are ready to go and your model is in the posing place, just say, "All right, we'll start now—just hand your robe to me."

5. Give posing instructions in a clear and matter-of-fact way, taking some of the poses yourself so that your model can see what you want. Don't touch the model unless it is very clear to both of you that he or she just doesn't understand your instructions; then it is all right to push an arm, leg, or hand into place.

As you see, this ritual is very artificial, almost like a heavily stylized dance. You can add to it or shorten it, depending on how at ease you and your model are. Consider yourself the main problem, however; when you relax your model will too. Bear in mind that the main purpose of the ritual is to lessen emotion, which it does by making the situation totally unlike a seduction scene and by constantly reminding both you and your model that your only purpose in being together is to produce fine photographs. Though the sexual tension very quickly drains out of a modeling session, it is wise to continue the ritual, anyway. So it is a bit phony? So it works, that's what.

• Backgrounds and Posing Environments

In deciding on a background it is usually a good idea to follow photographic tradition, which insists that the posing place should be simple, handsome, and very unlike an everyday environment. In addition, it should "look like art," i.e., like something in a picture that is generally assumed to be art. Following this rather restrictive covenant may introduce an air of self-conscious artiness to your work, but this can be overcome. You should permit yourself to be guided by it mainly for self-protection, because following the tradition will make it obvious to nearly everyone

that your intentions are to produce art, not pornography. If your work isn't very good it is especially important to make your intentions clear.

Earlier, I listed an everyday environment as one reason for calling a nude study pornographic, an idea that approaches the ridiculous. Well, some people think this way, so you ought to take it into account. The thing is that everyday environments may imply certain things about your models and yourself that people find unacceptable. For example, if a man photographs a nude woman in her living room (an ordinary one) the implications may be that she is a nudist, that the photograph recorded only part of a seduction scene on the couch, that a sexually promiscuous woman removed her clothes in order to beguile the photographer, that the photographer deliberately invaded her privacy, and so on.

Though it is possible to produce nude "art" in an ordinary living room, the odds are against it. If the room itself is "art," that is good for a start. That is, you can do anything you like in Buckingham Palace. This is pretty weird stuff, but one has to go along with public morality—or at least be aware of it.

Fortunately, there is a very easy way around the background problem and it has other important advantages, too. Use no-seam paper, which comes in rolls nine feet wide and is available in many tones and colors. You staple or tape the free end of the paper to the wall, up near the ceiling, then roll it down the wall and out across the floor. Then you have your models pose on the paper.

• No-Seam Paper

Since no-seam paper is by far the most popular background for nude studies, it deserves a section of its own in this chapter. It will also be discussed in the section on lighting.

An important factor in its usefulness and popularity is that it completely isolates the things that are photographed on it from everyday reality. In the resulting pictures they seem to exist in no par-

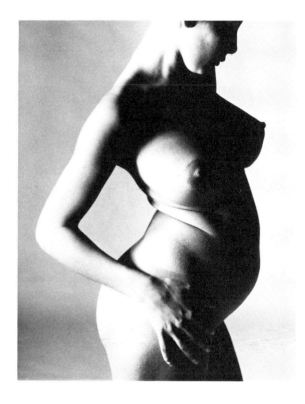

This girl has a splendid body (though her breasts are a bit large), yet it was possible to make her look gross and ugly. Though this might seem like a cruel and stupid thing to try, intentionally creating ugliness is actually a way of learning to see beauty better, for beauty and ugliness are two sides of the same coin. In the print below you can see that the girl's body is actually as healthy and handsome as I say.

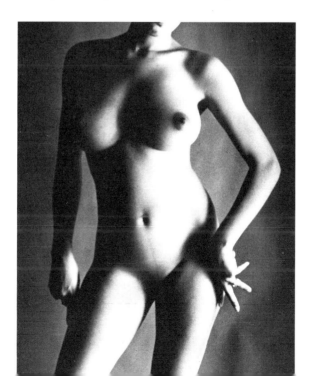

ticular place, and the paper itself doesn't even look like paper.

Since the paper background effectively represents no-place, it implies very few things about the people or objects that are photographed on it. However, one implication is fortunately quite clear: that the photographer's intention is to produce "art." Not journalism, sexual exposes, sociology, psychology, history, and so on—just "art."

Furthermore, using a no-seam will even help you in this effort, because it removes all environmental distractions so that you can concentrate on really seeing your models. And a well-seen human being always comes out as art—a well-seen anything does, for that matter. Since the human body is a very complex and aesthetically confusing structure, you need all the help in this direction that you can get. The body can be both beautiful and ugly; learning to see the difference is difficult; and a nondistracting background is a great help.

Though no-seams come in many colors it is best to stick to gray and white, even if you are using color film. The problem with color?—distraction. For example, with a red background—which you might wish to buy because it is very pretty—your eyes and emotions would be so overwhelmed by the sheer redness that you would have great difficulty in seeing the difference between Helen of Troy and a kangaroo. Because there was nothing else available, I once used a red background for some nude studies and thought I would go totally crazy before the session was over. However, color is pretty and you may insist on it. If so, you might try a pastel blue, which is the least distracting of colors.

The main problems with no-seam paper are finding a place that sells it, getting it hung without creases or tears, and keeping it clean while you are using it. It is usually sold in stores that supply artists, photographers, or window decorators. Experienced photographers can usually tell you where to get it.

With experience you will be able to hang a no-seam by yourself, but at first you should have an assistant—your model, perhaps. One trick is to lift up the whole roll when you are attaching the loose end to the wall. After it is *very* securely attached (the paper is heavy) you can start carefully unrolling it. To unroll it *before* attaching it is an invitation to disaster, for it tears easily and is extremely unwieldy.

The cleanliness problem is due mainly to dirty feet—yours and your model's. Put a chair, a bucket of warm water, soap, and a towel right next to the background and have your model very carefully wash his or her feet before stepping onto the paper. Make it very clear that one should step directly into shoes, slippers, or socks upon leaving the background, so as not to dirty the feet again. The cleanest of floors isn't clean enough, so bare feet shouldn't touch it. As for yourself, step directly out of your shoes onto the paper and work in your stocking feet. And when you leave the paper, step directly into your shoes again. With such precautions you can keep a no-seam clean for several modeling sessions. Without them you can ruin it in five minutes.

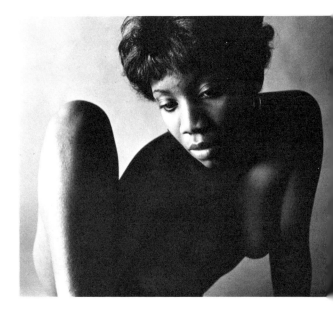

The leg is just one example of the phallic symbols that male photographers are always finding in female bodies. So be it. It seems to be one of the normal things for men to do.

● Abstracts of Nudes

Most people are extremely critical concerning beauty in the human figure, so most figures, including many very healthy ones, simply will not measure up to their standards. When you start shooting nudes you will probably feel the same way, but this is no cause for celebration. It means that in your ignorance and inexperience you are depriving people of their God-given right to be seen as beautiful. It also means that you will be deeply disappointed with all your full-figure shots, for you will undoubtedly work with bodies that are less than perfection or see really fine bodies poorly.

The thing is that our basic ideas of beauty and ugliness stem mainly from ourselves; we derive our concepts from human faces and bodies without really looking at them. We see nearly everyone as composed of both beauty and ugliness—physically, mentally, and emotionally. Though we

see ourselves hardly at all, we think of mankind as flawed.

Now, ugliness can be defined as "that which is not well seen." Thus ugliness in humankind is largely a fiction based on the inability to see, yet it has a powerful influence on most of us. And the fact that we persist in seeing the average figure as both beautiful and ugly at the same time makes figure photography difficult, because ugliness easily wins out in our minds. The solution is to learn to see all figures, from the gross to the gaunt, as beautiful, but this is far easier said than done.

We must work toward this solution in easy steps, one of which is to make abstracts of nudes rather than full figures. In this way it is fairly easy to see abundant beauty in even the most ill-proportioned bodies, whereas in full-figure studies we might see only ugliness.

Photographing the figure in sections helps us

see beauty and ugliness in the abstract in terms of tones, lines, contours, textures, and colors, which simplifies the perceptual problem considerably. When one is working with segments of the body, the beauty and presumed ugliness residing in these areas are relatively easy to see. In a full figure, even a splendid one, beauty and so-called ugliness are often so intertwined and complex that it is next to impossible for a beginner to sort them out; and he or she often ends up seeing only the ugly.

Working with sections of a figure does more than help you differentiate between beauty and presumed ugliness in abstract visual terms such as tone, light, texture, etc. It also helps you expand your mental-emotional concepts of beauty—which control your ability to see it—until you eventually see little in a human figure but beauty. Frankly, this is one of the main justifications for doing figure photography: to learn to see all people as beautiful.

When you are working with abstracts of nudes it is sometimes interesting (and quite easy) to work with two or more bodies; and people—both men and women—don't mind posing together. However, if you show whole figures people are likely to think you are purveying pornography, so stick to abstracts.

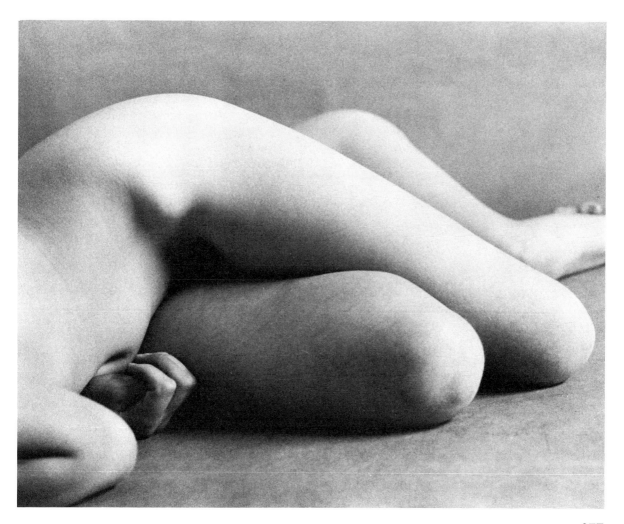

Learning to see the beautiful drains away the fear of ugliness, and when the fear goes away the ugliness goes with it, for fear and the concept of ugliness are very closely related. In essence, that which we fear is called ugly, though fear itself is the real culprit.

Now, with an expanded sense of the beautiful you will still be able to identify so-called ugliness (with much greater skill than before), yet you will tend to see it mainly for what it really is: a concept based largely on fear and ignorance.

The emotional charge (fear) will drain out of your perception of ugliness, enabling you to use it with dispassion in your photography. In truth, ugliness is only a tool for the artist; it is merely an aspect of the beautiful; and art without it isn't really art. These things are very hard to see and understand, but approaching the nude mainly through abstractions will help you a great deal. You think you already know all about beauty and ugliness—but wait and see.

Once you have a better idea of the endless dimensions of beauty you will be able to handle full-figure nudes with little difficulty. Until then you will tend to see human bodies only through your stereotypes, which means you will hardly see them at all.

● Posing the Nude

The best way to pose nudes is to not pose them at all, though one can pose them up to a point. The thing is that the beauty in human beings comes out best when they are behaving naturally by making themselves comfortable. However, giving people detailed instructions limb by limb on how to dispose themselves for your camera almost invariably makes them quite *uncomfortable,* which introduces too much of the ugliness factor.

The thing is that people will cheerfully move a limb at a time if you ask them to, but this is not the normal way to shift position. With every movement, no matter how small, the body as a whole wants to adjust position, for that is the way it was made to function. Thus having models move their parts piecemeal makes them look like badly built robots. However, if that is what you want, go right ahead.

The best way to get handsome poses is to give very generalized instructions to your models and encourage them to do as you wish in the most comfortable ways possible. For example, you might say, "Lie down here, curl up a little bit, and make yourself as comfortable as you can" or "Stand facing me, carry your weight mainly on one leg (like this), and brace your right hand on your hip (like this). Now, make yourself com-

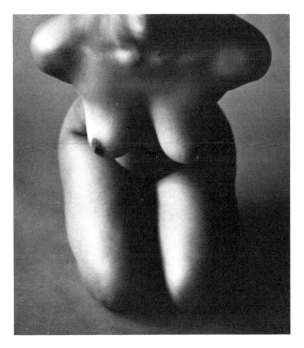

The objective here was to see the figure as an abstract sculpture, perhaps by Henry Moore or Jean Arp. Working with abstracts is the best way to refine your perception of beauty. With whole figures, personality problems tend to interfere with vision.

fortable, because you may have to stand there for a while."

Though the instructions for the standing pose are rather specific, they only ask a person to do what people normally do when they have to stand for a while. Such things as the position of the head, the tilt of the pelvis, the position of the left hand, and the placement of the leg that is not carrying weight are left strictly up to the model. Indeed, the less you have to tell a model the better off you are.

Unfortunately, some people don't quite believe it when you say you want them to be comfortable, so you have to continually reinforce the idea until they do. One way is to frequently tell them to break their poses as soon as they begin to get uncomfortable, even if this makes you miss a few pictures. Just tell them that there will be plenty more good poses to come and that you will get all the pictures you need. Even with such instructions, some models will hold poses until they turn to stone. So be on the lookout for signs of strain and ask them to break their poses as soon as you see it. And bear in mind that holding a pose can be very hard work.

Some models deeply enjoy following the instructions: "Make different shapes with your body just to see what they feel like. Hold each shape for a few seconds, then try another—or hold the shape longer if it feels good. I will take care of the photography end of it, so don't bother waiting for me to shoot." Doing this kind of thing is much easier than holding set poses for five or ten minutes at a time, so models don't tire so rapidly. It also gives you the opportunity to see many more poses than you normally would in a modeling session. If a particular pose is good, you can ask your model to hold it a while, or until it begins to get uncomfortable. For your model's morale you should photograph every pose (film is cheap), even if you don't like some of them very much. Later, you can study your contact sheets and figure out why you didn't like them, which is a good way to learn.

The morale factor is extremely important, incidentally. In order to let their natural beauty flow out, people must feel cared for and appreciated while they are being photographed. In order to be beautiful they must dare to think that they are, so you must help them. One way to do it is to welcome each pose with words such as good, fine, swell, wonderful, excellent, lovely, and so on— but it works best if you really mean what you say. If you don't like a pose think of something you *do* like (say your model's efforts to please you) and say, "Wonderful," anyway. Your affirmation will then be genuine.

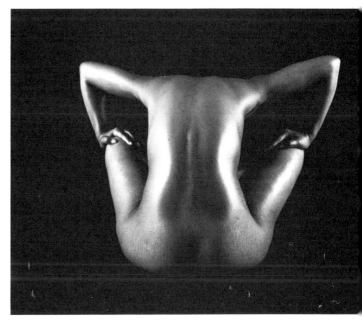

The objective here was to see the figure as akin to a sugar bowl with two handles, or perhaps to some winged creature. Seeing a human body as related to lots and lots of things is a way of comprehending how wonderful it is. And the related things are wonderful too.

● Lightings

Beginners should use only bounce lightings, for they are easiest to use and very flattering to the human body. In contrast, direct lightings bring in far too much of the ugliness factor, unless one is expert at using them. This is because they create sharp-edged shadows, which can make bodies look hacked-up, ill-proportioned, and stuck together with joints in the wrong places. This is all illusional, of course, but the magic is so strong that it can lead to very ugly pictures. Well, just to see for yourself you should try some direct light-

You don't always have to be dead serious in figure photography. Here Dorothy Grazes reveals that she has a heavy vein of natural ham in her. A welcome change from pious or preachy nudes.

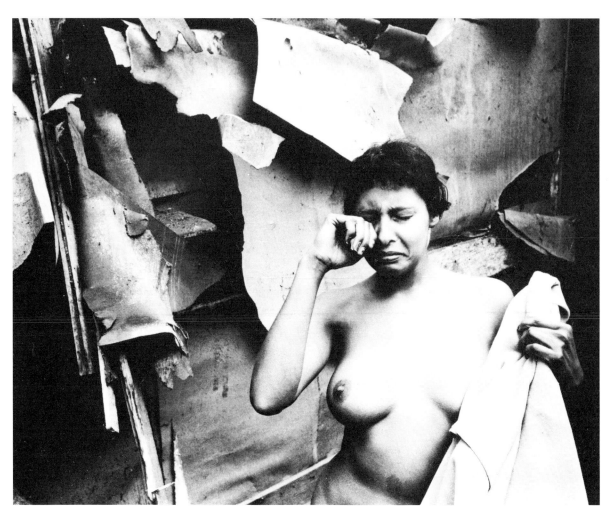

ings, anyway. But if your models come out looking like dead meat, don't be surprised.

Fairly contrasty side bounce lighting gives bodies a very sculptural feeling, that is, roundness, solidity, and realness. And it may actually make them look like sculptures. At the same time it creates very soft-edged form shadows on figures, gently bringing out all the beauty of the human form. The darker shadows (in prints) obscure certain areas, so that an element of mystery is added. Surely, one should approach human beings as mysteries, for that is the only intelligent thing to do.

For figure studies, side bounce light works best with a medium-gray no-seam paper background. Using bounce light from both sides of a model also works well, especially if the light from one side is slightly stronger. With this double bounce lighting you get highlights on both sides of a figure and very interesting and handsome shadows in the middle. You will surely see curves that you have been unaware of before and increase your awareness on what figure photography can teach you.

Side bounce can also be good with white no-seams, though gray is much easier to work with. However, you may have trouble in making your prints if the highlights on your model match the background in tone. Then parts of the figure will simply disappear into the background tones of the prints. The way around this is to position the model far in front of the vertical part of the white no-seam; about seven or eight feet is far enough.

With this distance to work with you can use your lighting to control the brightness relationship of model and white background and make them sufficiently different in tone so that they will not blend together in prints. This is called "getting enough separation." If you use overhead bounce light you will usually not have as great a separation problem with a white no-seam, but you will probably have printing problems, anyway. Your preconceptions will undoubtedly get in your way.

You see, many people think that white back-grounds should "logically" come out white in prints, because white is always white. So they print them white, but the pictures just don't look right. They simply "fall apart," the tones looking disconnected and shattered. Even so, white *is* always white—but only as an abstract concept.

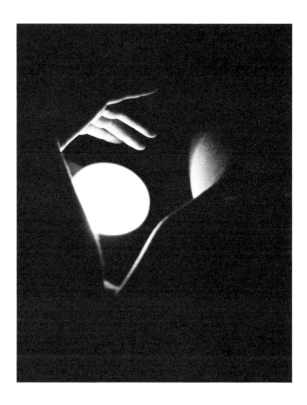

Here we see how very abstract a figure study can be—just three curves, four fingers, and the light source. Working this simply will help you refine your taste, whereas in working with full figures you might be greatly distressed at your inability to see the beauty in them. So stick to simplicity and save yourself suffering.

However, in the world *as we see it* the whiteness of something is mainly relative to the lightness or darkness of other things seen at the same time. Grayness and blackness are also relative. Another way of describing this tonal relativity is to say that lights *make* darks, darks *make* lights, and both can *make* grays. In other words, a thing is seen as light, dark, or gray only in comparison with other things, for vision is a comparative process. In a universe exclusively black, white, or gray there could be no human visual perception at all, at least not with our present perceptual equipment.

Now, we are not off on a digression, or detour, but are creeping up on the question of what figure photography is actually good for beyond producing pretty pictures of naked people, which is not really very important. So bear with me a while longer.

We will return to white paper, because it is a good teacher. When we exclude its surroundings, a white no-seam will also *look* white only if it reflects considerably more light than the model positioned on it (this is difficult to see in the studio, easier to see in prints). Whether this will happen depends on the reflectivity of the model's skin and the paper (the percentage of incident light that they reflect) and the relative intensity of light falling upon each one (there are other factors, but they are best ignored at this point).

For example, if the model and the white background receive the same amount of light the background will tend to *look* white because of its higher natural reflectivity. However, if we slowly change the lighting geometry so that the model receives progressively more light than the background paper, the paper will be seen to gradually change from light, to medium, to dark gray—or even to black. Though such a change should be obvious to anyone who sees it happening, it unfortunately is not.

To understand why it isn't obvious we must consider certain differences between seeing and perception. In the simplest terms, seeing means using the eyes to permit visual data (in the form of differential light energies) to enter oneself. In this sense, all people with normal eyes see extremely well. But perception is quite another matter. Perception refers to what the ego and the portion of the mind that it dominates do with the visual data received through the eyes. Since the ego is a highly fallible instrument it frequently garbles, or misinterprets, the data.

Among other things, the ego creates highly inaccurate mental images of the visual world from the splendid data transmitted by the eyes. That is, the ego's *perception* of this world is very poor. For example, it radically alters nearly everything, confuses memory with vision, ignores things it can't explain, automates perception with bad programming, and refuses to see changes in the constantly changing visual world around it. This is perception. Unfortunately, our awareness of the visual world is strictly limited to our perception of it. We *see* immensely more of it, but we are not aware of this. Another way of describing the situation is that our only contact with the visual world (our perception of it) is through ego-colored glasses, which is a very uncomfortable thought.

So, we return to the white background that people persist in perceiving as white, even when it happens to be gray. Why is this? Well, it is an ego problem, first of all. The ego insists on seeing whiteness (or grayness or blackness) as an unchanging (absolute) *characteristic* of certain things, not as a relativistic *quality* that they may sometimes display. White as an absolute is a comfortably simplistic concept, while the notion of whiteness as relative is not. The ego clings to the absolute simply because it always wants to move in the direction of its greatest comfort. Therefore, it persists in perceiving whiteness that isn't there, even though this contradicts the visual data coming to it through the eyes.

Considering the problems, you might suppose I am trying to tell you to never use a white no-seam for figure photography. Indeed, I consider it mandatory that you use one now and then to help you really understand the things you have just read. There is more to come, so bear with me still longer.

Though this is a section on lighting, backgrounds are a very important part of learning how to light things. The reason for this is that certain backgrounds will give you a greatly improved opportunity to perceive what light does to things and what things do to light. The great visual simplicity of neutral-colored no-seams eliminates all visual distractions (rugs, chairs, wallpaper, architectural details, etc.) and makes such perception much easier. And nude human models contribute greatly to the motivation.

The overall objective is to overcome the bad perceptual habits of a lifetime (ego habits, or self-conditioning) and make your perception as accurate as your seeing. In the arts this is called "learning to *really* see" or sometimes just "learning to see." Whatever it is called, it means developing acute awareness of what is happening in the visual world. And it happens that the human body has been studied for this purpose for millennia: to teach people to see.

Overcoming the habit of perceiving the tone of a background as an unchanging absolute is just a step along the way, yet it is an important breakthrough. The lightness or darkness of a thing is a relative quality. A larger step is to see that this also applies to human bodies. By careful choice of background and lighting, one can make a black person white, a white person black, or make either of them gray, but these are gross changes. Becoming aware of the subtleties of what light can do is what really matters, and doing figure studies can be a great help in this direction. More of this in a moment.

● A Primary Justification for Figure Photography

You may think that the best reason for photographing nudes is to simply make beautiful pictures. Not so. It is the process of making them and what experiencing the process does to you that count. The pictures as such are of relatively little importance. These truths have been known in the arts for hundreds of years. The main objective of figure studies has always been learning to see better.

Now, learning to see is a very heavy experience involving a good deal of suffering in the form of nausea, headaches, and despair. Any real artist can tell you this. Indeed, so great is the suffering that most people won't even try to learn unless they are powerfully motivated. So here is where the human body comes in: most of us are strongly motivated to see it well. As we are learning how we soon discover that seeing the body helps us see everything else, too, and this encouraging insight adds greatly to our motivation. Understand this: the urge to be truly aware of the visual world can be very strong.

Essentially, to develop motivation means to tap the forces within oneself, the sexual force being the strongest. People being what they are, it is not hard to understand that this force might provide photographers with abundant energy for figure photography. Psychologists like to call this "sexual sublimation," or the use of a lower force for a worthy purpose, such as the creation of art. More accurately, it is the use of the *highest* force for self-evolution, part of which involves learning to see. In learning to see we create ourselves, you might say.

In this so-called age of sexual enlightenment, one might wonder if interest in sex is still strong enough for it to perform its motivational function in the arts. Or has it gotten so commonplace that nobody gives a damn any more? Well, this sexual revolution of ours is mainly journalistic hot air, and people haven't really changed a bit in any fundamental way. Whether we like it or not we are programmed to be interested in sex and will be able to draw on its energies for artistic purposes as long as people are left on earth.

Usually, when we try to learn something we start out on the simplest possible level and try to build up to it step by step. In studying the figure, however, we do it the other way around and start out on the highest level of all. Following is a list of some of the difficulties encountered: figures are visually complex; we are greatly confused by seeing them as beautiful and ugly at the same time and unable to decide which is which; positive and negative sexual feelings badly impair our vision; our perception is badly warped by extremely ignorant notions concerning what healthy bodies should look like; and we are willing to look at them from just a few highly selective viewpoints, all others being considered as distortions. And this is not the half of it.

Considering the difficulties of learning to see a figure well, one might think that only an idiot would even try. Sure enough. If it weren't for the benevolent energy of the sexual force, figure photography would be much too hard for any of us. However, a little bit of this energy goes a long, long way.

Since there is a lot of heavy reading in this chapter, a simple summary of some of the main points may be helpful to you:

1. Learning to see is difficult.

2. Part of the process is to discover the things considered worth seeing, many of which are embodied or reflected in the human figure. This is because our aesthetic value systems are based on ourselves.

3. Learning to see the body will help us see things worth seeing elsewhere, for the body is visually related to the rest of the world. For example, its curves and textures are found in many places.

4. But learning to really see the body is extremely hard work, and this work involves a considerable amount of suffering.

5. However, the sexual force gives us direction, provides us with energy, helps us have staying power, makes our suffering bearable, and gives us hope, so that we can confront this otherwise overwhelming task.

6. In short, we can use the sexual force and the human body in a method for teaching ourselves to see. Though there are other methods, this one is fastest.

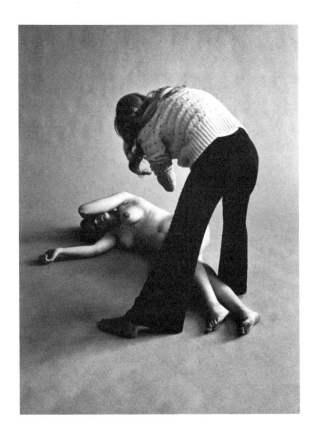

Scenes from my figure photography classes at New York's School of Visual Arts. The atmosphere was always casual, with people running in and out of the studios, and students didn't have to make pictures unless they wanted to. In one picture we see the boys persuading student Jan Cobb that he should be a nude model too.

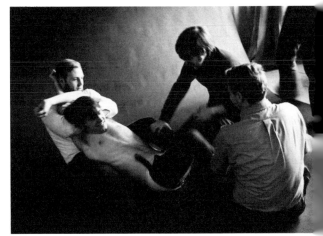

384

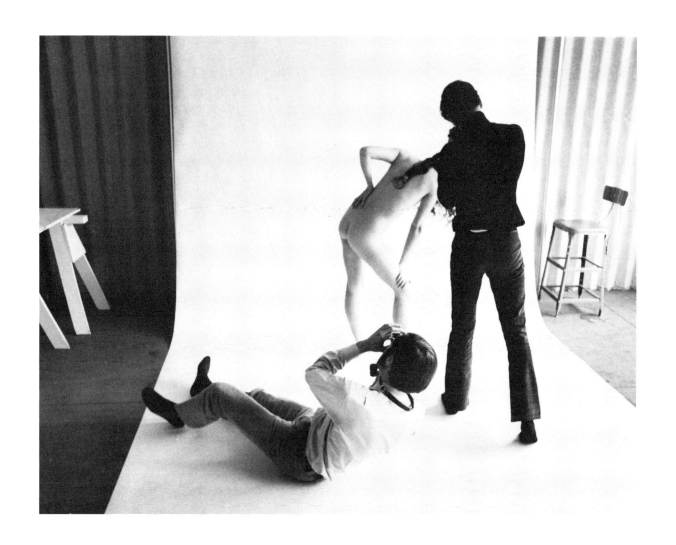

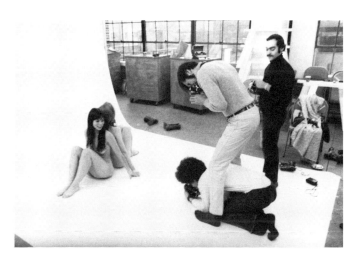

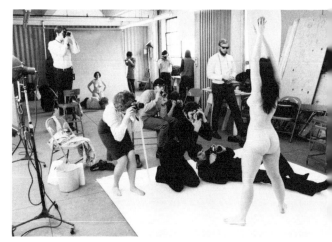

● Miscellany

Hand-held miniature cameras, especially 35mm single lens reflexes, are best for learning to see through doing figure photography. In comparison with larger cameras they encourage one to shoot more pictures, view models from more angles and distances, and make more prints.

Normal lenses are best for figure work. Though wide-angle distortions are very interesting at first, one soon tires of them. Telephotos won't let you get close enough and may limit the angles from which you can shoot—unless you have a very tall stepladder.

Model releases can be obtained from camera stores.

A roll of no-seam paper is long enough to provide you with either two or three backgrounds, depending on how far you stretch it out on the floor. To inhibit wrinkling in the paper, store the roll by standing it up in the corner of the room. If you like, you can buy special aluminum poles for hanging no-seams.

Don't use black no-seams, for they are psychologically very depressing to both photographers and models. Also, they make human skin look very dead and dreary.

To maintain your morale you should try to work only with handsome, well-built models while you are still a beginner. Even then you will find it quite a challenge to solve the beauty-ugliness problem. When you are quite advanced you may be ready to search for beauty in the gross and the gaunt, or you may never reach that level. Though beauty abounds in such people, it may be very hard for you to find, for that beauty must also be in the eye of the beholder.

Use either one or two 500 watt bulbs for your bounce lightings. They will give you enough light for both black-and-white and color films. However, 1000 watt bulbs are even better—if you can find them. A household electrical circuit will usually handle two of them at once.

As you have seen, studying the figure can be a way of learning to see. I used the method for five years at New York's School of Visual Arts, where I taught second year photography students. The required semester of figure photography worked very well for most students. The students in my last two years were so exceptional that I permitted them to work only with homely models. They were ready to see that these rather bedraggled men and women were also very beautiful. To their everlasting credit, a few of the students managed to see this. Their pictures were beautiful, of course.

HOW TO PHOTOGRAPH A GHOST

ESP and the occult have become such popular subjects nowadays that every supersensitive soul ought to know how to conjure up ghosts. Since live (or dead?) ghosts are hard to find and not dependable, you may have to stir up some fresh ghosts on your own. Let your friends furnish the bodies and photography provide you with the modus operandi. And as you work think, "Dracula will love me for this."

• How to Deaden Your Friends

Turning live flesh into ectoplasm is not a hard job —you do it by double-exposing film. Put your camera on a tripod and take a picture of your candidate for smoky oblivion. Then without moving the camera take another picture on the same film frame without him or her on it. In the resulting color slide or black-and-white print you will find a properly constituted ghost—it's as easy as that. However, ghosts can vary in quality from the truly horrendous to the merely banal, so we will look into some of the tricks of the ghost-making trade.

• Preparing Your Ghost

The average ghost is apparently like anyone else except for being a lot less dense—it doesn't have enough smoke or ectoplasm to fill a shot glass. Thus a very translucent picture of somebody ought to look ghostish enough, but some photog-

raphers won't settle for that. They think that ghosts ought to be hoked up like everything else. If you agree with them there is a lot of mischief that you can cook up.

There is catsup, of course, if a bloody ghost is your ideal. A sheet to make a ghost of your wife or husband, and a pillow case for the cat—wrap-around ghosts, you see. Some people think that ghosts should dress like nuns or monks, though genuine nun or monk ghosts are no more common than any other kind. Real ghosts wear ectoplasmic clothes, they say, but you may wish to fabricate a nude ghost. And you could get some good mileage out of Halloween masks and fright wigs. I personally prefer very ordinary ghosts, but that is what I am used to. If there is to be a brimstone ghost with three heads, snakes for hair, a forked tail, and teeth like a snark, I'm afraid that you yourself will have to create it.

• How to Make Double Exposures

Depending on the kind of camera you have you may or may not be able to make double exposures. Many cameras have built-in provisions for this, but you can get along if all you have is a shutter with a "B" (bulb) setting. A typical built-in arrangement is a little button you depress before rewinding your film. On some cameras, if you hold it down while using the film advance lever you will cock the shutter *without* advancing the film. That is, the film frame that you have just exposed will stay in place so that you can expose it again.

To use the bulb setting for double exposure you need a 5-inch sheet of black paper or cardboard. A cable release is extremely useful, though not absolutely necessary. When you have set your camera on "B" the shutter opens when you depress the shutter release and stays open as long as you hold down the release with a finger or a cable release. When you are ready to make a picture, hold the black card in front of the lens so that no light can get into it, then open the shutter and hold it open. As long as the card is there no light will reach the film. To expose the film, jerk the card away for a moment, then put it back in front of the lens and ask your ghost to get out of the way. Finally, jerk the card away again to make the second exposure, then put it back in front of the lens and let the shutter close itself.

This black card exposure method is classical in photography, incidentally. It was used with ancient cameras and lenses that didn't have shutters. With modern cameras it is a way of making sharp pictures by getting around camera movement caused by shutter vibration or by reflex mir-

Ghostly Bob and the mirror again—from another angle and distance.

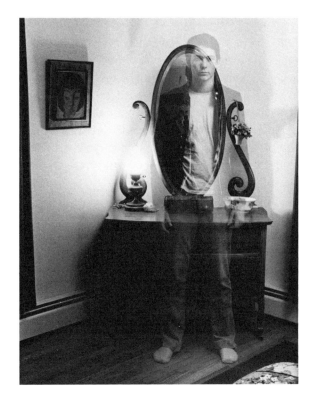

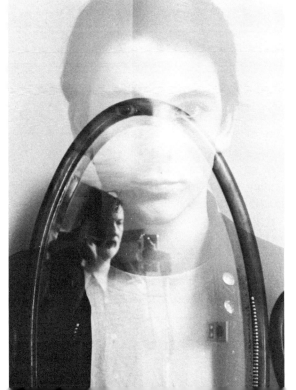

My younger stepson Bob Turner as a ghost. This was a simple double-exposure shot, with the mirror (and my reflection in it) getting two exposures, Bob getting one.

rors slamming into the "up" position. If the shutter is held open with a cable release, the method can also be used to get away from movement caused by a flimsy tripod or makeshift prop for a camera.

● Exposures

Since the background gets photographed twice, you should avoid overexposing it by giving only half of the correct exposure with each of your two shots. You can halve the correct exposure by stopping down an extra stop or by selecting the next fastest shutter speed. Thus the background will end up correctly exposed, while your ghost will be 50 per cent underexposed, which is mainly what will make him or her look like a ghost.

For the black card exposure system you need exposures that are long enough to be timed with reasonable accuracy by counting under your breath, with 1 second probably being the shortest usable time. Thus before being cut in half the correct exposure time would have to be at least 2 seconds. There are several things that you can do to get such slow exposure times—stop down your

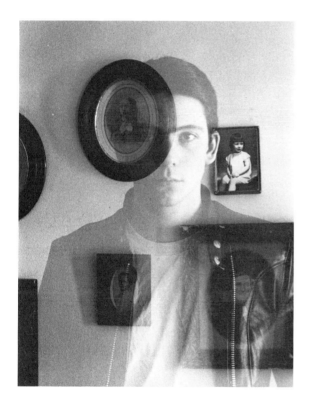

Ghost Bob Turner with ancestors, mainly mine. The little girl on the right is his mother as a child. She and Bob look very much alike.

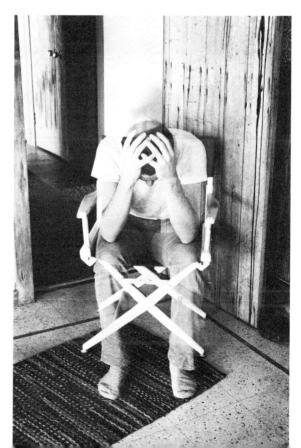

The ghost of the chair—again simple double exposure. Notice that Bob's head and hands look real enough, while his legs look quite transparent. How substantial a ghost looks depends primarily on how much exposure it gets in comparison with the total exposure.

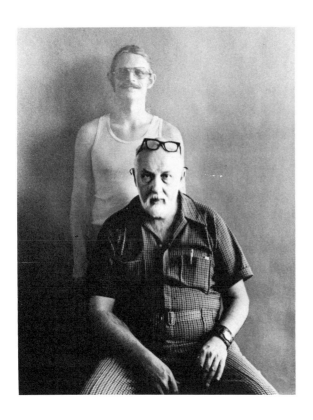

The author with ghost Mike Goodwin. Mike has the most erect posture of any man I know.

Mike and Claire Goodwin, a simple double exposure. Claire sat still for two exposures, while Mike only stayed around for one.

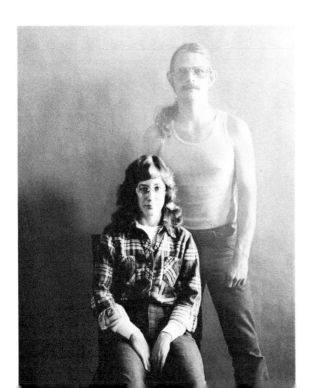

lens all the way, work in rather dim available light, or use a medium-to-slow film (ASA 125 or under).

You might think that exposures timed by counting wouldn't be accurate enough, but they usually are. Furthermore, inaccuracy as high as 50 per cent usually doesn't matter very much, especially with black-and-white films. With color films you will barely be able to see what difference it makes.

● Backgrounds

In order for your ghost to show up well in a color slide or a print, the area behind him or her in the picture should be from medium gray to black in tone. With light gray backgrounds ghosts show up poorly, with white ones not at all.

If there are objects (chairs, pictures, doorways, etc.) in the backgrounds behind your ghosts they will be visible through the ghostly bodies in your pictures, making said bodies look quite transparent, as proper ectoplasm should.

If your background is *really* black the ball game changes somewhat, because you can make as many shots as you like on the same frame without the film getting any exposure at all from the background. Thus you can make from 3 to 12 or more shots of the same ghost located in different parts of the picture.

By using a black background (black no-seam paper or the black sky at night, for example) you can use the same model as both a real person and a ghost in the same picture. For the real image, give the full correct exposure. For the ghost, cut the exposure in half. Your model should change position after the first exposure, of course. If you like you can make the ghost image even more wispy and ethereal by using only one fourth of the correct exposure when you shoot it.

Unfortunately, black no-seams aren't really black (just dark gray) unless you take pains to shade them from light. It may take a while to figure out how to do this, but you will come up with an answer if you try. In comparison, a black sky will stay that way, no matter what you do with your lights.

If your background is really black you can take several real images and several ghost images of the same person on a single frame of film.

• Ghosts and Non-Ghosts

You can make a ghost picture with just a ghost image, but it is often better to have two images— one to look ghostly, the other to look real. By having someone real to compare your ghost with it will look even more ghostly.

The technique is simple enough, though your real person will have to hold a long pose. The ghost has to be in position for just one of the exposures, but the real person must hold stock-still until both exposures have been made. However, if you are using a really black background you can photograph your models one at a time, exposing normally for one and underexposing the other. You won't get quite the same effects with the two methods, but your ghosts will look sufficiently ghostly.

• Other Tricks for Making Ghosts

You can turn a person into a ghost simply by photographing him out of focus. Or you can use selective focus and have the person out of focus and everything else sharp. Blurred movement also works very well. You get it by using a slow shutter speed and having your subject move during the exposure. Moving your camera instead of your subject will also give you blurred movement.

• Some Potentials of Photography

Though this chapter is mostly about ghosts it is also designed to help you see some of the many potentials of photography. You can do a great many things with double exposure, which you now know how to do. It is one of the standard creative techniques of the medium.

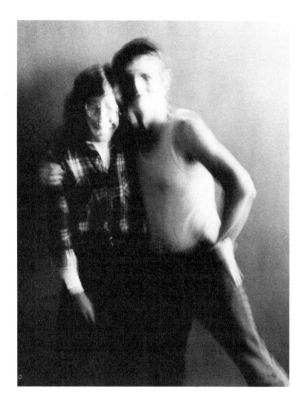

Ghosts made in another way, by blurred subject movement. Mike and Claire were jumping around quite a bit, and I photographed them with a slow shutter speed, their movement and the slow speed causing the blur.

Charles, holding a candle, spins to his left and becomes a ghost. A very slow shutter speed helped create the effect.

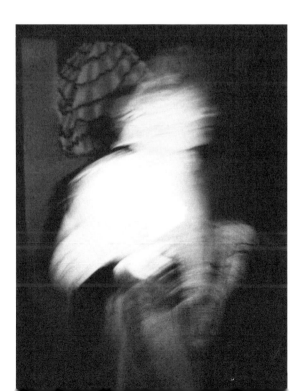

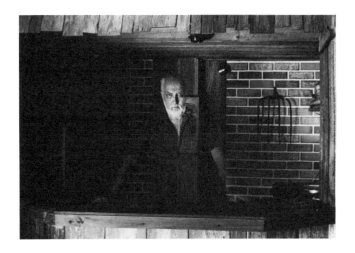

The ghostly bartender, your author himself. Notice that the central part of my figure—which was a dark jump suit—disappears almost entirely.

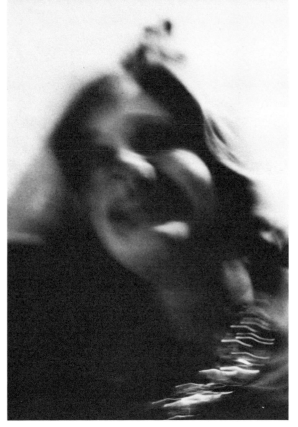

A statue of an ancient Egyptian princess turned into a ghost by selective focus. I shot at a wide aperture (probably f/2), which would give only a very limited depth of field. Then I focused on her headdress, letting her face go way out of focus. This makes it appear that my model was a live person.

Christine turned into a rather ghastly ghost by blurred movement. Here she looks like a cross between a troll and a grasshopper.

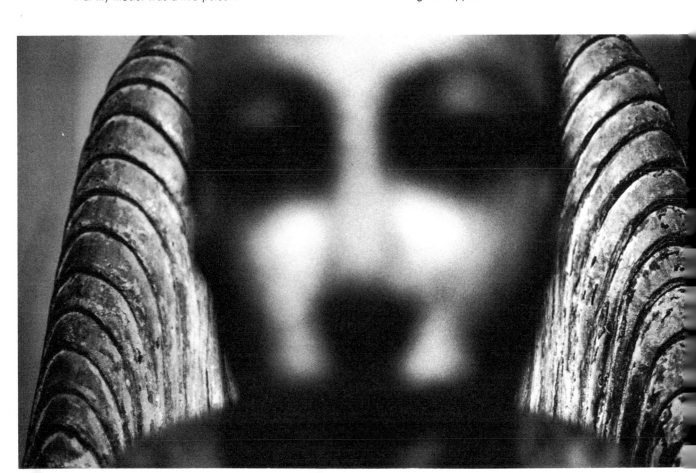

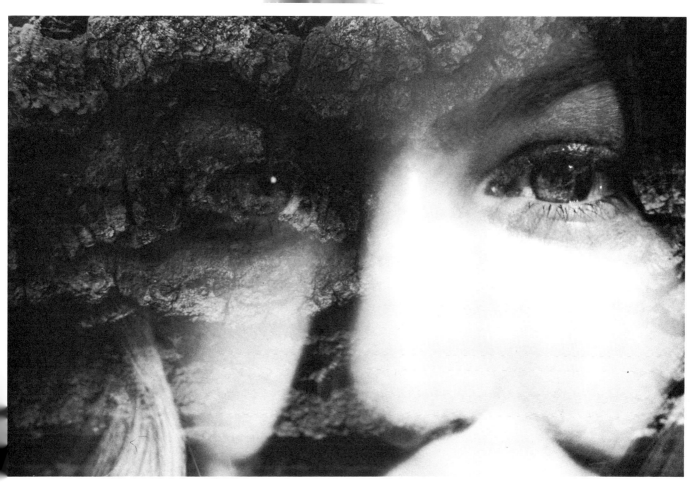

I exposed a whole roll of film with tree trunks, stumps, and knotholes, then re-exposed the roll with images of Anna, this being one of them. She's the nymph of the tree more than a ghost.

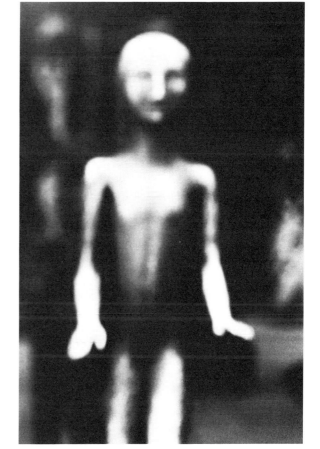

I changed a little statue into a ghost by racking it way out of focus and shooting it that way.

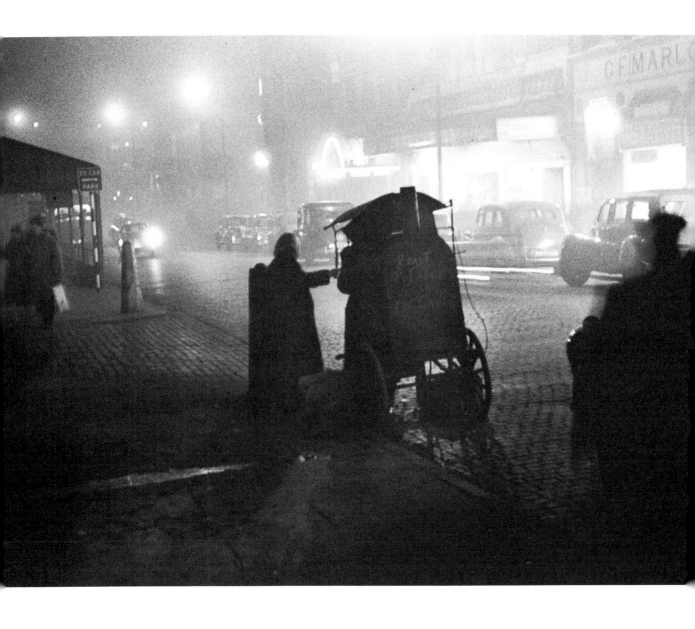

A typically foggy winter night in Birmingham, England.
I guessed a hand-held exposure, but it would have
been better to have a tripod and use extensive
exposure bracketing.

AVAILABLE LIGHT PHOTOGRAPHY AFTER DARK

Making pictures by available light after dark is a lot of fun, though you do have to concentrate on getting your exposures right. Fortunately, there are a number of ways around this problem. In this chapter we will take up the methods that are easiest to use.

• More Information for Sports Photography

Though this chapter is primarily designed to provide a general picture of the available light situation and the exposures involved, it is also an extension of the material on sports photography. For example, you will find estimated exposures (for a variety of ASA ratings) for many night sports events, including football, baseball, horse racing, boxing, wrestling, ice shows, swimming, basketball, hockey, and bowling. There is also additional information on speed pushing for both black-and-white and color films, including a list of film and developer combinations recommended for this purpose.

• If You Don't Have a Supersensitive Exposure Meter

For working at night it is desirable to have a supersensitive light meter such as the Gossen Luna-Pro. There are also supersensitive light boosters to use with meters built into certain cameras. Unfortunately, most meters—including built-ins and separate meters—won't give you good readings in dim light. Indeed, many of them

won't register at all when used in the ordinary way. To compound the problem, you may not even have an exposure meter. Don't despair: we will cover two very good ways for getting better readings with insensitive meters. And in the following section there is material that will help you solve the exposure problem without even having to use a meter.

• Available Light Categories and Exposure Chart

The things that people generally wish to photograph at night can be put into convenient exposure categories. This is because certain professional photographers and photographic technicians have spent a great deal of time photographing these things all over the country and have learned an immense amount concerning the exposures required. The thoroughly explored categories and exposures are usually printed on convenient exposure dials, charts, or information sheets included in film packages. Since the information has been tested again and again over a period of many years, you can get very good exposures by using it properly.

However, you must understand that some exposure information can only be approximated. For example, in the list of categories that follows you will find "bright downtown streets" (category E). Surely you realize that the brightness of streets will vary from city to city or from one part of town to another. For this reason you may not

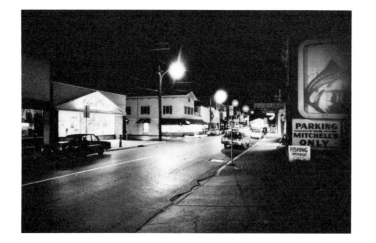

The tone of the street just below the car on the left seemed to be about the average tone of the scene, so I took an exposure reading from it, figuring that the other tones would take care of themselves. The exposure on Tri-X at ASA 400 came out right on the button (about 1/30 at f/2.8).

get a good exposure for a given street by following a recommended exposure too literally.

The thing to do in such a situation is to bracket the exposure, using the recommended exposure as the presumed normal exposure. For all the categories listed in this section it should be sufficient to bracket with only 3 shots—one normal exposure, one that is 2 stops overexposed, and one that is 2 stops underexposed. There is a very high probability that one of your 3 shots will be exposed just right.

For the overexposure, open up the lens 2 stops, *or* use a shutter speed 2 positions slower, *or* open up 1 stop *and* use a shutter setting 1 position slower.

For the underexposure, stop down 2 stops, *or* use a shutter speed 2 positions faster, *or* stop down 1 stop *and* use a shutter setting 1 position faster.

While you are doing the bracketing record all of your exposures in a little notebook. Then when your film has been processed mark the exposures that look best. Thereafter when you photograph again in the same places you can get the correct exposures from your notes; your recorded exposures will be more accurate than a dial, chart, or even a sensitive exposure meter.

Even if you have a supersensitive exposure meter the available light exposure chart should prove useful. It gives you a preview of the kinds of exposures you will probably use in various lighting situations and can be used to check your metering technique. If the exposures you get by using your meter differ considerably from the charted exposures you should begin to suspect your methods and carefully check them for errors.

Categories of available light at night

A   Early dusk shortly after sunset
B   Skyline 10 minutes after sundown
     Neon and other lighted signs
     Spotlighted subjects at ice shows, circuses, and stage events
C   Brightly lit theater and nightclub districts— Las Vegas or Times Square
     Burning buildings and campfires
     Night football, baseball, racetracks
     Floodlit circus and ice show subjects
D   Interiors with bright fluorescent lights
     Boxing and wrestling events in sports arenas
     Ground displays of fireworks
E   Bright downtown streets
     Basketball, hockey, and bowling
     Stage events with average lighting (not spotlighted)
     Hospital nurseries
     Color TV with black-and-white film
     Store windows

F Bright home interiors
   Fairs and amusement parks
   Interior swimming pools, above water
   Museum dioramas
G Amusement park and carnival rides
H School stage and auditorium events
   Church interiors
I Car-traffic light patterns (give long exposures
      to bring out the patterns)
   Average home interiors at night
J Indoor and outdoor Christmas tree lights
K Aerial displays of fireworks
L Illuminated fountains
   Lightning
M Subjects lit by streetlights
   Subject 6 inches from a candle
N Floodlit buildings and monuments
O White lights on Niagara Falls
P Light-colored lights on Niagara Falls
   Subjects lit by bonfires
Q Subject 1 foot from a candle
   Dark-colored lights on Niagara Falls
R Floodlit dark factory buildings
U Subject 2 feet from candle
W Full-moonlit snowscapes
X Full-moonlit marines and distant landscapes
Y Full-moonlit landscapes at medium distances

In order to condense the information as much as possible the exposures in the following chart were calculated for only two aperture settings—f/2.8 and f/3.5—f/2.8 being a regular f-stop and f/3.5 a half stop located on the aperture scale of a camera between f/2.8 and f/4. Thus f/2.8 and f/3.5 are a half stop apart. You can make both settings with most lenses fast enough for night photography, and they are very frequently used. If you wish to convert exposure times for use with other f-numbers there are two simple charts that will help you do this. Though experienced photographers usually make such conversions in their heads, you may need a little help at this point in your career.

The ASA numbers on the preceding chart may be considered as either rated film speeds or as push speeds, depending on how you use them. For example, if you use the ASA 400 shutter speeds for Tri-X you would be shooting it at its rated speed (the one given it by the manufacturer). However, ASA 400 would be a push speed for a film rated at ASA 100. Similarly, ASA 800 would be a push speed for Tri-X.

Though a rated speed and a push speed aren't the same thing, we preface both speeds with the letters ASA. You set both types of speeds on your exposure meter as ASA speeds. Furthermore, you use a push speed *as if it actually were* a rated speed. For example, you can expose Tri-X at ASA 1600 even though it is actually rated at ASA 400.

This is quite confusing, to be sure, but you can figure it out if you stick to it. The jargon of photography is often incomprehensible at first, but you will gradually get used to it.

An old hotel in my home town of Conrad, Montana (population 2,000, more or less). I took an exposure reading from the wall under the sign, expecting the windows, street lamp, and sky to take care of themselves, which they did. I forget what the exposure was—photographers usually do forget.

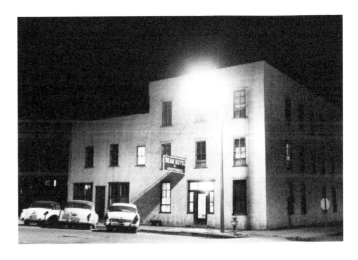

Available Light Exposure Chart

	ASA 100	ASA 200	ASA 400	ASA 800	ASA 1600	ASA 3200	f-number
A	1/125	1/250	1/500	1/1000	1/2000	1/4000	f/2.8
B	1/60	1/125	1/250	1/500	1/1000	1/2000	f/3.5
C	1/60	1/125	1/250	1/500	1/1000	1/2000	f/2.8
D	1/30	1/60	1/125	1/250	1/500	1/1000	f/3.5
E	1/30	1/60	1/125	1/250	1/500	1/1000	f/2.8
F	1/15	1/30	1/60	1/125	1/250	1/500	f/3.5
G	1/15	1/30	1/60	1/125	1/250	1/500	f/2.8
H	1/8	1/15	1/30	1/60	1/125	1/250	f/3.5
I	1/8	1/15	1/30	1/60	1/125	1/250	f/2.8
J	1/4	1/8	1/15	1/30	1/60	1/125	f/3.5
K	1/4	1/8	1/15	1/30	1/60	1/125	f/2.8
L	1/2	1/4	1/8	1/15	1/30	1/60	f/3.5
M	1/2	1/4	1/8	1/15	1/30	1/60	f/2.8
N	1 sec	1/2	1/4	1/8	1/15	1/30	f/3.5
O	1 sec	1/2	1/4	1/8	1/15	1/30	f/2.8
P	2	1 sec	1/2	1/4	1/8	1/15	f/3.5
Q	2	1 sec	1/2	1/4	1/8	1/15	f/2.8
R	4	2	1 sec	1/2	1/4	1/8	f/3.5
S	4	2	1 sec	1/2	1/4	1/8	f/2.8
T	8	4	2	1 sec	1/2	1/4	f/3.5
U	8	4	2	1 sec	1/2	1/4	f/2.8
V	16	8	4	2	1 sec	1/2	f/3.5
W	16	8	4	2	1 sec	1/2	f/2.8
X	32	16	8	4	2	1 sec	f/3.5
Y	32	16	8	4	2	1 sec	f/2.8

Chart for Finding Shutter Speeds (or Exposure Times) for Whole f-Stops Starting with the Charted Shutter Speeds for f/2.8

	Starting with the shutter speed (or exposure time) for f/2.8
f/1.4	2 shutter speeds (or exposure times) **faster**
f/2	1 shutter speed (or exposure time) **faster**
f/4	1 shutter speed (or exposure time) **slower**
f/5.6	2 shutter speeds (or exposure times) **slower**
f/8	3 shutter speeds (or exposure times) **slower**
f/11	4 shutter speeds (or exposure times) **slower**
f/16	5 shutter speeds (or exposure times) **slower**
f/22	6 shutter speeds (or exposure times) **slower**
f/32	7 shutter speeds (or exposure times) **slower**

Chart for Finding Shutter Speeds (or Exposure Times) for Half-Stops Starting with the Charted Shutter Speeds for the Half-Stop f/3.5

Set aperture at:	Starting with the shutter speed (or exposure time) for the half-stop f/3.5
f/1.4 ▼ f/2	2 shutter speeds (or exposure times) **faster**
f/2 ▼ f/2.8	1 shutter speed (or exposure time) **faster**
f/4 ▼ f/5.6	1 shutter speed (or exposure time) **slower**
f/5.6 ▼ f/8	2 shutter speeds (or exposure times) **slower**
f/8 ▼ f/11	3 shutter speeds (or exposure times) **slower**
f/11 ▼ f/16	4 shutter speeds (or exposure times) **slower**
f/16 ▼ f/22	5 shutter speeds (or exposure times) **slower**
f/22 ▼ f/32	6 shutter speeds (or exposure times) **slower**

Relationship of Film Speeds in Terms of f-Number Settings

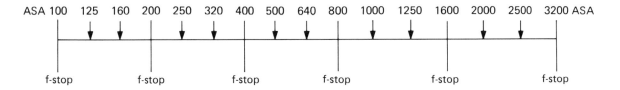

ASA 100   125   160   200   250   320   400   500   640   800   1000   1250   1600   2000   2500   3200 ASA

f-stop   f-stop   f-stop   f-stop   f-stop   f-stop

The vertical lines in the diagram above represent f-numbers spaced one stop apart. Immediately above them are the ASA speeds listed on the Available Light Exposure Chart. In between are other ASA speeds that are commonly given to films. If you are using a film with one of the in-between speeds you can safely use the shutter and aperture settings for the charted ASA speed that it is closest to. For example, if your film is rated at either ASA 160 or ASA 250 you can use the settings given for ASA 200. Since the listed exposures are only approximate anyway, the amount of error that will be introduced this way (about ⅓ stop) won't really matter. Furthermore, exposure bracketing will compensate for much larger errors and for the approximations in the Available Light Exposure Chart itself.

Because the information on the Available Light Exposure Chart has been highly condensed you will have to extrapolate (perform conversions) in order to get certain other information that hasn't been listed. This new information is implied by the list, but you have to know how to find it. To make your search easier, three supplementary charts have been provided. You might call them charts for interpreting a chart.

The chart above is to help you extrapolate for shutter speeds (or exposure times) for f-numbers other than f/2.8, which is one of the two f-numbers on the Available Light Chart. For example, you may have looked up a shutter speed for a certain available light category and ASA speed and found a shutter setting of 1/500 second for f/2.8. However, you wish to take your picture at f/5.6 instead. This means that you will have to use a *slower* shutter speed, because this smaller aperture won't let enough light through it in 1/500 second. The supplementary chart says to use a setting that is 2 speeds *slower,* which would be 1/125 second.

Perhaps it would be wise at this point to take a second look at the shutter speeds (or exposure times) for f/2.8 listed on the Available Light Exposure Chart. They range from 1/4000 second to 32 seconds. Starting with 1/4000 second the times for f/2.8 get progressively *slower* (or longer) by one-stop jumps (1/2000, 1/1000, 1/500, etc.). Working backward from 32 seconds we find the times getting progressively *faster* (or shorter) by one-stop jumps (16, 8, 4, 2, 1, 1/2, etc.).

When you are working with both fractions and whole numbers it is hard to keep track of which number is faster (or slower) than which. It will help if you use the shutter speeds marked on your camera or exposure meter as a guide.

The chart above has the same purpose as the chart preceding it, except that it is designed to help you make extrapolations from exposure times listed for f/3.5. For example, you may have looked up a shutter speed for a certain available light category and ASA speed and found 1/250

second for f/3.5. However, you wish to shoot at 1/500 second (one shutter speed *faster*). The above chart indicates that you should then open up the lens a little bit, setting it between f/2 and f/2.8. Getting the marker approximately in the middle is quite close enough.

Though it is unhandy to have to extrapolate from both f/2.8 (a whole stop) and f/3.5 (a half stop), there is a reason for this. The classical exposure categories are spaced exactly one-half stop apart. If this difference were to be expressed in terms of shutter speeds we would have numbers

Actor Bernard Kilby was sitting in a dark stairwell in the wings, waiting to go onstage. I already knew the exposure for this spot (about 1/8 at f/2.8 with Tri-X rated at ASA 400), having taken a white card reading earlier.

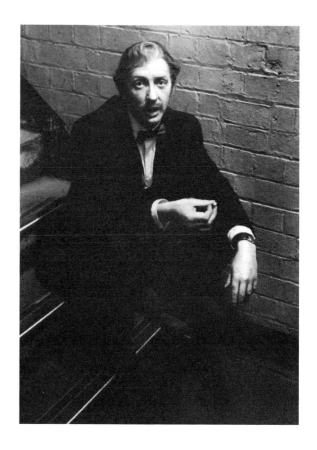

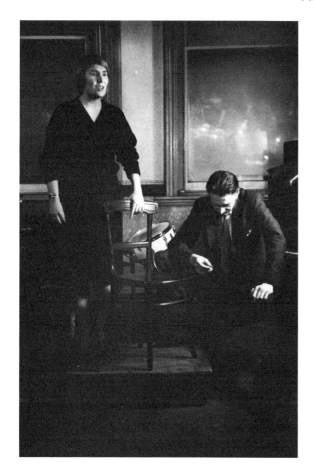

The performance area for these folk singers was so dark that I couldn't get a good reading with my meter (a Weston Master II), so I guessed 1/2 second at f/2 and lucked into a well-exposed negative. Guesswork can be an important part of available light photography after dark. Also luck.

such as 1/185, 1/375, and 1/750. They would represent "half-speed" shutter settings that cameras just don't have, though they could have if we really wanted them to.

The alternative adopted long ago in photography is to express a one-half stop difference by means of unmarked aperture settings located between whole f-numbers. Though we can attach numbers to these intermediate settings, it is easier

not to. However, it is wise to remember 3 half stops that are often marked on lens barrels— f/3.5 (about halfway between f/2.8 and f/4), f/4.5 (about halfway between f/4 and f/5.6), and f/6.3 (about halfway between f/5.6 and f/8). It would be less confusing if manufacturers didn't print half stops on cameras (to indicate the speed of a lens, or its maximum aperture), but we are stuck with what they sell us.

• Figure Things Out in Advance

Though the arithmetic involved in the preceding section is very simple (mainly multiplying and dividing whole numbers and fractions by 2), it gets people all mixed up anyway. Therefore, it is wise to work out all your exposures before you go out to photograph—assuming that you already know where you wish to make your pictures. Then write your data in a little notebook, all ready to use. If you try to figure everything out while you are actually shooting there is a good chance you will never know which way is up.

• The Kodak Exposure Dial

It would help you understand photography better if you were to thoroughly sort yourself out with respect to the Available Light Exposure Chart and the three supplementary charts which can help you use it properly. But such an understanding can come only in due time. In the meantime you may prefer to get your data from an exposure dial such as the one in the *Kodak Professional Photoguide,* which is available in most camera stores. Since a tremendous amount of information can be condensed into a dial (a very simple type of computer), you will find a lot of things you need to know in a very accessible form. In short, the dial is easy to use and informative.

If you can stand to use charts and dials, you will find all kinds esoteric and interesting information in this splendid little book—things you will need to know tomorrow and others that you will never use in a million years. But they are all nice to know about. When it comes to accumulating and compressing information about photography the Kodak writers are the very best.

● Using an Exposure Meter

For accurate metering you usually need to know just one general rule: read the thing you wish to photograph—not something else too. Not the background behind it or the foreground in front. And most certainly not a light source. In many cases you will have to walk right up to a subject —with your built-in or separate meter—in order to read only what you intend to photograph and not everything else in town. But you can then back up again and shoot your picture.

● Substitute Readings

You can't always walk right up to a subject, for it may be across the river, on a theater stage, or on the other side of a fence. Then you should use a substitute reading, which is simple enough to do. This is easiest when the same amount of light is falling upon your subject as upon yourself. Then

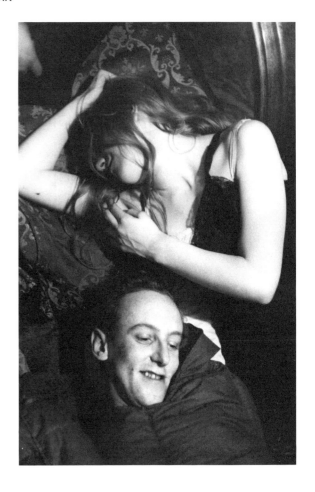

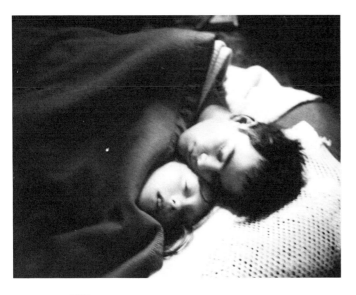

Anita sound asleep and Bartle bright and perky in his sleeping bag—another dim light exposure situation (about 1/8 at f/2.8). With practice you can learn to hold a camera steady with such slow shutter speeds. It mainly involves careful breath control.

Anita and Chris illuminated by a little light gently filtering in from the adjoining room—a very dark exposure situation. Lucky guesswork gave me 1/2 second at f/2, which turned out to be a good exposure. Don't be afraid to guess—you'll be right more often than not.

Actor Ian Richardson working on one of his musical compositions. Though it looks rather dark there was actually quite a bit of light here. I took a reading from Ian's face and exposed at 1/15 at f/4.

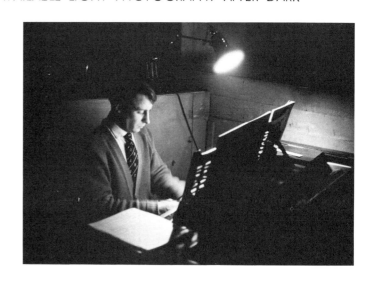

Loving partners at a dance—I had never seen them before, but they wanted me to take their picture. I took a substitute reading of my hand (so as not to poke a meter in their faces) and photographed them at 1/8 at f/2.8. The negative was very thin, but I printed for the darks and used ferricyanide bleach to get the highlights light enough—a standard trick for use with thin negatives.

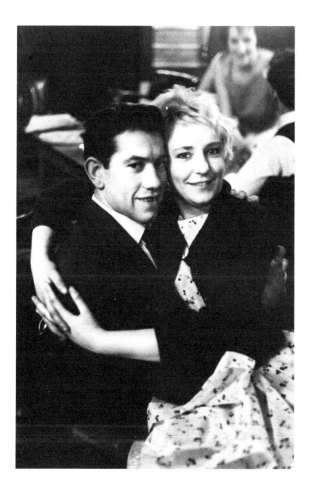

you find a convenient substitute for this subject (something that reflects the same amount of light), read the substitute, and make your picture.

For example, you may wish to shoot a telephoto picture of a person standing under a streetlight across the road from you, using a lens that is not coupled with your built-in meter. Walk to a streetlight on your own side and take a reading from the palm of your hand as a substitute for your subject's face. This will give you the correct exposure for both your hand and your subject, for they have the same degree of reflectivity and are positioned equidistant from nearly identical lights. Then set your camera, walk back to where you were, and shoot your picture. As long as they are of the same type it doesn't matter how far apart the lights are; they could even be in opposite sides of town.

If you and a subject aren't getting the same amount of light you can still take a substitute reading, but you should do it by sighting. Hold your palm in front of you as if it were a rifle sight aimed at your subject—your hand should overlap part of it. If you then close one eye you should easily be able to see which is darker, your subject or your own skin. Tilt your palm backward or

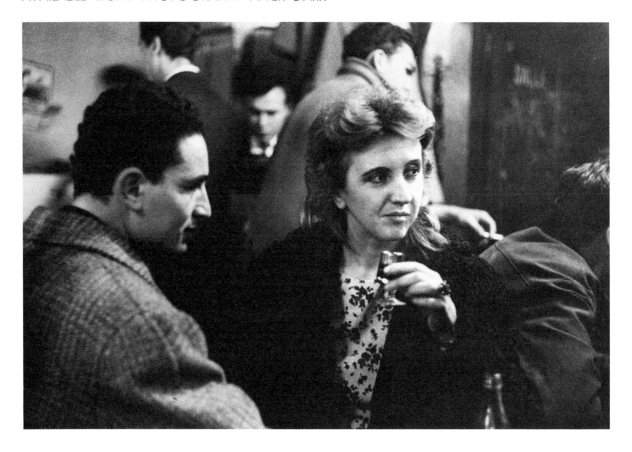

forward (which will change its tone) until your hand and your subject are matched in tone. Then take a reading from your hand, set your camera, and shoot your picture. The principle is that things reflecting the same amount of light generally require the same amount of exposure; when they are matched in tone this condition prevails.

If there is quite a bit more light falling upon a subject than upon yourself, there may be no way of tilting your palm far enough to make it light enough for a match. In this case do your sighting over (and take your reading from) an 8×10-inch sheet of white cardboard. Like your hand, the cardboard will also change tone when you tilt it. When you get the tonal match, take your reading, set your camera, and shoot. If the white cardboard is still not light enough to match your subject you may have to brighten it up a little with a penlight, which you should carry with you anyway when working at night. Don't worry about

404

People in an after-hours bistro in Paris. Sitting at my own table, I took white card readings (by sighting: see text), so that I knew the exposure for most of the people in the room without having to walk up to them. About 1/8 second at f/2.8. Now, f/2.8 is my favorite aperture setting for dim light photography. When you can stop down that far (which isn't very far) you are usually safe as far as depth of field (sharpness) is concerned.

Even with as much exposure as 1/4 second at f/4 I got a very thin negative, so I exposed the print to make the darks look good and used ferricyanide bleach to get the light areas light enough. In effect this technique adds the contrast that is missing in a thin negative.

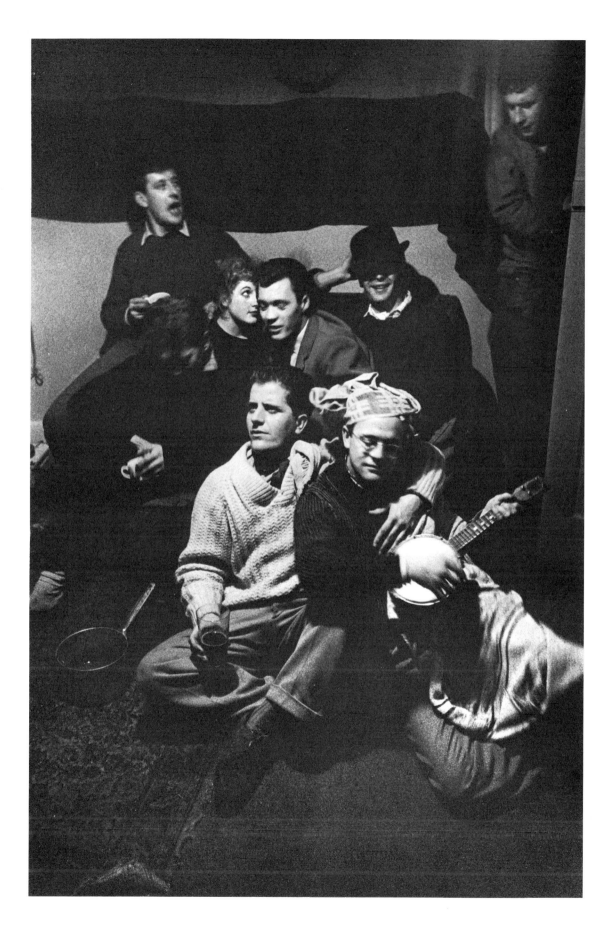

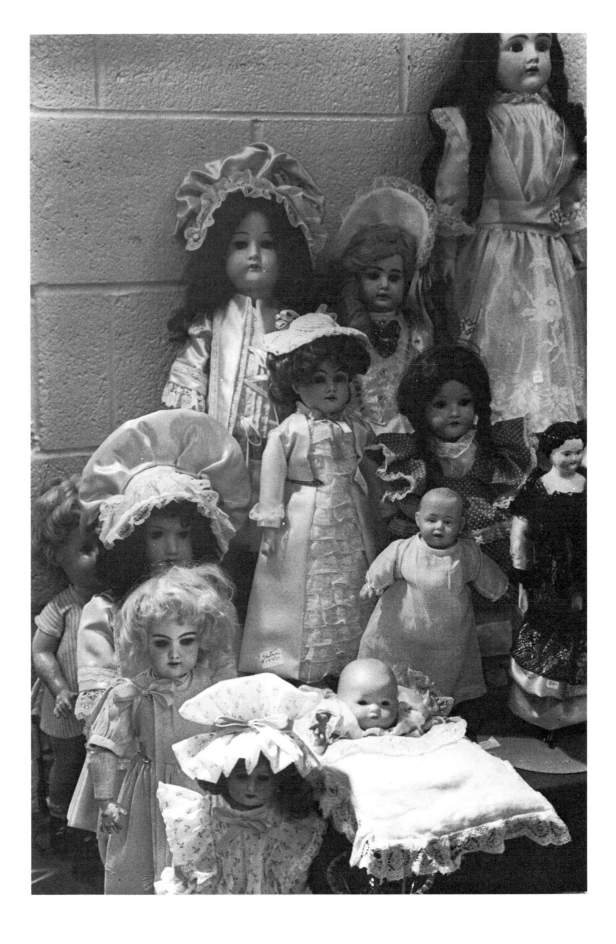

introducing an extra light source. The only thing that matters is that the cardboard (or your palm) be a tonal match for your subject. How you make the match doesn't really matter at all.

• The Commonest Nighttime Metering Errors

Because light may be very dim at night, people tend to point their meters or cameras (with built-ins) at whatever will give them the highest readings, for example white things (walls, tablecloths, shiny floors, rugs, etc.) or even light sources. Though it may give you comfort and pleasure to see your meter needle move in a positive way, this approach nearly always leads to serious underexposure. So read your subject as a whole. If you have to choose a *part* of a subject to read, pick one that is *average* in tone—not brighter than everything else.

Another serious error is in reading a subject that is surrounded by very dark tones at too great a distance. Since your meter will then read both the subject and the background it will be strongly influenced by the dark tones and tell you that there is very little light available for your picture. Thus you will compensate by overexposing heavily. So walk right up to subjects or use substitute readings.

An error of a similar type is to be at too great a distance when reading a subject surrounded by very light tones. This leads to underexposure, sometimes very serious. Though you can safely make direct readings at a distance with so-called spot meters, you probably don't have one. In such a meter the acceptance angle may be as small as two degrees, so you could reasonably call it a telephoto exposure meter.

At an indoor antique show, an exposure problem easily solved with an incident light reading with a Gossen Luna-Pro (1/30 at f/3.5).

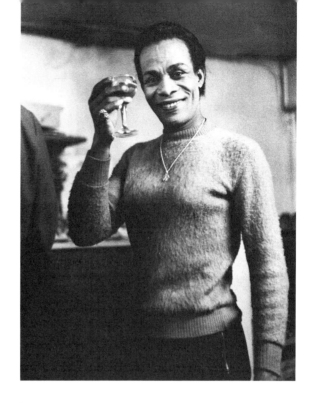

Having made substitute readings for the entire bistro, I knew the exposure for this friendly fellow without having to walk up to him. By pointing at my camera I signaled my request to photograph him. He responded with a toast and a smile.

This lady is friendly and seems determined to flirt with me. The ballroom was so dark that I could hardly see, so I was using exposure times from 1/2 to 1/8 second (at f/2). A couple of pints of goodly English beer helped steady my hand for such slow speeds.

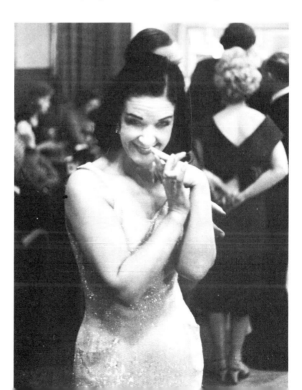

● Meter Stretching: the White Card Method

Because many meters—built-in or separate—aren't very sensitive they register poorly or not at all in dim light. In many cases you can get around the problem by using the so-called white card method in which a piece of white cardboard (for example, the reverse side of a Kodak Gray Card) is used as a substitute for the average tone of a subject (see page 29). Since it is white it will reflect quite a bit more light than the subject itself, perhaps enough to register on an insensitive meter. However, it can only represent the average tone of your subject in an indirect way.

Now, if you hold the gray side of a Kodak Gray Card (see page 28) in front of a subject so that the same amount of light falls on both card and subject, the gray will actually represent the average tone of the subject very well. Thus you can take a reading from the gray and get a very accurate exposure for your subject. Indeed, this is a classical way of determining exposure and the reason for the existence of Kodak Gray Cards.

Obviously, a white card won't represent this average tone very well at all—it is much too light—unless we throw in some kind of a metering factor, which happens to be 5. The factor of 5 is derived from the fact that a white card reflects 5 times as much light as the average tone of the average subject (most things happen to fit well in the average subject category).

When you decide to use a white card you must compensate for the fact that it isn't very average in tone. Do this by dividing the ASA speed of your film by 5 to get its "white card speed" and set this new speed on your meter. The factor is now included so that a white card reading will represent the average tone of your subject on your meter, provided that you hold up the card in the correct way.

The card should be held in the same plane as your subject. For example, if you are photographing a standing woman it should be held vertical to the floor, which will make its surface par-

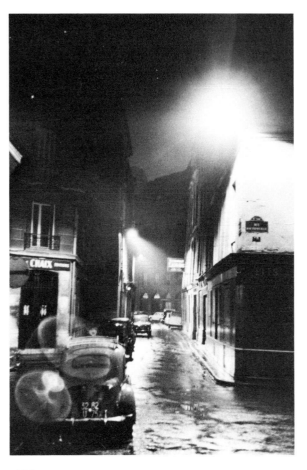

A back street in Paris well after midnight. Since the streetlights were very dim and the street itself darkened by rain I couldn't get a good reading with my old Weston Master II meter, so I guessed 1/4 at f/2 and came out on top. If you have a tripod (which I didn't) this is a kind of situation in which exposure bracketing is advisable.

allel to her. And the card should be held up in light of the same intensity as that falling upon the woman. Usually, the card should be almost touching her, but if the area is very evenly lit you can get a good reading when five or ten feet away from her. Distance doesn't matter at all as long as your subject and card are receiving light of the same intensity.

Let us go back to the factor and see how it would work with a specific film, say Tri-X (ASA 400). Dividing the speed by 5 gives you 80, which you set on your meter. Then read the white card, set your camera, and take your picture. Once the factor has been set into the metering system you no longer have to think about it.

Do not confuse the white card method with the sighting method mentioned in a previous section. When using a white card for the latter technique you don't divide the film speed by 5. Then the card actually represents directly the average tone of a subject, because you tilt it until there is a tonal match. However, when you use the white card method (this is its traditional name) the card will look considerably lighter, so a conversion factor is required. If it doesn't look lighter you are either reading a white subject or doing the reading incorrectly.

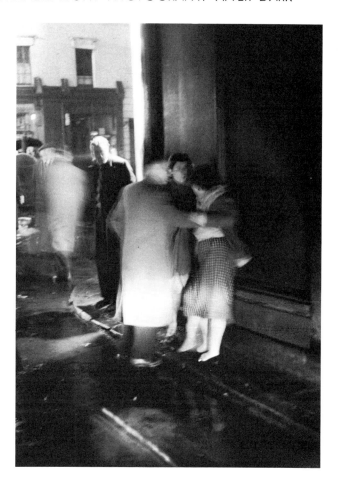

Coming out of my pub I could hear a fight nearby rather than see it clearly. Not wanting to get my ears beat off in a fight among strangers, I ventured a hand-held shot from where I was standing—1 second at f/2 (the maximum speed of my lens). When I saw the print later I discovered that it had been a drunken man giving two equally plastered women a hard time. The point is that you can get pictures even if you can barely see.

● Film and Developer Combinations for Film Speed Pushing

In the chapter on sports photography you read that film pushing should only be considered as an emergency measure because it generally leads to image degradation, especially with contrasty subjects. But when the emergency arises it may be the only way of getting your pictures, especially at night.

It was also suggested that you stick to just two developers for speed pushing black-and-white films—D-76 (diluted 1:1) and Acufine. Though this recommendation still holds, you may wish to know about other popular developers and the speeds they are said to be capable of producing with various fast black-and-white films. There is

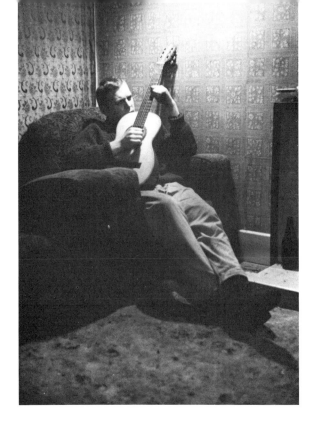

Though the party was going strong he was sitting in a corner by himself in light so dim I could hardly see him, but I got his picture anyway. Dim light need not impede your photography, especially if you do exposure bracketing or use a supersensitive light meter such as the Gossen Luna-Pro.

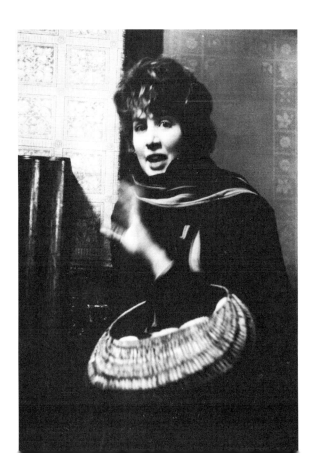

also more information on push speeds for color films.

In the following material I included wherever feasible the developer dilutions, temperatures, and developing times. However, there are cases in which it would be better for you to get your data from the information sheets that come with the developers listed, usually because the processing instructions are lengthy. In a few instances the data simply wasn't available to me, but you can work them out for yourself by running tests (see the chapter on sports photography, p. 117).

Fuji Neopan SSS (rated at ASA 200)
Ethol T.E.C. (1:15)—ASA 800—21 minutes at 70F
Ethol UFG—ASA 640—7 minutes at 70F
Ethol Blue (1:30)—ASA 1000—7½ minutes at 70F

GAF 500 (rated at ASA 500)
Acufine—ASA 1000—7¾ minutes at 68F
Diafine (two-bath)—ASA 1000
Edwal FG7 (two-bath)—ASA 1000
Ethol UFG—ASA 1000—4¼ minutes at 70F
Ethol Blue (1:30)—ASA 800—7 minutes at 70F
H & W Maximal Developer—ASA 1000—8 minutes at 68F

Ilford HP-4 (rated at ASA 400)
Microphen—ASA 650—5 minutes at 68F
Acufine—ASA 1600—8¾ minutes at 68F
Edwal FG7 (1:15)—ASA 2400
Ethol T.E.C. (two-bath)—ASA 1000—5 minutes in Solution A, 4 minutes in Solution B at 75F

Even in the dim light I could see that she was pretty, so I snapped a slow shot of her. How slow is indicated by the blur of her hand as she waves hello to her friends, who also happened to be my friends.

Ethol UFG—ASA 800—5¼ minutes at 70F

Ethol Blue (1:30)—ASA 1200—8 minutes at 70F

H & W Maximal Developer—ASA 1250—8 minutes at 68F

Ilford HP-5 (rated at ASA 400)

Microphen—ASA 3200—18 minutes at 68F, 12 minutes at 75F; ASA 1600—12 minutes at 68F; ASA 800—8 minutes at 68F

D76 (full strength)—ASA 1600—15 minutes at 75F; ASA 800—11½ minutes at 68F

Kodak Royal-X Pan—roll film, cut film, and film packs—(ASA 1250) DK-50—ASA 5000 (?)

Kodak Tri-X (rated at ASA 400)

D-76 (1:1)—ASA 800

Acufine—ASA 1200 and higher—5¼ minutes at 68F

Diafine—ASA 2400

Rodinal (1:50)—ASA 6400—22½ minutes at 68F

Edwal FG7 (two-bath)—ASA 3200

Ethol T.E.C. (two-bath)—ASA 1000—4 minutes in Solution A, 3 minutes in Solution B at 75F

Ethol UFG—ASA 4000—9½ minutes at 70F

Ethol Blue (1:30)—ASA 2000—6¾ minutes at 70F

Ethol 90 (1:10)—ASA 2000—9 minutes at 70F

H & W Maximal Developer—ASA 1250—8 minutes at 68F

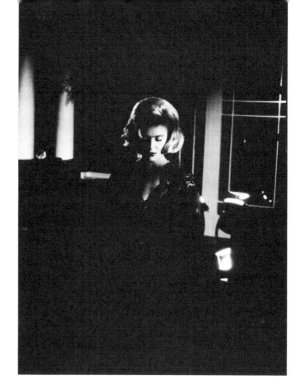

With strong spotlights there was enough light for an exposure of 1/30 at f/5.6 on this movie set. Shirley Eaton running through her lines before the cameras started to roll. In a lighting like this, read the highlights on the face and double the exposure you get. Equally good, take an incident light reading with the meter aimed halfway between the light source and where your camera will be positioned.

At the Beaux Arts Ball in Birmingham, England—the floor covered with broken bottles and everyone whooping it up. Anne kicked off her shoes and did a wild barefoot dance in the glass, sustaining not a scratch. In the dim light I had to use a very slow shutter speed (1/4 or 1/8 probably), giving us this blurred movement.

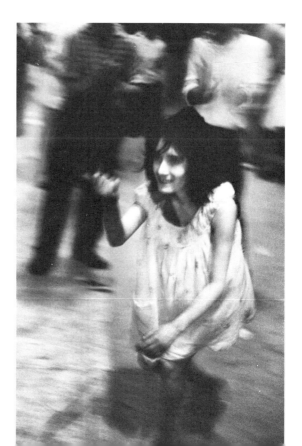

Kodak 2475 Recording Film (rated at ASA 1000)

DK-50—ASA 3200—8 minutes at 68F

Acufine—ASA 3200—7¾ minutes at 68F

Ethol T.E.C. (two-bath)—ASA 5000—7 minutes in Solution A, 6 minutes in Solution B at 75F

Ethol UFG—ASA 6000—16½ minutes at 70F

Ethol Blue (1:30)—ASA 2000—10 minutes at 70F

Polaroid Type 107 (rated at ASA 3000)

Polaroid Type 57 (rated at ASA 3000)

Color films

Fuji Fujicolor F-II (rated at ASA 400)

Kodak C-41 chemicals—ASA 1600

Fuji CN-16 chemicals—ASA 1600

Kodak High Speed Ektachrome, tungsten (rated at ASA 125)

Kodak E-4 chemicals—ASA 500

Unichrome chemicals—ASA 640

Kodak Ektachrome 160 Professional, tungsten (rated at ASA 160)

Kodak E-6 chemicals—ASA 640

Kodak Ektachrome 200 Professional, daylight (rated at ASA 200)

Kodak E-6 chemicals—ASA 800

At this writing I don't have push data for Kodacolor 400, though it will surely push as far as Fujicolor F-II and possibly even further.

The preceding material is designed to tell you how far you can push films and still get printable negatives and acceptable color transparencies. However, manufacturers vary considerably in what they see as printable or acceptable. And your methods of taking exposure readings may be quite unlike theirs. You should therefore run a test on any film and developer combination that you wish to use (see the chapter on sports photography, p. 117).

By now you should have seen that the main problem in available light photography at night is to get the correct exposures for various lighting situations. Though this chapter may puzzle you in places, you should stick with it until you have everything figured out. Thereafter, photography at night shouldn't give you much difficulty.

PAINTING WITH LIGHT

We think that we see *things,* but we don't. Our eyes can see only *light*—light that is reflected, transmitted, or emitted by things. Thus to see a thing means only that we are aware of the light coming from it; beyond that we have no visual contact whatever with it. Take the sun, for example—except for its light we wouldn't even know of its existence.

Photography is the art of using light to form images and applying chemistry to make them permanent. No light—no pictures. But we take such things for granted and do not think about light very much. We easily forget that photography as such is based entirely on the magical things that light can do. Not what *we* can do—what *light* can do. However, to be a photographer who is not acutely aware of light is like being a symphony conductor who has never heard a musical instrument. Such a thing is possible, no doubt, but who would do it by choice?

The chances are that you are *not* acutely aware of light at this point. If you are only concerned with having enough of it to correctly expose your film you have hardly started on the long and glorious path to photographic excellence. You must learn to *see* light, and then you will really be getting somewhere. Fortunately, there are things you can do that will give you a lot of help. For example, you ought to work with an interesting technique called painting with light, in which you use a light source as if it were a paint brush.

Though light sources of almost any size can be used for painting, it is advisable (and a lot of fun) to start with flashlights. Small as they are, they are extremely effective and, of course, very inexpensive compared with other photographic light sources. You can make very fine pictures with them. Most important, they make you very much aware of light when you are using them.

● The Gist of It

The idea of painting with light is very simple, though it hasn't even occurred to most people. You simply set your camera on a tripod in front of something you wish to photograph, then turn off the room lights so that everything is pitch black. Next, you open the camera shutter and keep it open, using the "B" setting. When the room is coal black you can leave it open for hours and nothing will happen to your film. Finally, you switch on a flashlight and start moving the light pattern over some of the things that are in front of your camera. When you are finished you close the shutter and turn on the room lights again. That's all there is to it—you have shot your picture.

If you like you can do the same kind of thing outdoors at night. Using larger light sources you can paint large buildings, streets, and so on.

● Darkness and Light

When you use a flashlight in a darkened room only a part of the room is illuminated, especially if you hold the light close to your photographic subject. When thus surrounded by darkness the light pattern stands out clearly as light and nothing else, which makes it easier for you to be aware of light as such. In comparison, it is difficult to be even vaguely aware of light *as light* in a fully illuminated room. We are so used to this condition that we no longer know how to pay any attention to it.

The flashlight is a miniature spotlight, and the nature of spotlights is to draw attention to light as such. Though this is mainly due to the surrounding darkness, another important factor is that we are unaccustomed to spotlighting in everyday life. Thus its unusual quality helps awaken our sleeping eyes.

Considering our terrible dependence on light, it may seem strange to be told that you hardly see it at all. In the sense that seeing involves awareness, this is true nevertheless. Thus you should consider the technique of working simultaneously with darkness and light as a golden opportunity to awaken yourself. Furthermore, you should look at the simple flashlight as a very effective piece of photographic lighting equipment.

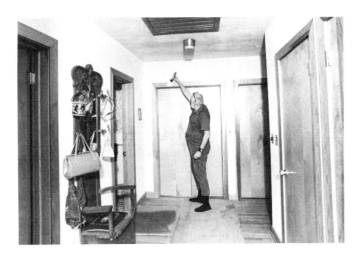

In the picture on the left we see how one does painting with light with a hooded flashlight, though it is done in a room that is entirely blacked out. Below the caption we see the results of the technique, a rather eery picture like an illustration for a Gothic novel. It certainly doesn't look like the hallway illuminated in the usual way.

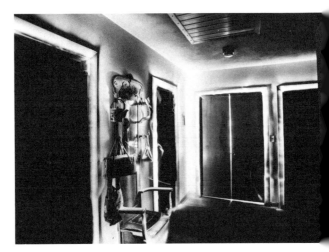

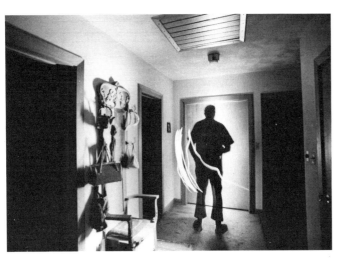

I just stood still and splashed the light around (from a flashlight) for ten or fifteen seconds. The camera (with a 19mm lens) was on a tripod with the shutter held open by my homemade remote shutter tripping device. Except for the flashlight, the hallway was entirely blacked out.

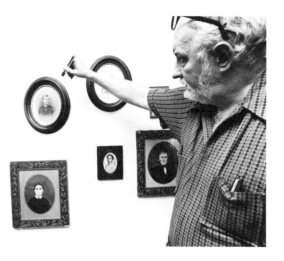

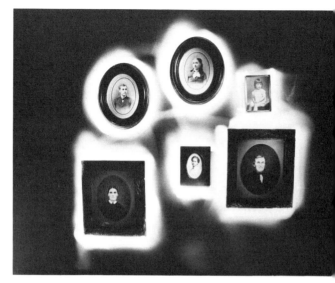

Above we see a hooded penlight held in the position in which it will be used for painting with light. Both the penlight and I will be within camera range, but it won't matter. The hood will prevent the flashlight from being visible to the camera, and so little light will reflect on me that I too will be invisible. On the right is the picture made by painting. Each picture was traced around with the penlight, then given a burst of light in the middle.

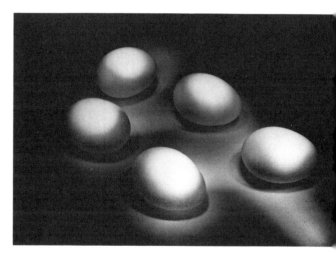

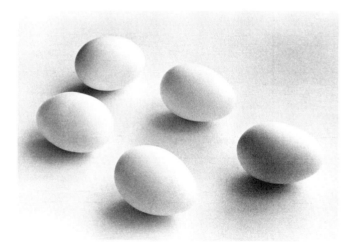

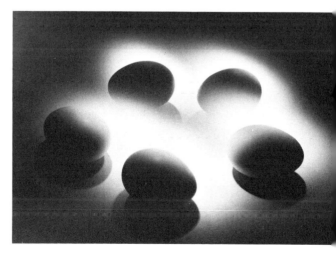

White eggs on a white mount board and two pictures made by painting with light, showing how much both the eggs and the mount board are changed with this technique. With ordinary photographic light sources there is no way of getting these effects.

● Holding the Shutter Open

For painting with light your camera must have a provision for holding the shutter open—either a "T" (time exposure) or a "B" (bulb) setting. The setting most frequently found on cameras nowadays is "B," so we will deal with that (there is no problem with a "T" setting anyway). With the camera set on "B," depressing the shutter release with a finger or cable release opens the shutter, which stays open until the shutter is released. Though you can use one hand to keep the shutter open and do your lighting with the other, this ties you to your camera, which can be very inconvenient. It is desirable to have some kind of a device that will hold the shutter open while you rove freely around the room doing your painting.

Such a device, powered by small rubber bands, is illustrated in the chapter on self-portraits, p. 89. Though originally designed as a remote release for making self-portraits, it works equally well for holding the shutter open when it is set on "B." It stays open until you lift up the top section of the release device. Since for painting with light you both open and close the shutter in absolute darkness, you don't really need a gadget this sophisticated. With masking tape, a couple of short sticks, and rubber bands you should be able to rig up something—a simple gadget to hold down the shutter release button. You could probably even use a small C-clamp or its equivalent.

Fortunately, there is still an easier and cheaper way to keep the shutter open when the "B" setting is used. Buy the kind of cable release that has a little lock-screw on it—it costs as little as two dollars. Then you depress the plunger, activate the screw, and the shutter stays open until you loosen the screw again. It's dead easy.

● Selecting Your Flashlights and Batteries

Though you can get by with a single flashlight it is much better to have three sizes—one with two D batteries, one with two AA batteries, and a light with *one* AA battery. The flashlights must be especially prepared for use (next section).

The large flashlight (two D cells) is used for large subjects—a whole room, for example. The smaller lights are good for such things as still life setups, creative print copying, and portraiture.

Oddly, the biggest problem is in having too much light to work with, which is why a light with just one AA cell is recommended. The thing is that you have to have at least a second or two of painting time (which you can count under your breath) in order to be able to control your exposures. Since your light may be within an inch or two of (or even touching) your subject, it may be just too bright.

If you have a lens that will stop down to f/32 or smaller, this will help a lot, but most cameras stop down only to f/16. Thus it is fortunate in a way that flashlight cells fade so fast—with a few partly shot batteries on hand you can get light dim enough for almost any purpose. Though you can accomplish much the same thing by using a fairly slow film such as Plus-X Pan or Verichrome Pan (both ASA 125), it would be better to stick with a fast film such as Tri-X (ASA 400). You see, you may wish to make certain pictures in which your lights are at a considerable distance from your subjects.

In addition to faded batteries you should surely have fresh ones, the so-called alkaline energy cells being the best. Though they cost a lot more than regular cells they also last a lot longer. Thus their rate of fading, which can constitute an exposure problem, is held back quite a bit.

● Preparing Your Flashlights

Unfortunately, flashlights project very irregular lighting patterns that have to be smoothed up by diffusion, which is easy enough to do. Though diffusion reduces the light intensity by about 2 stops, we have seen this doesn't matter—we have more of a problem with too much light than with too little of it.

The easiest way to diffuse a flashlight is to tape strips of Scotch Magic Transparent Tape over the end of it—one layer is enough. This brand of tape is made with a matte acetate base (so you can write on it), which diffuses light extremely well. The light pattern that results is very smooth and even.

Now, flashlight heads often bulge out, so that they give off light sideways as well as forwards. The result is that when you are painting with the light source within the picture area (say, with your hand right in front of the camera) the sideways light will reach the film, making dark spots and streaks. Since it is often desirable to use a flashlight within the picture area, the sideways light should be eliminated. Do this by taping a cylinder of black paper around the head of the light, allowing it to protrude about ½ inch. However, you should diffuse the light first. A flashlight thus shielded won't make light streaks if it is held sideways to your camera or pointed slightly away from it when it is within camera range.

● Making Exposure Readings

Painting with light poses certain exposure problems, one of them due to the fact that flashlight batteries—large or small, regular or alkaline—start to fade rapidly as soon as you begin using them. However, once you know this happens it doesn't have to be a problem at all; all you have to do is take a fresh light reading just before making each picture. In contrast, if you use the same reading for, say, six shots you will probably underexpose the last of them, perhaps badly.

A reading should be made in a fully blacked-out room, with only the flashlight turned on. The easiest way is to take an incident light reading, though it requires that you have a separate meter with an incident light sphere or attachment, for example a Luna-Pro, Metrastar, or Sekonic L-218 Apex CDS. You hold the light source at the same distance from the meter as it will be from your photographic subject, aiming the

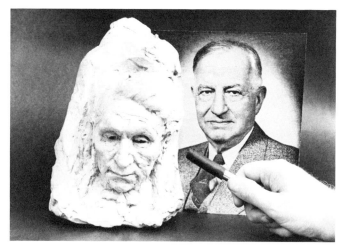

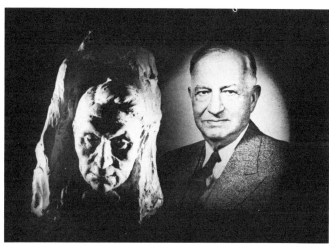

My father Judge Hattersley and his favorite piece of sculpture. On the top we see my hand and hooded penlight in the positions they will occupy during one of the several required exposures. As you see, they are well within the picture area. On the bottom is the picture made with the painting technique. Note how different the portrait and the sculpture look.

brightest part of the diffused light pattern right at the incident sphere. The reading will give you the exposure you should use with the light held at this distance from the subject—if you intend to hold the flashlight stationary or move it around in tight circles.

However, if you intend to move the light pattern through a considerable distance you must increase the total exposure time so that each illuminated part of your subject receives the required exposure. It is usually safe to simply guess the necessary extra time, especially when you use exposure bracketing.

Built-in meters pose a slightly more difficult problem, because they usually aren't very sensitive to light, and the technique to compensate for this is quite awkward, though effective. With a relatively weak light source such as a flashlight, you can increase the effective sensitivity of such a meter by taking white card readings (see the chapter on p. 155). Though people don't usually take white (or gray) card readings with built-ins, it is only because they don't know about this re-

markably accurate way of determining exposures. A little awkward but very good.

Remember to divide the film speed by 5 and to set the resulting "white card speed" on your camera. For example, ASA 400 would be converted to 80, which is the number you use. Now, open the lens all the way, say to f/2. Since you will be reading light of rather low intensity you want as much of it as possible to get into your camera from the white card. Hold the flashlight in your left hand, the camera in both hands (see illustration), and take a reading from the card. The flashlight should be the same distance from the card as it will be from your photographic subject.

Unless your camera has automatic exposure controls that cannot be operated manually, it

Indicated and adjusted exposure times at f/16 for Tri-X (ASA 400) with three different types of flashlights at various distances						
Light-to-subject distances		3 in	6 in	1 foot	2 feet	4 feet
flashlight with 1 AA cell	indicated exposure times	1 sec	4 sec	9 sec	1 min	4 min
	adjusted exposure times	2 sec	10 sec	32 sec		
flashlight with 2 AA cells	indicated exposure times	1 sec	1 sec	5 sec	12 sec	1 min
	adjusted exposure times	2 sec	2 sec	13 sec	25 sec	
flashlight with 2 D cells	indicated exposure times	1/15 s	1/4 s	1/2 s	2 sec	7 sec
	adjusted exposure times	1/15 s	1/4 s	1/2 s	5 sec	20 sec

probably has a "match-needle" system. That is, when the meter needle intersects a certain mark or indicator your camera is then set for the correct exposure. You get the needle to move into the correct position by experimentally setting your camera on various shutter speeds, until one of them does the job. Start with the slowest speed and work your way up.

In this manner you will get the correct exposure but not the exposure time and f-number that you will actually use. The time (shutter speed) that you get directly by reading is too short for any painting with light, so you have to convert it. That is, you have to find a much longer time (and a much smaller aperture) that will still give you the correct exposure.

We will see how this worked with an actual reading made with a built-in in a Nikkormat loaded with Tri-X (ASA 400), with 80 set on the camera as the white card speed, with the aperture set at f/2. The flashlight had two brand-new Ray-O-Vac AA Alkaline Energy Cells. It was positioned 6 inches from the white card. The correct exposure for this light when used for painting at this distance came out to be 1/60 second at f/2, which of course wouldn't give us sufficient time for painting. However, we can get an exposure time of 1 second (and still the *correct* exposure) by stopping down to f/16. Due to the reciprocity effect (which we will get to in a moment) we would actually use 2 seconds, which is even better.

I hope you have read my other books in this Doubleday series for beginners in photography, so that I don't actually have to tell you how I moved from 1/60 second at f/2 to 1 second at f/16 without changing the correct exposure. But maybe you haven't read the books and are more of a beginner than I have assumed. So I'll explain. The commonly encountered f-numbers are 1.4, 2, 2.8, 4, 5.6, 8, 11, 16, 22, 32, 45, 64, and 90, though most cameras leave off at f/16. Each number represents an area of the adjustable hole made by the iris diaphragm mechanism (aperture). The largest hole (called both the maximum

aperture and the lens speed) is on the left (above) and the smallest hole on the right. As we move from left to right the areas are progressively cut in half with each jump. Conversely, as we move toward the left they are progressively doubled.

Thus stopping down means to progressively halve the size of the hole that light must pass through in order to reach the film. However, if we double the exposure time at each step the total amount of light that gets through (the exposure) will remain the same. Let us return to the f/2 from which I started my Machiavellian maneuvers. Moving from f/2 to f/16 the area of the aperture is halved 6 times. To compensate for this I merely doubled the original exposure time (1/60 second) 6 times, ending up with 1 second. If you have trouble halving or doubling fractions, look at your camera or exposure meter, where the numbers are all printed in the correct order.

The foregoing paragraphs are not as much a detour as they may seem. Whatever your level of advancement in photography, it is time for you to memorize the common apertures (given above) and the common shutter speeds, which are 1, 1/2, 1/4, 1/8, 1/15, 1/30, 1/60, 1/125, 1/500, and 1/1000 seconds. Write all these numbers down and carry them in your wallet or purse. Unless you can learn to easily perform the kind of conversion just demonstrated you will be unduly restricted in your photography. If necessary, figure out conversions with pencil and paper.

To return to white card readings made with built-in meters. They are excellent for increasing the effective sensitivity of meters that register poorly or not at all in rather dim light, though sometimes even a white card won't help. It is easy to take a reading if the illumination is even, but the light pattern from a flashlight is bright in the middle and dim on the outside. The thing to do is move the light around to get the highest reading you can at whatever distance you have chosen. Remember that the light-to-card distance and the light-to-subject distance should be the same.

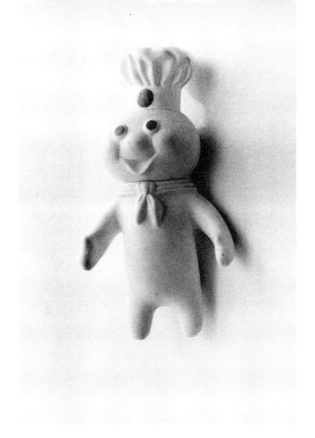

A white doll on a white background illuminated by
room light and the same setup lit by a moving hooded
penlight in a darkened room. We can see that the
second picture is very much more dramatic.

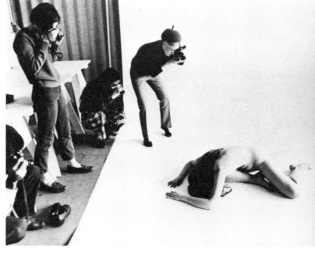

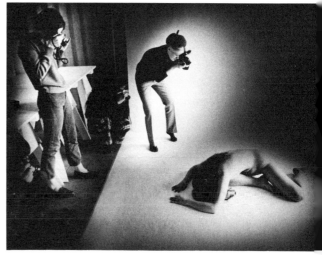

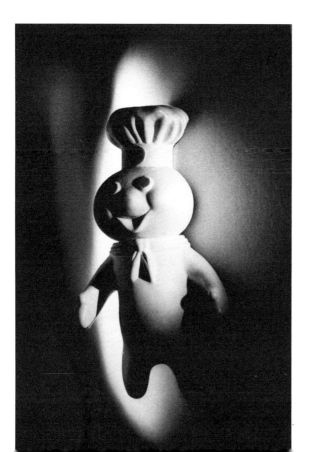

A straight copy print of a picture of some of my
students at The School of Visual Arts and a copy print
made from a copy negative made with three separate
exposures with a hooded flashlight. In the second print
we get the effect of spotlights, though they were
obviously not used for the original picture.

A hand photographed by painting with light.

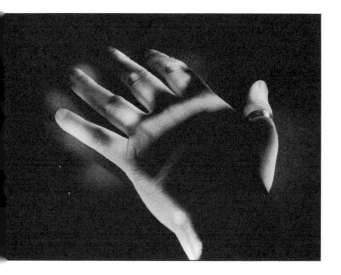

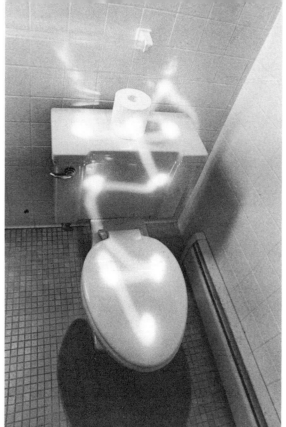

Two versions of a magical john lit with a flashlight. In one the room light was turned on for 1 second, the other being done in total darkness except for the flashlight.

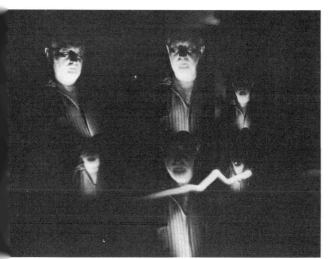

I took various positions in a darkened hallway, shining the light on my own face at each one. The camera was on a tripod, of course, the shutter remaining open for the whole sequence. The picture probably belongs in the chapter on ghosts, this being a multiple ghost.

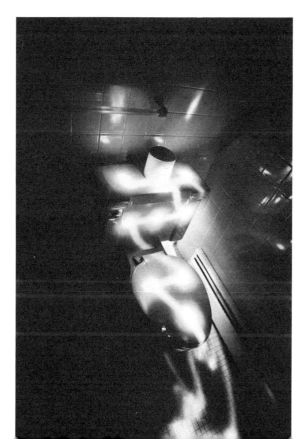

● Compensating for the Reciprocity Effect

The reciprocity effect relates to what happens to photosensitive materials when they cease to obey the so-called law of reciprocity, which we needn't discuss here. For our present purposes it is sufficient to say that when exposure times are long (or very short) the average film doesn't respond as much to an exposure as we would expect it to. For example, if your meter says that the correct exposure for a certain film and photographic subject is 1 second at f/16 you would naturally expect the meter to be right. However, the film will actually need 2 seconds (twice as much time), because with longer exposures it progressively loses much of its effective speed. Thus if your meter says 10 seconds the film begs for 40, and if the reading indicates 100 the film requires 1200 seconds, or 20 minutes. Failing to give the extra exposure time will lead to badly underexposed negatives. However, we need the extra time for painting anyway, so we welcome and use the reciprocity effect rather than worrying about it.

The following chart gives you some approximate exposure time corrections for the reciprocity effect, though they are accurate enough for our needs. Indicated exposure times are those you work from meter readings; you might call them uncorrected times. Adjusted exposure times take the reciprocity effect into consideration. The figures given here apply to 2475 Recording Film, Royal-X Pan, Tri-X Pan, Plus-X Pan, Panatomic-X, Verichrome Pan, and certain other films. However, you have to work out your own figures for high contrast and special purpose films.

(Ideally, you should cut the film development time 10 per cent for a 2-second adjusted exposure time, for the reciprocity effect increases image contrast with long exposures—and cutting the developing time reduces it again. For a 40-second adjusted time the cut should be 20 per cent, which is substantial. However, you can ignore the developing time cuts when painting with light, because you will be working with spotlighting, which is very contrasty anyway. That is, you both want and expect a lot of contrast.)

Compensations for the Reciprocity Effect

Indicated exposure times	1	2	3	4	5	6	7	8	9	10 sec
Adjusted exposure times	2	5	8	10	13	18	20	25	32	40 sec

Adjusted times are the ones you actually use in making your pictures, of course. The most convenient range is from 2 to 10 seconds, shorter times being too hard to work with and longer ones tedious. The way to arrive at an adjusted time within the recommended range is to take an exposure reading and figure out which f-stop would go with an indicated exposure time falling between 1 and 4 seconds. Then you simply convert this time to an adjusted time, using the chart. For example, from a reading you work out an indicated exposure of 2 seconds at f/16, which translates to an adjusted exposure of 5 seconds at f/16.

You will probably find yourself using mainly f/16 when you are using your flashlights within 12 inches or less of your subjects. If you get a reading that is too high (say, 1/4 second at f/16) use a smaller flashlight, switch to partly worn out batteries, or use a greater light-to-subject distance.

● A Flashlight Exposure Chart

If you don't have an exposure meter, built-in or separate, you can still do this project—provided that your camera has a "B" setting and that you have constructed a gadget for holding the shutter open. You merely use the chart on page 178, in conjunction with exposure bracketing.

You may have noticed that you have been getting a mental workout in manipulating exposure figures, which you should learn to do in your head—or at least with pencil and paper. Learning to do this will considerably improve your command of the photographic medium. However, if you are temporarily tired of such computations you may find it a relief to use a chart.

In the chart above, indicated exposure times are the kind you work out after taking meter readings. Adjusted times, which are the ones you should actually use in shooting your pictures, take the reciprocity effect into consideration. Tri-X is the film recommended for this project, though other films (including color) will work quite well if you make adjustments for their ASA speeds.

The times were given for f/16, because you will probably use this aperture setting most. However, if you wish to use your lights at quite a distance from your subjects you can open up the lens quite a bit. For example, by opening up to f/2 you would get an *indicated* exposure time of 4 seconds (instead of *4 minutes* at f/16) with a one AA cell penlight at 4 feet. This would give us a 10-second *adjusted* time, of course. For the betterment of your photographic education, work out how I arrived at these figures.

To obtain the charted data I made incident light readings from three flashlights with a Gossen Luna-Pro, a very reliable but not infallible instrument. The batteries were all Ray-O-Vac Alkaline Energy Cells that had never been used until the readings were made. The lights were all diffused with strips of Scotch matte acetate tape and were hooded with cylinders of black paper. The closer you can come to duplicating these conditions the more accurate your exposure will be when you follow this chart. However, batteries do fade rapidly—even alkaline ones—so you should consider using exposure bracketing as a safeguard.

Review the information on exposure bracketing in the chapter on p. 155. When your batteries are brand-new, bracket with 3 exposures that are 2 stops apart—under, normal, and over—obtaining

the normal exposure from the chart. After a light has been turned on for a total time of 5 to 10 minutes you can stop shooting underexposures with it, because the batteries will have faded quite a bit by then. Continue making 3 shots, however —a normal and *two* overexposures that are 2 stops apart. Even when the cells are rather far gone this should bracket the correct exposure easily enough. It will also compensate for errors in timing exposures by counting and for mistaken estimates of the light-to-subject distance.

You may have noted that there are some peculiarities in the flashlight exposure chart. For example, the flashlight with two AA cells produced the same reading for both 3 and 6 inches, which doesn't seem to make sense. And the light with one AA cell produced the same reading at 3 inches as the one with two AA cells. Since these results were repeatable, I attribute them to the way the flashlights were designed rather than to metering errors. Whatever be the case, you are safe in using these data, provided that you also do exposure bracketing. Incidentally, professional photographers tend to do a tremendous amount of bracketing, so you can see that the technique is highly regarded.

• Handling Your Lights

Though you paint with light in a totally blacked-out room, it is safe to use your flashlight itself to give you enough light to see what you are doing. For example, you can cover the end of it with your hand, turn it on, and let just enough light escape through your fingers to guide you to your subject—you actually need very little of it. Another trick is to hold the light midway between the camera and your subject and pointed either crosswise to the lens axis or down at the floor; then turn it on. Maintaining this crosswise relationship to both the camera and the subject, move the flashlight to the position at which you wish to paint with it. Then point it at your subject, count out the exposure, and swing it away again. With the light pointed at the floor, move

423

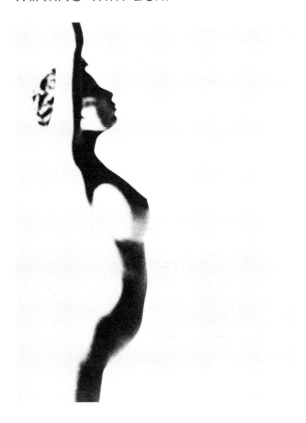

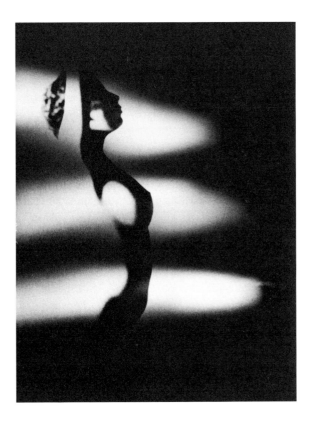

A copy print made from a copy negative made in the usual way (with flat light) and a copy print from a copy negative made by painting on the original print with a hooded flashlight. We get the effect of spotlighting.

back to your camera and close the shutter. The extremely small amount of light that falls on a subject from a flashlight in the crosswise position has a negligible effect on the picture, because flashlights are very directional, even when diffused.

You can light several parts of a single subject one at a time, covering the light or turning it crosswise between individual exposures. If you wish, you can turn off the light after each exposure, but you may then get disoriented in the dark.

A light that is moving will produce quite different effects than a light held stationary. With moving lights you can get an endless variety of lighting patterns in your pictures. You can also get shadows with very soft edges, if you wish. In comparison a stationary light produces a round or elliptical light pattern and tends to create shadows with very sharp edges—the greater the light-to-subject distance the sharper the edges.

It is useful to make one or more dry runs before shooting a picture. Turn out the room light and see what effects you can get with your flashlight, then use the ones that look best. This preview technique will also help you get a better idea of what light does, which is one of the main reasons for painting with light in the first place.

● **A Serious Business**

Because you can get all of your lighting equipment for less than ten dollars, you may not take this chapter seriously. In this consumer society, things are not held to be of any consequence unless they are very expensive. Please unburden yourself of this illusion, for it will limit your progress.

Perhaps you should think about Edward Weston, one of the greatest photographers who ever lived. He used equipment that today's average advanced amateur wouldn't even store in his dog house, much less use for making pictures. Yet time and again Weston used this "junk" to make pictures that have gone down in history. Another great photographer, Eugène Atget, also worked with extremely simple means. Many others have followed the same path. The point is that it isn't the equipment you have but what can be done with it that makes the difference.

Flashlights are real junk—anyone knows that —but they are also splendid instruments for developing your awareness of light and for making splendid pictures. Furthermore, solving the exposure problems involved will contribute substantially to your understanding of photography as a science.

In shooting the pictures the leaves were lit from behind, one after the other, the entire exposure sequence taking about two minutes.

In an entirely darkened room I lit my wife's face first from one side, then from the other. The picture hardly flatters this beautiful woman, but it does suggest some of the possibilities of the technique.

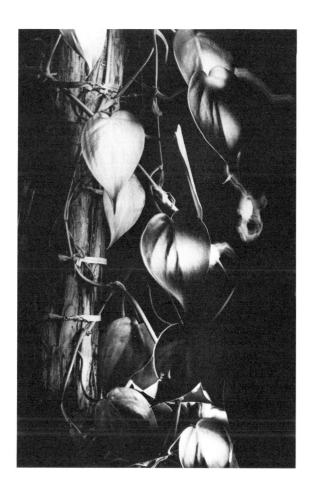

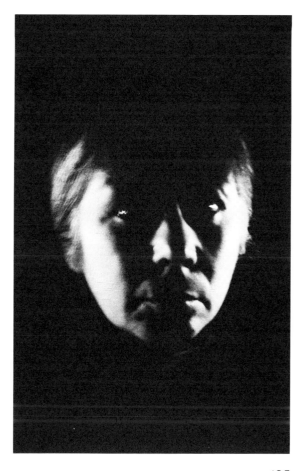

425

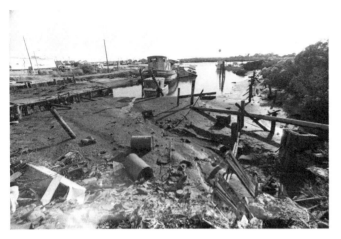

1: 19mm

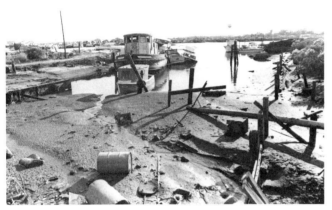

2: 28mm

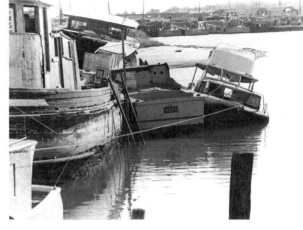

4: 135mm

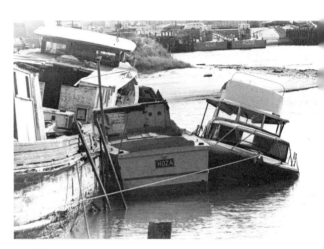

5: 200mm

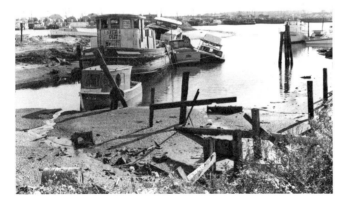

3: 55mm (a "normal" lens)

A series of pictures of the same scene shot from a single viewpoint with lenses of different focal lengths. As you see, the wide angle lenses compress a lot of visual data (visible things) into the picture area and make this little world seem much larger, more spacious, than it actually is. The telephoto lenses eliminate much visual data and compress the world from front to back until it seems strangely lacking in depth, with distant things appearing oddly near to faraway ones. In the text we see that using such lenses must surely have a psychological effect on the users and suggest new ways for becoming aware of one's own eyes and using them better.

WHAT LENSES DO

One of the fascinations of photography is in using lenses of various focal lengths, or perhaps the zoom lens, which has a built-in range of focal lengths. Many people play with lenses, but do they actually stop to figure out what they are accomplishing with them? Up to a point, yes. Anyone can see, for example, that a telephoto lens will make distant things seem closer or that a wide angle lens can distort things or make small areas seem much larger than they are. And everyone knows that telephotos make it possible to take pictures of people without their being consciously aware of it. Fair enough—these things are important in photography—but lenses do much more than this.

In this chapter we will deal with the things that lenses do—or seem to do—but not in terms of lens optics, which is a special study in itself. Instead, we will explore the idea that lenses of various focal lengths offer us different ways of seeing, recording, and responding to reality and that the lens used in making a picture has a considerable influence on the way people react to it. Lenses will also be looked at from a metaphysical, or occult, point of view, because they do many things that can't be explained in ordinary terms. Finally, I will say a few words concerning where lenses fit in when photography is considered as a language, which it most assuredly is.

Though this book is primarily about *how* to do things, there are times when you should ask yourself *what* you are doing. Indeed, we are entering an age in which the *what* of photography is becoming very important. A good start toward answering this question of what photography is up to is to take an imaginative look at what lenses are up to—what do they do?

● Telephoto Lenses

You know, of course, that telephoto lenses reach out and bring distant things near—with a long-enough lens you can park the moon in your own back yard. From watching baseball on TV you know that with a telephoto the distance between things is greatly compressed, so that when a pitcher winds up he seems to be standing on the batter's big toe. When you can see the ball it seems to be traveling at a very leisurely rate, which just isn't the truth of the matter.

Have you noticed the tableau quality in the telephoto image, especially in still pictures? A kind of frozen feeling, unreal and seemingly staged. Live creatures often look like puppets, carefully stuffed and anchored in place for an eternity. Even sports pictures, with all the action that they record, have this frozen tableau quality. Though much of it is due to high shutter speeds, the telephoto lens is also responsible.

Have you probed your fascination with the idea of sneaking portraits at a distance with a telephoto? Cowardice may be one reason for doing it, because most of us are afraid of confronting people close-up—but that is too obvious an answer. There must be others, too. For example, people who are at a distance and not consciously aware of being observed change somehow, become much more their real selves. At least we have grounds to think that they do.

So we may wish to capture their reality on film, for very good reasons. It happens that we must use the realities of other people in order to define our own. Experiencing others helps us define such things as self, sanity, good, and evil, so it is understandable that we would wish to see them well. But there is a great problem in seeing people accurately, for when we are close to them and they are aware of being observed, they defensively slide into various roles (fictional selves) that they are long accustomed to playing in the presence of others. However, when we view them through binoculars or telephoto lenses they don't play these defensive roles. They still play roles— all of the time—but at least they are private roles rather than public and are not so defensive. We can see them more for what they really are.

Earlier in the book I said that people at a distance always know when you are photographing them, though not necessarily at the ego level. They know by a process of unconscious telepathy shared by the entire human race. Remember, this unconscious knowledge can also move into consciousness and often does. The push button for this shift is mainly your attitude: if you telephotograph a person for negative, contemptuous, put-down reasons, conscious or unconscious, he may alert himself to what you are doing, cross the street, and punch you in the nose. On the other hand, if he unconsciously respects your reasons he will let you photograph as much as you like and will continue to reveal that side of his secret self that you prize so much.

We don't usually connect telephoto lenses with distortion, though they distort just as much as wide angles do. We just don't notice it, that is all. However, they distort only in the sense that they show us things in a perspective that we are not ordinarily aware of, which is a very good way of defining lens distortion. The perspective itself

conforms to all the rules. A part of the presumed distortion by telephotos is the near and far distance compression, or shrinkage, already mentioned. Another factor is that things decrease less in size than we would expect them to as they move away from us. The smaller the angle of coverage of the lens the less the decrease.

Perhaps with a hypothetical lens with no angle at all there would be no size decrease at all. Thus we could line up a sugar lump in New York with one on Alpha Centauri and have them come out exactly the same size in a photograph. Furthermore, they would appear to be in exactly the same place. Though we now have no such lenses, we are getting closer to it every day. However, with the lenses we *do* have, near and far things of equal size tend to hold that relationship in pictures. In a baseball picture, for example, the batter is nearly the same size as the pitcher.

Selective focus is still another possibility with telephoto lenses. That is, you can select the thing you want to come out sharp in a picture and let the background (or foreground) go completely out of focus. Or you can have sharpness in the middle distance and have both foreground and background out of focus. Selective focus is mainly used to get rid of, or tone down, things that you don't want clearly delineated in pictures, though it is also used for the soft feeling that it gives to out-of-focus areas.

Telephotos (usually from 90 to 135mm) are often used for portraiture, with the explanation that they give a better facial perspective than so-called normal lenses do. Mainly this means that telephotos don't make noses look too long—but neither do normal lenses. A more likely excuse is that a long lens prevents the photographer from getting too close to his subjects. The value of this extra distance is explained in a concept developed by Ken Heyman, a well-known professional (see page 32).

Heyman says that each person has an invisible emotional defense perimeter, an imaginary circle that he draws around himself. As long as no one penetrates this perimeter he feels safe, whereas intrusion creates anxiety or anger. Now, the problem with using a normal lens (e.g., a 50mm on a 35mm camera) to make a head shot is that you may have to violate your model's territory. His resultant anxiety may give rise to visible facial tension, rather frantic role-playing, and the appearance of being thoroughly miserable—things that don't look good in portraits. Thus increasing the subject-to-photographer distance by using a telephoto makes good sense.

Let us now go outdoors for a moment to consider the contrast problem with longer telephoto lenses. Due to atmospheric haze, even small amounts of it, the contrast between distant things may drop to almost nothing. Certain optical effects also contribute to this problem. To bring back the contrast you can develop your film from 50 to 100 per cent longer than usual or shoot your pictures through a red (haze cutting) filter.

Or you can simply use the flatness as a part of your pictorial designs. Perhaps the easiest solution is to simply photograph things that are closer to you.

Pictures taken with a 19mm lens and a 200mm, the former seeming gross and distorted. It is gross only in the sense that many people will dislike it, like the mating dance of a slime puppy, and distorted only in the sense that the perspective is unexpected. However, this is the way Bob Turner actually looks if you look at him with one eye from a distance of six inches. That is, the perspective as such *is not* distorted. In comparison, the picture made with the 200mm lens is very comfortable to look at. Though Bob's head has been compressed or flattened considerably from front to back this is very difficult to see and not at all disturbing.

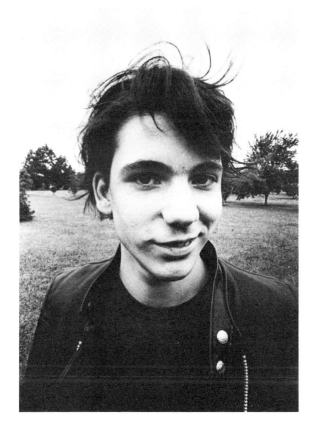
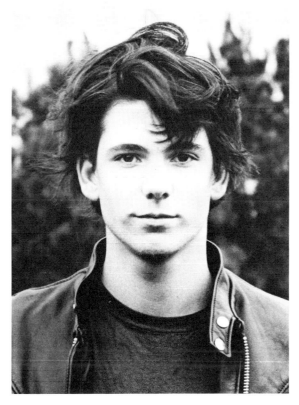

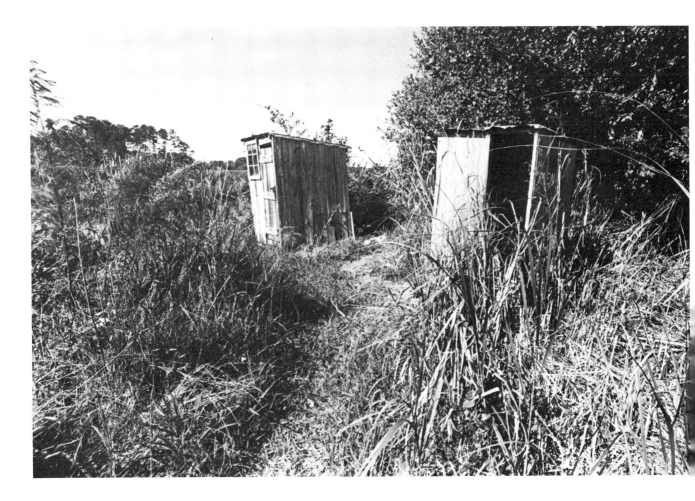

Though the grass and trees were probably greatly "distorted" by this 19mm lens picture, there is no easy way to tell that they were—so we don't notice anything odd at all. So it looks like a "normal angle picture" showing the way things "really are" to the eye, though it has actually made this little world seem very much larger. For example, I was standing nearly on top of the privies, though they seem to be a considerable distance away.

In our efforts to understand our own eyes better we should study the effects of lenses, for the eye can do anything that a lens can do, no matter what kind of a lens it is. Initially, we should study the wide angle lens, for its effects are most obvious to us. In this picture made with a 19mm lens, for example, you can tell that this wooden pier can only be about eight feet long. However, it looks very much longer, let us say *feels* that way. It would appear the same way to wide field vision (see text) when seen directly at the location where I found it.

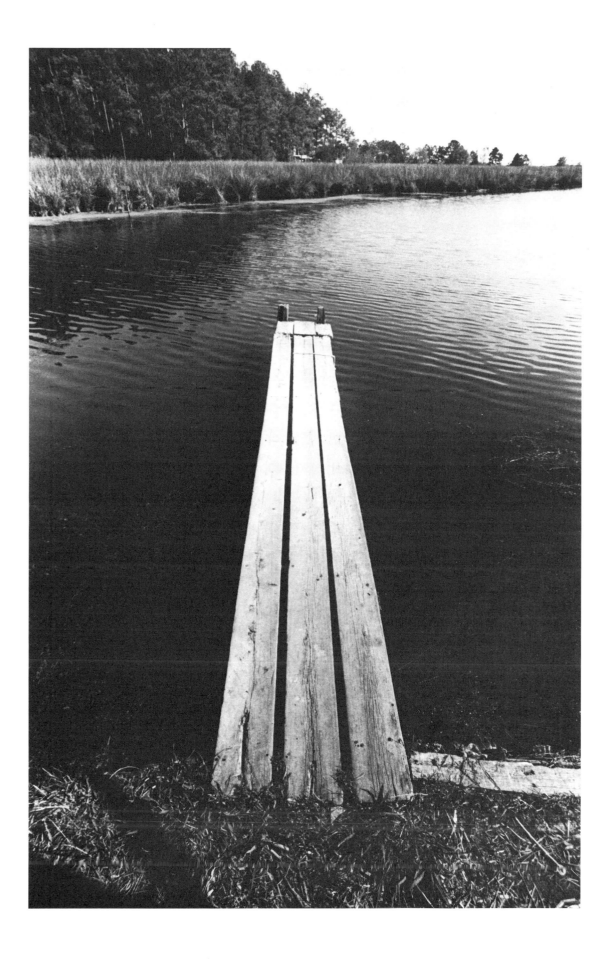

• Wide Angle Lenses

Perhaps the most obvious things about a wide angle lens is that it will include more of a scene or interior setting than will a normal lens and that it can apparently distort perspective considerably, though the perspective is actually normal. What is sometimes not noticed is that this inclusion can make things look considerably larger than they usually appear to be. The ordinary appearance of things can be explained by the way our eyes function.

Though our eyes actually take in a good deal, only the center of vision (foveal) is sharp, the rest being so fuzzy that we pay little attention to anything within it except movement. The result is that we live in a rather small visual world that is approximated only by the reality seen by a normal lens—but not a wide angle. The latter is psychologically a world expander, however, because it gives us the effect (in pictures or through the camera viewfinder) of having vision that is entirely foveal, or sharp. This in turn permits us to see the world as looking considerably larger than usual. It seems larger in height, width, and depth.

No doubt this has a profound psychological effect on people who use wide angle lenses, for by simple acts of will they can more than double the size of the familiar visual world. Certainly, this appeals to the common desire to be one with the gods, to be all-powerful. Similarly, shrinking or compressing the universe with a telephoto lens must also be felt as godlike.

Yes, wide angle lenses seem to expand the world, making it look wider and deeper. Oddly, as it gets steadily larger the objects in it get progressively smaller. On the other hand, telephotos seem to shrink the world, making it narrow and shallow. Strangely, as it gets more compressed the objects in it get larger. Such things surely have a psychological effect on people.

Another odd thing about wide angle lenses is that they create a strange physical tension in your eyes when you look through them with the help of a camera viewfinder. Though the sensation can't be described with accuracy, it is like having our eyeballs sucked out into the world. You can definitely feel this pull on your eyes if you are on the alert for it. Psychologically, it may represent your effort to encompass a larger than usual world with your eyes. Or it may come from a conflict between two opposed desires, both of them very basic. They are the desire to see much and the desire to see little.

This pulling effect can sometimes be experienced when you are looking at pictures made with wide angle lenses. Such a picture may seem to draw you into itself, as if it were some kind of a visual magnet. You may get the feeling of entering into another world, as represented by the photograph. In comparison, you are more likely to feel excluded from pictures made with normal or telephoto lenses. Though such feelings are subtle, they most certainly have a psychological effect.

With wide angle lenses the possibilities for so-called distortion are very obvious, and one may have a compulsion to play with them a lot. In a sense, to distort something is to re-create it, so the God syndrome comes into play: "I will re-create the world to my own liking." Since distortion is usually associated with ugliness (the unfamiliar seen as ugly), using it is also a way of getting revenge on reality, of holding it up to profound contempt.

We call it perspective distortion, but it really isn't. Perspective just happens to work that way, but we are not ordinarily aware of all the strange things that it does. Thus the so-called distortions of lenses often aren't distortions at all but things we could also see with our own eyes if we knew how to see better, which is something we can train ourselves to do.

Thus another reason for playing with "distortion," which is made easy with wide angle lenses, is to get a better idea of the capabilities of our own eyes. Remember that telephotos distort (appear to change things around) just as much, but that this may be more difficult to see. Because we frequently use our eyes as if they were telephoto lenses (psychological projection of vision), we are very familiar with the telephoto effect (up to a point) and therefore don't think of it as distortion. In fact, we just don't think of it at all. Though in peripheral vision we also use our eyes as if they were wide angle lenses, we are aware of this mainly on the unconscious or semiconscious level. Thus telephoto lenses and vision offer us few surprises (distortions), while wide angle lenses and vision offer many.

Even with the help of lenses, it is difficult to become aware of the wide angle capabilities of your eyes, because only the center of vision is sharp. Furthermore, your ego identifies very strongly with this sharpness, relegating unsharp peripheral vision to a state of semi-oblivion and surrender control of it to parts of your mind that are not easily accessible to you. Even so, it is possible to become much more aware of your wide angle eyes.

Wide angle lenses can help, because they can give you a preview of what may be possible for you. Learning how to look at things without focusing is another help. You should practice this in dim light when you are fully relaxed, trying not to think about the things within your field of vision. This is because thinking and focusing usually go together, and you should try to separate them. This is much easier said than done, of course.

Another trick—also a tough one to learn—is to intentionally make your vision passive, rather than active. That is, instead of projecting it outward into the world (tightly focusing on things is a sign of this), let the world come into your eyes in whatever way it wants to come in. Don't look for things; just let them come to you. Women, who as a rule see much better than men, often find this trick relatively easy, but for the average man it is extremely difficult.

When you are using unfocused and passive vision the world won't look very sharp, but you will be astonished at how much more you see that

Though this girl has a very handsome, normal, and healthy body a 19mm wide angle lens has made it look all out of proportion and ugly. However, this is very normal perspective for both wide angle lenses and wide angle vision, which we have yet to develop in any great numbers. Our fear of this presumed distortion probably helps inhibit this development. Overcoming this irrational fear of ugliness (of the unexpected) should help us free our vision.

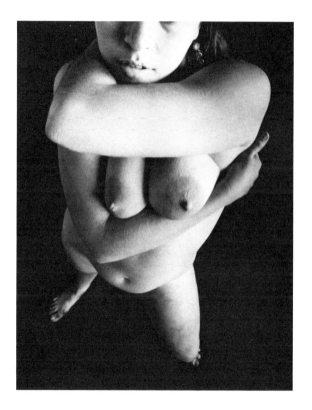

way. Persuading your ego to temporarily give up its desperate hangup on sharpness and sharp focus will open up a whole new world for you. Now, this hangup should be looked at briefly.

The ego's powerful attachment to sharpness may be the main reason we see a very limited reality instead of one infinitely complex, which is both good and bad. The attachment and resulting simplification of life contribute to personal and racial stability, which are highly necessary, but they limit us to perceiving a very small part of what is actually happening. Perhaps the modern fascination with the things that lenses will do indicates an unconscious racial desire to leave comfortable stability behind in an orderly way and to search for a more expansive reality. We may be using our photography, which includes all of television, the cinema, and all photographs reproduced in the graphic arts, to lead us to our innate capabilities in visual perception.

This would fit with the notion that photography per se is a giant analogue of the innate perceptual capabilities of man, filtered down to us piecemeal from the higher consciousness of the race, and intended for our use in expanding our awareness to (and beyond) the limits now described by what photography can do. We will come back to this idea later.

Let us return to the idea that the ego's identification with (attachment to) sharpness prevents effective use of the wide angle capabilities of our eyes. If photography is indeed a perceptual analogue of man, then our wide angle lenses clearly tell us of abilities we have not yet learned to use. Using such lenses and experiencing pictures made with them help lead the way, but we are doing other things, too.

One of the things we do to expand awareness is create certain compensatory physical defects in ourselves. For example, to counteract an undue attachment to sharp focus (which is apparently a major psychological affliction in itself) we deliberately develop specific eye defects, usually (but not always) relatively minor. Since such an idea sounds highly improbable, we will turn to the fields of medicine and psychology in search of a solid foundation for it.

Advances in psychosomatic medicine have made it seem likely that all (or at least most) physical defects and ailments originate in the mind. This includes visual defects, of course. That is, due to decisions made in our unconscious

minds we intentionally afflict ourselves in a wide variety of ways. Since disease of any kind whatever seems to have no purpose, it is no wonder that we tend to see the unconscious mind as a repository—admittedly vast—of superstition, stupidity, and ignorance. If this is true the notion of compensatory (and possibly necessary) defects just won't hold water. Then the explanation of our suffering would be that we are basically too stupid to stop inflicting it upon ourselves.

When we turn to the psychologists for enlightenment we find many of them tacitly supporting the idea that the unconscious is primarily a reservoir for discarded mental and emotional garbage. However, some do not, including the Jungians, who have discovered that the minds of all people link together in the so-called racial unconscious, which is a vast repository for all human thought from the beginning of the race up to the present. This means that, at a certain level of being, a single person shares the intelligence of all mankind. Furthermore, this intelligence is accessible to what we call the unconscious mind, which is really not unconscious at all. In truth, it is acutely aware of a vast number of things that we have never even heard of on the conscious level. We erroneously call it the unconscious simply because we have little conscious access to it.

The truth is that we are immensely more intelligent on the so-called unconscious level than we are in consciousness, which is ruled by the childlike ego, a rather recent development in man. To the super-intelligent and super-conscious part of ourselves that we ignorantly call the unconscious, all suffering has both meaning and purpose. Ailments and defects, all intentionally created, are intended for very specific curative, educational, or compensatory purposes. It is like the young doctor I met who cured a patient of deadly tetanus (lockjaw) by inflicting him with malaria, which would destroy the tetanus organisms. When the tetanus was gone the malaria was treated with relative ease. Had the patient unconsciously afflicted himself with malaria we would have the exact pattern of what goes on in man all the time: he creates inner afflictions in order to heal himself physically, mentally, and spiritually.

The promised foundation has been sketched. Though brief, it lends credence to certain ideas presented here, for example, the notion that photography (which includes all of television, the cinema, still photography, and the visual press) is an analogue of innate human visual capabilities, a vast self-teaching machine intentionally passed down to us from the higher reaches of the racial intelligence. Its objective: to teach us how to see. If our minds are indeed linked at a certain level, such a possibility shouldn't seem unlikely. This foundation also supports the supposition that we may intentionally create our ocular defects in order to counteract our bad visual habits, for example, an undue attachment to foveal awareness, or sharpness. That is, we may be inwardly intelligent enough to create our afflictions for very good reasons, though we may not be conscious of what they are.

Let us return to lenses for a moment. A while back I said that the wide angle lens is an analogue describing the eye's innate capability to function consciously for wide angle (broad field) vision but that the ego's attachment to sharp focus (to foveal awareness) permits broad field vision only on the unconscious or semiconscious level. The wide angle lens shows us that such an awareness is both possible and wonderful, and gets us accustomed to the idea of eventually developing such vision. By itself, however, it can't overcome our self-limiting attachment to foveal awareness, which has yet to be recognized as a serious psychic impairment. Thus stronger measures are needed.

Thus we return to the notion of compensatory eye defects that we may intentionally create in ourselves, some of which seem to be designed to wean the ego from its desperate attachment to strictly foveal awareness. They do this by simply making sharp focus impossible under certain conditions so that the ego can learn to do without it, at least temporarily. And without the sharpness the conscious visual field is broadened, for we can no longer lock our attention into foveal awareness to the exclusion of everything else. Though wearing glasses should ostensibly return us to the state of attachment, they don't really work that way. On the contrary, by frequently bringing our attention to the ways in which we use our eyes they help us erode the attachment, which is largely dependent on our not being aware of what our eyes do or of how we use them. Thus glasses as such are a part of the treatment for foveal attachment.

Though you may make your eyes defective mainly to counteract foveal attachment, there may be many other reasons for drawing your attention to your eyes in this manner. For example, you may be inclined to always see things in exactly the same way, which actually means not seeing them at all. Or you may have a serious mixup between memory and seeing, so that instead of really seeing things you are merely remembering them—and memory is always faulty, you know. Or you may use the visual world as a constant distraction from your spiritual duty to pay sufficient attention to the inner you. Eye defects of various kinds would tend to break up such habits. Though such notions aren't a part of the world as seen by Sigmund Freud, they are nonetheless very serious psychic and spiritual problems.

It may seem strange that a discussion of lenses should dwell so frequently on eyes, but lenses as such are simply substitute eyes. Put it this way: lenses are about eyes. Furthermore, to talk about lenses without mentioning eyes is to miss the whole point of photography, which is mainly a tool for our search for self-knowledge. In terms of both what it *is* and what it can *do*, photography is a mirror of man, as he is and as he can be. Thus it is wise to consider lenses as a study of eyes.

As you have seen, it is necessary to wade in rather murky waters when you ask what lenses really do, because the question boils down to what they do for us, which has never been explored. And you have apparently been asked to believe in some very improbable hypotheses, though this isn't quite so. Truly, all I ask is that you hold both belief and disbelief in suspension until you can figure everything out for yourself. However, one notion needs further explanation, because it is seemingly so absurd that suspending disbelief in it is nearly impossible. It is the idea that attachment to sharp focus (to foveal awareness) may be a serious limitation and psychic defect—who ever heard of such a thing? It seems to suggest that it would be better to be half blind than to have good vision.

Not so. It is surely better to have good vision —provided that you use it properly. Otherwise, one or more corrective defects might be in order. To cover this subject properly we should have a long book entitled *Sins We Commit with Our Eyes,* using the word sin in its ancient meaning (to sin meant to make a mistake, usually a spiritual one). The list of ocular sins is long and includes such things as voyeurism, visual aggression, distorting visual reality, visual possession, using your eyes in the service of fear, anger, or contempt, insisting on seeing only negative things, and refusing to see all that you are capable of seeing. Though these are sins of the spirit they nevertheless have physical correctives. We will take up only the last one, which relates to the problem of foveal attachment, or an addiction to sharp focus.

Remember that the fovea is the only part of the retina that forms sharp images and that the ego can become attached to them—to sharpness itself, as it were. Now, the problem with attachment to anything whatever is that it tends to blind you to everything else. Thus it is a form of partial suicide, even if we don't recognize it for what it really is. A person with this addiction pays too much attention to images in the foveal part of the retina, where things can be focused sharply, and hardly any attention to unsharp images in the periphery of the retina. Since the fovea will sharply register only a small fraction of the visual information streaming through the eyes, the foveal sharpness addict in a sense refuses to see all that

he is capable of seeing. That is, he excludes from conscious awareness most of what he confronts with his eyes.

● Sharp and Unsharp Foveal Images

It could be said of many people that they focus too much. Though the fovea will register sharp images, we shouldn't always use it for that purpose. When our eyes aren't focused, which should be much of the time, the fovea registers images that are semisharp to fuzzy. At the same time the conscious field of awareness expands considerably. In effect, we begin to approach a type of wide angle seeing exemplified by the wide angle lens. Though unsharp, the images can adequately stimulate a great many kinds of awareness, and that is really their essential function. We should use our eyes to serve awareness, not our awareness to serve our eyes. The unfocused eye, which sees well enough for a great many purposes, permits an expansion of awareness to a greater visual field.

However, an addiction to sharpness can lead us to constantly focus on things, which severely constricts the visual field and excludes most of visual reality from awareness. We might call this single-pointed vision and say that the person addicted to it always sees the tree but never the forest.

● The Fear of Unsharpness

There are numerous reasons for an attachment to sharpness, one of them being the fear of blindness. To put it simply, we equate unsharpness with incipient blindness, even though we experience unsharpness all of the time. True, we need the sharpness, and not being able to create it may indeed be a prelude to blindness, though it usually isn't. But we also need the unsharpness, which has a wide variety of functions. The fact that we are unaware of most of them, plus the fear of blindness unless we are almost constantly aware of sharp images, contribute greatly to the hangup.

With the help of lenses of various kinds it is easy to prove to yourself that you are afraid of unsharpness. For example, try wearing someone else's glasses and note the nausea it causes. Or try some rather extended periods of looking through the viewfinder of a single lens reflex camera without focusing the lens—same effect. And print some pictures with your enlarger lens out of focus —again you will feel the nausea, which is simply a fear reaction.

In order for us to take possession of our natural visual heritage, this fear of unsharpness must be overcome, for it shuts off our awareness of most of the visual data that comes to us through our eyes. Since these data are embodied in unsharp imagery, we are simply afraid to see them. Fortunately, it is possible to use photography to help undermine the fear. For example, the many intentionally out-of-focus pictures that you see nowadays have this psychological function, though you may not like them. If you are alert, your dislike may lead you to your fear, and an abnormal fear will tend to disappear once it has been well seen. Even if they don't lead you to your fear, such images can help you, because they help get you used to the idea of unsharpness as something that can be harmless. After all, the pictures don't bite you, do they?

Another help comes from using a single lens reflex camera, the most popular kind nowadays. Every time you focus the lens you unconsciously reassure yourself that unsharpness doesn't necessarily exclude sharpness, that you can have both. This is true of the camera, of course, but, more importantly, also true of yourself. You can have them one at a time or both at once, depending on where your attention is fixed. There are also certain lenses with which you can get both at once.

Now that I have mentioned this fear of unsharpness it is up to you to discover it in yourself and eliminate it. You will find that it is a very powerful fear indeed, because it is the fear of blindness in disguise. Considering its strength, it is no wonder that we permit ourselves so little

awareness of the unsharp peripheral events in our own eyes. Indeed, fear as such is the main limiting factor in human awareness of any kind. Thus we are afraid to "see" what we see.

• Zoom-and-Unzoom Lenses

If wide angle lenses describe a human capability for broad-field visual awareness that is used too little, zoom lenses describe the same capability when they are unzoomed (racked inward). The reason for our present inability stems largely from the previously described attachment to sharpness (to sharp foveal images).

The zoom lens describes rather well what we do when we focus sharply on something. In effect, we severely narrow our field of awareness and zoom our attention outward to the thing we are interested in. Though the eye's magnification doesn't substantially change, as it does with zoom lenses, it might just as well. The psychologically important factors are attention and exclusion, not magnification. When we focus on something (project ourselves out to it, as it were) we exclude everything else from our attention, severely limiting the field of awareness. We apprehend this process as magnification, though it isn't usually. However, it could be, for that is another capability of the human mind.

This limiting capability is very important, of course, for it enables us to visually cope with reality one thing at a time. Without this ability we would simply be overwhelmed by the unfocused and undifferentiated visual data streaming in through our eyes from an endlessly complex visual world.

Thus zooming a lens outward describes a survival capability of man, but what happens when it is unzoomed? (notice that its very name—zoom —indicates only one of its main capabilities). Well, unzooming describes an innate human capability that we haven't realized yet, though a few people have it in considerable degree.

To help you visualize what you are about to read, try to imagine a lens that hasn't yet been invented, one with a zoom range of about 15 to 200mm. This would give us coverage varying from a very wide visual field to a very narrow one and is roughly analogous to what our eyes will do. That is, the visual intake of the eye approximates such a range, though conscious awareness does not.

When unzoomed down to 15mm our hypothetical lens would maintain its awareness, so to speak. That is, it would continue to "see" everything in front of it, clear "proof" of this being the sharp image produced at 15mm. In the case of a lens we can say that the proof of awareness is sharpness—we can use any metaphor we like. However, we unconsciously apply the same idea to ourselves, making a permanent wedding of the two qualities.

This is not so good. In human beings, acute awareness (visual or any other kind) may have little to do with sharpness, because awareness as such (a faculty of the mind) can transcend all the perceptual mechanisms. Thus when we unzoom ourselves (which is like a lens unzooming itself out of focus) we should be able to maintain awareness of the whole visual field down to about 15mm, but the fact is that we don't. That is, most of us don't. When sharp focus disappears most of our awareness goes with it.

Yes, we disconnect all or most of our conscious awareness when we unzoom, surrendering the use of our eyes to unconscious forces (which happen to be aware *all* of the time) and occupying ourselves mainly with our own thoughts. As our eyes unzoom we simply disconnect the visual world, except for paying fragmentary attention to it. This capacity is, to be sure, a very important one, because it makes it possible for us to separate ourselves from exterior reality in order to think about it and assess our relationship to it.

Thus the ability to disconnect ourselves mentally from the broad visual field and its enormous supply of distracting visual data is both good and necessary, but like eating hot fudge sundaes, we like to overdo it. At any rate, using zoom lenses or experiencing their effects on television gives us the idea of trying to keep ourselves plugged in

when we unzoom and encourages attempts to do it. Since the experience of photographic unzooming is quite exciting, it suggests to us that maintaining awareness while unzooming our visual attention might be at least as rewarding.

This disappearance of awareness with sharpness is automatic and if noticed at all is thought to be normal. Yes, it is normal enough but also abnormal in the sense that it excludes other possibilities, which is something that habits very often do. The fact that a visual process is automatic doesn't make it divine. Indeed, human beings can automate themselves to do an endless number of things, normal, abnormal, and in between. In the case of maintaining conscious awareness of a broad visual field, it is normal to do it and equally normal not to—we can permit ourselves to do both. The two states—awareness and nonawareness—have quite different functions, and both should be given their due.

Earlier, I said that one of the primary purposes of photography is to help us gain conscious possession of our innate perceptual capabilities, an assumption surely open to debate. However, I will stand by it without outlining arguments against myself (a part of the so-called academic method), letting others disagree if they wish. Now, from what you have read so far you should suspect that this notion assumes a literally enormous human perceptual potential (on the order of what Jesus told his disciples: "Haven't I told you that you are gods?"). Obviously, your author has positioned himself well out on the limb. Though we are still far from realizing this potential, we are certainly making great haste to develop one of the primary tools with which to lead ourselves to it—the tool being photography, which is progressing in astronomical leaps.

Now, gaining free access to an enormous potential can't be done in a day. Indeed, if it were actually possible it would lead only to madness. Things must be done in turn in an orderly progression, day by day and year by year. We must prepare ourselves for them gradually. One of the first things in learning to see better, for that is really what this chapter is all about, is to learn how we see *already*. To get started on this it is necessary for us to get our own attention by stripping the veil from automatic visual behavior in order to learn what it actually consists of. When the veil has been lifted we know *what* we do and *how* we do it and find ourselves in a position to consciously modify our behavior and direct it toward a diversity of ends. Otherwise, we are helpless to change ourselves, human robots blinded by self-automation.

So what can the zoom lens and its effects do for us on this basic level?—forget for the moment the interstellar horizons of innate perceptual capacity. Why, it can draw our attention to the strong parallel between zooming a lens and zooming attention, and to the strange disparity when we unzoom both. Becoming aware of what we do with our eyes, even to this limited degree, is a tremendous leap in the right direction.

● How Large Is Photography?

Though I have called photography per se a system with which we are leading ourselves toward our innate perceptual capabilities, I have said little about its scope except to say that it includes television, the cinema, still photography, and the picture press. Thereafter, I concentrated on just a few of the abilities that will be ours in the future, for example, broad-field awareness. Such a severe delimitation was necessary for clarity and at least a modicum of believability. However, we have reached a point where we should see photography's enormous scope.

In its most basic definition, photography is the storage and communication of information by means of radiant energy. This definition immediately moves us into such fields as electron microscopy, radio astronomy, tensor mathematics, plasma physics, plamoid chemistry, mirror optics, systems analysis, trace element chemistry, hydraulics, microminiaturization, computer design, surfactant chemistry, electronics, business reproduction, theory of numbers, and so on. We find that science, industry, business, government, the military, and the space program depend heavily

on photography. In fact, they all might collapse without it.

Photography as most of us experience it—mainly through television—describes capabilities that the public as a whole is nearly ready to realize. The sciences listed above, and many that were not mentioned, describe innate abilities that will, for most of us, come into flower much later.

● From Science Fiction

If I were to make the improbable assertion that $E=mc^2$ is a variant of $E=IT$ (the law of reciprocity), saying that both explain what photography is really all about, this would surely get us nowhere. You surely don't have the slightest idea of what I am talking about, nor could I ever explain it to you.

At this point you don't need scientific (or pseudo-scientific) hypotheses, but your gray cells do need to be awakened and stimulated. Thus we will turn to science fiction, which has this as its primary purpose. The following entirely fictional material should give you an imaginative idea of what photography might really be up to, what lenses do being but a part of it. Some of it may even be true. As part of the game I will be as convincing as possible, writing as if I were telling the whole truth and nothing but the truth.

In the universe, all possibilities are probable; and everything that can be thought of is a possibility. Thoughts are *things* of infinite duration. Literally everything is real, including nothing. In reality, everything is happening at once. Thus can we describe the limits of science fiction.

All thoughts since the beginning of things still exist, stored, as it were, in the so-called Akashic Record. In the fairly near future there will be a photographic machine, controlled telepathically by the mind of its operator, for obtaining Akashic readouts. For the very first time we will have an accurate picture of the history of Man. From the beginning it has been written second by second, and we will finally have conscious access to it.

The typical camera of the future will not require film. Instead it will employ a cubical mercury mirror, one such mirror lasting its owner a lifetime. This cube will have a memory, so to speak, and used in a single simple camera will produce both still and motion pictures, including sound. The photographer will get readouts in his brain by holding the cube to his forehead and concentrating his will on the things he wishes to recover from his past. Other people who wish to inform him about their pasts will simply lend him their memory cubes. There will also be readout machines for this little mirror, which will be about the size of a pea. Oddly, one of the main functions of the cube will be in training people to take command of their will.

There will be a machine that will convert a single still photograph into a movie of any desired length showing what happened to the things in the still picture before and after it was shot. There will be no time limit to the coverage; if desired, the movie will extend into the infinite past, into the infinite future, or both. The future will be expressed as probabilities.

The cameras we already have that "see" in the dark by means of invisible radiant energy and/or electronic amplification are preludes to equipment with which we will lead ourselves to the conscious ability to do much better than this without any mechanical help at all. In doing this we will only be learning what we already know, which is usually the case in education. Information soon to be recovered from the Akashic will clearly prove that the ability to see well in absolute darkness was developed long ago in our racial history, then put aside for a few millennia while we worked on developing other talents, including daylight vision. However, an ability fully developed is never really lost again but stored in our genes and passed on through heredity. Thus night vision merely needs to be reawakened, which photography is already helping us do.

A favorite lens of the future will be a perfect sphere, flexible and liquid-filled. Due to reactions between submicroscopic amounts of gold and fluorine, which otherwise exist at quite different levels of reality and fail to react together, the liquid will be highly responsive to light pressure,

thought pressure, sound, and gravity. With the understanding gained in developing this lens we will banish trachoma and most other eye diseases from the face of the earth. The lens, which will be given as a toy to children, will be used mainly as a training instrument for conscious telepathy. As we are learning that vastly complex language art we will use the lens for such things as turning thoughts into pictures, converting data from the Akashic from the sound form into the visual, making permanent or temporary records of events in both the past and the future, and learning to understand the true nature of light (it is by no means what we now think it is).

Using a knowledge of language brought to us through experiencing photography in its many present and future ramifications, we will rather easily teach the blind to see, for it will be discovered that blindness is primarily a linguistic problem. Even people who entirely lack eyes will develop excellent vision. The very same visual language art will be used to communicate clearly and easily with autistic children.

There will be a photographic device, worn like glasses, that will enable us to see, usually one at a time, an infinity of worlds that exist parallel to our own. Some of them are very much like ours, others utterly different. Training with the device will help us remember an ability learned long ago. Eventually, the trainee will be able to see other worlds without mechanical help. He will also be able to enter them at will.

The electron microscope prophesies a time when we will have consciousness of our own bodies at all levels down to the subatomic. Actually, we already have this consciousness in full force, but it is locked up in that higher aspect of consciousness mistakenly called the unconscious. When we are ready for it, this ability will shift to the ego level.

By this time we will realize that ego conscious (being awake) has been a form of deep sleep from the very beginning. However, with the shift our egos will awaken, and consciousness will actually be consciousness for the first time. To prepare ourselves for a shift of such magnitude (which would be disastrous if it all happened at once), we will have a variety of photographic devices to help us gradually overcome our fear of looking into our own bodies, this fear being very powerful. With these gadgets, some of them already in existence, we will be able to comfortably examine ourselves piecemeal. Eventually, we will be able to put everything together without being shocked into catatonia by our own enormous complexity and diversity.

Very shortly we will discover that our efforts to teach photography to small children have been badly misdirected, because we have been asking them to do the wrong things. A child should be asked to take pictures of fairies. In the future we will get children started by asking them to record through projections instead of exterior reality, and they will find this quite easy to do. Since photosensitive silver compounds in use today are also thought-sensitive, children's photography on this level is already a possibility, though qualified teachers are lacking. However, we do need materials more sensitive than silver and will surely have them before long.

Through advances in trace chemistry and the chemistry of essences we will discover the element that we need. However, we will mistake it for a compound and call it helium sesquidioxide (an impossible compound of helium and oxygen), though it is actually an organic form of molybdenum. This is the most thought-sensitive element we will ever discover and the most powerful catalyst as well. Indeed, in extremely minute quantities it will catalyze image formation in certain base metals, which will take the place of silver in photography.

Though molybdenum has several organic forms we are mainly interested in helium sesquidioxide, which we will "grow" in molybdenum breeders by means of certain readily available organic substances and sound vibrations, mainly the wavelength G below low G. The key information leading to this technology will be provided by perfume chemists studying both garlic and the geranium blossom, each of which contains one of the organic forms of molybdenum.

With this powerful thought-sensitive element we will develop films and papers that will cost us next to nothing, so that our children will be abundantly supplied. A roll of film costing about five cents will produce either black-and-white or color pictures and will record either thought projections or exterior reality. The emulsion will be a peanut oil derivative. The camera, now foreshadowed by the Polaroid Land camera, will cost about two dollars. It will have a liquid lens. Models for older children will employ mercury mirrors.

The new equipment and materials will be used mainly for preparing children in a very direct way for conscious telepathy. As they are learning to project thought forms onto film they will also be learning to project them to one another. Most will start this training before the age of two. In truth, photography as it is today is already a training system for conscious telepathy, but its methods are still indirect.

By the time direct teaching is possible, photography will have developed far enough as a language to provide us with a framework for making sense of the telepathic experience. Otherwise, many would experience telepathy as chaos and be in serious danger of insanity. With small children, however, this is not a great problem—provided that they have good teachers. Already, photography as it is today is teaching the teachers.

So this is a taste of pure science fiction as it applies to photography. Take it seriously or not —it's up to you. But at least permit your gray cells to be stirred up a bit.

• Just a Beginning

As you have seen, this discussion of lenses, which expanded to include photography in general, has barely touched on the subject. Thus you can spend happy years figuring the rest of it out for yourself. Don't underestimate photography—and don't overestimate it either. Whatever you do, try to accept the possibility that there may be purpose underlying a cultural force of such magnitude.

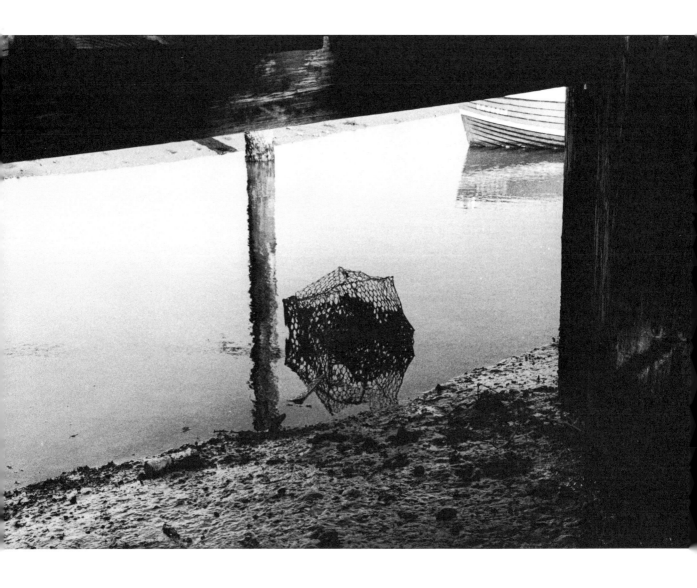

This rather strange picture could be used in meditation as a symbol of the hidden and unexplored self—if you can manage to think of yourself as a battered and beached lobster pot. Or you could just call it an artistic creation and let it go at that; many serious photographers would agree with you.

WHAT PHOTOGRAPHY CAN DO FOR YOU

Now that you have read most of this book and doubtless taken a billion pictures it is a good time to hear what photography can do for you. Had I told you earlier you wouldn't have been ready to listen. If you are a relative beginner, this chapter will help you look ahead a little bit. If you are more advanced it will help you review your experience and determine how far you have come.

You have probably discovered that it is very easy to get hooked on photography. If not, you soon will. Some people feel rewarded to find themselves hooked, but others have qualms about it. Is it a good thing? Yes, I think it's a good thing. I have taught photography to more than four thousand people and have yet to see one who wasn't substantially benefited by it, which is saying a lot for the medium. It has been kind of a hobby of mine to learn how many uses people will make of photography, and I discover more each day. Its personal usefulness seems to be nearly endless. This would explain why so many people regard it as a kind of gift from the gods.

If you are a beginner you will soon find yourself in unfamiliar territory, but don't let that worry you. Things will be explained simply and clearly, so that you will probably find that you have a taste for the unknown. Photography is a mysterious magical art, anyway, as you may have guessed from the preceding chapter. It is good to understand this from the beginning.

Though the things that photography can do for you actually overlap quite a bit, I am going to tell you about them one at a time, now and then repeating things said in earlier chapters. This should make for easier reading and can help you form your personal perspective of the whole subject, photography. It can also help you decide what kind of an involvement you want with it.

• An Aid to Memory

Everyone knows that photography helps us remember those whom we love. The fact that it has grown into a huge industry is based squarely on this truth. Remove this memory factor and photography would soon wither away, but since a divorce of photography from the memory problem is one of the things in the universe least likely to happen, there is no point in worrying about it.

Taking family pictures to bolster future memories should be the easiest kind of photography there is. All you have to do is take lots of them. It doesn't matter a bit whether they are aesthetically good, bad, or indifferent. However they come out, they will still do their job in bringing back warm memories. A well-made picture will have no more value in this respect than a poorly made one.

Oddly, those who do best by their family memory files are often those who know the least about photography. These are the people with their inexpensive plastic camera equipped with flashcubes. They know barely enough to get the film,

443

or film cassettes, into their cameras properly, and the flash cubes seated so that they will fire.

Beyond knowing how to depress the shutter release when the picture is framed in the viewfinder, these people know little else about what they are doing. But they do know what they want to remember, and that's what really counts. The technical or aesthetic quality of their pictures just doesn't matter to them, nor is there any reason why it should.

People with more experience in photography often have trouble in making memory-file pictures, many of them soon giving it up as a bad job. They want to make "good" pictures and to look good while they are making them. Though wanting goodness is surely a virtue, the desire to create it is easily taken over by the ego and used for ego purposes. And we can project our egos into photography, too, though it usually takes a while to reach this point.

So the advanced workers, believing that their egos are being displayed and publicly tested, feel that they have to come off like hotshots, both in their way of shooting and in their finished pictures. They can't take ordinary snapshots but feel impelled to produce "art," whatever that is. When you try that you may seriously impair the memory stimulation functions of your pictures; all you will remember is what your own ego was experiencing, which is only a part of what was going on. Instead of being the thrill it should be, looking back through your pictures becomes an orgy of embarrassment for your ego.

And you know how families are about egos! Why, the family could even be defined as the social grouping in which egos are given the hardest possible time. Thus a person who has advanced far enough in photography to identify his ego with it is really asking for a hassle, silent but deadly, when he brings out his camera. Small wonder that so many soon give up on family photography.

In itself, this projection of the ego is not a bad thing. Indeed, it is a spiritual opportunity, in that it can guide you toward seeing what your ego is up to. If you want to be an angel you have to separate your ego from all of its disguises, then bruise and batter it into line—which you can do with photography, if you like. But ego projection, for all that you can learn from it, does make simple memory-file shooting very difficult. How can you make simple snapshots when your ego insists that you have to become the greatest photographer who ever lived?

So you can see certain advantages in being naïve about yourself and photography: you can easily make memory pictures that are relatively undistorted by your own egotism. A monkey could do it too, but don't let that thought disturb you. It just happens that monkeys are greatly superior to people in some respects.

Many people lose their photographic innocence, then struggle for years to get it back, usually without success. There is even a so-called school of serious photographers devoted to this pursuit, and a few of them seem to have come close. It is a very rugged road, however, so let this be a warning to you. If you enjoy simply snapshooting around—family, friends, interesting places—you might be wise to let well enough alone and not dig into photography too far. There is no reason why you shouldn't cling to your innocence in this particular area. Lord knows, you have to give it up just about everywhere else.

Perhaps the best defense for your innocence is to stick strictly to the how-to-do-it side of the medium and stay very carefully away from the *why* side. If you start asking why, as we are doing in these last two chapters, you will soon learn that photography can be a very heavy game indeed. If heavy life games are your meat, hop to it, and be sure to help yourself to the gravy. But if you want to just snapshoot around happily, play it dumb—good and dumb. One of the most important things I ever learned in my life was when and how to play dumb, so I pass this secret on to you. Passing yourself off as a koala bear could even save your life some time, and I kid you not.

You may feed your need a rationale to bolster

you in your snapshooting innocence. Try this one: the only kind of photograph that people entirely believe is the snapshot. With other kinds they are intuitively aware that they are looking at ego projections, not reality as the race has agreed to see it. As for the memory question: there is no better way to assemble a fantastic memory-file than to be a productive, flat-out snapshooter. You will really capture your family and friends, not just self-centered projections of yourself. Thus going back through your pictures in later years will be an immensely gratifying experience.

• Involvement in a Creative Process

In our constant efforts to improve, heal, and create ourselves there is no better tool than a lively involvement with a creative art. The artistic history of mankind stands as a testimony to this. Artists and poets have long been considered those who have reached the farthest in self-evolution, in the search for human perfection. But we don't have to get grandiose about this: even those who have merely dabbled have usually found their lives improved.

It is the innate nature of human beings to be creative, and this process should go on all the time, night and day. Creation is our business, you might say, even if we don't know for sure *what* we are creating. It is life, it is movement, it is human nature and need. Indeed, we even create ourselves; and it is our spiritual responsibility to do the best job of it that we can.

In the business world there are many people who think they do us a favor by making individual creativity unnecessary, and we in our naïveté believe them. Thus we have number painting, screw-together sculpture, and a myriad of plastic parts waiting only a touch of model cement. The general idea of do-it-for-them has proliferated and expanded in every conceivable way, so that many of the arts have been nearly spoiled for the public.

But not photography. Though the spoilers have been at work since the beginning of the medium,

they have never managed to get a big enough bite of it to do any real harm. So we have an unspoiled medium to work with; thank the Lord for that. Whatever small damage was done is rapidly being undone. Though the do-it-for-them philosophy is very much with us in things like automated cameras, it is unlikely to do any real harm there. Indeed, it will mainly lead people further into personal creativity with the medium.

The protective shield for photography has always been the fact that people basically want to make their own pictures, not someone else's. Though many have been led into imitation, the majority are no longer interested in it. The do-it-for-them concept is surely a part of photography, embodied mainly in equipment and materials, but it is not likely to get out of hand. People resist it after a point. For example, it would be possible to market a little kit containing processing chemicals and exposed paper; develop the paper and you get an original print by a famous photographer.

Certainly this has been thought of more than once, but I can't imagine the public really going for it. For better or for worse, the majority wish to make their own pictures and couldn't care less for pictures by the famed. Such things guarantee that photography won't turn into a sterile medium, though you can use it that way if you insist. The nibblers are all around us, to be sure, trying to turn photography into a hobby for idiots. But if they were going to make any real progress we would have seen signs of it by now.

One of the protections against being forced or led into imitation is people's innate contempt for photographs made by others. The existence of this attitude is illustrated by the little success even our finest photographers have had in selling original pictures and portfolios. I have seen literally thousands of splendid photographs that the public wouldn't pay a nickel for. People just don't want them; they want their own pictures.

Unfortunately, this contempt that people have extends to themselves and to the medium itself. The feeling is that photography is a nothing art for nobodies. Though people experienced in photography worry about this they shouldn't, for it is an important part of photography's self-protection system. The professional spoilers won't deign to meddle with something they consider so unimportant. And the contempt goes away in time, so that people involved with photography can learn to appreciate one another's work. In the meantime, photography is kept unspoiled for them, protected by its overwhelming ordinariness, shielded by the contempt that so many feel for it. Incidentally, this is the only time in my life that I have had anything good to say about contempt. It is like saying that Satan accidentally does good in this world.

Another protection for the medium is that the spoilers, grammarians, and do-gooders just don't know what to make of it. It is like the halfwit Eskimo hunter confronted for the first time by an African elephant. He doesn't know whether to shoot it (which end?), forget it, or invite it home to tea.

So you have an unspoiled medium to work with. If you still find yourself happily making pictures, bringing them home from the drug store, or making your own prints, you are well ahead of the game in terms of what photography can do for you. You are functioning as people were intended to: creatively. You are bringing new things—images—into existence and reacting to them in a fruitful way. Though you may not feel like a great *artiste* in photography, this doesn't matter a bit, for the process of creation itself is the thing. You are now working on the cake, and the frosting can come later.

• Nonverbal Talking to Yourself

When we are children we are all experts at talking to ourselves, but as we grow older we tend to treat this lively and useful inner communion with skepticism and cynicism. As our egos develop they muddy up the water so much that we can't trust what we hear when we are talking to ourselves, so more and more we tend to deny our-

selves this inner reverie. But we feel the loss deeply.

Few realize that there are kinds of inner dialogue that can more or less sidestep that accomplished spoiler, the ego. Photography can be used in such a communion and very often is. However, we then listen to pictures with our emotions, not

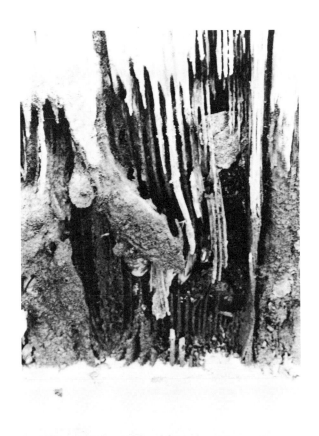

Say you are interested in photography as a visual language and wish to consider this picture as a statement of how you feel about things. This is a legitimate way to use your imagination. Well, how *do* you feel? Pretty negative, I would say. Again, feeling this way and seeing your negativity symbolized in a picture is a legitimate choice, though it is not especially good for you.

our intellects, sometimes trying to translate what we feel into words, usually not. With or without words, we know that there is real communication going on, because we can *feel* it. And this communication has value. As we gradually learn to trust our feelings this knowledge becomes a certainty. Women are usually best at this, because

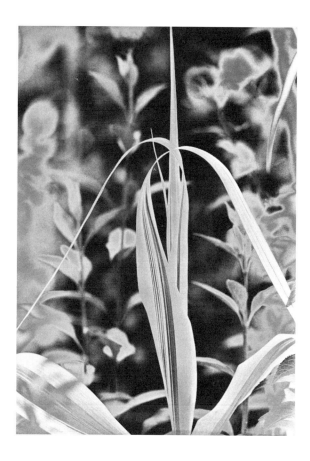

Poets sing of grass and bumblebees, but to me grass is mainly something to cut and bumblebees to run from. Well, photography can help you heighten visual perception, so this particular grass began to take on majesty and lyric form. Enough of that: let us say I merely noticed, for a change, that tall grass is kind of pretty.

they haven't spent their lives denying the very existence of their emotions.

Psychologists have provided us with some useful descriptions of the human self, which they see as a multi-level entity. Except for the ego, which dominates so-called consciousness, all the other levels are carefully hidden, though they are striving constantly to express themselves. As a way of continuing its domination over consciousness (which has turned it into a form of sleep), the ego constantly blocks expression from within, ordinarily doing a very thorough job of it.

However, when we get involved in creative work such as photography there is just too much going on for the ego to keep track of, so that higher and lower levels of the hidden self can sneak their messages through and give them expression in pictures. They are usually in the form of rather obscure visual symbols which we can feel but not understand verbally, though a verbal understanding is possible. This obscurity is necessary for outwitting the ever-vigilant ego, which was at one time called "the wolf of consciousness."

Thus our photographs are always full of symbols designed to catch our attention and help us consciously share knowledge from the higher reaches of our own minds. However obscure these symbols may seem, at one level of the self we know exactly what they mean, or we wouldn't have bothered to use them in pictures. To that super-self erroneously called the unconscious, everything whatever is a symbol, and the meaning of all of them is available to it through the racial memory. So you see that it has an abundance of symbols to draw upon and that there is no way whatever to avoid them when you make photographs. The fact that the ego is not aware of this vast languaging capability is one reason that the "unconscious" can sneak its symbols (very carefully selected) past the ego and into pictures.

With our minds (mind and ego aren't the same thing) we can step around our egos and open ourselves to what the symbols selected by the unconscious are trying to tell us about ourselves.

447

Remember that on one level of self we already know what they mean, so the process identifying them and deciphering them is not as terribly difficult as it might seem to be. Furthermore, the symbols selected are ones the ego is almost ready to be aware of anyway, often in the sense of being prepared to take it on the nose.

In some pictures the meaning is much closer to the surface than in others. You can often identify the more accessible types by your feelings about them, using the emotional extremes as indicators. For example, if one of your pictures makes you feel either very exhilarated or very upset you may be sure that it embodies a message, often an important one, that you are very nearly ready to be aware of. Now, your ego very definitely doesn't want to hear it, yet at the same time it does want to—for a very good reason. You see, messages from the inner you strengthen your ego and help

If you are a junk addict like myself this nostalgically corroded bicycle frame may bring back sweet memories of happy hours spent wandering up and down the beach looking for interesting flotsam and jetsam. Or it may remind you of the day your new bicycle was stolen and you fell down the back stairs and broke your elbow. Take your choice, sweet memories or sour.

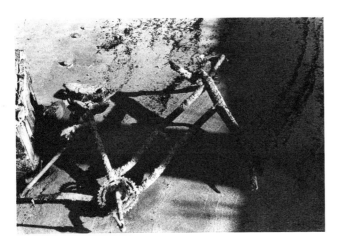

it expand and improve itself. Even so, the inner conflict goes on almost continuously.

One of the ego's problems is that it is definitely finite, while the self as a whole is infinite. Thus the ego is deeply terrified of being swallowed up in the immensity. That is, we are very afraid of ourselves, and well we should be. A sudden confrontation with his or her own immensity would be enough to give anyone a permanent case of the ravels. However, the manner in which we use art forms such as photography make it very certain that such confrontations will take place very gradually. The symbols delivered to the ego in pictorial form are chosen with very great care by the higher self so as not to be too overwhelming, because for its own sake it must strive to keep the ego healthy and intact, despite the endless crimes that the ego commits against it. Crimes against the self, as it were. For all its famous foolishness and stupidity, the ego is a high spiritual part of a human being. It just needs to learn a few things. For a reasonable perspective, think of it as mainly like a baby or small child, not so much like a willful adult criminal.

So you see that our pictures can have a lot to tell us, because there are many levels of the self speaking through each one—unless they are entirely blocked by the ego, which can happen. But listening well to oneself is a very high art not easily learned. It can only be mastered by learning to listen well to others, and you know how that goes. Since you are interested in photography, you should learn to listen well to what people say about pictures. Many people work very hard at this kind of listening.

That people intuitively know the royal road to the self is through others helps explain the enduring popularity of photography classes, seminars, and camera clubs. What people have to say about pictures—or the fact that they say anything at all —can be extremely hard to take, but people interested in photography sense the good in such groups and manage to stick it out.

My advice, then, is to join or help form such a group, with the primary goal of learning to listen well to other people in all the ways they communicate—with words, pictures, gestures, yawns, coughing spells, silences, sneezes, or whatever. One reason to follow this advice is that people will very frequently tell you very accurately what you are trying to tell yourself in your pictures. Thus when your ego blocks such knowledge, as it is very prone to do, you can get it from someone else.

Like dreams, your photographs can tell you who and what you are. Unlike dreams, they do not fade away and disappear, or get changed and distorted in memory. Photographs are telegraph lines to parts of the self that are much greater than the so-called consciousness that you know of. For both beginners and more advanced photographers this material on reading pictures ought to be spelled out a bit, so this is what I will do.

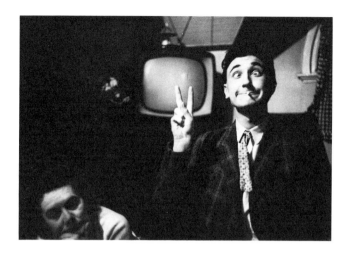

Though it isn't true, you could say that this picture shows accurately how I really feel about people, that I see half of them as crazy and the other half bogged down in despair. Well, this may be true enough, but it's not my way of seeing them. Or you can just call this a mildly nutty picture and let it go at that. Incidentally, if you want to know how your author actually sees people, look at the pictures in this book.

● **How You Really Feel About People**

One of life's problems is in keeping track of how we really feel about other people, because there is a lot of suffering, conflict, and confusion involved in not knowing. Recently, for example, I have been working with one of the country's finest portrait photographers, whose attitude toward his subjects is making him utterly miserable. He thinks he sees them coldly and cynically, but this is by no means the truth.

If you were to look at a group of his portraits you would almost instantly see that he adores the people he photographs—all of them without exception. I doubt if it is possible to love people more than he does, yet he actually thinks he despises them and condemns himself deeply for this. So it is left up to others to tell him the truth, which we are doing as swiftly and convincingly as we can. His life should then be considerably improved.

Helped by others, it is not all that hard to tell from your pictures what you think of people. This is because they function as mirrors when you are photographing them, reflecting back to you your own attitudes, emotions, and prejudices.

Since people are entirely unconsious of doing this they do it with great honesty and incredible accuracy. The reflections are messages from their super-intelligent higher selves. Because the human face is immensely more pliable than generally supposed, it makes a splendid tablet on which to write such messages.

In effect, when you photograph someone you ask him or her, "Who am I? How do I really feel? What are the main psychic problems confronting me?" You invariably get the right answers, though they may be hard to decipher because your ego does its best to mess things up by making the messages in your pictures obscure to you. Even so, with the help of others you can get a very complete and informative reading on almost any portrait you can make.

(When members of a discussion group analyze a picture they seldom find its message right away,

449

for this takes time and patience. Moreover, they must tentatively assume that the message is indeed there, which is a difficult assumption to make for people unversed in the ways in which the unconscious mind expresses itself. And much of the discussion is banal, irrelevant, and egocentric. Even so, the wheat can be winnowed from the chaff—by people of patience and good will.)

It needn't be said that people on an ordinary level often find it difficult to work together. Perhaps the important thing to realize, however, is that at the higher levels of self they are very cooperative indeed, though not consciously aware of it. These levels account for this helpful mirroring which people do for one another. This goes on all the time, whether or not you are making photographs. Thus if you are uncertain as to how you feel (unhappy, confused, angry, frightened, etc.), all you have to do is look at the people around you; their faces will tell you—provided that you will permit yourself to be aware of what your eyes are trying to tell you.

But sometimes we definitely don't want to see what faces tell us, not on the ego level at any rate. I once had a student, whom I will call Bill, who had the hardest time getting his own attention. A very productive photographer, he brought in dozens of new people-pictures every week, and every one of his subjects looked very angry. They were all trying to tell Bill—and he was trying to tell himself—that he had a very serious problem with repressed anger. Unconscious forces in himself, helped by similar forces in others, were trying to draw his attention to the difficulty so that he could begin to deal with it on the conscious level. Thus his pictures inundated him with the fact of his anger, contrary to his ego's wish to shove the whole problem under the carpet. If I had a nickel for every Bill I have had as a student, I would be a wealthy man today.

One reason why this mirroring works with such great accuracy is that at a higher level of the self we are all accomplished telepaths. Thus at this level you can make it very clear to others what you want them to mirror back to you for

your ego's enlightenment, egos not being telepathic yet. The mirror images will be excellent, though your ego may not wish to see this. If you don't like this explanation, which is a little far out, try to come up with a better one. If you have been around in photography it is hard to escape the fact that mirroring does indeed go on, and it can hardly be accounted for in an ordinary way. Stir up your gray cells and see what you can figure out.

● What Others Think of You

A few people use photography as a way of getting a better idea of what others think of them. Though this is a painful way to use the medium, it helps us along the arduous path to self-discovery. However, the mirroring makes interpretation difficult. How can you tell whether you

I would call this a really rotten picture, frankly, and it reminds me most of anger and fear. Ugly as it is, making such a picture can be useful, for it can help one track down the sources of these terribly negative and destructive emotions. Perhaps you don't get my imagery: try thinking of the charred driftwood as a brain cell rotted by anger and fear. Pretty lousy, what?

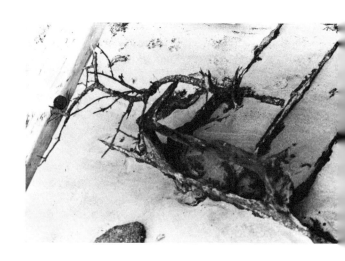

are looking at people functioning as mirrors or, instead, coming across as themselves? I can't give you an easy answer for this, because they do both things at the same time but in different proportions, which makes it difficult to sort things out.

Nevertheless, we can look at our pictures of people and get some pretty good clues concerning how they see us. We do this mainly by feel rather than intellection, so people who have strangled their feelings won't get very far. Fortunately, there are surface clues that we can look for, such as tensions in the eyes, mouth, neck, and shoulders of the person (or portrait) we wish to read. The hands communicate a good deal, as does posture. Consciously, people try not to communicate to you. On the ego level, they usually don't want you to know what they actually think of you. Impelled by higher forces in themselves, however, they are constantly giving them-

selves away to anyone who knows how to see. It is human destiny that people will eventually get to know one another well, so this is the general direction we are taking, despite ourselves (egos).

There is an ancient truism that makes interpretation a little easier: like begets like. For example, if you think a person a fool your attitude will breed similar thoughts in him or her with respect to you. If you then make this person look like a fool in a photograph you may be sure that you have made a self-portrait written on another person's face. This kind of thing happens all the time, incidentally, because like begets like is one of the higher laws of psychology, a law that never fails.

I remember a student who brought me a picture he had made of his best friend's father. He was terribly happy when I saw that he was portraying the older man as extremely egotistical. Though I was considerably less blunt than he, his fiendish delight disappeared when I told him that his subject undoubtedly reciprocated this attitude and that the picture showed this clearly. That is, the father saw the young man as an extreme egotist. It was a case of egotist vs. egotist.

So, if you want to know what people think of you, just figure out what you think of them. Having pictures of them will help a lot because they won't bite you and can't talk back when you are talking to them. As a guide for analysis, remember this rule: the characteristics that disturb you most in others are ones you share with them, though you may not be aware of it. If self-knowledge is one of your goals in life, photography can help you a lot—but it won't always be easy.

• Fear of Others

Quite a few people use photography to help them uncover, analyze, and dispel their fear of others. They do this mainly through making pictures of their friends and acquaintances, whom they also inexplicably fear. But the fear of friends isn't so strong that it can't be worked on and dispelled.

Now, you can use photography to increase your awareness of beauty. For example, every night for years I lay on the bed reading and could have seen this pretty little tableau (set up by my wife) had I bothered to look beyond the ends of my toes. But I rarely did, until one sweet day I got out my camera and decided to really look at what my wife had done to our apartment. I found it utterly charming.

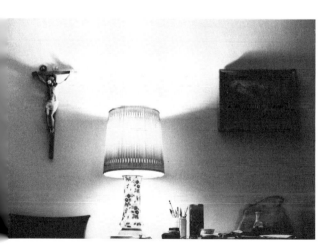

Just looking at people up close, and thinking the thoughts that naturally occur, can help a lot. However, we need an excuse for such close proximity, which photography readily provides. And people see no harm in having their pictures taken, so they don't make an issue of it. Finally, the very act of photographing someone gives the photographer the psychological position on strength, which helps him greatly in holding himself together.

It may seem strange that merely taking pictures of people will help you overcome your fear of them, but that's the way it works. Few people are able to verbalize what is happening to them as they photograph, though they usually know they are frightened. People who are determined to deal with their fear just dive into portraiture and wade their way through it, no matter how hard it is on the gut. Please don't construe this as a kind of masochism, because it is far from it. Indeed, it is a pathway through fear to the other side, which is a horse of a different color.

If you are an everyday coward, as most of us are, you might consider specializing in portraits of your friends and acquaintances for a while. You can even tell them what you are going through, and it may help a lot. Your camera gives you the only excuse you need for what you are doing, and your subjects are unlikely to question it. Indeed, they are just pleased to know that you want pictures of them, for it is a very nice compliment.

• Actively Experiencing a New Language

For unknown reasons there has been a great upsurge of interest in photography recently. Most obvious in Japan, where nearly everyone has turned into a photography nut, it is also making itself felt in this country and elsewhere. I would say that this interest has largely to do with language and the fact that photography, especially in television, has finally reached the point where it is functioning fully on the linguistic level. If this is true, it means that photography has become a cultural necessity, just like the spoken and written languages.

Earlier, I said that photography is unconsciously, but very skillfully, being used to prepare us for conscious telepathy. In itself it is becoming the exterior form of the language of telepathy. It is well known that people are fully telepathic on the higher levels of the "unconscious," but nearly forgotten that talents such as this can also shift levels, even into so-called consciousness. Considering all that is happening in the world of photography (which in its linguistic applications includes television, the cinema, still photography, amateur photography, the picture press, and so on), it shouldn't seem unduly strange that we might be unconsciously preparing ourselves for such a shift, even in the near future. Of course, this would help account for the unexplained surge of interest in the medium.

Photography's long period of development as the teachable form of the language of telepathy has been vitally necessary, and it must continue to develop at a constantly accelerating pace, into the distant future. The long years are necessary, because a true language is an organic growth arising slowly from the thought patterns and perceptions of those who use it. For them, it must be an all-encompassing mirror, though they may not be able to see themselves in it. Now, this developing language of telepathy is apparently destined for all the nations. As such, it must have the enormous breadth and flexibility that will make it an effective tool for coping with every conceivable linguistic event, both in exterior reality and in the human mind. Since everything that can be thought of is such an event (a symbol), you can see that a language is no small matter.

This developing language of telepathy (photography) must take within itself all the written and spoken languages, which photography (television) is rapidly proceeding to do. For example, in American TV we have both types of language represented in full force, though the written language is only implicitly present. However, since written words in the English language stand very explicitly for sounds, this kind of presence is quite adequate for our linguistic needs in terms of telepathy. This bringing together of pictorial, written, and spoken languages is also happening in many other nations, of course.

When telepathy is mentioned people generally look stupid and obviously haven't the slightest idea of what it is and what it would do for (or to) us. Fair enough, nobody really knows— unless he or she is a telepath. But imagine having a television set in your head, broadcasting programs from Lord knows where, with somebody else selecting the programs, doing the tuning, and obviously trying to communicate something to you. Now imagine six sets going along in your head at once, one of them following your best friend at the supermarket as she looks over the vegetables, another taking you on a guided tour of your own pancreas, a third showing you a burning passenger liner in the Mediterranean, and so on. Well, this is kid stuff, I suspect—for telepathy could be immensely more complicated and confusing than this. For example, you might have a helluva hard time even keeping track of who you are. At any rate, with such things going on in our heads we would need some kind of a linguistic structure that we could use to get everything sorted out, which is where photography comes in. It is coming along very well in its development in that direction. I can't say that I worry about our telepathic future (if it actually comes about), but I at least find it interesting. Indeed, if we need a language for telepathy, why then we will have it when we need it. The human race has better survival capabilities than some people suppose.

Let us now consider photography-as-a-language on a more down-to-earth level, letting the future take care of itself for a while. As a teacher for many years, I've put in thousands and thousands of hours working with groups in photography. Seminar stuff, mostly, where people come together to talk about their work. Years ago it used to be such a terrible grind for the teacher, because no one had a word to say. The teacher himself had to make up all the meaning that got attached to the pictures, fighting each point with the students, who were certain that photography didn't mean anything at all. Everyone thought that, including most professional photographers. I'm telling you, it was really hard on the gut, trying to convince all those people that their chosen lifework actually had meaning. Can you believe that they preferred to think it did not? Such is the perversity of man.

Well, quite a change has taken place since then. The groups you meet with now actually think that photographs can mean something (praise the Lord!) and that it is fully worth one's while to try to decide what it is. I have sometimes read about the group of famous literati who used to meet at the Hotel Algonquin in New York— Dorothy Parker and her crew. Frankly, I doubt if the discussions would hold a candle to the ones you can now get into with groups of photographers in almost any part of the country, although there are also groups in which pigheadedness and banality predominate. But the good ones—vive la différence, I say. We have even reached a point where people can be teachers of photography without sacrificing their sanity, solar plexi, and left hind legs.

These present-day groups usually have a terrific time together, though it can get very heavy, too. However, they tend to take the heaviness as part of the learning process and learn to suffer through a good deal of it without backing off. Indeed, many of the youngsters thrive on heavy and ask for as much of it as the group can give. In this sense photography groups are a lot tougher nowadays, much more inclined to suffer hearing people out than they used to be. Listening is very heavy duty stuff, you know. In the old days the big thing was for people to chop each other up and play the old "I win, you lose" game.

So this is what is open to you nowadays: if you work hard to make your pictures communicate something you can actually find people who will work equally hard to determine what it is. Since this can be a very heavy business, it means that they will even willingly suffer for you. And often your pictures will get through to them like the Red Ball Express, which is a wonderful experience. How nice to know that you have communicated well! Furthermore, you will almost invariably learn that your pictures say much more than you thought, which is equally rewarding. To be able to communicate fills a deep human need, and when it involves a new language you are mastering, like photography, it is outright thrilling.

A thing that happened in young people's music is also having a strong effect on photography. A few years ago the kids decided that all people should be permitted to make music, even if they sang off key or sounded like aardvarks in heat. Let people do their own thing, was the slogan. This was one of the most brilliantly revolutionary developments of the century. It meant that *everyone* could make music and not be criticized, not just the brilliantly gifted.

Fortunately, the very same young people brought this idea into photography, where it still has a powerful influence. Though there are still a few laceration specialists around, they no longer run the whole show. In a contemporary group the majority no longer huff and puff to tell you how bad your work is. Instead, they wait patiently to tell you what it communicates to them, if that is what you want. This is one of the recent developments that seems to portend a telepathic age. In such an age a person's communications will have to be heeded (just try keeping him out of your head!), even if they aren't spectacular and important. Furthermore, this patience with others that we seem to be seeing more of nowadays will be of great importance should the race decide to shift into the telepathic mode. Make no mistake of this: we will do it if and when we decide to do it.

And if we don't? Well, things will be a lot more simple. As Grandma said when she jumped into the washing machine, "It would have been easier not to!"

454

• What Things Look Like

When we are little we are very interested in what things look like and spend endless days soaking it all up. But as we move out of our teens many of us lose all interest and never get it back. Not caring what the world looks like is a deadened state of mind which contributes greatly to the general malaise that afflicts so many. You might even call it a psychological illness.

Fortunately, photography is a powerful tool for regaining an interest in the appearance of things. It presents reality to us in such a magical way that we find it nearly impossible to resist. When an image comes out of a Polaroid camera or pops up in a print tray it really gets to us, excites us. Only a very dull character can ignore such blandishments. And the magic continues to work through many a year.

So if you find that your visual world has lost its spice, photography may be the very thing for you. If you are already involved in it consider yourself lucky. Compare yourself to the millions for whom the world is just a vast monotony of nothingness and count your blessings.

• Heightened Visual Perception

It is not only possible to regain interest in the visual world but to learn to perceive it with an intensity never before experienced. For example, you may now think that the super-intense "fluorescent" colors are the liveliest ever—for they are extremely bright—but did you know that it is possible to see nearly all man-made colors that clearly? It is a wild and wonderful experience, to be sure, and some fortunate people see that way most of the time.

Some see the world as much brighter and cleaner than others do, sometimes to the point where they have to wear dark glasses to bring it down to a bearable level. You would be mistaken to think that people wear shades only if there is something wrong with them. Often, dark glasses

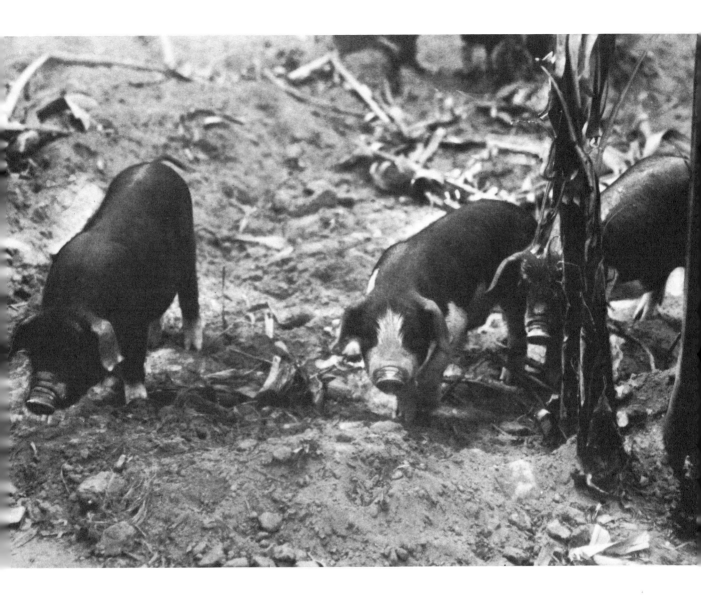

In the text I suggest that you can use photography for coping with such things as fear and anger, and I have my own special way of doing it—with pigs, of which I am extremely fond. When my brain feels like a badly burned roast and I feel like condemning the world to perdition, I think of photographing pigs and how much fun it would be to do it. Or even having a pet pig (a small one). It works amazingly well.

mask very superior sensitivity and awareness, for the very people who see brightly also see much more of the visual world than others do.

Now, the practice of photography moves one gradually but surely in the direction of heightened visual perception—and there is much more to it than has been suggested in this book. It is like moving into a new and unspoiled world—the fresh and vital world of childlike perception.

You don't especially need signs and guideposts for this journey. Just take your pictures and follow them where they lead.

• Awareness of Time and Space

Through working with literally thousands of photographers I have learned that they are fascinated by time and space, though I am unable to tell you why. The space part is easy enough to figure out, because all photographs embody space illusions of some sort, subtle or gross. We find positive space, negative space, shallow space, deep space, nonspace, or a mixture of different kinds in every picture. I've personally played endless hours with visual space and consider myself well-versed on the subject, but what about time? What has time got to do with pictures?

Talking to other photographers hasn't explained time. They can't seem to verbalize what they are up to, though their enthusiasm is communicated strongly enough. Most of them don't even try to translate from photography into words, yet they may be right. Perhaps photography, a nonverbal language, is a good way of intuiting time, not intellectualizing it. Though we are doing our best to translate all of photography into words, and vice versa, there will always be large and important areas that just aren't translatable. Perhaps time is one of these.

Oddly, photographers often relate pictures of stairways to time. Equally odd, some of my students have told me that when they are tripping or

stoned on pot they can see movement in still pictures, and when we have movement we have time. Well, you figure it out.

I have observed that people need little experience in photography before becoming enchanted with time, and that they don't seem to mind pursuing their interest on a purely intuitive level. They seem to relate time to tone and space, but communicate such ideas mainly by pointing, waving their hands, and shrugging, rather than by verbalizing. Whatever is going on, we seem to be racially involved in a growing awareness of some kind, which would help explain the enthusiasm for time and space in photography. It also seems clear that if you are interested in time and space you will find photography rewarding.

• Insights into Visual Communication

When we speak of the visual communication world we are usually referring mainly to television, which is a form of photography. We list TV first simply because it takes up more of our time than any other visual medium.

TV and still photography are undoubtedly more closely related than anyone supposes—if we knew more about the nature of time we could probably see this quite clearly. Even without this understanding, people in droves are intuiting the essential oneness of the two forms of the medium. As you will see, this would help explain the tremendous growth of interest in still photography.

Let us see what happens to people in this so-called visual world. For years we passively submit to a daily bombardment of TV images, only vaguely aware of how the visual language works. Eventually we reach the point where we feel ready to see the whole thing as a language structure and to become fully aware of how it functions. Intuitively, we grasp the fact that the grammar of this language is outlined best and most simply in still photography, so this is where we turn in search of understanding. Fortunately, all we learn from stills relates very directly to our experience of television.

Some general comments are in order. Nowadays, students have a much better idea of where they are going with their photography than they used to have. Many have established their goals even before starting school. Perhaps the most common goal is this: to put it all together, this vast puzzle of the so-called communication world. Some put it this way: "I want to find out what the hell TV has done to me," which means approximately the same thing.

Well, TV (photography) has done much more to us (actually, *for* us) than anyone suspects. As we've just seen, it drives people into a study of the visual language, which happens to be a good thing. Furthermore, it prepares them very well for this study, though the people in television certainly haven't had this in mind. Even so, the actors, producers, cameramen, directors, advertisers, and so on have served us well, mainly because they have had to. In order to stay in business (hold their viewers and sell them things) they have had to use the visual language with very great care, which is all that really counts. In comparison, the garbage they produce and the shenanigans they pull hardly matter at all.

Back to cloud nine for a moment: television per se is a gigantic teaching machine handed down to us piecemeal from the higher consciousness of the race for use in preparing ourselves for conscious telepathy, which demands that we have a language proper to it. The basic grammar of this language is embodied in still photography (as well as in TV and the cinema), giving us easy and economical access to it. People interested in photography may be mainly preparing a language for the future. On the other hand, the racial shift into telepathic consciousness could come soon and suddenly, overnight as it were. In this case, learning the grammar of the visual language could be seen as an unconsciously motivated step toward preserving sanity against the tremendous impact of telepathic consciousness.

And, of course, you can see this whole paragraph as hogwash, if you like.

Well, anyhow, back to Mother Earth for a while. For all their experience with images, people still have a lot to figure out concerning what makes visual communication work. So many of them are doing it; simple as that. Photography was just sitting there waiting for them, including thousands of fine teachers who just weren't available a few years ago—and thousands of fellow students with the same interest in sorting everything out and putting it all together. I would say that the setup is nearly impeccable—much to my surprise. This doesn't mean that learners won't have very heavy ups and downs, but such things are an important part of the growing experience. And if the situation looked *too* good we should be worried.

A development of special interest is that many of the people using photography to figure out the visual communication thing for themselves aren't asking for help. By themselves, or with a friend or two, they sail right into it, asking and answering all the questions for themselves. On a cultural level their ability to function independently is a very good thing. If we are indeed close to a shift or awareness levels (which is only an hypothesis) there just aren't enough teachers to help everybody, despite their great increase in numbers in recent years. But not to worry. My crystal ball (filled with hot chicken soup) says that TV itself is doing the major part of the teaching job, though few seem to suspect it.

• Hidden Levels of the Self

A few years ago if you told someone he had levels of himself quite unknown to him he would just sit there like a constipated oyster with not even a "So what?" expression on his face. I ought to know, because I have the world's record for the number of times I've told people this (Guinness Book of Records). But I'll never get

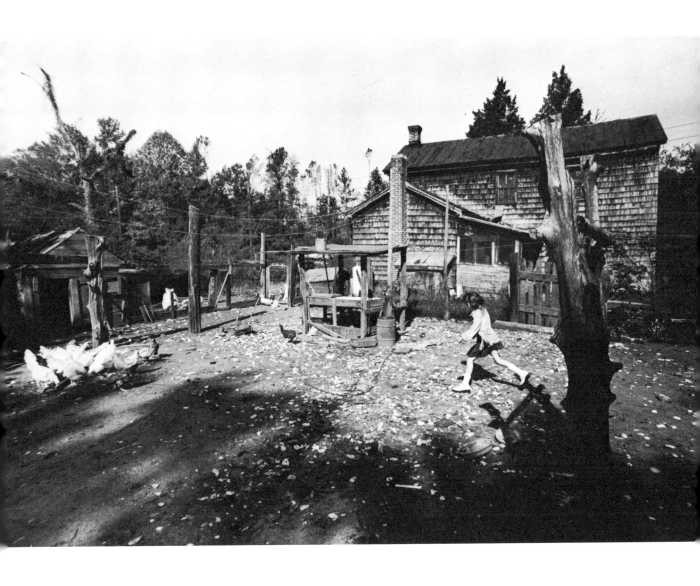

To me there is much time in this picture as well as space. The little girl running through her grandma's chicken yard carries me back to the days I spent on *my* grandma's farm, happy, carefree days. And age is also in the battered house and chicken coops, even in the ground strewn with oyster shells. And chickens are a gas, really such groovy little dumb creatures.

really used to those oysters sitting there without a burp.

Things have changed a lot in the last few years, and the average kid knows very well about these hidden levels and has done everything he could think of to gain access to them. This is what the Drug Scene was all about, of course, and explains why Don Juan reigned so long as America's Guru-in-Chief. After racking themselves up with the hard ways of trying to make higher contact with themselves, many of these kids have turned to gentler and more gradual routes, such as music and photography. There they can experience enough to keep themselves as spaced out as they like.

Essentially, being spaced-out means to be in contact with your higher self or with someone else's, which also happens now and then. It can also mean contact with a lower self. Many of the young—and their elders too—have become addicted to being spaced-out for its own sake and make no effort whatever to learn anything from it. But there are a few real heavy types who do want to learn.

Now, these real heavy types, many of them in photography, really want to put the whole thing together by figuring out, bit by bit, what is actually going on in themselves, why, and how it all works. These heavies are very strong people, though many of them are young. They will invite emotional punches in the gut that would fracture an elephant, then come back for more. Despite the suffering that it entails, they *really* want to learn about themselves, in fact consider it their spiritual duty. With this I totally agree.

We will see how the heavies use photography. If you assume hidden levels in yourself expressing themselves somehow through your photography you will not look at your pictures in the same way as people who don't make this assumption. They may assume that they completely understand their own photography, while you see yours mainly as a puzzle to be unraveled. As you look at your work you constantly ask yourself, "What does this mean? What am I trying to tell myself,

if anything? What am I *really* trying to communicate to others? And on what level?"

For a person aware of the existence of hidden levels of the self, looking at a picture becomes a subtle form of listening, too. As you look you listen to your own thoughts, trying to stay aware enough to pick out the ones that don't sound especially like you. These are the thoughts that may originate in your higher self. But don't be too sure of this, because your ego would like to take over this act and can peddle some very fancy blarney when it wants to. With time and patience, however, you manage to sort out which message comes from where. Best to stay alert for ego twinges, incidentally—for they are often caused by thoughts emanating from a higher level. Though the ego also shafts itself now and then, you can usually tell when this is happening.

Earlier, I said you can learn most about how to listen to yourself by learning to listen to others, so don't neglect this vital part of your education. Oddly, the harder a person is to listen to the more you can gain from forcing yourself to do it. This sounds like looking for misery, and in a sense it is, but it really cleans out the psychic channels. There is a trick to it, however: while your "friend" is putting you up the wall, very carefully banish all negative thoughts and attitudes from your mind and think only positive things with respect to him or her. This is a difficult task, but you can learn to do it with time and patience. If you use this "trick," listening will cleanse you. If you don't your suffering is wasted, turned into cheap food for egotism.

Perhaps you don't see any point in self-discovery; many people don't. If so, it is probably because you have no idea of how utterly marvelous the whole human self is, even your self. Seers have often pointed out that the human idea of gods is actually descriptive of an ordinary human self in its wholeness, and that is saying a lot for it. So if you should actually manage to discover yourself you are going to be onto something large and wonderful far beyond what you can now even imagine. Since your pictures can be a royal

459

highway to this unknown self, why not learn to listen to them? Once you start listening to them your inner self will put more and more into them for your uplift and education.

● Meditation While Printing

Quite a few people have noted that printing can be a form of meditation and that they enjoy this meditation deeply. It sounds deadly serious, but it doesn't have to be: you just let your mind wander wherever it wants to, which you probably do anyway. Given this chance, your mind can have a good time, because it loves to wander around.

Silly as it sounds, you might try talking to the people in your pictures when you are alone in the darkroom. Will yourself to believe that the real people (not the images) actually hear you, because in some far reach of the racial mind they probably do. And if they don't it doesn't matter. This provisional and temporary belief, imaginatively entered into as an act of will, can make printing portraits a real gas, especially if you really let yourself get carried away with your conversation. Memories will flood in by the ton and insights into your relationships with people will follow each other in rapid succession. So talking to pictures is a dumb thing?: do it anyway. Call it an exercise in imagination.

Pictures give you something to focus your attention on almost effortlessly, and the technical details that must be attended to provide exactly the right amount of distraction, which is very useful. In this case, distraction is a state of mind in which the ego is sufficiently sidetracked by technical matters to keep it from constantly interfering with whatever is going on in your head. Thus occupied, it will relax some of its desperate grip on the conscious mind and permit it to wander fruitfully. This productive wandering we call meditation. Don't tell your mind *where* to wander —that is your ego speaking. Just let it think whatever it thinks.

There are lots of formal ways of meditating which you can look up in books on Eastern religion and philosophy. However, they are not well adapted to the Western mind and can lead you around the barn or get you into serious trouble. They might even lead you to persuade yourself that you are a somebody. Better stick to your own style of meditation, whatever it may be, and just wing it. Let every printing session be a play, with you the director, stage manager, and all the actors. It surely won't make you any crazier than you already are.

● A Harmless Experience with Power

One of man's biggest problems is to learn how to handle power, even small amounts of it. It is said that power corrupts and that absolute power corrupts absolutely (Lord Acton). In international relations and our own government we see enough of this to accept it as a truism. Power is dangerous and not something to be fooled with blindly. However, learning how to handle it safely is an important step in human evolution. We also need the experience of power now and then to convince ourselves that we aren't quite as helpless as we are prone to think. Indeed, a normal human being is a real powerhouse, though his powers are held in stasis. Thus our main need for the experience of power is to learn to safely take possession of our own powers. But power can be a deadly thing.

One of the safe ways to experience power is in the practice of art, as people have learned through the ages. Those who can make good pictures have a strong effect on others, and that is what power mainly is. Though art can be misused it ceases to be art when it is. Most of us sense this and intuitively avoid such distortion, for the desire to be a true artist is very strong in us. The effect we mostly strive for in our work, insofar as it concerns others, is to open up people's heads and hearts to what we are trying to say to them. And getting through to them is power, a good kind of power. We assault them with our pictures, in a sense, and a by-product of this is a gradual but certain expansion of their perceptivities, which is a good thing. With it comes a breaking down of some of the communication barriers that hold people apart.

But we don't have to assault people all the time: we can woo them with lyricism and beauty. Here is where the *real* power is anyway, and we don't have to worry about the personal dangers of misusing it. Power used poetically is the glue that holds whole civilizations together, for it is not the nature of poets, whatever be their media, to misuse power. They use it only to heal. Only when man learns to use power poetically, learns to heal himself, can he come into possession of his own power. Let us come down from the stratosphere for a moment. When you personally make a picture that people really dig you will know what power is. And your chances of experiencing this power with your photographs are getting better and better, because the public is getting excited about photography and willing to look at what it does. This willingness is with us now for the very first time.

• Expanding Your Awareness of Beauty

It is said that seeing beauty is a basic biological survival function and that this defines the nature of beauty. Roughly, if a thing is edible, kissable, or wearable we call it beautiful and seek to possess it for our good health. But there is more to human existence than gross biological survival. We must also consider mental, emotional, and spiritual survival and come to understand that anything that contributes to them, in ourselves or others, should also be considered beautiful. We must also learn that it is extremely important to become aware of this beauty, that this awareness itself is a survival function.

We can turn to Islam and find a splendid formulation of the "beauty problem" from the spiritual point of view:

> "God is Reality.
> God is Beauty.
> Thus to see God
> We must see Reality as Beauty."

The problem, of course, is to learn to do this. And the eat-kiss-wear formula won't take us very far.

Fortunately, being really involved with any art form, photography included, gradually (yet dramatically) expands one's awareness of beauty. This is a natural by-product of trying very hard to see and understand. The beauty that we thus learn to see could be defined as follows:

> Anything well seen is beautiful;
> And anything well understood is beautiful.

Now understand this: though learning to see reality as beauty is one of our deepest human needs it is also a very long and tough row to hoe. However, if at this point you are already hooked on photography you have probably begun to suspect that it can provide you with most of the hard workouts you need. If you don't try to avoid the necessary suffering (the ego must be tamed), it can take you far along the road to beauty and reality.

• Expressing and Overcoming Repressed Anger

One of our greatest problems is repressed anger, which generates negative energy that is destructive both to self and others. Because it *is* repressed (pushed into the unconscious and confined there), we usually don't know *why* we are angry or even *that* we are. Thus our self-ignorance makes it difficult to cope with anger or even to see that we have a problem.

The negative energy generated by anger must be released or expressed, or it will eventually wreak havoc in our minds and bodies. However, it should be done in such a way as to convert negative energy into positive, because straightforward expression of unconverted negative energy is itself destructive. We see its grim effects in various neuroses and psychoses, bodily ailments, and societal maladjustments.

461

Merely expressing and converting repressed negative energy doesn't go far enough, for the anger that gives rise to it remains within us as a continuing source of physical and psychic infection. The repressed anger itself must be deprived of its many disguises and driven out into the open where we can see it clearly. Once well seen it will go away, often forever.

Now, the artist has purposes that the public doesn't see in his or her art, the main one being self-discovery. An important part of this is the recognition, use, and elimination of repressed anger. Our knowledge of hidden anger is at first intuitive: we feel its presence without actually knowing what it is. At the same time we sense that it is a powerful motive force that can be used for struggling with ourselves (our egos) as we strive to create art. This struggle converts much of the negative energy of anger into positive energy and eliminates some of the anger itself. The next step is to see this hidden anger in all its dimensions, so that it will entirely go away.

Learning to see repressed anger clearly is one of life's great challenges, for it is very well hidden indeed. You might say that it is buried in a mountain of symbols, each one designed to distort the anger's true nature or to even deny that it exists. However, this mighty mountain of self-deceit exists at a superficial level of the unconscious, and there are higher forces of the "unconscious" (the super-self, so to speak) that are always ready to help us pull it down by helping us understand what it actually is.

Roughly, what we must learn to do is listen to ourselves. This includes listening to our pictures, which invariably embody messages from our higher selves. With time and patience we can construct from these messages an accurate picture of our buried anger, finally free of disguise. But when we reach this point we are in for a big surprise: the problem is not anger but fear. Anger is nothing but fear in disguise. Once recognized for what it truly is, anger is much easier to cope with.

Now, I have known literally hundreds of people who were using photography as a primary tool for discovering anger, converting its negative energy into positive in the form of art, and trying to eliminate it altogether. Used in this manner, photography is a *very* heavy business, but many people find the goal worth suffering for. One reward, incidentally, is to tap into energy sources that are much greater than anger ever could be.

• Not the Half of It

It is truthfully said that a life in art is a means for creating oneself—the artist slowly awakens and turns himself into art. This is a very large order to fill, of course, but time and patience availeth much. Though the end may be far away, the knowledge of where we are headed gives us hope.

As both an art form and a language, photography is a splendid tool for conscious self-creation or self-evolution. It can take us to far horizons, provided that we use it well. Since art and language are very large subjects, this chapter isn't the half of what photography can do for you. However, it should stimulate thought and observation.

• Conclusion

This book for beginners tells you how to do a few things in photography. Furthermore, it provides you with a basis for personally discovering whether they are really worth doing. I hope you find it useful.

This tragic little picture works powerfully as communication, reminding us forcefully of the male condition—hung up on barbed wire by the you-know-whats. Well, Eddy Mole wasn't actually hanging from anything, but he sure put on a good act. Anyhow, a photograph can be language—that's the point of this whole story.

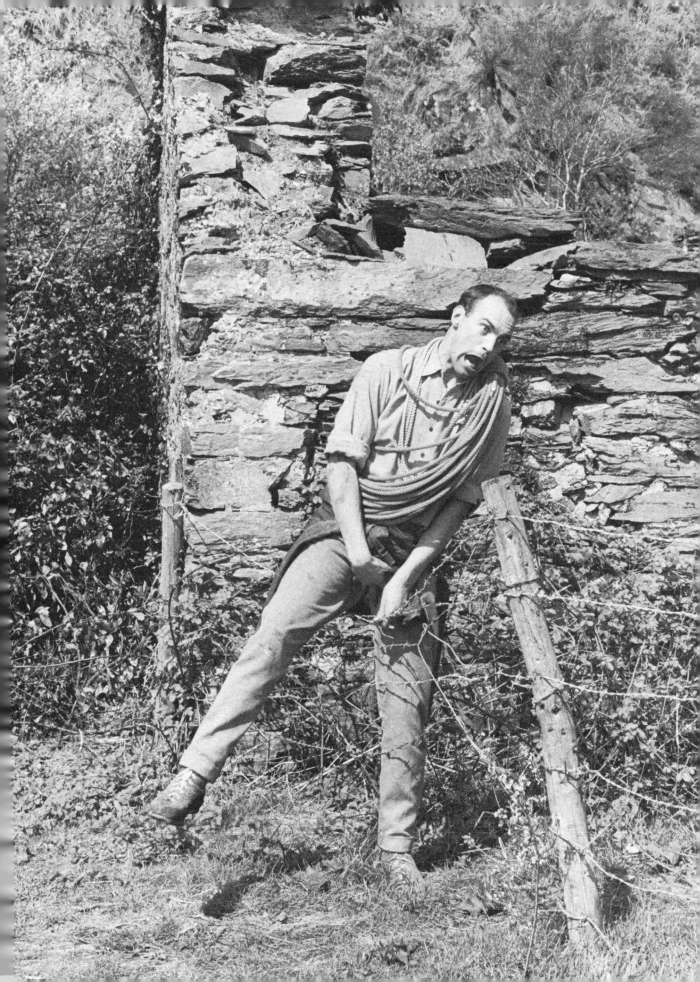